More praise for *The Courage to Heal:*

"The Courage to Heal is a wise and gentle book that should be read by all people trying to recover from having been sexually misused as a child, and by all friends, family members, and professionals with a genuine desire to understand both the experience of being a victim of sexual abuse and the arduous path to recovery. *The Courage to Heal* has helped countless survivors of sexual abuse in their efforts to confront the realities of their lives and to take charge of them in the present."
　　　　　—Bessel A. van der Kolk, M.D., associate professor of psychiatry, Harvard Medical School

"The Courage to Heal continues to be an invaluable resource for adults sexually abused as children. Ellen Bass and Laura Davis provide survivors with concrete and practical information about the healing process and its many challenges, including the current controversy about memory and delayed disclosure."
　　　　　—Christine Courtois, clinical director of the Post-Traumatic Disorders Program of the Psychiatric Institute of Washington, D.C. and author of *Recollections of Sexual Abuse: Treatment Principles and Guidelines*

"With scrupulous care, balance, and a clear political vision, Ellen Bass and Laura Davis have written a groundbreaking book that will stand as a classic for many years to come. Clearly a labor of both love and commitment to the healing of tens of thousands of women still suffering the deep wounds of their experience, *The Courage to Heal* will find a wide, appreciative, and altered readership."
　　　　　—Sandra Butler, author of *The Conspiracy of Silence*

Acclaim from survivors for *The Courage to Heal:*

"The Courage to Heal touched the deepest part of me, the part that has been walled off and silent for twenty-five years. You have spoken the words for me that I was unable to utter."

"When your book entered my life, it gave me the reassurance that one day I would be whole."

"Dealing with feelings that have been hidden, suppressed and unacknowledged for fifty years is an awesome task, and your book is helping to make the process bearable and possible."

"If there was any one thing that helped me to believe in myself, and helped to reconstruct my life, it has been this book. *The Courage to Heal* has not spent a day on the bookshelf—I utilize it so often that it is a waste to put it away."

"Thank you hardly seems like enough to say. You have changed the direction of my life in a *positive* way with as much impact as the incest changed my life in a negative way so many years ago."

"Thank you for helping me save my life and my sanity."

Other Books by the Authors

Ellen Bass

I NEVER TOLD ANYONE: WRITING BY WOMEN SURVIVORS OF CHILD SEXUAL ABUSE (COEDITOR, WITH LOUISE THORNTON)

FREE YOUR MIND: THE BOOK FOR GAY, LESBIAN, AND BISEXUAL YOUTH—AND THEIR ALLIES (WITH KATE KAUFMAN)

OUR STUNNING HARVEST (POETRY)

FOR EARTHLY SURVIVAL (POETRY)

I'M NOT YOUR LAUGHING DAUGHTER (POETRY)

I LIKE YOU TO MAKE JOKES WITH ME, BUT I DON'T WANT YOU TO TOUCH ME (FOR CHILDREN)

Laura Davis

ALLIES IN HEALING: WHEN THE PERSON YOU LOVE WAS SEXUALLY ABUSED AS A CHILD

THE COURAGE TO HEAL WORKBOOK: FOR WOMEN AND MEN SURVIVORS OF CHILD SEXUAL ABUSE

BECOMING THE PARENT YOU WANT TO BE: A SOURCEBOOK OF STRATEGIES FOR THE FIRST FIVE YEARS (WITH JANIS KEYSER)

Ellen Bass and Laura Davis

BEGINNING TO HEAL: A FIRST BOOK FOR SURVIVORS OF CHILD SEXUAL ABUSE

THE COURAGE TO HEAL

A GUIDE FOR WOMEN SURVIVORS OF CHILD SEXUAL ABUSE

Third Edition—Revised and Updated—
Featuring "Honoring the Truth:
A Response to the Backlash"

ELLEN BASS and LAURA DAVIS

HarperPerennial
A Division of HarperCollinsPublishers

Lectures and Training Seminars

Ellen Bass offers lectures for survivors and their supporters and training seminars for counselors. For a schedule of upcoming events, please write to the address below.

The authors welcome any feedback or responses to *The Courage to Heal* but regret that they are unable to answer individual letters.

> Ellen Bass and Laura Davis
> P.O. Box 5296
> Santa Cruz, CA 95063-5296

The Courage to Heal is available on audiocassette from HarperAudio, a division of Harper-Collins Publishers.

Copyright acknowledgments follow the Index.

A previous edition of this book was published in 1988 by Harper & Row, Publishers.

THE COURAGE TO HEAL (THIRD EDITION). Copyright © 1994 by Ellen Bass and Laura Davis. All rights reserved. Printed in the United States of America. No part of this book may be used or reproduced in any manner whatsoever without written permission except in the case of brief quotations embodied in critical articles and reviews. For information address HarperCollins Publishers, Inc., 10 East 53rd Street, New York, NY 10022.

HarperCollins books may be purchased for educational, business, or sales promotional use. For information, please write: Special Markets Department, HarperCollins Publishers, Inc., 10 East 53rd Street, New York, NY 10022.

FIRST EDITION

Designed by Laura Hough

Library of Congress Cataloging-in-Publication Data

Bass, Ellen.
    The courage to heal / Ellen Bass, Laura Davis.—3rd ed.
      p. cm.
    Includes bibliographical references and index.
    ISBN 0-06-095066-8
    1. Child molesting—United States. 2. Women—United States—Psychology. 3. Adult child abuse victims—United States. I. Davis, Laura. II. Title.
HQ72.U53B37 1994
616.85′822390651—dc20   93-48353

---

    04 05 06 DT/RRD 30 29 28

CONTENTS

Don't run away from it. Don't bury it. Don't try to produce a different reality getting all strung out on something, or eating your way through your feelings. Don't slash your wrists. Just deal with it, because it's going to keep coming back if you continue living anyway. It's painful, but you just have to keep going. It's just part of life, really.

—Soledad, 28-year-old survivor

Give as much commitment to healing as you did to surviving for the last ten or fifteen years.

—Dorianne, 35-year-old survivor

There's more than anger, more than sadness, more than terror. There's hope.

—Edith Horning, 46-year-old survivor

ACKNOWLEDGMENTS

We would like to thank the hundreds of survivors and partners who answered our ads, returned our calls, and shared their stories with us. We are also grateful to the participants in Ellen's workshops who generously allowed us to tell their stories and describe their struggles. Their courage and determination inspired us and deepened our own commitment. This book would not exist without them.

There are many people who've provided invaluable assistance to us in completing this project. Together, we'd like to thank:

Janet Goldstein, our editor at Harper & Row, for her incredible support, brilliance, dedication, and her unwavering belief in this book from the beginning.

Katherine Ness, production editor extraordinaire, whose care, thoughtfulness, and attention went beyond the call of duty; Laura Hough, whose creative attention to design made for a beautiful book; and to our literary agent, Charlotte Raymond, for her ongoing encouragement and support.

Sandra Butler, Lucy Diggs, Jeanne Mayer Freebody, Dorothy Morales, Nona Olivia, Kay Slagle, and Daniel Sonkin for their invaluable criticism of the manuscript as a whole. And Lucy Diggs for extensive line editing, and for cooking a fine Christmas dinner.

Lola Atkins, Janet Bryer, Jesse Burgess, Mariah Burton-Nelson, Pandora Carpenter, Lauren Crux, Carol Anne Dwight, Rashama Khalethia, Edith Kieffer, Ellen Lacroix, Donna Maimes, Wendy Maryott-Wilhelms, Rose Z. Moonwater, Pat Pavlat, Amy Pine, Robin Roberts, Helen Resneck-Sannes, Ariel Ellen Shayn, Roger Slagle, Deborah Stone, and Karen Zelin for their careful reading of portions of the manuscript.

Kristina Peterson, Margaret Hill, Pat Saliba, and Emily Joy Hixson, Laura's housemates, for love and patience all those days when Ellen slept in the living room and the dining room table was piled with papers.

Among the survivors we'd like to thank for their contributions are: Janice Avila, Rachel Bat Or, Shelley Bennet, Eileen Daly, Natalie Devora, Martha Elliott, Jill Fainberg, Ely Fuller, Ann Marie Godwin, Jayne Habe, Barbara Hamilton, Margaret Hawthorn, Rashama Khalethia, Edith Kieffer, Krishnabai, Dorianne Laux, Jennierose Lavender, Suzanne Leib, Cristin Lindstrom, Julie Martchenke, Erin May, Sharrin Michael, Janet Hanks Morehouse, Nina Newington, Kathleen O'Bannon and her daughter Maureen Davidson, Lynn Slade, Kay Slagle, Catherine Stifter, Teresa Strong, Josie Villalpando, and Diana Wood.

Others whose contributions have helped along the way: Jane Ariel, Beth Beurkens, Diana Bryce, Judy Butler, Don Cotton, Gabby Donnell, Linda Eberth, Sandi Gallant, Diane Hugs, Adrianne Chang Kwong, Julie Robbins, Kathleen Rose, Sue Saperstein, Theresa Tollini, Donna Warnock, Mary Williams, and Linda Wilson.

The Fessenden Educational Fund, for help with expenses.

Ellen Bass

I have received such abundant encouragement and support that I can't name everyone, but I would particularly like to thank:

All the workshop participants who taught me what survivors need in order to heal.

Mildred Bass, my mother, for giving me the wholehearted love and commitment every child deserves. And Sarah Wolpert, her mother, for giving that to her. So much of

what I have to give to survivors I received from them.

Josephine Clayton, for being a second mother to me, when I needed one very much.

Pat Pavlat, my therapist, for being a model of excellence. And for inspiring me to climb Angel's Landing.

Florence Howe, for teaching me the basics of facilitating groups: respect for each person's feelings and thoughts. And for opening so many doors.

Marty Bridges, for promoting the first I Never Told Anyone workshops; Pam Mitchell, for bringing them to Boston; and Becky Northcutt, for bringing it all back home.

Susan Bass, for vigorously encouraging me to write this book, against all my protestations.

Laura Davis, for pushing me past what I thought were my limits.

Saraswati Bryer-Bass, for making me care so much.

And Janet Bryer, for loving my eccentricities instead of my virtues and for teaching me to fool around.

Laura Davis

Writing my first book on an issue of such deep and personal significance has been possible only because of the tremendous love and support I have received. I'd like to thank:

Karen Zelin for being everything a best friend should be, Natalie Devora for many kinds of sustenance, Barbara Cymrot, Dafna Wu, and Ruby for being family, Nona Olivia for humor, encouragement, and wisdom, Aurora Levins Morales for cooking me duck and telling me to write, Roberta Rutkin for teaching me to honor my creativity.

Janet Bryer and Saraswati Bryer-Bass

for patience, love, countless wonderful meals, and always making me feel at home.

Abe Davis, my father, for creative inspiration, his quick wit, and most of all his unyielding faith in me.

Linda Eberth for teaching me that healing was possible, even for me.

Dagny Adamson, Marcy Alancraig, Ophelia Balderrama, Theresa Carilli, Kimberly Jane Carter, Lynn Chadwick, Diane Costa, Carol Anne Dwight, Brandy Eiger, Toke Hoppenbrouwers, Diane Hugs, Shama Khalethia, Wendy Maryott-Wilhelms, Helen Mayer, Jennifer Meyer, Nina Newington, Kathleen Rose, Paula Ross, Jane Scolieri, Ray Gwyn Smith, Catherine Stifter, Deborah Stone, and Cheryl Wade for friendship, encouragement, and belief in this project.

Irena Klepfisz, Sandy Boucher, and Tillie Olsen for inspiration, wisdom, and encouraging me to write.

Rick Eckel, Alan Burton, and all the reporters at *Youth News* for patience and flexibility.

Dorothy Morales for wisdom and generosity.

Melanie Joshua for helping me stay in my body.

And finally my coauthor, Ellen Bass, for a million things, but mostly for changing her mind and saying yes.

ACKNOWLEDGMENTS FOR THE THIRD EDITION

This third edition of *The Courage to Heal* would not have been possible without the generous help of the following people:

Our irreplaceable and irreverent research assistant, Shana Ross, for whom no job was too big—or too small.

Our editor, Janet Goldstein, for her commitment to ensuring that *The Courage to Heal* continues to address the needs of survivors with integrity.

Our agent, Charlotte Raymond, for her encouragement, advocacy, and dedication.

Our colleagues at *Moving Forward*, Lana Lawrence, Linda Palmer, and Susan Neill, for their hard work and willingness to make "Honoring the Truth" available prior to its publication here.

Our readers, whose careful critique of "Honoring the Truth" informed our thinking and infused our work with their collective wisdom: Sherry Anderson, Kathy Barbini, Sandra Butler, Christine Courtois, Abram Davis, Jill Freeland, Denise Gaul, Evelyn Hall, Mary Harvey, Judith Herman, Leslie Ingram, Jaimee Karroll, Richard Kluft, Dan Lobovits, Teri Ray, Shauna Smith, Maxine Stein, Mary Tash, Ellie Waxman, and Judy Wilbur-Albertson. Special thanks to the Dayenu Club—Lucy Diggs, Jennifer Freyd, Barb Jackson, Lana Lawrence, Susan Frankel, Larry Klein, Karen Olio, Nona Olivia, Anna Salter, Margot Silk-Forrest, and Roland Summit—who not only read the manuscript but shared their time and knowledge in countless other ways.

Many others contributed time, information, and resources: Brian Abbott, Patricia Alexander Weston, John Backus, Mary Jo Barrett, Pamela Birrell, Laurie Braga, John Briere, Jennifer Carnes, Teri Cosentino, Renee Fredrickson, Gail Gans, Faye Gorman, Jaime Guerrero, Cory Hammond, Val Hartouni, Lisa Lipshires, Elizabeth Loftus, Màiri Mc Fall, Chrystine McCracken, Kee McFarlane, Rebecca Northcutt, Jackie Ortega,

Sherri Paris, Judith Peterson, John Rhead, Margo Ross, Lynne Sansevero, Mark Schwartz, Jane Sinclair, Gary Stickel, Gayle Stringer, Patricia Toth, Heidi Vanderbilt, Charlotte Watson, and Linda Meyer Williams.

We also thank our partners, Janet Bryer and Karyn Bristol, for their love and moral support.

For the math we couldn't do ourselves, we thank Saraswati Bryer-Bass and Chantalle von der Zande.

And for loving care of baby Eli so Laura could go back to work, Laurel Wanner.

PREFACE TO THE THIRD EDITION

When we began work on *The Courage to Heal* in 1984, the climate for survivors of child sexual abuse was dramatically different than it is today. There was little understanding about the process of healing from child sexual abuse. There were few support groups or therapists knowledgeable about treating abuse. When survivors did disclose their abuse, they were most frequently met with denial, minimization, or blame.

An awareness of sexual abuse was dawning, but little real help or hope was available for those who'd suffered from it. There was just a staggering need. We wrote *The Courage to Heal* to offer survivors practical, empowering first-hand information and to provide respectful, compassionate guidance through the healing process.

We chose to avoid academic language, psychological theories, and statistics; in the tradition of speak-outs for rape victims, we wanted women to tell their own stories. By reading the words of other women who had been there, survivors gained inspiration and strength. They learned they were not alone, they were not to blame, and that healing was possible.

In the six years since its publication, we've heard from survivors around the world describing what *The Courage to Heal* has meant to them:

I've been in treatment since I was six. I've been in mental hospitals. I've been given shock treatments. I've been on meds. I've seen counselors up the wazoo, but [your book] is the first real help I've ever received.

At times, I've simply sat holding your book knowing that at last someone understands how I feel inside.

If you had written *The Courage to Heal* only for me, it would have been worth every hour, every tear, every frustration, every effort you have put forth.

The Courage to Heal has saved my life—literally.

For the first four years after its publication in 1988, *The Courage to Heal* was not considered controversial. Then suddenly in 1992, with the emergence of a highly publicized backlash against survivors, *The Courage to Heal* was among the individuals, groups, and books targeted for attack. As the most visible self-help resource for survivors, it was blamed for inducing "false memories," tearing families apart, and creating a climate of "hysteria" around child sexual abuse.

As authors, we have been criticized for our lack of academic credentials. But you do not have to have a Ph.D. to listen carefully and compassionately to another human being. In fact, our perspective as laypeople helped us to take the suffering of survivors out of the realm of pathology—and instead to present them as strong, capable people who'd been hurt.

In light of the criticism the book has received, we're frequently asked, "If you were going to write *The Courage to Heal* today, what would you change?" Actually, there are a number of changes we would make, but ironically, most of them don't have to do with the things we've been criticized for.

The Courage to Heal is, and has always been, in the process of evolution. Since its initial publication we have continually made changes—deleting outdated information, clarifying and incorporating new material based on feedback from our readers, and up-

dating the Resource Guide. The book has been strengthened by everyone who has taken the time to share insights, information, and suggestions.

If we were writing *The Courage to Heal* today, the biggest change we'd make is that we wouldn't write the book just for women. It has become clear that boys are also sexually abused in large numbers. Although *The Courage to Heal* does not specifically address male survivors, we are glad that many men have found it to be helpful in their healing.*

If we had known then what we know today, we would have included more stories of women abusers as well. Ten years ago we thought almost all abusers were men. Now we know that substantial numbers of survivors have been abused by women—and it is essential that their experiences be acknowledged.

We would have included more examples of milder abuse—abuse that is covert and harder to identify. And we would have included more about sibling incest, as well as examples of sexual abuse by clergy, counselors, doctors, and other helping professionals.

If we could have foreseen that therapists might someday assume abuse where there wasn't any, we would have included a caution about that in our guidelines for choosing a counselor. In this edition, we stress that you are the expert in your own life. Ultimately, no one else can tell you whether or not you were abused—not your therapist, not your parents, not your friends or your partner or *The Courage to Heal.* You are the one who

---

* A special section of the Resource Guide includes resources for male survivors. See p. 557.

must struggle to know and understand your history. As we advise in our chapter on choosing a counselor:

> If you feel your therapist is pressuring you to say that you were abused, you're seeing the wrong therapist. . . . Find someone who will follow your lead, not insist they know your final destination.*

There are other changes we have made in language and emphasis. We have modified some of the statements we originally made, in part because of legitimate criticisms. For example, in the original edition, we said:

> So far, no one we've talked to thought she might have been abused, and then later discovered that she hadn't been. The progression always goes the other way, from suspicion to confirmation. If you think you were abused and your life shows the symptoms, then you were.

Since writing that statement, we have talked to a small number of women who thought they might have been sexually abused but who found, after much exploration, that the pain they were suffering resulted from emotional abuse or other early trauma. In this edition, we have written instead:

> It is rare that someone thinks she was sexually abused and then later discovers she wasn't. The progression usu-

ally goes the other way, from suspicion to confirmation. If you genuinely think you were abused and your life shows the symptoms, there's a strong likelihood that you were. If you're not sure, keep an open mind. Be patient with yourself. Over time, you'll become more clear.†

We have rewritten our introduction to "Effects," in which we discuss the long-term effects of sexual abuse. This chapter was never designed to be a checklist of symptoms by which readers could determine whether or not they'd been sexually abused. In this edition, we've clarified our intention.

We've also added further information to the chapters "Remembering," "Believing It Happened," "Families of Origin," and "Counseling," as well as other small revisions elsewhere.

Because the original guidelines for counselors were so basic and there is now so much excellent information available, we decided to eliminate the section "For Counselors" and instead to provide a bibliography for professionals in the Resource Guide.

The Resource Guide has once again been updated, reflecting the abundant services, organizations, support groups, and books available to survivors and their advocates. We've also improved the Index.

And we've included two new voices in the section called "Courageous Women": a scientist who's a survivor of sadistic ritual abuse and a nineteen-year-old college student whose experience in the court system, in a women's hospital, and in a group home

---

* See p. 325.

† See p. 26.

reflects both the progress we've made and the distance we have yet to go.

The greatest change is the addition of a new section, "Honoring the Truth," in which we analyze the current backlash against survivors and their supporters, placing these attacks in a historical and political perspective. We present relevant research on memory and address the controversy over sadistic ritual abuse. We offer guidelines for survivors who are confused about their memories or angry about the current climate of disbelief in survivors' stories. Finally, we suggest future directions for moving forward in a positive and respectful way.

For those of you new to *The Courage to Heal*, we want to emphasize a truth that will hold fast regardless of any changes in the social and political climate: If you were sexually abused as a child, you can not only heal but thrive. In the years since *The Courage to Heal* was first published, hundreds of thousands of survivors have succeeded in creating lives rich with meaning, joy, and self-acceptance. The rewards of healing are available to you too.

—Ellen Bass and Laura Davis
January 1994

PREFACE TO THE FIRST EDITION

Ellen Bass

I first heard that children were abused in 1974, when a young woman in my creative writing workshop pulled a crumpled half-sheet of paper out of her jeans pocket. Her writing was so vague, so tentative, that I wasn't sure what she was trying to say, but I sensed that it was important. Gently, I encouraged her to write more. Slowly she revealed her story. In pieces, on bits of paper, she shared the pain of her father's assaults, and I listened.*

Shortly afterward, another woman told me her story. And then another. And another. There were no groups for survivors of child sexual abuse then. The word "survivor" was not yet in our vocabulary. But as they sensed that I could understand their stories, more and more women shared them with me. The psychologist Carl Rogers once said that when he worked through an issue in his life, it was as if telegrams were sent to his clients informing them that they could now bring that subject to therapy. Once I became aware of child sexual abuse, it was as if women knew that I was safe to talk to.

I was stunned by the number of women who had been sexually abused. I was deeply moved by the anguish they had endured. And I was equally impressed by their integrity, their ability to love and create through such devastation. I wanted people to know about this, about their strength and their beauty.

In 1978, three months after my first child was born, five women from my work-

---

* This woman, Maggie Hoyal, went on to become a fine writer, and her story, "These Are the Things I Remember," is included in *I Never Told Anyone* (see the Resource Guide).

17

shops and I began collecting stories for *I Never Told Anyone: Writings by Women Survivors of Child Sexual Abuse.* By 1983, when it was published, I had learned a great deal about the healing process. One of the things I learned was that writing itself was healing.

I decided to offer a group for survivors and designed the I Never Told Anyone workshops. I tried to create an environment safe enough for women to face their own pain and anger so they could begin to heal. At the first workshop, I mainly listened. I wanted to learn what survivors needed to talk about, what they needed to hear. Women wrote about their experience of being sexually abused, and read what they had written to the group. The simple opportunity to share with other survivors was profoundly healing.

The women who came to the workshops had no historical reason to trust. As children they had learned that their trust would be taken advantage of. And yet in the groups, they trusted.

This book, like the workshops, is based on the premise that everyone wants to become whole, to fulfill their potential. That we all, like seedlings or tadpoles, intend to become our full selves and will do so if we are not thwarted. People don't need to be forced to grow. All we need is favorable circumstances: respect, love, honesty, and the space to explore.

Since I began the I Never Told Anyone workshops, I have worked with hundreds of survivors across the country. I've facilitated workshops for partners of survivors and offered training seminars for professionals who work with survivors. I have solidified my understanding of what it takes to heal from child sexual abuse. This is the knowledge I want to share with you here.

I am not academically educated as a psychologist. I have acquired counseling skills primarily through practice. Since 1970, when I began working as a counselor and group facilitator, I've had the opportunity to train with a number of excellent therapists. But none of what is presented here is based on psychological theories. The process described, the suggestions, the exercises, the analysis, the conclusions, all come from the experiences of survivors.

I am also the partner of a survivor. In the beginning of our relationship we struggled with issues of trust, intimacy, and sexuality common to many couples and exacerbated by the effects of sexual abuse. Now, several years later, the problems that caused us both such anguish are no longer wrenching. Sexual abuse no longer overshadows our relationship. I want to tell you this because when you are in the thick of the pain, it's hard to believe that it will ever change. Yet it does. And it does not take forever.

As my grandmother used to say, "No one gets cheated from trouble." I was not sexually abused as a child, but I too have had pain to heal from. In the three years since beginning this book, I have made major personal changes. I live in the same house, with the same family, doing the same work. But I am not the same. Inspired by the survivors I worked with, I followed their example. Slowly, repetitively, step-by-step, little by little, my old fears, my desperate places, my limiting ways of coping, have receded. After saying "Healing is possible" to hundreds of survivors, it occurred to me that it was possible for me too.

Sometimes people ask, "Don't you find it depressing always to be thinking about child sexual abuse?" But I don't think so much about the abuse. I think about the healing. The opportunity to be a part of women's healing feels a little like assisting at a birth. It's awesome to touch the miracle of life so closely. When women trust me with their most vulnerable, tender feelings, I am aware that I hold their spirit, for that moment, in my hands, and I am both honored and thrilled.

I want to see us all become whole—and not stop there. As we become capable of nurturing ourselves and living rich personal lives, we are enabled to act creatively in the world so that life can continue—the eucalyptus trees, the narcissus, the sunfish, the squirrels, seals, hummingbirds, our own children.

—*Ellen Bass*

Laura Davis

I remember calling Ellen one day a few months after I'd first remembered the incest. I counted the rings—two, three, four—she had to be home! She had to be! Five, six, seven—if I didn't talk to her right now, I knew I couldn't last through the afternoon. Eight, nine, ten—well, maybe she was outside folding the laundry and was just slow getting to the phone. Eleven, twelve, thirteen—I cannot stand another moment of this pain. My heart hurts and I can't take anymore. Fourteen, fifteen . . .

"Hello, this is Ellen," she said, cheery and calm.

"Ellen, this is Laura. Look, you've got to tell me just one thing. Will I ever get through this? Is there ever an end? I can't take it anymore, and if you'll just tell me I can get to the other side, I'm sure I can last through the week." I was talking fast, my sentences piling up on each other.

"Hello, Laura. I'm glad you called." Her voice was smooth, reassuring. "And yes, you can make it. Healing is possible. You're already well on your way."

"Well on my way? How can you say that? I can't sleep, and when I do, it's all I dream about. I can't think about anything else. Every child I see on the street reminds me of incest. I can't make love, I can't eat, my whole body feels like a giant piece of rubber. I'm crying all the time. My whole life is flashbacks, going to therapy, and talking about incest. Half the time I don't even believe it happened, and the other half I'm sure it was my fault."

"It did happen, Laura. Look at what you're going through. Would anyone willingly choose to go through this torture? Why would you ever want to invent something this bad? You were just a little girl, Laura. He was what—seventy years old? You were a victim. You were innocent. You didn't do anything. It wasn't your fault."

Over and over, Ellen repeated those simple phrases: "It wasn't your fault. I believe you. Healing is possible. You're going to make it. You're going to be okay."

I expressed every doubt I could think of. Then I made up some new ones. I knew other survivors didn't make up this sort of thing, but I was the exception. I'd always been the exception, all my life.

"You can fight it all you want, Laura," she said finally, "but the door's been opened, and you're in the healing process whether you like it or not."

There was a long silence. Then I said, "Isn't there any way out?"

"The only way out is through, honey, I'm sorry."

I was quiet for a long time. "But it hurts, Ellen. It hurts so much."

"I know, Laura. I know. But there's a way through this stuff, and I know you're going to find it."

I wanted to write this book for probably the same reasons you are picking it up now—I felt a tremendous amount of pain in my life, and I wanted it to stop. Six months before I approached Ellen about collaborating, I had my first memories of being sexually abused by my grandfather when I was a child. Since that time, my life had fallen apart. My lover was leaving me. I was becoming increasingly estranged from my family. I was sure I was going crazy. I needed to understand what was happening to me. I needed to talk to other women who had been through it. Out of that need, my desire to write this book was born.

During the first year of our collaboration, it was my task to gather other women's stories. Ellen and I placed ads in papers, wrote to the women who'd come to her workshops, put out the call by word of mouth. I screened hundreds of calls and spent days on the phone listening to the stories of survivors, some of whom had never told anyone about their abuse before they read our ad, saw our poster.

Even though many of the women I interviewed had been actively healing for years, our conversations were never easy. One woman came to my house with a bag of food and ate from it for the whole three hours we talked. Another had to get stoned to tell me her story. A third burned sage and cedar, cleansing the room to make it safe. Sometimes the women cried. Sometimes we both did.

The honesty and courage of these women continually gave me hope. When I found it impossible to make love because of flashbacks, I'd ask a woman I was interviewing how she had healed her sexuality. When I started to wish I could shove the memories back where they came from, a woman would tell me that healing was the greatest miracle in her life.

As the months went by and the number of interviews grew, it became clear that there were tremendous similarities in the stories. The black ex-nun from Boston and the ambassador's daughter from Manila described the stages of their healing process the same way. A pattern started to emerge. What I was going through made sense.

As I moved along in my own healing, my relationship to the book changed. The acuteness of my own needs began to fade. It became increasingly important for me to communicate what I was learning. I began to talk more freely about the book with people I met. Within the first few minutes of any conversation, I'd be asked why I was writing it, and it would all be out on the table: "Because I'm a survivor myself."

Many people quickly changed the conversation or turned away. But an astonishing number responded with stories of their own: "It happened to me too." "My best friend says her swimming coach used to touch her." "My neighbor's kid reported her father just last week."

There are many phases involved in writing a book. For me, they have felt just like the stages of the healing process. With each new juncture I'd freeze, certain that I couldn't possibly jump over the next hurdle. I couldn't confront my family. I couldn't begin to write. Then I'd take that first terrifying step forward, and be set in motion again.

Throughout the first year, I wrote nothing about my own experience as a survivor. Ellen began the first draft while I kept busy transcribing and editing the interviews. Underneath, I knew that this book was as much about my life as it was about theirs, but I successfully avoided the inevitable moment when I, too, would have to speak my truth.

I remember the day very clearly. It started with a sentence I came across in one of Ellen's drafts. I was lying on the floor of her living room, reading through "Disclosures and Confrontations" with a red marker in my hand. Ellen was explaining the fact that family members may be sympathetic when first told about sexual abuse, only to turn on the survivor later on. She had used me as her example:

When Laura told her mother about the incest, her mother's first reaction was to send her one of her favorite nightgowns, so that Laura would be comforted; but after she'd thought about it for a while, she called Laura back and she said . . .

After that, Ellen had left a blank. She'd forgotten the exact content of the call.

When I read what she had written, my breakfast curled up into a tight little ball in my stomach. I started to tremble, and then I started to sweat. Anxiety shot from my stomach straight through my head. The fact that I was writing a book about my experiences in healing from incest could no longer be denied, abstracted, placed in a vague never-never land. There was the sentence, clear as day. "This is about me! This is about my life. That's *my* mother she's talking about."

"You'll have to rewrite that part," Ellen said with studied casualness. "It'll be much better in the first person."

I picked up the manuscript, and I crossed out the "Lauras." It wasn't easy to do it because I was holding my breath and my hand was shaking. Every time the word "Laura" appeared, I substituted the word "I." And whenever I saw the word "her," I put in

"my." Then I finished the sentence. When I was done, it read:

When I called my mother and told her I had remembered the incest, her first reaction was to tell me she loved me and supported me. She had an old favorite nightgown. It was cotton, well loved and broken in. She said she was going to send it to me in the mail, so I'd have something that smelled like her, since she couldn't be with me to comfort me in person.

A week after the nightgown arrived, my mother called me at four in the morning, waking me out of a sound sleep. She was screaming: "I've been up all night, and you're going to be up all night too! My father would never have done anything like that! You're just making this up to destroy me! You've just jumped on the incest bandwagon. You've always been into the 'in' thing. It's all because you're a lesbian. You all hate men. You all hate your families. You just want to kill me! You couldn't have done anything worse if you'd shot me."

The words flew out in a torrent, filling the whole side margin and curving around into all the available space at the top of the page. They wavered before my eyes, a field of red. "I did it," I said to Ellen, my voice high and tight. "Wanna hear it?"

"Sure," she said. "What have you got?"

I read it to her. She pretended not to notice the tremor in my voice. "Sounds better," she said. "Sounds a whole lot better."

For days after I wrote those words, I lived in a state of raw, unparalleled terror. I became convinced that Ellen did not really want to write the book with me. It was clear the whole collaboration was going to fall through. There was a conspiracy against me. Every day my anxiety increased, more and more out of proportion.

It wasn't until my friend Aurora, who is a very wise writer, invited me over for roast duck, fed me, soothed me and listened to me, that I quieted down enough to hear her say, over and over, in a hundred different ways, "Yes, Laura, it seems that you and Ellen will have to talk, *but what about those sentences you wrote?*"

It's been my experience that every time the subject of incest comes up in any kind of personal way, I reexperience the terror I felt as a child being abused. It's the same terror I saw in the faces of the women I interviewed when we finally sat down, small talk and tea finished, and I nudged them, my voice gentle: "What happened to you?" It's the fear I've seen flash across the faces of other women who ask what my work is, and who cannot bear to speak to me once they've heard the answer. It's the terror that's silenced us.

This book has been a way for me to break silence. But it has been more than that. It has been a steady source of inspiration and amazement for the past two and a half years. It has taught me that it is possible to take something that hurt me so deeply and turn it around. I hope it teaches you the same.

—*Laura Davis*

INTRODUCTION: HEALING IS POSSIBLE

He pulled his hand out of my pants and spit on his fingers and rubbed them together. He didn't even seem aware of me. The sound of his spitting made me sick. Then he put his hand back down my pants and started to say something in that singing voice he used.

The front screen door slammed and his hand ripped out of my pants like it was burned. Then he turned on me and whispered harshly, "Don't you say anything to your mother ever. If you do, you'll be sorrier than you've ever been in your life."

—Maggie Hoyal, from "These Are the Things I Remember"

I can't scream, I can't speak, I can't breathe. My mouth, my whole face aches from his thrusts. I cannot see him, only huge arms, only dark brown hair around a wet red penis, pushing and pushing. I kick at the chair. I scratch his arms and skin comes off in my nails. He laughs, pressing harder, pushing his penis down my throat. Kiss it, kiss it.

—Experience Gibbs, from "1952, and Other Years"

Then one afternoon when I was just waking up from a nap, he sat next to me on the side of the bed. He put his big heavy fingers in my pants and began rubbing my clitoris. I had no idea what he was trying to do. He asked, yet sort of told me, "It feels good, doesn't it?" All I knew was I couldn't say no. I felt powerless to move. I said Yes.

—Karen Asherah, from "Daddy Kanagy" *

If you have been sexually abused, you are not alone. One out of three girls, and one out of seven boys, are sexually abused by the time they reach the age of eighteen. Sexual abuse happens to children of every class, culture, race, religion, and gender. Children are abused by fathers, stepfathers, uncles, brothers, grandparents, neighbors, family friends, baby-sitters, teachers, strangers, and sometimes by aunts and mothers.† Although women do abuse, the majority of abusers are heterosexual men.

All sexual abuse is damaging, and the trauma does not end when the abuse stops. If you were abused as a child, you are probably experiencing long-term effects that interfere with your day-to-day functioning.

However, it is possible to heal. It is even possible to thrive. Thriving means more than just an alleviation of symptoms, more than band-aids, more than functioning adequately. Thriving means enjoying a feeling of wholeness, satisfaction in your life and work, genuine love and trust in your relationships, pleasure in your body.

Until now, much of the literature on child sexual abuse has documented the ravages of abuse, talking extensively about "the tragedy of ruined lives," but little about recovery. This book is about recovery—what it takes, what it feels like, how it can transform your life.

People say "time heals all wounds," and it's true to a certain extent. Time will dull some of the pain, but deep healing doesn't happen unless you consciously choose it. Healing from child sexual abuse takes years of commitment and dedication. But if you are willing to work hard, if you are determined to make lasting changes in your life, if you are able to find good resources and skilled support, you can not only heal but thrive. We believe in miracles and hard work.

---

* All quotes are from Ellen Bass and Louise Thornton, eds., *I Never Told Anyone: Writings by Women Survivors of Child Sexual Abuse* (New York: Harper & Row, 1983).

† For sources on the scope of child sexual abuse, see the "About Sexual Abuse" section on p. 545 of the Resource Guide. A number of these books cite recent studies to which you can refer for more complete statistics.

HOW CAN I KNOW IF I WAS A VICTIM OF CHILD SEXUAL ABUSE?

When you were a young child or teenager, were you:

- Fondled, kissed, or held for an adult's sexual gratification?
- Forced to perform oral sex on an adult or sibling?
- Raped or otherwise penetrated?
- Made to watch sexual acts?
- Forced to listen to excessive talk about sex?
- Fondled or hurt genitally while being bathed?
- Subjected to unnecessary medical treatments to satisfy an adult's sadistic or sexual needs?
- Shown sexual movies or other pornography?
- Made to pose for seductive or sexual photographs?
- Involved in child prostitution or pornography?*
- Forced to take part in ritualized abuse in which you were physically, psychologically, or sexually tortured?

---

* Between 500,000 and 1,000,000 children are involved in prostitution and pornography in this country; a high percentage of them are victims of incest. See *Sex Work: Writings by Women in the Industry,* edited by Frédérique Dellacoste and Priscilla Alexander (Pittsburgh: Cleis Press, 1987).

Some people are unable to remember any specific instances like the ones mentioned above but still have a strong feeling that something abusive happened to them. (See "But I Don't Remember," page 26).

Women who come to Ellen's workshops are often afraid that their abuse wasn't bad enough for them to be qualified to participate. They will say, "It wasn't incest—it was just a friend of the family," or "I was fourteen and it only happened once," or "He just showed me movies," or "It was with my brother. He was only a year older than me."

Such statements are a measure of the gross minimizing of abuse done in our society.

The fact that someone else has suffered from abuse more severe than your own does not lessen your suffering. Comparisons of pain are simply not useful.

There are many ways of minimizing sexual abuse. A particularly offensive one is to claim that if a man didn't force his penis into some opening of your body, you weren't really violated. This is not true. The severity of abuse should not be defined in terms of male genitals. Violation is determined by your experience as a child—your body, your feelings, your spirit. The precise physical acts are not always the most damaging aspects of abuse. Although forcible rape is physically excruciating to a small child, many kinds of sexual abuse are not physically painful. They do not leave visible scars.

Some abuse is not even physical. Your father may have stood in the bathroom doorway, making suggestive remarks or simply leering when you entered to use the toilet. Your uncle may have walked around naked, calling attention to his penis, talking about his sexual exploits, questioning you about your body. Your tennis coach may have badgered you into telling him exactly what you did with your boyfriend. There are many ways to be violated sexually.

There is also abuse on the psychological level. You had the feeling your stepfather was aware of your physical presence every minute of the day, no matter how quiet and unobtrusive you were. Your neighbor watched your changing body with an intrusive interest. Your father took you out on romantic dates and wrote you love letters.

Nor is frequency of abuse what's at issue. Betrayal takes only a minute. A father can slip his fingers into his daughter's underpants in thirty seconds. After that the world is not the same.

BUT I DON'T REMEMBER

Children often cope with abuse by forgetting it ever happened. As a result, you may have no conscious memory of being abused. You may have forgotten large chunks of your childhood. Yet there are things you do remember. When you are touched in a certain way, you feel nauseated. Certain words or facial expressions scare you. You know you never liked your mother to touch you. You slept with your clothes on in junior high school. You were taken to the doctor repeatedly for vaginal infections.

You may think you don't have memories, but often as you begin to talk about what you do remember, there emerges a constellation of feelings, reactions, and recollections that add up to substantial information. To say "I was abused," you don't need the kind of proof that would stand up in a court of law.

Often the knowledge that you were abused starts with a tiny feeling, an intuition. It's important to trust that inner voice and work from there. Assume your feelings are valid. It is rare that someone thinks she was abused and then discovers she wasn't. The progression usually goes the other way, from suspicion to confirmation. If you genuinely think you were abused and your life shows the symptoms, there's a strong likelihood that you were. If you're not sure, keep an open mind. Be patient with yourself. Over time, you'll become more clear.

GETTING SUPPORT

No matter how committed you are, it is extremely difficult to heal from child sexual abuse in isolation. Much of the damage experienced is the result of the secrecy and silence that surrounded the abuse. Trying to heal while perpetuating that lonely silence is nearly impossible.

It is essential that you have at least one other person with whom you can share your pain and your healing. That person may be another survivor, a member of a support group, or a counselor. He or she could be a nurturing partner or family member, or a sibling who was also abused. Ideally, you will have a combination of many resources. (For help in finding support, see "Counseling," page 321.)

WHERE ARE YOU NOW?

You may be reading this book at any point in the healing process. You may not yet have identified yourself as a survivor. You may be just starting to make the connection between sexual abuse and its effects in your life. On the other hand, you may be years into an active healing process. Or you may simply want an affirmation of how far you've come. This book can provide specific suggestions, support, and validation no matter where you are in the healing process.

WHAT READING THIS BOOK WILL BE LIKE

Reading this book can be a cathartic healing experience. As you begin to realize that your life makes sense, and that you are not the only one who has suffered, you may experience a tremendous feeling of relief. But relief is not the only response you may have.

In the course of writing this book, we shared parts of the manuscript with many survivors. In response, women have gone out and confronted abusers, renewed their commitment to heal, or shared honestly with their partner for the first time. Some have had breakthroughs in their sexuality. Others have stopped blaming themselves.

Women have also reported feeling terrified, furious, and anguished. Others have connected with forgotten pockets of grief and pain. Women reported having nightmares, flashbacks, new memories. One survivor, a recovering alcoholic, began to crave alcohol as she read. Another woman began fighting with her lover. Several went back to therapy. All said their lives were changed.

If you have unfamiliar or uncomfortable feelings as you read this book, don't be alarmed. Strong feelings are part of the healing process. On the other hand, if you breeze through these chapters, you probably aren't feeling safe enough to confront these issues. Or you may be coping with the book the same way you coped with the abuse—by separating your intellect from your feelings. If that's the case, stop, take a break, talk to someone for support, and come back to it later. It's important that you don't "bear" this book the way you bore the abuse: numb and alone. If you come to a part that stops you, you may be having a hard time with the material in that section. Don't force yourself to read it. Try a different chapter.

As you read, it's important to look inside, paying attention to your own thoughts and feelings. The idea of developing such a relationship with yourself may be foreign to you. As women, we've been taught to meet the needs of others, that focusing on ourselves is selfish. But healing requires a willingness to put yourself first.

The other morning, when Ellen listened to the messages on her answering machine, there was one that said, "I called to let you know that I really *am* healing. And this is the sweetest feeling I have ever known—to be whole."

You deserve this feeling.

ABOUT THE STORIES IN THIS BOOK

Over two hundred survivors volunteered to be interviewed for this book. Out of these, we talked to fifty women in depth. We could not tell everyone's story in its entirety, but we have included portions of each woman's experience.

We have also included stories from the participants of the I Never Told Anyone workshops, as well as workshops for partners and for counselors. All these women and men generously gave us permission to include their experiences.

The survivors presented here represent a broad range of women. You will meet women who vary in terms of age, economic background, race, and sexual preference. Some are in committed relationships, others are single; there are mothers and nonmothers; women who were abused under different circumstances and by different perpetrators. You will read about women who are at different stages of the healing process and women whose approaches to healing have varied.

The quotes and stories included throughout this book come from survivors and the partners of survivors. Throughout the text, you will see many unidentified quotes. Each quote stands alone and represents one person's experience. Sometimes two or more survivors speak on a single page.

We chose not to place a name with every quote because it would have been unwieldy. Yet when it was essential to the story or when someone specifically asked to be identified, we did use names. We wanted to respect each person's right to choose whether they wanted to use their real name, a pseudonym, or no name at all. (For more on the use of pseudonyms, see "Names or Pseudonyms: The Right to Choose," page 363.) As authors, we also had personal experiences we wanted to share. At those times we identify ourselves by our first names.

The creative writings are primarily by survivors or supporters of survivors—partners, friends, and counselors. The others are poems we thought would have significance for survivors.

Although we've included the experiences of male partners and supporters, we chose not to address male survivors directly. Many boys are abused, and male survivors need and deserve support in their healing, but we wrote this book for women because women's experiences were what we understood best. Since most of the healing process is universal, we hope men who read this book will find it helpful. There is a growing movement of support for male survivors, and we've included some references in the "For Male Survivors" section of the Resource Guide (page 557).

USING THE
WRITING EXERCISES

In the I Never Told Anyone workshops Ellen leads for adult survivors of child sexual abuse, ten to twenty women come together in an environment of support, confidentiality, and safety to explore their feelings, mourn their violation, gather their strength, and celebrate their survival.

Participants are asked to write about being sexually abused as children. So often survivors have had their experiences denied, trivialized, or distorted. Writing is an important avenue for healing because it gives you the opportunity to define your own reality. You can say: This did happen to me. It was that bad. It was the fault and responsibility of the adult. I was—and am—innocent.

By going back and writing about what happened, you also reexperience feelings and are able to grieve. You excavate the sites in which you've buried memory and pain, dread and fury. You relive your history.

WHY WRITING?

One handy thing about writing is that it's almost always available. At three in the morning, when you're alone or you don't want to wake your partner, when your friend's out of town, when your counselor's answering machine is on and even the cat is out prowling, your journal is there. It's quiet, cheap, and portable. A journal can help you figure out how you feel, what you think, what you need, what you want to say, how you want to handle a situation, just by writing it through.

ANYONE CAN USE WRITING

Using writing as a healing tool can be helpful whether or not you participate in an organized workshop with other survivors. You don't need to think of yourself as a writer or even like to write. You may have had a limited education. Perhaps you can't spell or think you're a terrible writer.

Some survivors have special blocks associated with writing. If your mother read your private diary, if your father was an English teacher and always criticized your written work, if your best friend passed your intimate letters around the junior high school cafeteria, then you may be wary of putting words on paper. But all of us have a deep need for self-expression. Yours may take forms other than writing, but if you'd like to try writing as one method of healing, even previous blocks need not stand in the way. Many women who have been reluctant to write have done these exercises—and benefited enormously.

TIME AND PLACE

Choose a time and place where you won't be interrupted. Though it may take some arranging, you deserve such a time. Half an hour is a good actual writing time for each exercise. Although you can write for longer if you want, setting a specific time can help you feel comfortable.

Since writing about sexual abuse can bring up strong feelings, don't squeeze in your half-hour of writing time between picking the kids up from school and starting dinner. Make sure you give yourself a little time afterward to absorb the impact of the writing.

BEING HEARD

Writing itself is very helpful, but sharing what you've written is important too. After you write, read your writing to someone who will listen attentively and be responsive. *Make sure you protect yourself by not choosing anyone who will reabuse you in any way.*

If there's no one you can read to right away, read out loud to yourself—at least you will be reading to one attentive listener. Just saying the words out loud can make them more real.

If you read your writing to someone who has no experience in listening to personal writing, tell that person what you need. You may say that you'd like them not to criticize or judge what you say. You may want them to ask questions, to help you talk about it more, or you may want them simply to listen quietly. You may want comforting and you may not. People usually respond in more satisfying ways when you tell them what you want.

THE BASIC METHOD

Try to forget everything you've ever been told about writing. What you're going to do is a kind of free writing, or stream-of-consciousness writing. It's not about making art or polished crafting or trying to make sense to someone else. Rather it's a way to short-circuit some of your censors to get to what you need to say.

Write without stopping. Go at a pace that's comfortable for you, and don't stop. If you get stuck or can't think of anything to say, you can write "This is the stupidest exercise I ever heard of," or "I'm hungry—I wonder if time's up yet." One woman who was writing about her abuse stopped every few lines and wrote "I cannot say any more," and then went on to say more. Allowing herself to refuse to go on, saying no, made it possible for her to go one more step each time.

You needn't use full sentences. You needn't spell or punctuate properly. It can be in English or in another language. Sometimes if another language was spoken when you were a child you will remember in that language. If you were abused before you learned to talk, your writing may come out as baby talk.

THE WRITING EXERCISES

PART ONE
TAKING STOCK

EFFECTS: RECOGNIZING THE DAMAGE

People have said to me, "Why are you dragging this up now?" Why? WHY? Because it has controlled every facet of my life. It has damaged me in every possible way. It has destroyed everything in my life that has been of value. It has prevented me from living a comfortable emotional life. It's prevented me from being able to love clearly. It took my children away from me. I haven't been able to succeed in the world. If I had a comfortable childhood, I could be anything today. I know that everything I don't deal with now is one more burden I have to carry for the rest of my life. I don't care if it happened 500 years ago! It's influenced me all that time, and it does matter. It matters very much.

—Jennierose Lavender, 47-year-old survivor

The long-term effects of child sexual abuse can be so pervasive that it's sometimes hard to pinpoint exactly how the abuse affected you. It permeates everything: your sense of self, your intimate relationships, your sexuality, your parenting, your work life, even your sanity. Everywhere you look, you see its effects. As one survivor explained:

It's like those pictures I remember from *Highlights for Children* magazine. The bicycle was hidden in a tree, a banana was growing from someone's ear, and all the people were upside-down. The caption underneath said, "What's wrong with this picture?" But so many things were disturbed and out of place, it was often easier to say, "What's right with this picture?"

Many survivors have been too busy surviving to notice the ways they were hurt by the abuse. But you cannot heal until you acknowledge the areas that need healing.

Because sexual abuse is just one of many factors that influenced your development, it isn't always possible to isolate its effects from the other influences on your life. Is your self-esteem low because you were an African-American child raised in a racist society? Because you grew up in a culture that devalues women? Because your mother was an alcoholic? Or because you were molested when you were nine? It's the interplay of hundreds of factors that make you who you are today.

The way the abuse was handled when you were a child has a lot to do with its subsequent impact. If a child's disclosure is met with compassion and effective intervention, the healing begins immediately. But if no one noticed or responded to your pain, or if you were blamed, not believed, or suffered further trauma, the damage was compounded. And the ways you coped with the abuse may have created further problems.

Not all survivors are affected in the same way. You may do well in one area of your life, but not in another. You may be competent at work and in parenting but have trouble with intimacy. Some women have a constant nagging feeling that something is wrong. For others, the damage is so blatant that they feel they've wasted their lives:

As far as I'm concerned, my whole life was stolen from me. I didn't get to be who I could have been. I didn't get the education I should have gotten when I was young. I married too early. I hid behind my husband. I didn't make contact with other people. I haven't had a rich life. It's not ever too late, but I didn't start working on this until I was thirty-eight, and not everything can be retrieved. And that makes me very angry.

The effects of child sexual abuse can be devastating, but they do not have to be permanent. As you read this chapter, you may find yourself nodding your head—"Uh-huh, me too"—recognizing, perhaps for the first time, the ways in which the abuse affects your life. Look at the following lists and ask yourself how you've been affected. Such recognition will probably be painful, but it is, in fact, part of the healing process.

When we ask "Where are you now?" we describe the range of effects that survivors of child sexual abuse experience; this is to help you look honestly at the impact of abuse on your life today. The lists are not a diagnostic tool and are not intended to serve as a way to determine whether or not you've been sexually abused.

Some of the effects of child sexual abuse are quite specific—such as intrusive images of the abuse while making love. Others are more general—such as low self-esteem or difficulty in expressing feelings—and can be caused by circumstances or events other than child sexual abuse. It is important to be aware that physical and emotional abuse can also lead to many of the symptoms listed here.

If you recognize your own problems in the following lists but are unsure whether you were sexually abused, don't feel you need to label yourself as a survivor before you're ready. Take care of yourself. Get support. Work on healing from the experiences you're sure of. And trust that over time your history will become more clear.

SELF-ESTEEM AND
PERSONAL POWER

When you were abused, your boundaries, your right to say no, your sense of control in the world, were violated. You were powerless. The abuse humiliated you, gave you the message that you were of little value. Nothing you did could stop it.

If you told someone about what was happening to you, they probably ignored you, said you made it up, or told you to forget it. They may have blamed you. Your reality was denied or twisted and you felt crazy. Rather than see the abuser or your parents as bad, you came to believe that you did not deserve to be taken care of, that you in fact deserved abuse. You felt isolated and alone.

Many abused kids are told directly that they'll never succeed, that they're stupid, or that they're only good for sex. With messages like these, it's hard to believe in yourself.

WHERE ARE YOU NOW?

- Do you feel that you're bad, dirty, or ashamed?
- Do you feel powerless, like a victim?

- Do you feel different from other people?
- Do you feel there's something wrong with you deep down inside? That if people really knew you, they'd leave?
- Do you ever feel self-destructive or suicidal? Or that you simply want to die?
- Do you hate yourself?
- Do you have a hard time nurturing and taking care of yourself? Are you able to enjoy feeling good?
- Do you find it hard to trust your intuition?
- Do you feel unable to protect yourself in dangerous situations? Have you experienced repeated victimization (rape, assault, battery) as an adult?
- Do you have a sense of your own interests, talents, or goals?
- Do you have trouble feeling motivated? Are you often immobilized?
- Are you afraid to succeed?
- Can you accomplish things you set out to do?
- Do you feel you have to be perfect?
- Do you use work or achievements to compensate for inadequate feelings in other parts of your life?

FEELINGS

As a child you could not afford to feel the full extent of your terror, pain, or rage. The agony would have been devastating. You could not have done arithmetic with other second-graders had you known the depth of your sorrow. And you could not think about killing your father when you relied on him to feed you.

Because your innocent love and trust were betrayed, you learned that you could not rely on your feelings. The feelings you expressed may have been disregarded or mocked. You were ignored, told you had nothing to worry about, molested again.

If the adults around you were out of control with their feelings, you got the message that feelings led to violence or destruction. Anger meant beatings or furniture thrown across the room.

You may have learned to block out physical pain, because it was too devastating or because you did not want to give the abuser the satisfaction of seeing you cry. But since you can't block feelings selectively, you simply stopped feeling.

WHERE ARE YOU NOW?

- Can you recognize your feelings? Tell the difference between them?

- Do you have trouble expressing your feelings?
- Do you value feelings or see them as an indulgence?
- Are you comfortable with anger? Sadness? Happiness? Calm?
- Do you feel confused much of the time?
- Do you experience a wide range of emotions or just a few?
- Are you prone to depression? Nightmares? Panic attacks?
- Have you ever worried about going crazy?
- Are you afraid of your feelings? Do they ever seem out of control?
- Have you ever been violent or abusively angry?

YOUR BODY

Children learn about the world through their bodies. When you were sexually abused, you learned that the world was not a safe place. You experienced pain, betrayal, and conflicting sensations of arousal. Children often learn to leave their bodies to avoid these feelings—or they numb themselves as best they can.

WHERE ARE YOU NOW?

- Do you feel present in your body most of the time? Or are there times when you feel as though you've left your body?
- Do you ever use alcohol, drugs, or food in a way that concerns you?

- Do you have a full range of feelings in your body? Or do you sometimes go numb?
- Are you aware of the messages your body gives you (hunger, fear, tiredness, pain)? Do you respond to them?
- Do you have a hard time loving and accepting your body? Do you feel at home in it?
- Do you have any physical illnesses that you think might be connected to your abuse?
- Do you enjoy using your body in activities such as dance, sports, or hiking?
- Have you ever intentionally hurt yourself or abused your body?

INTIMACY

The building blocks of intimacy—giving and receiving, trusting and being trustworthy—are learned in childhood. If children are given consistent loving attention, they develop skills for establishing and maintaining nurturing relationships. Unfortunately, if you were abused, your natural trust was skewed by adults who misused your innocence. You were told, "Daddy's only touching you because he loves you" or "I'm doing this so you'll be a good wife to your husband someday." You grew up with confusing messages about the relationship between sex and love, trust and betrayal.

WHERE ARE YOU NOW?

- Do you find it difficult to trust anyone? Do you have close friends?
- Can you imagine a healthy relationship?
- Is it difficult for you to give or receive nurturing? To be affectionate?
- Are you afraid of people? Do you feel alienated or lonely?
- Do you tend to get involved with people who are inappropriate or unavailable?
- Have you ever been involved with someone who reminds you of your abuser?
- Do you often feel taken advantage of?
- Do you find that your relationships just don't work out?
- Do you have trouble making a commitment? Do you panic when people get too close?
- Do you find you're able to get close to friends, but can't seem to make things work with a lover?
- Do you find yourself clinging to the people you care about?
- Do you repeatedly test people?
- Do you expect people to leave you?
- Can you say no?

SEXUALITY

When children are sexually abused, their natural sexual capacity is stolen. You were introduced to sex on an adult's timetable, according to an adult's needs. You never had a chance to explore naturally, to experience your own desires from the inside. Sexual arousal became linked to feelings of shame, disgust, pain, and humiliation. Pleasure became tainted as well. And desire (the abuser's desire) was dangerous, an out-of-control force used to hurt you.

Children often leave their bodies during sex with the abuser. You numbed yourself or disappeared. You disconnected from sexual feelings.

When abuse was coupled with affection, your needs for nurturing were linked with sex. You didn't learn to meet these needs in other ways.

WHERE ARE YOU NOW?

- Are you able to stay present when making love? Do you go through sex numb or in a panic?
- Do you try to use sex to meet needs that aren't sexual? Can you accept nurturing and closeness in other ways?
- Do you find yourself avoiding sex or going after sex you really don't want? Can you say no?
- Do you feel your worth is primarily sexual?
- Are you sexual with partners who respect you? Have you ever had partners who sexually abused you?
- Have you been a prostitute? Or used your sexuality in a way that had elements of exploitation?
- Do you experience sexual pleasure? Sexual desire? Do you think pleasure is bad?
- Do you ever think sex is disgusting or that you're disgusting for enjoying it?
- Are you turned on by violent, sadistic, or incestuous fantasies?
- Do you find you need to control everything about sex to feel safe?
- Do you ever experience flashbacks to the abuse?
- Do you have sex because you want to, or only because your partner wants it?
- Have you ever been sexually abusive?

CHILDREN AND PARENTING

If the abuse took place within your own family, or if your family did not protect and support you, you grew up in a dysfunctional family. You did not have the benefit of healthy role models. Until you actively face your abuse and begin to heal from it, you are likely to repeat the same kind of parenting you had as a child.

WHERE ARE YOU NOW?

- Do you feel uncomfortable or frightened around children?
- Have you ever been abusive, or feared you might be?
- Do you find it hard to set clear boundaries with children? To balance their needs with your own?
- Do you have a hard time feeling close to your children? Are you comfortable being affectionate with them?
- Have you had trouble protecting the children in your care?
- Are you overprotective?
- Have you taught your children to protect themselves? Have you talked to them honestly about sex?

FAMILIES OF ORIGIN

Relationships are distorted in incestuous families. The essential trust, sharing, and safety are missing, and in their place there is secrecy, isolation, and fear. If you were abused by a family member, you may have been made the family scapegoat, repeatedly told that you were crazy or bad. You may have felt isolated, cut off from nurturing contact with others.

Since alcoholism and other dysfunctional patterns often accompany sexual abuse, you may have had to cope with these problems as well. Adult responsibilities may have been forced on you.

If the abuse took place outside your family and you weren't adequately heard, you got the message that your pain wasn't important, that you couldn't rely on your family to protect or understand you.

WHERE ARE YOU NOW?

- Are you satisfied with your family relationships? Or are they strained and difficult?
- Is the sexual abuse acknowledged in your family? Do the people in your family support you?
- Do you feel crazy, invalidated, or depressed whenever you see your family? Have you been rejected by your family?
- Have you confronted your abuser or told other family members about your abuse?
- Do you feel safe when you're with your family?
- Do you expect the people in your family to change? To take care of you? To see your point of view? To believe you? Do you keep hoping?
- Does incest still go on in your family?

YOU CAN HEAL FROM THE EFFECTS OF ABUSE

If you feel overwhelmed reading this chapter, remember that you have already lived through the hardest part—the abuse itself. You have survived against formidable odds. The same abuse that undercut you has also provided you with many of the inner resources necessary for healing. One quality every survivor can be confident of having is strength. And with an understanding of what it takes to heal, that strength leads directly to determination. As one woman stated: "No one's gonna fuck with me no more."

WRITING EXERCISES: THE EFFECTS

(See the basic method for writing exercises on page 32.)

Write about the ways you're still affected by the abuse. What are you still carrying in terms of your feelings of self-worth, your work, your relationships, your sexuality? How is your life still pained, still limited?

Write about the strengths you've developed because of the abuse. Think of what it's taken for you to survive. What are the qualities that enabled you to make it? Perseverance? Flexibility? Self-sufficiency? Write about your strengths with pride.

COPING: HONORING WHAT YOU DID TO SURVIVE

My whole life has pretty much been coping.

—35-year-old survivor

Coping is what you did to survive the trauma of being sexually abused. There is a continuum of coping behaviors. You may have run away from home or turned to alcohol or drugs. You may have become a super-achiever, excelling in school and taking care of your brothers and sisters at home. You may have forgotten what happened to you, withdrawn into yourself, or cut off your feelings. With few resources for taking care of yourself, you survived with whatever means were available.

Many survivors criticize themselves for the ways they coped. You may not want to admit some of the things you had to do to survive. But coping is nothing to be ashamed of. You survived, and it's important to honor your resourcefulness.

While some of the ways you've coped have developed into strengths (being successful at your work, becoming self-sufficient, developing a sense of humor, being good in a crisis), others have become self-defeating patterns (stealing, drug or alcohol abuse, compulsive overeating). Often one behavior will have both healthy and destructive aspects. Healing requires that you differentiate between the two. Then you can celebrate your strengths while you start changing the patterns that no longer serve you.

As you read through these different ways of coping, you'll find some that are general, common to almost all survivors. Others are specific and may or may not be familiar to you. Identifying the ways in which you've coped is an essential first step in making satisfying changes in your life.

THE BASICS

MINIMIZING

Minimizing means pretending that whatever happened wasn't really that bad. It means saying "My dad's a little pissed off," when in fact he just smashed an armchair to bits. Kids growing up surrounded by abuse often believe that everyone else grows up the same way. Doesn't every father tuck his daughter into bed like that?

> Yeah, I minimized it. "Hey, so your dad puts his prick in your mouth? What's the big deal? Hey!" Up until five years ago, people would say to me, "Were you from an abusive family?" and I'd say, "No!" After all, I didn't die. I was in the hospital with broken bones, but I didn't die. There was blood all over the place but at least I made it.

RATIONALIZING

Rationalizing is the means by which children explain away abuse. "Oh, he couldn't help it. He was drunk." They invent reasons that excuse the abuser. "Four kids was just too much for her. No wonder she didn't take care of me." Rationalizing keeps the focus on the abuser:

> There's a part of me that always wants to figure out "Why the hell did he

What My Father Told Me
by Dorianne Laux

Always I have done what was asked,
　melmac
dishes stacked on rag towels, the slack
of a vacuum cleaner cord wound around my
　hand,
laundry hung from a line.
There is much to do always, and I do it. The
　iron
resting in its frame, hot in the shallow pan
of summer as the basins of his hands push
the book I am reading aside.
I do as I am told, his penis like the garden
hose, in this bedroom, in that bathroom,
　over
the toilet or my bare stomach. I do
the chores, pull weeds out back, finger
stinkbug husks, snail
carcasses, pile dead grass in black bags.
At night his feet are safe on their pads, light
on the wall to wall as he takes the hallway
to my room.
His voice, the hiss of lawn sprinklers, wet
hush of sweat in his hollows, the mucus
still damp in the corner of my eyes as I wake.
Summer ended. Schoolwork didn't suit me.
My fingers unaccustomed to the slimness
of a pen, the delicate touch it takes
to uncoil the mind.
History. A dateline pinned to the wall.
Beneath each president's face, a quotation.
Pictures of buffalo and wheat fields, a
　wagon train
circled for the night, my hand raised to ask
　the question
Where did the children sleep?

do it? What could have hurt this poor man so terribly that he would have to resort to these things?" That's a way of dramatizing his story instead of mine. It's a way of trying to forgive him, instead of allowing the real anger and fury I feel.

DENYING

Denying is turning your head the other way and pretending that whatever is happening isn't, or what has happened didn't. It is a basic pattern in alcoholic families. It's almost universal where incest is concerned. "If I just ignore it long enough, it will go away."

Denial can also be a way to avoid telling anyone about the abuse. It's often more comfortable for a child to deny reality than to face the fact that the adults around her won't protect her, and in fact may harm her.

One woman remembered the time a neighborhood boy told her everyone knew that her father had been beating her the night before. They'd all heard her screaming. "I told him, 'Oh, that wasn't me. My father would never beat me.' "

Some survivors acknowledge that they were abused but deny that it had any effect. "I told my therapist I'd already dealt with it," one woman said. "He believed me."

FORGETTING

Forgetting is one of the most common and effective ways children deal with sexual abuse. The human mind has tremendous powers of repression. Many children are able to forget about the abuse, *even as it is happening to them:*

> I had a visual image of a closet in my mind. I shoved everything that was happening to me into the back of that closet, and I closed the door.

This capacity to forget explains why so many adult survivors are unaware of the fact that they were abused. (For a more thorough explanation of this phenomenon, see "Remembering," page 77.) Some survivors remember the abuse but forget the way they felt at the time. One woman, repeatedly molested throughout her childhood by her stepfather and her brother, said, "I had totally and completely repressed that it had even been uncomfortable."

SPLITTING

We use the term "splitting" to describe two different feeling states. Although only the first usage fits the clinical definition, we use "splitting" both ways because survivors so often do.*

---

* Clinically, "splitting" refers to the tendency to view people or events as either all good or all bad. It is a way of coping that allows a person to hold opposite, unintegrated views. For example, the child separates the father whom she depends on for love and protection from the father who abuses her. This allows her to preserve an image of the "good" father, but at great cost. She is left identifying herself as "bad" in order to make sense of the abuse.

"Splitting" also describes the feeling the survivor has when she separates her consciousness from her body, or "leaves" her body.

LACK OF INTEGRATION

One of the by-products of forgetting is a feeling of being divided into more than one person. There is the little girl having the good childhood, but underneath there is the child who's prone to nightmares and sees people hiding in the corner of the room.

Many survivors continue this pattern into adulthood. On the inside you feel evil and bad, and know that something is very wrong, but on the outside you present a different front to the world. Laura remembers:

At twenty-one I was lying in my bed, unable to get up, watching the bugs march across my sheets, thinking I would either kill myself or go crazy. A half-hour later, I turned around and wrote my mother another cheery letter about how well I was doing. I was desperate to maintain the facade.

But the facade is often very thin. A fifty-six-year-old psychotherapist explains the way she acted out the split in her life:

Growing up, I did everything super-right. I was an overachiever. I was an A student all through college. I was a Fulbright scholar in London. I was considered a huge success.

I developed a total false personality based on what you were supposed to be, and hid myself. My interpersonal relationships were exchanges of displays, nothing more. I got by because of money and status.

I knew I was sick. I knew there was something hideously wrong with me. Underneath that false personality was a blankness, and underneath the blankness was a tremendous rage. I was sure that if I ever allowed my behavior to manifest any sign of the problems I had inside, everything would crumble entirely and I'd end up in an insane asylum or police lockup.

In cases of extreme abuse, this kind of splitting can result in the development of multiple personalities. (See "Multiple Personalities," page 438).

LEAVING YOUR BODY

Children who are abused or battered often numb their bodies so they will not feel what is being done to them. Others actually leave their bodies and watch the abuse as if from a great distance.

It's like I actually rise up out of my body. I could feel myself sitting in a chair, and I could feel myself floating up out of my body. That's exactly what it is, like being suspended in midair. I know that my body is in the chair, but the rest of me is out of my body.

(For more on this kind of splitting, see "From Splitting to Being in Your Body," page 219.)

CONTROL

Control is a thread that runs through the lives of many survivors:

I have a tremendous attachment to things going my way. It feels like I'm going to die if I don't get my way. There

Two Pictures of My Sister
by Dorianne Laux

If an ordinary person is silent
it may be a tactical maneuver.
If a writer is silent, he is lying.

—Jaroslav Seifert

The pose is stolen from Monroe, struck
in the sun's floodlight, eyes lowered,
a long-stemmed plastic rose between her
      teeth.
My cast-off bathing suit hangs in folds
over her ribs, straps cinched, pinned
at the back of her neck. Barefoot
on the hot cement, knock-kneed, comical
if it weren't for the graceful
angles of her arms, her flesh soft
against the chipped stucco.

The other picture is in my head.
It is years later.
It is in color.
Blond hair curls away from the planes of her
      face
like wood shavings. She wears a lemon
      yellow
ruffled top, denim cutoffs,
her belly button squeezed to a slit
above the silver snap.

She stands against the hallway wall
while Dad shakes his belt in her face.
A strip of skin has been peeled
from her bare shoulder, there are snake
lines across her thighs, a perfect curl
around her long neck.
She looks through him as if she can see
behind his head. She dares him.
Go on. Hit me again.
He lets the folded strap unravel to the floor
and holding it by its tail bells the buckle
off her cheekbone.
She does not move or cry or even wince
as the welt blooms on her temple
like a flower opening frame by frame
in a Disney film.
It lowers her eyelid with its violet
petals and as he walks away only her eyes
move, like the eyes of a portrait that follow
      you
around a museum room, her face a stubborn
moon that trails the car all night, stays
      locked
in the frame of the back window
no matter how many turns you take,
no matter how far you go.

are a lot of small, everyday interactions that make me feel tremendously out of control.

When survivors grow up in a chaotic environment they often go to great lengths to keep their lives in order:

> My shoes have to be put back in the same place at night. My room is always neat. When I come to work in the morning, I have this whole routine of putting the pen in a certain place, my keys in a certain place. Wherever I can maintain control, I do it, because there were so many places as a kid where I didn't have any control.

Such control can be positive. Good organization is an asset if you're a manager, a mother, or a worker. The negative side can be a lack of flexibility, and difficulty in negotiating or compromising.

CHAOS

Survivors sometimes maintain control by creating chaos. If your behavior is out of control, you force the people around you to drop what they're doing to respond to your latest problems. In this way, you get attention (though negative) and in effect become the person calling the shots. Laura's father always told her, "A family is a dictatorship run by its sickest member."

Like children of alcoholics, survivors are often good at both resolving and generating crises:

They say that humans tend to gravitate toward what is comfortable, what they know. If this is true, then it explains why more often than not you find survivors in the midst of chaos. Not only are they familiar with it, they handle it beautifully. I could handle any extraordinary circumstance and in fact felt in my element in those situations. But put me into the everyday world and I was very freaked-out. I have always been hysterical in the midst of normalcy.

Before I found out that I was a survivor, I wondered why my life was filled with traumatic situations. Not only did I not have any middle ground, I was terrified at the thought of it. Whenever my life would calm down, I would start wishing for something major to happen so I could feel at home. While other people were looking for ways to put

themselves on the edge, I could never get off it.

—Jerilyn Munyon

While this capacity to handle crises can make you a good emergency-room worker or ambulance driver, it can also be a way you keep yourself from feeling. If you are addicted to intensity and drama, you might make a dynamic, charismatic performer, but you may also be running from yourself.

SPACING OUT

Survivors have an uncanny capacity to space out and not be present. There are many ways to do this:

I walked into walls and doors and furniture a lot, because I wasn't in my body, but a few bruises were a small price to pay for oblivion.

Whenever something scares her, one survivor finds an object in the room and stares at it—just as she did when she was being molested:

I have total recall of the most intimate details of different rooms I've been in. I can't remember who I was talking to or what we were talking about, but I sure can tell you exactly what the window looked like!

The problem with this kind of distancing is that you cut yourself off, not only from pain but from the richness of life and human feeling. You avoid the pain but miss everything else as well:

I spent a lot of my life spacing out and disappearing. I pride myself on how slick I am. I have been known to sit there and be totally gone and then to come back and have no idea where I am in a conversation. I'll have been talking the whole time. And what's really weird is that most people don't even notice I'm gone!

During an interview, both Laura and this survivor demonstrated their abilities to space out. Laura says:

We were laughing about how good we both were at disappearing and I turned and asked her how much of the time she had been present during the interview. "Oh, about 70 percent," she answered. "What about you?"

"Oh, about 65 percent. I'm having a hard day." We laughed. There we were, two incest survivors doing an interview about healing and neither of us was fully there. We made a pact on the spot to stop at any point either of us started to disappear and to talk about what had triggered it.

BEING SUPER-ALERT

As a child, tuning into every nuance of your environment may have saved you from being abused. You may always be aware of where you are in a room. You may sit where you can watch the entrance, making sure no one can come up behind you. You might also be hyper-aware of the people around you, always anticipating their needs and moods. One woman said she was a confirmed gossip for just this reason. If she kept track of what

everyone was doing around her, no one could ever surprise her again.

Hyper-awareness can be an asset. Survivors have become excellent therapists, sensitive doctors, ground-breaking reporters, perceptive parents, compassionate friends. One survivor works in a crime lab analyzing evidence in sexual assault cases. She says her extra level of awareness makes her great at the job. Other survivors have developed psychic abilities from their sensitivity. Yet this state of constant alertness can be wearing. We all need to relax sometimes.

HUMOR

A tough sense of humor, a bitter wit or sense of cynicism, can get you through hard times. As long as you keep people laughing, you maintain a certain protective distance. And as long as you keep laughing, you don't have to cry:

For years I used humor to deflect the pain and the shame I felt talking about incest. The humor was, of course, the gallows variety. It often pointed out the absurdity of the American Ideal, the family surrounded by a white picket fence—with blood dripping down the painted slats where the daughters had been sacrificially skewered. It was my way of telling the truth about something I wasn't sure anyone would believe if they hadn't lived through it.

Once I asked my therapist about my use of humor. It didn't seem right to laugh about these things. He told me, "Humor is only one way of dealing with tragedy. Other people destroy themselves or others, or they start fires or drink themselves to death. Of all the possible ways there are to deal with deep pain, you have chosen one that is fairly harmless and that affirms life with laughter. Not a bad choice. Not a bad choice at all."

Humor can be an asset. People enjoy you. You may keep yourself from being depressed. You might even become a comedian or a performer. The goal is to use humor effectively, without hiding behind it.

BUSYNESS

Staying busy can be a way to avoid being in the present moment, to avoid feelings. Many survivors live their whole lives according to the lists they write first thing in the morning. As one woman remarked, "I often mourn for a pace of life that I've never had."

ESCAPE

As a child or an adolescent, you may have made attempts to run away. If you were more passive, there was escape through sleep, books, and television. Many adult survivors still read obsessively. One woman said, "I'd buy a junk novel and read it till I fell asleep, usually for a good thirty-six hours at a stretch." Others spend hours in front of the TV.

If you couldn't afford to believe the abuse was really happening, you could make believe something else was going on. Sometimes children create fantasies that explore their desire for power in a powerless situation. One woman dreamed of a little house she could live in all by herself, with locks on all the doors. Another spent her childhood dreaming of revenge:

I'd watch *Perry Mason* to get ideas about how to kill my father. It was really the best of times. Every day I would get a new method. However the person was murdered on *Perry Mason* that day, I would go to bed that night, and that's how I would kill my father. One time on *Perry Mason* this guy killed his wife by knocking an electric fan into the bathtub. I imagined electrocuting him like that. I remember really vividly fantasizing about putting ground glass in the meatloaf. I was the cook. I thought about stabbing him, shooting him. Every night I killed him in another way.

Many survivors continue an intense fantasy life when they grow up:

As an adult these changed to vindication fantasies, fantasies about having power in the world, revenge fantasies. I can work myself into a state of sobbing over something in a fantasy. I love fantasies about dying and everyone regretting all the wrongs they'd ever done to me. They're just an updated version of what I did as a kid. I can be lost in fantasy for hours. It's a lot safer to work things out in my head than to change things in the world.

Yet fantasies can be the source of a rich creative life. One teenager needed to escape so badly, she believed *Star Trek* was real. When the series was taken off the air, she began to hear the voices of the characters in her head and started writing her own episodes. Today she is a successful science fiction writer.

WHEN THE PAIN GETS TOO GREAT

MENTAL ILLNESS

Problems occur when the line between fantasy and reality blurs. For many survivors "going crazy" makes a lot of sense:

I've been mentally disturbed all my life. Mental hospitals were more like a respite for me because they got me away from my family. It was just an extension of the running away. I had no control in my life whatsoever. What my father didn't control, my mother controlled. It wasn't my life. I was in this body, but it was like I was this puppet, and everybody else pulled the strings. *I had to get sick to get away.* I just kept going further and further in my head, so I wouldn't have to deal with reality at all.

SELF-MUTILATION

Self-mutilation is one way survivors control their experience of pain. Instead of the abuser hurting you, you hurt yourself. One woman beat herself severely with a belt. Another carved into her leg with a knife:

I've wanted to hurt myself, to cause myself pain, and the way I usually think of doing that is cutting myself with a knife. It's a feeling that the pain inside is so bad, that if I cut myself, it'll come out. Lots of times I have images of putting my fists through glass, and I just think watching the blood go down the glass would make the pain go away somehow. It's like you're a balloon pushed full and you need to pop open a little. It seems like once you do it, it gets easier to do it again and again. It's like any other addiction.

Lots of times I get the urge when I have a new memory. I start to feel so out of control. If I cut myself, other people will know the pain I'm in. Otherwise they don't notice, especially since I try to cover it up emotionally.

The other thing is that physical pain distracts from the emotional pain. So I could focus on that instead of the emotional pain, which makes me feel so trapped and hopeless.

For information on stopping a pattern of self-mutilation, see "From Self-Mutilation to Self-Care," page 229.

SUICIDE ATTEMPTS

Suicide sometimes seems like the only option left in a life that feels out of control:

I've been suicidal many, many times and have been serious about it, but there is something in me that doesn't want to die. I've slashed a razor blade down a vein, and the blood just spurted out, but I didn't die. I took twenty-eight meprobamate, which is a strong tranquilizer. Half of that should have killed me but I didn't die. I have a very strong will to live.

Attempts at suicide are not always so overt. One woman spent her childhood saying the prayer "If I should die before I wake" with her fingers crossed. (If you're feeling suicidal, see "Don't Kill Yourself," page 212.)

ADDICTION AND ISOLATION

Addictions are common ways of coping with the pain of sexual abuse. They are usually self-defeating and self-destructive. You can be addicted to dangerous situations, to crisis, or to sex. You may have turned to drugs, alcohol, or food to keep the memories down, to numb feelings. Addictions must be curbed if you want to heal. (For more on fighting addictions, see "From Addiction to Freedom," page 226.)

Isolation is often coupled with addictions. If no one is close to you, no one can hurt you anymore. Survivors often shut others out, creating a half-life of their own making.

Before I Remembered the Abuse: Sunny's Story

I started drinking with my mother in the afternoons after school. Her cocktail hour started with *Merv Griffin*. She was disabled, so when I came home from school, she'd say, "Make me a drink." And then one day she started to say, "Make us a drink." It wasn't until I was seventeen and went away to college that I started having blackouts and getting more serious about my drinking.

I never was a party-goer. I rarely went to bars. I did my drinking alone at home. I drank until I passed out, or until the bottle was empty. It was always the last time I was going to do it, so why not finish it off?

I did the same thing with eating. I wouldn't eat anything in the morning, because every day started out with me on a diet. I might go till two or three in the afternoon, and then I'd start eating. Instead of eating a meal like a normal person, I'd buy half a gallon of ice cream or a dozen doughnuts, and consume a huge quantity of food in a short period of time. It never tasted good. I just felt bad about myself, and the eating would make me feel worse. I'd feel horrible, that I'd failed. And then I'd say, "Well, I'll start tomorrow."

Before I went to AA and got sober, I felt that I was the only person in the world who felt the things I felt, who did the things I did, who lived the way I lived. I lived like a rat. I dressed normal, and I had a job, and I had a nice apartment, but I would go home on Friday, shut the drapes, lock the door, watch old movies and drink and eat.

I wouldn't ever watch anything current —like the news, or a parade, or a baseball game. Only old movies that were fantasies. Or soap operas. The characters were like my family. I especially liked the fact that they aired on holidays, because I could have Christmas and Thanksgiving with *All My Children*.

I would only get dressed to go to the store. There was a liquor store one block from the house and I would drive the one block. Sometimes I wouldn't even make it home. I'd have to stop the car and get into whatever it was that I had bought. Sometimes I wouldn't even get dressed. I would put a coat over my nightgown and drive to the store.

I felt bad about living that way, but I tried not to think about my life. I knew there was something wrong with it, but I couldn't put my finger on it. I knew other people didn't live that way. I'd think that someday I'd do something about it. But not today.

I had no friends. I knew only a small handful of people. I remember thinking if I died, the first person to know it would be the landlady when I didn't pay my rent on the first of then month. There was really nobody in my life. No one I cared about. I was incredibly isolated. And I continued to feel that way until I went to Alcoholics Anonymous.

EATING DIFFICULTIES

Eating difficulties often result from abuse. Young girls who were sexually abused sometimes develop anorexia and bulimia. In a rigidly controlled family system where the abuse is hidden and all appearances are normal, anorexia or bulimia can be a cry for help. For girls who've been pressured into sex they didn't want, growing into a woman's body can be terrifying. Anorexia and bulimia can be an attempt to say no, to assert control over their changing bodies.

Compulsive overeating is another way of coping. Survivors may feel that being large will keep them from having to deal with sexual advances.

I've been overweight since I was nine. I remember exactly the day I started eating. It was the day my stepfather fingered me in front of other people. He took off my bathing suit and under the guise of drying me off, got his fingers inside of me. I felt completely exposed and I remember I started eating that day. And I really ballooned.

I frequently eat very consciously to gain weight to cover me, to protect me. When I lose weight, I feel totally exposed and naked. I can't stand it. There's a lot of heartache in being so overweight. It affects every part of your life, but I still need the protection.

Another survivor said, "I kept eating so I wouldn't have to talk about what had happened. I just made sure my mouth was always full."

Compulsive eating is not necessarily related to body size. Some large women are not overeaters and some thin women binge compulsively. In our culture fat is a stigma, but we all have naturally different body sizes. Being large is not necessarily an indication of anything emotional or problematic. An excellent resource on the oppression and liberation of large women is *Shadows on a Tightrope* (see the "Health" section of the Resource Guide).

For more on anorexia, bulimia, and compulsive overeating, see "Eating Difficulties," page 227.

LYING

When children are told never to talk about the abuse, or don't want people to know what's really going on at home, they become adept at lying. Sometimes this pattern of lying to cover up or protect continues into adult life.

STEALING

Stealing is a totally absorbing activity. It enables you to forget everything for a brief moment—including the abuse. It is a way to create distraction or excitement, to re-create the feelings you had when you were first abused—guilt, terror, the rush of adrenaline. Stealing is also a way of defying authority, an attempt to take back what was stolen, to even the score. It can also be a cry for help:

> I worked at being a thief for a year and a half. When I first quit drinking, it was a way of coping. I didn't steal because I wanted the stuff—I got a terrific high from it. Unfortunately, it only lasted for about thirty seconds, and so I kept having to repeat the act.
>
> I embezzled from the company I worked for. I worked an insurance fraud that was grand larceny. And I shoplifted. I accumulated so much stuff that I started throwing it away. My car was full of loot. I never got caught.
>
> I stopped stealing five years ago on Christmas Day. I hadn't had one day where I hadn't stolen anything in a long time. All the stores were closed that day, so it seemed like a good day to begin. I finally called someone from AA and told them I had this problem. Just telling seemed to release me.

GAMBLING

Gambling is a way to maintain the hope that life can magically change. It's a way to act out the longing that your luck will shift, that there will be justice: if you win big, you will finally get your due.

Gambling is also a thrill, a way to escape the difficulties and challenges of day-to-day life by entering another world—one that is totally consuming and in which the risks and payoffs are well defined.

WORKAHOLISM

Survivors often feel an overwhelming need to achieve, to make up for the badness they feel is hidden inside. Excelling at work is something that they can control and that's given a lot of support in our high-achieving culture. While working to excess can show a strong motivation to succeed, it can also be a way to avoid an inner life or a connection to the people around you:

> I became 100 percent work. I got into graduate school and just turned off to sharing or closeness with anyone. I was in a really intense MBA program, and I was determined to be perfect. If I wasn't at work with my job, I was working on school, which was supposed to get me further ahead in my job. During that two-year period, I raised my income $19,000 a year. It was all that mattered. It was the only place left where I could prove I was worth anything.

SAFETY AT ANY PRICE

While some survivors have felt compelled to go out and overcome every obstacle, others have chosen security. They are the obedient daughters, honor students, good wives, and selfless mothers. They take few risks, sacrificing opportunities for protection. Opting for security can provide you with grounding and stability, but it may mean giving up your ambitions and dreams.

One of the most common ways for

women to find safety is through their families:

> I married a man who would be stable, who wouldn't leave me, and above all, would not be intrusive. He was the rock. I felt myself to be on such shaky ground. We had a traditional marriage. I didn't really have to do anything. I just clung to my husband. He was a high-status high achiever, and I shone in his glory for a long time. I lived in his protectorate for twenty-two years and that's how I survived.

AVOIDING INTIMACY

If you don't let anyone close to you, no one can hurt you. As one woman said, "You can't be in an abusive relationship if you don't get in relationships." Another added, "I kept myself safe *and* alone."

Survivors go to great lengths to limit intimacy. One woman said, "I can stop being friends with someone and never think twice about it." Another had relationships only with men who lived a great distance from her: "One of them was a plane ride away. The other one didn't have a car. That was really good."

Some survivors avoid intimacy in less overt ways, seeming open and friendly on the surface but hiding real feelings inside. One survivor had a "Ten Official Secrets List" which she freely shared:

> I'll tell people things about myself that seem too personal to share, but I don't really trust them or get close to them. They don't know what I feel inside. I hardly ever share that.

While avoiding intimacy keeps you safe—and sometimes leads to positive traits such as independence and autonomy—it also means missing out on the rewards that healthy relationships can bring.

GIVE ME THAT OLD-TIME RELIGION

Safety can also be found by attaching yourself to a belief system that has clearly defined rules and boundaries:

> I'm addicted to religion and theology. I was married in a Chasidic Jewish wedding. I can "do" any ethnic group that you like. I am addicted to groups. I am a sponge. Put me somewhere where people are nice to me, and I'll learn their whole scene better than they can do it themselves.
>
> I converted to being Jewish when I was twelve. I did Orthodox Chasidic Jew for nine years. Kept a kosher house, kept Shabbos, all of it. Eventually, I got bored with doing Jewish, and I switched over to Swami Satchidananda. I did yoga. I went to India and lived in an ashram.

More traditional religion can provide an anchor as well. The lure of divine forgiveness can be a powerful pull for the survivor who still feels the abuse was her fault.

Marilyn's Story: Being Born Again

I found some security in a born-again Baptist group when I was about fifteen. The evangelist talked about how bad we all were and how our sins could all be forgiven.

Everybody went to Bob Jones University with the pink and blue sidewalks, where the boys walked on the blue and the girls walked on the pink. We all wanted to go to Bob Jones. It was the ultimate. We were always out on the streets, evangelizing, handing out tracts, witnessing to all our friends.

Church was a release. It gave me the structure—if you do this and this, then you will be okay. There are formal do's and don'ts that you get from the pulpit, and then there are informal ones you get from your friends. You know which stores to buy your clothes in and which clothes to buy. You know which kinds of nightgowns to wear. You know which kinds of sexual activities with your husband are all right, which ones are not allowed. You all cook the same things. You raise your children in the same way. The point being that if you do those things, you're going to be all right.

I thoroughly believed that God intervened in the details of everything I did, including grocery shopping. I believed that as long as I was walking in the Light, nothing was going to happen to me that God wouldn't allow. I knew that if I couldn't make a decision, all I had to do was wait and God would tell me. I took no responsibility for my life—it was wrong for me to do so. What I had to do was find God's will in everything I did. I'd go to the store, and the sofa I had been looking at would be on sale, and it was God's will that I buy it.

I used to teach Bible studies for women. The teachings I lived by and taught for so many years were *Fascinating Womanhood* and *The Total Woman*. I just cringe when I think of those women, and I hope they have discarded what I taught them. One of them

would be a little rebellious, and I would tell her she'd better knuckle under to her husband. I would quote scripture and verse.

I allowed no doubt. None. I just lapped those things up because they gave me great security. I knew I'd be forgiven for what a bad person I was.

COMPULSIVELY SEEKING OR AVOIDING SEX

If abuse was your sole means of getting physical contact when you were a child, you may continue to look for closeness only in sexual ways. You may become promiscuous or try to meet nonsexual needs through sex.

While some survivors use sex as an escape, or experience it as an addiction, many go to great lengths to avoid sexuality.

I intentionally married a man who was basically asexual. He was the three-time-a-year man, and he was absolutely perfect. When we wanted to get pregnant, I took my temperature. The conception of my children was as close to artificial insemination as you can get.

Others numb their bodies so they no longer respond:

Part of the way I coped with the fact that some of the incest felt good was by saying, "It will never feel good. Sex will never feel good, because it felt good when it shouldn't have." So I don't ever feel. I don't pay attention to sex. I don't care about it and it doesn't make me feel anything. The other person is happy when it's done. And I can't wait until I'm out of the situation so I don't have to do it again.

YOU CAN CHANGE

When you were a child, you did not have many options. Now you have more resources. You can recognize self-destructive patterns. You can pick and choose among your coping behaviors. You can discard the ones that no longer work for you and keep the positive skills you've developed. (See Part Three for specific suggestions for changing patterns of coping.)

Not everyone has the same opportunities. If you coped in a way that gets positive recognition—by being super-nurturing or successful in work—your options may be broader than if you turned to drugs as a way to get by. If you are incarcerated in prison or a mental hospital, you clearly will not have the same control over changing your life. If your health has been ravaged by eating disorders, you will face real limitations. And of course your economic and social status, race,

and sexual preference all influence your opportunities.

The starting point for everyone, however, is to look at the ways you coped and to forgive yourself. You have no reason to be ashamed. You did the best you could as a child under impossible circumstances. You have earned the name "survivor." Now you are an adult with the power to change. From a place of acceptance and love you can do so.

WRITING EXERCISE: COPING

(See the basic method for writing exercises on page 32.)

You've read about different ways that people have coped. Some of these you will identify with. There may be others not mentioned that have been recurring themes in your life. This is an opportunity for you to write about your experience of coping—how you remember it, how you're still doing it, how it's affected your life. Write with as much detail as you can, always from the perspective of honoring what you did.

Take half an hour to write.

PART TWO

THE HEALING

PROCESS

AN OVERVIEW

"Don't give up." That's the best thing I could tell somebody who just remembered she was a survivor. That's the most important thing right in the beginning. There are people who have lived through it, and as trite, and as stupid, and as irrelevant as it sounds to you right now, you will not be in so much pain later. Even not so far in the future. If you made it this far, you've got some pretty good stuff in you. So just trust it, no matter what outside messages you get. You're the only person who can tell yourself what you need to do to heal. *Don't give up on yourself.*

Survivors often come to Ellen's workshops expecting to pay their money, invest one weekend, and be healed. One woman said, "I thought once I told someone what had happened to me, that would be the end of it. I wanted to get well, and of course it was going to happen overnight."

We live in a society of instant mashed potatoes, microwave ovens, one-hour dry cleaning. We are taught to expect results immediately. But deep change takes time.

The healing process is a continuum. It begins with an experience of survival, an awareness of the fact that you lived through the abuse and made it to adulthood. It ends with thriving—the experience of a satisfying life no longer programmed by what happened to you as a child. And in between is the subject of this book: the healing process.

Until recently, survivors have had to

make the journey with no map, no guarantees, and few role models. These women have been pioneers. Their courageous acts of healing have taught us much.

We have learned that healing is not a random process. There are recognizable stages that all survivors pass through. The next chapters will provide you with a map of those stages, enabling you to see where you are, what you've done already, and what's yet before you.

We've presented the stages in a particular order, but you will probably not experience them that way. Few survivors finish stage #1 and then move on to stage #2. Healing is not linear. Rather, it is an integral part of life. As one survivor said, "No matter what happens, I can turn it into my healing."

THE STAGES

Although most of these stages are necessary for every survivor, a few of them—the emergency stage, remembering the abuse, confronting your family, and forgiveness—are not applicable for every woman.

The Decision to Heal. Once you recognize the effects of sexual abuse in your life, you need to make an active commitment to heal. Deep healing happens only when you choose it and are willing to change yourself.

The Emergency Stage. Beginning to deal with memories and suppressed feelings can throw your life into utter turmoil. Remember, this is only a stage. It won't last forever.

Remembering. Many survivors suppress all memories of what happened to them as children. Those who do not forget the actual incidents often forget how it felt at the time. Remembering is the process of getting back both memory and feeling.

Believing It Happened. Survivors often doubt their own perceptions. Coming to believe that the abuse really happened, and that it really hurt you, is a vital part of the healing process.

Breaking Silence. Most adult survivors kept the abuse a secret in childhood. Telling another human being about what happened to you is a powerful healing force that can dispel the shame of being a victim.

Understanding That It Wasn't Your Fault. Children usually believe the abuse is their fault. Adult survivors must place the blame where it belongs—directly on the shoulders of the abusers.

Making Contact With the Child Within. Many survivors have lost touch with their own vulnerability. Getting in touch with the child within can help you feel compassion for yourself, more anger at

A common analogy for the healing process is that it's like a spiral. You go through the same stages again and again; but traveling up the spiral, you pass through them at a different level, with a different perspective. You might spend a year or two dealing intensely with your abuse. Then you might take a break and focus more on the present. A year or so later, changes in your life—a new relationship, the birth of a child, graduation from school, or simply an inner urge—may stir up more unresolved memories and feelings, and you may focus in on it again, embarking on a second or a third or a fourth round of discovery. With each new cycle, your capacity to feel, to remember, to make lasting changes, is strengthened.

your abuser, and greater intimacy with others.

Trusting Yourself. The best guide for healing is your own inner voice. Learning to trust your own perceptions, feelings, and intuitions forms a new basis for action in the world.

Grieving and Mourning. As children being abused, and later as adults struggling to survive, most survivors haven't felt their losses. Grieving is a way to honor your pain, let go, and move into the present.

Anger—the Backbone of Healing. Anger is a powerful and liberating force. Whether you need to get in touch with it or have always had plenty to spare, directing your rage squarely at your abuser, and at those who didn't protect you, is pivotal to healing.

Disclosures and Confrontations. Directly confronting your abuser and/or your family is not for every survivor, but it can be a dramatic, cleansing tool.

Forgiveness? Forgiveness of the abuser is *not* an essential part of the healing process, although it tends to be the one most recommended. The only essential forgiveness is for yourself.

Spirituality. Having a sense of a power greater than yourself can be a real asset in the healing process. Spirituality is a uniquely personal experience. You might find it through traditional religion, meditation, nature, or your support group.

Resolution and Moving On. As you move through these stages again and again, you will reach a point of integration. Your feelings and perspectives will stabilize. You will come to terms with your abuser and other family members. While you won't erase your history, you will make deep and lasting changes in your life. Having gained awareness, compassion, and power through healing, you will have the opportunity to work toward a better world.

THE DECISION TO HEAL

If you enter into healing, be prepared to lose everything. Healing is a ravaging force to which nothing seems sacred or inviolate. As my original pain releases itself in healing, it rips to shreds the structures and foundations I built in weakness and ignorance. Ironically and unjustly, only I can pay the price of having lived a lie. I am experiencing the bizarre miracle of reincarnating, more lucidly than at birth, in the same lifetime.

—Ely Fuller

The decision to heal from child sexual abuse is a powerful, life-affirming choice. It is a commitment every survivor deserves to make. Although you may have already experienced some healing in your life—through the nurturing of a foster family, the caring of an intimate partner, or the satisfaction of work you love—*deciding* to heal, making your own growth and recovery a priority, sets in motion a healing force that will bring to your life a richness and depth you never dreamed possible:

For the first time I'm appreciating things like the birds and the flowers, the way the sun feels on my skin—you know, really simple things. I can read a good book. I can sit in the sun. I don't ever remember enjoying these things, even as a little kid. I've woken up. If this hadn't happened, I'd still be asleep. So for the first time, I feel alive. And you know that's something to go for.

****

I am here now. I don't have my thoughts and feelings planed off into the future, or wasting away because of some memories. I am here right now. I am experiencing every bit of my life and I'm not wasting any of it.

****

This has given me the opportunity to look at me. I am emotionally more open. I've learned so much. It's not all bad. You do heal. And you do become stronger. I don't know what it would take to flatten me, but it would have to be something really big. I am, in fact, a survivor.

The commitment to heal rises from a different set of life circumstances for each survivor. A young girl who turns her father in for molesting her may be ordered by the court to go to therapy. A twenty-five-year-old woman may get married and suddenly find that she can't maintain the intimacy she felt with her husband before their wedding. A thirty-year-old may start to feel crazy when her daughter reaches the age she was when her own abuse began. An older woman might decide to heal at the funeral of her abuser.

Other women describe themselves "bursting apart at the seams," or "hitting bottom" before they decide to heal. One woman didn't get help until she was hospitalized for eating difficulties: "I actively avoided getting a therapist for years. I didn't start dealing with it until I couldn't *not* deal with it." Healing isn't always a matter of choice:

It was a compulsion. I think everybody has a compulsion to grow and to be whole. I think everybody has a compulsion to seek relief from pain.

A single human interaction may be the impetus to heal. One survivor decided to heal because a friend told her, "I don't trust you, I never feel you're telling me the truth. I can't trust you with my feelings because I don't know what you're doing with them." The survivor was shocked. First, because it was true, and second, because she thought she'd done a good job of faking it. "I felt she'd crawled inside my head and seen what was really there. She put words to what I'd been feeling all my life. So I went to therapy."

Another woman decided to heal when her younger sister killed herself. "She didn't make it. I had to understand what had happened to her, and give myself the tools to make sure it couldn't happen to me."

One young survivor said she was motivated to heal because of a class assignment:

I was twenty years old. I was in a psych class doing a research project on the aftereffects of incest on survivors. Now, most people just wouldn't choose that kind of subject! But the stuff was pushing up from the inside. I wanted to annihilate my grandfather. I just wanted to castrate him by the time I finished this paper. I thought writing the paper would heal me from it, but my feelings were just erupting all over the place. By the time I presented the paper, I fell apart. I'd been contemplating therapy for a while, and a few days later I found a therapist.

A survivor who'd been a Carmelite nun described her decision to heal as a need to clarify her reasons for living in the convent.

"I loved the convent, but somehow I distrusted my choice to be there. Until I worked out the sexual abuse, I felt I would never know if I was really choosing this life out of health, and out of all the good things that religious life should be chosen from. I wanted to believe that whatever I chose to do, I was doing it for all the right reasons."

IT'S NOT EASY

While it is always worth it, healing is rarely easy. Choosing to work on abuse-related issues will raise questions you never planned to ask and will give answers you didn't expect. Once you commit yourself, your life won't be the same:

My therapist was not the kind of person who would lie to me. He would say, "I can't give you any guarantees. I don't know if you're going to feel better after you talk about this. You could feel a lot worse." And it was hard to make that leap, to decide that it didn't matter which way it went, that the leap itself was the important thing.

I was giving up a person who was really a very viable, powerful, self-reliant human being. There were a lot of positive things about those negative aspects of my personality. And I didn't want to give them up. Maybe it wasn't the best way of coping, but at least I was used to it. I felt incredibly vulnerable having to let go in order to make the room to create a new person. Into what void would I be thrown if I let go of this stuff? I felt like a raw muscle walking around for a long time.

to my friend, jerina
by Lucille Clifton

listen,
when i found there was no safety
in my father's house
i knew there was none anywhere.
you are right about this,
how i nurtured my work
not my self, how i left the girl
wallowing in her own shame
and took on the flesh of my mother.
but listen,
the girl is rising in me,
not willing to be left to
the silent fingers in the dark,
and you are right,
she is asking for more than
most men are able to give,
but she means to have what she
has earned,
sweet sighs, safe houses,
hands she can trust.

You may wonder if it's worth it to take the risk. But as one survivor simply put it, "Taking that risk was the most promising choice I had."

Often the decision to heal wreaks havoc with marriages and intimate relationships, dealings with parents, other relatives, sometimes even your children. It can be hard to function, to go to work, to study, to think, to smile, to perform. It can even be hard to sleep, to eat, or simply to stop crying:

If I'd known that anything could hurt this much or could be this sad, I never would have decided to heal. And at the same time you can't go back. You can't unremember. I spent so many years not hurting at all. It's like I don't have the coping mechanisms for hurting. I have the coping mechanisms for *not* hurting. And that's been real hard.

Sometimes the early stages of healing are so filled with crisis that women have a hard time accepting the fact that they made a choice at all. When Laura remembered her abuse and made her first call to a therapist, she made the decision to heal. But it didn't feel that way to her:

For a long time, I felt like a victim of the process. This was something I'd chosen? No way! Remembering the incest was something that had happened *to* me. The memories were like one of those plastic raincoats that come in a two-inch package. Once I opened them up, I could never fold them neatly back inside. The whole thing felt out of my control, like being swept up in a hurricane.

There are certain major decisions we make not really knowing what we're getting into. Healing from sexual abuse is one of them:

Though sometimes I want to crawl into a dark place and hide from reality, and other times I want to give up completely, I go on. I don't know where this "healing" will lead me. I live on other people's hopes. I live on other people's faith that life will get better. I continue to wonder whether it is worth it, but I go on. This, then, is healing.

Deciding to actively heal is terrifying because it means opening up to hope. For many survivors, hope has brought only disappointment.

Although it is terrifying to say yes to yourself, it is also a tremendous relief when you finally stop and face your own demons. There is something about looking terror in the face, and seeing your own reflection, that is strangely relieving. There is comfort in knowing that you don't have to pretend anymore, that you are going to do everything within your power to heal. As one survivor put it, "I know now that every time I accept my past and respect where I am in the present, I am giving myself a future."

EVERYONE DESERVES TO HEAL

Aside from the obstacles we've already mentioned, some women face additional factors that hinder their commitment to naming their abuse or healing from it. Age, race, religious background, and other factors all influence the decision to heal.

They'll Use It Against Us: Rachel Bat Or's Story

Rachel Bat Or is a forty-one-year-old lesbian who lives in Oakland, California. She works with abuse survivors, helping them reclaim their strength. Born to Jewish parents, she was abused by all four members of her family—her mother, father, brother, and grandfather. Through the course of her own healing and her work with other survivors, Rachel has seen a reluctance on the *part of many Jewish women to acknowledge that they were abused, and therefore to commit to healing.* *

Compared to many of our parents' lives of poverty or escape from anti-Semitic countries, whatever happens to us gets played down. As long as we have a roof over our heads, we have clothes and food, then nothing that happens to us can be as bad, because they lived with rats, in incredible poverty, the families often separated in traveling to America. And so no matter how awful we feel inside of us, we feel we can't say that out loud because our parents had it so much worse.

Then the stereotypes of Jewish women are that we're loud and pushy and that the men are gentle and hardworking. And so we're taught to feel sorry for the men and blame the women. So if the men—our fathers or brothers—are abusing us, there isn't that instantaneous hatred, because they're so exalted in the religious teachings and the culture. So it's very hard for us to hold on to that anger.

And then there's the myth that Jewish men are not alcoholics or batterers. So if our family is different, that can't be admitted.

The next thing is, "What will the neighbors say? We're Jewish." Because we have to protect our religion from being criticized, we ignore whatever happens in our family. If there are any problems, it's the whole religion that gets looked on, not just our family. We know that. It's not some myth.

And then there's the last thing that puts us in a real quandary: There's the us/them dichotomy. If we do tell about whatever happens to us, it's usually to the "them," someone who's not Jewish, who's outside the family, who doesn't respect our family, and so we lose the "us" security. It's hard to go to a "them." And maybe we can muster our courage and do that, but then we lose any of the benefits we do get from being an "us."

It's Never Too Late: Barbara Hamilton's Story

Barbara Hamilton is sixty-five years old. She was molested by her father in childhood. She grew up, married, raised six children, and now has grandchildren and great-grandchildren as well. Unknown to Barbara until a few years ago, when she started talking about her own molestation, some of her children and grandchildren were also molested, either by her father or by other perpetrators. She talks about the difficulties older women have in making the commitment to heal.†

When you get older, especially as a woman, you deal with rejection on all sides. Society devalues you, and you fall right into that as a victim. Being a survivor ties right into that sense of isolation. It went underground for all those years I was raising my

---

* Survivors of other racial and ethnic groups have faced similar problems in naming their abuse. When a group of people has been oppressed and discriminated against, there is a need to maintain a united front. This can make it more difficult to acknowledge abuse within the group. See Soledad's story on p. 384 for another example.

† Barbara Hamilton has published her story in a compelling book, *The Hidden Legacy: Uncovering, Confronting, and Healing Three Generations of Incest.* See p. 547 of the Resource Guide.

family, but as I got more and more alone, and as the insecurity in my life increased *because* I was an older woman, it all came back up. I had to realize that it hadn't been resolved. All I'd done is acknowledge that it happened. It hadn't really been touched. And I had fifty years of pushing it away.

Don't wait. Don't wait, because it won't go away. It always comes back, and it gets harder. But older woman deserve to heal too. There must be thousands like me who are living under it just like I was. And though the focus of all the books is toward younger women, I don't think you're ever too old. You may be infirm. It may be too hard that way. You won't have the same experiences as a young person. As an older woman, you probably won't ever be able to confront your abuser. But it's worth it. I feel so much better about myself.

In spite of the horror, in spite of the tragedy, in spite of the weeks of sleepless nights, I'm finally alive. I'm not pretending. I feel real. I'm not playing charades anymore. I wouldn't go back to the way I was for anything. I'm really like a different person. I'm where I am, and I'm making the most of it. I *know* I'm courageous now. I found out I had it in me to face this. It's just not ever too late. Look what Grandma Moses did at ninety-five. There's still hope.

It's like going from black-and-white to color, and you never even knew you were in black-and-white. We all thought black-and-white was great all those years that all we had was black-and-white. Do you remember the first time you saw Technicolor? The first time you wore those 3-D glasses? Eventually you get to where life is Technicolor, and it's worth it.

If you say "Why should I bother? I've coped this far," I'd say to you, "You *haven't* coped. You haven't even lived a fraction of yourself. You may be smothering an artist. You may be smothering all kinds of self-expression that needs to come out for your sake, and for others. Why not give it a chance?"

THE EMERGENCY STAGE

Q: Was your healing process an obsessive one?

A: Are you kidding? In the beginning, I'd go to an incest conference for two days and then sit up all night reading Michelle Morris's book *If I Should Die Before I Wake.*

The emergency stage feels like this: You walk out the door to go to work, and you fall on the steps and break your leg. Your spouse tries to drive you to the hospital, but the engine of your car blows up. You go back to the house to call an ambulance, only to find you've locked yourself out. Just as a police car pulls over to give you some help, the big earthquake hits, and your home, your spouse, your broken leg, and the police car all disappear into a yawning chasm.

Many women go through a period when sexual abuse is literally all they can think about. You may find yourself talking about it obsessively with anyone who will listen. Your life may become full of practical crises which totally overwhelm you. You may find yourself having flashbacks uncontrollably, crying all day long, or unable to go to work. You may dream about your abuser and be afraid to sleep:

I just lost it completely. I wasn't eating. I wasn't sleeping. I did hold down a job at Winchell's Donuts. But I was afraid to stay in the house alone. I would go out in the middle of the night and hide somewhere, behind a Dipsy dumpster or something. I had terrible nightmares about my father. I was having all kinds of fantasies. I'd hear the sound of my father's zipper coming down, the click of the buckle. Then I'd imagined all this blood. Physically, I was a mess. I had crabs. I hadn't bathed in a month. I was afraid of the shower.

Total obsession with sexual abuse is more likely if you've forgotten your abuse. When Laura had her first memories, the shock alone was enough to fixate her on incest for several months: "I hadn't had many real memories of my childhood, it was true, but I had created a picture I could brag about, of those early golden years. It's not that all those good things I remembered hadn't happened. It's just that I had somehow forgotten the fact that I had been sexually abused too.

"Breaking through my own denial, and trying to fit the new reality into the shattered framework of the old, was enough to catapult me into total crisis. I felt my whole foundation had been stolen from me. If this could have happened and I could have forgotten it, then every assumption I had about life and my place in it was thrown up for question."

Remembering, for Laura, was a veritable earthquake. Women often describe the early stages of their healing as a variety of natural disasters: "It was like being lifted up in a twister." "It was like being caught in an avalanche." "It was a volcano erupting."

I felt like I was standing in a room, looking at the floor. I was shattered all over it, and I had to go through and pick up the pieces and put them back together. Look at each one and say, "This is me," put it on, and say, "This is where it goes." Or, "Nope, wrong place." Then I'd have to find the place

where it really fit. I was picking up pieces of my life and looking at them, saying, "Do I want to keep this? Is it of any use to me anymore? When will the pain stop?"

The emergency stage is not something you choose, yet it must be ridden through to the other side. It cannot be ignored. As one survivor aptly remarked, "It's like learning a new word. Within days, you start seeing it in everything you read, and you never saw it before in your life."

The Emergency Stage: Catherine's Story

Catherine first faced the fact that she had been sexually abused in a therapy group for alcohol co-dependents. She called a therapist and said, "I need to come to therapy because I'm an incest survivor."

Three months later Catherine quit her job. She had a verbally abusive boss and decided, "I was going to eliminate any stress I could, and so I quit."

At that point, the emergency stage kicked in with full force. "I didn't have any daily responsibilities anymore. I didn't have to be personable for anyone. That's when the despair really had a chance to surface. I started feeling this uncontrollable sadness.

"I dropped everything else in my life. It was like there were large six-foot-high letters in my living room every day when I woke up: *INCEST!* It was just so much in the forefront of my mind that I felt that everyone knew I was an incest victim. I thought I looked like one. I was sure everybody would know the real reason why I was such a creep. I was in constant fear of telling anyone that's what I was in therapy for, because I was so ashamed."

Catherine also disconnected from most of the people in her life. "I had no energy to deal with other people or their problems. My reserves had been drained dry. I withdrew my social time with acquaintance-type people. Then I started to rely more on the people I felt were really true friends. I told them more about my therapy and what I was discovering. The people I used to call up and say, 'Hi. Let's go roller skating,' I didn't bother to call anymore."

Catherine felt completely drained and slept ten or twelve hours a night. "For a long time, all I cared about was going to sleep and being able to wake up the next day."

There were certain emergency things she did to take care of herself during these early stages. "I had to find people who would sit with me no matter what I felt like. I had one friend who'd been beaten when she was a kid. She understood. I could call her up when I felt horrible, and she'd let me come over to just eat and watch TV. It was okay to go over there and feel shitty. She knew what was going on, but we only discussed it if I brought it up.

"I also had to find a safe place to be alone. I went for walks in the woods. I ran a lot. I'd go for twenty- or thirty-mile bike rides. I spent a lot of time outdoors by myself. It felt a lot safer than being at home where someone might need something from me."

Catherine's self-esteem was also hard hit. Like many survivors, she experienced a profound sense of disorientation. "It was the most awkward feeling, to have to try out everything I'd been familiar with. I had to

prove to myself that I could go to the store or drive my car, *and* be an incest victim, all at the same time. I had to spend time in my own house thinking, 'Now I know I'm an incest victim, and yes, I still live here, and yes, my cats still like me.' Outside, it all looked the same, but inside, it was just scrambled. I felt like I was in a vacuum for a whole year, and all that was in front of me were flashbacks and crying."

An essential lifeline for Catherine during the emergency stage was her connection to her therapist. "The only thing that saved me when I felt totally cut off from everything was that I had my therapist's phone number written many places, all over my house. I had it up on the mirror in the bathroom. I had it in my journal. I had it in books that I was reading. I'd stuff it in there on little pieces of paper. I just burned it in my memory, so at any time I could stop and call her. And many times, just making the call and getting her answering machine, and being able to leave a message in my real voice, in my cracking, crying voice, that I needed her to call me, let me know that I could reach out. It reminded me that there was actually something other than my pain and depression. There was actually somebody up on the ledge and I could reach out to her. I knew she would call me eventually, and I could hold out till then."

In Catherine's life, it took many months before the pressure lessened. "After about a year, something shifted for me. I was able to lift my head up a little bit and notice that the season had changed. I started to realize that even though I was an incest survivor, I could go on with my life. I wanted to pick up all the things I had dropped the year before. I was able to say, 'I'll only go to therapy once a week and think about incest twenty hours a week, instead of going twice a week and thinking about incest one hundred hours a week.' I had a choice. I could stop myself from thinking about it at times. It was a tremendous relief."

SURVIVING THE EMERGENCY STAGE

The important thing to remember is that the emergency stage is a natural part of the healing process and will come to an end. The nature of crisis is that it overwhelms you; while you are in it, it is all you can see. But there will be a time when you will not think, eat, and dream sexual abuse twenty-four hours a day. And if you are in the emergency stage, that time will not come a moment too soon.

- **Don't hurt or try to kill yourself.** You deserve to live. If you start feeling suicidal or self-destructive, reach out. (And read "Don't Kill Yourself," page 212 and "Reasons to Not Kill Yourself," page 436.)
- **Know that you're not going crazy.** What you're going through is a recognized part of the healing process. (If you find yourself in a panic, read "Panic," page 211.)
- **Find people you can talk to.** Don't try to bear it alone.
- **Get skilled professional support.** (If you don't know where to look, see "Counseling," page 321.)
- **Get support from other survivors.** It's unlikely that anyone other than another survivor can listen as much as you'll need to talk.
- **Allow yourself to obsess.** Don't make things worse by hating yourself for being where you are.

- **Do as many nice things for yourself as possible.** (For suggestions, see "Nurture Yourself: The Teddy Bear's Picnic," page 197.)
- **Drop what isn't essential in your life.** Release the pressure any way you can. This means dropping unsupportive people, quitting activities, lightening your work load, getting extra child care.
- **Create a safe area in your home.** You need at least one place where you feel safe. (For suggestions, see "Create a Safe Spot," page 213.)
- **Watch your intake of drugs and alcohol.** Repeatedly numbing your feelings will only prolong the crisis.
- **Get out of abusive situations.** If you're currently in a situation where you're being abused, get out of it. (If you have an abusive partner, see "Recognizing Bad Relationships," page 244.)
- **Sit tight and ride out the storm.** Your decision-making capability is limited right now. Except for getting out of abusive situations, the emergency stage is usually not a good time for making major life changes.
- **Remind yourself that you're brave.** This is a challenging, scary, difficult period. You don't have to do anything but live through it.
- **Remember to breathe.** Stay as connected to your body as you can. (See "Exercises for Connecting with Your Body," page 224.)
- **Develop a belief in something greater than yourself.** Spirituality can give you inspiration and strength.
- **This too shall pass.** Your experience tomorrow, or next week, or next year will not be the same as it is right now. (Pay special attention to "Why It's Been Worth It," page 179.)

HEALING CRISES OVER TIME

Although you won't experience the same intensity of crisis once the emergency stage is over, you may go through other crisis periods in the course of your healing. Though these times can be agonizing, we like to call them healing crises, because they offer an opportunity for deep growth.

Some women have experienced so much trauma in their lives that they go through an emergency stage that lasts several years, with only short breaks in intensity. Even though they may be making excellent changes in their current lives, they still feel suicidal, self-destructive, or obsessed with abuse much of the time. If this is the case for you, get all the support you can, and know it won't last forever.

WHAT GAVE ME HOPE

"I had this vision one day of me at the end of the tunnel, and I could look out and I could see the blue sky. I was standing on this very thin ledge, not holding on to anything, just balancing there, and I had my arms spread out and I was going to fly."

"I was a nun in a contemplative order. Because I had lived that lifestyle, I knew that things took a long time. I was geared to an interior life. I knew that the process of becoming holy, of knowing God, was very slow. Day by day, I just knew I was growing closer to God. And I felt the same thing applied to dealing with the incest. I just trusted that something was happening, that there was a hidden growth going on."

"When I'm sure I'm about to be locked up as a crazy woman, the thing that gives me hope is remembering what my therapist kept saying to me, over and over: 'This is part of the change process.' I held on to that when there was really nothing else to hold on to: 'Oh, this is a recognized part of the change process.' "

"My friend Patricia gave me hope. She would basically talk me into wanting to live. She would tell me all the wonderful things there were about life in general, and I would believe her, because I loved her and I cared about her, and I knew she cared about me."

"My sister inspires me through her struggle. She had it a lot worse than I did. She went through absolute Nazi horror, and she is struggling to live. It's an amazing thing to see what people can live through, and still want to live."

"Reading gave me a lot of inspiration. I fell in love with the beauty of the human spirit through reading literature."

"Knowing another survivor who's been in a successful relationship for seven years gave me a lot of hope."

"My own inner strength gave me hope. I just won't quit. Period."

"Music. Spirituals have really helped me. Nina Simone. 'Ooooh child, things are gonna get easier. Ooooh, child, things'll get brighter.' 'The Need to Be Me' by Esther Satterfield."

REMEMBERING

I've looked the memories in the face and smelled their breath. They can't hurt me anymore.

The experience of remembering abuse varies greatly from survivor to survivor. Many women have always remembered their abuse. They may have minimized its importance, denied its impact on their lives, or been numb to their feelings, but they have never forgotten the events themselves. One woman explained, "I could rattle off the facts of my abuse like a grocery list, but remembering the fear and terror and pain was another matter entirely."

Other survivors have selective or partial memory. They remember some occurrences but not others:

I always knew that we had an incestuous relationship. I remember the first time I heard the word "incest," when I was seventeen. I hadn't known there was a word for it. I always remembered my father grabbing my breasts and kissing me.

I told my therapist, "I remember every miserable thing that happened to me." It seemed like I remembered so much, how could there be more? I didn't remember anything *but* abuse. But I didn't remember being raped, even though I knew I had been. I categorically told my therapist, "I don't want to remember being raped." We talked about the fact that I didn't want to remember that for months. Yet I knew my father had been my first lover.

Survivors sometimes remember physical or emotional abuse but not the sexual assaults. Or they may remember the context in which the abuse took place but not the specific physical events.* Others remember part of what happened—such as sitting in a bedroom crying—but don't remember what happened to make them cry. There are also survivors who don't remember anything about their abuse until the memories come crashing—or seeping in:

I'd had clues all along, but I chose to ignore them. I concentrated on my goals, achievements, things I could make, do, produce. I didn't think about how I felt. How I felt was like a sewer—somewhere you wouldn't want to go. Then I got pregnant. It was an accident. I didn't love the man. I'd never loved anyone—I couldn't afford to. I thought about an abortion. It was the sensible thing. But I couldn't.

I loved my baby so intensely, even before she was born, that I couldn't stop myself from feeling. The love was too strong to block out. And along with the love came, of course, the other feelings. All the feelings I'd kept buried—and the memories.

Remembering is a unique experience for every survivor. Although some survivors remember almost all of the abuse they experienced and others remember almost nothing, most fall somewhere in between. Whether you recall your abuse vividly or are just beginning to sense that something terrible may have happened to you, you are engaged in a process of exploration and discovery which will ultimately help you know and understand more of your history.†

WHAT REMEMBERING IS LIKE

There is no right or wrong when it comes to remembering. You may have numerous memories. Or you may have just one. When you begin to remember, you might have new images every day for weeks. Or you may experience your memories in clumps—several in a matter or days, then none for months. Sometimes survivors remember one abuser or a specific kind of abuse, only to remember, years later, another abuser or a different form of abuse.

Remembering sexual abuse is not like remembering ordinary, nonthreatening events. When traumatic memories return, they may seem distant, like something you're observing from far away.

The actual rape memories for me are like from the end of a tunnel. That's because I literally left my body at the scene. So I remember it from that perspective—there's some physical distance between me and what's going on.

---

* See Rachel's story on p. 524, in which she describes growing up in an environment full of pornography, sexualized talk, and emotional abuse.

† Recently there has been much controversy about memories of child sexual abuse. We address some of the disputed issues in "Honoring the Truth," which begins on p. 473.

Those memories aren't as sharp in focus. It's like they happened in another dimension.

Other times, memories come in bits and pieces.

I'd be driving home from my therapist's office, and I'd start having flashes of things—just segments, like bloody sheets, or taking a bath, or throwing away my nightgown. For a long time, I remembered all the things around being raped, but not the rape itself.

If memories come to you in fragments, you may find it hard to place them in any kind of chronological order. You may not know exactly when the abuse began, how old you were, or when it stopped. The process of understanding the fragments can be like putting together a jigsaw puzzle or being a detective.

Part of me felt like I was on the trail of a murder mystery, and I was going to solve it. I really enjoyed following all the clues. "Okay, I was looking at the clock. It was mid-afternoon. Why was it mid-afternoon? Where could my mother have been? Oh, I bet she was at . . ." Tracing down the clues to find out exactly what had happened was actually fun.

Ella is a survivor who remembered piecemeal. To make sense of her memories, she began to examine some of her own strange habits. She started to analyze certain compulsive behaviors, like staring at the light fixture whenever she was making love:

I'd be making love and would think, "Why would somebody lay here, when they're supposed to be having a pleasurable experience, and concentrate on a light fixture?" I remember every single lighting fixture in every single house we ever lived in! Why have I always been so obsessed with light under doors, and the interruption of light? That's a crazy thing for an adult woman to be obsessive about—that someone walks past and cracks the light. What's that about?

Ella realized she was watching to see if her father's footsteps stopped outside her door at night. If they stopped, that meant he'd come in and molest her. Once Ella started to pay attention to these kinds of details, the memories started to fit into place.

All memories may not be literal representations of what happened. Some may be symbolic or may represent an aspect of the trauma, but not be wholly accurate. Yet there is an essential emotional truth to our memories which can tell us a lot about how the experience has affected us. (For more, see "The Essential Truth of Memory," page 89.)

FLASHBACKS

Flashbacks are memories that are so vivid that you feel as though the original experience is happening again *now*, rather than just being remembered. Flashbacks may be accompanied by the feelings you felt at the time, or they may be stark and detached, like watching a movie about somebody else's life.

Frequently flashbacks are visual: "I saw this penis coming toward me," or "I couldn't see his face, just the big black belt he always

WHY CHILDREN FORGET

Although there is a great deal we don't yet know about memories of trauma, there are some concepts we can clearly understand. Why, for instance, might the survivor of an earthquake, a shipwreck, a war, or a concentration camp retain a conscious awareness of these ordeals while a survivor of child sexual abuse might not?

To begin with, earthquakes, wars, shipwrecks, and even concentration camps have names. When the room starts shaking, the walls buckle, and objects fall, we know what to call it. Even children too young to recognize the event as an earthquake have it named for them. An older person explains, "This is an earthquake. We run to the door frame to be safe; there may be little earthquakes that follow," and so on. But after being raped, assaulted, or violated sexually, it is unusual for this event to be explained to the child: "You've just been sexually abused; the perpetrator had no right to do this to you; it's important that you get help." Until very recently, such acknowledgment and confirmation of abuse has been exceedingly rare. Most children who are sexually abused do not have a name for their experience.

Publicly acknowledged events are more likely to be remembered than events that are never discussed or are denied or ignored. Yet even sexual abuse which has public confirmation is more likely to be forgotten than an earthquake because of other factors, such as shame. There is no shame or stigma associated with an earthquake. If a person remembers being in an earthquake, it will not affect her sense of self-worth or self-esteem. She will not be blamed for the earthquake or told that she asked for it. And earthquake victims are not threatened with violent consequences if they talk about what happened.

Also, survivors of child sexual abuse were, by definition, children when the abuse took place—often without any trusted adults to turn to even for sympathy. Except in families where siblings stuck together, these children frequently were isolated in their trauma—unlike soldiers in a war, who had a group to belong to and to bond with, and unlike concentration camp prisoners, who had at least some awareness of who was on their side and who was the enemy. For many abused children, the person who was supposed to be on their side *was* the enemy.

We know that even survivors of recognized events such as wars or disasters can have amnesia for particularly painful aspects of their experience. When we consider the plight of an isolated child, unable to name her suffering, even to herself, unable to speak of it or to comprehend it—with no means of escape except in her mind—we can see why this process of burying the abuse might have been necessary to survive.

DISSOCIATION

To comprehend how someone can "not remember" traumatic events, it's useful to understand the process of dissociation. In situations of overwhelming pain, terror, and violence, when our minds cannot bear to endure what we are forced to endure, we separate ourselves—or a part of ourselves—from the experience. We dissociate. Survivors of child sexual abuse frequently report that they watched themselves being raped: "I left my body and looked down at myself from the corner of the ceiling." Your consciousness split, separated from what was unbearable.

Under these conditions, our brains do not function as they do under conventional circumstances. In fact, the entire physiology of the brain works differently. When our minds are this overstimulated, we can become physiologically incapable of absorbing and storing information in a normal way. Instead, we dissociate these experiences, split them off from our conscious knowledge. Later fragments may return in the form of visual images, body memories, sensations, and intrusive feelings or thoughts.*

Survivors of child sexual abuse who separated from themselves at the time when they were being abused may have perceived and remembered their experience only in bits and pieces—feelings, body sensations, sounds, smells, visual images—not in a coherent, chronological story that can easily be told.

Paradoxically, although trauma may lead to amnesia or to a disjointed remembering, it may also fix memories indelibly in our minds. We may be unable to know the whole story of what happened to us for the same reason that we may not be able to get away from fragments of what happened to us. In both situations, our minds have been unable to integrate the memory of our trauma into the whole of our lives. So even while we may not be able to understand or to tell the story of our abuse, we may also be bombarded by feelings, body sensations, and images of terrifying scenes.

Recalling the actual events, talking about them, feeling our feelings, and integrating these events into our life histories is a part of the healing process that can enable survivors to move beyond, past suffering and into the future.

---

* For further information on the processing of traumatic memories, including the biological aspects of traumatic memory, see "Survivors' Memories and the Denial of Abuse" on p. 554 of the Resource Guide.

wore." These memories can be very dramatic:

> My husband was just beginning to
> initiate some lovemaking. I had a flash
> in my mind. The closest way I can de-
> scribe it is that it was much like viewing
> slides in a slide show, when the slide
> goes by too fast, but slow enough to give
> you some part of the image. It was
> someone jamming their fingers up my
> vagina. It was very vivid, and enough of
> the feelings came sneaking in that I
> knew it wasn't a fantasy. There was an
> element of it that made me stop and
> take notice. I lay there and let it replay
> a couple of times.
>
> I felt confused. I was aware that it
> was something that happened to me. I
> even had a recollection of the pain. I
> scrambled around in my mind for an
> explanation. "Was that a rough lover I
> had?" Immediately I knew that wasn't
> the case. So I went back into the flash
> again. Each time I went back, I tried to
> open it up to see a little more. I didn't
> see his face, but I could sense an essence
> of my father.

But not everyone is visual. One woman
was upset that she couldn't get any pictures.
Her father had held her at knifepoint in the
car, face down in the dark, and raped her.
She had never *seen* anything. But she had
heard him. And when she began to write the
scene in Spanish, her native language, it all
came back to her—his threats, his brutality,
his violation.

Flashbacks can involve any of the senses.
What you heard, saw, smelled, tasted, felt, or
thought can return with such immediacy that
you actually relive the original experience.

SENSE MEMORY

Often it is a particular touch, smell, or
sound that triggers a memory. You might remember when you return to the town, the
house, or the room where the abuse took
place. Or when you smell a certain aftershave
the abuser wore.

Thirty-five-year-old Ella says, "It's all
real tactile, sensory things that have brought
memories back. Textures. Sounds. The smell
of my father's house. The smell of vodka on
somebody."

Ella had a magic purple quilt when she
was a little girl. Her grandmother made it for
her. It was supposed to keep her safe—nothing bad could happen to her as long as she
was under it. The quilt had been lost for
many years, but when Ella finally got it back,
at twenty-one, it triggered a whole series of
memories.

Touch can also reopen memories.
Women have had images come up while they
were being massaged. You may freeze and
see images from your past when you're making love. Your lover breathes in your ear just
as your abuser once did, and it all comes spilling back:

> Sometimes when we're making
> love, I feel like my head just starts to
> float away somewhere. I feel like I lit-
> erally split off at my shoulders, and I
> get very lightheaded and dizzy. It's as if
> someone was blowing a fan down on top
> of my head. There's a lot of movement
> down past my hair. It's like rising up out
> of my head. I get really disoriented.
>
> The other thing I experience is a
> lot of splitting right at the hips. My legs
> get very heavy and really solid. They
> just feel like dead weight, like logs. No

energy is passing through them. Then I get real sick to my stomach, just violently ill. I find the minute I get nauseous, whatever it is is very close to me. And if I pay attention to it, I can see it, and move on.

THE BODY REMEMBERS WHAT THE MIND CHOOSES TO FORGET

Memories can remain stored in our bodies—in sensations, feelings, and physical responses. Even if we do not know what took place, fragments of what we suffered endure. You may be assailed by unexplained physical pain or arousal, fear, confusion or any other sensory aspect of the abuse. You may physically reexperience the terror, your body may clutch tight, or you may feel that you are suffocating and cannot breathe.

I would get body memories that would have no pictures to them at all. I would just start screaming and feel that something was coming out of my body that I had no control over. And I would usually get them right after making love or in the middle of making love, or right in the middle of a fight. When my passion was aroused in some way, I would remember in my body, although I wouldn't have a conscious picture, just this screaming coming out of me.

TIMES WHEN SURVIVORS REMEMBER

Memories come up under many different circumstances, often with some event or situation setting off the process. Sometimes women remember abuse when there is sufficient safety for the memories and feelings to emerge. For example, you might remember when you're finally in a relationship that feels safe.

On the other hand, difficult or painful times may precede remembering. You may experience a loss, such as divorce or the death of a loved one, and feel as though everything in your life is unraveling. A contemporary event that resembles the original abuse can also trigger memories. Some women, for instance, have recalled childhood abuse when they were raped or attacked in adult life.

But memories don't always surface in such dramatic ways. While talking with a friend, one woman suddenly heard herself talking about being abused as a child for the first time. "It's as though I always knew it," she explained. "It's just that I hadn't thought about it in twenty or thirty years. Up until that moment, I'd forgotten."

WHEN YOU BREAK AN ADDICTION

Many survivors remember their abuse once they get sober, quit drugs, or stop eating compulsively. These and other addictions can effectively numb your feelings and block any recollection of the abuse, but once you stop, the memories often surface. Anna Stevens explains:

At the point I decided to put down drinking, I had to start feeling. The connection to the abuse was almost immediate. And I've watched other people come to AA and do the same thing. They have just enough time to get through the initial shakes, and you watch them start to go through the memories. And you know what's coming, but they don't.*

WHEN YOU BECOME A MOTHER

Mothers often remember their own abuse when they see their children's vulnerability, or when their children reach the age they were when the abuse began. Sometimes they remember because their child is being abused. Dana was court-ordered to go for therapy when her three-year-old daughter, Christy, was molested. Dana first remembered her own abuse when she subconsciously substituted her own name for her daughter's:

I was in therapy talking about Christy, and instead of saying "Christy," I said "I." And I didn't even catch it. My therapist did. She had always suspected that I was abused too, but she hadn't said anything to me.

She told me what I had said, and I said, "I did? I said 'I?'" I hadn't even heard myself. It was really eerie.

What came out was that I was really dealing with Christy's molestation on a level of my own. The things that I was outraged at and that hurt me the most were things that had happened to me, not things that had happened to Christy. Part of the reason I fell apart and so much came back to me when I found out about Christy was because

my husband was doing the same things to her that my father had done to me.

AFTER A SIGNIFICANT DEATH

Many women are too scared to remember while their abusers are still alive. One woman said, "I couldn't afford to remember until both my parents were dead, until there was nobody left to hurt me." A forty-seven-year-old woman first remembered a year and a half after her mother died: "Then I could no longer hurt my mother by telling her."

MEDIA COVERAGE OF SEXUAL ABUSE

Jennierose, who remembered in her mid-forties, was sitting with her lover one night, watching a TV program about sexual offenders in prison. The therapist running the group encouraged the offenders to get very emotional, at which time a number of them remembered traumatic events from their childhood.

In the middle of the program, Jennierose turned to her lover and said, "I wish there was a therapist like that I could go to, because I know there's something I'm not remembering." As soon as she said that, Jennierose had a vision of the first time her father sodomized her, when she was four and a half and her mother had gone to the hospital to have another baby. "It was a totally detailed vision, to the point of seeing the rose-colored curtains blowing in the window."

Sobbing, Jennierose said to her lover, "I think I'm making something up." Her lover simply said, "Look at yourself! Look at yourself! Tell me you're making it up." And Jennierose couldn't. She knew she was telling the truth.

---

* For more of Anna's story, see p. 398.

FEELING THE FEELINGS

Although remembering sometimes feels emotionally detached, when you remember with feeling, the helplessness, terror, and physical pain can be as real as any actual experience. You may feel as if you are being crushed, ripped open, or suffocated. Sexual arousal may also accompany your memories, and this may horrify you, but arousal is a natural response to sexual stimulation. You don't have to be ashamed.

You might remember feeling close and happy, wrapped in a special kind of love. Disgust and horror are not the only way to feel when you have memories. There is no *right* way to feel, but you must feel, even if it sends you reeling.

When I first remembered, I shut down emotionally right away. I climbed all the way up into my mind and forgot about the gut level. That's how I protected myself. For a long time it was just an intellectual exercise. "Oh, that's why I have trouble with men and authority. That's why I might not have remembered much about growing up." It took nine months after I first remembered for the feelings to start bubbling up.

I found myself slipping into the feelings I'd had during the abuse, that hadn't been safe to feel at the time. The first was this tremendous isolation. From there, I moved into absolute terror. I got in touch with how frightening the world is. It was the worst of the fear finally coming up. I felt like it was right at the top of my neck all the time, just ready to come out in a scream.

I was right at the edge. I had an encounter with my boss, who said that my performance had been poor. I finally told him what had happened, which was really heavy—telling some male authority figure that you remembered incest in your family. He is a kind and caring person. The best he could do was back off and leave me alone.

I was then carrying around all this external pressure—my job was in jeopardy, my life was falling apart, and I was having all these feelings I didn't know what to do with. In order to keep myself in control, I started compulsively eating. Finally I decided I didn't want to go through this stuff by myself anymore. I got myself into therapy.

Having to experience the feelings is one of the roughest parts of remembering. "It pisses me off that I have to survive it twice, only this time with feelings," one woman said. "This time it's worse. I'm not so effective at dissociating anymore."

Another woman said, "I started off very butch [tough] about remembering. I kicked into my overachiever thing. I was going to lick this thing. I believed getting the pictures was what was important. I got a ton of memories, all on the intellectual level. It was kind of like I was going to 'do' incest, just like I might take up typing."

It was only after a year of therapy that this woman began to realize that *she* was the one who'd been abused. "I finally realized, I finally *felt,* that this was something that had happened to *me,* and that it had been damaging. I had to realize that just getting the memories was not going to make it go away. *This was about me!*"

While Making Love
by Laura Davis

It was a sunny Sunday morning. We had not made love for a long time. We lay in bed, curled together like spoons. I was half-asleep, half-awake, feeling her warm weight curve into mine, her knees fitting smoothly against mine. Her musky breath touched me, warm and familiar on my neck, her fingertips gently searching my back, a question: "Can it be now? I want you."

I turned to face her, to study the green-gold eyes I loved. To wonder at this miracle woman who had crashed through all my defenses and disarmed me. She had made it all the way in and I trusted her. Finally, at twenty-eight, I felt safe in love. Before, I'd been a loner, too busy achieving, too busy living in my head, afraid of loving, a terror I could not name keeping me distant, just out of reach. There'd been other lovers, surely, others whom I dismissed when they got too close, others who skirted my edges. But she was the first who'd reached all the way through those walls. She was the one I'd dreamed of but never thought possible, the one whose soft presence beside me still surprised and awed me these slow weekend mornings. I was happy, happier than I'd ever been.

So to answer the question of her searching fingers, I looked up and smiled at her, inviting her caresses, and reached to stroke her face. She pressed her belly up against mine, and I felt the sudden jolt of passion flare skin to skin. "I love this woman," I thought. "And we have our whole lives to share it."

She was kissing me now, teasing and slow, waiting for me to answer, for me to rise, for me to catch the rush, like winds in a sail, to fly with her. "So far, so good," I thought, my tongue answering, responding, my body firm against hers, passion rising.

There was a gleam in her eyes. She'd been waiting for this for a long, long time. "I want you," she said, her fingers reaching in, her body on fire against me. "I want you."

And then I felt it. Subtle, unmistakable. Painfully familiar. A small spark of terror and then the screen. An impermeable wall suddenly cast between us, my body cut loose, my mind floating free. I tried to call myself back, but already it was too late. I was gone.

"Well, there's not enough eggs for waffles," I thought. "But there are those leftover baked potatoes. And they'd make great home fries." I closed my eyes, tried again to reel myself in. "C'mon, Laura. You want to be here. You want to do this. Get back in your body. C'mon! This is the

LETTING MEMORIES IN

Few survivors feel they have control over their memories. Most feel the memories have control of them, that they do not choose the time and place a new memory will emerge. You may be able to fight them off for a time, but the price—headaches, nightmares, exhaustion—is not worth staving off the inevitable.

Not everyone will know a memory is

woman you love!"

But it didn't work. My mind was already far above my body, spinning, dancing intricate loops. I felt totally out of control. My body lay on the bed beneath, still going through the motions. God, how I hated this! The old grief, this lack of presence, surged through me.

I slowed down my caresses, pulled my mouth away. I grew quiet, solitary. Looked back at her face, drawn tight and hard with disappointment. "I'm sorry, honey," I said after a moment. "I just can't." She looked stung, tears frozen in her eyes. We'd come so close.

This was not the first time I'd "disappeared." Nor the second. This was old, familiar territory, a vast chasm spreading between us, wider and wider the closer we got.

"Where the hell do you go?" she screamed at me then, months of patience suddenly giving way. "Where the hell are you? Just what is wrong with you anyway?"

Then silence. Her words reverberating, burrowing in, digging deep into my center. I felt them choking me. Nothing else was real. I didn't know where I was, who I was looking at. Her face wavered before me. I couldn't breathe. I stopped seeing. Stopped doing anything but feeling those questions probing deeper and deeper inside.

I must have looked stricken because her face softened then, and she held me, her eyes deep with concern and tender with love. "Breathe, honey," she said. "Go ahead and breathe."

That's all I remember. I know there were moments passing, quiet pensive moments. Something was happening to me. I could feel it—a tiny bubble of truth rising up from deep inside, a knowing coming from an unnamed core, the kind of knowing that pierces through years of fog and cannot be denied.

I started sobbing. Deep, wracking sobs that scared me and confused me, leaving me helpless and hurting, a child in pain. I had never cried like this. What was happening to me? Someone had hurt me very badly.

She stroked my forehead, peppered it with kisses. "Sweetheart, what is it?"

More sobs, more shaking. A terror, a truth, a knowledge too awful to utter, was finally breaking free. I did not recognize the words until they spilled from my lips. I knew I was going to say something, but I did not know what it would be.

"I was molested," I finally said, a tiny child's voice at last managing those three small words. As I heard them cut through the quiet of the sunny morning air, I knew that they were true. "I was molested."

starting, but many survivors do get warnings, a certain feeling or series of feelings, that clue them in. Your stomach may get tight. You may sleep poorly, have frightening dreams. Or you may be warned in other ways:

I always know when they're coming. I get very tense. I get very scared. I get snappy at things that ordinarily wouldn't make me angry. I get sad. Usually it's anger and anxiety and fear that come first. And I have a choice. It's a real conscious choice. It's either I want it or I don't want it. And I said "I don't want it" a lot. And when I did that, I would just get sicker and sicker. I'd get more depressed. I'd get angry irrationally.

Now I don't say I don't want it. It's not worth it. My body seems to need to release it. The more I heal, the more I see these memories are literally stored in my body, and they've got to get out. Otherwise I'm going to carry them forever.

REMEMBERING OVER TIME

Sometimes when you've resolved one group of memories, another will make its way to the surface.

The more I worked on the abuse, the more I remembered. First I remembered my brother, and then my grandfather. About six months after that I remembered my father. And then about a year later, I remembered my

---

IF YOU THINK A MEMORY IS ON ITS WAY:

- **Find a place where you will be safe.** If you're at work, try to get home. Go to the safe place in your house (see "Create a Safe Spot," page 213), or go to a close friend's house.

- **Call a support person.** You may want to be with a supportive partner, friend, support group member, or counselor before, during, or after your memory. Or you may prefer being alone.

- **Don't fight it.** The best thing to do is to relax and let the memory come. Don't use drugs, alcohol, or food to push it back down.

- **Remember, it's just a memory.** What you're experiencing is a memory of abuse that happened a long time ago.

Your abuser is not really hurting you in the present, even if it feels that way. Reliving a memory is part of your healing, not an extension of the abuse.

- **Expect yourself to have a reaction.** Recovering memories is a painful, draining experience. It may take you a while to recover. It's best to give yourself that time and not expect to run off and do something else right away.

- **Comfort yourself.** Having a memory is a very vulnerable experience. Do some special things to take care of yourself (for suggestions, see "Nurture Yourself: The Teddy Bear's Picnic," page 197).

- **Tell at least one other person.** Even though you may prefer to be alone when you have a new memory, it's important that you tell someone else about it. You suffered alone as a child. You don't have to do it again.

mother. I remembered the "easiest" first and the "hardest" last. Even though it was traumatic for me to realize that everyone in my family abused me, there was something reassuring about it. For a long time I'd felt worse than the initial memories should have made me feel, so remembering the rest of the abuse was actually one of the most grounding things to happen. My life suddenly made sense.

The impact new memories have will shift over time. One woman who has been getting new memories for the past ten years says that remembering has become harder over time:

My first flood of memories came when I was twenty-five. The memories I get now are like fine-tuning—more details, more textures. Even though there was more of a feeling of shock and catharsis at first, remembering is harder now. I believe them now. It hurts more. I have the emotions to feel the impact. I can see how it's affected my life.

Laura also says new memories are harder:

Just when I felt that my life was getting back to normal and I could put the incest aside, I had another flashback that was much more violent than the earlier pictures I'd seen. I was furious. I wanted to be finished. I didn't want to be starting in with incest again! And my resistance made the remembering a lot more difficult.

Other survivors say memories have gotten easier to handle:

As I've come to terms with the fact that I was abused, new pictures, new in-cidents, don't have the same impact. The battle of believing it happened is not one I have to fight each time another piece falls into place. Once I had a framework to fit new memories into, my recovery time got much faster. While my first memories overwhelmed me for weeks, now I might only cry for ten minutes or feel depressed for an hour. It's not that I don't have new memories. It's just that they don't dev-astate me anymore.

And new memories don't take anything away from the healing you've already done. Paradoxically, *you are already healing from the effects of things you have yet to remember.*

THE ESSENTIAL TRUTH OF MEMORY

Memories of child sexual abuse can be exceedingly accurate. In situations where abusers are willing to relate their version of the events, the abuser's story often matches the survivor's memory quite closely. Also, when siblings or other family members share what they witnessed, there is often a striking correlation. And when the abuser is outside the family, other victims of the same perpetrator frequently report remarkably similar abuse.

Yet memories of child sexual abuse, like other more ordinary memories, are not to-tally objective recordings of what took place and are likely to exhibit some degree of dis-tortion. The sequence of events may be re-arranged, or multiple incidents may be telescoped into a single instance. Sometimes the way you experienced the abuse leads to distortions. A common example is in the description of size. A small child may remember the abuser as being huge, or the abuser's genitals as filling her whole field of vision. One survivor who was abused by a teacher remembered that the school was enormous, with extremely high ceilings and wide corridors. When she went back as an adult, she was shocked at how small it really was.

Another survivor originally thought she'd been sexually abused with a lollipop. When she went back to her parents and told them what she was remembering, they reminded her she'd been sexually abused by her pediatrician during routine appointments. At the end of each visit, he'd given her a lollipop. Even though this woman had talked about the abuse as a child, and even though her parents had responded appropriately, she had forgotten the abuse entirely. It wasn't until she was an adult in therapy, trying to make sense of images of lollipops and flashes of vaginal pain, that she started to remember.

Sometimes distortion in survivors' memories works as a shield against a more disturbing memory. One survivor thought her babysitter had abused her. Later she discovered it was actually her mother.

Another survivor described witnessing her father forcing oral sex on her adolescent sister. She remembered that after he'd finish with her sister, he'd come and kiss her goodnight and that "his kiss would hurt." But she felt sure he didn't actually abuse her. Over time, however, she recovered the fuller memory that what hurt was not only his kiss, but that he had violated her through oral sex as well.

Although inaccuracies may exist in your memory, you can still work with what you remember as an indicator of what you felt and experienced. One survivor related that she remembered her abuser putting a knife up her vagina. But she went on to explain that she didn't think that's what actually happened. There was no blood, no scarring, and she had no memory of the knife. She assumed that he penetrated her vagina—perhaps with a finger or his penis—and the feeling was so painful, so cutting, that she, in her child's mind, had no concept for it other than a knife.

The way these women worked with their memories is a good model. It's okay to shift your understanding of your childhood as you incorporate new information and learn more. Discovering, understanding, and integrating your past is an ongoing part of the healing process. (For more about the accuracy of memories, see "What We Do and Don't Know About Memory," page 513.)

BUT I DON'T HAVE ANY MEMORIES

Usually when women say they feel they were sexually abused but don't have any memories, they mean that they can't tell a cohesive story about the abuse. However, when they begin to talk in detail about their childhoods, they frequently relate events that are covertly sexual or even blatantly abusive.

I remember the first time I told my therapist how my mother would give me enemas. She would lay me down on the bathroom mat and talk really sweet to me. She was usually abrupt, like we kids were in her way and she wished she didn't have to bother with us, but at enema time she'd turn all her attention on me, stroking me, telling me what a good girl I was. She'd rub my legs and my thighs and my buttocks, saying she just wanted to relax me.

When I told my therapist about this, she asked me how often it happened. I told her every day as soon as I got home from school. I'll never forget the look on her face. She didn't have to say a word.

You may not recall particular incidents such as the one this woman describes, but you're likely to discover that you know more than you think you do about the environment in which you grew up. Specific incidents of sexual abuse don't usually occur as isolated blotches in an otherwise healthy family. You may clearly remember times when you felt used, humiliated, undermined, manipulated, or smothered.

I've always remembered the violence—Dad beat Mom. It wasn't that often, but you never knew when it was going to happen. He was seething *all* the time. We kids would cower in the bed, covering our heads with pillows and singing TV jingles to drown out the noise. We were never allowed to have friends over. My sisters and I fought all the time. I was desperately lonely.

As you explore what you *do* know about your childhood, you will sometimes remember more.

There are also times when women don't have memories of sexual abuse because no specific incidents took place. Instead you may have been subjected to an environment of inappropriate boundaries, lewd looks, sexually suggestive behavior, or emotional incest.

My father made me his wife. After my mother died, he put me in her place. He'd send me bouquets of flowers addressed to "My darling," he'd bring me fancy chocolates, he'd dress me up. He even bought me a ring with a diamond chip and put it on my finger. Everyone thought he was so devoted, so charming. But it was sick and it left me hopelessly confused. What little girl wouldn't lap up that attention? I worshiped him. But the underside of all that adoration was a kind of possession. It's affected every relationship I've ever been in.

I was in therapy for three years, searching, expecting to uncover some rape or instance when he actually molested me. But he didn't do any of that. It was all emotional.

Many women never recall all of what happened to them. There may be gaps and unknowns that become clear as your healing progresses, but it's also possible that there will be aspects of your experience that you never fully recover.

Fortunately, it's possible to heal from the effects of childhood abuse even if your memories are incomplete. One thirty-eight-year-old survivor described her relationship with her father as "emotionally incestuous." She has never had specific memories of any physical contact between them, and for a long time she was haunted by the fact that she couldn't come up with hard data. Over time, though, she's come to terms with her lack of physical memories.

Do I want to know if something physical happened between my father and me? Really, I think you have to be strong enough to know. I think that our minds are wonderful in the way they protect us, and I think that when I'm strong enough to know, I'll know.

I obsessed for about a year on trying to remember, and then I got tired of sitting around talking about what I couldn't remember. I thought, "All right, let's act as if." It's like you come home and your home has been robbed and everything has been thrown in the middle of the room, and the window is open and the curtain is blowing in the wind, and the cat is gone. You know somebody robbed you, but you're never going to know who. So what are you going to do? Sit there and try to figure it out while your stuff lies around? No, you start to clean it up. You put bars on the windows. You *assume* somebody was there. Somebody could come along and say, "Now, how do you know someone was there?" You don't know.

That's how I acted. I had the symptoms. Every incest group I went to, I completely empathized. It rang bells all the time. I felt like there was something I just couldn't get to, that I couldn't remember yet. And my healing was blocked there.

Part of my wanting to get specific memories was guilt that I could be accusing this man of something so heinous, and what if he didn't do it? How horrible for me to accuse him! That's why I wanted the memories. I wanted to be sure. Societally, women have always been accused of crying rape.

But I had to ask myself, "Why would I be feeling all of this? Why would I be feeling all this anxiety if

something didn't happen?" If the specifics are not available to you, then go with what you've got.

I'm left with the damage. And that's why I relate to that story of the burglar. I'm owning the damage. I want to get better. I've been very ill as a result of the damage, and at some point I realized, "I'm thirty-eight years old. What am I going to do—wait twenty more years for memory?" I'd rather get better.

And then maybe the stronger I am, the more the memories will come back. Maybe I'm putting the cart before the horse. Maybe I've remembered as much as I'm able to remember without breaking down. I don't want to go insane. I want to be out in the world. Maybe I should go with that sense of protection. There is a survivor in here and she's pretty smart. So I'm going with the circumstantial evidence, and I'm working on healing myself. I go to these incest groups, and I tell people, "I don't have any pictures," and then I go on and talk all about my father, and nobody ever says, "You don't belong here."

The process of remembering is different for every survivor. If you remember very little of your abuse—or of your whole childhood—it may be hard to define your experience clearly. But if you are in deep pain, there is a reason for your distress. It may not be sexual abuse, but there's something for you to identify and address. You're not crazy to be feeling so much pain.

Although the desire to know and name your experience may feel urgent, it often takes substantial time to explore and discover your past. Try to be patient with yourself.

Don't rush. You can move forward in your healing in important ways, even if you can't pin down exactly what happened.

SURRENDER
by Molly Fisk

When the truth came to me,
slipped into my house in its white
robes, its face open as my face,
its heart obvious and trusting,
I stood calmly in the front hall
and did not move to bar the door.

When the truth laid its cool hand
on my sleeve and said,
Come with me, it's time, I went
quietly. She led me into the past,
through the backyards I once
knew, bedrooms and kitchens;
we sat in my father's car and talked.

I was shivering in my thin skin
and crying readily by this time: terrified,
furious. She offered her own consolation—
no false pats on the hand and no shoulder
to lean on, I had to learn to stand upright
or bend on my own. In her clear voice
the truth offered all she has to give us:
Herself, and the stern comfort
of belonging to this world.

WRITING EXERCISE: WHAT HAPPENED TO YOU

(See the basic method for writing exercises on page 32.)

Write about your experience of being sexually abused as a child.

Many women have found it very difficult to tell people that they were sexually abused. When they do tell, it is often in very generalized terms: "I was molested by my brother," "I was raped when I was ten." Rarely do you share the details, partly because it's hard to tell even the general facts and partly because you want to spare the listeners. You don't want to impose.

But the tight statement "My stepfather abused me" is not the way you live with the abuse, not the way you experience flashbacks. That's not indicative of the creepy feelings you get when something triggers your memory. What you remember is the way the light fell on the stairway, the pajamas you were wearing, the smell of liquor on his breath, the feel of the gravel between your shoulder blades when you were thrown down, the terrifying chuckle, the sound of the TV downstairs. When you write, include as many of these sensory details as you can.

If your abuse covers too much time and too many abusers to write it all in half an hour, just write what you can. Don't worry about which experience to start with. Begin with what feels most accessible or what you feel you most need to deal with. This is an exercise you can do over and over again.

If you don't remember what happened to you, write about what you do remember. Re-create the context in which the abuse happened, even if you don't remember the specifics of the abuse yet. Describe where you lived as a child. What was going on in your family, in your neighborhood, in your life? Often when women think they don't remember, they actually remember quite a lot. But since the picture isn't in sequence and isn't totally filled in, they don't feel they have permission to call what they know "remembering." Start with what you have. When you utilize that fully, you usually get more.

If you come to things that feel too difficult to say, too painful or humiliating, try to write them anyway. You don't have to share them with anyone if you don't want to, but in order to heal you must be honest with yourself. If there's something you feel you absolutely can't write then at least write that there's something you can't or won't write. That way you leave a marker for yourself, you acknowledge that there's a difficult place.

If you go off on tangents, don't pull yourself back too abruptly. Sometimes what may look irrelevant leads us to something more essential. Although you want to stay with the subject, do so with loose reins.

There is no one right way to do this exercise. Your writing may be linear, telling your story in chronological order. It may be a wash of feelings and sensations. Or it may be vague, weaving together scattered bits and pieces. As with all the writing exercises, try not to judge or censor. Don't feel that you should conform to any standard, and don't compare your writing with others'. This is an opportunity to uncover and heal, not to perform or to meet anyone's expectations—not even your own.

I Give Thanks for the Sky
by Teresa Strong

Teresa Strong's poetic response to this exercise is vivid and deeply moving. We hope it inspires you to tell your own story.

It's morning twilight, gray world, dreamworld, non-world time. I'm asleep, or at least I think I am. I'm dreaming, or maybe I'm crazy like my grandmother. I'm sleeping in the back room and hear my grandfather (and know he's *not* really my grandfather) coming in. He sits down beside the bed I used to sleep in—the one my niece sleeps in now. (Get her *OUT* of the fucking bed. It should be burned and chopped and destroyed. No one should sleep in that bed.)

He sits down beside the bed and starts easing me from sleep by rubbing his hand over me on top of the covers (the whole world is asleep), and under the covers and under my nightgown and over and all around me. And his touch is soft and he strokes and I don't know what is going on but it feels like a charge, like Life going through me. And it feels good to be touched and sometimes I pretend to be asleep and sometimes I am asleep and he just keeps touching and stroking and gliding and then somewhere in the tingling and feeling like Life going through me flashes *DANGER! DANGER! DANGER! STOP!* And that's when he starts moving faster and he's not stroking or touching anymore. He's grabbing and rubbing and holding me down and leaning over me. And all I see are cold steel balls where his eyes used to be. And he's over me and all I can see from the corner of my eye is the sky and a leaf. I hold on to them.

That's the sky. I know that's sky. That's a

piece of the sky, and that's a leaf. I know that's a leaf. And I'm clinging to the sky with my eye and he's whispering in my ear. "Oh Honey, see how much you like this and the best is yet to come."

I hear his zipper unzip. My body is jerking and writhing under him. *I* say it's because I'm trying to get away and he's almost giggling (these are the only times I see him smile big smiles), telling me how much I love this. His touch isn't a human touch anymore. He just presses and grabs. And then his penis is in front of my face and I know I'm either dreaming, crazy, or about to die, and my only hope is to hold on to the sky. And I do.

That's the sky and that's a leaf and he shoves his penis in my mouth. I die looking at the sky and he pushes and shoves and it feels like the roof of my mouth has to split open soon. And it feels like he's all the way down my throat. I can't breathe! I can't breathe! I need to throw up! *WHERE* is the sky? *WHERE* is the leaf? I can't see anything. I'm going to be sick. I want to *DIE*. I leave my body. I hide in my forehead and then in the sky. My throat is burning. He comes half in my throat, half in my face. I gasp for breath. He holds my jaw shut and I lose sight of the sky. I *HAVE* to see the sky—it's my only hope of getting out of here alive.

Sometimes he wipes my face clean and sometimes he forces me to eat it. Sometimes he grins and sometimes he strokes for a long time. Sometimes I completely lose sight of the sky and pass out. And when I wake up to the sounds of breakfast being prepared, the world is ordinary and fine.

As time goes on he doesn't bother to stroke or hold or touch me. I'm not even there. But each time before he leaves, he leans down, his nose brushing against my ear, and whispers, "Just remember, Honey, nothing happened." And being eager to please, I remember perfectly.

Once I ask my mother to let me sleep in a different room and she refuses because I'm now four and a big girl. My grandfather's story changes. Sometimes he tells me that if I tell, everyone will know I'm crazy and I'll be sent away. But, unlike my grandmother, he'll make sure I never come back. He also tells me that because I like this so much (and here he'll stroke me again like he hasn't for a long time and I do like the touch), if anyone finds out I'll really be in trouble because only whores/bad girls/crazy people like being touched like this. And besides, he tells me, we come to his home every year on my father's vacation.

So when early morning comes I pretend to be asleep as long as I can until he shakes me awake. And when I can't do that I look for the sky. And I keep the secrets that I like being touched and that I'm crazy. I fool people by getting good grades so no one knows I'm crazy. And I don't let anyone touch me, so they don't know I like it. And I hold on to the sky.

BELIEVING IT HAPPENED

Up until three months ago, I didn't *really* believe it happened: "It was hypnosis." "I only imagined it." I was acting as if it really happened. I'd go to an incest survivors' group. I'd freely tell people. But when I was alone, I'd say, "Of course it didn't *really* happen."

To heal from child sexual abuse, you must face the fact that you were abused. This is often difficult for survivors. When you've spent your life denying the reality of your abuse, when you don't want it to be true, or when your family repeatedly calls you crazy or a liar, it can be hard to stay clear in the knowledge that you were abused.*

Some survivors have no trouble believing it happened. Corroboration can make it easier to accept the truth. You may have a sister or brother who remembers. A mother who said, "But honey, we had to stay with him." Physical scars from a rape at age four. A doctor's report. Court testimony. An abuser who says, "Yes, I did it." A neighbor who remembers. Another child you told.

What cemented it for me was when I told my mother what I remembered. I watched her face go blank, like she was in shock, and then she said, "That's

---

* The recent surge of public attacks on survivors' credibility has made believing it happened more difficult for some survivors. For a thorough discussion of the backlash and its impact on survivors, see "Honoring the Truth," p. 473.

your old room on the farm in Kentucky."

But even survivors who have confirmation of their abuse sometimes struggle with believing it happened. For many survivors, denial has been a way of life. You may have grown up in a family where many things were denied, not just abuse. You may have learned by example to numb your feelings, to dissociate from painful or confusing experiences, to deny any troubling realities. These long-standing patterns don't just evaporate, even when there's clear proof of abuse.

And for many survivors, such proof is not available. Nor is support or validation from family members. Yet even if your memories are incomplete, even if your family insists nothing ever happened, you still need to face your own experience.

THE ROLE OF DENIAL

Survivors sometimes go to great lengths to deny their memories. One woman convinced herself it was all a dream. Another dismissed her memories by saying, "Oh, it's just a past life." When Laura was getting her first pictures of the actual abuse, she did not want to believe what she saw:

I did not want to believe with a passion. Even as part of me recognized the truth, another part fought to deny what I had seen. There were times when I would rather have viewed myself as crazy than acknowledge what had happened to me.

I had come from a wonderful family. *I* couldn't have been raped as a child. *I* couldn't have been molested by the grandfather I had revered and loved. I remembered all the wonderful things he did. That he had abused me was out of the question! It couldn't be!

This type of denial might seem surprising, but in reality it is a self-protective way to deal with traumatic pain. Denial gives you a respite when you cannot bear to align yourself with that small, wounded child for another minute. It allows you to go to work, to make breakfast for your kids. It is a survival skill that enables you to set a pace you can handle.

Often in the beginning stages, belief in your memories comes and goes. One woman explained:

It's like being in a fog and the clouds go away. I'd have a memory. I'd relive the experience. Then I'd know it was true. "That was real. I don't want it to be true. But it happened." Then as soon as I said that, I'd deny it: "But I love my father. He couldn't have done that." But there'd be these little things inside that would say, "But what about the mysterious bladder infections I had when I was eight? He never could look me in the eye when I was in the hospital."

A dramatic example of this touch-and-go belief in memories occurred in one of Ellen's workshops. During a writing exercise, one woman wrote about the abuse she experienced when she was very young. When she read it aloud to the group, she experienced a complete regression, sobbing, stuttering, and

There Are Things
by Lisa Schweig

I. Facts and Figures	II. Confusion and Doubt
There are facts and figures	There is confusion and doubt
Dates and times	Frustration and denial
True statements	Questioning
There are things I know.	There are things I don't know.
I know what I was wearing	I don't know why
I know what I wasn't wearing	or how
I know where I was	it really
I know who was with me	happened.
I know his body over me	I don't know when
I know his hand on my breast	it started
I know his hand going down	where
I know there is more	he stopped
I know I felt scared	I don't know who
I know I curled up	he is
I know I tried hard	if
I know I said no.	I love him.

shaking as she relived the experience. Everyone in the group was deeply moved.

Later the same day, the same woman asked, "Do you think I really could have been abused? Maybe I was just acting." Another woman in the group turned to her and said, "Could you have acted joy and happiness as convincingly? If you're such a great actress, why do you only act out the same scene again and again?"

It is natural to have periodic doubts about your experience—accepting memories is painful.

WHEN DOUBTS PERSIST

For some survivors, disturbing doubts about their abuse persist for a long time. One survivor, Emily, grew up in a family where her reality was so severely tampered with, it's no wonder she has trouble trusting her perceptions:

At night, before I went to sleep, my mother would tell me that what went on during the day when I was awake was

First Light
by Aurora Levins Morales

This is an excerpt from a longer, unfinished piece. The character, a nine-year-old girl, has just been raped by her uncle.

She lay on the narrow bed in the very early morning light and felt herself dying. She kept herself very still until she could feel nothing at all, and then she knew the process was complete. She was dead. Now, she knew, came the washing of the corpse, and this one needed it. The monster that had killed her had left blood on her. It was a strange thing, being killed in your own bed like that, in such an ordinary place. Nothing looked different, but it was all unfamiliar. Like the kind of bad dream where after you wake up, for a few minutes the clothes draped over the chair still look like a wolf and you're afraid to move.

Only she couldn't remember waking up after this dream. The events were seamless. She had paid close attention, but the only waking she remembered was when the door opened and the monster came in her room.

So it must be real. As she thought this, she felt the cold in her body deepen. Because what if they insisted it was a dream? Insisted she was still alive? What if they made her walk and talk and go to school and eat, when really she was dead? What if they told her it was just pretend?

Suddenly, small and clear, like a picture on a very tiny far-away television screen, she remembered the afternoon with her aunt Luisa. They had been playing that she was a wicked witch and her aunt was the evil creature who tagged along. In the middle of the game her aunt got tired and said she wasn't an evil creature at all.

Disappointed that the game was ending so soon, she had insisted, "You *are*, you *are*, you *really* are!" Aunt Luisa had made her sit down on the floor for a serious talk, and her face—long and stretched tight around the eyes and mouth—had scared her.

"It's okay to play and make up stories, but you mustn't believe in what you make up. You have to know the difference between real and pretend. Otherwise people think you're crazy." Then she whispered, "And maybe they'd be right!"

Now her aunt was in the hospital and all anyone would say was that she didn't feel well.

So if this was just a dream and she couldn't tell the difference, then maybe she was crazy. But even if she wasn't, even if the monster was real, what if no one believed her? They would think she was crazy anyway, and put her in a loony bin. She imagined a loony bin. It had smooth white sides like the bin her mother kept onions in, and the crazy people were dropped in with tweezers and lay in a heap on the bottom of it. She would hate that. It would be much better to pretend, to go along with them and act alive.

The first thing was to wash. When you washed a dead person, later people went to look at them and said "She looks just like herself," "She looks like she's only sleeping." She would pretend she was only sleeping from now on, and she would look like herself.

It was growing lighter now. She could see the blood on her thigh, but none of it was on the bed yet. She got up quietly and went to the bathroom, closing the door gently so as not to wake up her grandmother. Using wet toilet paper she began to wash herself between the legs, and being dead, it hardly hurt at all.

really a dream. And that what happened in my sleep, that was real. She turned reality and dreams, awake and asleep, exactly opposite.

This is an extreme example, but some distortion of the truth is common in families where sexual abuse takes place. If you've grown up unsure of what to believe, if your perceptions haven't matched what you were told, you may find it particularly hard to trust your own reality when it comes to sexual abuse.

However, consistent doubt can also be an indication that you're on the wrong track. If you're genuinely unsure about what happened to you, don't rush yourself—or allow anyone to rush you—into giving it a label. Take your time. Explore your history, your feelings, your concerns. Trust yourself. Eventually you will come to a fuller understanding of your experience.*

LOOK AT YOUR LIFE

One practical way to validate your abuse —and to learn more about what took place— is to look at your life now. Your feelings, your responses and interactions, hold clues to your past experience. You may find that as you face and work through the trauma of abuse, your behavior changes in healthy ways:

The hardest part was accepting and believing that it really happened. Being

---

* For more on this, see "If You're Doubting Yourself," p. 523.

in the group really helped. I was able to see other people who had gone through sexual abuse, and my symptoms were similar. I have all the classic symptoms of sexual abuse—feeling suicidal, running away, a high pain tolerance, spacing out, not being able to succeed at anything, denial, always being isolated.

Another thing that helped me believe it was watching my own behavior change. Like my paranoia going away. I used to think the Mafia was out to get me, and that someone was going to set fire to a place I was in. When I remembered the incest, I realized those were threats my father had made. He used to lock me in the cedar closet and sodomize me. Then he'd threaten to set fire to it. He said if I ever told anyone, the Mafia would come and get me. As soon as I made those connections, my paranoia went away.

YOU NEED VALIDATION

Some survivors grow up in families where abuse is such a part of their daily lives that they believe what happened to them is normal (see Kyos on page 405). For these survivors, beginning to heal involves learning what to expect in a healthy family. As one survivor explained:

I would talk with my therapist about what people had done to me in my family. And she would say to me, "That's abuse. It's terrible that that happened to you." And I was shocked, because I thought I'd had a normal childhood. I only knew it was abuse because other people would mirror it back to me. I would walk around saying, "My family abused me." I had to say it a lot to really believe it. My first year and a half was spent just accepting the fact that I had been abused.

Believing It Mattered: Vicki's Story

Many women believe their abuse doesn't count because it happened only once. But as the following story shows, all abuse is harmful.

There was always a creepy feeling in my house of my father being really inappropriate. He'd just be too affectionate, too close. He was always kissing me too long. It got worse when I was a teenager. He had a more difficult time containing himself. My girlfriends felt weird around him and he was really hostile to my boyfriends.

My father only molested me once, when I was twelve years old. I was asleep in bed. He came into my room and lay down next to me. He put his hand down my pajamas and started playing with my vagina. It woke me up. I turned away from him. I pretended I was turning over in my sleep. He must have gotten frightened that I would wake up, and he left. I remember watching his shadow outside the door. He never did it again.

Before he molested me, I felt very free in my body. I felt wonderful. I was coming into the height of puberty. I was outgoing and friendly. I had boyfriends. Everything was awakening. And my first intimate sexual experience was with my father. He was the first man to ever touch my genitals.

It was very upsetting and confusing to me. I loved my father. We had a really strong relationship. After he molested me, I went into a deep depression. I shut off communicating with the outside world. It was like this veil just came down, and that was it. It took me until I was twenty-two to even realize something was wrong. I've had to find out what my real personality was underneath.

I never forgot what happened. It sort of went underground. I didn't think about it a lot, but it's had long-lasting effects. I've had a really difficult time getting close to my lovers. I need a disproportionate amount of control in relationships.

I've been estranged from my father for the last five years, ever since I confronted him. Our relationship has basically fallen apart.

I never compared what happened to me to what other people went through because I really felt the hell inside myself. I knew it was wreaking havoc in my life and in the lives of my lovers. You don't have to have it happen over and over to know "This is really terrible." It doesn't take much for a child to feel the devastation of a parent crossing over those boundaries.

If I was talking to someone and she said, "Oh well, he just fondled me a little bit. It's not such a big deal," I'd ask, "When you connect with another human being in a deep way, how does it make you feel? Does it make you feel scared? Like closing down? Or like being completely one with that person?" Really check it out with yourself. In the deepest part of you, how are you connecting with people? Then reassess if you were affected.

It counts if it keeps you from being close to another person. It counts if it's devastated your life, if you're missing a part of yourself. Even if it only happened once, it counts.

BELIEVING DOESN'T HAPPEN ALL AT ONCE

Even when you know the facts are true, you may still, at a deep emotional level, have trouble believing it happened. Believing doesn't usually happen all of a sudden—it's a gradual awakening.

At first, I had regular doubts that the abuse had happened at all. Once I became more steady, I still thought of it as something that had happened to someone very far away from me. Over time, I've been able to incorporate it more into the texture of my life. I include it when I tell people about my life. I talk about it freely, much as I would the fact that my family went to museums a lot when I was a kid. It's no longer a shameful secret, separate from the rest of who I am. I used to feel I had this good childhood, and then off to the side was this horrible, shameful abuse. But now I know there was only one child and she lived through it all.

BREAKING SILENCE

What would happen if one woman told the truth about her life? The world would split open.

—Muriel Rukeyser, from "Kathe Kollwitz"

An essential part of healing from child sexual abuse is telling the truth about your life. The sexual molestation of children, and the shame that results, thrive in an atmosphere of silence. Breaking that silence is a powerful healing tool. Yet it is something many survivors find difficult.

I feel very lonely and isolated. I've always had so much to say, and I've never said it. What's hindered me the most is being so skilled at being silent. Incest has had so much to do with being silenced and silencing myself.

HOW YOU WERE SILENCED

The first time you tried to talk about your abuse, you may still have been a child. Under ideal circumstances, you would have been believed, protected, and assured that the abuse wasn't your fault. You would have been given age-appropriate counseling and placed in a support group with other children. If the abuser was a family member, he would have been the one sent away, not you.

Unfortunately, this was probably not the response you got. More likely, you were threatened, blamed, or called a liar. You were accused of "asking for it" or were called "a little whore." You may have been warned not to tell during the abuse itself: "It would kill your mother if she knew," or "I'll kill you if you tell."

Sometimes telling led to further abuse. One child confided in her best friend. That girl told her father, who asked for the details. He then took both girls into the garage and did to them all the things he'd just heard about.

Telling frequently ignites the wrath of the abuser. Eleven-year-old Carey was abused by both her mother and her stepfather.

When I was eleven, I went horseback riding with my best girlfriend. I told my girlfriend what I was doing with my stepfather. She told her mother, who called my mother. When I got home, my mother came tearing out of the house, crazy angry. She grabbed me and pulled me off my horse. Kicking me and hitting me, she dragged me into the house, up the steps, across the porch, into my bedroom. She threw me on the bed, screaming at me about telling stories.

I was sobbing and saying, "They're not stories, they're true, and you know they're true." And she started to choke me. My stepfather was standing right behind her, watching, with no expression on his face.

I couldn't breathe. I believe she would have killed me. It was the third time she'd tried. Finally he pulled her off, saying, "You know nobody's going to believe her. Nobody believes anything she says."

If your case was taken to court, you may have been subjected to brutal testimony procedures, grilled by insensitive defense attorneys, or repeatedly forced to face your abuser.*

---

* Recently some states have begun to amend the legal codes to meet the special needs of child witnesses. These changes are slow in coming, but pioneering programs have been introduced. In some jurisdictions, judges no longer wear formal robes or sit on an elevated platform. Instead everyone sits around a table at eye level with the child. More support people and family members are allowed in the courtroom. Some courts appoint a special child advocate to wait with the child before and after the court appearance, to make sure the child does not see the offender beforehand, and to be a supportive friend to the child.

Washington State has actual children's courtrooms. Children sit on the floor with toys and the judge sits on the floor with them, taking their testimony. The room is equipped with a one-way mirror and the defendant is on the other side, so the child never has to face him.

Videotaped testimony is used throughout the country, even where it is not yet admissible evidence in court. Videotapes of a child's testimony are used to con-front offenders, and are often enough to elicit a guilty plea.

There are proposals in various states for a "hearsay law" which would enable a second party, such as the child's therapist, to testify on behalf of the child. Such a system is used in Israel, where children never appear in court in incest cases. A youth counselor is assigned by the police department to get the child's statement, in accordance with legal code, and that person then testifies for the child.

In response to these positive changes there has been a very strong backlash. Accused abusers, defense attorneys, and expert witnesses for the defense have stepped up their efforts to discredit the testimony of children in sexual abuse cases. It is imperative that we continue to advocate for children so that the gains we've made on their behalf are not lost. (For information on organizations formed to protect the rights of children, see "Organizations" on p. 577 in the "Safe, Strong, and Free" section of the Resource Guide.)

If your mother divorced your father because he was abusing you, you may have felt guilty for breaking up the marriage, for separating your family, or for ruining a "happy home."

Children not slapped with an actively cruel response are often met with devastating silence or told never to speak of it again. Families often go on as if nothing happened, never mentioning it. In that case, children get the message that their experience is too horrible for words. And, by implication, that *they* are too horrible.

In this way, children learn there is no one they can trust, that sharing leads not to help but to harm or neglect, that it's not safe to tell the truth. In other words, they learn shame, secrecy, and silence.

HOW CHILDREN TELL

Children do not generally say "My brother molested me six times," but in their own way, all children "tell" that they've been abused. They tell in vague terms: "I don't like Mrs. Johnson." "I don't want to go to Boy Scouts anymore." For a child, "Don't make me go Poppa's house anymore" is a very clear message.

If children don't tell with words, they often tell through behavior. They wet their beds. They steal from a parent's wallet. They are terrified to go to sleep, and wake up screaming from nightmares. They regress to more babyish behavior. They don't want to be left alone. They develop asthma. They stop eating. They have trouble in school. They cry hysterically every time a particular babysitter comes over. They demonstrate a precocious interest in sex. They act seductively to get things they want.

Sometimes older children or teenagers act out by disobeying or getting into trouble with authorities. They become depressed, take drugs, or engage in self-destructive behavior. They are trying to get someone to pay attention, but their behavior is usually misinterpreted. They are labeled "bad" or "stupid." These messages make them feel even more hopeless. "Perhaps they're right," the kid thinks. "I am no good. No wonder he does that to me."

Perceptive parents notice changes and respond. They listen, no matter how their children express themselves. But until recently most abused children had no one who would listen.* No one wanted to know. Stuck in an abusive situation, often with an unrealistic sense of responsibility, they carried this secret burden alone.

If you believe you didn't tell, look again. In your own way, you reached out for help—and were denied.

TELLING: IT TAKES A LEAP OF FAITH

It's not only children who have been met with insulting or insensitive responses when they tried to talk about their abuse. Adult

---

* As parents and professionals become more aware of the need for compassionate responses when children are abused, this is changing. Hopefully survivors years from now will find this statement false. They will have received prompt, skilled, and sympathetic help and so will have much less compounded trauma to heal from.

survivors have also been blamed, ridiculed, or shunned. Yet in spite of these negative experiences from the past, it is necessary to take a leap of faith—and tell.

Telling is transformative. When you let someone know what you have lived through and that person hears you with respect and genuine caring, you begin a process of change essential to healing.

Catherine was in a therapy group when she first told about her abuse:

I had to get up and talk about what my parents had done to me, and why it was hard for me to grow up in my family. I remember being in the group and crying, and saying, "I can't tell this to you. My parents are going to get me if I say this to you!" It was horrible. People encouraged me to tell my story, and I finally did.

When it was over I went home and laid in my bed, and literally waited to die. I had never told anybody before. I knew my parents would find out that I had told on them, and would get me.

And that's when I decided I was going to become a person who could talk, instead of being a person who had to keep secrets.

In workshops, when a woman tells her story the effects are often dramatic. She no longer feels so different or alone. She knows she is understood because she has been listening to other survivors' stories and she understands them. She learns that she is important, worthwhile, and lovable because she feels the compassion of the other women as they listen and respond to her. She feels authentic because she allows herself to feel her real feelings. She experiences release because there is relief in the telling.

When I talked about the incest with my counselor, it stayed almost as big a secret as when I hadn't told anyone. Going to group and speaking to all

---

WHY TELLING IS TRANSFORMATIVE

- You move through the shame and secrecy that keeps you isolated.
- You move through denial and acknowledge the truth of your abuse.
- You make it possible to get understanding and help.
- You get more in touch with your feelings.
- You get a chance to see your experience (and yourself) through the compassionate eyes of a supporter.
- You make space in relationships for the kind of intimacy that comes from honesty.
- You establish yourself as a person in the present who is dealing with the abuse in her past.
- You join a courageous community of women who are no longer willing to suffer in silence.
- You help end child sexual abuse by breaking the silence in which it thrives.
- You become a model for other survivors.
- You (eventually) feel proud and strong.

those people was important. It was a real coming out.

After telling in a group, you may feel as though being a survivor, with all its difficulties, is not all bad. As one woman said, "We're a beautiful, courageous bunch of women—and I'm proud to be one."

THE LEVELS OF TELLING

There are many levels of telling, ranging from the first time you dare to broach this subject to when you have told so many times and in so many ways that you can talk about it naturally, as just another part of your life. Each time you tell is a different experience. Telling your therapist or your support group, telling your partner or a new lover, telling a friend, telling publicly, telling in writing, will all feel different.

You may tell with detachment, with sadness, with anger, or occasionally even with humor. Participants in a recent summer I Never Told Anyone group nicknamed the workshop "Incest Camp," and one woman sent everyone T-shirts with "I.C. Survivor" printed across the front.

Jude Brister, a co-editor of *I Never Told Anyone*, said that each time she talked about her abuse, it put more distance between herself and the pain. The more she talked about it, the less she identified herself as a victim. She saw herself instead as a strong, capable adult.

Ella, another survivor who has told her experiences many times, described her process in detail:

For me there were at least three different levels of telling. The first was telling the story and not feeling anything. Telling it as a third-party story. Saying "I" but not really meaning it happened to me. At that point I still didn't really believe it happened. And part of that telling was that I was really angry. It was a way to get back at them. Like "I'm going to tell on you." It's kind of like "I couldn't get anybody mad at you then, but watch this!"

Then there was a really painful, scared level of telling. The tone of my voice changed and I looked like I was seven years old. My language was more simple. And it hurt. That's the place I discovered my feelings. And usually people got sad when they heard it that way. They felt sorry for me. The people I told that way included my therapist, my close friend, people in caretaker positions, paid or unpaid. It included the people in my support group. I told not like a victim, but like a little kid that hurt.

The last way I've told has to do with stepping back and seeing the bigger picture. I looked at family dynamics and got the rest of the story. I saw what happened and why it happened. I put the abuse through a sieve and was able to see parts of it I couldn't see when I was only hurt or angry.

So I went from anger to pain to a fixing. In Hebrew there's a word, *tikun*, that means a fixing, a healing. That way of telling was a *tikun*.

BREAKING THE SILENCE: ABUSE BY WOMEN

Although the majority of sexual abuse is committed by heterosexual men, women do abuse children. Both girls and boys have been abused by their mothers, aunts, grandmothers, or other women.

Since much of the incest literature has focused on father-daughter incest, or solely on abuse with a male perpetrator, those survivors who were abused by women have felt even more isolated than those abused by men.

At an incest art gathering in Los Angeles in 1980, one woman played a videotape in which she talked about the incest she'd experienced with her mother. The response she got was one of shock and disbelief:

A woman who'd written a major book about incest stood up in the audience and said, "There is no incest between mothers and daughters." So I walked away thinking, "I must be crazy."

This unwillingness to acknowledge women as offenders has slowly started to break down. Support groups for survivors abused by women are beginning, but many women still find themselves discounted:

I find that when I tell my story, a lot of people are uncomfortable. People have all these squirmy reactions. It's almost as if they don't quite believe it. I can't just tell my story— I have to tell my story and then explain it.

People like to think in categories. So when you talk about women as sexual abusers, it blows a lot of myths: Women aren't sexual. Women are gentle. Women are passive. How could a woman do that to a child?

But people need to hear it. They need to hear, "I'm an incest survivor, and it was my *mother*." Women do abuse, and if it's not put out there, the healing can't happen.

Most of the issues explored in this book apply equally to all survivors, but there are some unique problems faced by survivors of abuse by mothers.

Since children frequently bond most closely with their mothers, abuse by mothers can leave a child with a severe lack of boundaries between herself and her offender.

For a while I didn't know where my mother left off and I began. I thought she had a psychic hold on me. I was convinced she knew every thought I had. It was like she was in my body, and she was evil. I felt I was possessed, that I was going to be taken over. I've had a real fear that if I look at all that stuff that I don't like about myself, it would be my mother inside of me. And I've had to do a lot of growing over the last few years to know that she's not inside me anymore.

Other women have had a hard time maturing, watching their bodies grow similar to their mothers'.

For a long, long time, I didn't call myself a woman. When I left home at eighteen, I continued to call myself a girl because I couldn't stomach the associations with "woman," which meant being sexual. My mother was a woman, but I was a girl. If being a woman meant being like her, that's not what I wanted. It took a long time for me to get rid of that self-hate.

Like abuse by male perpetrators, abuse by women can be overtly sexual or violent and it can also be subtle and covert. Frequently, abuse by mothers begins when the child is very young, sometimes masked in cuddling or daily caretaking. And in many families the father is also sexually abusive, either separately or in conjunction with the mother, creating a devastating double jeopardy for the child.

It is essential not to discount the pain and betrayal experienced by survivors of abuse by women. Every survivor deserves to heal. (For more on healing from abuse by a mother, see Anna Stevens's story on page 398 and "Abuse by Women" on p. 556 of the Resource Guide.)

CHOOSING SOMEONE TO TELL

If you are in counseling or a support group where you feel safe,* that's an excellent place to begin to talk about your abuse. Telling for the first time can feel scary, and it helps to be in a context where you know someone will listen compassionately.

Telling your partner, lover, or close friends is also important. You need to let the people around you know why you are sometimes sad, angry, upset, busy, needing to be alone. Your friends need to understand why you may not trust them readily. Your lover needs to know why you may have difficulty with sex, why you withdraw or cling. There is a lot of work involved in building healthy relationships, and you need the people in your life as allies. Although it is not necessary —or even appropriate—to tell every single person you meet, it is important that you share with the people you want to be close to.

I don't run around telling every soul I meet that I'm an incest victim, because I don't want that to be my definition, but I went through a period of time when it was just about like that. That was the first thing I would tell people, almost anybody. "Did you know I was an incest victim?" "Oh really, thank you for sharing that." It's like any movement, whether it's black power or gay rights, you need time to try that identity on and claim it. I needed to do that, but that need has faded over time. Now I just do what I feel like doing. If I feel like telling someone, I do. If I don't, I don't.

For some women, telling goes even further. They see it as a political choice, a necessity. Dorianne Laux, who runs workshops on sexual abuse for teenagers and has read her poetry about incest extensively, explains:

So many women still feel they have to hide the fact that they were molested. I can just see it in their bodies, that they're real frightened that somebody might find out. Well, I don't like that. I don't have to be frightened that somebody's going to find out.

I always use my first and last name when I talk about incest. It's a political statement for me. I don't have anything to be ashamed of. I don't have to be anonymous. Even though it could affect my life in some way, it shouldn't. It should affect *his* life.

And the whole idea of the secret is perpetuated when I keep my name out of it. Incest doesn't need to be hidden. It needs the exact opposite. People need to come out and say, "My name is so-and-so, this happened to me, and I'm angry about it."

Also, I'm a fairly well-adjusted person, and I make a good role model for the young people I work with. So speaking out and saying who I am is real important to me.

---

* If you don't feel safe enough with your counselor or support group to talk about these issues, read "Counseling," on p. 321, to determine whether your counselor is safe and it's just hard for you to trust, or whether you would do well to seek a different counselor.

HOW TO TELL

Talking about your abuse with a skilled counselor or supportive group of survivors needs no planning. They should be able to hear you however you get the words out. But if you are telling friends or family for the first time, it's best to make the circumstances as favorable as possible. (This applies only to telling family members you expect to be supportive. If you're planning to tell unsympathetic or unpredictable family members, read "Disclosures and Confrontations" on page 144. That's a whole different kind of telling.)

You can maximize your support by choosing wisely. When you're considering talking to someone, ask yourself the following questions:

- Does this person care for and respect me?
- Does this person have my well-being in mind?
- Is this someone I've been able to discuss feelings with before?
- Do I trust this person?
- Do I feel safe with this person?

If you can answer yes to all of these questions, you're choosing someone who's likely to be supportive.

Tell your friend (lover, partner, cousin) that there's something personal and vulnerable that you want to share and ask if this is a good time to talk. Suggest that it if it isn't, you could make it another time. By asking, you ensure that your friend doesn't need to leave for work in five minutes. You also give that person a chance to either postpone the talk or prepare to listen.

If there are certain responses that you want or don't want, say so. You may want your friend to listen but not to give a lot of advice. You may want to be asked questions, or you may want to be listened to silently. You may want to be held or you may not want to be touched at all. Often people want to support you but don't know how (or how to ask). A good friend will welcome your guidance.

And if you want what you say to be kept confidential, say so. Although it is important to break silence, do so at your own pace, with people *you* choose.

WEEDING

Listening to the truth of someone's life is a privilege and an honor. When you tell someone your history, they should receive it as such. But because this is not always the case, you need to be prepared for possible negative responses.

Some people may be threatened. Some will go blank or be shocked. These people may be reminded of their own abuse. If they have not yet recovered their memories, all their defenses may ring in alarm, trying to protect them from their own remembering. Some people will be horrified. Some may not even believe you initially. Others may be incredibly rude. One woman waited until after she had had three children to finally tell her husband about the incest. His response: "You mean I wasn't the first one?"

One survivor was reluctant to tell: "I have been afraid of people's reactions. People like victims. There's an animal part in people, and they get excited, and they'll just jump on you." Other people have been titillated by the stories of survivors and have asked for "details." In a society where the sexual abuse of children has been eroticized, this is not surprising.

Although you will meet up with some of these hostile, insensitive, or insulting responses, it is still important to tell. There is a weeding out that goes on in relationships when you start to share who you really are, how you genuinely feel. You may find that some relationships cannot stand this challenge and you will grieve for them, along with your other losses. Or you may choose to continue the relationship on a more superficial level rather than abandoning it altogether.

Although it is likely that you will get some unsatisfying responses, it is also likely that you will get some supportive, sympathetic ones, as Laura described:

When I first remembered my abuse, I was overwhelmed. I stopped calling my friends and when they called me, I was distant and preoccupied. Karen, my closest friend, was hurt and angry. She was about to write me off totally. Finally, I told her about the abuse. Once she knew what was going on, she was wonderful. She became my most devoted supporter.

It is important that you have some relationships in which you can be your whole self —with your history, with your pain and anger—and the only way to create those is to share honestly about yourself. When you are met in that honesty, then you feel real intimacy.

One Hundred and Fifty-Seven Ways to Tell My Incest Story
by Emily Levy

Tell it in Spanish
In Sign Language.
Tell it as a poem
As a play
As a letter to President Reagan.
Tell it as if my life depended on it.

I was not molested as a child.
I feared, when I was three years old, that a man would come into my room in the middle of the night and Get me. Where did that idea come from?
I wonder why I hate my father so much. The explanations I've developed don't add up to the amount of anger and hatred I feel.

There's a vague possibility I was molested as a child.

Tell it as a court case
As a congressional debate
As if the power of children were respected.
Tell it as domestic terrorism
As a national sport.
Tell it as a jump-rope game:

A my name is Annie
He stuck it up my Anus
Now I am Angry
And I want Action.

B my name is Betty
The penis was my Brother's
I wrote a Book
'Cuz I want to get him Back.

C my name is Carla
He said he'd give me Candy
I told my Cousin
And her Dad got Caught.

D my name is Doris
I was still in Diapers . . .

Tell it as graffiti
As a religious service.
Tell it as a classified ad.

Why is it that when I see Dad I make sure to
wear a long scarf that covers my chest?
There's no way he could have molested me.
I'd remember it. I have a great memory.
Everybody in my family says so.
Why did I suddenly start hating him when I
was eleven years old?
I think my father might have molested me
when I was a child.

Tell it as a TV commercial
As a science experiment
As a country western song.
Tell it as ancient history
As science fiction.
Tell it in your sleep:

This time I decided to get him instead of
letting him get me. I jerked him off
angrily, scratching his cock with my
fingernails, digging them into his flesh as
deep as I could. I kept going at it, trying
to make him ejaculate. Then I realized it
would be meaner to stop. As soon as I
stopped, my mother was there again.

Tell it as a bedtime story
As a bumper sticker.
Tell it as if we liked it.

When I was young, I used to say, "Don't touch
me, I'm alive!" Why did I make up that
expression?

Tell it as justification for nuclear war
As justification for never having another war.
Tell it as a greeting card:

To A Beloved Niece—

On this day I think of you
A girl with virtue always true
A sweeter thing I ne'er did see
No wonder Pop molested thee.

Your rosy breast and dangling tongue
What heaven in a girl so young!
Your beauty now is crowned with luck
His love shown by a family fuck.

One wish for you, now, if I may:
Happy Molestation Day!

Tell it as a gossip column
As a last will and testament
As an exhibit at Ripley's Believe It Or Not.

Am I making this up as an excuse to hate him?
If I falsely accused him, I'd never forgive
myself.

Tell it as a soap opera
As a telephone answering-machine
message.
Tell it as a board game:

"Snake eyes. Damn it, I rolled snake
eyes."

"Ha, ha. You get molested by your twin brother. Your nightmare quotient goes up 60%, your therapy sentence up three years, and your sexuality goes into the shop for repairs."

"Hey, give me that marker! I can put my own sexuality in the shop!"

"OK. My turn now. Three. One, two three. All right! 'Doctor Feminist'!"

"Pick a card."

" 'You go to a three-day workshop where you cry, talk about why you cried, and talk about why you talked about why you cried. Take six months of therapy off your sentence.' All right!"

"How come you get all the good ones? My turn."

Tell it as a "How To" book
As a newscast
As instructions on the box it came in.

Why do the muscles in my vagina tighten when I hear his name?

Tell it as a fairy tale
As a magic trick.
Tell it as of this moment:

Kissing your lips is like walking into a lush garden. I watch each emotion bud within your dark eyes.

My palms engulf your breasts, your fingernails cruise across my belly. We rock until you lie on top of me. You press your knee against my cunt, whisper I want you Baby, and suddenly you become him. You are pinning me down, holding me so tight I cannot breathe. You are pushing your prick into me, insisting I want it. I wrestle with your body and with the voice inside my head saying Calm down. This is different: you choose to be here.

Hey, where are you, you ask. What happened. My eyes clearly describe to you the fear my mouth cannot speak. You sigh and hold me gently. Finally I cry.

Tell it as a healing ritual
As an epitaph
As discovered and interpreted seven
    generations from now.

Maybe my family named me The One Who Remembers so they could believe that anything that I don't remember didn't happen.

Tell it as a map of the world
    As if I were still forbidden to speak the words.

My father molested me when I was a child.

Tell it so it will never happen again.

UNDERSTANDING THAT IT WASN'T YOUR FAULT

I know I was only five years old, but I was an extremely intelligent five-year-old. I should have been able to figure out a way to escape.

Victims often believe they are to blame for being sexually abused. Many adult survivors continue to hold this belief. Although large numbers of children and adolescents are abused, it is never the fault of any of them. Yet there are many reasons why survivors assume that blame.

Some survivors were told explicitly that it was their fault. The abuser said: "You're a bad, nasty, dirty girl. That's why I'm doing this." "You really want this to happen. I know you do." "You're such a sexy little girl. I just can't help myself."

You were punished when someone did find out. If you said anything, you may have been told you made up horrible lies. Or the subject was never discussed, giving you the message that it was too terrible to talk about.

Your religion may have told you that you were a sinner, unclean, damned to hell. You may have become convinced you were unlovable, even to God. One woman said: "That little incested girl inside of me is still waiting for the lightning to strike because I told people what happened to me. If I say, 'I think it was my Dad,' I'll burn up in hell-fire."

One small child was even begged by her abuser to stop him. He kept telling her how wrong it was and that she must not let him do it ever again—and then he'd force her once more.

I felt I was really evil. It's almost like those child-devil movies, like Damian. Inside this innocent little child is this evil seed. I used to think that just my presence made people feel bad and made bad things happen. I used to think that if only I did something, then everything would change. If only I got straight A's, then my Dad would stop touching me. I felt I could control things by my behavior. No one around me seemed to be controlling anything. I still have this really warped sense of what I can do with my presence or my actions.

There are also less obvious reasons why survivors blame themselves. It is a stark and terrifying realization for a child to see how vulnerable and powerless she actually is. Thinking that you were bad, that you had some influence on how you were treated, gave a sense of control, though illusory. And perceiving yourself as bad allowed for the future possibility that you could become good, and thus things could improve.

In truth, nothing you did caused the abuse; nothing within your power could ever have stopped it. Your world was an unsafe place where adults were untrustworthy and out of control, where your well-being and sometimes your very life was in danger. This perspective, though realistic, is more distressing for many children than thinking that they were bad and somehow responsible for the abuse. For if there is no hope that the people whose job is to love and protect you would do so, where could you turn?

Recognizing that you were not to blame means accepting the fact that the people you loved did not have your best interests at heart. In one workshop, a woman blamed herself because at the age of twelve she said no, and her father stopped. "Why couldn't I have done that right away, at four, when he started?" she chastised herself. "I *did* have the power to stop him."

Another woman answered her: "I said no and my father never stopped. I fought and kicked and screamed no. But abusers don't stop because you say no. They stop when they're ready to stop. By the time you were twelve your father was ready to stop. Maybe he only liked small children. You had less control than you think."

Women blame themselves because they took money, gifts, or special privileges. But if you were able to get some small thing back, you should instead give yourself credit. One woman in a workshop was given a bicycle by her abuser. On it she was able to ride away from her house, out to the woods, and there feel the safety of the trees. She blamed herself for having taken the bicycle. Instead, she should be commended for taking what she could get in that wasteland.

BUT I WANTED TO BE CLOSE

Many survivors hold particularly shameful feelings if they needed attention and affection and did not fight off sexual advances because of those needs. Or if they sought out that affection. The closeness may have felt good to you. You may have adored your abuser. You may have loved feeling like Grandpa's special little girl. Women say, "I'm the one who asked for a back rub," or "I kept going back," or "I climbed into bed with him."

But you were not wrong. Every child needs attention. Every child needs affection. If these are not offered in healthy, non-sexual ways, children will take them in whatever ways they can, because they are essential needs.

BUT IT FELT GOOD

Although some women felt only pain or numbness when they were abused, others experienced sensual or sexual pleasure, arousal, and orgasm. Even though your experience of abuse may have been confusing, frightening, or devastating, you may also have felt some degree of pleasurable feelings. For many, this aspect of the abuse is one of the most difficult.

Some of it felt good, and ugh! It's still hard for me to talk about it. When I think back on some of the times I was close to my mother in a sexual way, where I was getting turned on, there's a lot of shame there. It feels real yucko! It feels really embarrassing.

Another woman was gang-raped as a teenager and had an orgasm. "For a long time I thought it was a cruel joke that God had made my body that way. I forgot what had happened because of the shame of having liked it." When she first remembered the rape, this woman spent a night frantically skimming *Voices in the Night* cover to cover to see if anyone else had had an orgasm while being abused.* She urgently needed to know that she wasn't the only one.

* Toni McNaron and Yarrow Morgan, eds. (see the "Survivors Speak Out" section on p. 546 of the Resource Guide).

It is important to recognize that it is natural to have had sexual feelings, and that even if you had sexual responses to the abuse and those responses felt good, it still doesn't mean that you were responsible in any way.

Our bodies are created to respond to stimulation. When we are touched sexually, our whole physiology is designed to give us pleasure. These are natural bodily responses over which we do not always have control. When we eat a sandwich, our stomachs digest the sandwich. We can't stop our stomachs from digesting the sandwich. In a similar way, when we're stimulated sexually, we can't always stop our bodies from responding.

The girl or woman who is sexually abused and experiences orgasm does not want to be abused. The fact that she responds sexually is not a statement that sexual pleasure is bad. And—very important—it is not a betrayal of her body. Her body did what bodies are supposed to do. You were betrayed not by your body, but by the adults who abused you. For Saphyre, it's taken a lot of self-love to overcome the shame:

I had to realize I didn't get off because I liked it, but because I have a woman's body that is made to experience passion. My body responded to touch. That was all. And they had no right to mess with that. That anger helped me get over the shame.

BUT I WAS OLDER

When children are abused, their capacity to say no and set limits is severely damaged. So even if the abuse continued into your adult years, you are still not to blame. There is no magic age when you suddenly become a responsible, cooperative partner in sexual abuse. Even if your father is still having sex with you when you are thirty, it is not your fault. You may be an adult in age, but you are still responding from the perspective of a small, powerless child.

Mary spent her childhood being regularly abused by her stepfather and brothers. When she was twenty-one she went on a weekend trip with her twenty-two-year-old brother and some of his friends. The two were asked to share a room. "I spent the night sleeping on the bathroom floor, because my brother would not leave me alone. He begged to make love with me. He kept grabbing at me. Finally I locked myself in the bathroom."

For a long time, Mary felt guilty about what had happened. He was her brother. He was only a year older than she was. She was an adult and should have known better. She should never have agreed to go on the trip in the first place. It was all her fault.

It wasn't until Mary went to therapy that she began to accept the real facts of the matter. "What happened when I was twenty-one was exactly the same thing as being eight years old and having to take a bath with my father. I just hadn't been trained to say no."

If your boundaries have always been violated, then it is unfair to expect yourself to be able to set them all of a sudden. You don't become assertive and powerful just because you grow up and leave home. No matter what age you are, no matter what relationship you have with the abuser, if someone with more power is pressuring you into a sexual relationship, then you are being abused.

IT'S NEVER YOUR FAULT

It is unfair to expect children to be able to protect themselves. Children do a lot of testing. They test limits. They test attitudes. This is their job. They develop a sense of what the world is all about through this testing. And it is *always* the responsibility of the adult to behave with respect toward children.

Even if a sixteen-year-old girl walks into her living room naked and throws herself on her father, he is still not justified in touching her sexually. A responsible father would say, "There seems to be a problem here." He would tell her to put clothes on; he'd discuss it with her, get professional help if necessary. Regardless of age or circumstance, there is never an excuse for sexual abuse. It is abso-

lutely the responsibility of the adult not to be sexual with children.

As a child, you did not have the skills or power to protect yourself. Today at least there are child assault prevention programs in schools, which teach children to be "safe, strong, and free." (For more information on these programs, see the footnote on page 291.) Now many parents are teaching their children that they have the right to say no. But it is only recently that children have been provided with even these few basic tools. No woman we know was told, as a child, that she had the right to control her body. Even those of you who did try to resist or fight back often encountered increased coercion.

Bubba Esther
by Ruth Whitman

She was still upset,
she wanted to tell me,
she kept remembering
his terrible hands:

> how she came, a young girl
> of seventeen, a freckled
> fairskinned Jew from Kovno
> to Hamburg with her uncle
> and stayed in an old house
> and waited while he bought
> the steamship tickets
> so they could sail to America

> and how he came into her room
> sat down on the bed, touched
> her waist, took her by the
> breast, said for a kiss
> she could have her ticket,
> her skirts were rumpled, her
> petticoat torn, his teeth were
> broken, his breath full of
> onions, she was ashamed

still ashamed, lying
eighty years later
in the hospital bed,
trying to tell me,
trembling, weeping with anger

OVERCOMING SHAME

A key sign of healing is that your shame becomes less. Instead of looking at somebody's watch while you tell them what happened, you can look at their face. And then eventually you can look in their eyes and tell them, without feeling they can see what a creep you are. You can just look at someone, tell them, and say, "And I'm okay" without having to ask, "Right? I am okay, aren't I?"

There are many ways to overcome shame. The most powerful is simply talking about your abuse. Shame exists in an environment of secrecy. When you begin to freely speak the truth about your life, your sense of shame will diminish.

You know how they say, "Speak the truth and the truth shall set you free." Well that's how it really is. I'm not in a cage anymore. I have no bars. The best part is there are no more secrets. And it's the secrets that kill you. It's not the poison and the hate that kill you; it's keeping secrets. Because you live in fear that someone will find out. Secrets destroy people, and they destroy them unnecessarily. It's like being reborn when you shed the secret, because you have no more fear.

JOIN A SURVIVORS GROUP

Being in a group with other survivors can be a powerful way to vanquish shame. When you hear other women talk about their abuse and are not disgusted, and when you see those same women listen to your story with respect, you begin to see yourself as a proud survivor rather than as a conspiring victim. As one woman said, "When your counselor says, 'It wasn't your fault,' that's one thing. But when you have eight people saying it to you, it's a lot more powerful."

SPEAK OUT IN PUBLIC

Speaking publicly—doing outreach to other survivors, working on child assault or rape prevention programs—is a powerful way to transform shame into a feeling of personal effectiveness and power. For Jennierose, who'd been a prostitute and a thief in her twenties, speaking out was a way to let go of shame, once and for all:

After I'd been working with the incest for a while, I felt the need to help other people. I did it by going out talking to kids in school, and talking to professional training groups. One of the training programs I did was for police officers. All these years, I'd been sure that people still thought that I was a prostitute. And that was twenty years ago! I stood up before all those cops and I said, "I'm not a thief. And I'm not a prostitute." It was one of the most rewarding moments of my whole life. I faced the enemy.

LOOK TO THE CHILDREN

Spending time with children can provide you with convincing evidence that the abuse wasn't your fault. Children help you remember how small and powerless you actually were. One mother said:

Watching my daughter grow up gave me a sense of "How could anyone do that to a kid?" that I couldn't get just in relation to myself. I had been able to rationalize the mistreatment of kids for a long time. But when I saw how little power she had, how small she was when I put her to bed, I got a real picture of how small and vulnerable *I* had been. I got it in my heart that abuse was not okay. And that I had not been responsible for what had happened to me. I started to forgive myself.

At the workshops she does for teenagers on child sexual abuse, this woman passes around a picture of herself at three years old. "I tell them, 'This is the child that my father was having sex with, the one with the rubber pants and the little lace-up shoes.' I always show that picture to let the kids know it wasn't my fault."

Even if you don't have children of your own, you can still find opportunities to observe children. The next time you're near a schoolyard or at a mall where kids hang out, look around for kids who are the age you were when your abuse began. Watch the way they interact. Listen to the pitch of their voices. Look at their actual size. Do you honestly think one of those children deserves to be abused?

If you still believe the abuse was your fault, you have lost touch with the simplicity of a child's longing to share love. One woman told the following story:

When my daughter was about six, we were riding in the car on our way to visit friends and she told me she wanted to be my lover. I knew her concept of lover was somewhat fuzzy, but she had enough idea to feel she wanted that. I responded gently that it wasn't possible.

She quickly added, "I know I'm too small, but when I'm grown up."

"No," I explained. "Even when you grow up, I'll still be your Mom and you'll still be my daughter. We have a special relationship that will never change. We can never be lovers, but we will always love each other in our own special way."

"Yes," she assented, "that will never change." Then, as we got out of the car she turned to me. "Mom, don't say anything to them about what we talked about, okay?"

I took her hand as we walked to the house. "Of course not."

This is the innocent love that abusers exploit.

THE CHILD WITHIN

When I first heard people talk about forgiving the child within, I raised my left eyebrow and thought, "California." There was no little girl inside of me. And if there was one, she was too weak and helpless for me to want to know her. She was the one who'd gotten me into this. She was a troublemaker and I wanted nothing to do with her.

Many survivors have a difficult time with the concept of the child within, even though forgiving that child is an essential part of healing. Too often women blame her, hate her, or ignore her completely. Survivors hate themselves for having been small, for having needed affection, for having "let themselves" be abused.

You may feel split, caught in a real schism. There is the "you" that's out in the "real" world, and then there's the child inside you who is still a frightened victim: "I felt like all my successes had been one big fake, because

I ignored the little child who never got over it, and who lives her life in humiliation and pain because of it." This survivor pictured herself as a successful career woman, carrying a briefcase and walking out the door to work. Beside her she'd imagine a little child whining over and over, "You can't go to work! You have to stay home and take care of me."

For a long time the briefcase-carrying woman could only respond in one way: "I can't stand being around you. I hate your guts, and I don't want to sit and look at your sad little face all day!"

Yet as long as you ignore that child's frozen pain, you won't feel whole.

Coming to terms with the little girl was really hard. I had to see all along that I'd had the enemy in the wrong place. And when I started to see what she had to deal with, and how well she did, I began to see how amazing it was that she survived whole. It took me a long time to accept and love her, but I finally was able to start cutting her some slack.

WHY IT'S HARD

It is helpful to know why it's so difficult to open yourself up to the little girl. To begin with, your survival depended on covering up her vulnerability. Even acknowledging the fact that you once *were* a child can be very threatening. It means remembering a time when you did not have the power to protect yourself. It means remembering your shame, your vulnerability, and your pain. It means acknowledging that the abuse really happened to you.

One woman had a terrible time accepting the fact that the incest wasn't something she'd conjured up in her adulthood. Even after years of therapy, this woman, like many survivors, couldn't remember being a child at all. It wasn't until her therapist asked her to bring in pictures of herself at various ages that she began to realize that she was the same person as that child who'd been molested. "See," her therapist would say, pointing to the photos, "*this is you.* This is something that happened to you. Do you see that this child is only *this* tall? Can you see that this child is you?"

Survivors who are mothers often say that seeing their own children's vulnerability is what enabled them to connect with the child within. Laura's reconnection to the inner child came about in a similar way:

I have always loved children, but for months after I remembered the incest, it was too painful to be around them. I'd see them playing or running down the streets, little girls flipping up their skirts and showing white cotton panties, and I'd cringe inside. "They're too vulnerable," I'd think. "They're too little."

I spent Halloween at my friend's house, just a few months after I had my first memories. I'd fled the trick-or-treaters in my neighborhood. It still hurt too much to see those innocent little faces. They'd say, "Trick or treat," and all I could think was, "Who's going to ruin you?" Every child seemed like a target.

The doorbell rang. My friend asked me to get it. I opened the door to a mother and a little girl. The girl was dressed as an angel, in a flowing white dress with gold trim. She had straight blond hair cut in a pageboy. Set on her head was a halo made of aluminum foil and a bent wire hanger. I asked her how old she was. "Five and a half!" she answered proudly.

I couldn't take my eyes off her. She looked exactly like I had when I was her age. It was like looking in a mirror back twenty-five years. I just stared at her, until her mother put a protective arm around her shoulder, and glared at me.

I gave the girl a Snickers bar and turned away. I shut the door slowly and sat down in the living room, dazed.

All I could think was, "That's how small I was! I was that little when he forced himself on me. How could he have done that?" I felt tears of outrage and grief. I had been innocent! There was nothing I could have done to protect myself. None of it had been my fault. "I was only a child," I screamed into the empty living room, the sudden reality of what a child of five is flooding through me.

MAKING CONTACT

Not having that little girl in your life means you have lost something. You have not had access to her softness, to her sense of trust and wonder. When you hate the child within, you're hating a part of yourself. It is only in taking care of her that you can really learn to take care of yourself. And although you may start with feelings of mistrust and ambivalence, part of healing is accepting her as a part of you.

I had to make a real commitment to the child inside myself. I had to say, "What do you need today? What can I do to make you feel safe? No, I'm not going to just tell you to go away." I had to make a literal commitment to do that. I had to say, "Okay, you need for me not to talk to so many people about what's going on." Or, "Okay, today you need for me to take five minutes at lunchtime to talk to you."

It was really wonderful, because suddenly I felt a real loyalty to this child. I began to feel that I wanted her to be a part of me. I wanted to help her feel all right. And I had never felt that before. What I had felt was, "Get this fucking brat out of my way, and let me get on with my life!"

Feeling that I had the ability to parent her was amazing. I had always said that I would never have children because I didn't want to do to them what my parents had done to me. So the fact that I could develop parenting skills toward myself was real important.

Coming into an intimate relationship with the child means hearing the depth of her pain, facing her terror, comforting her in the night. This will not be easy. But embracing the child inside is not all painful. It also means giving yourself extra pampering. Julie Mines gave herself birthday parties:

When I turned twenty-five, I began a countdown to thirty, anticipating an approximate five-year healing time. Starting with my "fifth" birthday, I have been counting down to my first. I celebrated my "fifth" over children's stories and chocolate cake. Friday I'll be celebrating my "third" birthday with the women in my life who help me heal. I'm going to build a tent out of bed sheets and we'll sit inside and read stories by flashlight. There will be glow-in-the-dark stars on the tent ceiling too. Oh, I love being little!

Another woman set up whole playrooms for the injured children who lived inside her.

Getting to Know the Child
by Eleanor

When I communicated how dependent I feel on being fat to keep me safe from men, my therapist asked me to imagine what it would take for the little girl inside of me to feel safe. When I closed my eyes, I saw myself as a young girl walking down the road, with a machine gun, a shoulder sash full of bullets, a couple of grenades, and a knife in my cowgirl boots. My therapist noted that my child believes she has to take care of herself, whereas it is my job to become the kind of adult who can protect her from harm. That way she won't have to do it herself with excessive body weight and other defenses.

In a later fantasy, I approached the little girl to tell her that I would keep her safe. She was playing in a sandbox with toy soldiers and tanks. She had on khaki shorts, a T-shirt, and an army helmet. She never looked at me. In utter sarcasm, she said, "Yeah, right." But she believed me. When she knew that I knew she believed me, she said, "But don't think this means I'm going to put on a dress or be nice to company." I told her not to worry, she doesn't have to do anything to get my protection.

Later the same day, she let me see tiny glimpses of her, sometimes tough, sometimes vulnerable, soft, feminine, pretty, scared. Once when I approached her she was in her jeans and T-shirt, with a camouflage army cap on. Long, soft tendrils of her beautiful hair had escaped her hat and were falling along her back and shoulders. I asked her if there was anything I could do for her.

Without a moment's delay she answered, "Well, you *could* stop stuffing me with food!"

"What do you mean?" I asked, shocked. "It's you who demand all that stuff."

She made a loud smack with her tongue. "*Somebody* has to be the adult around here, you know. Just because I ask you for it doesn't mean you have to give it to me. You don't let your son eat all that junk, no matter how he acts to try to get it. Don't you love me as much as you love him? What's the matter with you anyway?"

I am so delighted with her. She's intimidating too, though. I told her that I'd think about what she's saying, but that I don't have any magic solutions and she's going to have to be patient while I learn to parent her. She seems satisfied with that. She doesn't trust adults, but she thinks I'm a lot better than most grown-ups. She likes me. Maybe not full-out, but she does like me. She has seen me parent my son and she trusts me to proceed with integrity. I'm educable, she has decided.

She's such a smart, alive, spunky little thing. If she thinks I can do it, I can do it. She's an excellent judge of character. I'm hopeful. I have a new chance. I begin now.

She created safe places for each one, complete with age-appropriate toys, stuffed animals, postcards sent and received, drawings, and lots of affirmations.

You can draw pictures or play hide-and-seek in twilight. One woman got her husband to read her children's books every night before going to sleep. Another sat down before she went to bed and wrote a letter to the child within. "I'd tell her all these nice things. And then I'd get up and read it in the morning."

Your job is to give that child pleasure and to listen to the stories she has to tell. As one survivor, Gizelle, explained:

I began to listen to her and honor her, to do nice things for her. I needed to be her mother. That awakened my own healing energy. And I began to respond to that child: whether she needed to wear soft clothes, or eat an ice cream cone, or watch *I Love Lucy*, or sit out in the flowers. She knew what she needed to heal.

And this I'm discovering more and more. She will guide me. She's the one who's been wounded. She knows if she needs to be held. There may be times she just needs to have her hair brushed. She *knows* and I do as much as I can. I hold myself. I stroke myself. Or I rock. I comfort the child.

(For more of Gizelle's story, see page 461.)

WRITING EXERCISE: THE CHILD WITHIN

(See the basic method for writing exercises, page 32.)

This is a chance to talk to the child within. If you're capable of loving and comforting the child within, if you can let your adult self express the compassion you have for this child, write to her now and let her know. You can write a letter directly to her. Or you can engage in a written dialogue with her, first writing as the adult, and then as the child responding.

If you don't feel any allegiance, tenderness, or connection with the child yet, start with how you honestly feel. You can't write "I love you, I'll take care of you" if that's a lie. Start with: "I'm willing to sit down and write to you even though I'm not quite sure you exist," or "I don't sympathize with you yet," or even, "I hate you. You got me into this mess to begin with." Any point of contact is a start. You can't have a loving relationship until you make contact. Take the first step.

If you feel totally alienated from the child in you, imagine another child the age you were during your abuse. Try writing to her instead.

This is a good exercise to do more than once, particularly if you're not starting from a place of compassion. Eventually you'll be able to tell the child she's not to blame, that she's innocent, and that you'll protect her.

TRUSTING YOURSELF

What I've had to tell myself again and again is "Trust yourself." When my body tells me to stop, I stop. When my body tells me to go, I go. I used to push myself beyond my limits, and I'd always get sick. Now I've learned to listen so I don't have to go to that point. I trust myself because I'm my own greatest healer. Even the best therapist can't help me heal unless I listen to my body.

When children are abused, their perceptions become threatening to them. To acknowledge that the neighbor who pushed you on the swings and gave you birthday presents was also the man who made you suck his penis was unbearable. To admit that your father, who went to work to support you and stayed up late to make you a dollhouse, had a scary smile on his face when he touched your genitals was too terrifying. So you pretended they weren't doing these things or that these things were really all right. The lengths to which children go to distort their perceptions are striking.

When my father would come into my room at night, I would think, "That's not my father. That's an alien being." I'd look at these people doing these things to me and think, "Invaders have taken over their bodies." And these invaders were doing things to me. The original was still out there somewhere and why wouldn't they come back? I'd think, "Daddy, why did you let those aliens take your body over?"

If the significant adults in your life told you that your experiences didn't really happen, or that they happened in ways radically different from the way you perceived them, you probably became confused and distressed, unsure what was real.

A father can touch his daughter's breast and explain it away by saying, "I'm just tucking you in." A daughter can tell her mother that her stepfather touched her in a funny way. The mother can respond, "Oh, honey, that was just a dream."

Family members aren't the only ones to perpetuate this invalidation. Many young girls try to tell teachers, counselors, ministers, or other adults, only to be told, "You must be mistaken. Your Uncle Jimmy is a deacon in the church." Survivors have gone to therapists for help and been told, "You should be over that by now," or "It was just your brother; all kids do that."

It can also be terrifying to trust your inner voice if you're afraid of what it will tell you. One survivor explained: "My greatest fear is that if I listen to my insides, I will become crazy like my Mom. She's often said to me, 'You have the same kind of powers I do.' So the message is if I listen to my insides, I will really become off the wall. If I listen to my inner voice, I will drift into my own inner world, which is really crazy."

Although you may find it difficult to have faith in your own perceptions, it is possible to develop the capacity to trust your inner voice.

THE INNER VOICE

Within all of us, there is an inner voice that can tell us how we feel. If it's been covered over, or if you are not practiced at listening to that voice, it may be very small, just a pipsqueak. Yet it is there. And the more you listen and act on it, the stronger and clearer that voice will grow.

In child assault prevention programs, children are taught to identify the voice inside that warns them that something isn't right. They refer to this voice, intuition, as the *uh-oh* feeling. With encouragement, children easily recognize this feeling as danger—uh-oh, something's wrong here.

The uh-oh feeling is the one that tells you if you're in danger on the street. It tells you to cross the street and walk the other way. It's the sixth sense that warns you that something is about to happen.

Everyone experiences her inner voice differently. You may have bad dreams. You may get headaches. You may become exhausted. You may have a sudden urge to binge on crackers. Or you may notice you've cleaned the house twice in two days. The important thing is not what you experience, but that you recognize it as a message.

Ellen discovered a few years ago that every time she was about to make a poor decision for herself, she'd get a tight, anxious feeling in her stomach:

Looking back, I could see that that simple physical warning had been there throughout my life, but I'd never before given it a hearing. I'd never stopped and said, hey, what is this squeamish feeling in my stomach telling me? Once I began to listen and to respect this feeling, I began making much better decisions for myself. Now, whenever I feel it, I stop what I'm doing and take a minute to trace where the feeling originated. This information has been immensely valuable.

For more on getting in touch with your inner voice, see "Feelings," page 201.

GRIEVING AND MOURNING

Sometimes I think I'm going to die from the sadness. Not that anyone ever died from crying for two hours, but it sure feels like it.

As a survivor of child sexual abuse, you have a lot to grieve for. You must grieve for the loss of your feelings. You must grieve for your abandonment. You must grieve for the past and grieve for the present, for the damage you now have to heal, for the time it takes, for the money it costs, for the relationships ruined, the pleasure missed. You grieve for the opportunities lost while you were too busy coping.

And sometimes the losses are extremely personal:

I don't remember ever being a virgin. It wasn't fair. Everybody else got to be one. It has always really hurt me. I still have a real anger that that was taken away. Nobody asked. It was just gone. I didn't have that to give. I know that's just "The American Dream," but I heard that dream the same as any other woman did. Whether it's important now or not, it was to me.

If you maintained the fantasy that your childhood was "happy," then you have to grieve for the childhood you thought you had. If your abuser was a parent, or if you weren't protected or listened to, you must give up the idea that your parents had your best interests at heart. Part of grieving is replacing the unconditional love you held for your family as a child with a realistic assessment. Your childhood may have been completely awful. On the other hand, there may have been a lot of good times mixed in with the abuse. If you have any loving feelings toward your abuser, you must reconcile that love with the fact that he abused you.

You may have to grieve over the fact that you don't have an extended family for your children, that you'll never receive an inheritance, that you don't have family roots.

You must also grieve for the shattered image of a world that is just, where children are cared for, where people respect each other. You grieve for your lost innocence, your belief that it's safe to trust. And sometimes, you must even grieve for a part of you that didn't make it:

> I went down to see the children inside me. The first one I noticed just sat on the curb in my abdomen. She'd sit there with her head in her hand, looking very sad, or she'd be jumping up and down, being manic. Then there was one in my heart who would sit in a room behind a door. She'd open the door and peek out, and then shut the door, 'cause she got scared. Then there was the one who was dead. I'd been waiting for her to wake up. And one day I was lying in bed crying, and I said, "Okay, it's time for you to wake up," but she was dead. I sobbed and mourned that a part of me had died. The part of me that had really wanted to believe in the good of the family and the good of everyone just died.

Some survivors grieve not just for themselves, but for the abuse that was done to the people who abused them, for the generations of victims continuing to perpetuate abuse. A woman who was abused by her mother explains:

> There was a lot of grief, lots of tears realizing I didn't have the kind of family I thought everybody else had. It really hurt. It still hurts. It comes in waves. Those kinds of tears go real deep. It's a sadness for what I didn't have; it's also a sadness for my mother. It hurts that she's so sick. It hurts that she never realized her beauty, and still doesn't. Because she had so much self-hate, she had to abuse me. For a long time I was angry about that, but then there was a stage of grieving for her because she *is* beautiful, she is loving; it's just that her sick side is overwhelming to her.

BURIED GRIEF

Buried grief poisons, limiting your capacity for joy, for spontaneity, for life. An essential part of healing from traumatic experiences is to express and share your feelings. When you were young, you could not do this. To fully feel the agony, the terror, the fury, without any support would have been too devastating to bear. And so you suppressed those feelings. But you have not gotten rid of them.

To release these painful feelings and to move forward in your life, it is necessary, paradoxically, to go back and to relive the experiences you had as a child—to grieve, this time with the support of a caring person and with the support of your adult self.

What you need to heal is not fancy or esoteric. It is remarkably simple, though for many survivors it has been hard to find. All you need is the safety and support that enable you to go back to the source of your pain, to feel the feelings you had to repress, to be heard, to be comforted, and to learn to comfort yourself.

And in this way, a transformation takes place. Once you have fully felt a feeling, known it and lived in it, shared it, acted it, given it full expression, the feeling begins to transform. The way to move beyond the grief and pain is to experience them fully, to honor them, to express them with someone else, thus assimilating what happened to you as a child into your adult life.

ABOUT GRIEF

You may feel foolish crying over events that happened so long ago. But grief waits for expression. When you do not allow yourself to honor grief, it festers. It can limit your vitality, make you sick, decrease your capacity for love.

Grief has its own rhythms. You can't say, "Okay, I'm going to grieve now." Rather you must allow room for those feelings when they arise. Grief needs space. You can only really grieve when you give yourself the time, security, and permission to grieve.

After I had been in therapy for several months my whole self began to respond to that environment, within which I could allow my feelings. There were weeks I entered the building, went up the stairs, checked in with the receptionist, all with a smile on my face and cheerfulness in my step. Then I'd enter the office, my therapist would close the door, and before she'd even get to her chair, I'd be crying. Deep within me I held those feelings, waiting until I knew there would be time and compassion.

THE ROLE OF RITUAL

In order not to stifle your feelings of grief, take this period of mourning as seriously as if someone close to you had died. One survivor, whose abusive parents were still very much alive, spent many months dressed in black, telling everyone her parents had died. Another woman wrote a eulogy for her abuser, imagining herself at his grave, telling everyone exactly what she would remember him for. A third held a wake. Rituals such as these can be powerful channels for grief.

I wrote a divorce decree from my mother, because I kept having these dreams of wanting to cut the umbilical cord and her not letting me. I just couldn't figure out how to separate from her. We weren't talking. We weren't seeing each other, but I was still feeling too connected.

You may not be inclined to ritual or ceremony. You may simply cry a lot. As one woman put it: "I hadn't cried in years. It's only recently that that's been restored. I'm not sure I'm happy about it. It's like Niagara Falls at times."

However you grieve, allow yourself to release the emotions you have struggled all your life to smother. Grieving can be a great relief.

Own Your Own Pain
for Alana and Irma

by Patricia Roth Schwartz

Own your own pain.
Why not? It's yours.

You've hawked it, pushed it, pimped it—
     now,
Your body, breathing, life, guts, luster,
     sweetness, softness,
Pays the price.

So own your own pain. Why not?

You've eaten it for breakfast,
Sung it to sleep at night,
Rinsed it out in the basin,
Watched it rise with the bread.

So—take it, turn it,
Let it slither,
Into blood-beat, breast-bone, cell-song,
     skin.

Give it a name.
What you possess
Cannot possess you.

WRITING EXERCISE: GRIEVING

(See the basic method for writing exercises on page 32).

Write about what you lost, what was taken, what was destroyed. Write about the extent of the damage. Write about the things you need to grieve for. This is a chance to give voice to your pain, and to write about how you feel about your loss.

ANGER— THE BACKBONE OF HEALING

When I'm angry, it's because I know I'm worth being angry about.
—Shama, 25-year-old survivor

Few women have wholeheartedly embraced anger as a positive healing force. Traditionally women have been taught to be nice, conciliatory, understanding, polite. Angry women are labeled man-haters, castraters, bitches. Even in new-age psychotherapy circles, anger is usually seen as a stage to work through or as something toxic to eliminate. And most religious or spiritual ideologies encourage us to forgive and love. As a result, many survivors have suppressed their anger, turning it inward.

I'm albino and I get severe sunburn whenever I'm exposed to the sun. As a kid, I'd get really pissed about what was happening at home. But you weren't allowed to get angry at my house. So rather than say anything, I'd purposefully go out on a sunny day without a hat or any other protection. I'd come home blistered and with a fever.

Other survivors have been angry their whole lives. They grew up in families or circumstances so pitted against each other that they learned early to fight for survival. Anger was a continual armoring for battle. And sometimes the line between anger and violence blurred, and it became a destructive force.

I saw men and women angry and rageful when I was growing up. Both of

133

my parents, and other relatives too. I remember my mom slapping the shit out of this woman in the bar because the woman said, "We don't allow dirty Mexicans in this bar." But then my parents would turn it on each other, and on us. Anger, violence, and self-defense are all mixed up for me.

But anger doesn't have to be suppressed or destructive. Instead, it can be both a healthy response to violation and a transformative, powerful energy.

DENYING AND TWISTING ANGER

Anger is a natural response to abuse. You were probably not able to experience, express, and act on your outrage when you were abused. You may not even have known you had a right to feel outraged. Rather than be angry at the person or people who abused you, you probably did some combination of denying and twisting your anger.

One way survivors cut themselves off from their anger is to become so immersed in the perspective of the abuser that they lose connection with themselves and their own feelings. This approach is enthusiastically endorsed by most of society. Many people find it easier to sympathize with the abuser than to stand up as a staunch advocate for the victim. This is particularly true once time has passed and the abuser is an older man and the child a grown woman. People will feel sorry for him, perceive even weak attempts toward reconciliation on his part as major efforts, and blame the survivor if she continues to be angry.

But if you are unable to focus your rage at the abuser, it will go somewhere else. Many survivors turn it on themselves, leading to depression and self-destruction. You may have wanted to hurt or kill yourself. You may feel yourself to be essentially bad, criticize yourself unrelentingly, and devalue yourself. Or you might stuff your anger with food, drown it with alcohol, stifle it with drugs, make yourself ill. As Adrienne Rich writes: "Most women have not even been able to touch this anger, except to drive it inward like a rusted nail." *

Having been taught to blame yourself, you stay angry at the child within—the child who was vulnerable, who was injured, who was unable to protect herself, who needed affection and attention, who experienced sexual arousal or orgasm. But this child did nothing wrong. She does not deserve your anger.

LASHING OUT

Many survivors have also turned their anger against partners and lovers, friends, coworkers, and children, lashing out at those who (usually) mean no harm. You may find yourself pushing your child against the wall or punching your lover when you get mad.

I had a lot of physically abusive relationships. I didn't know how not to fight. My first impulse when I got angry

---

* Adrienne Rich, "Disloyal to Civilization," in *Lies, Secrets, and Silence* (New York: W. W. Norton, 1979), p. 309.

was this [she smacks one hand hard on the other], because that's what I saw growing up. Whenever I started to get upset with someone, I would literally feel the adrenaline running up and down my arms. My muscles would get really tight, my fists would clench, and I would break out into a sweat. I'd be ready to smack the person around. I'd want to fight.

If violence has been part of your life and you find yourself expressing your anger in abusive ways, you need to get help right away. It's okay to be angry, but it's not okay to be violent. (For help, see "Controlling Abusive Anger," page 210.)

If you don't physically fight, you may pick verbal fights or look for things to criticize. You mean to tell your son to do his homework and you find yourself yelling or calling him names. Your husband forgets to put oil in the car and you tell him he's a stupid idiot. Even though it isn't physically violent, verbal abuse is destructive.

DIRECTING YOUR ANGER WHERE IT BELONGS

It is time to direct your anger accurately and appropriately at those who violated you. You must release yourself from responsibility for what was done to you and place the responsibility—and your anger—clearly on the abuser.

I had a hard time directing the anger at my Dad. My therapist would say, "Well, how did you feel when your Dad picked you up and threw you against the wall?"

And I'd say, "Well, I pretty much felt like he was an asshole."

And my therapist would say, "Hmmm."

One time, after years of therapy, when he asked me something about my father, I was holding this pencil, and I just threw it across the room and said, "That bastard!"

It was the first time I was ever clearly angry at him. Sure, I'd been mad at my Dad. But it was directed in all the wrong directions. And this was the first time in all those years that I was just mad at him, period, without laughing about it, without being sarcastic or defensive. Just full on, "That shit!"

GETTING IN TOUCH WITH YOUR ANGER

If you're willing to get angry and the anger just doesn't seem to come, there are many ways to get in touch with it. A little like priming the pump, you can do things that will get your anger started. Then, once you get the hang of it, it'll begin to flow on its own.

It's often easier to get angry for someone else's pain than for your own. That's fine for a beginning. Imagine a child you love being treated the way you were treated. Read the writings of other survivors in anthologies and feminist journals. You can listen to their stories at conferences, workshops, and in small support groups. You can look at the expressions of grief on their faces and be touched.

WORKING THROUGH MOTHER BLAME

Although our culture usually criticizes women for being angry, it does not hesitate to direct anger toward women. Women, and specifically mothers, are frequently designated as the recipients for whatever anger needs a target. This is sometimes evident in the extreme, as when a mother is blamed for the father's abuse of their child.

Fathers have habitually blamed their wives for the fact that they abused their daughters. Many psychologists and sociologists have endorsed this position as well. They cite the wife's failure to meet the husband's needs for nurturing or sex. They refer to her drinking illness, working nights, or being otherwise unavailable. "And so," the father pleads, holding up his hands in a gesture of helplessness, "I turned to my daughter."

This is preposterous. It is never anyone else's fault when a man abuses a child. Regardless of how inadequate a mother may have been, no behavior on her part is license for any man to sexually abuse a child. It's time to stop blaming women for what men have done.

The role of mothers in father-daughter incest has traditionally been misunderstood and misrepresented (see page 482 for this history). It has been assumed that the mother knew the abuse was going on —and if they didn't, it was because they didn't want to. Mothers have been labeled collusive, contributing, weak, passive, withholding, and inattentive. And certainly some mothers have been. More than one survivor has described literally being handed over for sex by her mother.

But not all mothers are the same. Some genuinely didn't know the abuse was going on. And sometimes even a mother's best efforts are insufficient to stop it. Mothers have lost custody cases, been dismissed as vindictive, paranoid, or unfit by judges and social workers. Against what can be formidable odds, some mothers have succeeded in protecting their children. A number of mothers have gone underground with their children to shield them from abusive fathers. And a few have gone to jail rather than comply with court orders to hand over their children.*

Children have a right to be protected. And you have a right to be angry if you weren't protected. If your mother did not listen when you tried to tell her, did not leave an abusive or alcoholic man, did not offer the warmth, attention, or understanding that you needed, you have a right to hold her responsible.

Although some women direct all their anger at their mothers, others are afraid to get angry at them at all. You may identify so much with your mother's oppression that you minimize or negate your own. You may feel allied with her as women in a patriarchal society and think that acknowledging your anger would threaten that bond. But if your mother didn't protect you, looked the other way, set you up, or blamed you, you are inevitably carrying some feelings of anger. It is necessary to experience, validate, and express those feelings. This is not only your right; it is essential for your healing.

However, unless your mother was your abuser, you must not direct *all* of your anger toward her. Remember: the abuser *always* holds the ultimate responsibility for sexual abuse, and thus he deserves your legitimate anger.

---

* One highly publicized example is Dr. Elizabeth Morgan, who served two years in jail rather than send her daughter on court-ordered visitations with her ex-husband. Resources for protective parents begin on p. 574 of the Resource Guide.

You can hear their fury and be incited. Know that any time you cry or get angry for someone else, it taps your own grief and anger as well.

Getting into an angry posture also helps. Physically taking an angry stance, making menacing gestures and facial expressions, invites genuine anger to rise. One woman, who described herself as much more prone to feeling hurt than angry, was quietly weeping during a therapy session. As she relates:

My therapist scooted her chair toward me so that her knees almost touched mine. Then she put out her hands, palms facing me, and instructed me to put my palms against hers. "Push," she said. "Push against me." I pushed against her palms and she pushed back. As I pushed harder, she met me with equal pressure. It took all my strength to maintain. Within seconds I was angry. The tears were long gone. I was mad! And it felt powerful.

Therapy and support groups can be ideal places for stirring up anger:

I felt incredible anger, but I never allowed anger my whole life. It was really a difficult thing to let out. One day my therapist got up out of her chair, and she said, "Your father's in that chair." And she handed me a rolled-up towel and she said, "I want you to hit your father."

It took me a long time to psych myself into doing that, but once I started, I couldn't stop. I pounded and screamed until I couldn't move anymore. It was such a relief.

That was an important turning

point for me. After that, I did a lot of pounding on beds and screaming and writing angry letters to my dead father. I even worked with a punching bag.

Another way to get in touch with your anger is to role-play a situation that made you angry in the past. A therapist, friend, or group member can play the part of the person with whom you are angry. You describe the body language, gestures, and words that made you angry originally, and then you re-create the scene. This time you can respond with your genuine anger, and experience release and relief.

In order for this kind of exercise to be safe, the people involved have to be trustworthy and able to handle strong feelings. There must be guidelines for the expression of anger—for example, no hurting people, no hurting yourself. Also there should be an agreement that you can stop whenever you've had enough.

If you prefer to work with your anger alone, there are a number of writing exercises that can rouse your ire. Make a list of all the ways you're still affected by the abuse. If you do this in detail, you can hardly avoid at least some anger. You can also write a letter to your abuser. Try beginning with "I hate you."

Eva Smith arranged a satisfying outlet for her anger (for more of her story, see page 373):

I had a friend who made ceramic things, and if they were cracked or whatever, he'd set them aside for me. I'd come around at midnight. I'd go around the back and throw them against the fence. It was a miracle no one called the police because I'd be out there throwing stuff.

Piggybacking your anger at your abuser to more accessible anger is a good, sneaky way to bring it past your internal censors. If international issues like apartheid in South Africa easily inflame you, let yourself get worked up over those problems, and then, when you're really angry, remind yourself that the mentality that allows whites to torture blacks is the same mentality that allowed your abuser to vent his twisted, uncontrolled needs, fear, and ruthlessness on you. You can slide your own trauma in with the rest of the ills of the world, and you'll find yourself finally angry.

FEAR OF ANGER

Many survivors are afraid of getting angry because their past experiences with anger were negative. As one survivor put it, "I don't get the difference between anger and violence yet. When I hear loud noises, I think they're coming after me." In your family, you may have witnessed anger that was destructive and out of control. But your own anger need not be either. You can channel your anger in ways that you feel good about and respect.

Even women with no history of violence are often afraid that if they allow themselves to feel anger, they're liable to hurt or kill someone.

I know the anger is there. I'm too scared to let myself experience it. I'm scared that I won't be gentle with myself. That I'll turn the anger on myself.

And I'm so used to watching other people hurt people. I don't want to be a perpetrator. I don't know how to discharge my anger in a way that's safe.

It is extremely rare for women to violently act out their anger toward the people who abused them as children. And for women with no history of violence, the fear that you might hurt someone with your anger is usually unrealistic.

Anger is a feeling, and feelings themselves do not violate anyone. It's important to make the distinction between the experience of feeling angry and the expression of that anger. When you acknowledge your anger, then you have the freedom to choose if and how you want to express it. Anger does not have to be an uncontrolled, uncontrollable phenomenon. As you welcome your anger and become familiar with it, you can direct it to meet your needs—like an experienced rider controlling a powerful horse.

ANGER AND LOVE

Another aspect of anger that is often misunderstood, and thus keeps women from releasing their dammed emotion, is the relationship between anger and love. Anger and love are not incompatible. Most of us have been angry, at one time or another, with everyone we love and live closely with. Yet when you've been abused by someone close to you, with whom you've shared good experiences, it can be difficult to admit your anger for fear that it will eradicate the positive aspects of that relationship or of your childhood.

But getting angry doesn't negate anything you want to retain of your history. What's good can still remain in your memory as something from which you've benefited.* You forfeit nothing of your past by getting angry, except your illusion of the abuser as innocent.

Often survivors are afraid of getting angry because they think it will consume them. They sense that their anger is deep and fear that if they tap it, they'll be submerged in anger forever, becoming bitter and hostile. But anger obsesses only when it is repressed and misplaced. When you meet your anger openly—naming it, knowing it, directing it appropriately—you are liberated.

I'D LIKE TO KILL HIM

At one point or another, many survivors have strong feelings of wanting to get back at the people who hurt them so terribly. You may dream of murder or castration. It can be pleasurable to fantasize such scenes in vivid detail. Wanting revenge is a natural impulse, a sane response. Let yourself imagine it to your heart's content. Giving yourself permission to visualize revenge can be satisfying indeed.

---

* It is fine, of course, if you do not love your abuser. This should be obvious, but because many women carry a sense of responsibility for loving everyone, it is necessary to reinforce again and again your right not to love your abuser—even if he bought your food, taught you to ride a bike, read you bedtime stories.

If you start to think about acting on your fantasies, you need to consider how your actions would affect your own future. It's not wise to seek violent revenge in this society; you'd most likely perpetuate your own victimization.

What I say to myself is, "Wait a minute. I don't want to go to prison. I don't want the cops to come." I grew up with the cops coming. I don't want to go back to jail for being violent.

You also have to decide if you want to perpetuate abusive behavior further or if you want to break the cycle. As Soledad put it, "I've learned to respect human life." (For more of her story, see page 384.)

There are nonviolent means of retribution you can seek. Suing your abuser and turning him in to the authorities are just two of the avenues open. One woman threatened her abuser with the following telegram:

> YOU HAVE WONDERED WHY I DON'T WANT TO BE IN TOUCH WITH YOU ANYMORE. NOW I KNOW WHY, AND I HAVE PEOPLE WATCHING YOU. IF YOU EVER MOLEST ANOTHER LITTLE GIRL, EVEN LOOK AT HER IN THE WRONG WAY, I WILL TAKE YOU TO COURT AND WIN.
> BARBARA LITTLEFORD
>
> YOUR MESSAGE WAS DELIVERED BY TELEPHONE AT 2:19 PM PST ON 1/21 AND WAS ACCEPTED BY JACK.
>
> THANK YOU FOR USING OUR SERVICE.
> WESTERN UNION

Another woman, abused by her grandfather, went to his deathbed and, in front of all the other relatives, angrily confronted him right there in the hospital.

Some survivors feel revenge is something that's not in their hands. One woman, a devout Christian, said simply, "God will take care of him. It's not my job." Another woman said she couldn't do anything to her father that was worse than what he was doing to himself. He was dying of testicular cancer.

And sometimes the best revenge is living well.

THE POWER OF ANGER: THREE STORIES

Barbara Hamilton, a sixty-five-year-old survivor who has written a book about her abuse and her healing, describes the first time she really got in touch with her anger.*

I went racing back and got a hold of my therapist before she left. I started to rage and the whole mental health department of Napa heard me, because I raised the roof. Everything came up. All the obscenities and everything were connected. The male assaults of me and my kids all went together. I had been intellectually angry at my father before, but this time I just blew. I just screamed my fury all over the place. I threw my glasses against the wall. I was just beside myself. I can't say that it felt good, but it was a turning point. It was so clear where the rage was coming from. It was

the beginning of me not blaming myself.

If you've suppressed your anger for many years, it can be explosive. But even torrential anger doesn't have to be dangerous. Esther Barclay was able to trust her anger with striking results:

As I regained more memories, I moved through terror to a period of such intense anger toward my parents that I fairly radiated. . . . One night I was awakened by a loud screaming. At that moment just preceding full consciousness I was aware that I was the person screaming and that it was coming from the soles of my feet. As I became fully awake, I put my arms around myself and sobbed with relief. I did not know where this was leading, but soon after an especially heavy counseling session in which I worked intensely on anger toward my father, two things were apparent: (1) my vision changed; colors were bright and clear in a way unusual to me, and (2) for several days my back and legs were sore and tender in a way that can best be described as an enormous taproot being pulled out with all the little branches following.

And Edith Horning's experience clearly illustrates the dramatic healing effects of anger:

I had my therapist on one side of me, and a man I was very close to on the other. My therapist had me imagine I was in the balcony of a movie theater,

---

* Barbara Smith Hamilton, *The Hidden Legacy: Uncovering, Confronting, and Healing Three Generations of Incest.* See p. 547 of the Resource Guide.

POSITIVE EXPRESSIONS OF ANGER

Whether you express your anger directly to the abuser or you work with it yourself, it's essential that you give it some outlet. You can:

- Speak out.
- Write letters (either to send or purely for the chance to get your feelings out).
- Pound on the bed with a tennis racket.
- Break old dishes.
- Scream (get a friend to scream with you).

- Create an anger ritual (burn an effigy on the beach).
- Take a course in martial arts.
- Visualize punching and kicking the abuser when you do aerobics.
- Organize a survivors' march.
- Volunteer at a recycling center and smash glass.
- Dance an anger dance.

The list is endless. You can be creative with your anger. And ultimately, you can heal with anger.

---

and that quite far away my father was up on a tiny movie screen. I did this scenario where I imagined him coming closer, getting larger and larger, and as he did, the people on either side of me encouraged me to stop him, to do whatever I had to do to make him powerless. They encouraged me to say no. It took me two or three tries before I could get the nerve to shout. Suddenly I got this tremendous surge of feeling from inside. I screamed, "No! You get back! Just stop it!" And in my mind, I could see my father getting smaller and smaller and smaller. And I pounded on him until he was really tiny, just a shrimp.

That's when my father stopped being more powerful than I was. That's when I stopped protecting my mother or father. I no longer felt sorry for them. They made choices as they went along, just like I have. And when you make the choices, you pay the price. I did. They are. And that's the way it is.

SUPPORTIVE ANGER

In the introduction to *I Never Told Anyone*, Ellen wrote about her experience as a child being protected by her mother's anger when a deliveryman tried to molest her:*

My mother got furious at him. Then she fired him. She cared about me. Not the delivery man. She didn't tell me to take his feelings or his bad past experiences into consideration. She

---

* Ellen Bass and Louise Thornton, eds. (see the "About Sexual Abuse" section on p. 545 of the Resource Guide).

didn't care if he had trouble getting another job. She cared about me. I internalized the message that I was important, worthy of protection, worthy of her outrage.

Even if you are not yet in solid contact with your own anger, you may welcome a show of supportive anger. Although counselors are traditionally trained not to show more emotion than their clients, and parents are warned not to "overreact" when their children are abused, someone else's anger can help you experience your own. Women say things like, "It's still too scary for me to get angry at him myself, but it feels good to see you get so angry." Ellen has seen this frequently:

> Anger fuels my work. The women with whom I've been privileged to work have felt the power of my fury and it has been a shelter, a spark, a breath of fresh air, a model, an exciting if scary possibility, an affirmation.

Similarly, one woman's anger can clear the path for another. At a workshop, one survivor, Patricia, was rationalizing her father's abusiveness. Another woman kept quiet for a long time and then burst through in a passionate torrent, saying that she couldn't understand how anyone could not be angry, that she was so angry, all the time so angry, that she felt alone in the intensity of her anger. Rather than being overwhelmed or feeling criticized by this outburst, Patricia rushed across the room and took the hands of the outraged woman. She said that by overstepping the normal bounds of tidy, well-contained anger, this woman gave her permission to reach her own hidden anger.

Patricia was grateful, receiving that strong anger as a valuable gift.

ANGER AS AN ORDINARY PART OF LIFE

As you become more familiar with experiencing and expressing your anger, it can become a part of everyday life. When it's not so pent up, it stops being a dangerous monster and takes its place as one of many feelings.

> I'm learning that I can let people know when I'm angry without it being this terrible traumatic thing. I can say, "No, that upsets me," without feeling like the world is going to end.

Anger can be so safe that even children aren't scared by it. In Ellen's family, they have an enormous stuffed frog that a friend bought for two dollars at a garage sale:

> When one of us gets really angry, we stomp all over it. Even as a very small child, my daughter would explain, "It's okay to beat up Big Frog because he's not alive. It doesn't really hurt him." And at times when I was crabby she would encourage me: "Go get Big Frog, Mom. You can yell all you want. There's nobody here but me and you, and I don't mind."

ANGER INTO ACTION

Our task, of course, is to transmute the anger that is affliction into the anger that is determination to bring about change. I think in fact that one could give that as a definition of revolution.

—Barbara Deming, "On Anger"*

In Ellen's story about her mother protecting her from the deliveryman, her mother experienced her anger, expressed her anger, and then acted on her anger. She fired the deliveryman. She threatened to tell his wife if he ever spoke to Ellen again. She demonstrated her power to take action. This part is critical.

One woman in her late thirties described her realization that action is necessary:

In the early seventies, when I began participating in growth and therapy workshops, we were encouraged to express our anger. I had, it became apparent, plenty to express. I ranted, broke chairs, pounded pillows, slammed doors, screamed and raged for a number of years. I had married a

man with whom I was incompatible and we both expressed great quantities of anger toward each other, often in emotionally abusive ways. Yet none of this helped me feel better.

It took a long time for me to realize that experiencing my anger and expressing my anger were not enough. The last critical step, acting on my anger, was missing. Finally I gained the courage and clarity to act. I left my marriage and was no longer filled with rage.

Action, using the anger as a motivating force, is a critical part of healing. If you listen to what your anger is telling you, if you allow it to be a guide, then it becomes a valuable resource moving you toward positive change.

Women's anger has inspired them to cut ties with abusers, never again to have to endure pinches, inappropriate jokes, and drunken advances while they try to chew their Thanksgiving turkey. Women's anger has catalyzed them to quit jobs with domineering bosses, to divorce battering husbands, and to break addictions to drugs and alcohol. Focusing anger precisely—onto the abuser and away from yourself—clears the way for self-acceptance, self-nurturance, and positive action in the world.

---

* Barbara Deming, "On Anger," In *We Are All Part of One Another: A Barbara Deming Reader,* edited by Jane Meyerding (Philadelphia: New Society Publishers, 1984), p. 213.

DISCLOSURES AND CONFRONTATIONS

If you feel you need to talk to your mother about it, if you feel you need to confront your molester, do it. Because the next thing you know, that person's going to be dead, and you're going to be wishing for the rest of your life that you had. It's those unvoiced cries that haunt you forever.

Everyone has a right to tell the truth about her life. Although most survivors have been taught to keep their abuse a secret, this silence has been in the best interests only of the abusers, not the survivors. Nor does it protect the children who still have contact with the abuser.

Many survivors have a compelling desire to speak out. Yet whenever you consider breaking the taboo of secrecy, you are apt to feel fear and confusion. You may question your right to tell or criticize your motives. In order to understand the strength of these feelings, you must remember that you are

emerging from a context of severe cultural and personal repression. You are challenging the secrecy that is the foundation of abusive family structures. You are taking revolutionary steps toward self-respect and respect for all children. You are exercising your power.

There are many motives for wanting to confront or disclose. You may want validation that these things actually happened, perhaps from a sibling who experienced abuse or witnessed yours. You may want factual information to help piece together your memories. You may want to make the abuser, nonprotecting parents, or others feel the impact of what happened to you. You may want to see them suffer. You may want revenge. You may want to break the silence. You may want financial reparations or payment for your therapy. You may want to warn others that there are children still at risk. (*And they are.* We have heard countless stories of survivors who didn't think the abuser would hurt anyone but them, only to find he had also molested their own children, nieces, nephews.) You may want to explore whether it is possible to establish an honest relationship, to get support. If you choose to speak out, it is probably for several purposes, some more attainable than others.

There is no right course of action in disclosures and confrontations. There is no right time to tell, no right way to tell, and no right decision whether to tell. It is very important not to be pressured into confronting. Although some stages in the healing process are absolutely necessary, confronting abusers and telling family members are not.

Be clear that whatever you do, you are doing it for yourself. Consider your decision thoroughly, and whatever your choice, carry it out in a way that will best allow you to assert your own rights to honesty and visibility.

MAKING THE DECISION

There are some questions you can ask yourself to help you make up your mind:

- Whom exactly do I want to talk to? Why?
- What do I hope to gain from this confrontation? Are my expectations realistic?
- What are my motives for confronting or disclosing?

- Is there anyone who can give me the information I need?
- What do I stand to gain? To lose?
- Would I be risking something I still want from my family? A job in the family business? An inheritance?
- Could I live with the possibility of being excluded from family gatherings?
- Am I willing to take the risk of losing contact with other family members with whom I want to stay connected?
- Am I stable and centered enough to risk being called crazy?
- Could I maintain my own reality in the face of total denial?
- Can I withstand the anger I am likely to face?
- Could I handle no reaction at all?
- Do I have a solid enough support system to back me up before, during, and after the confrontation?
- Can I realistically imagine both the worst and the best outcomes that might result?
- Could I live with either one?
- Have I prepared for the confrontation?

THE WORLD DOESN'T FALL APART

If you decide not to disclose, make sure it's not because of shame or because you still think it's more important to protect the abuser or the family than to take care of yourself. There are some good reasons not to tell, but shame and protecting a sick family system are not among them (see "If You Don't Confront" on page 153).

Celia is a poet. As she began to write about the incest and to go public with her work, she was terrified. She was convinced that her words would destroy her family.

Like many abused children, she had grown up with an unrealistic sense of her own power. "I had this ridiculous feeling that any little thing that I said or did could blow the whole world apart and destroy all its inhabitants. What I had to realize was that my family stayed intact through all those years of incest. Me opening my mouth and talking about it now was not going to break those bonds."

When Celia finally began to read her work in public, her mother was afraid that Celia would end their relationship. But Celia chose to keep visiting her family. "In doing so," Celia said, "I was saying to my mother, 'I don't have to only hate you. I don't have to only love you. I can do both.' I was setting an example that these things can be talked about and the world doesn't fall apart."

NOW HE'LL FINALLY LOVE ME, I JUST KNOW HE WILL

In thinking about confronting or disclosing, you need to be realistic about the kinds of responses you might get. If someone has abused you in the past, it is unlikely that person will suddenly become sensitive to your needs. Although you may get some sympathetic, supportive responses, the disclosure of abuse usually disrupts a family system of denial. Often family members find the exposure so threatening that they turn the survivor into a scapegoat, denying her experiences, minimizing them, or blaming her. One survivor who told her mother that she had been abused by her father received a letter back from her mother saying that, although it was hard, she forgave *her* (the survivor) for having sex with her father!

Another woman, whose grandfather violently attacked her while she was playing cops and robbers in the basement, told her mother about the abuse. Her mother retorted, "You wanted it. What else would you have been doing playing in the basement? You must have been looking for sex."

This kind of extreme defensive reaction is common. If your mother knew that you were being abused and didn't take steps to protect you, it is unlikely that she will be understanding now, unless she has made some significant personal changes.

Often other members of your family also have been abused and have either repressed it entirely or want to avoid feeling the pain around it. Unearthing these feelings can be so threatening, or can imply such changes, that the family will reject the survivor altogether rather than deal with her. Therefore it is essential that you approach any confrontation focused on yourself, what *you* want or need to say, how *you* want to handle the situation, rather than on any response you may hope to get.

With the increasing public attacks against survivors' credibility, the private denial within families has been bolstered. Now, in addition to all the old lines, survivors are being told that they are victims of therapists who have implanted "false memories" into their brains. And some families have retaliated, going to the media with their claims of innocence or harassing or suing the survivor's therapist.

You should never proceed naively expecting that finally, now that you are telling, you will get everything you didn't get as a child. Or that if you tell in the "right" way, you'll get the support and love you're entitled to. Yet many survivors hope, secretly or openly, for just such a response. You need to be very clear about this so that you don't set yourself up for another betrayal. When you confront the abuser or disclose your abuse, you are deciding to give up the illusions in order to determine reality. You must be willing to relinquish the idea that your family has your best interests at heart.

If, on the other hand, your parent, other relative, or even the abuser can genuinely hear you, extend understanding, and be willing to support you, then you have the real benefit of that relationship.

It Brought Us Closer Together: Vicki's Story

The way I told my mother that my father had abused me was during a therapy session I arranged with her therapist. I'd set it up that way because she was the hardest person for me to tell. I called her up and said, "Mom, I have something really important I want to talk with you about. Is it okay if I fly down and go to your therapist with you? It would probably be a lot easier."

Her first reaction was, "Are you okay?"

And I said, "Yeah, I'm okay." She told me to go ahead and call her therapist. So I did. I told her therapist what I wanted to do and we set up an appointment two weeks later. I talked to my mother a few times during that period. She never once said, "Tell me what it is! You're driving me crazy." But she was terrified.

I flew down and she picked me up at the airport. In the car, on our way to the session, she said, "I want to ask you two questions. Are you dying of some terrible disease?" I thought my heart would break.

Her second question was, "Are you in very deep trouble?"

I said, "Neither one of those."

She said, "I feel better now."

When I finally told her that my father had abused me, her reaction was what I'd always wanted the whole time I was growing up. She looked at me and said, "I'm so sorry." She reached toward me and just held me, like a mother holds a child who's been hurt. It wasn't thought out. It was genuine. She just came toward me with raw emotion. Twenty years flashed in front of me. I said, "My God, why did I wait so long to tell her?" She was totally sympathetic.

She had no denial whatsoever. And it wasn't until halfway through the session that she started in on what a bad mother she must have been. Then she got fiercely angry at my father. She wanted to go over to his house and shoot his brains out. She wanted to kill him. I loved it.

Telling her has brought us much closer together. We're much more honest with each other now.

CONFRONTING OUTSIDE THE FAMILY

If the person who abused you was not a close family member, you may find it easier to enter the confrontation purely for yourself, not longing for reconciliation. Your family may find it less threatening to be supportive as well. Obviously it will be easier for a mother to hear that a neighbor or a teacher abused her daughter, than it will be to hear that her husband, father, or son did the abusing.

But whatever your situation, it is important not to minimize the effects the process can have on you. One woman, who'd been abused by her teacher, found herself shaking and unable to sleep all night just from looking up the man's name in the phone book and finding him listed. Breaking the taboo of silence is never something to take lightly. It can shake your whole world.

PREPARING FOR A CONFRONTATION

Although it is impossible to predict the response you will get, the odds are that it won't be satisfying, compassionate, or responsible. If it is, that's terrific. But it can't be counted on. Instead you must say what you have to say for yourself and assess how you feel about the confrontation in terms of what *you* did, not the reaction you get.

It is important that you prepare yourself for defensive and aggressive reactions. As a child you were violated without any adequate way to shield yourself. Now you do not have to be so vulnerable.

There are many ways to protect yourself. You may want to talk to family members individually rather than all together. You also may want to talk to some family members and not others. You may want to begin with one person at a time, starting with those most likely to be allies. Respect your own inner timing.

However, once you begin to tell, you have set the ball rolling. Although you may tell someone and ask them not to tell others, they may not honor your wishes or follow your guidelines. In dealing with families in which there has not been adequate respect, don't underestimate the betrayal you may experience.

WAIT UNTIL YOU'RE CLEAR

Usually it's a good idea to work through some of your own feelings before you talk with family members who may not be sympathetic. If you're still doubting that it could have happened, unsure that it was really all that bad, still believe it was your fault, then it's not the best time to try to deal with people who are likely to challenge or attack you.

If your memories of the abuse are still fuzzy, it is important to realize that you may be grilled for details. Laura received a letter from one of her relatives, full of demands for proof:

> Rape and incest are among the most heinous of all crimes and he does not become guilty on the basis of 25-year-old flashbacks. . . . These are very serious charges and you had better present some factual evidence to back it up.

Of course such demands for proof are unreasonable.* You are not responsible for proving that you were abused. However, you need to assess whether you feel solid enough to withstand such attacks. It helps if you seek out people who can support you rather than undermine you at this stage. In this way you build your own foundation first.

---

* See "Legal principles do not apply to healing," p. 505.

PUT YOUR OWN NEEDS FIRST

In preparing for a confrontation or disclosure, it's important to remember that, except for the protection of children, confrontations are for you. Take the time to prepare. The terms are yours: you set the boundaries, you pick the timing, you choose the turf.

After a long silence, Louise made contact with her father. She confronted him about his abuse, and they began a painful correspondence. After a year or so, it became clear that he was not able to communicate through letters, that if Louise wanted a satisfying confrontation, she'd have to do it in person.

When Louise told her husband about this, he suggested she talk to her father with a mediator or a therapist present. Louise responded, "But I don't know if there's anybody down there who could do that."

Her husband almost hit the roof. "Down there?" he exclaimed. "You'd actually think of going down there? Why would you leave your whole support system behind and go there? Let him come here."

"Oh," Louise replied. "I didn't think of that."

Like Louise, many survivors have trouble figuring out how to take care of themselves. But when you're considering a confrontation, it's essential to put your own needs first. Where and when the confrontation takes place is of primary importance.

Preparation for an actual confrontation can be as important as the event itself. You can role-play possible scenarios in therapy or with supportive friends. Practice saying the things you want to say and responding to different reactions. You can write out the things you want to get across and memorize the essential points. That way, if you get nervous, you'll be able to remember what you wanted to say.

Talk about what it is that you want. What do you want to say? What do you want to achieve? Assess what is definitely possible (I want to tell my mother that my father raped me), what is unpredictable (I want her to listen to me; I want her to care about my feelings), and what is probably fantasy (I want to feel totally taken care of by her; I want her to divorce him).

Look at several possible outcomes, some of them unsupportive or hostile. Imagine the worst reaction you could get. Can you live with that?

When one woman was preparing to tell her mother that her father had abused her, she was afraid her mother wouldn't be able to handle it:

> I knew she wouldn't attack me or reject me, but I was afraid she'd stop eating and sleeping, get sick, have a heart attack, and die. My therapist asked me to consider whether I could live with that, her death. That was a difficult session, but what I came to was that I would not have been the cause of my mother's death. That if she got sick and died, that would be her choice. There were many other ways that she could respond to the information that I'd been abused, and if she chose death that was beyond my responsibility. I would be deeply distressed, of course; it would be hard to keep from shouldering the blame. I would feel terrible not to have her alive, but I would not die myself. I would recover. That would be my choice.

As it turned out, this woman's mother did not get sick or die. But in order for the daughter to speak her truth, she needed to confront the worst and know she could handle it.

STAY CENTERED

Dealing with abusers or close family friends can flip you into childhood insecurities. You can begin to doubt your own reality. Therefore it is important that you provide yourself with ample support when you approach abusers or family members. You need people who can offer a contemporary mirror, who can remind you of who you are now and affirm that your reality makes sense.

Another practical aid in staying centered is to keep a record of your interactions. If you write letters, keep copies; record phone calls or make notes after the conversations; during visits, keep a daily log. If you're going for a visit, bring things with you that remind you of your current life: photographs, your pillow, a favorite memento or a present given to you by a friend. You can also call home for reality checks while you're away. Or better yet, take a friend with you as a witness. Be careful about whom you pick to do this. Choose someone who won't get drawn in by your family. (Another family member is usually not the best choice.) Be clear with that person about your expectations. Make sure they can come through for you.

THE CONFRONTATION

In confrontations, say what you want to say and ask for what you want. You may not get it, but you can at least have the satisfaction of knowing that you spoke up for your-self. If there are things you want, say so. You may want an apology, an acknowledgment of responsibility, an admission that what you say is true, an expression of willingness to make reparations or payment, or a change in your present relationship (such as, don't hug or kiss me anymore). You may want the abuser to read certain books about sexual abuse or to go into therapy. Chances are the abuser will not make major psychological changes as the result of a confrontation, so it's usually more effective to ask for specific behaviors rather than changes in attitude. And it's easier to see whether you're getting what you've asked for if you've been concrete.

There are many ways to confront or disclose. You can do it in person, over the phone, through a letter, in a telegram, or through an emissary. Twenty years ago, a woman went to her grandfather's funeral and told each person at the grave site what he had done to her. In Santa Cruz, California, volunteers from Women Against Rape go with rape survivors to confront the rapist in his workplace. There they are, ten or twenty women surrounding a man, giving tangible support to the survivor, as she names what he has done to her. This makes for a dramatic and effective confrontation.

The initial confrontation is not the time to discuss the issues, to listen to your abuser's side of the story, or to wait around to deal with everyone's reactions. Go in, say what you need to say, and get out. Make it quick. If you want to have a dialogue, do it another time.

BUT HE'LL COME AND GET ME

You may fear that your abuser will further hurt you if you speak out or confront him. One woman was sure her father would appear on her front steps and try to kill her. In actuality, he hid from her after that, avoiding her totally. *He* was scared of *her.* You may not realize it, but you hold a lot of power when you choose to disclose and confront.

Of course there are some instances where there is danger. In those cases it is essential that you take measures for your safety. You need to set up adequate protection for yourself so that the confrontation does not lead to further assault. For example, you may want to meet only in a public place, not give out your present address or phone number, or have witnesses along. You may even choose not to confront at all because the person is too violent or unpredictable.

AFTERWARD

The aftermath of a confrontation can feel horrible, great, or anything in between. Women often fear that a disclosure will cause a cataclysm: their mother will go insane, their father will kill himself, their aunt will divorce their uncle, the principal will fire the teacher. And sometimes such extreme reactions or major upheavals do happen. But it is also possible that very little will change. Whole families may pretend nothing was ever said.

Or you may get a sympathetic response initially, and then, when the implications sink in, all support may be withdrawn. You may get a negative initial response, but as time goes on, your family may come to terms with what you are telling them and become more supportive. Sometimes one family member will support you and another will reject you. Alicia wrote to her parents and told them her uncle had abused her:

My mother wrote me back, accusing me of being spiteful. It was a handwritten letter, and she must have used the word "abuse" twelve times in two pages. It was over and over again, how *I* was abusing *her.* It was clear that *she* wanted to be the abused child in this interaction.

My father, on the other hand, was wonderful. And this was his brother we were talking about. When he first got my letter, he sent me a note. He said, "I don't feel defensive for Steve. What I feel is for the little girl, and I just want to pat her on the head and say, 'There, there.' It was just the perfect response. There was no question at all that he believed me. I know I was really lucky.

I went to visit them a couple of months after I sent the letter. He and I were alone in the car together, and at one point he said, "Can I ask you something about the incest?"

And I said, "Yeah." I expected him to ask me factual things.

All he wanted to know was, "Are you going to be okay? Is there an end point in sight?"

It was so moving. He didn't care about his brother. He didn't say, "Are you sure?" He just wanted to know I was going to be okay, and then he wanted to know how he could help. He offered to help me pin down factual stuff. He said he'd find out when my uncle was and wasn't in the country, to help me get external timetables. My dad actually sat down and helped me figure out how and when it could have happened.

All he said to me about my mother was, "We feel very differently about this. Don't assume we have the same reaction."

(For more of Alicia's story, see page 421.)

Confrontations and disclosures can be difficult, frightening, painful, and demanding. Yet they are also opportunities to express your feelings directly, to break the twisted pact of secrecy, to assert your own needs and boundaries, to overcome your fears, and to act for yourself. All these are potent steps in working through the victimization of abuse.

Whatever the consequences, it's common to feel some sense of relief mixed in with your other emotions. There is no longer a secret in the air. There is no longer hiding. If you don't want to trim the Christmas tree, share Chinese New Year, or attend a cousin's wedding because you don't want to be near the abuser, you don't have to lie about it.

After the confrontation or disclosure,

PROTECTING OTHER CHILDREN

Many women were molested by abusers who work professionally with children—teachers and counselors. A growing number of these survivors have confronted their abusers and alerted the schools or institutions where the abuse took place, in order to protect other children.

Whether the abuser is a person who works with children, a neighbor with access to children, or a family member, protecting children in the present and future is an important consideration. Child sexual abuse thrives in a climate where people let the past be past and hope for the best. As adults we all have a responsibility to children—to confront abusers, to warn parents of children the abuser has access to, to alert supervisors in camps and schools, to let children know that we will listen if they need to talk.

Sometimes it is difficult to weigh your own needs to be silent or to go at a slower pace against the pressing need to protect children presently at risk. Just as you are opening up to your own pain, feeling overwhelmed with your own experience, you remember a niece or a grandson.

I'd had no contact with my father for fifteen years when my sister called up, finally furious about what he'd done to her. He'd molested both of us since early childhood, and she'd been forgiving ever since. In the course of that conversation, she told me our half-sister was leaving her daughter with him for babysitting. We realized that he might be molesting this little girl, and discussed calling our half-sister to warn her. At first my sister was worried that we'd be calling for the wrong reason—because we wanted revenge. I said, "So what if we are vengeful? He took his revenge out on us for years. Besides,

you will need to decide what kind of contact, if any, you want to continue, either with the abuser or with others. You may choose never to see your abuser again. You might want to try to rebuild shattered relationships. (See "Families of Origin," on page 299, for more suggestions.)

IF YOU DON'T CONFRONT

Choosing not to confront your abuser or your family is a reasonable option if the choice is made from strength rather than fear. Sometimes women have felt pressured by other survivors who've done particularly painful confrontations: "We went through it. You can go through it too." This kind of peer pressure is damaging. You are not "more healed" if you confront than if you don't.

There are many reasons for not confronting. You may be in actual danger. You might not have enough support to back you up. You might not want to take on the additional stress. You may not feel firm enough in your own sense of reality. You may not be ready to risk a total break with your family. Your parents may be paying your tuition at school, and you can't yet afford to be eco-

---

we have to protect this child.''

So we called our half-sister and told her that our father had molested us and other foster kids for years, and that we were concerned for her daughter's safety. She took it all in very calmly and thanked us for telling her. We felt frightened and empowered at the same time. Mostly we felt we had done something for that little girl that had never been done for us —we told, we protected, we valued her safety over the secret.

Although it is not good to sacrifice yourself to save others, children need and deserve protection. Deciding what to do in this kind of situation requires taking into account all the factors:

• How immediate is the risk to the children?

• How much time do I need to prepare myself?
• Are there ways I can inform the children's parents before I'm ready to confront the abuser?
• Is there a step I can take now, knowing that more is required later?

There may be more options than you think. You can call Child Protective Services and anonymously report abuse. You can talk to the child's teachers or the family doctor. One woman thought her brother was abusing his children. She sent them child abuse prevention books that encouraged telling. Another woman knew that her neighbor's children were being abused by their paternal grandfather. Instead of talking to the father, who she knew would be defensive and possibly hostile, she chose to talk to his wife. Since she was not a blood relation, she was more receptive.

nomically self-sufficient. Or perhaps you just don't want to be discounted, or once again told that you're crazy.

The thing about confronting my abuser is that I don't think it would be very satisfying. He's a real reality manipulator. He's been married a whole bunch of times, and each time he gets a divorce, he justifies it by saying how crazy his wife is, using all this medical terminology. I decided I didn't want to hear that crap turned on me.

It hasn't felt like there'd be a whole lot of satisfaction talking to most of my family. If I'm not going to get validation, it doesn't make sense to put energy into talking to people who are probably going to dump a lot of junk on me. I decided to talk only to the people in my family who were either going to give me additional information or give me validation.

Whatever your reasons, if you're not ready for a confrontation, or if it's not right for you, don't feel obligated to do one. You can heal without it.

WHAT IF HE'S DEAD OR GONE?

You may not have the option of confronting your abuser or disclosing to family members. If your abuser was a stranger or someone you no longer know, you may be disappointed that you don't have the opportunity to confront him. If your abuser is dead, you may be furious that there's no chance for confrontation or reconciliation. At the same time, you may feel tremendous relief that you don't have to go through the ordeal you see other survivors face, that you don't have to carry around the hope that someday (if you're good enough, wait long enough, pray enough) things will change.

If your abuser has died, you may be glad he is dead. This is a perfectly reasonable feeling to have. One woman said she couldn't wait for her father to die so she could spit on his grave. Another said:

I went through periods where I knew my father was lucky he was already dead because if he was alive I would have killed him. I would have beaten him to a pulp. He would have been eighty-something years old and I would have demolished him. I can imagine him denying the whole thing, me flying into a rage, and not even having the awareness of what I was doing until I did it, and ending up behind bars.

This woman probably would not have actually killed her father, but it felt good to think about it. Imagining the confrontation gave her a place to direct her anger, a way to feel powerful. Her father's death hadn't stopped her from actively engaging in resolving her own feelings. It only meant she didn't have the option of meeting him directly.

The fact that your abuser or other significant people are no longer around doesn't mean you can't (and won't need to) resolve your relationships with them. Although you can't interact face to face, you still need to deal with your own unresolved feelings.

YOU CAN STILL LET GO

Even without a direct confrontation, you can experience the satisfaction and catharsis of a confrontation. There are many symbolic ways to face your abuser or sever your ties. You can write him a letter and not mail it (see the exercises at the end of this chapter for suggestions). You can write a poem or draw a picture about your abuse and publish it in a survivors' newsletter. You can donate money to an organization that helps survivors. You can design your own ritual.

> One time I buried my uncle and sent him out to sea. It was a ritual Indians do. I chanted and I cried about it. I put him and all the things he had done to me into this litter box and visualized him going away. I took a picture of him and burned it.

There is also a lot you can do in a workshop or therapy setting. Psychodrama is a particularly useful tool for acting out confrontations. In a psychodrama, you choose people to act out certain people in your life. You tell them what the person is like and what they might say, so they can respond to you in character. Then you set and enact a scene with them. Psychodrama can often be quite realistic, and it is a dramatic and powerful tool for resolution when real-life confrontations are impossible.

Doing It: Catherine's Story

Catherine is a twenty-eight-year-old West Coast radio producer. She grew up in a rural midwestern town, the child of alcoholic parents. Her father was a doctor, her mother a psychiatric nurse. Catherine was abused by her father from early childhood, and began to recover her memories a year before she did this confrontation.

I was beginning to want to tell one of my parents. My mother called one weekend. She said she'd been worried about me, that she knew I'd been depressed. She was concerned that I had been avoiding the family. She asked me what was wrong.

I had just gotten out of bed, and I thought, "Well, I might as well do it now." So I just said, "I'm an incest victim, and I think it was Dad." Then I said to myself, "Oh my God! Why did you say that? You're half asleep! What have you gotten yourself into?"

I could hear my mom choking on the other end of the phone. It was awful. She cried while I told her the story. I cried also.

At first she was very comforting. The first thing she said was, "I believe you 100 percent. You were a trustworthy child. Mothers usually side with the fathers in this kind of thing, and I'm not going to do that."

A couple of days later, I got a letter in which she asked me how she could possibly go on living with him. Her attitude began to shift from that point on. And now she denies it even happened.

TALKING TO MY FATHER

I had specifically asked her not to tell my father. I said I wanted to be able to tell him in my own time. But she told him everything and he called up a week later, extremely angry, demanding, "What's this incest shit you're talking about?"

And at that moment, I decided to tell him the whole story and we spent the next two hours on the phone, screaming at each other about whether or not it had been him, why I hadn't said anything before, and why I hadn't been able to remember. He said it was just like me to accuse him. He said he'd never touched me in my life. He demanded that I

WHAT WAS THE HARDEST AND SCARIEST?

Laura says: Every time I sat down to write another section of this book, I found myself thinking about the topic at hand and saying, "That was the hardest part of dealing with the abuse." Believing it happened was the hardest. No, reliving memories was the hardest. But then again, dealing with my family was really the hardest. The truth is, the hardest stage was whichever one I was currently in.

WHAT DID OTHER SURVIVORS THINK WAS HARDEST?

"The hardest part was going back to therapy every week."

"The collective wrath and the collective lie of my family has been the hardest thing to deal with. I see them as an embodiment, kind of as a big shadow hanging over me, telling me I'm making a big deal out of nothing."

"The hardest thing was accepting the fact that someone I loved and cherished—my father—could have violated me so deeply. That and the fact that he died three years ago, and I will never be able to go up to his face and say, 'Why did you do this to me?' "

"The hardest thing is still having this confrontation thing with my father hanging over my head."

"Dealing with my mother, dealing with her absolute refusal to hear about it."

"The hardest part was getting in touch with my feelings, allowing myself to feel sad and to cry."

"That he was *still* interfering with my body was very, very hard. That years after he had ever touched me, I still couldn't feel things, that I still couldn't make love and feel safe, that it didn't stop when he stopped touching me."

"Letting myself feel the absolute isolation, how absolutely lonely I had been, to remember how frightening the world had been."

"Patience has been the hardest thing for me."

"The hardest part for me still is being involved in an intimate one-on-one relationship with a man. It just doesn't go easy for me, and it has nothing to do with the man. It is something I do all by myself."

"Sex—because there's only so much

you can do on your own. Then you need another person to cooperate."

"The hardest part of my healing process has been trying to end it."

WHAT WAS THE SCARIEST?

"The scariest part for me was that I had to do this all by myself, that no matter how many people expressed their caring for me, or told me I'd get over it, I had to be the one to do the work. And to face that has been almost more than I could bear."

"The scariest thing has been intimacy. It's terrifying."

"The scariest part was when it actually happened. Nothing in the healing compared to that."

"The scariest part was that I might remember I was a whore, that I'd find out that it really had been my fault. And if I had been bad, then I would have to die."

"The scariest part was wanting to hurt myself or kill myself."

"It scared me when I thought that therapy was an endless process and that I wasn't making any progress."

"The scariest part is the panic. It's like you're dissolving and there's nothing to hold on to. There's just this terror and there's an incredible impulse to do something and there's nothing to do."

"Telling."

"The scariest thing was talking about my psychosis and giving up my medicine, being able to give trust one more chance."

"The scariest thing has been not fogging over. Committing to being present has been very scary."

"Telling a male authority figure 'No, I'm not going to do that' was really scary."

"The scariest part has been resigning myself to the fact that my mother loves my father and has chosen him, and that I've lost her."

"The scariest part is that I might be crazy like my mother."

"The scariest point was when I didn't know whether I was going to make it or not, when I felt I'd rather die than know anymore, or feel anymore, or even have it be true. I really felt he could succeed in killing me."

"It's a circular answer, but the scariest thing is facing my fears."

come up with proof and that I meet with him. I said I didn't know whether I wanted to meet with him at this time, and that when I did, it would be on my time and on my turf. Turning him down and maintaining my own power was really really hard. I'm proud I did it.

I hung up. The whole time I'd been on the phone, I had successfully maintained my position—that this had been done to me, that I was hurt, that I was angry, that there was no excuse for it. I had cried to him and I had given him the facts. I kept both my intellect and my feelings intact. And the truth of that was real powerful.

FAMILY THERAPY

I asked my mother and father to do a family therapy session with me. I met with them for two hours. We both drove about a hundred miles to get there. There was a very tense scene while we waited for my therapist to get there, a lot of suspicious glances between us.

Once we got in the session, my therapist introduced the topic. She said we were here to talk about my feelings, about having been abused. She said we had to walk a fine line between honesty and kindness and if we were to err, we would err on the side of honesty. She said the session would dwell on the bad things that had happened, but that didn't mean there hadn't been good in our family life.

Then she turned it over to me. My goal was to show my parents how hurt I was, to cry in front of them, and to tell them what had happened. It was hard for me to let myself be vulnerable to people who I felt had a lot of hatred for me.

My worst fear was that my parents were going to come off being the sweetest, nicest, most rational people, who never could have abused anyone, and that my therapist would know what a liar I was. Within five minutes they played out their whole relationship right in front of her—yelling, screaming, running all their usual numbers. It was a relief to have someone else see what had gone on my whole life.

The thing that changed for me the most since that family session was my level of hope that they would ever change. It dropped dramatically to about minus ten. Part of the session, I think, was to destroy the hope that maybe they really weren't the people who had done this to me.

Listening to them, and watching them during the session, I saw how abusive they were. And that perception has certainly changed how I went about dealing with them. It helped me to focus on my own work, not to drag them into it, because they certainly weren't out to help me.

WHY I'M GLAD I DID IT

I'm really glad I told my parents. It was one of the most unpleasant things I've ever done in my life. But the freedom of telling the truth to the people who abused you is really amazing. It feels rotten before you do it, it feels rotten while you're doing it, and it feels rotten after you've done it, but at least it's not hanging over your head anymore.

I would like to tell people who are considering doing a confrontation about the attitude I took in my family session which really helped me, and which was absolutely terrifying for me. I would recommend it for anyone who is afraid they might waffle and not say everything that they have to say. Just think that they're going to die the minute you end the session. I pictured them dead, and me still alive, living a miserable life, wringing my hands, saying, "Why?" Oh, why didn't I tell

WRITING A CONFRONTATION

Sandra Butler, the author of *Conspiracy of Silence*, does trainings for therapists and leads workshops for survivors, using writing as a tool. In her Writing As Healing workshops, Sandra uses a powerful series of exercises to help survivors get in touch with their feelings. These can also be an excellent vehicle for preparing for a confrontation.

She asks participants to choose a significant person from their childhood about whom they have unresolved feelings. "Now," Sandra continues, "write everything that has been unsaid in the relationship. The person can't interrupt or threaten you, but must simply sit and listen. Just say everything—the rage, the disappointment, the betrayal, the sadness, the loss. Start with the sentence 'There are some very important things you need to hear.'"

After ten to fifteen minutes of writing time, Sandra interrupts and says, "Now write as you imagine the other person would respond. Get under their skin and speak as you think they would. Let them respond just as powerfully to what you've said."

After another ten minutes, Sandra interrupts again and says, "Now, return to your own perspective and set some ground rules for any further communication. Begin with the sentence 'While I never imagined that this conversation would resolve a lifetime of history between us, I need to set some basic ground rules. There are a few things we need to get straight.'"

Ten minutes later, she stops the writing again. "From this point on," Sandra instructs, "keep going back and forth in the two voices until you feel the interaction is finished, staying as dramatic and powerful as you can."

them?" It really helped me to be bold and to say the worst, and to say it in a way that didn't protect them.

WRITING EXERCISE: DISCLOSURES AND CONFRONTATIONS

(See the basic method for writing exercises, page 32.)

Write a letter to your abuser. Do not be reasonable. This is not a letter to send, although you can send it when you're done, or you can modify it and send a variation. Write it as if you weren't sending it so you can say exactly what you want to say without having to think about possible repercussions. Be as angry and hurt and blunt as you want. Let it be a cleansing.

You can write this letter more than once. You may have had more than one abuser. Your feelings about your abuser may change over time. You may want to write to a nonprotective parent or other person as well.

FORGIVENESS?

I'll never forgive my father. It would be a lot different if he had come to me at any point in time and said, "I'm sorry for what I've done. I've hurt you terribly. I'm going to get myself in therapy. I'm going to work this out." But he's never done anything like that.

He'd have to work awfully hard to get me to forgive him. He'd have to work as hard as I've worked from the time I was seventeen until now and he doesn't have enough time left in his life. He's going to die soon. So the chances of me forgiving my father are real slim.

When talking about the stages in the healing process, the question is inevitably raised: What about forgiveness? The only necessity as far as healing is concerned is forgiving *yourself*. Developing compassion and forgiveness for your abuser, or for the members of your family who did not protect you, is *not* a required part of the healing process. It is not something to hope for or shoot for. It is not the final goal.

Although there is a need for you to come eventually to some resolution—to make peace with your past and move on—whether or not this resolution encompasses forgiveness is a personal matter. You may never reach an attitude of forgiveness, and that's perfectly all right.

Forgiveness? I have my doubts. Acceptance, maybe, but not forgiveness.

Acceptance of who he was and what happened to me. Because there's no way of changing that. But I can't forgive him. He robbed me of twenty years of my life.

Many women try desperately to forgive. Survivors have often said how stuck they feel. They despair for their complete healing, because they can't foresee forgiving the person who abused them. But, as Ellen says in her workshops, "Why should you? First they steal everything else from you and then they want forgiveness too? Let them get their own. You've given enough."

WHAT IS FORGIVENESS AND WHO BENEFITS FROM IT?

To find out exactly what forgiveness is, we looked in the dictionary and found these definitions: (a) to cease to feel resentment against an offender; (b) to give up claim to requital from an offender; to grant relief from payment.

There are, then, two elements in what we call forgiveness. One is that you give up your anger and no longer hold the abuser to blame; you excuse them for what they did to you. The other element is that you no longer try to get some kind of compensation from the abuser. You give up trying to get financial compensation, a statement of guilt, an apology, respect, love, understanding—anything. Separating these two aspects of forgiveness makes it possible to clarify what is and what is not necessary in order to heal from sexual abuse.

It is true that eventually you must give up trying to get something back from the abuser. This process need not be hurried. It is appropriate and courageous to fight back in any way you choose. However, at some point, trying to get from abusers what they aren't going to give keeps you trapped. There comes a time when what you feel about the abuser is less important than what you feel about yourself, your current life, and your future. The abuser is not your primary concern. You say, "*I* am my primary concern. Whether the abuser rots or not, I'm going on with my own life." You recognize that many of your current problems stem from past abuse, but you also recognize that you have the power to make satisfying changes.

This stance is not incompatible with anger. And none of this pardons or excuses the abuser.

When a friend inadvertently hurts our feelings and apologizes, we forgive her. We no longer blame her. The relationship is mended. We are reconciled and we continue with trust and respect, without residual anger between us. This kind of forgiveness—giving up anger and pardoning the abuser, restoring a relationship of trust—is not necessary in order to heal from the trauma of being sexually abused as a child. You are not more moral or courageous if you forgive.

"OH, HONEY, JUST FORGIVE AND FORGET"

It is insulting to suggest to any survivor that she should forgive the person who abused her. This advice minimizes and denies the validity of her feelings. Yet the issue of forgiveness is one that will be pressed on you again and again by people who are uncomfortable with your rage or want to have you back under their control. While you don't have to stay angry forever, you should not let anyone talk you into trading in your anger for the "higher good" of forgiveness.

If you have strong religious ties, particularly Christian ones, you may feel it is your sacred duty to forgive.* This just isn't true. If there is such a thing as divine forgiveness, it's God's job, not yours. If feelings of compassion and forgiveness rise naturally and spontaneously during the course of healing yourself, fine. They can be a powerful part of your healing, but not if they're forced into being because you think you should feel them.

Trying to forgive is a futile short-circuit of the healing process. Trying to speed things along so you can "get to the forgiveness" is one of the fastest ways to undercut yourself. No one forgives by trying. If forgiveness of others is to be part of your healing (and it does not have to be), it will take place only when you've gone through all the stages of remembering, grief, anger, and moving on. It is not the grand prize. It is only a by-product. And it's not even a very important one.

Healing depends a lot on being able to forgive yourself, not on being able to forgive your molester. I don't think any time spent trying to forgive your molester is worthwhile time spent. You don't try to forgive Hitler. You don't sit around and work on that. There are a lot of other things to be doing with a life.

Forgiveness of yourself is what's important and when you start to feel that forgiveness, it just naturally extends itself to other people in the world. You start to get an understanding of what humanity is all about. You become able to see when somebody does something right. You can respond to a humane, loving act. And that's what forgiveness is really about.

AND WHAT IF COMPASSION SNEAKS UP ON ME?

If it does, let it. Experiencing compassion for another human being feels good. Often it rises out of the fact that you are feeling compassionate toward yourself, or because you have begun to view a particular family member in a different way.

Sometimes I feel forgiveness toward my brother because he was just as mixed up as I was. He really cared for me a lot.

One woman came to forgive her nonprotective mother as she gained more perspective on her mother's position in the family.

My mother was no more empowered than any of us. She was very much

---

* For an excellent analysis of the role Christian forgiveness plays in healing from child sexual abuse, read *Sexual Violence: The Unmentionable Sin* by Marie Fortune. The author combines a theological perspective with a feminist analysis of sexual violence. (See the "Religious Concerns" section on p. 561 of the Resource Guide.)

the victim. There's a picture that stays in my mind of my mother standing in the hallway with all of us kids when my father was in the bathroom, beating one of my brothers, and we're all crying and saying "Daddy, Daddy! Daddy!" And my mother's saying "Don, don't! Oh, Don, don't!" And she's right there crying with us. And to me she was as much a part of the helplessness as we were. I really believe she did the best she could do. It wasn't very good but it was the best she could do.

Laura had a similar experience as a result of doing a creative exercise: *

I was at a two-week writing workshop. One of the assignments was to take an incident in my family history that I could never really find out about, and to make up the story of what really happened, based on the few facts I did have. I wrote the story of my mother's childhood.

I had very little to start with—I knew she'd been the smart one in an immigrant family, the one sent to the door when people came over and had to be answered in English. I knew she'd been ashamed of her home, that she'd escaped into the world of the movies, a nickel a shot, at the Roxy. I knew my grandfather had been her father, that she'd had to live with him every day. And I'd seen a photograph of her. I

knew how she looked, a scared, shy little waif. I created the rest.

It was an amazing exercise. It allowed me to start thinking about my mother as more than just my mother, as a woman with a whole life before I was ever conceived, and a whole life afterwards. I started to understand, from her point of view, why she'd responded to me the way she had. The pieces started to fit together. I felt compasion for her and I liked it.

This attitude of compassion is something that happens naturally, often when you least expect it. One woman who was abused by all four members of her family swore she would never forgive them. She'd written them off and gone on with her own life. Months later, she had an impulse to go to temple for Yom Kippur, the Jewish Day of Atonement. Yom Kippur is the one day of the year when Jews let go of the wrongs they have done and the wrongs others have done to them. Without trying to, or expecting to, this woman suddenly started sobbing and much to her surprise found herself not only deeply forgiving herself but forgiving her family as well. "From that day on my life was mine. For the first time in my life I had an experience of being separated from them." This woman's experience of forgiveness transformed her, but it wasn't something she set out to do.

Women who have naturally come to feel compassion or forgiveness often have a new sense of freedom:

After the grieving and the anger and the loss, somehow came forgiveness. It's not okay what she did, I can't excuse her, but I forgive her from my

* This exercise can be an effective healing tool in other ways as well. See "Writing Exercise: Reconstructing Family History," on page 165.

heart. I've let go of the anger and by doing that I'm not carrying it on my back as much. I can walk straighter. Forgiving her is a way of healing myself.

****

One of the things I find is that a lot of the intensity in my feelings is gone since I've forgiven him. I don't wake up feeling like if I had his picture I'd throw daggers at it. In fact, I have been able to see him in dreams again after not being able to visualize his face for years. I was able to say "Your face no longer scares me. Your name no longer puts me in fear."

If you do come to feel forgiveness, the important thing is that forgiveness *has* to be for you. You cannot absolve someone else for what they have done in their life. If abusers are to heal, it will only be because they've acknowledged what they've done, made reparations, worked through their own pain, and forgiven *themselves*.

Not all survivors will feel compassion for abusers and family members. Depending on what someone has done, it may not even be appropriate.

I don't forgive him. He was an adult. He is ultimately responsible. I can't forgive anyone who does anything like that to a child, particularly anybody that did it to me. If someone tried to do that to my kids, I would flat out kill them. He deserves to die a lonely, miserable man. Let it die with him. I'd be glad to see it kill him. It's not going to kill me.

BUT THEY HAD A BAD CHILDHOOD

Laura remembers her mother coming home from her job as a social worker and telling stories about all the crazy, misguided people she worked with:

She'd take us to Burger Chef, and over the french fries she'd tell us a particularly juicy story about a sixteen-year-old murderer or a fifteen-year-year-old rapist. We'd always look up from our Cokes and ask the same question: "But why, Mom? Why would somebody do something like that?" My mother's answer never varied. She'd pick up her double hamburger and say, "They had a bad childhood."

While it's true that many abusers were abused as children and that sexual abuse ravages generation after generation, those facts alone are not enough to forgive the horrible things adults have done to children. Many women have been abused, and the vast majority of them have not become abusers. Regardless of childhood pain, there is no excuse for abusing children.

Bastard. He took my soul, and I don't give a shit that it might have happened to him. It happened to me, and I didn't do it to my kids! That excuse is bullshit. It's pure shit.

****

I would never in a million years forgive my father. He had a choice. He made a choice. I've had choices in my life that were just as difficult. Sometimes I've failed. But for the most part I try very hard not to. And I don't think he tried one bit. I think he gave in every single time to his impulses.

FORGIVING YOURSELF

The only forgiveness that is essential is for yourself. You must forgive yourself for having needed, for having been small. You must forgive yourself for coping the best you could. As one woman said, "I've had to forgive my genitals for responding. I've had to forgive myself for not being able to second-guess my father and avoid the abuse."

You must forgive yourself for the limitations you've lived with as an adult. You must forgive yourself for repeating your victimization, for not knowing how to protect your own children, or for abusing others. You must forgive yourself for needing time to heal now, and you must give yourself, as generously as you can, all your compassion and understanding, so you can direct your attention and energy toward your own healing. *This* forgiveness is what's essential.

WRITING EXERCISE: RECONSTRUCTING FAMILY HISTORY

Irena Klepfisz, author of Keeper of Accounts *and a gifted teacher, developed an exercise that enables you to piece together things you can't possibly know about your history or the history of your family. This form of "remembering," which she calls "imaginative reconstruction," can be a valuable tool in coming to terms with people and patterns in your family. Although you write about things you couldn't realistically know, the result often seems chillingly realistic:*

Take an event in your family history that you can never actually find out about. It could be your father's childhood or the circumstances in your mother's life that kept her from protecting you. Using all the details you do know, create your own story. Ground the experience or event in as much knowledge as you have and then let yourself imagine what actually might have happened.

SPIRITUALITY

There was some voice in me that just said, "You'll get there." And I took hope and courage from the voice inside of me. Somehow, I felt sure there was a process, that there was a reason for all of this, and that I was going to get to the end of it. And I believe that was my spirituality.

Finding the spiritual part of yourself can be an important aspect of your healing process. This has long been recognized in the twelve-step programs (Alcoholics Anonymous, Al-Anon, and others, which have helped millions of people overcome their addictions). Yet the very word "spirituality" turns a lot of people off. You may imagine people with shaved heads, forced processions to church, the hypocrisy of piety in an abuser who molested you. You may think of stiffness and formality. You may have been abused by a minister or priest.* Like many survivors, you may have lost your faith.

I was in a very conservative religious group for twenty years. For a long time I thought Jesus could heal me. When I was thirty-eight, I went to hypnotherapy as a last resort to cure the intense migraines I was having. That's when I started remembering the sexual

---

* There are now many excellent resources available for survivors struggling with religious concerns and for those who've been abused by clergy members. See "Religious Concerns" and "Abuse by Clergy" on p. 560 of the Resource Guide.

abuse. And the first thing I thought was, "What kind of God have I been believing in?"

A little girl had been beaten and raped and no God did anything about it. I got real angry. So I went to my minister and he gave me this cock-and-bull story about how God wasn't responsible. It was all man's badness. He told me I shouldn't be angry at God.

The more I remembered, the more I realized that God didn't care for me at all. If He didn't care for me, He wasn't who I thought He was. And who was He?

It's been an incredible loss. The spiritual side of me, which had been nurtured all my life, doesn't have a place to go. It's been very painful. I lost my sense of roots, my sense of purpose. All my friends in the church rejected me. I haven't been able to find a God I can believe in.

A healing spirituality is the opposite of this alienation. It's a passion for life, a feeling of connection, of being a part of the life around you. Many people experience this in nature, watching the ocean roll in, looking out over a vast prairie, walking in the desert. When you are truly intimate with another human being, when you are uplifted through singing, when you look at a child and feel wonder, you are in touch with something bigger than yourself. There is a life force that makes things grow, that makes thunderstorms and mountain ranges and perfect avocados. The fact that you can create a baby and give it birth, watch it roll over, then sit up, and then crawl, is a miracle of life. There's a part of everything living that wants to become itself—the tadpole into the frog, the chrysalis into the butterfly, a damaged human being into a whole one. And that's spirituality: staying in touch with the part of you that is choosing to heal, that wants to be healthy, integrated, fully alive. The little part of you that is already whole can lead the rest of you through the healing process. It's the inner voice that you learn to trust again.

A BREAK IN THE CLOUDS

Laura once spent a couple of years in Ketchikan, Alaska, the rain capital of North America, where annual precipitation averages thirteen feet a year. "It was always raining. We were on an island and it was gray and stormy and overcast all the time. I'd forget what the sun even felt like. But every time I flew out of there, I'd have the most incredible experience. The plane would take off. As usual, it would be raining. But seconds later, we'd break through the cloud cover into the most brilliant sunlight. It had always been there. It's just that I couldn't see it from the ground."

It's the same with healing. That person you want to become is already with you; you just can't always see her. If you stay focused on how far you have to go, rather than turning around to see how far you've already come, you stay caught in the storm and forget that the sun is just overhead. You lose your sense of perspective. Getting in touch with the stillness inside is a way to gain it back, a way to remember that you are more than just the abused child crying out in pain. It's not that you transcend your abuse or get rid of the "bad" parts of yourself—rather you enlarge yourself to include everything.

You start to see a self separate from the struggle.

KEEPING THE FAITH

One way to lose perspective is by focusing exclusively on your problems, your process, and your pain. While a certain amount of obsessing is inevitable, and in fact sometimes helpful, beyond a certain point it can be self-defeating. Obsession often comes from a lack of conviction that you've already set the healing process in motion through your own hard work and determination. You think you have to be vigilant at every moment. But that doesn't work.

If you have an injury and you press on the wound, insisting that it heal *now,* it will not heal. But if you take care of it and then direct your attention somewhere else, healing naturally takes place.

Breakthroughs often happen that way. You work and you work, and then suddenly, when you stop trying, you grow. But letting go takes faith. You have to trust your capacity to heal yourself. And each time you do, you move forward just a little farther. You gain confidence that you're going to be all right.

If you have an established religious path, faith will probably play a strong part in your healing. Mary, a survivor who spent several years as a nun, told the following story: "I had this picture of Jesus. And I used it like you'd use a candle, to center me to pray. And I looked at this picture, and I said, 'It's too much! No more. You have to make this stop. My heart cannot bear any more pain. They say you don't push a person beyond, but I'm telling you, this is it. This is as much as I can

bear.' And somehow that particular moment of anguish passed, and I felt less burdened."

But no matter how much faith you have, it's not going to work for you unless you roll up your sleeves and do your share. Having a relationship with God doesn't mean He—or She—does all the work. Mary explains: "I really believe I received the grace of God to do this work and to stick with it. I've always believed I've been blessed with a strong mind to survive what I survived. I chose to go back to therapy week after week. I chose the grace. I could have not gone back and just said, I'd rather suffer this quiet way I've always suffered. But then I had the grace to choose. I'll give God 65 percent and my guts 35 percent."

Whether you have a fixed concept of a God, believe there is a life spirit coursing through us all, or simply trust your own intuition, having faith in something more powerful and constant than your shifting emotions and ideas can be a great comfort to you as you heal.

FINDING OUT WHAT YOU ALREADY KNOW

When you're about to make a decision and a friend says, "Sleep on it," what they're really saying is, let the implications settle down past your conscious mind. And it often works. We go to sleep unresolved about what to do, and we wake up with a clear idea about the course of action to take.

Getting in touch with the spiritual part of yourself is a way to find that clarity, a way to back off from trying, a way to take a mini-vacation. It's a way to find a place of stillness, of calm inside, a neutral corner in which you can stay centered and watch the rest of the action. This enables you to see what's essential, to let other things fall away.

There's comfort in that space. It's the quiet place that can come right before sleep, the peaceful stillness you sometimes feel when you wake, before all the thoughts of the day crowd in. It can be soothing, a place to lay down your burdens for a moment. A place you can go for reassurance before diving into the fight once more. Like an oasis. A place of nourishment, of regeneration—what a baby feels at its mother's breast, what it feels like to be held and comforted when you're scared.

TAPPING THE LOVE

All survivors healing from sexual abuse have a tremendous need for love and support. Many women feel that they're always working at a deficit, trying to make up for the love and security they missed out on as children. A spiritual connection can be a way to connect with a deep source of love.

I think, like most incest survivors, I have kind of a bottomless pit of need inside me. I no longer believe human beings alone can fill it. Nobody can give that sort of thing. If there's a source of love in the universe that can fill that, it's not another person.

"I don't have to say the hole will never be filled," one survivor explained. "Love doesn't only come from the two people who raised me. I can parent me. Other people can love me. God can love me."

With this love comes a feeling of belonging, a sense of safety, a deeper experience of faith in your capacity to heal. And this love is not people-oriented. It's based on a relationship within yourself that no one can take away.

SPIRITUALITY IS NOT ESCAPE

The whole point of getting in touch with your spirituality is to enhance your healing, not to escape it. Spirituality is not a shortcut through any of the stages of the healing process. It's not an alternative to feeling your anger, to working through the pain, to fully acknowledging the damage done. Rather it should be an enrichment to healing, a source from which you can draw comfort and inspiration.

Certain religions and spiritual practices encourage you to avoid emotions, particularly anger. They stress forgiveness and are not likely to support you in confronting your abuser. These attitudes do not promote healing. If you are involved in a practice that denies your needs as a survivor in an active healing process, you are not helping yourself.

A PERSONAL THING

A spiritual connection is a very personal thing. You may feel it's all hogwash and want nothing to do with it. You might have a vague sense of longing for something you can't

Remember the Moon Survives
For Pamela

by Barbara Kingsolver

Remember the moon survives,
draws herself out crescent-thin,
a curved woman. Untouchable,
she bends around the shadow
that pushes itself against her, and she

waits. Remember how you waited
when the nights bled their darkness out
like ink, to blacken the days beyond,
to blind the morning's one eye.
This is how you learned to draw
your life out like the moon,
curled like a fetus around the

shadow. Curled in your bed,
the little hopeful flowers of your knees
pressed against the wall
and its mockery of paint,
always the little-girl colors
on the stones of the ordinary prison:
the house where you are someone's
daughter, sister, someone's flesh, someone's

blood. The Lamb and Mary
have left you to float in this darkness
like a soup bone. You watch
the cannibal feast from a hidden place
and pray to be rid of your offering.
The sun is all you wait for,
the light, guardian saint of all the children
who lie like death on the wake
of the household crime. You stop
your heart like a clock: these hours
are not your own. You hide
your life away, the lucky coin
tucked quickly in the shoe
from the burglar, when he

comes. Because he will, as sure
as shoes. This is the one

with all the keys to where you live,
the one you can't escape, and while
your heart is stopped, he takes things.
It will take years

to learn: why you hold back sleep
from the mouth that opens in the dark,
why you will not feed it with
the dreams you sealed up tight
in a cave of tears; why
the black widow still visits you,
squeezes her venom out in droplets,
stringing them like garnets
down your abdomen,
the terrifying jewelry of a woman
you wore inside, a child robbed

in the dark. Finally you know this.
You have sliced your numbness open
with the blades of your own eyes.
From your years of watching
you have grown the pupils of a cat, to see
in the dark. And these eyes are
your blessing. They will always know
the poison from the jewels that are both
embedded in your flesh.
They will always know the darkness
that is one of your names by now,
but not the one you answer to.
You are the one who knows, behind
the rising, falling tide
of shadow, the moon is always

whole. You take in silver
through your eyes, and hammer it
as taut as poems in steel
into the fine bright crescent of your life:
the sickle,
the fetus,
the surviving moon.

quite identify. Or you may have a precise discipline to practice. You may feel at peace in nature or you may feel inspired by your weekly support group. The important thing is that no one can tell you how to do it right. Your experience of spirituality will be unique.

I like to think this is my last day on earth. If this was my last breath, what would be important to me? I think of the song "Gracias a la Vida," which is about the simple things in life. That song says, "Thank you for the alphabet. Thank you for words. Thanks for being able to hear music. Thanks for being able to see." Taking time each day to notice the simple things I have to be grateful for has been one of the most healing things for me. Let today be enough. For peace of mind, I have to stop all my doing and be content with the simple things.

RESOLUTION AND MOVING ON

I feel like I'm home free. I still have a lot of work to do, but I know it can be done. I know what the tools are and I know how to use them. When I talk about the incest now, a lot of it is about the healing and the success and the joy.

—Saphyre

Jean Williams, an incest survivor and the adult child of an alcoholic, has worked on healing from child sexual abuse for many years. Recently she had an experience that dramatically shifted her focus:

I went to live in Mexico for a few months, and I really learned a lot by living in another culture. When I came back here my mail was full of circulars and fliers about human growth workshops and self-improvement programs. And I thought, "My God! I don't want to improve myself anymore. I don't want to go to therapy anymore. I'm good enough the way I am! For eleven years, I've been improving myself. It's time to realize *I'm already there*." I want to do things because I enjoy them, not because I'm going to fix myself in some way. I *am* healed. I'm whole. I'm ready to go.

Moving on is a tricky business for survivors. It cannot be rushed. It cannot be pressured from the outside. And there will be pressure. From the moment you first speak up, people will tell you to forget it, to "let the past be the past." But moving on to please someone else will not help you.

Most survivors reach points in their healing where they want to "move on" simply because recovery is such a painful process. When you're motivated by the fact that you don't want to face your rage, your parents, your abusers, or your vulnerability, moving on is an escape, not a liberation.

Authentic moving on is a natural result of going through each step of the healing process. It comes slowly and sometimes takes you by surprise.

> Knowing I'm not against the wall means I can get up in the morning, look in the mirror, and not have to say, "Oh God, incest again!" It's being able to brush my teeth and get through half my breakfast before I remember. Or I went to a movie and laughed through the whole thing, and didn't think about abuse one time.

STABILIZING

Resolution comes when your feelings and perspectives begin to stabilize. The emotional roller coaster evens out. You no longer doubt what happened to you. You see that your life is more than just a reaction to abuse.

> You can look at my life and say there've been some real tragedies, and there have been, but there've also been some exquisitely beautiful times. To me those far outweigh the others.

One survivor, whose childhood had good times mixed in with the abuse, sat down

Morning Meditation
by Lee Whitman

This morning my clothes are strangers
I take a sweater, green and white squares
from the shelf
pull on jeans   oddly loose
startle to see my hand veined and rough
not chubby   not
gripping the blanket tightly

Rain sighs down
foreign rhythms from the radio
cinnamon tea
hand on my belly   grateful for
dry shelter   warm clothes
sea glass palely glinting on the sill

most of all glad
that you can no longer draw breath
out of my lungs to fill your own

with a calculator and figured out the number of minutes she actually remembered being abused as a child. She multiplied this number by five, figuring there was probably a lot she'd forgotten. Then she took that total and compared it to the total number of minutes in her childhood. The nonabused hours far outweighed the abusive ones. "It helped me realize that there were other, more positive forces that had shaped me as a child. I had other things I could draw on."

Moving on means affirming the strengths you've developed. You recognize your own resiliency and drive to be healthy. You stand up for what you know to be true. You face your demons and come out alive. And finally, you make the changes you can, letting go of the things that aren't in your power to change.

RESOLVING RELATIONSHIPS WITH ABUSERS AND FAMILY

Resolving relationships with the people who abused you, didn't protect you, or don't support you now is essential to moving on. You come to your own sense of clarity in what you think and feel about each of these people.

As long as you continued to hope they would change, apologize, or understand you, you lived in a fantasy. Now you stop basing your life on that hope. When you stop longing for rescue from unlikely sources, you open the way to realistic richness in your life.

When you come to a place of resolution with your family or your abuser, the effect is often enormous. It's as though all the energy you'd been funneling into that old longing is suddenly released and you are catapulted into the present. Your identification with the abuse and its effects is greatly diminished and you are freed to enjoy a new and much more satisfying relationship with yourself and with the world.

It's taken me a long time to integrate the fact that people who were supposed to love me and care about me could have molested me and made my life miserable, and then deny that to my face. To try to squeeze that reality into the happy American home scene that's in my head has been very hard.

But it's worth it because it's a quantum shift in my perception of the universe. It's put me back on the track of creating my own life. As long as I held on to those fantasies and ideas that never were and never will be, it really limited me. As long as where I came from was clouded, it was very hard for me to take steps in another direction. If I hadn't come to terms with the reality of my family, the only option I would have had was to repeat it all over again.

LETTING GO OF THE DAMAGE

There may be times in the healing process when sexual abuse is all you see, times when you lose touch with the fact that *you are investing all this time and energy in healing so you can move on to something else in life.* There may even be a part of you that doesn't want to get through it.

Survivors often complain about how long it takes to heal, but there is an identity in being a committed survivor of sexual abuse. That identity has been closely linked to your survival, and it can be hard to give up.

A lot of people get stuck in that rage and that hatred and that fear. But I realized I didn't have to hang on to it. I started to think of it like a big wad of mucus that I had to cough up. I decided, "Okay, I've had enough of walking around like I'd like to brutalize everyone who looks at me wrong. I don't have to feel like that anymore." Then I thought, "How would I like to feel?"

I wanted to feel safe in the world. I wanted to feel powerful. And so I focused on what was working in my life, in the ways I was taking power in real-life situations.

I stopped sitting there picking open wounds, saying, "If I only pick deep enough, I can see some real blood and gore here." I started to function like I didn't have to carry around that baggage anymore. There was a point where I simply stopped carrying the bags.

Every now and then the porter brings it up to me and says, "Here's your baggage, ma'am." And I open it up and go through it again. And then I say, "I've seen enough of you for now. I want to go on with my life again." And life feels much better. It's a tremendous relief to stop suffering all the time.

And it's not a question of denial. It was an organic change. It wasn't like there was a road sign that said, "Leaving Guilt. Entering New Zone of Healing." It was almost like looking in a mirror after you get out of the shower, and it's all fogged over, and as the moisture begins to dry up, you see more of yourself. Things just got clearer.

I began to relate more to the person who I was becoming, rather than the person I had been. When I leave that baggage over to one side and step into that new self, I recognize her. She's not a facade. She's real. She's the person I was before I ever got abused.

REASSURING THE CHILD

One thing that can make moving on difficult is the feeling that you are somehow betraying the child who was injured. If you have had to struggle to get in touch with your childhood pain, you may be surprised by a reluctance to let it go. Evie Malcolm explains:

Emotionally, for me, and I'm not defending this, letting go of the damage would mean abandoning that eleven-year-old girl who's still alive in me, who nobody was there for, who wasn't listened to. If I get better, if the bruise heals, then there's going to be no sign of it, and it'll be as if she never got heard. And that would be an incredible disloyalty, a betrayal of that little girl.

So I'm trying to get myself healed and over the symptoms of the damage without denying that it happened. This is the intellectual "me" talking. This is not the eleven-year-old girl. She doesn't want to let go. It's an emotional feeling. And emotions are very powerful. You can have all the right intellectual thoughts, and emotionally you can be very childlike. And the fearful child in me doesn't want to be forgotten. So I have to reassure her that my getting better doesn't mean I'm abandoning her or denying her pain.

(For more of Evie's story, see page 392.)
There is no need to leave the child behind. Rather, by healing, you are creating a safe, healthy place where she can thrive.

INTEGRATION

A big part of moving on is integration. You see yourself as whole, not compartmentalized—your body, your sexuality, your feelings, and your intellect as interconnected parts of a whole. You start to accept the gray, the fuzzy in-between places that make us all human.

The last thing someone from our kind of family can do is learn to accept paradox. It's not black and white. It's not all neat. It's not all going to work out perfect. Learning to hold paradox is a real sign of healing to me. It's been very hard for me to accept that I'll still feel bad. I thought when you were healed everything felt good, but it's not true. You still feel shitty, though not all the time. I wanted to select certain things—humor, warmth, love, fun—I didn't want to feel scared, angry, or any

Reconciliation
by Cheryl Marie Wade

Thirty-seven years of denying my father's sexual abuse has taken a toll: massive deterioration of all my joint tissue. I use an electric wheelchair for mobility and my almost boneless fingers are as fragile as a cat-mauled wing. The medical establishment calls this rheumatoid arthritis. I call it my body's eloquent expression of my incest story.

I wheel my chair through Mojave sands
until I sink
There I sit
sun baking my spongy bones
so brittle
that when I stand
instead of feeling shin
push into ankle
ankle press
into heel
heel slam into a shoe of nails
my pelvic bones
snap
and I fall
slow motion
onto the warm
warm grains
I am bleached
white
nothing but a heap
of white sprigs
He comes
with his little girl
Holding her hand
he guides
her eyes to the lizard
a flicker of iridescent pink
but her interest is the white twig
at her feet
She bends and with a small
perfect hand
lifts what once had been
my aching finger
Look Daddy
a treasure
He leans down to admire her find
She puts it in the pocket of his plaid shirt
and the two of them walk on
My skull
opens wide
swallows the desert
and sings hosanna to the dry dry air.

"negative feelings." But they're all part of being human.

Integration means gaining perspective on growth over a lifetime. Susan King found a wonderful image for her healing journey:

I think of a Russian nesting doll my sister had. It fascinated me. A brightly painted wooden doll. I could twist her apart at the waist, and there was another smaller doll inside her. And another inside that, and another, down to a tiny diapered baby. And each Susan inside me has other little Susans inside her, and I am, at this moment, inside a wiser gray-haired Susan that is yet to be. Like the Russian doll, I am round—and complete.

LETTING GO OF CRISIS

It's easy to get used to the tangible anguish and turmoil of healing. Being in constant crisis means that you don't have to look at the changes you need to make in your life. Those survivors who are accustomed to crisis know just how hard giving it up can be.

I'm an intensity junkie. I feel a letdown whenever I come to the end of a particular cycle of intensity. What am I going to cry and throw scenes about now? What am I going to obsess about now? What is going to lend my life that particular tinge of stormy skies and wuthering heights?

I see it as almost a chemical addiction. I became addicted to my own sense of drama and adrenaline. Letting go of the need for intensity has been a process of slowly weaning myself. I've gotten to a point where I've actually experienced bits of just plain contentment, and I notice it, and I enjoy it.

Letting go of stress and turmoil as compelling forces in your life is a major milestone in your healing. You may be excited, proud of yourself. Yet after the initial victory, you may also feel hollowed out inside. You have cleared space so that new things can grow, but at the same time you may enter an unsettling limbo, just you with no trappings, ground zero.

It may take some time before you begin to get the first inklings of who you are becoming. Those empty in-between times can be scary, but you will regain your bearings. You will come through, in fact, more solid than you've ever felt before.

LIFE IN THE PRESENT

When you let go of the need for crisis, you make room for the rich and varied texture of ordinary living. You discover new, less stressful sources of excitement—challenging work projects, creative ventures, or greater risks in intimacy.

Part of moving on is learning to balance the excitement in your life with quiet, peaceful times. With practice, you can find contentment in small things—listening to music, cooking dinner, taking walks. From a calm place, you can assess what you want and take steps to get there.

If you don't yet know what you want in your life, this is a time to explore possibilities. Make a list of things you've dreamed of doing or becoming. This kind of self-discovery is something no one can take away from you. It is more rewarding than any crisis. And as you leave the effects of the past behind, the future becomes open possibility.

I lived a hard life on the streets. I was in and out of mental institutions. I don't know what's going to happen now. So much has changed, and I'm seeing myself differently. I am forty-seven years old, and there are not a lot of options at forty-seven like there are at fifteen. But I'm not closing any doors. I'm opening up a lot of doors in fact.

HOW HEALED DO I HAVE TO BE?

Healing is not about eternal struggle, the kind where you push the boulder up the hill, only to have it roll back down on top of you. There is a point when you will stop feeling like a victim, either of the abuse or of healing itself.

Recently Ellen was talking to a young woman who has been in therapy for the past two years, actively working on her healing. Because the work was so demanding, she cut back on many other activities early in the process in order to devote her full energies to healing. Gradually, as she became able to handle both the healing work and more commitments, she added school, a part-time job, and a lover to her life.

Now this woman had the opportunity to move to another city, join her lover there, and enter a school program that she very much wanted to be in. "But," she said to Ellen, "I think maybe I should wait until I'm all better. I'm not finished with therapy. How healed do I have to be to do what I want?"

Ellen laughed and told her to go. Part of healing is doing what you want to do, those things that will give you both fulfillment and pleasure. You don't have to wait.

THERE IS NO END OF THE LINE

There is no such thing as absolute healing. You never erase your history. The abuse happened. It affected you in profound ways. That will never change. But you *can* reach a place of resolution.

I don't know if I will ever be completely healed. It's like there was a wound and it healed over, but it was still infected in there. It needed to be lanced and cleaned out so that good healthy scar tissue could grow over it. I knew that once that scar tissue grew, it wouldn't be very pleasant to look at, but it wouldn't hurt anymore. It would be raised, and you would know it was there, but you could touch it and it wouldn't be painful. And I think that's how it is. I have scars, but they don't hurt. They're cleaned out now.

That doesn't mean every scar is. I'm sure there are still some I will discover as the years go by. That's one thing you can say about people like us, there's always going to be something that comes up. I don't think I will ever be completely healed, because it really cut to the core of my trust in the world. I don't believe in complete transcendence. I think people are too complex for that.

You need to accept the fact that the healing process will continue throughout your

WHY IT'S BEEN WORTH IT

"I feel like Rip Van Winkle sometimes, like I'm just waking up. Things like crying—I find myself crying now. I had given it up when I was eight. Or laughing. Giggling. Roughhousing with my kids and having it be safe. Playing. Getting angry at somebody I love. Telling the truth. Feeling something in the moment it's actually happening, instead of five minutes later, five years later, always *later*. Taking risks I never would have taken before. Just kind of waking up. It's a silly metaphor, but it's what flowers do. They just come out."

"Solitude has become important to me. I used to feel terribly lonely. I don't have to be lonely anymore."

"I'm not afraid of people like I used to be. I have a phone list that's incredible, and I really talk to these people. A lot of the barriers I've always put up between myself and other people are gone."

"These are the ways I've turned things that have damaged me into things that work. They're survival tools, and I've sharpened them up to use in real life. I'm proud of them."

"I feel life more intensely. Pain, but good things too. I can take a walk in the park and be really upset, and I can still see how beautiful everything is."

"I feel more peaceful. I feel like I'm normal now. Like I don't have to carry around this burden anymore."

"I'm thriving as opposed to surviving. There's all the difference in the world in how I look at life. I like myself so much better. And I'm happy most of the time. I'm more completely myself almost all the time. In fact, I am myself all the time."

---

life. One woman spent years resisting and hating herself every time the incest resurfaced in a new way:

Finally, I had to realize it was part of me. It's not something I can get rid of. The way I work with it will change, but I think it will always be there. And I think I have to get to the point where I love it, because then it's really loving me wholly. If I'm going to really love myself totally, then I had to love all of me, and this is part of who I am.

Many survivors make the decision to heal out of pain, shame, and terror, and at the outset the work frequently feels like a burden. But by the time you reach the stage of resolution and moving on, you come to an appreciation of the deep healing you have done. You recognize that healing has brought you more than just the alleviation of pain. You may, in fact, see your healing as the beginning of lifelong growth. As one survivor put it, "I have no intention of stopping. I fully intend to grow until I die."

A BROADER COMMITMENT

As you heal, as you feel more nourished, balanced, and whole, you will find that you have energy available to direct in creative and life-affirming pursuits. No longer struggling just to cope day-to-day, you can begin to make an impact in the world.

What really amazes me is that survivors can be out in the world completely functional using maybe 20 percent of their capacity. Can you imagine what we'll be able to do when we let the other 80 percent out? If we were able to recover, stop the abuse, and heal everyone, the world we live in would be so phenomenal.

If you think of all the ways in which you have been stunted, all the energy you have consumed simply to keep hanging on by your fingernails, all that you might have created or accomplished or simply enjoyed had you not had to stagger under the burden of abuse, you may have a formidable list.

If you multiply that times the number of other women similarly struggling—not only now, but back through the decades and centuries—the result is awesome.

Now, imagine all women healed—and all that energy no longer used for mere survival but made available for creativity, nurturing relationships, freeing political prisoners, ending the arms race. The effect on the world would be monumental.

We have never in recorded history lived in a time when women were, as a whole, empowered. We can only begin to imagine the riches.

HEALING MOVES OUT FROM THE CENTER

Your first allegiance must always be to yourself. If you race out to do good deeds without attending to your own needs, it's easy to create more problems than you solve. Women have been expected to sacrifice themselves while they help everybody else for too long.

It's a little like using oxygen masks on an airplane. If you're traveling with small children, the flight attendants tell you to secure your own mask first, and then to assist the child. Your initial reaction might be to help your child first, but if you pass out while trying to help your child, no one survives. When you ensure your own stability first, then you can help others, and everyone can be safe.

Although your responsibility toward healing begins with yourself, it does not stop there. Child sexual abuse originates from the same fear, hatred, deprivation, selfishness, and ignorance that lead people to abuse and assault in other ways. These attitudes are woven into the very fabric of our society and oppress on a large scale. We get nuclear waste, inhuman conditions for migrant farm workers, the rampages of the Ku Klux Klan.

Part of your healing is the healing of the earth. As you affirm your own worth, your own integrity, you become increasingly capable of taking positive, life-affirming action in the world.

It is you—who know something about both justice and injustice, about abuse and respect, about suffering and about healing—who have the clarity, courage, and compassion to contribute to the quality, and the very continuation, of life.

PART THREE

CHANGING

PATTERNS

THE PROCESS
OF CHANGE

For a long time I felt like damaged goods. I was obsessed with the question "What is wrong with me?" But I just kept doing the work. A part of me knew that I was not locked into anything. My cells replace themselves completely every seven years. How could I still be damaged goods? Of course I could change.

—Saphyre

When you first remember your abuse or acknowledge its effects, you may feel tremendous relief. Finally there is a reason for your problems. There is someone, and something, to blame. But eventually you realize that things are not that simple—or fair. As one survivor said: "My grandfather was dead and gone and I was still alive with the same problems I'd always had. I had to face the fact that if I wanted a different life, I was going to have to do something about it."

One woman went to ten years of incest-related therapy before she realized she was the one responsible for changing her own life:

I had to go from dealing with the incest an hour a week in therapy to dealing with it in my real life. I realized I had to stop talking at forty dollars an hour and start doing. It's a lot cheaper to fix yourself on your own time than to depend on an hour a week to get better. I could talk therapy with anyone who had the lingo, but I had to realize I wasn't taking care of myself in real life.

I decided to change my life and take responsibility for what was happening to me. I started asking myself questions like "What did I do to immobilize myself? Why did I stay in an abusive relationship?"

And then I started taking care of my own life. I *changed* my relationship. I *changed* my job. I *changed* my home. I started taking care of business! I filed a suit against my ex-lover for assault. I got money back that I had loaned out. I fought a custody battle against my ex-husband. I started getting angry. I started to cry. I've really changed. I *look* different. I *sound* different. I changed my life intentionally.

HOW TO CHANGE

The basic steps to making changes are:

- **Become aware of the behavior you want to change.**
- **Examine the reasons you developed that behavior to begin with.** When do you first remember feeling or acting that way? What was going on then? Try to understand why you needed that behavior.
- **Have compassion for what you've done in the past.** Even if you didn't make the wisest, healthiest choices, you took the options you saw at the time. And now you're making better choices. Focus on that.
- **Find new ways to meet your needs.** Although every change doesn't expose an unmet need, many do. By taking such needs seriously and finding new ways to

meet them, you make it possible to maintain the change.

- **Get support.** The environment in which you live—the people you see—affects your ability to make changes. People who are working to grow and change in their own lives will support you with encouragement and by example. People who are living out the patterns you're trying to break will continually suck you back in. Respect the power of influence.
- **Make several tries.** Although sometimes you can soar, usually making changes is a plodding process that doesn't look very heroic or exciting. Yet those everyday steps lead to real change and a more rewarding life.
- **Be persistent.** Most of the changes we make in our lives require repetition. If not smoking *one* cigarette were sufficient, it wouldn't be so hard to quit smoking.

OBSTACLES TO CHANGE

We do not change in a vacuum. Your new choices have repercussions on those around you. Your determination to change can be threatening to them because it means they will have to change too. Even though it's change for the better, people don't always willingly make the commitment to healthier living.

A forty-six-year-old survivor described the way her second husband responded when she got into therapy: "I made change after change after change. John was terrified. What happened to the woman he married? I looked like a little widow lady with three kids. All of a sudden, I wasn't. I was this woman who was just taking off."

Change requires support and community. If you do not get it from the people closest to you, seek it elsewhere, whether through new friends, a counselor, or a group of other survivors.

ACKNOWLEDGING FEAR

It helps to name your fears. Naming things gives them less of a hold. One woman, who suffered from continual depression and immobility, made a list of what she would have to face in life if she actually healed. Her list was extensive. She'd have to face the possibility of success—or failure—in her career. She'd have to risk greater intimacy with her lover. She'd have to stop blaming her family for her problems and would have to give up their image of her (that she was a loser). She'd lose her identity as a sick person, as a victim. She'd have to learn to deal with her real feelings instead of masking them with hopelessness and anxiety. She'd have to attract people on her own merits, not because they felt sorry for her. When she looked over her list, she could see why she was afraid.

FEAR DOESN'T HAVE TO STOP YOU

Often fear accompanies the unfamiliar and exciting leaps we take in life. It's the feeling that makes your knees shake the first time you sing in public, when you confront the person who abused you, or when you apply for a job you really want. When you do something new and challenging, you need that energy. It's adrenaline. Often women feel this kind of fear when they are taking absolutely the right steps for themselves.

Fear doesn't have to stop you. Even if you're afraid, you can still go ahead and make the changes you want. You just do it anyway. You do it afraid. You do it nervously, awkwardly. You shake or sweat. You are not graceful or composed, but you do it.

THE PATTERN FIGHTS BACK

A pattern is any habitual way of behaving. By its nature it is deeply entrenched, set by repetition, and brings a familiar result. Even if that result is not, ultimately, what you want, its predictability is part of its grip. Patterns usually start unconsciously as a way of coping when your options are limited. They serve you, but at a cost.

Patterns have a life of their own, and their will to live is very strong. They fight back with a vengeance when faced with annihilation. Once you recognize a pattern and make the commitment to break it, it often escalates. Laura remembers:

I decided I wanted to be more present in my life, that I no longer wanted to space out every time a strong feeling surfaced. But the pattern fought back with a frenzy. Things got much worse than they had ever been. I was spaced out all the time. Then just when I thought I couldn't stand it anymore, that I would never, ever get through it, it broke. I'd earned the scary miracle of being able to stay present.

Another woman, who'd had a whole series of abusive intimate relationships, worked toward changing this pattern. But just as the pattern was about to give way, she said, "I had a three-week affair in which I replayed every screwed-up relationship I ever had. I went through all my patterns in real rapid motion. It was like a Charlie Chaplin movie."

It's important that you don't give up at this critical point. It's likely the "I can't stand it anymore" feeling means you're close to the change you're working so hard to achieve.

A LITTLE SELF-LOVE GOES A LONG WAY

Be kind to yourself. Be patient. Babies do not go from crawling to walking in a single day. We are not impatient or angry when they totter and fall. In fact, we delight in their first forays, even when they end in a plop.

Forgiving yourself when you backslide, being gentle with yourself, may be a pattern-breaker in itself. One survivor related how her attitude toward herself has softened over time:

> When I slip into an old pattern, I see it almost as if I'm putting on a pair of shoes that don't fit anymore. I've put them on again, and here I am trying to tap-dance, and it's not working. At first I'd whip myself: "Why did you put those stupid shoes on again?" I'd get really despondent that I'd never change.
>
> As I've gotten further along in my healing, I've been able to be gentler with myself: "Oh God, I slipped again." I'll congratulate myself on recognizing it so quickly, and then I'll ask myself, "What happened this time to trigger it?" Instead of beating myself up, I tell myself I'll take care of myself the next time and I figure out ways to do that.

GIVE YOURSELF CREDIT

Often people are acutely aware of how difficult something is before they do it. You are scared, you vacillate, you collect all your strength and courage, and somehow you manage to do what you set out to do. Then, as soon as it's over, you jump in with "Okay, what's next?" Or worse, you frown at yourself and say, "I don't know why I had to make such a big deal out of that. It wasn't much."

It was much. And you need to acknowledge that.

One woman, who was in counseling with Ellen, was upset with herself for being in a relationship with a man she really didn't care for. Afraid she'd never find anyone else who wanted her, afraid to be lonely, she hung in. Now and then she'd try to work up her courage to break off with him, but each time she'd waver and stay. Finally, after many months, she ended the relationship. That week in counseling she talked about other things for most of the session and then mentioned that she had broken up with this man. In the same sentence she went on to say that she was feeling bad about herself because she was still ambivalent and wondered if she should go back.

"Wait," Ellen interrupted. "You broke up with him?"

"Yes, but I don't feel strong about it. I've—"

Ellen interrupted again. "But you broke up. Even if you decide at some time that you want to go back, you still did this thing that you really wanted to do and were very afraid to do. You did it! You don't even give it a sentence of its own."

Finally this woman slowed down enough to experience her achievement. She was willing to hear that many people feel unsettled when they act in unfamiliar ways, even if those ways are in their best interests.

CELEBRATE

When you accomplish a goal, when you make a change you have worked hard to make, celebrate. A celebration can be anything that feels right to you, from raucous to serious. Eat lobster, buy a lovely card and mail it to yourself. Light a candle. Do what's special for you.

WRITING EXERCISE: CHANGING PATTERNS

(See the basic method for writing exercises on page 32.)

1. Take some time to assess how far you've come in your healing. Are you at the beginning, or have you made some progress? What have you accomplished already? What do you have to be proud of? What obstacles have you broken through? What small (and large) successes have you achieved? Give yourself credit. In detail.

2. You've already done a lot of work—and there's still more to do. What are your goals for your healing now? What are some ways you may be able to work toward these goals? Write about the things you still need to do to move ahead in your personal life.

These can be general, such as "I need to be more compassionate with myself," or as specific as "I need to burn the picture of my abuser that still hangs in my living room."

Change
by Ellen Bass

This is where I yank the old roots
from my chest, like the tomatoes
we let grow until December, stalks
thick as saplings.

This is the moment when the ancient fears
race like thoroughbreds, asking for more
and more rein. And I, the driver,
for some reason they know nothing of
strain to hold them back.

Terror grips me like a virus
and I sweat, fevered,
trying to burn it out.

This fear is invisible. All you can see
is a woman going about her ordinary day,
drinking tea, taking herself to the movies,
reading in bed. If victorious
I will look exactly the same.

Yet I am hoisting a car from mud ruts
half a century deep. I am hacking
a clearing through the fallen slash
of my heart. Without laser precision,
with only the primitive knife of need, I cut
and splice the circuitry of my brain.
I change.

SELF-ESTEEM AND PERSONAL POWER

I remember saying in fits of depression, "You think I'm a good person, but I'm not. I'm a bad person." Deep inside, under all this cheerleader, straight-A bullshit, there is this little kernel, this bad seed, that's forced me to become perfect on the outside. Beause if I keep pretending that I'm good, it will make up for the awful person I really am.

Self-esteem is a basic issue for women. Because our culture devalues women, we often fight feelings of inadequacy or struggle with self-doubt. For survivors, these issues are heightened. You were damaged early. Something was broken at a core level. The reality that you were precious, that you deserved love, that you were capable, that you were okay just the way you were, was denied you as a child. You weren't given a chance to feel good about yourself. Instead, you were abused. You were left feeling dirty, somehow at fault. And the ways you were forced to cope may have left you feeling even worse about yourself, more ashamed.

You may experience low self-esteem as a constant feeling of worthlessness, a nagging voice that tells you you didn't do enough, you didn't do it right, you don't deserve it. Or your feelings about yourself may fluctuate. You may feel good about yourself most of the time, self-critical feelings lying dormant until you have some kind of setback—a loss, a period of change, an argument with someone you love. Then you suddenly lose touch with the good things about yourself. The self-love you've nurtured so carefully seems out of reach, unattainable.

Feelings of self-hate can erupt seemingly out of the blue. A small interaction can trigger a whole avalanche of self-doubt and uncertainty. You get one problem wrong on a college exam and you say to yourself, "I'm a stupid idiot. I'll never amount to anything." You stop dating someone because you decide that person isn't good for you, and instead of feeling proud of yourself for setting limits, you feel abandoned, sure you'll never love again. Even though you are taking care of yourself, you somehow end up feeling wrong—again.

Self-esteem is experienced in the moment, and your sense of yourself will fluctuate as you move through the healing process. When you're first recovering memories, struggling to accept the truth of what happened to you, or dealing with your abuser, you may feel worse than you felt before. Often feelings of shame, powerlessness, and self-hate are bottled up with the memories, and as the memories come through, these feelings do too.

Yet healing isn't just about pain. It's about learning to love yourself. As you move from feeling like a victim to being a proud survivor, you will have glimmers of hope, pride, satisfaction. Those are natural by-products of healing.

This whole book is about improving your self-esteem. Whether you are contacting the child within, discovering your anger, working on sex, or grieving for your past, you will be forging a more gentle, loving relationship with yourself. This chapter will give you some specific tools that can help you feel better about yourself along the way—on your own, in relation to others, and in the work you do.

INTERNALIZED MESSAGES

When you were abused, it's likely that you were told, directly or indirectly, that the abuse was your fault. You may have been told you were bad or stupid. You may have been humiliated or called a liar. Many survivors were told that they would never amount to anything. You may still be receiving this message. One survivor whose poem was published in a local newspaper sent a copy of it to her mother. Her mother replied, "It was just beginner's luck. You'll never write another one."

Another woman, elected homecoming queen in high school, had such a distorted image of herself that she was convinced her friends had chosen her only because they pitied her.

Even if you weren't given such messages directly, the very fact that you were abused taught you that you were powerless, alone, not worthy of protection or love. If you were ignored or neglected, your basic value was denied. You learned you were undeserving, unable to have an impact in the world.

When our own worth is negated often enough, we begin to believe there's something wrong with us. As a result of these childhood messages, you may believe you're only good for sex, that you're unlovable, that nothing you do matters, or even that you don't deserve to live. As Ellen says, "Survivors were programmed to self-destruct. You learned to put yourself down so effectively that the abusers don't even have to be around any more to do it. They can go off and play golf while you do yourself in."

This self-destructiveness often is at war with the positive, sustaining self-concept you are trying to build.

I have often felt like two different people. Wednesday I was going to buy a gun to kill myself. The gun store closed at 6:00. We had a sales meeting at work, which I didn't go to because I figured it was going to take me a half hour to get to the store from downtown.

All day I'd been going through this bullshit with the gun, but I'd also made this list of things that make me feel good. And then on my way to the store, I decided I didn't really want to buy the gun. So I bought a teddy bear instead. I made an appointment for a massage. And I bought myself a ticket to a show I really wanted to see.

A lot of times there's two people operating. There's this person inside who's really striving to be healthy. And then there's this other person who's been beaten so much, she just takes up where my father left off.

CHANGING INTERNALIZED MESSAGES

At the beginning of your healing, you may be experiencing negative messages constantly. But as time goes by and your basic self-image starts to shift, these messages will come less frequently. They will stand out more distinctly against a background of basically liking yourself.

While you may think such thoughts come without cause, the fact is that they are always sparked by something. Each time you feel bad about yourself, try to isolate the thought or event that set off the feeling. At first this won't be easy, but with practice you will be able to ask yourself a few quick questions to identify the source:

- When did I start feeling this way?
- Did I have a disturbing conversation with someone? Receive a disturbing phone call or letter?
- Did something scare me or make me angry?
- Is there a reason I'm feeling particularly vulnerable right now?
- When did I stop feeling good about myself?

Once you find the event or thought that started this feeling, ask yourself, "Is this feeling familiar?" Search back to find the first time you felt that way, the first time you were told that particular lie. What was the context? Who told you you were selfish? Who implied you were in the way? When did you decide it was you who was bad?

Allow yourself to feel the pain of the child you once were. Allow your compassion for her, your anger at those who hurt her, and any other feelings to rise. Recognizing and expressing these feelings helps to release the grip of negative internalized messages.

As you identify the lies you were told about yourself, you can get rid of them. One woman, who called the voices in her head "the committee," set about killing them off, one at a time:

Whenever I start to feel bad about myself, I say, "Okay. Who is that talking? Who on the committee is saying, 'You're no good. You can't do that?' Is it Daddy? Is that Mommy? Is that the scared kid? Is that the hurt kid? Is that Grandmom Jean?"

When all the committee members are sitting in my head making it so that I can't see and I can't feel, I need to identify and silence their voices. I iso-

THE MOST COMMON ONE-LINERS

I hate myself.

"I felt like I had an oil slick oozing goo inside me. I knew I was filled with something evil, and that evil rubbed off on everyone I came into contact with. So I didn't let anybody really get near me."

I don't deserve it.

"Struggle is my middle name. The basic pleasures other people enjoy—companionship, relaxation, fun—have always seemed out of reach to me. Underneath all my flirting and bravado, I don't believe anyone will ever love me. I know I'm really meant to be alone."

I can't do it.

"When I was a little kid I was expected to be the adult. I had to cook, keep up the house at some maintenance level. I was left in charge as early as nine, ten years old. And how good can a kid be at keeping together a household? I was always blowing it. They were always criticizing me. Now, I don't even try. What's the point? I can't do anything right."

It has to be perfect.

"In my family they were generous with failures, but they were very stingy with acknowledging success. So when someone says, "You did a really great job," I say, "Yeah, but look up there, there's a flaw." It's hard for me to see the good. I still see the wrinkle in the left-hand corner."

Whatever I do, it'll never be enough.

"I know I'm smart. I know I have a lot of skills. If I say I'll do a job, I have no doubt I'll get it done—and probably in half the time it would take someone else. My problem is that I don't feel I deserve anything for it. Why should I get money or recognition or stability? Everything I do, great as it is, is only making up for what happened when I was a kid. My achievements only bring me up to zero."

It's not worth trying.

"I've always had a real lack of ambition. I have a terrific business mind and I always use it for someone else's advantage instead of my own. Why? I've never looked for anything more than to just get by. I never wanted more than survival. I never wanted to be more than normal. And there's so much more to life than that."

What I want doesn't count.

"I was brought up as the receptacle. There were four people living in my house and every one of them abused me. All I learned was to accept abuse. I was never in my body long enough to know: Did I want to write? Did I want to draw? Did I want to play? I never learned to know what I wanted to do. So later, whatever came along job-wise, I took."

late the committee member and kick 'em out. I say, "Stop. Get out! This is my head! *I* get to decide. You don't have control over me! *Get out!*"

Just paying attention and discovering the roots of your negative thoughts will dramatically interrupt your tendency to feel lousy about yourself. By seeking the origins of these negative images, you are acknowledging that they did indeed come from somewhere. You are affirming that you don't feel this way because it's true, but because you were conditioned to feel that way.

After rejecting the lie, replace it with the truth about yourself. If you think you don't deserve love, say to yourself, "I am a beautiful, deserving human being. Just because I'm breathing, I deserve love. Just because I'm human. I don't have to do anything." This is the truth. If you don't believe it yet, say it anyway. In time, you will believe it. (See "Affirmations and Visualizations," on page 194).

Sometimes, especially in the beginning, a friend's perspective can really help. Laura worked out a unique system with her best friend:

Whenever one of us says something self-hating, that doesn't reflect our healthiest, most adult self, the other one lovingly interrupts the conversation with our secret code word, "Tomato!" If I start to say "Oh, it'll never work out. I couldn't possibly do that," she yells out, "Tomato! Tomato!" until I give it up and start laughing. If I'm having a really bad day, she'll explain to me, like you would to a child, *why* my tomato statement isn't true. Then she replaces it with the truth as she sees it: "Laura, you're a powerful woman, my best

friend. Of course you can do it." Having a friend like her really helps.

SETTING LIMITS AND BOUNDARIES

The capacity to set limits is essential to feeling good about yourself. Many survivors have not known how to define their own time, to protect their bodies, to put themselves first, to say no.

I've always given my time over to whoever asked for it because I didn't think it was mine to deal with. When I was little, if anybody wanted anything from me, they took it. I have poor boundaries. It makes me ridiculously easy to get along with. I'll do anything anyone asks me to do. If you do that, everybody likes you. And it's very important for me to be liked.

Although learning to say no is a difficult challenge, it is a relief to be able to stop doing what you don't want to. By setting limits, you protect yourself and give yourself freedom at the same time. As you say no to other people, you start to say yes to yourself.

But saying no isn't easy. As women, we've been taught to please others, to put their needs first.

I went to a workshop on dating. We were paired up and told to ask each other out on an imaginary date. Those of us being asked were instructed to say no. We were supposed to turn down the invitation. But when the women reported back to the group, a surprising number had said yes anyway. One even offered to cook dinner.

If you can't imagine saying no, set up some practice situations. Get a friend to role-play with you. Try a scene in which you are asked—or told—to do something you don't want to do. Then say no. Pay attention to the feelings that come up, but say no anyway. If you find yourself thinking "I just can't say no," ask yourself why not. What would happen if you said no? Do you think you or the other person couldn't handle it? If so, why? Talk about your feelings, and then say no anyway. Try reversing roles. Listen to the way your friend says no. Try out her style.

Then watch for situations in your life in which you want to say no. Start with what's easiest and build up to the harder ones. When a friend wants you to go out to lunch but you've set aside time to play the piano (and playing is what you *really* want to do), say no. When your six-year-old tells you to get her the milk, tell her she's capable of getting it herself, and that you're sure she can do a good job of it.

If you've never (or hardly ever) said no, your first attempts may feel awkward or even rude. When you feel you don't have the right to say no, or when you're new at it, you may add cumbersome explanations or refuse more strongly than necessary. Yet saying no doesn't have to be loud or hostile (although it can be if you want it to). As you feel more secure in your right to say no, you'll be able to do so with a simple statement: "No, I don't want to." "No thanks." "No, I'd rather not."

If you've been taking care of other people and saying yes all your life, you may encounter some angry resistance when you start to say no. People may say you were nicer before. They may say you're being selfish, that

Autobiography in Five Short Chapters
by Portia Nelson

I

I walk down the street.
    There is a deep hole in the sidewalk.
    I fall in
    I am lost . . . I am helpless
        It isn't my fault.
It takes forever to find a way out.

II

I walk down the same street,
    There is a deep hole in the sidewalk.
    I pretend I don't see it.
    I fall in again.
I can't believe I am in the same place.
        But it isn't my fault.
It still takes a long time to get out.

III

I walk down the same street
    There is a deep hole in the sidewalk.
    I see it is there.
    I still fall in . . . it's a habit.
        My eyes are open.
        I know where I am.
It is my fault.
I get out immediately.

IV

I walk down the same street.
    There is a deep hole in the sidewalk.
    I walk around it.

V

I walk down another street.

they prefer the "old" you. On the other hand, you might find that your honesty and clarity is respected by friends who are glad that you are finally taking care of yourself.

Although it's sometimes scary to say no, the rewards are worth it. You feel safer because you are protecting yourself from situations you don't want to be in. You get more of what you want, more of the time. You don't feel like a victim. You experience more confidence, power, and self-respect. Your self-esteem will rise.

CREATING A POSITIVE SELF-IMAGE

LIVE FOR YOURSELF

We all have the right to make choices that we believe will bring us satisfaction. We have the right to determine our own values, lifestyle, and priorities. If you are still trying to please others, if you are still hoping for someone else's approval, then you will never be smart enough, thin enough, successful enough.

Try approaching your life from your center rather than from external considerations. Try putting aside your father's expectations. Stop comparing yourself to your best friend. Think about what you like to do, whom you like to spend time with, what you find worthwhile.

Approach these changes gradually. Thinking for yourself and making your own decisions can be terrifying. Letting go of other people's expectations can leave you feeling empty for a time. And yet, seeing yourself as an independent adult who can stand up for your own choices frees you to accept yourself as you are. As you begin to trust your decisions and pursue your own goals, your self-respect will naturally increase.

DO THINGS YOU'RE PROUD OF

It's impossible to feel good about yourself if you are doing things that you aren't proud of. If you are gambling compulsively, not spending enough time with your children, or avoiding therapy, you're not going to feel good about yourself. To improve your self-esteem, it's essential that you stop doing things you don't feel proud of and start doing things you can respect and admire.

AFFIRMATIONS AND VISUALIZATIONS

Many women have found affirmations to be helpful in creating a positive self-image. You can say things like "I am a worthwhile, deserving person," "I like myself," "I am lovable," "I can trust my perceptions." By repeating these daily—out loud or in writing—you consistently affirm your positive qualities.

Some women prefer to phrase the affirmation to reflect what they hope to become, even if they don't fully feel that way yet. For example, you may want to feel powerful and effective in your life. At present, perhaps you feel more powerful than you used to, but still not all that powerful. By making the affirmation "I am powerful and effective," you create an image of yourself as you will be, and in doing so, you bring about what you wish for.

Visualizing how you want to be is another effective way to move toward your goal. You can imagine different scenes that show you as a more capable, powerful person: you may be brilliantly arguing a case in front of a jury, receiving your black belt in karate, or simply walking along the street with your back straight and your head held high. You can visualize yourself in a healthy relationship or even having fun. You can imagine whole scenarios. One woman who felt as if she was dirty, as if she was covered with shit, imagined scraping off all the shit and throwing it back at her abuser. Afterward, she reported feeling great.

ACCENTUATE THE POSITIVE

If you're used to seeing yourself as ineffective or worthless, you may not notice the wonderful things about yourself. Try making a list of all the things you do well. Include everything. "I make perfect fried eggs. I can whistle on pitch. I'm good at untying knots." Make another list of the things you like about yourself: "I like that I'm a good listener. I like my feet. I like my stubborn determination." Read your lists to yourself when you're feeling self-critical. Find an appreciative friend and read the lists aloud. Or ask friends what they like about you. Listen and take notes.

It's important to acknowledge both small and large changes. Eva, a survivor and former battered wife, was inspired when she saw how much her self-image had changed:

I used to feel like nothing I said counted, that people wouldn't listen to me. I didn't like myself. I think I went out of my way to find things that happened in my life that reinforced the things my ex-husband said about me, that I believed about myself. It took a long time for me to acquire the characteristic of being my own woman, of not letting other people dominate me and dominate my ideas.

All those things have changed tremendously. I'm more confident about who I am now. There were parts of me I liked when I was young. Now I've reclaimed them. I have a certain boldness. I was the boldest woman I knew. There was a time when I was afraid of what people would say, and now I don't give a damn. I'm gonna be who I am and if other people can't hang, that's their tough luck.

(For more of Eva's story, see page 373.)

FIND A TASK

If you find that you're sinking into the quicksand of self-hatred and desperation, it can help to get planted in the present by taking on some manageable task that you can handle competently. You might want to clean house, cook a pot of soup, or plant some flowers. Ellen says that when she feels miserable, accomplishing something helps:

I often go to my desk and answer mail, pay bills, clear the mass of papers that accumulate. Throwing things out always helps. And doing dishes—the warm water and the clarity of the task. After doing such routine tasks, I may not feel great, but at least I can feel good that I got something done.

TAKE BREAKS

When you're immersed in working through the trauma of sexual abuse, it's easy to feel that all you are is a person who has been sexually abused. You're in therapy, going to survivors' meetings, crying, raging, struggling with your partner, breaking addictions, reading, talking, and dreaming sexual abuse.

Although a time of intense involvement is often inevitable, as well as useful, it helps if you stop and appreciate how far you've come. When you feel that you haven't healed, that you still have the same basic problems, you need to remind yourself this is only a partial assessment. In reality, the severity of your problems may have lessened, and the way you handle them may be radically different.

Taking breaks can help you see that you are more than a reaction to abuse. Acknowledging the other parts of your life affirms that you are a complex, multifaceted person and that abuse issues, even if they loom over much or even most of your life, still do not gobble up every bit of it.

SELF-ESTEEM IN RELATIONSHIPS

An important part of creating a healthy self-image is being with people who mirror you positively, who believe in your strengths, your goodness, your capacity to manage your own life.

It's necessary to structure your life so that you are in contact with people who respect you, who understand and take you seriously. This is what you did not have as a child, and what you need now in order to construct healthy feelings of self-worth.

It's important to stop being with people who make you feel bad about yourself, whether it's your husband or lover, the neighbor who always takes advantage of you, someone in your original family, or your abuser. In their place, plant and nourish relationships with people who respect you and understand you.

Those who appreciate you can be friends or even just acquaintances. They can be counselors, co-workers, teachers, family, other survivors, members of a support group.

Consider yourself valuable enough to be discriminating about whom you relate to. Although you are not always in a position to cut off contact completely with people who don't respect you (for example, a teacher in a required course), weed out the ones who put you down as much as possible. Then you will hear positive things about yourself. Listen. Take it in.

I am hearing from people around me that I'm a courageous person, and that often surprises me. I don't feel that what I'm doing takes guts, just that I've *had* to do it. Hearing people say I'm courageous has made me take another look at it.

Ellen has grown to like one of her clients very much. Recently, when this woman was feeling bad about not having a lover or many close friends, Ellen reassured her that as she began to feel better about herself, she would connect more deeply with others. "You're a likable person," Ellen told her. "I like you."

The woman continued talking as though

NURTURE YOURSELF: THE TEDDY BEAR'S PICNIC

There are a million ways to nurture yourself. Choose things that make you feel good and do them often. This is not optional. It's an essential part of feeling good. Once a day, at least, do something nice for yourself.

"I love sushi. So I go out and have sushi."

"I love movies and I love to buy books. So I do a lot of both."

"I go away on the weekends to places I like."

"I set aside times in my week when I plan to come home and *not* think about incest. Or I go out with a friend and we agree not to talk about it."

"I go to a lot of hot tubs and get massages."

"I've been exercising more."

"I surround myself with people with whom I can discuss the whole of my life, that I don't have to keep any secrets from. I worked very hard to get the secret out of my life. I need to be able to talk about it with the people in my life as easily as I can ask them what kind of coffee they want."

"I'm in a support group. I have close contact with the other group members. We talk every other day. And when one of us is feeling real bad, like wanting to hurt herself or something, we call. We support each other a real lot."

"I have affirmations all over my room. They say things like: 'I do not deserve to be hurt.' 'There's nothing wrong with my body.' 'I love myself.' 'I am gentle and patient with myself.' 'I am good.' 'I forgive myself.' "

"When I come out of a heavy therapy session, no matter what it feels like, I always buy myself flowers."

"I eat a good breakfast. I try to look after myself with food. It's the least I can do."

"I write."

"I make myself a big cup of tea and curl up with a book. Or I take a really hot bath with some nice bath oil, and stay in there with a book till the water gets cold."

"I've gotten clothes that are far more colorful and flattering. I went out last year and bought myself this absolutely gorgeous emerald green dress that was very fashionable. I look very good in it, and that was a real gift for myself. That was a real step for me, not to just buy it because it was on sale."

"Working in my garden is a wonderful healing metaphor for me. I'd never done anything like that before. When we bought our house, the garden was totally overgrown. I went out with pruning shears and cut back twenty loads of debris we took to the dump. Each time I turned over a shovelful of dirt or planted something new, it felt like I was doing that for myself."

"I try to get into nature and walk and hike and ski as often as I can."

Ellen hadn't said anything. "Did you hear me say 'I like you'?" Ellen asked.

The woman looked at Ellen quizzically. "No."

"Well, let's try it again," Ellen said. "I like you."

"You're different. I pay you to like me," the woman protested.

"No," Ellen responded. "You pay me to help you, to support you in your healing, to care about who you become. You can't pay me to like you. I just happen to feel that way."

The woman looked at Ellen again and nodded, taking it in just a little.

At first, the simple genuine appreciation of who you are can be so unfamiliar that you don't even notice it. Train yourself to hear the positive things people reflect back to you. They shouldn't go to waste.

THE NURTURING PARENT EXERCISE

In her book *Solving Women's Problems,** Hogie Wyckoff presents a group exercise called "The Nurturing Parent," in which women write on a big sheet of paper what they would like their ideal nurturing parent to say to them: "I love you." "You're beautiful." "I like you just the way you are." "I'm proud of you." They use crayons and their "other" hand (the left if you're right-handed, and vice versa) to write the sentences, so they are more childlike. When their lists are finished, each woman gets up and reads these things aloud in the way she would like to hear them: warmly, lovingly, slowly, tenderly. Next, each person gives her list to a partner,

who cuddles her in her lap and reads the list over and over to her in a nurturing way. Then the partners switch.

This is a beautiful way to experience some of the nurturing you need. You can do this in groups. You can also do it with a trusted partner, friend, or counselor.†

A Name of My Own: Rachel Bat Or

Some women have changed their names in order to establish their own definition of themselves. This is an ancient way that many cultures have used to mark major transformations. Rachel Bat Or, who gathered her friends together to share in a naming ceremony, experienced empowerment and renewal both from the name change and from creating the ritual.

I changed my name. It was the most healing thing I've ever done for myself. My old name was Ruthann Theodore. And I never liked it. I wanted a name that reflected who I really was. Picking "Rachel" was easy. That was my grandmother's name, my name in Hebrew, the name I should have gotten. Then a friend of mine, who

---

* This book is currently out of print.

† When considering this (or any) exercise, be aware that what may be helpful to one person may feel threatening to another. For some survivors this kind of physical holding may not feel safe—and some groups may not have developed clear guidelines for nonsexual touch. As in all group activities, there should be room for each member to participate or not, without judgment. Also, it's usually possible to modify an activity to meet different needs—such as listening to positive statements without being held physically.

speaks Hebrew, said Bat Or meant "daughter of the light," and that felt right. The light, and by that I mean my inner enlightenment, has kept me alive and has gotten me to heal myself. And I wanted to be someone's daughter. I felt like I had lost my parents. And that was very sad to me. So I changed my name to Rachel Bat Or.

I invited nine friends, women who I've known over the last nine years. Together we were a minyan.*

The first thing we did was cast a circle. We turned to each direction and invited the spirits of that direction to join us. The person facing each direction just sat where she was and said, "Welcome the spirits of the east." The east is air and dawn and springtime, the beginnings. And then each person said how I reminded them of that direction and what was in me that was strong in the same way. South is fire, noontime, summertime. It's the real burst of energy. The west is water, emotions, twilight, and autumn. It's the beginning of the ending, when things are calming down. And the north is very dark, and the earth, and the night and winter. It's the place we settle into when we take things into ourselves, the place of death and rebirth.

We read "The Sisters of Rachel," which I had written:

> And the sisters of Rachel gathered around her to celebrate the naming. Long had she waited for this moment. Dreamed of it. Planned it. Sometimes doubted it would ever happen. Each sister stood and one by one spoke aloud to

Rachel and the other sisters. And when they spoke, their true feelings emerged.

Rachel, you have worked hard for this moment. You have been valiant and now you shall be rewarded.

Rachel, you have survived years of not being able to feel who you are. Today you allow yourself to feel.

Rachel, you have taken care of others for many years and helped them grow. Now it is your time to be cared for, to be nurtured.

Rachel, you have not permitted the joy and pain of love to reach you. It is time to feel that love flowing out of and into yourself.

Rachel, you have often thought of death as a reason to live. You now know that life is the only way to live.

Rachel, you have often been alone. From today on, we will be with you. You will carry our love, nurturance, feelings, life. We acknowledge and witness your valiant struggle to survive and applaud its success.

Rachel, you are now whole again.

It was very powerful to have everybody facing me, reading one of these sentences. And then the friend who helped me find the name read the Hebrew prayer used when girls are named. In English, it was:

> Sustain this woman for herself,
> for her friends, her lover, and
> for her son;
> And her name shall be called
> in Israel

---

* In Jewish tradition, a *minyan* is the minimum number of men required to hold religious services.

Rachel Bat Or.
Let us rejoice in this beautiful
and strong woman.

And then I read "I am Rachel, daughter of the light":

I am Rachel, daughter of the light.
I renounce my mother's claim to my being.
But I am not alone or motherless.
I have the light to nurture and comfort me in times of distress.
I look to the light for the answers to my dilemmas and I trust that the light will never lead me astray.
Within the light I am able to express strength and weakness; love and hatred; fear and comfort; spontaneity and rigidity; thoughtfulness and rashness; patience and impatience.
All of my dualities are acknowledged and honored.
There is no part of me that is not holy in the light.
I am Rachel, daughter of the light.

After that we all talked about our names. Everyone had some feelings about her name. Either she had changed it, or she had thought about changing it, or she really loved it.

Finally, I asked everyone to write my old name on a piece of paper and to throw it into a moving body of water. I didn't want to destroy the name, but I didn't want it. I wanted to pass it on. Then we opened the circle and had a party.

When everyone left I really felt that I had a new name. I'd been struggling beforehand with "What did the name mean to me? Was I really worthy of it?" But after the ritual, I felt my sisters had given me that name and it was truly mine now.

FEELINGS

Four survivors when asked about feelings:

"Feelings? What feelings? Are they in this room with us?"
"What did you say? Huh? I didn't quite hear you right."
"Mostly I have feelings with my head."
"I think one feeling a day is all I can handle."

We have feelings all the time, whether we're aware of them or not. Feelings arise in response to whatever is happening in our lives. A threat makes us fearful. When someone injures us, we feel hurt and angry. When we are safe and our needs are met, we feel content. These are natural responses. We may not always have the ability to recognize and understand our feelings, but they are there.

For a long time, I thought I didn't feel. I had ignored my own internal cues for so long that I was sure I didn't have any feelings to be in touch with. I thought of feelings as some mystical thing I had to concoct, rather than as an already functioning part of me I had to uncover. Any feelings I did have were something separate from me that I had to hurry up and get over, so I could shift back into the safety of neutral—being numb and in control.

When you were a child, your feelings of love and trust were betrayed. Your pain, rage, and fear were too great for you to experience them fully and continue to function, so you suppressed your feelings in order to survive.

Certain feelings just went under. I stopped having them at a really young age. I stopped having physical sensations. You could beat me and it literally didn't hurt. By the time I was thirteen, I no longer felt angry. And once I stopped feeling anger, I never felt love either. What I lived with most was boredom, which is really not a feeling but a lack of feeling. All the highs and lows were taken out.

But we all need feelings. They are useful messages from which we gain insight and the ability to make wise choices. Feelings, even painful ones, are allies, telling us what's going on inside and, often, how to respond to the situations in our lives.

FEELINGS ARE A PACKAGE DEAL

When you open up to your feelings, you don't get to pick and choose. They're a package deal. One of Ellen's clients was abused by her father over the course of many years. When she and Ellen began working together, she said she felt numb; she wanted to have feelings. After a few months she was crying through every session, crying at home, crying when she went out with friends. One day she came in, started crying, and then laughed, "Well, I sure got what I asked for."

Yes. She was feeling. And the way feelings work is that you can't feel selectively. When you decide to feel, you feel what there is to feel. For this woman, there was a great deal of pain and sadness. And after that, a lot of anger. And some fear. But slipped in among these difficult feelings were pride, hope, pleasure, self-respect, and a growing contentment.

To feel, you have to be open to the full spectrum of feelings.

When I first started to grapple with the concept of feeling—and in the beginning it *was* only a concept—I ranked all the possible emotions in two lists: good feelings and bad feelings. Every time I had a feeling, I'd think, "Is this a bad feeling or a good feeling? Is this a feeling I can allow myself to have?" Then I'd either feel it or suppress it. It's been hard for me to accept that there is no right or wrong to feeling.

The more you can accept your feelings without judgment, the easier it will be for you to experience them, work with them, and learn from them.

GETTING IN TOUCH WITH FEELINGS
YOU FEEL IN YOUR BODY

Getting in touch with feelings requires that you live inside your body and pay attention to the sensations that are there. Feelings are just that—things that you feel in your body: tightening in your throat, trembling, clutching in your stomach, shortness of breath, moistness behind your eyes, moistness between your legs, warmth in your chest, tingling in your hands, fullness in your heart.

If you have ignored your body for a long time, tuning in to these sensations may seem strange and unfamiliar. Or you may be able to objectively report the sensations you feel in your body but not know what they mean.

When children are very small they don't have the conceptual ability to say "I feel scared." They say, "I feel yucky in my stomach." When adults give that sensation a name, the child learns to connect the feeling with the emotion.

If no one paid attention to what you felt and you never learned to name your feelings, you will be starting at the beginning, teaching yourself to read the messages your body gives you. (For a powerful example, see Krishnabai's story, on page 440.)

PAY ATTENTION

All of us feel in different ways, with different levels of intensity. Getting to know your feelings is part of getting to know yourself as a unique person.

Many survivors have spent their lives racing to stay just one step ahead of their feelings. Slow down enough to ask yourself, "How do I feel?" Whenever you notice yourself gliding on automatic pilot, stop and check in with your body. Are you in your body? What sensations are going on? What might those sensations be telling you?

Pay attention to your behavior also. If you are acting inappropriately, slamming around the kitchen or crying at something small, you may be having a feeling you haven't yet acknowledged. Laura remembers:

When I first started to pay attention to my feelings, the thing I felt most often was the sensation that I was lost in a dense fog. Or I'd be overwhelmed by things like boredom, confusion, desperation, hopelessness, or anxiety. What I gradually learned was that these were not actually emotions, but lids I kept on my emotions. As soon as I'd have a glimmer of the raw feeling, I'd throw a big thick blanket over it to cover it up. If I scratched beneath the boredom, there was usually anger. Anxiety covered up terror. Hopelessness and depression were rage turned inward. And so on.

If you have habitually covered your feelings, this may take place so quickly and automatically that you don't even have a chance to feel the initial emotion. When you begin to feel happy, you slide into anxiety. When you're angry, you immediately hate yourself. These patterns are different for everyone, but if you are overwhelmed by states such as depression, confusion, or guilt, there's probably a specific emotion, triggered by a specific event, underneath.

Sometimes it's a thought pattern that intercedes when you start to feel something. If you catch yourself in an old line of thinking that makes you feel bad about yourself, it probably has a feeling underneath. Thoughts like "I'll never change" or "People don't like me" usually indicate buried feelings. As a child you couldn't afford to say "I hate my father; I want to kill him," so you hated yourself instead, finding a hundred reasons why you were bad, why the abuse was your fault.

EXERCISES FOR GETTING IN TOUCH WITH YOUR FEELINGS

CREATIVITY

All the creative arts can help you connect with your feelings. Put on music and move with your feelings. Sing the blues. Cut words and pictures out of magazines and make a collage. You do not have to be an accomplished artist, dancer, or musician to express your feelings in these ways. This isn't about performance—it's about expressing yourself.

Draw Your Feelings

Amy Pine, a creative-arts therapist in Santa Cruz, California, suggests trying to draw a feeling you have. Use color, shape, texture, degree of pressure, use of space, as well as literal pictures to help you express this feeling. Stick figures are also fine. Then draw the way you want to feel. Share these drawings with someone. What do they represent? What do you notice when you look at them? Then draw a third picture that takes elements of the first through a transition that brings it to the second. What had to happen to connect them? How did you do it? Is there any correlation with what you might do in your life?

USE YOUR MIND

If you can't readily identify a feeling, your intellect can sometimes help. Say to yourself, "My lover just left me and I don't feel anything. What would someone else be feeling in this situation? What have I learned from books, movies, and friends about the feelings that might be common in this circumstance? Could it be relief? Anger? Grief? Could that be what this knot in my throat is about?"

The next two exercises, from *Learning to Live Without Violence* by Daniel Sonkin and Michael Durphy, can be helpful in beginning to identify feelings.

By this time it's like a rut in an unpaved road. Hundreds of cars drive on a dirt road. Each car travels the same path, until it becomes automatic for the tires to follow the tracks. The same is true for thoughts. If you've had a lifetime of practice diverting the first glimmer of anger into "I'm bad," you need to explore the feelings underneath that habit, consciously changing the track. (For more on changing negative thought patterns, see "Internalized Messages" on page 189.)

HONORING FEELINGS

When you first become aware of the simple, pure emotions that move through you, all you have to do is be aware: "I'm feeling a feeling." If you're sad, let yourself feel sad—without worrying, without panicking, without needing to take any action. It's okay just to feel sad. Your feelings aren't dangerous. And most people find that once they get

FEELING vs. THINKING

People commonly confuse feelings with thinking or observation. For example:

"I feel it was unfair."

"I feel you are going to leave me."

These statements are "I feel-thinking" statements rather than "I feel-emotion" statements. A good test for whether a statement is an "I feel-thinking" statement is to replace "I feel" with "I think." If it makes sense, then it is probably more of a thinking statement or observation than a feeling statement. If we change the above "I feel-thinking" statements to "I feel-emotion" statements, they might read:

"I feel hurt by what you did."

"I feel afraid that you might leave me."

WHAT ARE FEELINGS?

The following is a list of feeling words. Say them out loud. Try out different tones of voice for each word, or say it louder or softer. Pay attention to your feelings as you say each word. What sensations does it stir up? How does your body feel? Do some words fit you, but not others? Write in any other words that especially describe you. When you are finished, underline the three words that you respond to most strongly.

excited	frustrated	hurt	_____
tender	frightened	jealous	_____
sad	contented	loving	_____
lonely	depressed	elated	_____
edgy	timid	happy	_____

started, feeling isn't as bad as they feared it would be.

The more I felt, the easier it got. Feeling became less and less scary. Even though I lost my capacity to just put things aside and I felt a lot of pain, my main feeling was one of relief. I found that the fear of feeling and the stress of suppressing my feelings were more painful than the feelings themselves.

Some of the feelings—especially the old ones I had to relive—were just as awful as I thought they'd be, but they didn't last forever.

Feelings exist in and of themselves, but when you're not used to them, having an emotion you can't tie to a concrete event can be frightening.

Whenever I have a strong feeling, I think, "There has to be a reason I'm feeling this way." And when I do figure it out, I'm incredibly relieved. "Oh! So that's what made me so angry." It's less scary for me to have feelings when I can understand them.

It is reassuring to understand why you feel a certain way or where that feeling originates, but that's not always possible. Even if you don't figure it out, the feeling still counts.

Valuing and believing your feelings takes time. But eventually you will stop seeing feelings as something separate from yourself.

I've integrated emotions into my life. I no longer have to take time out to feel. If I'm walking down the street and I feel sad, I can start crying. I don't have to wait until I get home and plan the time to do it. My emotions are a part of who I am, they're not split off from my body. I don't have to make a date to feel my emotions anymore.

It's the nature of feelings to ebb and flow, to change. You can be furious one hour, sad the next, full of love an hour later. Pain turns into rage, and rage into relief. If feelings are not jammed up, they shift with a natural rhythm that matches your experience in the world. Paradoxically, the best way to get rid of a feeling is to feel it fully. When you accept and express a feeling, it often transforms.

It's like a fire hose. When it's plugged up, the internal pressure is explosive; water bursts forth in a torrent. But when the water is flowing and the pressure is even, the water rushes steadily out through the hose and does its job.

When you're working with long-denied feelings, the transitions won't happen as quickly as they will with contemporary feelings, but all feelings, once released, eventually change.

GET SUPPORT FOR FEELING

If your feelings were denied or criticized in childhood, it may take a while before you feel safe enough to express your feelings. Many women first experience this safety with a counselor.

One day my therapist said to me, "I won't leave you no matter what you do." Before the session was over I got angry at her for the first time.

Being with people who respect your feelings and who are in touch with their own can also speed the learning process. Through feedback, example, and tenderness, you can learn to connect with your own emotions.

At first I didn't know how to have feelings by myself. I'd be numb until I saw my lover, my therapist, or a really good friend. They would draw me out, help me figure out what I was feeling. When they held or talked to me, I would squeak out a few tears or have a quiet moment of anger. I needed comforting and permission from someone else to be able to feel.

Although it's good to have loving, supportive people around when you start to connect with your feelings, over time you'll feel safe enough to open up by yourself. In your mind or out loud you can tell yourself the comforting things others have told you: "It's okay to cry." "You have a right to your anger." By calling on the part of yourself that is able to nurture you, to stand up for you, you provide a wise and kind mother for the frightened, hurt, or angry child within. You can stroke your own hair, rock yourself in a rocker, make yourself a cup of warm milk and honey, or set out pillows to punch. You become your own catalyst, midwife, permission-giver.

COMMUNICATING YOUR FEELINGS

Once you start to feel your feelings, you still may have a hard time expressing them:

My facial expressions didn't match what I said. I was always grinning. I might be down in the dumps, three feet depressed, but I kept smiling no matter what, so the outside world wouldn't know how much pain I was in, couldn't guess my secret. That way, they wouldn't fuck with me.

Or as Laura recalls:

All my life I've had this problem. I'd be overwhelmed with feeling and no one would believe me because it didn't show. A big expression of heartfelt grief for me would be several tears rolling down my cheeks. I'd be suicidal, sure I was going crazy, and my friends would maybe think I had a little something bothering me—a flea bite maybe? For a long time I thought something was wrong with me, that I had to become

dramatic in the way I expressed my feelings before they counted. I wasn't really angry unless I tore up phone books with my bare hands. Being happy without ecstatic leaps in the air didn't count.

There's no single way to show emotion. Everyone has her own individual style. But it's important to be able to express what you feel in a way that's satisfying and that communicates.

Certain ways of communicating feelings increase the likelihood that you will be heard. If you say, "I'm upset. When you are late and you haven't called, I worry. Please call me next time," you'll probably get a better response than if you say, "You're the most thoughtless person I've ever met. You never care about my feelings."

Timing is important too. If you have something to say that's important or vulnerable, don't undermine yourself by picking a time that is not conducive to real listening. Give yourself—and your friend—the benefit of a fair start.

DEVELOPING DISCRIMINATION

In an ideal world, you could express your real feelings anywhere, any time. Since we don't live in such a world, you need to make a balanced decision each time you consider whether to express your feelings. Balanced decisions take into account feelings, intellect, and judgment.

Getting angry at a police officer who pulls you over for a ticket isn't strategically sound. If you want to be intimate with someone, you have to express your feelings. But not all relationships are intimate.

EMOTIONAL RELEASE WORK

Recognizing and expressing contemporary feelings is often easier than getting in touch with buried feelings from childhood. Yet part of the healing process entails going back and feeling those feelings. (See "Grieving and Mourning," page 129.)

One useful tool for clearing out old feelings is emotional release work. Because memories and feelings are stored in the body, working through feelings physically can provide a powerful adjunct to talking. With proper safeguards and a responsible helping person to support you, emotional release work is a powerful and active way to get rid of emotional baggage.

Some therapies such as bioenergetics, rebirthing, primal therapy, and psychodrama include cathartic emotional release. Because this kind of work is active and intense (and sometimes takes people back in time to the original abuse), it is important to have the supervision of an experienced support person who is comfortable with the expression of deep pain.

EMOTIONAL RELEASE EXERCISES*

For anger: With a support person present, take a tennis racket and whack it against a mattress or piled-up cushions. Use sound and words if you feel them. Let them out. You can start with your full strength or start easy and work up to it. The support person

---

* These exercises were contributed by Amy Pine.

LEARNING TO LIVE WITHOUT VIOLENCE

An excellent book, *Learning to Live Without Violence* by Daniel Jay Sonkin and Michael Durphy, gives sound, practical guidelines for changing abusive patterns of expressing anger. Although it is directed toward men, it is useful for women as well. (See the "Battering" section on page 570 of the Resource Guide.)

RECOGNIZING YOUR OWN ANGER

There is a difference between anger and violence. Anger is an emotion and violence is one of the behaviors that can express that emotion. Many people do not know when they are angry until they reach the explosion point. Learning to identify your own anger cues will help you control your violence. (You can modify these questions to learn to identify other emotions as well, such as sadness or fear.)

Body Signals

- How does your body feel when you are angry? (Sad? Afraid? Happy?)
- Are the muscles tense in your neck, arms, legs, face?
- Do you sweat or get cold?
- Do you breathe deeper, faster, lighter, slower?

- Do you get a headache? A stomach-ache?

Behavioral Signs

How do you behave when you're feeling angry? Do you:
- Get mean? Blame others?
- Act extra nice?
- Start laughing?
- Become sarcastic?
- Withdraw?
- Break commitments? Arrive late or leave early?
- Have difficulty eating or sleeping? Eat or sleep more?

TIME-OUTS

Time-outs are a basic tool for controlling violence. They provide a structure that allows you to break abusive patterns. Time-outs not only stop the violence, they also help to rebuild trust. The rules are simple:

- **When you feel yourself beginning to get angry, say, "I'm beginning to feel angry. I need to take time out."** In this way, you communicate directly. You take responsibility for your own feelings and assure the other person you're committed to avoiding violence.

- **Leave for an hour.**

- **Don't drink, take drugs, or drive.**

- **Do something physical.** Take a walk, go for a run, or ride a bike. Exercise will help discharge some of the tension in your body.

- **Come back in an hour (no more, no less).** If you live up to your agreement, it will build trust.

- **Check in and ask the person you were angry with if they want to discuss the situation.** If you both agree, talk about what made you angry and why you needed the time out. If it's still hard to discuss, come back to it later.

ALCOHOL AND DRUGS

Alcohol and drugs do not cause violence. However, if you already have a problem with violence, they can make it worse. Alcohol and many drugs suppress feelings. You may be less aware that you are getting angry, and thus less able to take a time-out or direct your anger appropriately. Your ability to control violent impulses may also be lessened. If alcohol and drugs are a problem in your life, it is essential that you deal with your addiction if you want to stop your violent behavior.

can encourage you and cheer you on, as well as talk over your feelings with you afterward.

For grief: If you feel like crying but are stuck, allow your breath to help you connect your feelings with their expression. Exaggerate the breathing pattern—for example, long exhales, shaky inhales, adding sounds if you can. If tears do not come, it's still okay. Notice the feelings, thoughts, and sensations you do have.

For tension: Use your body. Wrestle with a friend. Chop wood. Swim.

FEAR OF FEELING

Many survivors fear that if they open up their feelings, they'll suddenly go out of control.

> I was terrified of my anger. I knew that if I didn't laugh about what had happened to me, I'd go stark raving mad and kill everybody who was in my way.

Although you may indeed be very angry or very sad for a long time, those feelings don't have to be overwhelming.

> As I've allowed myself to feel a little at a time, I learned that the valve to feelings was neither totally open nor totally shut—totally overwhelming or totally suppressed. I could feel bad without wanting to kill myself. I could be scared without being terrified. There was a whole range of gradations. Once I stopped trying to rein my emotions in, I had more control than I thought.

When you've repressed feelings for a long time, it's natural to be wary. But just because you have strong feelings doesn't mean you'll be unable to control yourself. Pounding pillows furiously does not mean you've gone berserk. In fact, actively expressing intense feelings in a safe, structured way makes it less likely that you'll explode. Very few murderers kill their victims after coming out of a pillow-pounding session with their counselor or support group.

CONTROLLING ABUSIVE ANGER

If you find yourself slapping your children, yelling at your co-workers, furious at your partner for the small trespasses of daily life, you're probably misdirecting your anger. Although it may be anger triggered in the present that is appropriate to the current situation, you may also be tapping into the wells of old rage from childhood. When the two blur, you tend to react in ways that are out of proportion to what's going on now.

As soon as you become aware that your feelings do not fit the present, take a break. Excuse yourself from the situation and try to separate the old from the new. If this is difficult, it will help to do some emotional release work so you have the opportunity to express your old rage in an active and focused way. (This is true for other feelings as well, such as feeling rejected, abandoned, or hurt.)

Violence is a way to assert power over others. It's effective in the short run but at too great a cost. You cannot heal from the effects of child sexual abuse while continuing to perpetrate abuse on others. If you're in a situation where you are battering or being battered, or if you find yourself repeatedly fighting or in dangerous situations, you need to stop now and get help.

PANIC

Panic is what you feel when you get scared by your own emotions and don't have the skills to calm yourself down. Or when you're trying like mad to suppress feelings or memories. Although panic sometimes seems to come out of the blue, there is always a trigger. Often it is a reminder of your abuse that you aren't consciously aware of.

Randi Taylor panicked whenever she stopped at a red light. The feeling of being boxed in and unable to move reminded her of the trapped feeling she had when she was being molested. (For more of Randi's story, see page 416.)

In a panic attack you are usually not aware of these connections. You simply feel out of control. Your heart is racing, your body feels as if it's going to explode, you want to run. Even your vision may change. You fear you're going crazy. And not understanding what is going on only makes things worse.

Laura had her first anxiety attack when she was twenty years old:

I was scared. I was scared about being scared, and the whole thing kept snowballing out of control. I was getting more and more terrified by the minute and I didn't know how to find the release valve. Somehow I had the sense to call my best friend. I remember telling her on the phone, "I feel like either I'll realize God, go insane, or kill myself." She gave me a priceless and simple piece of advice. It got me through that attack of panic and many other tight situations in the years that followed. "Breathe, Laura," she said. "Just breathe."

If you start to feel panicky, breathe. Sit with the feeling. Often women think they have to do something quickly to get away from the scared feeling, but this frenzy to escape can escalate your fear rather than relieve it. Don't rush into action. Instead, reassure yourself that this is just a feeling, powerful though it may be.

Acting out of panic makes for poor choices. Putting your hand through a glass window, driving too fast, screaming at your boss, can have long-term negative consequences.

You need to call on your judgment (what you know to be true when you're not scared) to guide you. Expressing feelings when you're extremely frightened can free you from that fear, but only if you're in a setting that's safe. A therapy group is a good place to get in touch with deeply buried feelings. Driving home isn't. You could probably drive safely while feeling some sadness or even yelling into the night, but not if you're reliving the terror of being raped. If you decide it isn't a good time to express or act on your feelings, take steps to calm yourself down.

CALMING DOWN

The most effective way to deal with panic is to catch it early. Once the panic spirals out of control, it's more difficult to stop, but at least you can keep yourself focused in a positive direction so you don't hurt yourself or others.

The important thing in calming down is to do whatever works for you, even if it seems silly or embarrassing. Through trial and error, you can develop a list of things that help. Try including comfort for as many of the senses as possible (feeling, hearing, sight, taste, smell). Actually write a list and keep it handy. You don't think as clearly or creatively when you're in a panic. If it's all written out, you only have to pick up your list, start at the top, and work your way down.

A sample list could look like this:

THINGS TO DO WHEN I'M DESPERATE

1. Breathe.
2. Get my teddy bear.
3. Put on a relaxation tape.
4. Get in my rocking chair.
5. Call Natalie. 555-9887.
6. Call Vicki if Natalie's not home. 555-6632. Keep calling down my list of support people. [Put their names and numbers here.]
7. Stroke the cat.
8. Take a hot bath.
9. Write a hundred times: "I'm safe. I love myself. Others love me," or "It's safe for me to relax now."
10. Run around the block three times.
11. Listen to soothing music.
12. Pray.
13. Breathe.
14. Yell into my pillow.
15. Watch an old movie on TV or read a mystery novel.
16. Eat Kraft macaroni and cheese.
17. Start again at the top.

DON'T KILL YOURSELF

I've been very suicidal in the process of remembering, to the point where I've had to say to myself, "You will not go to certain places because you couldn't resist the urge." I felt like the last things in my life that were important and gave me strength had been devastated. So there wasn't anything to look forward to. It's only been in the last few months that I've started to make plans again. Which means I've decided I want to live.

Sometimes you feel so bad, you want to die. The pain is so great, your feelings of self-loathing so strong, the fear so intense, that you really don't want to live. These are your authentic feelings and it is important not to deny them. It is also essential not to act on them. It's okay to feel as devastated as you feel. It's just not okay to hurt yourself.*

We have lost far too many women already. Far too many victims—both adults and children—have lacked adequate support and, out of despair, have killed them-

* Many of the women whose stories appear in "Courageous Women" have felt suicidal at some point in their healing. Their words can reassure you that it's worth staying alive.

Your list will be different, but try to include reaching out to others. And you can change your list over time. As long as everything on it is safe, it will help you calm down. If you get all the way to the bottom and still

selves. We can't afford to lose more. We can't afford to lose you. You deserve to live.

Reread the chapter on anger. You have been taught to turn that anger inward. When you feel so bad that you want to die, there's anger inside that you need to refocus toward the person or people who hurt you so badly as a child. As you get in touch with that anger, your self-hatred will dissipate. You will want to sustain your life, not destroy it.

All this takes time. In the meantime, don't kill yourself. Get help. If the first help isn't helpful, get other help. Don't give up. When you feel bad enough to want to die, it's hard to imagine that you could ever feel any other way. But you can. And will. As one survivor wrote in her journal:

> *I HATE LIFE!* I hate myself! I hate what I do to myself. I want to crawl into the dark earth and cover myself up. I hate that I need to remember! That I need to go through the abuse over and over again in order to let it go and find life. Why should I want to live again? How do I know it won't just be more pain? How can anyone expect me to continue working toward something so unknown and intangible?
>
> And yet I do. There is something inside me that must have incredible strength, because it has survived three major suicide attempts and lots of disillusioned and desperate times. And it's still there, keeping me going, making me work, urging me to remember and fight the guilt, to get angry, to cry, to feel, and share . . . and share . . . and share! Pushing me on toward that unknown which they call life.

If you start feeling suicidal or compelled to hurt yourself, get help right away. Make an agreement to call a counselor or a friend if you feel you can't control your actions. Call your local suicide prevention hotline. (Find the number *before* you need it).

The feelings will pass. You may think the feelings will consume you, will be absolutely unbearable. But you can learn to wait them out. It's like a difficult childbirth. The laboring woman thinks she can't handle another contraction, but she does. And then it passes.

Each time you are able to bear the pain of your feelings without hurting yourself, each time you are able to keep safe, to reach out for help, to befriend yourself through the anguish, you have built up a little more of the warrior spirit. You have fought the brainwashing of the abusers and won the battle. You have not let them destroy you.

don't feel better, you can start again at the top.

When all else fails, it may help to remember something that Laura's father always told her when things were hard: "This too shall pass."

CREATE A SAFE SPOT

It's a good idea to create a safe spot in your house, a place you can go when you're scared. Make an agreement with yourself that as long as you're in that spot, you won't hurt yourself or anyone else—you'll be safe. And make an agreement that if you start to feel out of control and afraid of what you might do, you'll go to that spot and stay there, breathing one breath at a time until the feeling passes.

Your safe spot might be a window seat on the stairway, your bed, or a favorite reading chair. Or it might be a hiding place where no one can find you. One woman spent the night sleeping in her closet on top of her shoes, something she'd done as a small child to comfort herself in a house where no place was safe.

Take your own nurturing seriously, no matter how odd it may look. When all else fails, Laura's been known to head for bed with her teddy bear and a baby bottle full of warm milk.

CHANGE YOUR ENVIRONMENT

Consciously changing your environment can sometimes snap you out of panic. This can be as simple as leaving your bedroom and walking into the kitchen to make tea. Or you can leave your house and take a walk down the block. If you're out in nature, looking up at the stars or trees can give you a sense of perspective.

Sometimes the things that upset you are sensory reminders of past abuse. The smell of a certain cologne, the tone of someone's voice, the sound of corduroy rubbing together, can trigger real anxiety.

One day I was in the kitchen, getting more and more depressed. I started trying to calm myself down, telling myself, "Okay, you're doing fine. This'll pass. It always does." That didn't help at all. I'm beginning to know how to take care of myself, so I just went back to the basics. I reminded myself to breathe, asked myself when I'd eaten, started cutting up vegetables for dinner —and felt worse. Finally I noticed that the light in the kitchen was really dim. I turned on an overhead light and felt better right away. That kind of dim light always makes me feel terrible. It reminds me of the house I grew up in.

By becoming aware of these cues, you will be better equipped to take care of yourself when you encounter them.

REACH OUT

Sometimes it's hardest to reach out when you need it the most, but give yourself a loving push to break out of your isolation. If you're with a trustworthy person, you can ask for a hug or to be held. If you're alone, call someone. It's a good idea to arrange this beforehand. When you're in that panicky place, you sometimes feel alienated, unsure why anyone would want to know you, let alone help you. If you're in a support group or in therapy, arrange to call a group member or your therapist. Make a contract with a friend that you'll call each other when you're in need. This may be the last thing you feel like doing, but remind yourself that you made the agreement for just this kind of circumstance, that it really is a good idea (even if you can't remember why), and then pick up the phone and dial.

SOME THINGS TO AVOID

Almost anything that works is fair game in dealing with panic, but there are a few things you should avoid.

- Don't enter stressful or dangerous situations.
- Stay off the road.
- Don't drink or abuse drugs.
- Avoid making important decisions.
- Don't hurt yourself or anyone else.

AFTER YOU COME DOWN

When you're on the other side of an attack of panic, self-hatred, or despair, relax and rest a bit. Such emotional intensity is exhausting and you need to replenish your energy. When you feel balanced again, try to determine what triggered it.

- What was the last thing you remember before you felt overwhelmed?
- Where were you? Who were you with?
- Was there anything disturbing that happened to you in the last day or two? (An upset at work? With a friend? A lover? Did you get a disturbing phone call? Piece of mail?)
- Was there a glimmer of any other kind of feeling before you lost touch with yourself? Is this something you've felt before?
- Are you under any unusual stresses? Time pressures? Money pressures?
- Were there thoughts in your mind that you quickly pushed away because they were uncomfortable? Were they old, familiar ones?
- Do any of these things remind you of your abuse in any way?

Sometimes questions like these can help you find the roots. It may take a series of episodes with similar dynamics before you are able to pinpoint the source, but it's worth the work. This kind of analysis can help you avoid getting swept up in the same cycle the next time. (For in-depth examples of how two survivors dealt with panic, read Evie Malcolm's and Randi Taylor's stories in the "Courageous Women" section.)

POSITIVE FEELINGS CAN BE SCARY TOO

Over time, your positive feelings will increase. Happiness, excitement, satisfaction, love, security, and hope will appear more frequently. Although these are "good" feelings, you may not be comfortable with them at first.

For many survivors, positive feelings are scary. As a child, happiness often signaled a disaster about to occur. If you were playing with your friends when your uncle called you in and molested you, if you were sleeping peacefully when your father abused you, if you were having Sunday dinner at your grandparents' when you were taken by surprise and humiliated, you learned that happiness was not to be trusted. Or if you pretended to be happy when you were suffering inside, happiness may feel like a sham to you still.

Even the idea that you might, at some time, feel good can be threatening. One woman said she dared not hope. As a child she hoped day after day that her father might come home cheerful, might be nice to her, might stop abusing her. And day after day, she was disappointed. Finally, out of self-preservation, she gave up hope.

Sometimes peacefulness and contentment are the most disconcerting feelings of all. Calm may be so totally unfamiliar that you don't know how to relax and enjoy it. Unexpected good feelings can be hard to come to terms with.

I'd been unhappy all my life. When I remembered the incest, I finally knew why, but I was *still* unhappy. Healing was a terrifying and painful experience and my life was as full of struggle and heartache as it had always been. Several years after I started therapy, I began to feel happy. I was stunned. I hadn't realized that the point of all this work on myself was to feel good. I thought it was just one more struggle in a long line of struggles. It took a while before I got used to the idea that my life had changed, that I felt happy, that I was actually content.

Learning to tolerate feeling good is one of the nicest parts of healing. Once you get started, you may find that you want to do it a lot. Take all the opportunities that come your way. A quiet moment drinking tea in the morning. Reading your child a bedtime story. A totally engrossing movie. A call from a friend just to say hello. An omelette that turned out perfect. Notice these things. Take the risk of admitting that you feel good—first for a moment, then for longer.

Being liked, loved, and appreciated has felt threatening for many survivors. Visibility is a kind of exposure. Appreciation can bring up feelings of shame. The contrast between someone's high opinion of you and your own self-hatred can be wrenching. And feeling positive about yourself—feeling worthy, deserving, and proud—may seem fantastically out of reach. But again, these feelings are so pleasant that you'll find it's worth getting used to them.

When someone pays you a compliment, try saying "Thank you" instead of immediately rattling off a list of your faults. If you receive a present, say "This makes me feel really good." If you get a raise, say "I like being acknowledged for my work."

Although you've experienced a lot of pain in your life, you have a multitude of opportunities for experiencing wonderful feelings as well. Take them. You deserve to feel good.

YOUR BODY

If someone said, "What do you feel in your arm?" I would have had no idea what they were even talking about. If I touched it, I felt my arm with my hand. But I couldn't get inside of it. I could only touch the skin from the outside. I couldn't have felt my heart beating. I couldn't experience anything from inside my body, because *I* wasn't inside my body.

—Rachel Bat Or

When you talk about your experience of abuse, when you share your feelings verbally, you are doing important releasing. But to fully heal, this release must happen in your body as well. The way you breathe, the way you eat, the way you feel, in fact your entire relationship to your body was affected by the abuse. You were abused on many levels, and healing must take place on many levels as well.

Children initially learn about themselves and the world through their bodies. Hunger, fear, love, acceptance, rejection, support, nurturing, terror, pride, mastery, humiliation, anger—all of what you know as emotion —began with sensation and movement on the body level. As a child, your body was the means by which you learned about trust, intimacy, protection, and nourishment. But when you were abused, you learned that the world was not a safe place where your needs would be met.

When children experience the world as unsafe, they do things to adapt. All the problems survivors experience with their bodies—splitting, numbing, addictions, and self-mutilation, to name a few—began as attempts to survive.

You cut off from your body for good reasons, but now you need to heal that separation. You need to move from estrangement from your body to integration, to move from self-hate and rejection of your body to self-love and acceptance.

FROM HATING YOUR BODY TO LOVING YOUR BODY

Sexual abuse was done to you through your body. Since many survivors blame their bodies for responding, for being attractive, for being womanly, for being small, for being large, for being vulnerable, for being susceptible to stimulation and pleasure, even for feeling anything, learning to love your body is a major element of healing.*

THE ONE-INCH EXERCISE

Sandra Butler, who leads Writing As Healing workshops for incest survivors in San Francisco, has a wonderful exercise for beginning to accept and nurture your body:

---

* It's not just survivors who have trouble loving their bodies. Most women have been taught to hate themselves. For help in this area, we recommend *Transforming Body Image* by Marcia Germaine Hutchinson. See the "Health" section on p. 565 in the Resource Guide for more information.

the one-inch exercise. If switching from self-hatred to self-love seems impossible to you, begin one inch at a time. Think about one inch of your body that you feel is quite lovely. It doesn't need to be a sexual part, but simply one inch you feel good about. It may be your throat, your knee, the skin behind your ear. Find a small part of your body that you can love. For the next week, pay attention to that part of your body. Stroke it. Buy it gifts—perhaps a bit of satin fabric or a jar of oil. The following week, expand that inch to an adjacent inch and do the same thing. Repeat this process, slowly increasing the reclaimed territory of your body, inch by precious inch.

AFFIRMATIONS

Try writing a sentence that feels both true and positive about you and your body. You can begin with ones most easy to embrace and then move to harder ones as you gain confidence. Some examples:

"My body is strong and healthy and serves me well."

"I appreciate my legs for taking me wherever I want to go."

"My hands are competent and can do many things, like hold my baby, type, make egg rolls, dig in my garden. I am grateful for such good hands."

"I am radiant. My loving spirit shines through my face."

"I have a well-shaped head. My short hair looks good on me."

You can say these affirmations to yourself, write them in your journal, tape them to the wall, or slip them into your wallet.

LOOK IN THE MIRROR

Another way to counteract the distorted messages you received is to look in the mirror —and really look. Take a little time for yourself when you won't be interrupted. Look at your face and also at your body. Don't look in order to criticize. Look simply in order to be introduced, to make the acquaintance of your body, to see this body in which you live. This time look with *your* eyes, not through the eyes of the abuser, the society, the lover, the mother, the judge. Look as if you were an artist, a painter. Look to see, not to judge. Do this five minutes a day and then write about the experience.

DRAW YOURSELF

Another way to reconceive your image of your body is to draw it. Artemis is an artist (her story is on page 446). While she was remembering her abuse, she drew an extensive series of self-portraits. "At first, the agony was drawn all over them, but bit by bit, they became softer. In the beginning, the lines were hard and black and angular, but then I would force myself to sit in front of a mirror and draw my own body nude, and try to draw it with all the sensual softness of a female body. I would use charcoal, which is very soft, and I'd keep drawing until I could draw my body very soft and very sensuous. And I learned to love my body through that."

NURTURE YOURSELF

Treating your body with care is another way to love yourself. Relax in baths, soak in hot tubs, or take saunas. Build a sweat lodge. Use bath oil, body lotion, powder.

Just paying attention to your body while you wash can make a difference. One woman began to feel more sensual this way. "My therapist suggested that when I take a shower in the morning, not to treat myself like I'm scrubbing the kitchen table—that I take some pleasure in my body, to feel the curves of my body with the soap and the water."

You can buy yourself warm socks, cozy pajamas, flannel sheets, silk underwear— whatever feels good. You can also wear things that are soothing to areas of your body that have been especially traumatized. One woman, who survived being strangled, felt particularly tense and vulnerable in her neck. Wearing soft, lovely scarves was a way she took care of herself. She liked the feeling of the extra warmth and gentle protection.

FROM SPLITTING TO BEING IN YOUR BODY

One of the common ways children deal with the unbearable experience of being sexually abused is to flee from the experience, to split.* Most survivors have experienced this at least to some degree. In its milder form, you live exclusively on the mental level, in your thoughts, and aren't fully present. At its most extreme, you literally leave your body. This feat, which some yogis work for decades to achieve, comes naturally to chil-

---

* See the footnote on page 47.

dren during severe trauma. They cannot physically run away, so they leave their bodies. Many adult survivors still do this whenever they feel scared.

> I do feel a good part of the time that I'm not present in my body. It's as if inside, from my neck down, it's hollow, and there's this ladder, and depending on how things are going, I'm climbing up the ladder, and this little person that is me is sitting in my head, looking out through my eyes.

Many survivors describe splitting as a sensation of floating above themselves, looking down at their bodies from the ceiling:

> It's like I'd actually rise up out of my body. I could feel myself sitting in a chair, and I could feel myself floating up out of my body. That's exactly what it is, like being suspended in midair. I know that my body is in the chair, but the rest of me is out of my body.

Others go somewhere they can't identify: "I can't tell you what happens when I leave my body because I'm not there."

You may consciously choose to split, but sometimes splitting happens spontaneously when you don't want it to—when you're in the middle of a serious conversation, for example, or making love.

TO STAY IN YOUR BODY

- **Remember to breathe.** Often when we're scared, we stop breathing. The simplest and most basic way to stay in your body, or to return once you've split, is to breathe.
- **Pay attention to when you split.** What's going on? What's the last thing that hap-

pened before you split? What feelings arose that were threatening?

- **Be willing to feel.** Listen to your fears and your needs. Be gentle and responsive to yourself. This makes it safer and more possible to stay present.
- **Make the commitment not to split unconsciously.** Make every effort to notice when you're splitting, and consciously decide whether you want to do so or not.
- **Reach out.** Splitting is a lonely, solitary condition. Telling someone what's going on can bring you back. Make an agreement with your close friends that they will notice when your attention seems to wander, and will ask you what's happening.

FROM NUMBNESS TO FEELING

Numbness is another way not to feel. During the trauma of sexual abuse, children often numb themselves, just as surgery patients are anesthetized to avoid excruciating pain. Like splitting, numbing physical sensations was a sensible and effective defense at the time. You blocked out pain, as well as conflicting sensations of arousal. But numbing no longer serves your needs.

To experience more feeling in your body, start paying more attention to physical sensations. Watching your breathing is a good place to start. Just allowing yourself to feel the breath entering and leaving your body, to feel the air through your nostrils, to feel your chest and abdomen expand and contract, to feel the small sensory components of breathing, can bring your body back to life.

Extend this awareness of detail to any common activity: walking, brushing your teeth, petting the cat, drinking a glass of water. Starting with the less threatening physical experiences, you can pay attention to how your body feels. You can register cold and hot, texture, thirst, taste, pressure, tingling, the pumping of your heart.

NURTURING TOUCH

Self-massage is a wonderful way to become aware of body feelings, to release tension, and just to feel good. Try giving yourself a foot or neck massage.

You can also seek safe, nonsexual touch from others. Everyone needs touch. You can talk forever, but some wounds are in a place more primal than words. You need circumstances that are safe enough to allow you to begin to let go of your protective numbness.

You can receive safe touching with friends who are comfortable holding or stroking you in nonsexual ways. It's also possible to share safe touch with members of a support group. Take time to establish beforehand that the touch will be strictly nonsexual, and agree to let each other know if something doesn't feel right or if you want to stop.

If you haven't received a massage by a sensitive, skilled practitioner, this can be a powerful way to wake up your body. Be sure to find someone who is trustworthy so that there's no chance of inappropriate touch or reabuse.

If you tell your masseuse that you are healing from child sexual abuse, you may feel more free to cry, to stop the massage, or just to breathe into your feelings. You can set limits, saying you don't want to be touched in a certain way or in a certain place. Although it may feel awkward at first, stating your needs directly is a mature way to take care of yourself.

Massage sometimes releases intense feelings. Some women have felt overwhelmed either during or after a massage, especially if they aren't accustomed to the vulnerability of being touched deeply. If you're planning a massage for the first time, you may want to start with a foot massage or just neck and shoulders. You may also want to arrange a session with your counselor or a supportive friend shortly afterward, so you will have a chance to talk about your feelings.

If you start to go numb when you are touching yourself, or when someone else is touching you, stop and try to isolate your thoughts or feelings at the moment the numbness started. Talk about your feelings or write them down. It's important not to continue the touching while you are numb. That's what happened during the abuse, and it won't help to repeat that same pattern.

FROM IGNORING YOUR BODY TO LISTENING TO YOUR BODY

Many survivors have decided that their bodies are more trouble than they're worth and have chosen to ignore them. Ignoring body needs includes working when you're sick, failing to put on a sweater when you're cold, or waiting to pee until you've finished just one more task.

This kind of negligence can have serious consequences. A former deputy sheriff, who had to retire early because of a back injury, describes the events that led up to her disability:

I never was in touch with my body. The reason I ended up having back surgery is because I completely ignored serious symptoms for six months.

I had a doctor. I had medical coverage. There was nothing keeping me from the doctor except that I didn't want it to be true, because I had something else I wanted to do at that time, and as far as I was concerned, my back was betraying me. I wanted to go to school and I wanted to graduate. And I did.

It wasn't until years later that I realized I believed my body had betrayed me by having pleasurable feelings when my brothers were abusing me. Therefore I hated my body, and if it did anything I didn't want it to do, like be hungry at an inappropriate time, or be in pain at a time that was inconvenient to me, I would simply ignore it. And I did that to the point of nerve damage in my leg and a ruptured disk.

Our bodies are a great source of wisdom. Listening to body messages is not only critical for maintaining physical health, it is also necessary for being in touch with your feelings and your needs. Our bodies are our essential connection to life.

To listen to your body, you have to be willing to feel. Although sometimes this means being willing to feel fear or pain, it also means being willing to take the time to feel good. If you're used to ignoring your body, this can be a radical, yet pleasant change.

I always took a shower the very last thing at night before sleep. Showers for me are a total pleasure. Unless something very serious is bothering me, I feel relaxed afterwards. But even if I needed a shower earlier in the day, even if I was tense, chilled, or irritable, I wouldn't take one until I had done all my work.

One evening around seven o'clock I decided to take a shower even though I still had a lot of homework to do that night. I showered, put on pajamas and a robe, made myself a cup of tea, and sat down to study. It was so pleasant. I was warm, relaxed, and productive. Feeling good wasn't incompatible with working. And feeling good didn't always have to come last on my list.

EXERCISE

Our bodies are designed for motion. You don't have to be a marathon runner or an Olympic swimmer to enjoy moving. Even simple walking is good exercise. Moving stimulates your circulation, massages your internal organs, stretches and strengthens your muscles, and energizes you. Exercise is also a great way to discharge tension, work through emotional blocks, release anger, and gain self-esteem. As Jayne Habe relates:

I swam again today. It feels so good to be back in the water, to be pushing my body to get strength. I look at it as being in training for my life.

If you're not accustomed to exercising, choose an activity you think you might enjoy, and start with just a little. It's more inviting to start small and work up than it is to set unreasonable goals, strain muscles, exhaust yourself, and give up. Exercise is not another ordeal to be endured. Rather it is a healthy part of living in your body.

INSOMNIA

Insomnia is common for many people under stress, and survivors are certainly under enough stress. Added to that, many survivors were abused when they slept, as they were falling asleep, or in their beds. Many have nightmares or recover terrifying memories in sleep.

If you suffer from insomnia, there are ways you can help yourself:

- Drink warm milk or chamomile tea before going to bed.
- Take a warm bath before bed.
- Exercise early in the day, rather than in the evening.
- Don't do upsetting things right before bed.
- Don't go to bed before you're tired.
- Give yourself thirty minutes early in the day as your worry time. Write down your obsessions in a room other than your bedroom.
- Put on quiet, soothing music or relaxation tapes, or turn on the television very low. Visualize sleepy, relaxing things.
- Make the environment feel safer. Put locks on your windows. Hang pictures of your friends on the wall next to your bed.
- If masturbation or sex is not anxiety-filled for you, it may help you relax.

If all these fail and you still can't sleep, don't fight it. Don't get mad at yourself, tell yourself how badly you need your sleep, or remind yourself of all you have to do the next day. Decide that lying quietly and listening to soft music will at least rest your body and that you won't die by missing a few nights' sleep. Or get up, put on a bathrobe, and read a book you really like (or something really bor-

ing). Write in your journal. Draw a picture. Call someone in another time zone. Do your income tax. Sew your child a Halloween costume. The night can be a quiet, special time just for you.

Insomnia is a result of stress, and it can lead to further stress. The important thing is to respond to it in ways that soothe and nurture you, even if you're not sleeping. In time, as you heal, you'll sleep more easily.

FROM PHYSICAL ILLNESS TO A HEALTHIER BODY

Some survivors were abused in ways that have left them with physical illnesses. For others, the ways they coped led to illness. Migraines, environmental illnesses, pelvic disorders and problems with sexual organs, asthma, arthritis, and many other illnesses can result from early trauma and stress.* Sometimes an area of your body that was injured will develop problems later—such as pain in your jaw if you were orally raped. You may also experience more subtle problems such as chronic tiredness, low resistance, susceptibility to colds and flu.

However, illness does not necessarily stem from abuse. People who were not sexually abused develop arthritis, and environmental illness is increasing dramatically because of the increase in toxic pollution. Some schools of alternative healing "blame the victim" by insisting that any physical ill-

---

* Read Gizelle's story on page 461 for a dramatic example.

EXERCISES FOR CONNECTING WITH YOUR BODY

Some of the exercises in this section require a partner. Others can be done alone.*

BELLY BREATHING

Belly breathing is a great thing to do when you panic—when you're scared that you may stop breathing altogether, or close to it. Your breath becomes shallow, uneven, and catches high up in your chest. To belly breathe, lie on your back and place one hand on your stomach, one hand on your chest. If the hand on your chest is the one moving up and down, you're breathing from your chest. Practice sending your breath deeper into your belly, until the hand on your stomach begins to rise and fall. Consciously blow the air out of your mouth, and let your belly refill with air.

RELAXATION EXERCISES

I. Lie on your back, or in any other comfortable position. Make sure your clothing isn't constricting you in any way. Take off your shoes; undo your belt. Take a few deep slow breaths and release the air. Starting at your feet, focus your attention there and feel any tension in your feet. With your next natural exhalation, let the tension go, and let your feet relax. Next, move to your ankles. Notice any tension there. As you exhale, release any tightness. Continue the same exercise, working your way up your body—feet, ankles, calves, thighs, buttocks, genitals, stomach, chest, back, shoulders, arms, hands, neck, face, head —until your body becomes more and more relaxed. This is wonderful just before sleep.

II. Find a comfortable position, sitting with your feet on the floor or standing. Turn your attention to your breathing, watching the inhale, the exhale, and the space in between. Don't force any change in your breathing, just watch it. Feel your body expand away from the center and release back toward the center. In time, allow your breath to deepen, moving deeper down into your abdomen. Let your belly be soft. Take in good things as you breathe in (hope, self-love, courage) and let go of things you don't want as you breathe out (fear, tension, self-criticism). Do this for five or ten minutes.

GROUNDING EXERCISES

I. Imagine that you are a tree sending your roots deep into the earth. Imagine these roots reaching down through your legs, through the bottom of your feet, into the earth, all the way to its center, where they're firmly planted.

II. Walking, especially without shoes (weather and terrain permitting), can be very grounding and centering. The beach and the woods are both good places. Your neighborhood is also fine if it's safe.

---

* Most of the exercises in this section were contributed by Amy Pine, a creative-arts therapist in Santa Cruz, California. We would like to thank her for helping to identify and conceptualize material throughout this chapter.

Breathe deeply and feel your contact with the ground. See what is around you. You can decide ahead of time how long you want to walk, and experiment with the pace.

III. Stand facing a partner and place your hands together, palm to palm. At a signal "go," push against each other as hard as you can. Take turns trying to back each other up to the end of the room (or yard). (Make sure there are no obstacles behind you.) Either person can stop the exercise if he or she feels uncomfortable. Afterward, check your body and see what you notice. Discuss your reactions. Try the same exercise back-to-back. This is not a competitive exercise. It should be done in a spirit of support, the goal being for each person to feel solid and grounded. This can also be a good exercise for getting back into your body.

TO GET BACK IN YOUR BODY

I. Sit or stand with your feet solidly planted on the floor. Make eye contact with a partner and really see her. Don't space out. Squeeze your partner's hands if your attention starts to waver. Simply be there together, with the partner mirroring (following and imitating) your breathing pattern as it changes. Talk about how you feel as you do this exercise. Notice any changes.

II. Explore the full range of movement in your joints. Beginning with your fingers, wrists, and elbows, moving to your shoulders, spine, hips, knees, and so forth, move through the joints in your body.

CONNECTING WITH BODY SENSATIONS

I. Begin a movement journal. Pick a body part and spend five to ten minutes allowing that part to move in any way it wants. The rest of your body may join in, but keep your primary focus on your chosen part. There is no right or wrong way to do this—the movement can be very small, almost still, and silent. It can also be large or connected to a sound. You can choose a toe, a hand, wrist, eyes, mouth, or pelvis—any part. Give your attention to what the movement feels like or has to say to you. After five or ten minutes, write down what happened for you. Share your writing with a trusted person.

II. Choose a theme that is relevant in your life—being open/closed, strong/weak, hiding/reaching out, depression/elation, centered/off-centered. Ask a partner to sit with you as a witness while you explore this theme through movement. You don't have to be a dancer—everyone moves. Afterward, talk about it together, sharing your feelings and observations. (The witness should be careful not to interpret the mover's experience.)

III. Give your body parts a voice; let them talk. A partner can ask questions in order to get more information and explore with you. For instance, the stomach might say, "I'm all knotted up. I've been tense for the past week. I'm sick of everything!" Your friend might ask, "What are you sick of?" Allow the stomach to answer. If you don't know for sure, guess. Give yourself permission to improvise. See what comes out.

ness is a result of some emotional attitude, and claim that if the patient would only work through the emotions, she would no longer be sick. This is simplistic and damaging.

Yet there sometimes is an emotional component to illness. If you are suffering from an illness that you suspect has its roots in your abuse, becoming aware of its origins gives you a chance to work with those aspects. Although traditional doctors are sometimes skeptical about the emotional component of illness, too many people have experienced a direct correlation to ignore the potential benefits of emotional work on physical healing.

There are many alternative means of healing available today, many of which work well on both the physical and emotional levels. Acupuncture, chiropractic, homeopathy, massage, meditation, and visualization all can be valuable. If you are under the care of a physician, you may want to discuss some of these possibilities. Doctors are becoming increasingly open to the benefits of less conventional treatments. Sometimes you can design a treatment plan in which you utilize both traditional and nontraditional methods.

FROM ADDICTION TO FREEDOM

Addictions are ways to escape, to find relief, to protect yourself, to gain control, to feel better. Addictions can also destroy your body, cut you off from your feelings, tear down your self-esteem, interfere with relationships, and sometimes kill you. To break an addiction, you must *want* to change. You must be honest about the extent of the problem, identify the purpose it serves, and see it as both a survival tool and a self-destructive pattern. Then get help and break the habit.

ALCOHOLISM AND DRUG USE

Many survivors are addicted to alcohol or drugs. Drugs and alcohol are temporarily effective ways to numb feelings, suppress memories, and escape from pain. Yet healing requires that you experience your feelings and look clearly at your life. *You can't do this if you're addicted to alcohol or drugs. To heal from child sexual abuse, you will have to break your addictions.*

Even if you are not addicted, you may still be using drugs or alcohol as a way to avoid feelings. This too will block your healing.

Breaking addictions is very difficult to do in isolation. Alcoholics Anonymous and Narcotics Anonymous have been tremendously effective in helping people break their addictions to alcohol and drugs. Depending on how far your addiction has progressed, you might also need the help of a residential treatment program.

If you are the child of alcoholic parents (as many survivors are), meetings for Adult Children of Alcoholics can help you identify patterns common to alcoholic families. If you are the partner of an alcoholic (or addict), Al-Anon can offer valuable support. For more on these and other twelve-step programs, see the Resource Guide.

QUITTING SMOKING

Quitting smoking is not a requirement for healing from child sexual abuse, but it can be a potent way to affirm your own power and choose to have a healthier body. Since smoking suppresses feelings, quitting is a good way to get more in touch with yourself. It's also a very tangible goal. So much about healing from sexual abuse is not concrete. Quitting smoking has visible results that can do wonders for both your body and your self-esteem.

It is difficult to break more than one addiction at a time. So if you are dependent on both alcohol (or drugs) and tobacco, tackle the alcohol and drugs first. They interfere directly with your healing in a way smoking does not. But do consider quitting cigarettes as one more way to choose life and health.

EATING DIFFICULTIES

Before we begin to talk about problems with eating, it is essential to say that there is no ideal size or shape for a woman's body. Some of us are tall, some are short; some are angular, some are rounded; some are small, some are large; some are firm, some are soft. And none of these qualities are better or worse in themselves.

Our culture sends out a strong message that women should look a certain way. That way has numerous characteristics, ranging from light-colored skin to long eyelashes, and one of its most relentless characteristics is thinness. The mass media today praise thinness and condemn large women. This is oppressive to anyone who isn't slim. We don't want to perpetuate that standard.* What we are talking about are problems *with eating— how we eat or don't eat, and what that means to us. We are not talking about body size.*

---

* We recommend *Shadows on a Tightrope* by Lisa Schoenfielder and Barb Wieser, a powerful anthology from the Fat Liberation movement. See the "Health" section on p. 566 of the Resource Guide.

COMPULSIVE EATING

Survivors eat compulsively for many reasons. Some women binge in order to numb their feelings. While they are totally involved with eating, shoveling spoonful after spoonful of ice cream into their mouths, other pains, fears, and hungers recede. Compulsive eating is an escape. Although you may hate yourself in an hour, you get relief in the moment.

If you are hurting, eating compulsively may be the only way you know to nurture yourself. You need to be held, you need time alone, you need more fulfilling work. But you're not accustomed to recognizing these needs and responding to them, so you eat. You give yourself food as a substitute for other needs.

Some women overeat for protection. Our culture perpetuates the myth that large women are less sexually desirable. Some women do experience less sexual attention when they are large and thus feel less vulnerable. Also, children are small. When you were a child you were abused, so now you may feel safer in a large body. However, size alone cannot protect you. Women of every size experience sexual advances—and sexual assault.

Although body size is not necessarily related to how or how much you eat—many women are naturally large or small regardless of their eating patterns—some women purposefully eat large quantities of food to make themselves larger. One survivor decided in her late teens that the only way to avoid sexual abuse was to get fat. She didn't like sweets very much, but she forced herself to eat them—and everything else—until she got to be a size that she thought was large enough to be unattractive.

Look at why you eat the way you do.

What does it give you? What needs does it meet? Don't condemn yourself for having tried to meet those needs through food. Instead, begin to honor them in healthier ways.

If you eat in order to be larger so that you'll feel safe or have more power in the world, think of other ways you might gain that same protection or power. If you eat to avoid unwanted advances, it's essential to learn to say no. "No" is simple and direct. Practice saying it frequently. In most situations, a firm "no" will protect you at least as well as eating, and usually better.

ANOREXIA AND BULIMIA

Anorexia and bulimia thrive in our culture, which exalts thinness and despises fat. Girls and women internalize this attitude and are terrified of being large. Sexual abuse then compounds the problem.

Many girls who have been sexually abused begin to suffer from anorexia when they go through puberty. They falsely believe that if they don't grow breasts, develop full hips, become curvy, they won't be attractive, and then no one will force them into being sexual. For these girls, it's understandable that it would be especially frightening to become a woman. They think, if this is what happens to children, how much worse will it be as a woman?

Anorexia, like compulsive eating, is an attempt to protect yourself, to assert control. By strictly controlling what you do and don't take into your body, you are trying to regain the power that was taken from you as a child.

Not eating, or eating too little to sustain health, is also a way of saying no to life. If life has given you abuse, fear, pain, and humiliation, this attitude is understandable. With anorexia, you are not instantly killing yourself, but you eat only enough not to die. And sometimes not even that.

Bulimia is a pattern of eating and throwing up, or bingeing and throwing up. You may have begun this pattern because you didn't want to gain weight, or you may have felt a compulsion to vomit that you've never understood.

Bulimia, like anorexia, is an attempt to control what happens to your body. Throwing up is a way of saying no. As children,

---

RESOURCES FOR ANOREXIA AND BULIMIA

AABA
American Anorexia/Bulimia Association
165 West 46 St., Suite 1108
New York, NY 10036
(212) 575-6200

AABA was founded in 1979 to counteract the silence associated with anorexia and bulimia and to offer help. They provide information and national referrals to more than 35,000 callers a year. They also offer support groups, recovery panels and outreach workshops in schools and community programs, and educational programs and professional training.

many survivors had fingers, penises, and objects shoved into their body openings. You may have had a penis shoved into your mouth. You may have gagged or vomited. If you're still vomiting, you may be trying to get those things out of your body.

The problem, of course, is that food is actually nourishing to you. And repetitive throwing-up robs your body of important nutrients, as well as damaging your teeth and digestive system. Ultimately, it can kill you. It is essential that you establish the ability to say no in other ways.

In a workshop for survivors who also had eating problems, Ellen helped one woman make a dramatic breakthrough in her struggles with bulimia:

After one survivor read her writing, some painful and humiliating memories began to surface. She felt a strong urge to vomit. If this had been a woman who rarely vomited, I would have grabbed a bowl and told her to feel free. Vomiting, if we do it *very* rarely, can be a cathartic release. But since this woman was bulimic, vomiting would have been just one more repetition of a self-destructive behavior. Instead, I encouraged her to get that penis out of her mouth another way. She was terrified and shaking, recoiling into a small childlike bundle. But with encouragement, she gradually sat up and began to say no. Bit by bit she got louder, until she was pounding the pillow in front of her with passionate force, screaming, "NO! Get that out of me! You can't put anything in me that I don't want! NO. NO. NO!" She screamed and pounded to exhaustion and then leaned back. Sweating, trembling, and smiling, she

looked at us and said, "That felt a lot better than throwing up."

Anorexia and bulimia are dangerous, life-threatening patterns. If you're caught in either one, you need immediate skilled help so that you can sustain your body while you heal your emotions and your spirit.

FROM SELF-MUTILATION TO SELF-CARE

Many survivors have hurt themselves physically—carving into their bodies with knives, burning themselves with cigarettes, or repeatedly injuring themselves. It is natural that survivors struggle with self-abuse. As children they were indoctrinated to abuse, and now they continue the pattern themselves, never having known other choices.

Self-mutilation provides an intense feeling of relief and release that many survivors crave. It is also an attempt at control, a type of punishment, a means of expressing anger, and a way to have feelings. Self-abuse is a way to re-create the abusive situation, producing a familiar result.

One woman suffered from severe nighttime attacks of terror and vaginal pain. When she could stand it no longer, she would insert objects into her vagina and hurt herself. Immediately afterward, she would feel relief and fall asleep.

At first glance this might seem incomprehensible, but like other coping mechanisms, it had its own intrinsic logic. When this woman was a child, she went to bed every night terrified that this would be one of the nights when her father would abuse her. She would lie sleepless until he did come in—and torture her by putting objects in her vagina or by burning her. Only after he had left could she sleep, knowing that her agony was over for that night.

This woman had no explanation for her actions. She only knew that after the pain came relief and sleep, states of being she was able to achieve no other way. Once she began to understand the connection to her childhood abuse, she took the first steps in stopping this self-destructive compulsion.

Self-mutilation is not always obvious. One survivor hid it under the guise of accidents:

> One of the only ways for me to get attention and be taken care of was to be sick or injured. I intentionally injured myself playing sports. Later, when I worked as a contractor, I'd slice my hand. Because of my work, there was always a reason for the injuries. I was not a wrist slasher. One thing about me, I'm subtle to the max. But these things were clearly intentional.

Self-mutilation is a source of great shame and humiliation. But it is important to talk about it because, like child sexual abuse, self-abuse grows worse in a climate of secrecy.

To stop self-abuse, you need to get help. A skilled counselor can provide essential support. It's no longer necessary to hurt yourself. You deserve kindness both from others and from yourself.

> To keep from cutting myself, I write affirmations. I do it right on my wrist. I'll write things like "I love myself," "I will not hurt myself," "I am

> good," "It's okay to be in pain. It's okay to say it." There was a while I'd change it every day. And then I tell people about what I want to do. I tell my group members. I tell my therapist.

One survivor went so far as to write loving messages all over her body. As a child she had carved "help" into her arm. Now, wanting to make peace with her body, she gently wrote love notes to all her body parts.

Once you decide that hurting yourself is no longer an option, you need to find healthier ways to gain that feeling of release. Physical activity and emotional release work can both be effective alternatives (see "Emotional Release Work" on page 208).

Stopping a pattern of self-mutilation requires that you express feelings directly. If you are angry, refocus your anger where it belongs—at the person or people who abused you (see "Anger—The Backbone of Healing" on page 133). If you hurt yourself when you get scared, practice responding to feelings of terror in a different way (see "Panic" on page 211).

SELF-DEFENSE: FROM VICTIM TO VICTOR

All women are targets of violence. Even if you use good judgment, have solid self-defense skills, and firmly believe you have the right to protect yourself, you are not immune to assault. For survivors, the risks are even greater.

A high percentage of women who were sexually abused as children have been revictimized in adulthood through assault, rape, and battering.* When this happens, the adult survivor frequently blames herself or feels she somehow deserved it. This is completely false. The reasons so many survivors experience violence as adults is that they were trained to be victims. The effects of childhood abuse leave them especially vulnerable to attack.

If you are unable to identify your own feelings or gauge other people's intentions, you may not recognize danger. If you space out, you may be oblivious to warning signals. And if you freeze when you're frightened, it will be harder to act appropriately. More generally, if you have been indoctrinated to believe that you deserve abuse, if you expect to be a victim, it's less likely that you'll be able to defend yourself.

In order to feel comfortable and relaxed in your body, you need to know that you can protect yourself. Usually the ability to say no firmly and to move out of a threatening situation is enough to keep you safe. But sometimes an assailant will not be repelled by words alone. Then you need to use additional self-defense skills to keep you from further violation—shouting, yelling, kicking, hitting, making use of your wits and intuition. Women in this society are not encouraged to be fierce on their own behalf. But you have the right and responsibility to take care of yourself.

There are many forms of self-defense that are helpful in increasing your determination to fight back against assault and in gaining the confidence to do so. Many rapists and assailants will be frightened away by a vigorous show of opposition, even if your skills are less than perfect.

Of course, there will always be situations in which you can't fight back successfully, or in which you judge it more dangerous to do so. But if you have basic self-defense training, if you feel powerful and entitled, you can protect yourself much more of the time.

SIMULATED ASSAULT SELF-DEFENSE

The simulated assault form of self-defense training† was originated in 1970 by a group of martial artists who realized that traditional martial arts did not meet the needs of women. Women are usually attacked differently than men. Women's bodies have different strengths than men's. And most women are conditioned not to hurt others in a way that can inhibit their total commitment to protecting themselves. The simulated assault approach is designed to enable women to develop strong fighting skills and spirit in a short time.

Women from all walks of life learn to deliver full-force strikes and blows in simulated rape situations. The course is team-

---

* Many of these women have no memory of their childhood abuse when they are attacked as adults. Often the adult victimization brings up a woman's first memories of the earlier abuse.

† The simulated assault form of self-defense training exists under different names. For criteria for evaluating the quality of individual programs, contact KIDPOWER•TEENPOWER•FULLPOWER, P. O. BOX 1212, Santa Cruz, CA 95061, (831) 426-4407. They also have a list of high-quality full-force programs throughout the country.

taught by a woman instructor and a male instructor who is specifically trained to be a mock attacker. The male instructor dresses in extensive, head-to-toe protective gear. He attacks each woman in a realistic scenario—approaching her with obscene and insulting comments at a bus stop, waking her from a sound sleep while she is lying on the floor, physically attacking her. He continues his attack until the woman delivers a knockout blow (one that would knock out someone not dressed in protective gear).

Coached by the instructor, students actually experience fighting back against the mock assailant. Their bodies learn the feeling of delivering a knockout blow. For most women, it is the first time in their lives they have used their full force to fight.

The simulated assault form of self-defense is an intense, exhilarating, and effective way to move toward further safety and empowerment. Survivors who have participated in the course often re-experience the fear and pain of their old victimization. The difference this time is that they are the victors. With the support of the instructor and the other students, they win. They knock out the assailant and walk away to cheers and applause.

An age-appropriate simulated assault program is also available to children through KIDPOWER,* a nonprofit organization dedicated to teaching children self-protection skills. Survivors report that having their own children learn how to prevent and escape abuse is an important part of their own healing process. And the children themselves gain tremendous empowerment through learning these skills.

Whether you take advantage of a simulated assault program or choose other forms of self-defense, learning to protect yourself is an important component of taking back your power. And age, health, or disabilities don't necessarily have to stop you. There was a story in the newspaper recently of an eighty-year-old woman in a wheelchair who scared a young rapist so with her spirited defense that he jumped out the window.

---

* KIDPOWER was formed in 1989 to help children become safer and more confident through teaching abuse and abduction prevention and escape skills. Family workshops include training for parents as well as children, with the opportunity for full-force practice of self-defense techniques with a padded instructor. For more information write P.O. Box 1212, Santa Cruz, CA 95061-1212, or call (408) 426-4407.

INTIMACY

I have beautiful things and people in my present. I have beginning friendships with women who understand from inside what I'm going through, unlike the friends I had a few years ago. I have a lover who supports me in my healing, who is not afraid or enraged to see me, and sometimes be with me, in the hellish place I must go in my deeper remembering. I do not have to lie to them. I do not have to keep up appearances for them, I do not have to regain perspective (their perspective). I am not alone.

—Ely Fuller

Intimacy is a bonding between two people based on trust, respect, love, and the ability to share deeply. You can have intimate relationships with lovers, partners, friends, or family members. Through these relationships you experience the give-and-take of caring.

Most survivors have problems with trust. If handling things alone and taking care of yourself was what you had to do as a child, it may feel unfamiliar and scary to be in a close, committed relationship. Many survivors describe intimacy as suffocating or invasive. They feel claustrophobic when someone gets close. Learning to tolerate intimacy, to feel safe with deep sharing, is a challenge.

One survivor, Saphyre, had no love in her life for many years:

I had nobody who cared about me, nobody who touched me, or who I touched emotionally. I didn't know how to be emotional. I'd go into total anxiety if there was a hint of connection with anybody. It's hard to explain how severe that is. It's really a critical problem. People die from it. I think "shy" has got to be the biggest euphemism for pain.

On the other hand, you may cling to those you love, unable to tolerate a healthy level of independence. Or you may find yourself too absorbed in your own problems to pay attention to anyone else.

I needed relationships with people who would allow me to be close when I needed to be close, and in another world when I needed that. Since I needed to be close a lot less of the time than I needed to be in my own world, I never got what I needed. I ached for it. I can remember feeling like I would do anything in the world to have the kind of friend who would just put their arms around me and hold me and love me and care, without me having to give anything back. Some nights I would cry all night long, just wishing for that.

You may not know how to give or receive nurturing. Physical closeness may be threatening or confusing to you. You may be able to establish intimacy with friends but not with lovers. You may sexualize every friendship or run away when sex enters the picture. Or a certain level of intimacy may be okay, but when you start to get more involved or the relationship starts to feel like family, you panic.

You may sabotage relationships or repeatedly test them to the breaking point. You may find yourself alienated, lonely, or trapped in relationships where your basic needs are not being met. You may not be able to say no, to set boundaries and limits. You may have no idea what a healthy relationship is like.

These may seem like insurmountable problems, but it is possible to teach yourself the necessary skills to have good, supportive loving in your life. The capacity for intimacy lives inside you. As a child, you started out with a perfect sense of trust and closeness. It was stolen from you.

Healing is the process of getting it back.

A WORKING RELATIONSHIP

Intimacy isn't something you can do alone. By its very nature, it assumes a relationship. And a relationship means risk. The other half of any relationship is a person you can't control. But being hurt or disappointed by someone you love can never be as devastating as it was when you were a child. If your trust is broken, it will hurt, but such a breach need no longer annihilate you. You can recover. You are building a more complete self to fall back on.

In order to develop a working relationship, you don't have to marry someone or be lovers. You can learn a tremendous amount about intimacy in the context of a close friendship.

If you are already in a partnership or friendship you consider intimate, assess the quality of that relationship. Ask yourself the following questions:

- Do I respect this person?
- Does this person respect me?
- Is this a person I can communicate with?
- Do we work through conflicts well?
- Do we both compromise?
- Is there give-and-take?
- Can I be honest? Can I show my real feelings?
- Do we both take responsibility for the relationship's successes and problems?
- Could I talk to this person about the effect child sexual abuse is having on our relationship?
- Is there room for me to grow and change in this relationship?
- Am I able to reach my own goals within this relationship?
- Is this person supportive of the kind of changes I am trying to make?
- Is this person willing to help me?

If you can answer most of these questions with a yes, it's likely you have a solid working relationship. If you aren't sure of the answers, either the relationship is very new or you're not asking enough of the relationship to know what is or isn't available to you. If you answered mostly no's, you should seriously consider changing or ending the relationship (see "Recognizing Bad Relationships," page 244).

THE IMPACT OF CHANGE ON RELATIONSHIPS

When one person changes in a relationship or a family, the whole equilibrium shifts. Although sometimes people appreciate the changes you make, upsetting the status quo usually causes reactions designed to keep things as they were:

As I got more in touch with my needs and my rights, I got more assertive. And of course, I brought it all right home to my relationship. Like with anything, when we get a new skill or a new tool we almost bludgeon people with it until we're comfortable enough to back off and relax. So I said, "I'm not going to whimper through life. I'm going to start having some expectations of my own."

And my partner said, "I liked you better before you were in therapy. You used to want to please me all the time. I don't get my way now, and I don't like it."

I got very assertive and she got very angry. Her feeling was "Okay, take care of yourself, but this is ridiculous!" And my feeling was that I was barely taking care of myself.

As you heal, you will change and your loved ones will be challenged to change along with you if you are to create healthy, meaningful relationships. This is often stressful, but if both of you are committed to growing personally, you will be more likely to see changes as positive and to welcome—or at least tolerate—them.

My lover has had to change a lot for our relationship to work. But mostly they've been changes he wanted to make anyway. He knew he needed to be more independent, less desperate about sex, less tense in general. The fact that I needed him to be that way just pushed

236 / CHANGING PATTERNS

him to move a little faster than he would have done otherwise.

Your changes make demands on the people close to you, but when they are changes toward health and fulfillment, ultimately they can enhance your relationship, as well as your individual lives.

CALCULATED RISKS

Learning to be intimate isn't comfortable. As one woman said, "I kept myself safe, but I also kept myself alone." Becoming intimate means peeling back the layers of protection to let someone in. It means going to the place where you're comfortable, and then taking one step more. One step, not twenty.

Instead of spilling out all your innermost thoughts, say "I'm frightened" one time. Instead of moving in with your lover, try spending the weekend together. It's the little steps that have staying power.

There's no fixed goal. Intimacy is experienced in the moment as part of a changing, fluid relationship. Learning to be intimate is a slow process, involving mistakes, small successes, and backsliding.

To break through to a deeper level of intimacy, you need to be willing to take calculated risks. A calculated risk is different from a blind leap. With a blind leap, you shut your eyes and lunge forward, hoping that things will work out magically. You start an affair with a married man, positive he'll leave his wife. You get pregnant, hoping a baby will save a faltering relationship. You tell a friend your deepest secrets a week after you've met. Blind leaps rarely pay off.

Calculated risks are different. With a calculated risk, you weigh your chances and step out onto the ice only when you're relatively sure it's solid. With intimacy, nothing is 100 percent sure, but with forethought and a responsive partner, you maximize your chances for communication, increased closeness, and satisfaction.

LEARNING TO TRUST

Survivors tend to see trust as an absolute, either not trusting at all or trusting completely. You may bounce between the two, not trusting until you are so desperate for contact that you throw your trust at the first likely target. Since most people can't handle that kind of desperation, you end up disappointed or abandoned, thus proving your original beliefs—that people aren't trustworthy, that you aren't lovable, that love isn't worth it.

Before you can trust anyone, you have to trust yourself (see "Trusting Yourself," page 127). If you know you can take care of yourself, you won't need to blindly fling your trust out in the hope that someone will take care of you. That kind of absolute love is what a child feels for its parents. It's not what two mature adults feel for each other.

I've come up against the issue of trust again and again. The more I love myself, the more that allows me to love someone else. And the loving is getting stronger than the fear.

In a healthy relationship, you vary your level of trust according to what's actually happening between you and the other person.

You experience gradations of trust, periodically assessing whether your needs are getting met, whether you're growing in the ways you want to grow. And if you see that the relationship warrants it, you open up more. Trust accrues over time. It's earned.

EXPERIMENT WITH TRUST

As you come to trust yourself, you build a foundation for trusting someone else. You can always go back to not trusting if you want to, but at least give it a try. The basic premise of this experiment, whether you believe it yet or not, is that under some circumstances, and with some people, trust is safe. Given that, try trusting in small doses.

Choose simple situations that give you a good chance of success. Instead of saying "I trust that you never betray me in any way," ask your partner to make dinner for you on a night you work late. Trust a woman in your support group to hold you in a nonsexual way for five minutes. Or call a friend when you're feeling sad and ask if she'll spend a little time with you.

Say that you are experimenting with trust and that this is important to you. Then, if they come through for you, let that affect your world view. Let it enter in on the tally. Maybe trusting is not as dangerous as it was when you were a child.

If the experiment fails and you are let down, try to analyze what happened. This is a learning experience. Ask yourself:

- Whom did I pick to trust?
- How long did I know the person?
- Did we have good communication?
- What kind of thing did I trust the person with?

- Did I explain what I was doing, letting them know it was very important to me?
- Did I make my expectations clear?
- Were there any elements in the interchange that paralleled my original abuse?

Use the answers to these questions to learn about when it is and isn't appropriate to trust. Then try again. Jerilyn Munyon is one survivor who learned to trust through trial and error:

I didn't know how to trust—not others, not myself, not the world. I always thought trust was something you either had or you didn't, like a talent. It took me a while to figure out that trust is a skill, a skill that even I could learn. I really didn't know what trust felt like or how to get it, but I did know I wanted and needed it. For a long time I either couldn't trust or I'd trust the wrong person, or the right person for the wrong thing.

Eventually, as I found out more about myself and accepted myself more, took more responsibility for myself, I began to see that I could actually make choices that would affect the outcome of situations. I hadn't known there were right—or at least better—times, people, and places for trusting. I had learned from my conditioning that I had to take everything that came along, good or bad. That was a lie. It was true when I was three and had no choice, but now I was in my thirties and for the first time, I really began to take my life in hand and make some choices. At first they were pretty mixed, but as time has passed I find that my choices get better.

TESTING

It's healthy to do some testing in a new relationship, but many survivors carry this to extremes. You may taunt your partner, waiting to see if he hits you. You may sleep with your lover's best friend to see if she'll get disgusted and leave. One woman never shows up for the first three dates. If someone makes it to the fourth date, she'll begin to consider that person a potential friend.

In the early months of the relationship I'm in now, I can't think of anything I didn't do to test Malcolm. After three years it's just starting to ease up, because he's stuck it through. He's passed the major tests.

It's legitimate to test people to see if you should trust them or if they can meet your needs, but if you find yourself excessively testing your friends or lovers, you may be reenacting the familiar betrayals of your childhood. If you set up tests that no one could possibly pass, then you're not testing. You're saying goodbye.

Instead, try designing tests that are fair: "I'm going to wait and see if you really take care of the kids two afternoons a week like you promised," or "I need to see if you stay open with me if I tell you what I'm going through."

Discuss your needs with your friends and lovers to make sure that you've set up reasonable assessment points.

CONFUSING THE PAST WITH THE PRESENT

You may have a partner or friend who genuinely loves and respects you, but you don't experience it that way because you expect relationships to be abusive.

I was very frightened of being abused again. And it didn't take much for me to think someone was being abusive, either. Until you get clear, you judge men from the standpoint of what you've learned in life, right? My experience was that 95 percent of men are abusers. So all I had to figure out was, "How do they do their abuse? Is it physical, mental, or emotional?"

Of course if someone *is* abusing you, you need to get out of that situation (see "Recognizing Bad Relationships" on page 244). But if you only *think* you're being abused, you must learn to make the distinction between the people who care about you now and your abuser.

One way to break this identification is to create reality checks for yourself:

- My father never listened to what was important to me. Bill usually listens.
- My mother always said things were going to change and nothing ever did. With Maureen, although we've still got a way to go, our relationship *has* changed.
- My friend John has straight brown hair and wears sloppy clothes. My uncle's hair was black and curly and he always dressed immaculately.

Reinforce these distinctions so that you can stay aware that the people in your life today are not your abuser.

DON'T COME NEAR ME

It is common for survivors to keep distance between themselves and the people they love. If you feel threatened by closeness, you pull away. You tear the other person down because you're scared and want a reason to leave. Or you stay present in body, while your mind is whirring a million miles away.

I knew I was going to get a divorce. No matter how hard I tried, this just wasn't going to work. I didn't want to be close to him, period. I just wanted out. And that statement, "I just wanted out," is a direct result of the child abuse. The way I kept myself safe all through my childhood was by getting out. I got out of the house. I got out of the bedroom. I got out of the basement. I spent half my childhood in the orchards, up a tree, over with the horses, anywhere that was out, away from people. I only felt safe when I was alone. There was no safety with people. Not ever.

Sometimes creating distance is a good thing to do. It's important to be able to separate from someone you're close to, so you can nurture other aspects of your life and keep your relationship in perspective. Being close, and then returning to yourself, and then being close again is a natural cycle in a healthy relationship. But if you withdraw every time you feel uncomfortable, it's a problem.

Notice when and why you pull back, and in each situation assess whether it's what you really want to be doing, whether it's appropriate, or whether it's a carryover from childhood that is no longer useful. If you decide you do want to be more separate, practice moving away in healthy ways. Picking a fight or having a secret affair is not a good way to create separation.

If you decide what you really want is to be close and not to withdraw, you will have to force yourself to reach out, even if your natural habit is to retract. Instead of saying "I'm leaving you; this will never work," say "I'm scared; let's talk." Tell your friend "I'm having a hard time," instead of not calling for weeks at a time. The key to greater intimacy is honestly expressing what's going on, instead of covering your panic and running away.

And if you need to build in a cushion of safety, strike little bargains with yourself— "I'll let myself be close tonight, but tomorrow night is just for me to be by myself."

If the distancing you do is in your head, the triggers may be harder to pinpoint. Try to watch where and when your thoughts stray. Enlist the help of the people close to you. Ask them to watch for the telltale signs —a lack of focus in your eyes, a drop in your voice, the sneaking feeling they get that you're just not around anymore. If you're caught, or if you catch yourself, stop and look at the reasons why you withdrew when you did (see "Spacing Out" page 50).

FEAR OF LOVE

If the people who said they loved you abused or neglected you, it can feel terrifying to love again.

I had a hard time telling anyone I loved them. My father, you see, was always gentle and loving to me. He always told me, "I love you. I love you in a way I can't love your mother." He'd say that to me while he was doing these horrible things to me. So I've had real fears of saying "I love you."

Commitment or love with a family feeling can be scarier still. The child in you still equates commitment with being locked into a situation where there's no escape. So as you get closer, you may become paralyzed by all your old defenses and memories.

When my therapist started telling me that she loved me, I hated her for it. I screamed at her. I wouldn't talk to her. For her to tell me she loved me meant that she was going to leave me or abuse me. That was all that I could believe about it. It wasn't until she kept sitting there, week after week, saying "But I love you" with this complete open heart that I stopped being so terrified and let it in.

Try talking to those close to you about what love and commitment mean to them. And if the word "love" sticks in your throat, try saying how you feel in your own words: "I am so glad I know you." "You make me feel special." "I get happy just thinking of you." One woman who refused to use the word "love" told her new lover, "I'm in serious like with you."

Love is a terribly misused word.* Eileen, a workshop participant, began to feel hopeful when she discovered there was more to love than she had experienced as a child:

I felt a lot of sadness when I realized that "love" was not what I was getting when I was a kid. The funny part is that the awareness comes as a tremendous relief. It gives me the opportunity to say, "Well, if that wasn't love, maybe it's not love that I'm terrified of." Hence the new beginning . . .

STATIC CLING

Our culture sanctions an image of women as dependent, unable to take care of themselves, and incomplete without a relationship. In addition to this societal conditioning, you may not have gotten the nurturing you needed in childhood. Or you may have been smothered, not allowed to separate from your family in appropriate ways. Now you find yourself clinging, afraid to be alone.

Overcoming this state of unhealthy dependency is much the same process a two-year-old goes through in learning to play independently. The toddler will spend a few minutes with a toy and then run back to the living room to make sure her mother is still there. Once reassured by a pat or a smile, she

---

* See "But Honey, I Love You," page 311.

ventures out again, until a few minutes later she needs to see her mother again. Learning to feel secure while spending time alone requires much the same thing: practice, positive reinforcement, and more practice.

Take time alone in small increments, doing things you actively enjoy. Ask your friend or partner to say encouraging things: "I'll still be here when you get back" or "I'm proud of you." Planning ahead is a big help too. You can arrange to have dinner with your husband after spending the day alone. Expand your sources of nourishment to non-people sources: pets, nature, creativity. If you spread out the ways you take care of yourself, you will be less dependent on any one person.

MERGING

Merging is a state of extreme dependency. Not having a strong enough sense of your own identity, you confuse your thoughts, feelings, and needs with those of others, until it's hard to tell where you stop and they begin.

My former husband and I were so desperate for intimacy that we totally fell into each other's lives. We capitalized on the things we genuinely had in common and denied our real differences. We wore the same kinds of clothes, went on the same health food diets, and read the same books. We used to make a joke that you could tell us apart because I was the one in the green sweater.

If you are lonely or afraid to be alone, this kind of closeness is seductive. It's also unhealthy. A strong relationship is made up of two individuals sharing together. For that you need an independent self.

WALK ALL OVER ME, WHY DON'T YOU?

Survivors often have trouble setting limits in relationships, because they didn't learn about healthy boundaries as children. You may do all the giving. Or you may feel you don't have the right to say no. But if you are one half of a relationship, you deserve to do half the decision-making and to exercise half the power.

In balanced relationships both people contribute to making it work. You don't have to be all-giving to merit love. Total self-sacrifice is not a virtue.

If you haven't had much practice setting limits, start with something small: "I don't want you to call me after 11:00 p.m. because my roommates are sleeping." Or, "If you use up the milk, please replace it."

Once you've had a little practice, go on to something bigger. If you've been expected to cook the family dinner every night and you no longer want sole responsibility for that job, make an announcement: "I will no longer be cooking on Tuesdays and Thursdays." Talk it over with your partner and children and help them come to terms with their new responsibilities. If they won't cooperate, you can still say no.

The fact that someone doesn't like a limit you set doesn't mean you have to back down. When 5:00 p.m. on Tuesday rolls around, head up to your room with an apple and a good book. And if you don't want to hear complaints from the kitchen, a walk in the park might be nice.

Your family may grumble. They might even make a lot of noise, but they won't starve. Your oldest boy might even find out he likes to cook. And you might find that you like setting limits a lot.

DEALING WITH CONFLICT

Conflict is threatening to many women, and especially to survivors. If you grew up in an environment where conflicts exploded into violence or where they were suppressed entirely, you may feel at a loss when it comes to dealing with conflict in a healthy way. Instead you may freeze, withdraw, or try to manipulate the situation to meet your needs without a direct confrontation. You may be afraid that if you assert yourself, you'll be abandoned. You may fear getting hurt or hurting someone else. Or you may escalate the disagreement until you say or do things you really don't mean.

But conflict is normal—and inevitable. It's a basic part of intimacy. As Ellen's mother says, "If two people always agree, one of them is superfluous."

Talking directly, with respect for both yourself and the other person, is a healthy way to air problems. Try to share your feelings as soon as you recognize them so you don't store up a backlog of resentments and disappointments. Say how you feel and what you want. Then listen to your friend or partner without interrupting.

To keep a conflict from spiraling out of control, you can agree beforehand on some basic guidelines, such as no violence and no name-calling. You can agree to stick with the present issue and not trash the relationship as a whole. Ground rules like these can help you feel safer.

Until now, I've had trouble sharing when it had to do with anger. I think, in a sense, anger is the ultimate intimacy. If you can feel safe enough to express anger with a significant person in your life, then you've got a real measure of intimacy. My relationship now is the first one where I've felt free to do that.

Not all conflicts involve anger. Sometimes you simply see things differently or have different desires and need to work out a compromise that's acceptable to both of you. Either way, it's important to hear each other's perspective. If this isn't happening naturally, set a timer so that each of you can talk for five minutes while the other really listens. Or try reversing roles—pretend that you're the other person and say what you think he or she is feeling.

In most situations there's at least one—and usually more—solution that could meet both people's needs. It's not necessary to back down from what's important to you or to invalidate your friend's or partner's needs. Negotiating respectfully and successfully is a skill you can learn.* And as you resolve conflicts in ways you feel good about, you build trust.

---

* There are a number of excellent books on nonviolent conflict resolution and successful negotiation. We recommend *Getting to YES: Negotiating Agreement Without Giving In* by Roger Fisher and William Ury of the Harvard Negotiation Project (New York: Penguin Books, 1986).

GIVING AND RECEIVING

There are two sides to intimacy: giving and receiving. You may have a hard time with one or with both. The way to learn either is to practice. If you have been unable to give, start by giving someone what's easiest for you—perhaps a compliment or a favorite food. Ask the person to acknowledge and thank you for what you've done. Recognition goes a long way in reinforcing behavior.

As time goes on, work up to giving things that are harder. You may find it relatively easy to give on your own terms—what you want to give, when you want to give it. Children often pick out presents, for instance, that reflect their own interests rather than the interests of the recipient. But as an adult, you need to work toward being able to give people what *they* need, when *they* need it. Your lover may want to be accompanied to an important event, not cooked for. Your friend might need to talk to you even though you want to treat him to the movies. This doesn't mean you can't say no, only that you become capable of stepping out of yourself to meet the other person halfway.

Receiving feels wonderful once you get used to it. But first you must acknowledge how scary it is to be open. If, as a child, you were left to fend for yourself or there were strings attached to getting what you needed, you learned that nurturing was either unavailable or unsafe. But now, receiving doesn't have to mean owing something back.

Start asking for at least one thing you want every day. It can be as small as "Would you make me some tea?" or "Can you drop this off to the Sales Department on your way out?"

Tell the people close to you that you're learning to ask for what you want, that you're learning to receive. You never know—your partner might spontaneously put love notes in your lunch bag. Your daughter might pick a flower for you on her way home from school.

In healthy relationships, there is a balance to giving and receiving. If you've always leaned heavily one way, you will need to focus more on the other aspect, but eventually, as you feel safer, both giving and receiving will develop a relaxed natural rhythm.

IN TIMES OF CRISIS

During certain crucial periods when healing from child sexual abuse demands all your attention, you may be unable to give anything. You may be so self-absorbed that you become temporarily unable to meet (or even pay attention to) the needs of your family and friends.

This kind of self-absorption is a natural side effect of engrossing emotional work, but you can't immerse yourself in it all the time and expect to maintain intimate relationships. You need to make an effort to keep relationships reciprocal.

If you can't give quality attention, at least apologize. Acknowledge that you can't do more just yet, but that you intend to be more present and available as soon as you can. Express your appreciation for your friend's loyalty in continuing to love you even when you can't give much back. Then see if there's something small you *can* give. Perhaps you can do your lover's laundry even while you're obsessed with your own thoughts. If you can't give fully, give what you can.

This doesn't mean you should fake it.

There may be legitimate times when you absolutely can't give anything. If this is the case, acknowledge your limitations and take responsibility for them, instead of putting down the other person for having needs.

Generally, the deeper a foundation you have with someone, the more the relationship is able to withstand trying times. (See "For Partners," page 337, for more on working through hard times.) Sometimes a healing crisis actually helps a relationship grow in depth and commitment. But even if you have a solid relationship, the demands of healing will still be hard on your partner and friends.

RECOGNIZING BAD RELATIONSHIPS

We all have the tendency to repeat childhood patterns. For survivors, this often means leaving a family situation that was unsupportive, distant, or abusive only to get involved with a partner who embodies those same qualities.

> I'd be talking to a man I was in a relationship with and suddenly I'd hear him talking to me like my father or acting like my ex-husband, who abused me. It wouldn't be obvious until a month or two into the relationship, but then one thing would happen and it would all click into place. I picked men like my father over and over again.

When women are in bad relationships, they frequently try not to notice, and hope things will change. Or they think that because nothing overtly abusive is going on, the relationship is okay. But relationships that lack life, inhibit trust, or are simply boring are unfulfilling too. If your partner is unwilling to relate to you as a courageous, vulnerable, strong woman, then you must question the nature of that relationship.

IS MY RELATIONSHIP ABUSIVE?

Because many survivors grew up in homes where abuse was the norm, they often have a hard time identifying and acknowledging abuse in their adult lives. In *Getting Free*, Ginny NiCarthy gives some guidelines for recognizing abusive relationships.* Has your partner done any of these things to you?

PHYSICAL ABUSE

- pushed or shoved you
- held you to keep you from leaving, or locked you out of the house
- slapped, bit, kicked, or choked you
- hit or punched you
- thrown objects at you
- abandoned you in dangerous places
- refused to help when you were sick, injured, or pregnant
- subjected you to reckless driving or kept you from driving
- raped you
- threatened or hurt you with a weapon

SEXUAL ABUSE

- made demeaning remarks about women

---

* See the "Domestic Violence, Rape, and Sexual Harassment" section on p. 567 of the Resource Guide.

If you have a partner who belittles you, a husband who hits you, or a friend who doesn't respect your values, you can't count on them to change. Everyone changes—that's a fact of life—but you can't expect them to change in any particular direction or at any particular pace. The only thing you can do to change a relationship is to change yourself.

You can act. You can develop alternative

- treated women as sex objects
- been jealously angry
- insisted you dress in a more sexual way than you wanted
- minimized the importance of your feelings about sex
- criticized you sexually
- insisted on unwanted touching
- withheld sex and affection
- called you names like "whore" or "frigid"
- forced you to strip when you didn't want to
- publicly shown interest in other women
- had affairs with other women after agreeing to monogamy
- forced sex
- forced particular unwanted sex acts
- forced sex after beating
- committed sadistic sexual acts

EMOTIONAL ABUSE

- ignored your feelings
- ridiculed or insulted women as a group
- insulted your valued beliefs, religion, race, heritage, or class
- withheld approval or affection as a punishment
- criticized you, called you names, shouted at you
- insulted your family or friends

- humiliated you
- refused to socialize with you
- kept you from working, controlled your money, made all decisions
- refused to work or share money
- taken car keys or money away
- regularly threatened to leave or told you to leave
- threatened to hurt you or your family
- punished the children when he (or she) was angry at you
- threatened to kidnap the children if you left him
- abused pets to hurt you
- manipulated you with lies and contradictions

Although some items are clearly more dangerous than others, almost all of them are potentially dangerous, and all show a lack of respect and an effort to intimidate and control you. One problem with accepting a certain level of abuse is that there's a tendency for the abusive person to interpret it as permission to escalate the assaults into more dangerous and frequent acts. You're the only one who can decide how much is too much and what you're ready to do about it, but it's important to recognize what's being done to you and to know that you don't have to take it.

support networks. You can forgive yourself for not knowing better in the past, and start saying no in the present. If you make all the changes you can and still aren't getting your needs met, consider leaving the relationship.* It is better not to be in a relationship at all than it is to be in one that continues to link closeness to betrayal, abandonment, and violation. (For information on leaving an abusive relationship when children are involved, see "Protecting Your Children," page 289.)

SEPARATING

Separating from an unsatisfying relationship can be very difficult. Sometimes the very fact that the relationship has never met your needs makes it even harder to leave. You've been trying to make it work for so long, it's frightening and foreign to think of doing something different. And you may have compelling reasons for staying. Financial dependence, the need for security, reluctance to give up hope, all can play a part in keeping you where you are. Sometimes women take on the mission of rescuing a partner. Other times you may find yourself repeating a pattern of caretaking or negative relationships from your past.

The first step in giving up an unhealthy relationship is to honestly assess what's going on, how *you* feel in the relationship. Ask yourself how much of the time you're living in the future, waiting for things to get better or for your partner to change. Also be willing to hear some feedback from people who love and know you as an individual, separate from your coupled relationship.

Start doing some things on your own: Take a class. Get involved in a project that interests you, make a friend, go on a short vacation by yourself. Independent activities give you a chance to become more comfortable on your own and help you to gain a clearer perspective on your feelings and your situation.

No relationship is perfect and many relationships go through difficult periods, but staying in a relationship that is abusive, unhealthy, or fundamentally unfulfilling is not in your best interests. This is true of friendships as well as marriages and romantic relationships. And although leaving may be very hard, over time your decision will open the door to more rewarding intimacy and greater contentment.

Sometimes the process of weeding out people who are no longer good for you is spurred by a decision you make about changing your lifestyle. If part of your recovery from sexual abuse involves getting sober, for instance, you will have to leave your old drinking buddies behind. Or if you have a friend who tells you you're lying every time you talk about sexual abuse, you may need to end that friendship.

All these changes can be hard. You may feel lonely or lost. Even if you know you are making room for something better, there's still loss—the loss of the familiar, the loss of the good qualities in the people you leave behind. This can be a painful and awkward time for you, a kind of limbo when you have let go of the old but have not yet grabbed hold of the new.

---

* Seal Press has published an excellent series of step-by-step guidebooks for women on getting out of abusive relationships. We recommend them highly. (See the "Domestic Violence, Rape, and Sexual Harassment" section on p. 567 of the Resource Guide for more information.)

When I feel lonely, I find that several things help me—telling someone how I'm feeling, knowing that the feelings will pass, and remembering a parable an old friend told me once: it's only when you have an empty cup that it can get filled with fresh, life-giving water.

YOU DESERVE TO HAVE ENRICHING RELATIONSHIPS

If you've previously chosen relationships for the wrong reasons, it's possible to break that pattern. For instance, if you find yourself repeatedly attracted to older, authoritative men who remind you of your abuser, and you know from past experience that you feel powerless with that kind of person, turn away and look elsewhere. However, sometimes you know what you *don't* want, but don't yet know what you *do* want. A woman in her mid-fifties said:

I realize I need to know more about men. I really don't know much about them. My father was so distant and so abusive. My uncles were distant. My husband was distant. And I didn't get along with my son, naturally. I don't have any models from my past of what it's like to be warm and friendly with a nice man. So I've been working on developing that. And it's funny, my perception of men is changing—they're seeming nicer all of a sudden!

You may feel you have no choice about the people you get involved with.

I believed if someone was nice to me, or wanted me, I had to comply. It was a miracle that someone wanted me at all! So what if he didn't respect me or even like me? I might never have another chance. At the time, I couldn't afford to say no.

As your self-esteem increases, it will seem natural that other people will like and love you. You will realize that you can say no to some people and actively choose others.

Try looking at new relationships as places to practice intimacy. We have all been conditioned to judge relationships on the basis of their length—a good relationship is one that lasts forever and everything else is a failure. But relationships can be worthwhile even if they are short or don't give you everything you need. If a relationship seems to provide a context in which you can practice communication, trust, and the give-and-take of caring, then you have a healthy basis for growth and intimacy.

ARE WE HAVING FUN YET?

A women's band in Santa Cruz sings a song about relationships that has as the chorus:

Work on it, work on it,
I don't wanna work on it.*

Whenever they play it in concert, the audience roars. We can all recognize the feeling of having worked at relationships to the point of overkill.

---

* From "Work On It" by Wicked Stance.

If you add to that the work of healing from child sexual abuse—memories and confrontation, rage, and grief—and then throw in the laundry, the kids, and earning a living, life can be overwhelming. When you're running on empty, trying to catch up, fun is the first thing to go. But that's a mistake.

If you see your partner only when you crawl into bed, exhausted, at the end of the day, you're both liable to forget what brought you together to begin with. If you talk only about sexual abuse when you see your friend Carol, Carol may stop calling. And even if you're fortunate enough to have friends and lovers who stick by you, you'll be missing out on fun times together.

If healthy relationships are important to you, structure your life to allow for quality time with the people you love. Laura did this quite successfully with a friend who is also a survivor:

When we first met, we'd get together and spend the whole evening talking about heavy, depressing things. After a few months, it wasn't so exciting to see each other. So we decided to make a change. We made a contract to do something fun once a month. Last month I took her on the carousel in Golden Gate Park. This month we're going bowling.

Fun is not an optional part of the healing process. It's one of its chief rewards.

SEX

Q: "Have you ever made love while working on incest issues?"
A: "Well, I have . . . and I haven't!"

The perspective on sexuality that is presented here applies to both lesbian and heterosexual women. Although there are some differences in the difficulties these groups face, they are far outweighed by the similarities. (If you're not sure about your sexual preference or want more information, see "On Being a Lesbian and a Survivor" at the end of this chapter.)

We use the word "lover" in this chapter to describe any sexual partner. This includes someone you are casually dating, someone you are deeply committed or married to, and any relationship in between. Healing takes place on many levels, and whether you are celibate, dating, in a short-term relationship, or in a committed partnership, you can heal sexually.

(If you are the partner of a survivor, see "For Partners," page 337.)

Survivors are not alone in needing to heal sexually. Our culture leaves little room for any woman to develop a healthy, integrated sexuality. Almost from birth, girls are given mixed messages about their sexuality. They are alternately told to hide it, deny it, repress it, use it, or give it away. The media flaunt sex constantly as a means of power, seduction, and exchange. As a result, most women grow up with conflicts around sex. For women who were abused, these problems are compounded.

Survivors face a wide spectrum of sexual

difficulties, all of which are natural and reasonable results of being abused (see page 39). For some women, these problems connect directly to the abuse. If your softball coach pinched your breasts in the locker room after every game, you may not want your lover touching your breasts today. If your stepfather violently raped you, you might experience pain in your vagina today, or you might be scared of intercourse.

Your problems may not be tied to specific abuse. You may feel an overall terror whenever you're in a sexual situation. You may try to meet all your needs through sex. Or you may find yourself unable to stay present when you make love. There is nothing crazy about you if you have these problems. Your sexual problems, like the abuse itself, were forced upon you. Fortunately, it is possible to experience your sexuality in a dramatically different way.

For a long time I felt like a sexual failure, like I was damaged beyond repair. Yet something in me wouldn't give up. And it just amazes me. Problems that seemed insurmountable five years ago, I can hardly relate to anymore. I haven't had a flashback in years. And now I regularly initiate sex. I can actually say I like sex. No, in fact, I love it. I'm not afraid of my passion anymore. It's an exciting part of my relationship.

Reclaiming your sexuality is slow and painstaking work. As you allow yourself to remember and open up to repressed feelings, you may find that making love is even harder than before. You may question your wisdom in trying to heal, wondering if it wouldn't have been better to just stick with your old ways of getting by. But you deserve more.

YOU DESERVE TO FEEL GOOD

Experiences of sexual pleasure and intimacy often raise conflicting feelings:

I'm afraid of feeling too much pleasure in my body. Do I really deserve it? I'm afraid if I feel that much, I'll burst open, that my body can't contain that much pleasure. It can contain that much pain, but can it contain that much pleasure?

Although many survivors experienced only pain or numbness when they were abused, others felt sexual arousal or orgasm. Because these good feelings were entwined with fear, confusion, shame, and betrayal, they grew up feeling that sexual pleasure was bad. As one woman said, "It hasn't been until recently that I even thought of putting the words 'sex' and 'pleasure' together."

Some survivors do not feel any pleasurable sensations when they make love. Others have orgasms but feel tremendous guilt about enjoying sex. And some feel conflict or distress: "Pleasure doesn't feel like pleasure to me. I want to throw up every time I have an orgasm. I feel disgusted, and all I can think about is my uncle."

It was a terrible violation that your body's natural responses were exploited. However, sexual pleasure in itself is not bad, not intrinsically connected to your abuse. And now, as an adult, it's safe to feel good. You can make choices about where, when, how, and with whom you want to be sexual, and within those choices, you can give yourself permission to feel pleasure. Sexual feelings are not inherently dangerous or destructive. Like fire, their qualities and effects depend very much on who is using them and to what purpose.

TIME OUT FROM SEX

Taking a break from sex is not necessary for every woman, but it can be a clarifying beginning. If you experience fear, disgust, or a lack of desire for sex, or if you have been unable to say no to sex, this is a wonderful opportunity to set your own boundaries and to get to know your body without the pressure of sex. If you have been sexual in addictive or abusive ways, taking a break from sex offers a chance to examine and change your behavior. It is up to you to say how long this time of celibacy should last. You may want to take a year or years. Or a month may feel sufficient.

LEARN TO SAY NO

Around the age of two, children learn to say no. They practice it all the time. They are asserting themselves, making it clear that although some things are okay with them, not everything is, and they are going to make sure they have some say about it. Toddlers often say no to almost everything. This is healthy. Unless you can say no clearly and effectively, yes is meaningless and cannot give you full satisfaction.

To heal sexually you must learn to say no to unwanted sex. It is important to make a commitment to yourself that you will never again grit your teeth and endure it when you really don't want sex. Every time you have sex when you genuinely don't want to, you add another layer of abuse, repeat the pattern of victimization, and thus delay your healing.

THERE'S MORE TO LIFE THAN SEX

One woman said she not only wanted to say no to sex with lovers, she wanted to say no to sex with herself. She established a hands-off policy that applied even to touching herself, recognizing that she needed a break from any kind of sexual stimulation.

Many survivors were given the message that they were useful only for sex. All your other qualities and skills, your needs and aspirations, were minimized while sex was emphasized. By allowing sex to recede for a time, by saying no to the pressure of it, the problems of it, and even the pleasure of it, you can begin to recognize that there is more to life, and to your worth, than sex.

If you are in a relationship, an extended period of celibacy can cause a lot of strain. You may need to consider compromises in order to include your lover's needs. But it is important not to deny your own needs in the process. If you absolutely need more time without sex and you push yourself to begin sex when it's not right for you, it won't do your relationship much good in the long run and it will certainly not help your healing.

START WITH YOURSELF

When you are ready and you want to begin the process of experiencing yourself sexually, start slowly and with awareness. Many women find that they are their own best lovers in these early stages. As one woman said, "If I can't have sex with myself, there's no point trying to do it with anybody else."

If you've never been comfortable touching yourself, you're not alone. Most of us have been told that touching ourselves is wrong, dirty, and shameful. Although you are supposed to enjoy it when your lover touches you, you are not supposed to touch yourself.

This attitude is not in your best interests. Who has more right to your body than you?

Many survivors carry disgust for their bodies. Some were told directly that they, or their genitals, were disgusting. One woman hates her right hand because her grandfather forced her to masturbate him with that hand. For others the whole experience of abuse was so disgusting that everything connected with it still carries that feeling.

But your body is not disgusting. It is rich and marvelous. And it belongs to you.

MAKING LOVE TO YOURSELF

The way you masturbate is very important.* Many survivors have approached masturbation, like sex, from a disconnected place. One woman explained: "Using my vibrator doesn't have anything to do with sex or intimacy. It has to do with tension and it's about release. It doesn't take that long. If I turn it on high it takes even less time."

Another woman said she would start out with a good warm feeling, be unable to come

to orgasm, and keep frantically masturbating just to have a climax. "It's as if I become the rapist. I don't even enjoy it anymore. It's the angry, compulsive part of myself."

If you avoid touching yourself altogether, or if your past experience with masturbation is quick stimulation and release, take some time to be with yourself in a relaxed, attentive way. (You might first try the exercise on page 224.) Run a hot bath, light candles, listen to Nina Simone. Put clean sheets on the bed, light incense, place fresh flowers in your bedroom, take your time. Maybe you'd like to smooth oil or lotion on your body. Feel your skin, your muscles. Don't start out by touching yourself genitally. Begin by holding hands with yourself. Stroke your arm. See what kind of touch feels good to you, what you like. Many women have gone through sex numb or in a panic, never taking time to notice how touch actually feels. Maybe on the first date with yourself you'll only touch one shoulder. That's fine. There's no rush. Make another date. Touch the other shoulder.

Over time you can allow yourself more and more feelings, more sensation. Perhaps you will feel sexual arousal, perhaps not. Whatever you feel is fine. When you're ready, but not too quickly, you can touch your breasts, your vulva, your clitoris, your vagina. The object here is not to do it fast and be done. The object is not orgasm. It's to feel your feelings, to give yourself pleasure, to know your body. Stop any time you want to. Notice when you want to stop, what makes you uncomfortable. Stay aware. Stay in your body.

If you find yourself spacing out—thinking about what you're going to wear tomorrow, splitting from your body—stop. Slow down, back up, breathe back into your body.

---

* We recommend *Sex for One* by Betty Dodson, a wonderful sex-positive guide to maturbation. See the "Sexuality" section on p. 568 of the Resource Guide.

Do whatever it takes to reconnect with yourself. Sex is about connection—in this case, your connection with yourself.

> I consciously try to connect my whole body. I have this meditation I do, even in the middle of making love. I imagine my body filling up with fluid or light. I imagine it coming all the way up from my feet and washing over me. Somehow that circular thing helps me feel like I'm all in one piece.

FLASHBACKS

If you have flashbacks to the original abuse while touching yourself, don't panic. Flashbacks can be an opportunity to understand your experience as a child and can yield valuable information and insight. They can give you a chance to release long-held feelings. (For more on flashbacks, see "Remembering," page 77, and "Flashbacks with a Partner," page 259.)

If you get too upset, open your eyes and ground yourself in the present. Tell yourself that touching yourself here and now is not abuse even though it may bring back memories of abuse. Tell yourself that touching yourself in a loving way is your right, that you deserve touch, you deserve pleasure. It is neither harmful nor shameful nor wrong. This is fine. This is healing. And you deserve it.

ORGASMS

For women who have difficulty having orgasms, it can be helpful to take some time deliberately avoiding orgasms when you make love to yourself. You might set aside a period of time to masturbate as often as you want, but rather than having orgasms (or trying to), allow the sexual energy to build and then contain it, holding it in your body. If you get close to an orgasm, back off a little, lessen the stimulation, let the energy subside. In this kind of lovemaking there's no prescribed time to end. You stop when you want to.

Touching yourself without striving for an orgasm can be a tremendous relief. There's no longer any pressure to "achieve" orgasm. There's nothing to strive for, nowhere to rush to, no "trying." Instead, there's a spaciousness to experience whatever feelings arise, to become aware of the gradations of arousal as you feel them, to stay in the moment, to experience pleasure, and to get to know your own responses as they are, rather than as you think they should be. This kind of exploration can clear some of the obstacles to experiencing orgasms. It can also be very exciting. (This is effective with a partner too. In that case, neither of you has an orgasm.)

While the point of this exercise is to take the pressure off, you may instead feel it's putting pressure on. One woman had a hard time not having an orgasm, because having an orgasm as a child signaled the end of that particular episode of abuse. "For me, sex without an orgasm is incredibly threatening because the sex becomes endless. I panic when there's no clear end in sight."

If you've never had an orgasm, there are some excellent suggestions for becoming orgasmic in the books on sex in the Resource Guide. If you've never tried a vibrator, we suggest you get your hands on one (see page 568 for mail-order sources).

Some women say that their orgasms have changed as they worked out their sexual abuse issues. Old blockages were loosened and stored emotions were released, allowing room for a fuller body experience. One woman found that doing emotional release work changed her orgasms from tight pin-pointed bursts to a much more powerful whole-body sensation.

MAKING LOVE WITH A PARTNER

How long you explore your sexuality alone is up to you. No one can tell you how much time you need. Listen to your body and your feelings to know if you feel ready or pushed. If you have a lover and have taken a break from sex, it is essential that you don't start again solely because you feel pressured, want to avoid conflict, or are afraid your lover will leave you. Making love for the wrong reasons will backfire on both you and your relationship.

WHAT'S YOUR MOTIVATION? *

Be honest with yourself about your reasons for wanting to work on sexuality at this time. You might make a list of the things you want to change about your sexuality. Then make a list of the reasons you're willing to do so. In one column list the reasons you want to change for yourself, and in another, the reasons you want to change for your lover's sake.

---

* This concept is drawn from the work of JoAnn Loulan, author of *Lesbian Sex* (see the "Sexuality" section on p. 569 of the Resource Guide).

Although it's often hard for survivors to separate their own needs and desires from those of others, it's essential that you have your own reasons for beginning to make love. Such reasons might be: "I feel that I'm missing out on an important part of life." "I want to feel pleasure," "I don't want my past to rule me," "I want to experience an intimate sexual relationship."

Lasting changes are made only when we have a deep desire to change within ourselves. At first you may be motivated by your acute awareness of your lover's impatience or your fear of losing the relationship, but eventually you must come to see sexual healing as something you're doing for yourself. If you force yourself to be sexual before you're actually ready, it's likely you'll experience struggle and disappointment, but little growth.

When my memories first came up, I turned off sexually right away. I told my lover I wanted to take a few months off from sex. He refused. I didn't want to lose him, so I backed down. We struggled over sex for six more months. He got more and more angry. I withdrew more and more. Finally we broke up over it. Those last six months were devastating. If I'd followed my own intuition and just held firm to my no, the relationship might have ended, but I wouldn't have felt like such a hopeless failure.

If it becomes clear that you're not ready to tackle your sexuality, and you're doing it solely because of the outside pressures, then this isn't the right time for you to focus on sexual healing. As a child you engaged in sex because someone else wanted you to. It is essential that you break this pattern. Sex is for you first, and there is no sense forcing yourself through a deep and painful process of change if you don't want it for yourself. It's okay if you're not ready yet. Someday you will be. Focus on other aspects of your healing now. There is more to life than sex.

WHAT IS SEX, ANYWAY?

Making love while healing from child sexual abuse will probably not fit the description in a popular romance novel: You fall into your lover's arms, your clothes magically drop away, you have no need to talk about fears or discomforts, and you come together in a burst of spontaneous passion.

Before you start sharing sex with a partner, it's important to reconceive lovemaking. Too often sex is seen as a series of events that takes place in a prescribed order. Survivors often go through the motions either not feeling at all, not liking what they do feel, or absolutely panic-stricken. You (and your lover) must give up the idea that sex is a series of events: first you kiss, then you touch, then you get genital, then you have orgasms, then you go to sleep. Instead, try looking at sex as an experience in loving, loving both yourself and another person—sex as an experience of honesty, pleasure, and intimacy. It starts, it changes, eventually it's over. But other than that, anything can happen.

IF YOU'RE STARTING A NEW RELATIONSHIP

Most sexual healing requires at least a minimal level of commitment between you and your lover. Finding a sensitive, understanding lover is difficult for many women, not just for survivors. If you feel frustrated or impatient, you are not alone.

You may feel burdened at the beginning of a new relationship by your problems with sex. One woman said it was actually harder to start new relationships the further along she got in her healing:

The more aware I am of the problems I face sexually, the less confident I feel with someone new. In the old days, when I was out of my body, things were much easier. If I was scared or disconnected, I never knew about it and neither did my lovers. Now I can't fake it anymore. Even though I'm more healed, the ways I'm damaged are a lot more visible. Couples who've been together for years have a hard time with this stuff. How can I expect a new person to deal with it? Sometimes I feel like I'm giving my relationships a death sentence before I even start.

It's important to remember that everyone comes into a new relationship carrying unresolved problems. No one is perfect. While it's true that you might have a difficult time having an orgasm or you might experience flashbacks, bear in mind that your lover might have a hard time with other things, like initiating sex or talking about feelings. Everyone has difficulties they need to work out.

If you feel too damaged to be in a sexual relationship, work on your fears with someone besides your new lover, so you don't drag the relationship down unnecessarily. Focus on your strengths. The person who is falling in love with you is noticing your good qualities. Pay attention. Those qualities are just as much a part of you as your problems.

Going slow can help if you're afraid your problems with sex will overwhelm a new lover. If you make love right away and then shut down sexually, there won't be much basis for sticking it out. But if you get to know each other first, without sex, you will have a basis of friendship that can sustain you through a rocky period later on.

Couples often use immediate sexual closeness as a way to obscure the fact that they are starting a relationship with someone they barely know. Opening up to a new person can be terrifying. Passionate sex creates a comforting illusion of safety. But sex alone is not a lasting or substantial basis for intimacy. The fact that you need to go slow may seem to be a hindrance now, but actually it can be an asset. When you're forced to develop trust and closeness before leaping into sex, it gives you and your lover the opportunity to build a solid foundation.

Try some old-fashioned courtship. Go out for a few dates where you only stare at each other with lingering looks. Let the excitement (and the trust) build. When you're ready to touch each other, start with some hand-holding, a few goodnight kisses, or even some heavy petting before jumping into genital sex. And when you're ready to make love, acknowledge that you're ready. Savor every moment.

One couple even designed a lovemaking ritual. They knew they were going to make love, but they took the time to acknowledge the rising passion between them. They talked about their feelings for each other, about their hopes and expectations for the relationship. They lit candles and proceeded very slowly, honoring the specialness and vulnerability of the moment. In doing so, they were able to ease each other's fears, build trust, and celebrate the beauty of coming together.

COMMUNICATE

Talking to a New Lover. With the proliferation of highly contagious and sometimes life-threatening sexually transmitted diseases, it is absolutely essential that you talk with a new lover before having sex. Although these conversations are awkward and difficult, there is an up side: they open the door for talking frankly about sex. You can slide a little information about sexual abuse right in there next to the herpes.

Be direct and straightforward when you talk to a new lover. Keep it simple. Give your lover an idea what he or she can expect from you sexually. If you're scared or uncertain or want to go slow, say so. Explain your limits. If you've made a commitment to yourself never to make love when you don't want to, or to stop when you have a flashback, say so. Tell your lover what you need. Give as much information as is necessary so that you don't feel alienated or that you need to fake it.

Women have said, "But I don't know him/her well enough to talk about things like that." If you don't know your lover well enough to talk, consider getting acquainted first. As one survivor said:

> You shouldn't be sexual with someone that you can't talk to, because that's a pattern. If you're in a relationship where you can't say no, then you're sleeping with Daddy.

At the same time, don't overwhelm your lover with more history or detail than is appropriate. Don't make things sound horrendous if they're not. Remember to say that you're actively healing, and that things will change over time. Set the basis for talking if problems come up.

Your dialogue can be a two-way street. The fact that you are being open gives your lover a valuable opportunity to talk about his or her sexual fears, needs, and wants. Honest communication may not burden your lover at all; it may be a welcome relief from the assumption that satisfying sexual intimacy should just magically happen.

Talking in an Established Relationship. If you haven't told your lover what you really experience when you make love, he or she may be stunned when you first start talking. If you admit you've been faking it, don't feel desire, or are often disgusted by sex, your lover is likely to take it personally. He or she may think you've fallen out of love, feel responsible for your sexual problems, be furious that you never said anything before, or fight to deny what you're saying so that things can remain the same.

Although you risk a negative reaction in being honest, you also stand the chance of gaining your strongest supporter. Lovers often feel relieved, having sensed all along that something was wrong. They may grieve for your pain and become allies in your healing. Honestly confronting problems deepens intimacy.

Whatever your lover's reaction (and it may shift over time), healing requires that you stop pretending and tell the truth about your experience.

Lay the Groundwork First. Whether you are talking to a new or an old lover, there are certain things you can do to make difficult conversations about sex easier:

- Think about what you want to say ahead of time.
- Practice. Role-play the situation with your counselor or a friend. Imagine your lover's reaction. Keep practicing until you can say what you want to say.
- Work with your own feelings. Deal with your own fears outside of the relationship so you don't overwhelm your lover.
- Talk out of bed. You're both less vulnerable with your clothes on. It's easier to listen and talk on more neutral ground.
- Pick the time carefully. Don't initiate this conversation when your lover is on the way to work or otherwise preoccupied.
- Don't talk as a way to push your lover away. The goal of this conversation is to make you closer.
- And remember, you're worth it. You deserve loving support, an ally in your healing.

Pillow Talk. Communication doesn't always have to be heavy or serious. You can talk sweet talk, make jokes and laugh, or just share your feelings as you're going along.

One day about a month ago, Nancy was hugging me and being very affectionate, and she said, "This is how I feel when I am making love to you." Her words gave me a completely new sense of lovemaking. Something clicked in me, and I said, like a child, "Say it again." She did. Laughing and delighted, I said, "Say it again and again so it won't disappear."

A few nights later, we were making love and I asked her to repeat those words. She did, which was very moving to me. For the rest of the lovemaking, she expressed her feelings a lot, instead of stressing how turned on she was, which is what she had done in the past. I felt much more connected to my body and my feelings and to her, and the lovemaking was wonderful. I was able to stay in the present without having a flashback, and without fear.

Even if you don't have a specific problem to discuss, talking is a way to feel close and reassured.

I've always needed to talk, to hear a voice during lovemaking, but I think men can get thrown by this. I'd sometimes ask for a glass of juice or an extra blanket, just to make contact.

You may have felt uncomfortable asking to talk directly, but the need to connect is a real and valid one. Talking is another way of making love.

TAKE YOUR TIME

In exploring sexually with a lover, it's important to remember that you can stop anytime. You must allow yourself the freedom to do only what feels good, to go slowly enough so that you can feel, and to take breaks, just as you did with yourself.

If you get scared, tell your lover you're scared. This gives your lover the chance to slow down and connect with you, to offer comfort, to talk, to learn more about what scared you. At that point you might be ready to continue making love or you might want to get up and do something else.

If your lover does anything that makes you uncomfortable, say so. If you start to make connections between the way you respond now and what happened to you as a child, let your lover know. These realizations are an essential part of healing.

I always pee a little when I am very aroused. One time when this happened, I suddenly realized that when my brother molested me, peeing was my only line of defense. I used to think it might save me from making love. When I remembered all of this, I had to say to my lover, "I need to stop." And then we talked about it.

Often there are some sexual acts that feel okay, but others that don't; some places you're comfortable being touched and some that you're not. Tell your lover. Just because you say yes to one thing doesn't mean you're saying yes to everything possible. And just because you say yes once doesn't mean you have to say yes every time.

Talk. Share. Experience the level of closeness and touch that you can handle now. You can feel good with someone even if you don't sail through sex, even if you don't "finish." There *is* no finish, no goal except intimacy, honesty, and pleasure.

SPACING OUT

To me, making love is a duet in solos. It's nice that someone's there with me, but I'm not there with them. I'm there as an observer. I'm there all by myself, and I don't like it, and it's scary. I have a flight reaction: "I *have* to get out of here." And the more someone likes me, the more they're turned on to me, the more scared I get and the faster I'm out of my body. I start looking up and making patterns out of the cracks on the ceiling.

I would make love with my husband and be totally detached. I'd look over his shoulder and watch the football game: "Oh, it looks like they made another ten yards." I'd find as many ways as I could to space out during The Act. I'd look out the window and think, "God, aren't you done *yet?*" I don't remember much about it. I just wasn't there. And the thing I find incredible is that I so rarely got caught, that I could be in this relationship and I'd be the only one who knew I wasn't there. *Don't they know I'm gone? Can't you even see that I'm not here anymore?*

If you find yourself spacing out or splitting while you're making love, stop or slow down. Talk to your lover. Look your lover in the eyes. Say your lover's name. One woman kept a jar of potpourri on her night table and stopped to smell it when she felt herself drifting. That strong sensory jolt helped her stay present.

But don't keep going through the motions while you are disconnected from your feelings. Even though you may be scared, awkward, or embarrassed, come back. Give yourself—and your lover—the respect of honest communication.

FLASHBACKS WITH A PARTNER

I had flashbacks making love. Frequently. One time the light was a certain way in the room. My lover got up to go to the bathroom. I looked up and she was standing in the doorway. I knew it was her. But what I saw was my father standing in the doorway watching my brother molest me. It didn't matter that I knew it was my lover. It *was* my father. It *was* my brother.

If you find yourself bombarded by flashbacks, talking helps. One woman and her husband developed the code word "ghosts," which she would say whenever she had a flashback. This would alert him that they were no longer in present time and he could then respond appropriately.

What is appropriate will vary. Sometimes you may want your lover to leave you alone, so you can stay with the flashback and open it up, so you can gain information about the past. Other times, you will choose to stay in the present. At those times, you can say to your lover, "I want to stay here, with you. I don't want to go back to the past. Help me stay here. Talk to me. Call my name. Remind me who you are."

One woman had a lover who helped her stay in the present just by saying, "Open your eyes, Edith. Open your eyes." When she opened her eyes, she saw him, saw her own room, and was able to slip into the present, away from the flashbacks.

You have a right to feel good in your present experience, even if it means regular reality checks to remind yourself that the abuser is no longer in your bed. Even if you start off with, "Sex? Uh-oh," you can talk to yourself and say, "No. Now sex is fun. This is James. This is not my cousin."

BE CREATIVE

In a relationship in which one person is actively healing from sexual abuse, sex is rarely something that just goes on conventionally. By talking with your lover, you can explore possibilities that will work for both of you. There may be times when your lover wants to make love and you don't. You have the right to say no. But you can't simply say no every time.

If you do not want to make love, you might be willing to suggest alternatives: a massage, kissing and cuddling, a walk holding hands, sharing a bath, an intimate talk. Although these don't meet the specific desire for sex, they can fulfill the longing for closeness and intimacy. Many lovers will appreciate being able to share in *some* way, rather than being totally shut out. You may find yourself appreciating the closeness as well, once you know the touching is within safe, nonsexual boundaries. Often when survivors say no to sex, they are so enmeshed in their own guilt that they push their lovers further away. Finding other ways to be close is an opportunity to build intimacy and trust instead.

Variations on mutually involved sex can help ease the process of working through sexual difficulties. Sometimes you may not want to be touched sexually—you don't want that stimulation or intrusion. But you may be comfortable touching your lover. Or you may not want to touch your lover, but you would be open to being touched. Other times you may not want to give or receive, but would feel fine about holding your lover while he or she masturbates:

When I finally remembered the incest, it was as if this tidal wave hit me. I really didn't want to be touched. But I'd struggled so hard to get to a point where I was a little bit free sexually that I didn't want to stop. So I decided even though I didn't want to be touched, even though I didn't want to have sex, I wanted to find a new way to make love, so my lover's needs could get met, so that I could have my needs met, so we could still be intimate, and so I could still feel safe.

We explored that. We found safe ways to make love. Sometimes I didn't want to do anything. I needed to write, or to cry, or just to be quiet. Sometimes I didn't even want to be hugged while working on incest, but that wasn't too often.

What you want or don't want sexually will vary. Perhaps you could enjoy watching your lover, or talking to your lover on the phone, saying provocative things. Or sending a letter describing a lovely sexual fantasy you'd like to enjoy together someday. If you expand your preconceptions a bit, you'll find that more is possible than you thought:

We're the vibrator queens. They're great. I don't think it requires intense intimacy to have an orgasm. Sometimes you don't want to make love, you just want to have an orgasm. We've had a lot of fun. We've had dueling vibrators.

Being sexual in a couple doesn't mean you have to do it with them. Often what will happen is that she'll just hold me and I'll buzz off. I didn't know that you got to do that with someone else there. And it's great. It's terrific. It works.

TRY A LITTLE TEENAGE SEX

Sometimes survivors find they are blocked at a certain age sexually, as if they haven't been able to grow up beyond a particular stage. When you were abused, you either had sexuality thrust upon you before you were ready or you were exploited in the process of coming into your sexuality. If adult sexuality still feels overwhelming, it can be helpful to give yourself the opportunity to redo your sexual awakening, this time at your own pace.

Try proceeding slowly and from your own inner promptings. Don't kiss until you feel the desire to kiss in your lips. Don't pull someone closer until your body yearns for that. As Kyos tells us, the results can be quite nice:

I started a sexual relationship with a friend who is a survivor. When we touch, there's space for me to explore, to learn about touch. It's okay for me to be whoever I am, and for her to be whoever she is. It's like reclaiming the child on a sexual level. I learn by doing.

Whatever I feel when she touches me is the important thing, not how it matches some sexual idea. We're not there to get off on each other. We're there because we love each other. If I start sobbing right before I come, that's okay. If I suddenly get angry, that's okay. If I have a flashback, that's okay. It doesn't matter. It's in the safety to stay in the present moment with whatever is happening that the healing takes place.

Sexuality is not a problem anymore. It's an exciting process. We're exploring our passion together. Once I realized that my sexuality was my power, I was able to embrace it. I'm looking forward to a lot of fun practice for the rest of my life.

(For more of Kyos's story, see page 405.)

YOUR LOVER CAN BE YOUR ROLE MODEL

If sex is an exciting, rich part of life for your lover, free of conflicts and problems, you can hold this not as a threat to your limitations, but as a vision of what sex can be.

Making love was special for her. She wanted to know how to please me. She had so much patience. It was new. People really feel this way about sex? My God! I'd never seen anyone that passionate. I watched her for a year and a half. Eventually I decided I wanted to learn to be that free. That's what it was —freedom. So I slowly started to say, "It's okay."

She would do or say something, and I'd say, "Oh, that's nasty!"

And she'd say, "That's not nasty. It's a lie. Who told you that?"

I'd say, "Yeah, it's not nasty," but in my mind I was still saying, "That's nasty!"

Eventually I got to the point where I could say, "Well, maybe it's not *that* nasty." I started to relax.

SEE YOURSELVES AS ALLIES

Lovers can become allies, united in solving a difficult and painful problem, rather than adversaries blaming themselves or each other. When your needs and the needs of your lover differ, it does not mean that either of you is wrong or to blame. It is helpful if you can see yourselves as caring partners facing a mutual challenge.

Working It Out with My Lover: Catherine's Story

A lot of times what I wanted to do sexually and what I could do were light-years apart. I wanted to maintain a pleasant, fun, playful sexual relationship with Barbara. At the same time, our lovemaking became tense, nearly impossible, and finally impossible. It became burdened with so much meaning. If she didn't get off, I couldn't just chalk it up to one time and see that it wasn't so important. It was "Because I'm an incest victim, you don't like making love to me anymore." *Everything* was my fault. I blamed myself for all our sexual problems. I was hyperaware of every little change in our usual routine.

She had to reassure me constantly. I needed her to validate my decision to look at incest material, that it was worth going through a period of changed sexuality in order for me to be able to integrate what had happened in my life. She needed patience and more patience.

I needed a lot of affection that wasn't sexual. I needed a lot of verbal expressions of love so all the pressure wasn't sexual. I needed to know she didn't love me only because I fulfilled her sexual needs. I needed to know she wanted the person inside the body, not just my body. I needed reassurance that I was still the person she wanted to be with. I needed to know she wasn't eager for me to get over it.

We decided that if sex felt bad to either one of us, we would stop. I felt, "Phew! Now I don't have to do that anymore." I started saying no all the time. Barbara got furious: "You're *always* saying no! You're always the one that doesn't want it! What am I doing wrong? I'm sick of you going through your goddamn incest stuff! I'm not your Dad! I'm not your Mom! I'm not the people who hurt you!" That would just make it worse. I'd feel like I was a terrible person.

That started to turn around when I said, "Look, it's not my fault. I know you're angry. I'm angry too. I want there to be sexuality. Yes, you're angry. But go deal with it somewhere else. And if you can't take it, leave!" We had to start from scratch, rebuilding our sexual relationship from zero. It's scary. But we're doing it. And it's been worth it.

MAKING ROOM FOR DESIRE

There is no set amount of sexual desire that is "normal." Some people have sexual feelings many times in a day, others once a week, once a month, or once a year. And everyone experiences changes in their level of desire. These fluctuations can result from stress, accompany feelings of grief or depression, or coincide with major life changes (sobriety, the death of someone close to you, moving in with a lover). Such shifts are a natural part of life.

Survivors often experience a lack of desire as a direct result of their abuse. Your lack of desire might be a defense against unwanted sex, a sign of sexual fear, a symptom of being disconnected from your body, or a reaction to the fact that you see desire as dangerous.

I've never had a sexual desire. It's amazing that someone can have screwed as often as I have, and as many as I have, and in as many places as I have, and had no desire. People ask, "Well, why did you do it?" I did it to get rid of them. I thought it was appropriate to sleep with your husband. I had a multitude of reasons, and one of them was never because I wanted to.

You may never have had the chance to feel your own desire. When children are forced to be sexual at an early age, their natural sexual feelings don't have a chance to emerge. This pattern often continues into adulthood.

When I began to get in touch with the earliest abuse, I could no longer feel desire of my own, only desire called up by the needs and desires of someone else, in this case my lover. This was so terrifying that I would space out, feel pain, or fear, or just not want to make love in the first place. I wanted loving and affectionate and sometimes sensual closeness, but I wanted these to have their own integrity, and not just be a prelude to sex.

As a child, you experienced the desire of your abuser as being out of control. You were forced to comply with your abuser's needs. Desire was a weapon used against you. And so today you may be threatened by your own desire, afraid it too may be abusive.

I got to a point where I allowed myself to get very turned on when I was making love. I was being very aggressive and in touch with my passion. I was on top of my lover, and all of a sudden I had this creepy feeling that I'd become the abuser. I just froze and turned off right away. The next thing I knew,

I started having flashbacks of being raped as a child. It was horrible. I didn't have a sexual feeling for months afterward.

The fact that you have flashbacks or painful feelings while making love may eliminate your desire for sex. People want to have sex because it makes them feel good, connected, and whole. If sex for you dredges up pain, grief, and anguish, it makes sense that you experience a lack of desire.

If you never (or rarely) experience sexual desire, taking a break from sex can give you room to see if those feelings emerge naturally when you are not having to perform for somebody else (see "Time Out from Sex," page 251). One woman who'd opted for a period of celibacy said she was feeling sexual desire for the first time in her life, but added that the feelings began to arise in an embarrassing way:

Recently, I've just started to have sexual feelings like "God, I'd really like to make love with my therapist." God, am I attracted to her! I've told her. We talk about it. She's the keynote speaker in my sexual fantasies.

BROADEN YOUR CONCEPT OF DESIRE

JoAnn Loulan, author of *Lesbian Sex,* has creatively reshaped traditional concepts of desire in a way that is enlightening for all women.* Loulan says desire can be felt on an

* See the "Sexuality" section on p. 568 of the Resource Guide.

intellectual, emotional, or physical level. Intellectual desire is a decision that you want to make love. Emotional desire is wanting to make love with someone because you feel close to them. And physical desire is a specific feeling in your body that says you want to make love. These three types of desire can exist together or separately. All three are valid.

Loulan suggests making a list of things that the culture defines as desire (being turned on by your lover's naked body, wanting sex whenever you can get it, and so on). Then make a list of what desire is for you. Compare the two. It's likely there'll be differences. That's because the cultural stereotype doesn't have much to do with people's real feelings. What's important for you to focus on is your own internal experience of desire.

If you let go of the expectations you have for yourself and broaden your concept of desire, you may find that you have more sexual feelings than you thought.

Sex for me used to be what I did when I went into the bedroom with my husband. Now everything can be a turn-on. Like ice cream. I'm not talking about wanting sex ten times a day. It's how I respond to things, visually and tactilely. I'm much more in touch with my senses now. Life is so much more of a turn-on now.

WILLINGNESS

One of the most pervasive myths about sexuality is that you have to feel desire or excitement to enjoy making love. Loulan exploded this myth in her revised version of the female sexual response cycle. Previous models of women's sexual response cycle

(Masters and Johnson, Helen Singer Kaplan) cite either desire or excitement as the necessary starting point for sex.

In Loulan's model, the sexual response cycle begins with neither of these. It begins with the willingness to have sex. Willingness simply means that you are willing to enter into the sexual realm with yourself or another person and to be open to what you might find there. Willingness is an attitude. It doesn't commit you to anything more than beginning.

The concept of willingness as a legitimate entry point for sexual activity makes sex much more accessible to women who don't experience desire. It means you can have sex even if you're not feeling physical longing, emotional excitement, or desire of any kind. This is a radical and liberating approach to female sexuality.

The reasons you are willing may vary. You might be willing because you want the pleasure sex brings, because you know you will enjoy it once you get started, because you want to work on sexual issues with your lover, or because you want to practice making love to yourself.

For many women, the idea of willingness is a tremendous relief. Instead of asking yourself "Do I want sex?" or "What's wrong with me that I don't feel desire?" you can ask instead "Am I willing to begin?" The concept of willingness gives you the permission to explore sexually from exactly where you are. Instead of trying to generate desire out of nowhere, you can simply say, "Yes, I'm willing to try."

EXPANDED PLEASURE

In Loulan's model, willingness leads to any of the other stages in the sexual cycle—

shutting down, desire, excitement, engorgement, orgasm, or the final stage, pleasure. In this view of women's sexual response, pleasure is not dependent on orgasm, physical excitement, or arousal. Rather, it is a unique experience determined solely by the woman involved.

You may experience pleasure because you took the time to touch yourself in a loving way, because you were willing to engage in sexual activity after a long period of celibacy, or because you took good care of yourself when memories of your abuse came up. All these are reasons to feel good about sex. If you expand the acceptable reasons for getting into sex and widen your expectations of what you can get out of it, your pleasurable experiences will increase considerably.

SEXUAL FEAR

Many survivors are afraid of sex:

I'm fifty-three and I've never married. I have close friends, but as soon as somebody wants to be sexual with me, I get absolutely terrified. I've had sex twice in my life, not counting my uncle. The first time the guy couldn't penetrate me. With the second guy, I felt disgusting and dirty and couldn't wait for it to end. I never wanted to see him again. I feel really, really angry—not about the rape, but about my life! I'm fifty-three years old and I don't even know what it's like to have somebody be intimate with me, to have sex that I love.

As an abused child, your sexual feelings were wired directly into fear. Every time you felt aroused, you also felt afraid. Now you can't become aroused without fear. Or you might be terrified of the painful feelings that come up whenever you make love.

It seems to me that the memories are stored at the same level the passion is. If I don't make love, I don't connect with them. But whenever I open myself to feelings of passion, the memories are right there. It's a little like opening Pandora's box.

You might be afraid of being hurt or hurting someone else.

There's some kind of connection between passion and anger for me. As soon as I start feeling passionate, somehow anger gets involved, and I get afraid of being aggressive in a hurtful way. So often when I start feeling passionate, I shut right down, because I'm afraid of hurting my partner.

Or you may not want anyone that close to you, because you fear you'll be suffocated or overwhelmed by such intimacy. You may be afraid of losing control, losing touch with yourself or your own boundaries.

These fears are the natural result of being abused, and there are ways to work with them:

- **Go slow.** Back off to whatever is more comfortable.
- **Find a place in the middle.** Many survivors fluctuate between extremes—shutting down totally or trying for complete sexual abandon.
- **Stay in the present.** Pay attention to the sensation of touch.

- **Listen to your fear.** What is it trying to tell you? Is there something unsafe in your current environment? Or is this an old fear you want to overcome?
- **Find ways other than sex to connect deeply to yourself.** If you start to confront painful feelings and memories in other settings (like therapy), sex will no longer be the only access point for connecting deeply with yourself, and you will gradually break the connection between passion, letting go, intensity, and abuse.
- **Check in with your lover.** If you're afraid you're being abusive when you have strong sexual feelings, ask your lover if he or she feels abused. (Your lover probably likes your passion.)
- **Push yourself a little.** If you want to make love and you're afraid, push yourself a little. Stay in touch with yourself and your partner. Communicate like crazy. Be prepared for a lot of feelings. Don't expect simple sex.
- **Stop if you need to.** Sometimes the gap between what you *want* to experience and what you *are* experiencing gets too wide. If your terror is too great, take a break. Find another way to be close.

UGH, GENITALS!

If you were abused by a man, you may find male genitals scary or repulsive, as Gizelle did:

When I start making love again, I have a feeling it's going to be difficult. You know, in my fantasies, when I imagine having a lover, I'm making love to him and everything is going along beautifully until he takes out his penis.

And then I vomit all over the floor. Literally, in my fantasy, I vomit all over the floor!

So whoever I'm with is going to have to have an understanding of that and a secure enough sense of his own maleness that he isn't going to take it personally. He's going to have to be someone who can help me very gently work through my sexuality.

(For more of Gizelle's story, see page 461.)
It may help to set aside a quiet time, perhaps just to look at your lover's body.

I find playing doctor really helps: "Oh look, it curves to the left," or "I wonder what'll happen if I touch it this way." When I look at his penis when it's not erect, it's small and soft, not so much like a weapon ruling him and me.

Try giving your lover a whole body massage, genitals included. This is not as a prelude to sex, but rather an opportunity for you to feel and explore his genitals in a safe way—a chance to realize that although his genitals are constructed in the same way as the genitals that violated you as a child, they are *not* those same genitals and will not violate you now. If your lover becomes sexually aroused, back off from touching, talk about your feelings, and continue to share in this exploration, which can help you to diffuse your fear in a safe, controlled way.

If your lover is a woman, you can get to know her body just as you have been getting to know your own. If you were abused by a woman, the same process applies. Become familiar with your lover's body. Learn about it, demystify it.

I HAVE TO LOVE THEM TOO?

Although many survivors manifest difficulties sexually, the more basic issue is often trust. As one survivor put it, "It's difficult to talk about sex without talking about intimacy. That's one of the problems."

I've always had the physical and the emotional separate, so I can always fuck men. I like to call it that because I like to call things what they are. I always knew I wasn't making love to them.

If you were abused by someone you loved and trusted, sex, love, trust, and betrayal became linked in profound ways. Many women have been able to maintain sexual relationships with some satisfaction until they fell deeply in love. Then the bottom dropped out and their fear rose like crazy. Sex was okay when they kept their feelings out of it. But sex with deep feeling brought back all the ancient pain. It was too much like the original abuse.

The image I have of my husband is that he reached through some sort of window in my life and pulled me out. He was being nonjudgmental. He was loving me unconditionally. Here was love coming at me without any expectations. We were really good friends. We got along well. I liked his temperament.

After we met, I went into a two-month anxiety attack. My stomach was always in knots. The closer we got emotionally and the more vulnerable we were to each other, the less I could be present when we were making love. There were points when the sexuality

was very present, but then we were communicating less. I felt that if I gave all of myself over, I'd lose myself and I wouldn't be able to get me back. So I kept parts of myself inaccessible.

Some women have not even remembered the abuse until they were in a loving, trusting relationship. They needed that much security to allow themselves the memories.

I met my husband eight months after my father died. I'd never had a constructive, positive relationship before. He was someone I'd really been waiting for. And it was about a year later that I had my first memory.

Understanding these patterns is essential. Then you can stop breaking up as soon as relationships become meaningful. You can see your difficulties as signs that this is, indeed, an important relationship in which you feel deeply, a special opportunity to restore your trust and inner security.

CONTROL: "WE HAVE TO DO IT MY WAY"

One common element among survivors is the need to control the sexual experience, sometimes to the extent of controlling every detail. You may feel comfortable only if you are in certain positions, if the lights are on, if you initiate, if it's morning, if it's *not* morning, and so on. Although this is limiting and sometimes difficult for your lover, it is essential for you. You need to set your limits. You need to be in an environment in which you can feel secure enough to relax. In short, you need control.

> Sex is the act of being out of control. It's wonderful, but it terrifies me to give up control. It's the approach that stops me. I have to stop and think, "Do I want this to be happening? Or is it because someone is approaching me and I'm letting it happen?" If I initiate it's much easier. Then I'm the one feeling sexual, I *know* I'm feeling sexual, and I'm pretty sure I'm not being molested.

Recognizing and fulfilling your need for control, without criticizing yourself, gives you power.

> It was very threatening for me just to have a male reaching out and touching me. The fact that someone was coming to me wanting something was hard. Our therapist suggested that he ask my permission before he touch me. We did that for a while, and then it felt less like an attack. It allowed me to make the differentiation: "This isn't my father coming after me. This is my husband."

As you feel more able to be both sexual and protected, you will find that some of the elements you once needed to control absolutely are no longer as critical.

YOU'RE NOT IN THIS ALONE

While there may be short periods when you need to exercise total control over sex, ultimately you have to engage in some give-and-take with your lover.

One day, our therapist asked Roger, "How do you feel when Karen's not responding to you, when she's closed off?" And he started talking about being flat-out terrified. To hear him talk about being terrified that our relationship was going to end made me stop and realize that I wasn't the only one who was going through terrible, awful feelings. Here was another human being, who I loved very deeply, who was bleeding, and some of that was a wound I had inflicted by being so wrapped up in myself.

While there may be essential stages in your healing when you are oblivious to the needs and feelings of anyone but yourself, the fact is that your pain—and your healing—affects everyone close to you. Nowhere is this more apparent than in the realm of sexuality. Lovers are often confused, hurt, frustrated, and furious with the sexual changes survivors go through. They may be enraged at having to deal with sex in such a conscious way. They may take your sexual problems personally. Or they may pressure you, threatening to leave the relationship.

> All along my lover has felt rejected by my sexual fears, rejected and angry. Her anger has become a steady bass, louder and more relentless and ready to lash out, to which my burgeoning sexual self-awareness became a weak treble. She asks too frequently, "How long will it be? *Promise* me it will be better soon. I don't see why you can't be better now. You don't know what you are missing. You don't understand what I am going through." In the face of these questions, I felt less like making love.

She got angrier. Now I don't feel like making love at all. Two nights ago she told me she wants a nonmonogamous relationship, she wants to look for someone else.

While you'd probably like an all-giving, totally understanding, completely patient lover while healing sexually, this is not realistic. Even the most supportive lover has personal feelings and needs. Although you can't force yourself to be sexual, you do have to make room for your lover's feelings, as fully as you possibly can. This is essential if you want the relationship to survive.

- **Be willing to listen.** Although your lover should have other people to talk to, you need to hear his or her frustrations and anger at least some of the time.
- **Validate your lover's feelings.** Your lover has a right to have needs, to be hurt, angry, or frustrated. You would too, if the situation were reversed.
- **Put yourself in your lover's shoes.** If you can't imagine being upset about not having sex, think of something important to you —like communication—and imagine how you'd feel if your lover wouldn't talk to you, and wasn't sure when he or she might feel like it.
- **Don't condemn your lover for wanting sex.** The fact that right now you see sex as a problem or a threat doesn't mean it is. Your lover's desire is a healthy, vital part of life.
- **Don't blame your lover.** This is all the abuser's fault, remember?
- **Be as consistent as you can.** At times this may be impossible, but it helps if you keep your limits as clear and consistent as possible, so your lover doesn't feel like a puppet on a string.

- **Communicate.** Let your lover know what's going on.
- **Let your lover know you're committed to changes over time.** Say it a lot. Reassure your lover that you want your sexual life to change.
- **Say the good things.** If you'd like to be able to make love, if you find your lover attractive, say so—frequently.
- **Give as much as you possibly can.** Then stretch just a little bit more. If you can't give sex, then give something as close to sex as you can.
- **Take breaks from dealing with sex.** Don't forget—there's more to life, and to your relationship, than sex.

USING SEX TO MEET OTHER NEEDS

While most survivors' sexual difficulties have to do with not wanting sex, others experience another range of problems: wanting sex all the time and trying to use sex to meet all needs, including nonsexual ones.

After my divorce, I was really into frantic fucking. I think that what I felt was some kind of release, some feeling of being held or comforted. But it was so fleeting I had to keep doing it over and over again.

When you want closeness, intimacy, or communication, when you want to feel you are loved and worthwhile and cared for, when you're unhappy, disappointed, or angry, you ask for sex instead. It makes sense that survivors who received all their attention and affection sexually as children now sexualize even nonsexual needs.

Anyone who ever loved me had a sexual relationship with me. So if you didn't make a pass at me, you didn't love me.

Abusers used sex irresponsibly to avoid their real feelings and needs. And a lot of survivors have learned that lesson all too well.

I've noticed that whenever I felt lonely or scared or had a need to connect with my husband, I would immediately interpret it as a sexual need, even though it was clearly an emotional need. I wanted to be made love to all the time. I was very seductive, trying to get sex I really didn't want at all. I would feel real stormy and out of control and freaked out if I couldn't get it. It felt like a powerful way to behave, but it really came from a distorted sense of my own desires.

It is possible to stop using sex to meet all your needs. Begin by paying attention to how you feel when you want sex. Ask yourself if the need or longing you feel is a desire for sex specifically, or whether it might be one or more other needs that you habitually try to meet through sex. Try to assess exactly what you want. Is it closeness, intimacy, relaxation, approval, validation, power, the gratification of pleasing someone, distraction from worries or problems, security, good feelings in your body?

In *Getting Free,** Ginny NiCarthy breaks sexuality down into five components: affection, sensuality, eroticism, intimacy, and ro-

mance. Of the five, eroticism (which she defines as "orgasm and the explicitly sexual arousal and tension associated with it") is the only need that can't be approached in ways other than sex itself.

If your pattern is to try to fill a wide variety of needs sexually, it will be difficult, but rewarding, to try other approaches. Sometimes just cuddling will actually give you more of what you want than sex. Sometimes an honest talk is more satisfying. Sometimes you'll feel better swimming, dancing, going to a concert, or painting a picture. The idea here isn't to stop enjoying sex, but to broaden your repertoire of ways to meet your needs, thereby giving you more freedom and more creativity.

It is also a clear message to yourself that you are more than just a sexual being. Although sex can be a wonderful and amazing aspect of life, it is only one aspect. You are a whole person, of many aspects, and you deserve to have access to them all.

REPEATING THE ABUSE

Many survivors have repeated their victimization. Some have married abusive lovers or had sex with many lovers in contexts that ranged from dangerous to humiliating to dull. Survivors have allowed others unlimited access to their bodies, and have been hurt again and again.

PROSTITUTION

Over a million women in the United States earn all or part of their income by

---

* See the "Domestic Violence, Rape, and Sexual Harassment" section on p. 567 of the Resource Guide.

working as prostitutes. Many of these women are victims of sexual abuse.

Prostitution was another way of becoming a victim. At the time, I was doing it because it was the only way I could see to earn a living and support my babies. I was too young to be emancipated. I wasn't getting public assistance. I had kids who needed diapers and food, and prostitution was the only way I could think to get it.

When survivors become prostitutes, strippers, or topless dancers, they are repeating an abusive pattern.* You may feel sex is all you're good for. You may reason that now you'll get paid for what was once stolen from you. But once again, you find yourself in a role where your value is solely sexual and in which you are sexual, not basically for your own gratification, but for someone else's.

After I left my second husband and my children, I came to California and within three weeks hooked up with a

very violent pimp who turned me out on the streets. I was twenty-four at the time. I was a prostitute for five years. They were very abusive years. I ran away from my first pimp, but I couldn't run away from the street. When I look back, it's hard for me to understand how I did that to myself. *I didn't know I didn't have to.* It was too close to my childhood.

Women say they're on the streets by choice, but it's not really a choice; *it's their only option.* I'd been set up for it. My father was abusive and he would pay me for sex. He would give me something afterwards that I wanted, something he hadn't let me have before. He taught me, "That's all you deserve. That's all you're good for." Being out on the streets was just a continuation of the same pattern.

If you are currently working as a prostitute, there are areas in which you can actively move forward in your healing. However, your sexual healing will be severely limited until you stop.

VIOLENCE AND SEX

For many women who were abused in violent circumstances, the connection between sex and violence is strong.

When I was little, my mother would start yelling and screaming and throwing things from one end of the room to the other. And what that usually meant was that I could count on my father

* Many prostitutes have organized politically to gain the protections they need so desperately in their work. Groups such as C.O.Y.O.T.E. (Call Off Your Old Tired Ethics) have worked hard to make prostitution a reputable, safe profession. While some prostitutes see their work as positive and nonvictimizing, for women with a history of child sexual abuse, prostitution is inevitably going to repeat aspects of the abuse.

The Council for Prostitution Alternatives provides direct services, financial assistance, counseling, and advocacy to women escaping prostitution. They can be reached at (503) 282-1082, 1811 NE 39th Ave., Portland, OR 97212.

being in my room later. So there was a connection established between violent scenes and sex. And that's been repetitive in my adult life. It's the "break up to make up" syndrome. Sex is always better after a fight. That feels really familiar. I know when I was beat up by my last lover, one of the things that really frightened me was that when I was on the floor and she was kicking me, I flashed back on my mother. I had no idea who was hitting me. My lover pulled me up by the hair, and I knew at that very moment that it could only end in two ways. One was me taking the door to the right, which was outside. Or I could take the door to the left, which was to the bedroom.

Changing this pattern is essential to creating a healthy sexuality. If you are in a relationship where violence and sex are linked, you will need to break the connection between the two. Or you may need to leave the relationship altogether. If the combination of sex and violence is exciting to you, it will require systematic work to change your orientation. (See "A Truly Chosen Sexuality," page 273.)

ABUSE AND FANTASIES

Many survivors can feel sexual arousal or have orgasms only if sex incorporates some aspect of abuse. One woman could climax only if she imagined her father's face. Another only if she imagined being bound or raped. Another only if she was stimulated in the way her neighbor stimulated her as a child. Another only if she fantasized being the abuser herself. Many masturbate while reading incest literature.

For weeks on end I compulsively read about incest—*If I Should Die Before I Wake* in one hand and my vibrator in the other.

Most women feel ashamed to admit they have such feelings or fantasies. A fifty-six-year-old psychotherapist, who was tortured with enemas when she was a child, explains:

I felt grossed out by my own sexuality. At times I've felt that my sexuality was grotesque and that it was sick and that it would land me in the hospital. When other people bring up the grosser details of their sexual abuse, I'm fascinated. Everything else just pales and I go right straight to it like a starving dog.

I have tremendous sado-masochistic fantasies which are just beginning to come out after seven and a half years of therapy. That's because of the intense shame. I have hospital fantasies, concentration camp fantasies, slicing people's bodies up fantasies. So naturally I had to keep my sexuality, my life energy, bottled up, because I felt so ashamed and terrified of where that stuff would take me.

When the fantasies first came up in therapy, I experienced a lot of destructive rage at myself. I wanted to kill myself. I was so horrified that those were the things that turned me on. I just wonder if that isn't really the hard core, the pivot of this whole thing—the shame and horror and utter self-despair about being turned on by terribly abusive, sadistic situations.

If abuse and sadism turn you on, you aren't to blame. You did not create these fantasies out of nothing. They were forced on you just as intrusively as those hands, penises, and leers were forced on you during the original abuse.

The context in which we first experience sex affects us deeply. Often there is a kind of imprinting in which whatever is going on at the time becomes woven together. So if you experienced violation, humiliation, and fear at the same time as you experienced arousal and pleasurable genital feelings, these elements twisted together, leaving you with emotional and physical legacies that link pleasure with pain, love with humiliation, desire with an imbalance of power. Shame, secrecy, danger, and the forbidden feel thrilling.

SM

Some women have acted out these linkages in sado-masochistic (SM) scenarios, claiming the right to feel sexual excitement and release by whatever means works. Advocates of SM argue that in mutually consensual SM, one can experiment with power. But for women who are working to heal beyond their conditioning to abuse, participating in SM—sex that involves pain, humiliation, or a situation in which one person wields power over the other—makes no sense. It would be like an alcoholic trying to heal from alcoholism by drinking only in special environments created for that purpose.

Saphyre, who was involved in SM for a while, says it felt to her like a self-betrayal:

At the time I thought SM was opening me up to my sexuality, but in retrospect I can see it wasn't. People talk a lot

of propaganda about SM. I believed a lot of the rhetoric. Looking back, it was counterproductive to healing. It contributed to me *not* dealing with my sexuality because I didn't have to stay with what I was feeling in the moment. I was playing a role.

People say SM is about taking risks and having trust. It wasn't a risk to me, being a bottom. I'd already been there in real life. I'd already been at someone's mercy in reality. How could playing a game be a risk? What's a risk for me is being in the moment with what I'm feeling when someone touches me. That's a risk for me. That's what takes a lot of trust. Not SM. I think SM is a way of avoiding sexuality.

I don't think SM is ever confined to the bedroom. In my relationship, it went from being a game that was fun to a game that trapped us. It's got to affect the rest of the relationship. When you're doing SM, you're practicing how to treat your lover like shit. How can that be healing?

Whether you're into SM or you're not into SM, you can still get into society's game—one kind of sex is good and the other kind of sex is bad. I'm going for something that's different: being in the present moment when someone touches me, accepting my own passion without having to role-play to do it.

A TRULY CHOSEN SEXUALITY

You can release yourself from the linkage of pain, humiliation, and sexual excitement. It is possible to change your conditioning, to disconnect those associations, to create an authentic, truly chosen sexuality that embodies passion and excitement.

- **Make the commitment that you want to change.** Saying "I don't want to do this anymore" is a powerful beginning.
- **Back up your commitment with action.** Stop engaging in sex that is abusive in any way.
- **Start with yourself.** Work with your fantasies as Saphyre did (see below).
- **Practice staying present in the moment.** Allow yourself to actually feel your feelings without using fantasies to take you somewhere else. Remember, there is no goal.
- **Talk honestly about your experience.** Even though it's difficult to talk about these things, it is essential to do so if you are to overcome your shame and move on. Talk to your therapist, a trusted friend, and your lover.

Changing the Tapes: Saphyre's Story

When Saphyre started working on incest, her only way of getting turned on was through rape and SM fantasies. She decided she wanted to get rid of them.

I don't believe we're born with our sexuality that way. I knew I had to start from a place of not feeling guilty about the fantasies, in the same way that I stopped feeling guilty about the incest. They were both coming from the same place. Letting go of the guilt was really important. But I wanted to take it further than that. I wanted to stop having them.

I started masturbating more, paying attention to exactly what the core feeling was that made me come. The characters could change, the costumes could change, but what was the core feeling? It was "I'm totally overcome by passion. I'll do anything you want." It was the only way I knew how to deal with my passion. I couldn't afford to take responsibility for it without being overpowered.

I kept working with those fantasies until I could really identify that feeling. The next step was learning to isolate the orgasm, the passion, the intensity, from the fantasy. I had to undo the programming. It was hard to separate the two. I didn't have any support. I was doing this in isolation. I didn't know what the outcome would be, and I wasn't even sure of what I was doing, but I wasn't about to wait till someone came along and told me what to do. I had the belief that I could change.

It helped for me to feel that I *deserved* to have passionate feelings, and that they didn't have to be linked to those fantasies. I came to the point where I really understood that they weren't *my* fantasies. They'd been imposed on me through the abuse. And gradually, I began to be able to have orgasms without thinking about the SM, without picturing my father doing something to me.

Once I separated the fantasy from the feeling, I'd consciously impose other powerful images on that feeling—like seeing a waterfall. If they can put SM on you, you can put waterfalls there instead. I reprogrammed myself. Instead of having to say "I'll do anything you want," I would see a waterfall and have the same intensity of feeling.

The Gift of Water
By Jeanne Marie Vaughn

This sexual fantasy began as a conscious attempt to replace old negative images with new nurturing and healing ones. I picked the thing that absolutely gave me the most pleasure, and that was water. My favorite place to have sex with myself is in the bathtub. This piece unfolded as I took the positive aspects of what worked for me and tried to reinforce them. The excerpt that follows is a portion of a short story which I wrote for myself. More than just a sexual fantasy, it has become a meditation.

I am in a rowboat in the middle of the ocean. It is early morning. The water is a brilliant turquoise blue. There is a calm which pervades the day and I comfort in the slight rocking motions of the boat. I am seated bare-chested in the small craft, wearing a loosely wrapped cloth garment around my waist. I feel the salt in the air, on my skin, in my mouth. A breeze gently scatters a strand of hair across my face. My nostrils widen as I fill my lungs with the salt sea air.

I notice the rhythm of my muscles rowing, the slap of the oars. The sun is warm on my nipples, the length of my back, my shoulders. Small beads of sweat begin to form under my arms and then roll slowly, teasingly, down my sides. My lungs swell with the exertion and I rejoice in the light, the sound, the smell of the morning.

I am nearing the island. I have come here before and I will come here again. It is a place to which women return over and over.

I gather up the fabric of my sarong, tying it between my legs, and step into the water, pulling the boat behind me onto the shore. I head into the jungle. The air is humid and hot, the aroma of the vegetation thick and heady. Barefoot, I wonder momentarily if I need to watch for thorns on the trail. The earth itself answers me—the path is well trodden. Here I am safe.

I continue on for a while and then emerge into a clearing. Before me is a small grotto encircled by a pool. Overhead a thin stream of water flows from a bamboo tube to a solitary point below; it spills over an ancient slab of stone partly submerged in the water. This is an altar, a place of offering, and I have come to offer myself.

Dropping my garment on the moss, I wade into the pool and position my body on the stone. As I continue breathing, I lower myself until I am reclining on the stone. It is warm and rounded on my back, molded over the centuries by the bodies of the women who have lain here in this spot.

Slowly I spread my legs, opening myself up, positioning myself under the stream of water which falls down, caressing my vulva. I feel the heat, the fire of life, creep into my solar plexus, spreading warmly into my thighs and buttocks. The water laps at my clitoris like waves nibbling and rolling against the shore. I take in the water as it mingles with the light of the sun; they fill me completely, cleansing, healing, empowering. I surge and swell with these gifts of water and light.

TAKE A BREAK AND LIGHTEN UP

Sometimes as you work to change sexually, the process seems grim. You're fed up with "trying to do it." Words like "spontaneity" and "enjoyment" sound foreign. This is when it helps if you can dig out your sense of humor and lighten up.

Sometimes we take on this real hardworking approach to making love, so sincere and serious and lacking in spontaneity. We focus in a very narrow way. We don't laugh. We don't tickle. We don't play. It's very cut-and-dried. And that can be terribly boring and frustrating. What we're trying to do now is consciously lessen that, to be more playful in bed, to just have fun.

SEXUAL HEALING OVER TIME

Sexual healing takes a long time, but gradually it happens. What you experience sexually today is not what you'll experience a year or two years from now. What seems like a terrible problem now may be just a minor annoyance later on. Or sex may get easier for a time, and then hard again, when you hit a deeper layer.

Sex also has a lot to do with the level of intimacy in your relationship, the dynamics in the relationship, even the particular lover you have. Adrienne has had several lovers since she started working on sexual abuse issues, and her experience has been dramatically different with each one:

Before I met Alan, I'd had lots of lovers. The sex wasn't fantastic, but I enjoyed myself, and it was never a big issue. But Alan was the first man I really fell for, and somehow the combination of love and sex did me in. I started to have a hard time with sex, and since sex was really important to Alan, he got more and more upset. He pressured me a lot and the pressure just shut me down entirely. It got so bad, we broke up. I felt like a failure.

After Alan, I was afraid to get involved with anyone. I felt like I wasn't good enough, that something was really wrong with me. But then I met Lance, and after being friends for a while, we became lovers. I'd warned him about my problems, but he didn't seem to care. Lance was a wonderful lover and never pressured me, and the sex was great between us. He gave me lots of room to explore and let me control the whole thing. I did a lot of healing with him, and left the relationship feeling good about my sexuality.

I thought I had this sex thing licked then, so when I got involved with John, I didn't even tell him. We got into it hot and heavy, and I opened up to feelings of passion I'd never allowed before, and then, boom! Two months later I started having new memories. And sex was the furthest thing from my mind. It was bad. I thought I was finished with all this stuff. But there it was again. At least I didn't hate myself this time. I had a better idea of what to do.

Your experience of sex can change within a single relationship as well. With a new lover, there's often a passionate rush that obscures problems. But as the relationship settles, sexual issues may need attention again. As you risk more emotional intimacy, you may start to shut down sexually. Or you may find that as your trust grows and deepens, you heal on a deep body level, surpassing even your own expectations.

Because it takes a long time to heal sexually, you may wonder whether you're making progress. But even though the process has ups and downs, you are headed in the right direction. If you are putting steady, consistent effort into developing a fulfilling sexuality, have patience, accept where you are, and trust your capacity to heal.

I've had to learn to accept myself. I know I've had experiences that maybe made me a little different, and that might have made my sexual appetite more, might have made my sexual appetite less, it might have made my sexual appetite different, but so what! It's me! Let me enjoy who I am! I feel that within every woman there are a thousand and one women, and it's okay to let each one of them out. The partner will just have to deal. That's all there is to it. Sexuality is not just about getting up and humping every night. It's about exploring who you are and not being afraid of that.

Although sex was used against you in bitter ways, you can reclaim your sexuality and shape it to reflect your own deepest values.

Sex can be a powerful surge toward creation, like writing a song or choreographing a dance. All of these require absolute attention and presence; all have that great intensity; all bring something new into existence. If you choose to share that opening with a lover, it's a risk, a thrill, and a deep affirmation of trust. You affirm vitality, joy, connection. Your passion becomes a passion for life.

Even without a lover, reclaiming your sexuality is worth it. One older survivor went through a long period of struggle before she realized why:

I don't expect I'll ever be in that kind of relationship again. And just thinking about having a sexual feeling makes me practically want to kill myself. But there's a way I've been looking at it recently—that sex is a part of life, part of being alive. It's a kind of life energy. And even if all I ever do is just feel the feelings in my own body, even if I never act on them, it's still worth it. Can you understand? It's like saying yes to life, yes to being alive.

ON BEING A LESBIAN AND A SURVIVOR

I've heard forever and ever, "Oh, you're a dyke because your Daddy did this to you." It's a comment that makes me mad. It's a way that people take choices away from me. Maybe if I was a murderer, you could say that was connected to the incest. If there was going to be a correlation, it would be between the incest and my capacity for violence or hatred, not with my capacity for love.

If you are a lesbian, what you are trying to heal from is the destructive effects of having been sexually abused, not the fact that you're a lesbian. This should be obvious, but some survivors still believe that there is something wrong with them that caused them to be lesbian—that if they hadn't been damaged sexually, they'd be heterosexual. And that it's better to be heterosexual.

I had believed that I was a lesbian because I had been so badly abused by my father. I thought maybe it was a point of being stuck in my emotional growth. I thought that until I met a lesbian who came from a happy home, who had never been abused in any way. She was well balanced. Her family accepted that she was a lesbian. She never had any problems with it, and that's when I realized my lesbianism didn't have to have a cause. It's got nothing to do with what happened to me.

It is true that being abused by men has influenced some women to relate sexually and emotionally to women rather than men. However, no one becomes a lesbian solely because she was abused by a man. After all, many heterosexual women were abused by men, and they continue to choose men as their mates and sexual partners. If abuse were the determining factor in sexual preference, the lesbian population would be far greater than it is now.

I'm a lesbian because I love women, not because I hate men. I'm not a separatist. I have a male child who I think is terrific. There are men in my life I care a great deal for. I'm not a man-hater. In fact, I think heterosexual women have a lot more reason to hate men than I do.

Being a lesbian is a perfectly healthy way to be, not another effect of the abuse you need to overcome. One workshop participant commented wryly on this search for the pathological reasons behind lesbianism: "If I'm a lesbian because I was abused, at least something good came out of it."

If You're Not Sure

If you're not sure about your sexual preference, give yourself some time for things to settle. It's okay not to know, or to be in transition.

If you haven't been in touch with yourself sexually—because you've been splitting, pretending, or not very conscious—it may take some time to find out what your true responses are. Try to tolerate the ambiguity of not having a set sexual orientation for a while.

Sexual orientation is a continuum. A small percentage of people are exclusively heterosexual or homosexual. Most are somewhere in the middle. Some lesbians say they were born that way; others that it was a choice they made. Women explore their attraction and love for other women at many times in their lives—in adolescence, in early adulthood, after years of marriage, after menopause. The decision is up to you.

However, if you hope becoming a lesbian will magically solve all your problems with sex and intimacy, this isn't the case. While becoming a lesbian may make things possible for you that weren't possible before, it's not a panacea.

If you are rethinking your sexual preference, consider what you want in an intimate relationship. Whom do you seem to get that from? See what it's like to relate to individual people. Stay open to how you feel moment by moment. Gradually you'll get an indication.

If you think you might be a lesbian but the idea scares or disturbs you, what you're feeling is natural. It's common to have doubts and questions in the coming-out process. Try reading about lesbians who are comfortable with themselves. Read coming-out stories. Talk to people you know to be unbiased, who will support you in whatever choice you make.

The most important thing is to take your time. Don't pressure yourself. It's better not to label yourself prematurely. And if you don't want to, you don't have to label yourself at all.

If You're Not Comfortable Being a Lesbian

You may not be comfortable being lesbian because it's a sexual identity, and you're not comfortable with sex. You feel that being a lesbian puts more emphasis on the sexual part of you than you want. But there is more to be a lesbian than sex. There's music, art, politics. There's a culture, a supportive community. There's an emotional, philosophical, and spiritual connection to women.

The context of your life can also make you uncomfortable about being a lesbian. Are you in the closet, surrounded by homophobic people (people who are afraid of lesbians and gay men)? Do you have role models—lesbians who are comfortable and relaxed in their sexual identity? Are there places you can go where it's safe to be visible as a lesbian? Hold hands with your lover? Feel that you're not the only one?

If you're uncomfortable, it may be because you feel you can't afford to be open with anyone around you. While this is stressful for any lesbian, it can be particularly painful for survivors. The secrecy, isolation, shame, and fear of exposure are very close to the feelings you had when you were abused. So if being a lesbian is the second secret you've had to keep, it can bring up unresolved feelings of terror, isolation, or pain.

Even if you don't come out publicly, there are things you can do to counteract your isolation, no matter where you are. Subscribe to lesbian journals and magazines. Get on the mailing list for women's music festivals and conferences (see the "Lesbians" section of the Resource Guide for resources). Reach out. You're not alone. For many women, their lesbian identity is a strong, positive anchor in their lives:

When I first started dealing with the abuse, I questioned everything. I mean *everything*. The only thing I was sure of was my choice to be a lesbian. That felt like the one healthy, sane thing about me. It was a relief to have something that felt solid!

CHILDREN AND PARENTING

My kids gave me hope. My kids would laugh, be crazy and stupid, and pull me out of it: "Okay, back to the future." Feeling totally responsible for these kids has really been an incentive to get better. I wouldn't have made it without them. I wanted them to have a responsible adult taking care of them, to be able to say, "This is where it stops. This is the end of it."

Parents are not the only adults who have nurturing family relationships with children. Many of the concepts in this chapter also apply to extended family and to friends who are chosen family.

Being around children can be an inspiring and challenging part of healing. Children can teach you that the abuse wasn't your fault. They can help you get in touch with the child within. They can motivate you to heal, to keep on keeping on. They offer you an opportunity to have a positive experience of family life. But children also bring up unresolved feelings. They can restimulate memories, put you face-to-face with the ways you're like your parents, or remind you of your own vulnerability.

CHOOSING TO HAVE CHILDREN— OR NOT

For many women, motherhood is not a choice. Yet increasingly, women are consciously deciding whether or not to have children. For survivors, this choice sometimes relates to their own healing.

One survivor, who is trying to get pregnant, says: "I think having a child is going to be really healing in itself. I'll be able to interrupt the cycle."

Another has made a definite decision not to have children:

> Here I'd been meandering around my entire life in a gray fog and only living half a life, and the idea of stopping my life to have a child, now that I'd finally come back to life, was more than I could bear. It's too exciting being alive now. So my husband had a vasectomy.

And another isn't ready yet, but may be in the future:

> If I did have kids I'd want to make sure it was many more years into my healing process. I don't feel capable of giving enough love and attention. I'm wrapped up in trying to nurture my own child. I already have a child, and it's me.

You may find that your feelings change as you move through the healing process. Coming to terms with your own childhood can radically alter your perspective. You may have always wanted children, but come to realize that what you were really longing for was the healing of your own childhood pain. Or you may have been afraid of kids, only to find that now you enjoy them.

CHILDREN AS TEACHERS

One of the most delightful parts of being a parent is the way children are always trying to snag you into playing.

> The real reason I decided to have kids now is that I get to have fun! I never had that in my own childhood.

Many survivors never really had a childhood. You were expected to assume adult responsiblities or to meet unreasonable demands. Even when you were allowed to play, you may not have felt very playful, carrying your secret burden. But now you get a second chance at fun. You can romp in the park, swing on the swings, dress up for Halloween.

For thirty-five-year-old Ella, having children has been a integral part of her healing process:

> I nurture them and I get it back. They love me, and you can't coerce that out of a kid. You can coerce sex out of kids, but you can't coerce something as pure as love. That's what keeps me going all the time. I look at my kids and know that I really *am* a survivor. Being able to parent gives me a perspective on how well I really am. Just the way they are shows me that I'm okay. It makes me feel that I'm a real winner. I can have anything I want. I can do absolutely anything. Being around them shows me that all the time.

Children challenge you to grow. Steps that you may hesitate to take on your own behalf, you will sometimes take for your child.

I have to learn how to do it first, so I can say, "See, watch Mommy. Mommy's strong. She can do it. You're strong. You can do it too." Things like expressing anger. Things like letting myself cry. Talking about someone hurting my feelings. Learning to reach out for comfort. I used to keep it all inside, and so did Christy. But we're changing now. Both of us.

Some women who were abused, neglected, or poorly parented have comfortable relationships with children and face basically the same problems that anyone faces in trying to be a good parent. For other survivors, the difficulties are more formidable. They have problems setting appropriate boundaries, or they repeat aspects of the inadequate or abusive parenting they experienced as children. As parents, they often feel confused, resentful, or overwhelmed.

The best way to learn parenting skills is through example. If you had supportive parents yourself, good parenting tends to come more naturally. But even if your parents weren't good role models, you can still learn to be the kind of parent you want to be.

LEARNING TO PARENT

When Ellen had her first child, she had no idea how hard it would be:

The lack of sleep, the twenty-four-hour-a-dayness of it, the shift of putting another person's needs before my own, just stunned me. And no one was applauding me. I'd gotten enormous recognition for publishing a few books of poems. People thought that was such a great feat. But writing poems is easy compared to being a mother. Yet the world just went on as if it were no big thing. Immediately I felt a kinship to parents everywhere. And the injustice that our work is so discounted.

Parenting is one of the most complex and demanding jobs anyone can undertake. Under the best circumstances, it's hard. If you have to teach yourself from scratch, it's even harder.

I wasn't sure of myself and what I was doing with my boys. I didn't have a memory of the right things to use as a base in my parenting. The base I had was of the wrong things, the things not to do. So I couldn't go with what I *felt* was right; I had to do what I *thought* was right. I had to be awake all the time to make sure I didn't hurt my kids. I had to be very aware.

Though demanding, this awareness has its advantages. Our culture doesn't give much thought to the ways we interact with children, often assuming that raising children just happens naturally. Survivors who approach parenting with a commitment to pay attention are able to make clear choices instead of working out of unconscious patterning.

I parent my kids very intentionally. I knew what kinds of things kids needed, that I didn't get—things like good touching, good physical contact, talking to them like real people—but I didn't know how to provide them. I had to teach myself to do those things. I watched how a couple of good families worked. I did a lot of reading. I actively fantasized about what a good family would be like. Initially it was awkward, but now it feels natural.

If you're unsure of yourself, you can join a parents' support group, take Parent Effectiveness Training,* read books, or talk to a friend whose parenting you respect.

Other parents who can listen, share their own experiences, and offer suggestions are an invaluable source of support and guidance. Laura and Ellen, and their respective partners, are members of a mothers' group that has been meeting monthly for seven years. As Ellen explains:

Whenever my partner and I are unsure how to handle a difficult situation, or one of my kids wants permission to do something and my partner thinks one way and I think another, we ask the Moms for advice. The collective wisdom of that dozen women is formidable. We rarely bother to argue over parenting questions anymore. Instead, when in doubt, we simply "take it to the Moms."

Making mistakes and trying out new approaches is a natural part of parenting. As your children grow, you grow too. While it's not easy, learning to become a good parent —in your own estimation—is a rich and rewarding experience:

Parenting is something I conquered. At first I thought I would be a wonderful parent and that I could undo all the wrongs my parents had done to

---

* For information on classes in your area, write P.E.T. Inc. 531 Stevens Ave., Solana Beach, CA 92075-2093, or call (800) 628-1197.

me. And then I realized that was an absolute farce. And I was able to really pull out and say to myself, "You can do it. It's not going to be as easy as you thought it was, but you can just plod through it, day after day, and have little tiny victories along the way." That's real affirming to me as a human being, that I was able to do a right thing. I committed to it, and I was actually able to carry it through.

FACING YOUR STRENGTHS AND WEAKNESSES

Honestly facing your strengths and weaknesses is essential. No one is a perfect parent. The goal isn't perfection. It's a healthy, growing relationship.

Ask yourself:

- What works? How do I feel successful as a parent?
- What am I proud of?
- Do I feel inadequate in any way? How?
- What would I like to change in my relationship with my kids?
- Are there areas where I feel confused? What are they?
- Are there patterns with my kids that remind me of my family of origin? Are there things that push my old buttons?
- Where do I feel stuck?
- When do I feel out of control?
- Am I able to protect my children adequately?
- How do my partner and I work out our differences about parenting?
- Do I have a support system of other parents I can talk to?

It's very difficult to be objective about your relationship with your children. You may feel defensive ("I'm doing the best I can"), or you may feel that any criticism of your children reflects badly on you.

> My best friend told me I was letting my son walk all over me. "He's spoiled," she said. "The way you let him talk to you!" I was devastated. I was aware that my son did have kind of a snotty tone of voice recently, but I didn't know what to do about it. And he's a really sweet kid. Didn't she know that?

If someone points out a problem in your parenting, try not to get too defensive. Instead, ask yourself if you think there's truth to what they're saying. If not, disregard their opinion. But if their criticism resonates with your own inner feeling that there's something wrong, then it's time to make changes that will benefit both you and your children.

> When my daughter was five, we lived in a very small house, and the way it was set up, she had to walk through my bedroom to get from her room to the rest of the house. I thought it was important for kids to have privacy, so I gave her the room with the door. Anytime she had to go to the bathroom in the night, she passed right by my bed. The rooms were so small she had practically to crawl over my bed. So she crawled in instead—and went back to sleep.
> I had a new lover at the time and she stayed over with me a lot. Finally, she got fed up. She got angry. I had no idea why. She explained that I should have *my* privacy. That she wanted privacy with me. That she didn't want my daughter always climbing into the bed.
> At first I was furious. How dare she come and criticize my mothering? But by morning I recognized that she was right. It was time for my daughter to get out of my bed. And for me to have the room with the door. That night I rearranged the furniture.

OPEN COMMUNICATION

Honest communication is an important part of any healthy relationship. Sharing your thoughts and feelings and listening to the thoughts and feelings of your children builds an environment of trust, safety, and intimacy.

> I don't lie to my kids. We talk about what's really happening. And in my family, we never talked about what was real. Never.

Even painful or frightening subjects need to be talked about. A few years ago, Ellen was asked to speak at a conference about being a parent in the nuclear age:

> As I was getting ready to leave, my daughter asked me where I was going. I told her and asked if there was anything she thought I should tell the parents. I said, "They'll want to know if they should talk to their children about bombs. They may be worried that they'll scare them if they do. What do you think?" Without hesitation, Sara answered, "Tell them, 'Talk to your children or they won't talk to you.'"

This sound advice applies to all the difficult issues in our lives. As a survivor, you know too well the danger and pain that silence carries.

TALKING TO CHILDREN ABOUT YOUR ABUSE

Children are very perceptive. If you are angry, distracted, or in crisis, they will sense it. Pretending nothing is wrong will only make them feel crazy and confused. Without facts, children draw their own conclusions, generally assuming that they are the cause of the problem. Let your children know they're not to blame.

In telling children about your own abuse, talk to them in ways that are appropriate to their age. They do not need detailed descriptions. Instead, make a general statement that reassures them and speaks to *their* needs: "I was hurt by my father when I was a little girl. That's why I've been going to so many meetings and crying a lot. I want you to know that if I seem sad, it doesn't have anything to do with you. I'm getting help now so I can feel better."

If your children want to know more, they will ask. For example, if a six-year-old asks, "How were you hurt?" you can respond with a little more information, such as, "When I was a little girl, my father made me touch his penis. That scared me a lot." If a fourteen-year-old asks, "What did Uncle Bobby do that was so awful?" you can say, "He raped me and beat me."

Answer questions honestly, always providing just the information they need at the time instead of overwhelming them with aspects of the abuse they might not want to hear or be able to deal with.

If you're not comfortable answering certain questions, communicate that in a respectful way, such as, "I'm not ready to talk about it more now, but I really did want to tell you a little about how I've been feeling, so you won't think my upset has anything to do with you. As I become more comfortable with my feelings, I'll answer more of your questions."

If your children are adults, it's still important to talk. A mother of five grown children describes the impact of her disclosure on her family:

I told my kids about the incest when I was working at the rape crisis center. My kids were surprised and supportive and then mixed up in their feelings toward their grandfather. "I can't believe he did that." Or, "He's real nice to me." And they've continued to be mixed in their feelings toward him.

Two of my daughters live in the same town as him and he takes them out to breakfast. They know all about the incest. They say, "Granddaddy's been good to us. We don't like what he did, but we're willing to see him." So they visit him, and at the same time they've been understanding about why I don't.

How much they want to talk is different for each of them. My son won't talk about any of it now. But my other kids do. I try not to impose on them. If they're not ready, I back off and respect that, and we connect however we can. I treasure my relationships with each of them more now.

If your children say they don't want to hear any more about your abuse or your healing, don't force it. Perhaps it will take some time for them to assimilate the fact that you were abused. This doesn't mean you should censor every word when they're around. But don't expect them to support you or to be sympathetic listeners. It's enough that you tell them the basics and then take your cues from them.

As with all important issues, abuse and its effects aren't things you can bring up once and be done with. Talking with your children is an ongoing process, part of creating a family environment of openness and sharing.

Incest is no longer a secret in our family. I'm committed to having as real a relationship with my kids as I can, to deal with as much of this with them as they're willing to at any point in time. Incest is not the only secret that needs to be talked about. In most families, a lot of things are treated as secrets. I've talked to them about the incest, their Dad's alcoholism, the breakup of my marriage, my lesbianism, all of it.

SETTING BOUNDARIES

If your own boundaries were violated as a child, you may have difficulty maintaining appropriate boundaries with your children now, or you may be confused about what is appropriate.

When I had my children, I experienced real bonding for the first time— a physical, sexual, emotional bond with these babies. It was just overpowering and I was scared to death that I was going to engulf them. For years it frightened me.

EMOTIONAL BOUNDARIES

Clear emotional boundaries enable you to experience yourself as separate from your children. You realize that they don't think and feel as you do, nor should they. Their interests and needs are different from yours and don't necessarily reflect on you. Assuming your own individuality and allowing your children theirs is respectful and healthy, though not always easy.

I believe in dressing for comfort. I always wear casual clothes. My daughter, on the other hand, is extremely finicky about what she wears. She loves ruffles and bows and is very dainty. She hates getting dirty and takes forever getting dressed. Sometimes I get impatient or wish she'd go out and play in a puddle or two, but that's not who she is.

Children have a right to their own ideas and beliefs. They have a right to time alone, solitary thoughts, and private places. Parents who establish their own right to privacy often find their children imitating this behavior. Your three-year-old may go to his room for "alone time" with his teddy bear, or he may ask you to knock before entering his room. If your children don't have their own rooms, they may find a place in the house or yard where they feel especially comfortable. Respect their need for solitude—to read, to be involved in their own projects, even just to daydream.

It's not appropriate to use your children as confidants or to look to them for sympathy or advice. Your emotional intimacy with them should be to meet *their* needs, not yours. If you're unsure about your emotional boundaries with your children, pay attention to their responses. If your children are pushing you away, let them move out from you a little more. Be available if they want to come close, but don't hold them to you.

SEXUAL BOUNDARIES

Parents often have sensual feelings toward their children. Caretaking, especially of small children, is very physical and it's not unusual for mothers to feel an occasional sexual response. If these feelings are neither consistent nor compelling, they are probably within a normal range. If, however, sexual desire for your children is strong or persistent, get help for yourself immediately.

Don't act on these feelings. And don't talk about them with your child. If you do, you will be sexually abusing your child.

Be aware that children often test limits, sexually as well as in other areas. They experiment with boundaries regarding intimacy, closeness, and physical affection. They might try to touch you in sexual areas or try to get you to touch them. If your child is testing you in these ways, set limits firmly while staying affectionate.

When my son was eight he kept trying to French-kiss me. I guess he saw me kissing my lover and was interested. Also, on TV there's plenty of all that and it's made to look pretty exciting. I had to tell him over and over that he couldn't do that with me. I said I knew he was really curious and wanted to try it out but that he'd have to wait until he was a little older and then experiment with kids his age. He was incredibly persistent until finally I insisted he stop asking. He even cried and begged, "If you let me do it just once, I promise I'll never ask again." I told him absolutely no, but said he could ask for something else—he could have three wishes. He asked for a roll of Scotch tape, a lullaby at bedtime, and Play-doh.

This story illustrates the innocence of a child's "sexual desires," and underlines the need for the adult to be clear about what is and isn't appropriate physical contact between parent and child.

FEAR OF BEING ABUSIVE

Some survivors go through a period of discomfort around children, when they fear they will act inappropriately or be unable to set proper limits.

I have to be constantly aware of my boundaries. Whenever I'm being physical and affectionate with a little kid, I have to think, "Is this okay? Am I crossing over his boundaries? Is this getting into anything sexual?"

If you've been abused and had your own boundaries violated, these are natural fears. You may, in fact, have had abusive thoughts or feelings. But once you are actively engaged in healing, it is extremely unlikely that you will *start* abusing children *if you haven't already done so.* (If you have been abusive to children, read "If You've Been Abusive" on page 296.) If you continue to be afraid, see a counselor to determine if there's a danger or if you're just scared. Being scared is okay. And common. Acting out isn't.

HEALTHY TOUCH

Children have a right to say no to touch, even if it's yours. Let your children know that their bodies are their own and that no one should touch them without permission. Unless you're sure your child wants a hug, ask, "Can I give you a hug right now?" Or say, "Tell Uncle Fred goodnight," instead of "Give Uncle Fred a kiss." These are ways of giving a child control. Affection should meet their needs, not the needs of the adults around them.

On the other hand, don't be so cautious that you deny children their basic need for human contact.

I don't touch people, and I don't like being touched. When it came to my kids, I had to make a conscious decision that they were going to get the benefit of the physical contact that I didn't get.

STRONG ENOUGH TO BE GENTLE

Essential to ending child sexual abuse is raising children in ways that will influence them to value each human life—including their own. In a society that glorifies violence, perpetuates prejudice, and reinforces rigid sex-role stereotyping, this is a staggering job. Through the media, advertising, and general cultural conditioning, boys are encouraged to be tough and insensitive and girls to be passive and compliant. Both are taught to bury painful feelings and ignore genuine needs. As parents, we struggle to instill value and attitudes in our children that will help them be both strong and sensitive, respectful of themselves and of others.

Pray For The People
For Evy

by Denise Low

My sons ignite Chanukah candles
one, two, three, four flames
and our friend recites Hebrew blessings.
Black solstice night cloaks the windows.

Flickering light ends this hard year.
We still see
    the Cheyenne people at Sand Creek
    the Jews of the Holocaust
    the murdered Cambodians
and our friend beside us
    raped by her insane father
    all through her growing years
    and bullied and beaten.

Somehow the candles are a healing.
Her voice rises over my sons,
over their slender, fragile bodies.
Soon they will grow and thicken into men
sure and strong enough to be gentle.
The first word we taught them,
while touching the cats, was "gentle."

May they live this next year as children.

May this Chanukah heal us all.

Once I decided they would, I had to say, "Okay, who's going to do it?" And it looked like it had to be me. So that became part of my healing, having these babies and touching them.

As you learn to nurture yourself, you will find you are better able to give to your children. As you begin to trust your capacity to set appropriate boundaries, you will feel more comfortable giving them the warm, safe touching they need. And you'll be able to experience the pleasure of being close too.

Sometimes at night when I'm reading to my daughter before bed or kissing her goodnight, I'm so touched by how good she feels. Snuggled up soft against me, with that sweet child smell. I love the physical closeness of mothering.

PROTECTING YOUR CHILDREN

If a survivor hasn't remembered her abuse or acknowledged its effects, she may not be able to recognize signs that her children are in danger or may not be able to respond effectively. One woman, who'd forgotten her own abuse, described an incident that happened to her daughter when she was six:

A young man in church started paying attention to her and of course she ate it up. He'd come over to the house and ask to take her out on rides. They'd go to his house and he'd take pictures of her. We always let her go with him. This went on every day. Then we'd see the pictures. She'd be up a tree, her dress pulled up, her panties exposed, in a very seductive pose. I'd feel uncomfortable looking at the pictures, *but my husband and I knew absolutely nothing about child molesting.*

It wasn't until a friend called to say he was doing it with her daughter, too, that we went to a deacon in the church to put a stop to it. He put us in touch with a psychologist who said, "The man's a child molester. Get your kids away from him." I did, and that was many years ago, but to this day I cannot talk to my daughter about it. I'm afraid something happened, that I didn't protect her. That would be an almost unbearable burden.

When survivors are forced to confront the fact that their children are being abused, they sometimes freeze and are unable to act.

When I heard that my brother had molested one of my girls, I blanked out. I was a total zombie. It was like I was back in bed as a nine-year-old. It was like trying to run in a dream. I could hear myself saying, "He did? Isn't that terrible?" My daughter was screaming at me, "You've got to do something!" And I didn't know what to do. All I knew how to do was avoid.

Situations don't have to be blatantly abusive for your child to need protection. You may let your child play at a friend's house where there's inadequate supervision. You may not take action when your child has an overly harsh music teacher, a neglectful baby-sitter, or a problem at preschool.

I'm disturbed to realize that I've been passing victimization along to our daughters by failing to resolve an unpleasant child-care situation. They're not being hit or molested, but they're not treated with love and respect. The message I'm giving them is that I won't (am afraid? don't know how to?) protect them. It has forced me to forgive my parents, because I see how easy it is to become immobilized, to hope a situation isn't really bad or that it will just go away.

As a victim the thing I've been trained to fear most is confrontation. I'm beginning to grasp why we need to confront our abusers and those who failed to protect us. I need to confront my nameless fear, my fear of standing up for myself and for those I love most. Yet here is a situation where I have a chance to confront, to experience growth and healing, and I'm still hiding my head, wishing the problem would magically disappear.

It's essential to do your own emotional healing so that blocked memories or fears don't obscure your vision or keep you from acting on your child's behalf. As difficult as it is to break lifelong patterns of ignoring, denying, and hiding, this is what is required of us as parents. And as with all growth, the rewards exceed the challenge. Not only are your children protected, but you emerge a more courageous, capable person.

OVERPROTECTION

Overprotection is an exaggeration of the healthy desire to keep children safe. If you're afraid, especially if you're unaware of the source of your fears, it's easy to become obsessive.

I always scrutinized anyone I left my children with. If just a hair was out of place, I wanted to know about it. I wouldn't leave my kids if I could help it. I never let my husband bathe my kids. I didn't think then that I didn't trust him, but I clearly didn't. All this was before I remembered anything. I never knew why I took all those precautions. I just did.

You may try to keep your children safe by limiting their activities, but children should have the mobility and freedom appropriate for their age. You need to overcome your fears, not pass them on.

I remember going through this thing about my daughter wearing shorts and trying not to let her do that. Luckily I have this friend who is like my brother, and he told me how unreal I was being about this whole thing. He said, "Now we know you have a certain amount of things that bother you. Do you want to give her a trip about her own sexuality because you won't let her wear those shorts?" He's really helped me keep on track with my children on little things like that.

If you're uncertain about the limits you're setting, talk with other parents. Getting feedback from others is a useful way to gauge if you're being overprotective.

Although wanting to protect your children is a valid desire, you need to distinguish what you can protect them from and what you can't. No matter how careful you are, you cannot regulate every aspect of your child's life. Children spend time in situations and with people you cannot control. For this reason, it is essential that you teach your children to protect themselves. Children need to be educated and empowered. You must prepare them as best you can, take a deep breath, and let them go.

TEACHING CHILDREN TO PROTECT THEMSELVES

Parents sometimes hesitate to talk to their children about sexual abuse because they don't want to frighten them. But in reality, children are aware of danger. With the extensive coverage of sexual abuse in the media and the faces of missing children appearing daily on milk cartons, children are already afraid. And fear does not make powerful children. You were scared when you were a child, and fear did not save you from being abused.

Teaching children personal safety skills so they can protect themselves will replace their fear with self-confidence. Some excellent books and programs are described under "Safe, Strong, and Free" in the Resource Guide.*

Children need to know that they have choices, that they can say no, and that they are capable of protecting themselves in a variety of ways.

When my daughter was little, I told her that she should tell me if she ever felt funny about the way anyone talked

---

* See the "Safe, Strong, and Free" section on p. 574 of the Resource Guide.

to her or touched her, and that she had a right to her own body. I told her no one should ever touch her body in a way that was uncomfortable, even her mom or dad.

And she did have an incident happen to her. She and a girlfriend were playing outside, and a man offered them some candy and asked them to get into the car. As it turned out, they both ran in the house and told me. Later the police came. They identified the man, and he was indeed a child molester they'd been looking for for a couple of months. So they were instrumental in getting him caught and sent to jail.

I made sure they were very proud of what they had done, of how strong and brave they had been. I told them they had saved a lot of other kids, and that they were the heroines of the block. My daughter still talks about it, about how she did the right thing. She helps other kids now. She's very strong.

DEALING WITH YOUR FAMILY OF ORIGIN OR YOUR ABUSER

If you were abused by one of your relatives, you may wonder if you have a right to deny your children access to your family (or your family access to your children). If your children already have an established relationship with your father, for instance, you may not want to spoil their image of Grandpa. Or you may feel it's okay to take your children to visit the abuser as long as you don't leave them alone. But maintaining family ties solely for the sake of tradition—or out of guilt—

does not help your children. You do not owe the molester an opportunity to have a relationship with your child, just as you do not owe your child the opportunity to bond with a child molester. Let the abuse have the repercussions it merits.

In the rare case when an abuser has sought therapy and has truly transformed his life, *carefully supervised* visits may be an option.

It's your responsibility to make decisions about your child's relationships with your abuser or family of origin (see "Families of Origin," page 299). If you do decide to break ties, this can be very painful. As one woman said, "I don't have grandparents for my children. I ache for an extended family."

If you discontinue your children's visits with their grandparents (or if they never visited in the first place), tell your children why. Tell in a way that is appropriate for their age, but do tell. Maintaining an illusion about the abuse protects the abuser and reinforces secrecy as a family pattern.

And if your relatives are unsuitable as a healthy extended family, consider surrogates —friends who can be loving companions and role models for your children. (See "Families of Origin," page 299, for more on dealing with your family now.)

YOU'RE THE PARENT NOW

In visiting members of your family who haven't been abusive, you may still encounter behaviors that aren't acceptable to you. Your relatives may want to give your children more sweets or money than you want them to have. They may tell your children not to cry, force them to eat everything on their plates, ridicule them, or slap them.

If these are the same behaviors that you

experienced as a child, your initial reaction may be to respond the same way you did then. If you froze, withdrew, or complied, denying your real feelings, it will be important to remind yourself that you're the parent now. You get to set the rules for yourself and for your children. It's your responsibility to take control and use your appropriate power.

We were at my parents for dinner and my son spilled his soda. My mother started in yelling at him—how he sat it too close to the edge, how he should pay more attention, how clumsy he was. It was so familiar, for a minute I just sat there, looking at the soda, like when I was a kid. Then I looked up at his face —scared, eyes wide, about to crumple— and I came to. I told her it wasn't okay to yell at him, that everyone spills sometimes, and that it was just an accident. Then I took him in the kitchen with me to get a towel, and I hugged him and told him he didn't do anything wrong and no one had a right to yell at him like that, even his grandmother.

IF YOUR CHILD IS BEING ABUSED

If your child tells you he or she has been abused, believe it. (For information on how children tell, see page 105.) Children rarely lie about sexual abuse. If you suspect that your partner, the person who abused you, other family members, or your child's caretakers are being abusive, take action immediately. Countless women have been sure they were the only ones to be abused, only to find out years later that their own children, or

YOUR CHILDREN SHOULD KNOW

This information is taken from Your Children Should Know by Flora Colao and Tamar Hosansky, an excellent resource for teaching children how to recognize and escape from dangerous situations, how to protect themsevles from assault and abuse, and how to feel both safe and empowered.

In order to teach children the skills to protect themselves, it's necessary to talk frankly. Personal safety strategies can be presented in the same manner as fire and traffic safety—with straightforward, practical information and explanations.

Self-defense is anything that enables children to escape dangerous situations. It can be crossing the street if being followed; not answering questions over the telephone; refusing to open the door to a stranger; saying no; screaming and yelling; making a scene; calling for help; running away; talking calmly to an attacker; pretending to cooperate with an attacker; or physically resisting an assault. It is a state of mind and body that allows children to feel comfortable and secure. It's the belief that their own safety is more important than the feelings of the assailant. And it's the knowledge that they're in control of their own well-being.

Children need to be given rights over their bodies and feelings in order to prevent abuse effectively. The following rights are crucial.

A CHILD'S BILL OF PERSONAL SAFETY RIGHTS

1. The right to trust one's instincts and funny feelings.
2. The right to privacy.
3. The right to say no to unwanted touch or affection.
4. The right to question adult authority and to say no to adult demands and requests.
5. The right to lie and not answer questions.
6. The right to refuse gifts.
7. The right to be rude or unhelpful.
8. The right to run, scream, and make a scene.
9. The right to bite, hit, or kick.
10. The right to ask for help.

When introducing these rights to children, be simple and concrete, using language they can understand. Encourage children to think for themselves by using imaginative or what-if games, role-playing, fantasies, or incidents from your own childhood. Always acknowledge the children's contribution, thus helping them to develop the ability to do spontaneous problem solving in unexpected situations.

grandchildren, or even great-grandchildren had become victims as well.

Barbara Hamilton was in her late fifties, at the start of her own healing process, when she discovered that there had been extensive abuse in her family:

My own healing came to a screeching halt when I heard about my daughters. The pain of that whole thing, I don't know how to describe it. I just felt so much worse about them than I did about me. That's the trap you're in as a mother. I felt flattened by the news. It just knocked me out. I didn't have the *umph* left to deal with my own abuse.

These men, starting with my father, were stealing my childhood, and were stealing my children's childhood, and were stealing everything about us, even our memories. I felt like there was some big force trying to obliterate us from the earth. It was all one great big river of male abuse. We were all just tumbling down the rapids together and there was no possible way I could separate myself from them, because they were littler, and they were going to drown sooner.

Even though it is devastating to find out that your children are being abused, *it is essential that you muster the strength to protect them.* * Take your son out of day care. Stop visiting your father. Don't let your brother baby-sit anymore. Don't think the abuse was an iso-

---

* *Helping Your Child Recover from Sexual Abuse* by Caren Adams is an excellent book. For this and other resources, see "If Your Child Is Abused," on p. 579 of the Resource Guide.

lated incident that won't happen again. It will.

Your family is in crisis and you must break the silence to get help. Call the National Child Abuse Hotline: (800) 422-4453. They can refer you to support services. Call your local women's shelter. Call a supportive neighbor or friend. Report the abuse to Child Protective Services. (They are listed in the state or federal listings of your phone book.) While reporting the abuse may be frightening and traumatic for you, it is important for your child, for your family, and even for the offender.

The job of the people to whom you report is to stop the abuse and keep it from recurring. Reporting will serve to protect other children. It will make a clear statement to the child that he or she is not to blame and deserves protection, and that the abuser will be held accountable. Also, reporting the case and having it go to court is often the only way the offender will get into treatment.

GETTING AWAY FROM THE ABUSER

I remember when I was a kid saying, "I'll never be like my mother. I'll never let those things happen to my kid. I'll stand up to my husband." But in retrospect, I can see that I was doing exactly the same thing. I thought I had broken away from all of them, that nothing was ever going to happen like it had to them. Yet it did. I was so blind. I married someone exactly like my father. He battered me and molested our daughter.

If you're living with a molester, the only responsible option is to have the molester leave the home, or to leave yourself with the child. *Children should not have to live with an abuser.*

Leaving can be terrifying. It goes against all the social pressure that says the family must stay together. You also may be in desperate financial straits. But economic dependency and fear do not justify sacrificing your children.

Some organizations that deal with incest encourage reunification of the family as the ultimate goal. This can be very dangerous. Reuniting the family is acceptable only if it is truly in the child's best interests, and this is unusual. Abusers do not become safe caretakers of children after a few counseling sessions and a little group therapy. It is far better for a child to live in a difficult—or even dire—economic situation with one nurturing, protective parent than to live with an abuser. (See "Recognizing Bad Relationships" on page 244 and the "Domestic Violence, Rape, and Sexual Harassment" section on page 567 of the Resource Guide for practical help in leaving an abusive situation.)

Breaking the Chain: Dana's Story

Dana, the daughter of a survivor, the mother of a survivor, and a survivor herself, took her ex-husband to court after he molested their daughter, Christy. She talks about the resistance she met in her family and the isolation she felt when she took action to break the cycle of repeated abuse. (For more of Dana's story, see page 304.)

My mother-in-law and I were in court one day and she said, "Dana, why are you making such a big deal out of this?" And I said, "Do you know what he's done?"

"Look," she said, "Jack slapped me around and he slapped the kids around and I'm okay." She refused to connect the fact that her son was doing it to his wife and to his child with the fact that she had allowed it to happen to her and her children.

Then when I was having dinner with my grandmother, my mother's mother, I was trying to get her to tell me more about when I was little. And she said, "Why do you have to bring up these things? Does it really make a difference?"

And I said, "It really does make a difference." And then I asked about what happened in her family when she was young. She said, "Well my mother and father fought a lot. My mother was always antagonizing my father and he would have to hit her to make her stop. She really brought it on herself."

Those are the two women who are the matriarchs in the families that came together and created Christy. There's so much complacency. No one is willing to look at the fact that abuse formed the way we behave now, the way we react in relationships, the way we treat our children, and the messages we give our children about their self-worth. No wonder it'sgoing on generation after generation.

And I can't believe that I'm the only one in these two families that include my grandmother, who had nine children, and my mother-in-law, who was one of eleven children, and my father-in-law, who was one of eleven children, who is saying anything. Of all those people and all those people's children and grandchildren. I'm the only one who's saying, "Hey, you think maybe we have a problem here?" It makes me feel incredibly alone. But someone had to stop the cycle. And I did.

IF YOU'VE BEEN ABUSIVE

When I was fourteen I was baby sitting for a little girl who was around two. I was diapering her, and she was lying there were her legs spread, and I felt furious with her for how vulnerable she was. "You can't do that! You can't be a little girl in the world like that!" And what I ended up doing was touching her vagina and putting my finger inside. I did it for a minute or two, and I was furious at her the whole time. I hated her for being vulnerable. And I had this warped feeling that I was protecting her. "You can't go around being this vulnerable, so I'm going to do something to make you less vulnerable. That way, when the *real* child molesters come along, you won't be hurt by it."

I had the assumption this happened to every little girl, and that didn't stop me from hurting a child. I had to smash the vulnerability I saw in her. It frightened me. It was that simple.

Women and girls do abuse children—emotionally, sexually, and physically. When a woman's own experience of child sexual abuse remains buried, there is a chance that she will repeat the pattern.

My earliest memory of my mother is her trying to drown me when she was washing my hair. She was holding my head under the faucet, crying, saying "I can't love you. I'm sorry. I can't love you." I have no reason to believe I received any warmth or comfort from her as an infant. She was always drunk and beat me all the time. When I was eigh-

teen she told me she'd never loved me. My grandmother said my mother openly hated me while I was in her womb.

I got pregnant at seventeen to get away from home. I had a baby boy and settled down with my husband to raise him. Less than a year later, I got pregnant again. This time it was a daughter. And I hated her while she was in my womb. I didn't want her. I was desperately ill the whole pregnancy. I vomited all nine months. I kept trying to miscarry.

She was born and I still didn't like her. I just knew I couldn't love her. I never held her close. I wouldn't care for her. She cried constantly. I started abusing her right away. I'd take my daughter and slam her down on the sofa. The rage was uncontrollable. I never made the connection to what my mother had done to me. At that point, I hadn't even remembered it. And all the time I was abusing her. I was being a great mother to my son.

Admitting that you have abused a child is terrifying. This is why abusers almost always deny it. Yet, if you have abused a child, it is imperative that you acknowledge the seriousness of your actions, get yourself into counseling right away, and take responsibility for the implications of what you've done. If the child is still under your care, it's important to get that child into therapy with someone trained to work with abused children. Don't assume the abuse won't have a lasting effect. You have only to look at your own life to know that abuse keeps affecting you until you deal with it. Good early intervention can help children heal now and save them from carrying damaging effects into their adult lives.

IF YOU'RE FEELING SHAKY

If you haven't abused a child but feel you're on the verge—either sexually, physically, or emotionally—get help right away.

One day when I was taking Jerri to her baby-sitter's, she started crying that she didn't want to go. I was already late for work. She was screaming and throwing a fit. I finally got so angry, I picked up her box of crayons and threw them at her. She was absolutely terrified.

I took her to the baby-sitter and when I was about a minute away I turned back, got her, sat down with her on the step and said, "What I just did was really terrible and no mother should ever treat her daughter like that." I told her I knew I'd been mean to her for a long time, and that I was going to get help so I wouldn't do it anymore.

I got in touch with a family counselor who would see Jerri alone for play therapy and then would see the two of us together. It really helped our relationship a lot. The pressure was let out.

Many communities have groups for stressed parents. Ending your isolation can dramatically improve your capacity to cope. Don't be ashamed to ask for help. Admitting your need and dealing with your problem is an honorable way to protect your child and take care of yourself.

If you still feel you can't control yourself with your children, consider placing them in a temporary safe home away from you. Leaving them may be necessary for their safety or for your healing. Living in a nurturing environment without you is better for your children than living in an abusive or neglectful one with you. Wrenching as it is, sending a child to live with a safe relative or even with warm strangers in a foster care situation is sometimes the most responsible thing to do. Protecting children has to come first. As Jennierose relates:

I left my children with my second husband when they were four and a half and eleven months old. I couldn't have taken care of them. I was extremely disturbed. Looking back, I now know why I left them when I did. Because four and a half was when the worst part of my life started. And a few days before I decided to leave, I found myself hitting my son for the first time. I was pounding on his back and I knew that I could really injure him, like my parents had injured me, if I stayed. So really, I left because I loved them and didn't want to damage them, and I would have damaged them.

IT'S NOT TOO LATE

Children challenge us to change and grow—no matter how old we are, no matter what mistakes have been made. For years after Jennierose left her children, she was full of guilt. She repeatedly tried to find them, but every time she came close, their father and stepmother moved. Finally her children came to her:

When my eldest son was eighteen, he came looking for me. He stayed for a week. And then my younger son, who was fourteen, came and stayed for a couple of weeks.

We had years when we weren't in contact, but in the last few years we've gotten really close. My older son asked me to tell him my life history: "I just want to know about you." And I wrote him a whole series of letters. I told him everything. Since then we've developed a real closeness, because I don't have to protect what I say. They know who I am.

I've asked them if they were angry that I left them. Both of them said they were, but they're not anymore, because they understand. There was no way I could have cared for them. I left to protect them.

Their stepmother has since died. I'm grateful to her for raising my children, but her death has made it more possible for me to be their mother again. Since my first granddaughter was born, I've stayed in close contact with both my sons, and that's been really wonderful. I have my children.

Even when children are grown, you still have an impact on their lives. The opportunity to be nurturing and supportive, to be an inspiring role model, and to contribute to your children's healing continues. And for some survivors, healing the pain with their children is part of coming to a resolution with their own abuse:

I'm standing in the middle between the generations. I can't face my parents and heal it that way. Maybe I can turn to my children and heal it in the other direction. That would be making an end to it.

FAMILIES OF ORIGIN

I saw this picture. I was standing in the sunlight and my family and ex-husband's family were all back in this dark cave. They were crowded in there, and I was in the sunlight with fresh air all around me. They wanted me to come back in and I wouldn't do it. I'd finally made it out into the sunshine and I wasn't going back. And I had no sense that they were going to come out either. I knew for the first time that I didn't have to make them come out, that I didn't have to save them.

If you were abused within your family or if your family is generally unsupportive, critical, or withholding, continued relations can be difficult. Sometimes survivors receive genuine support and understanding from members of their families. Others experience a mixture of positive interactions and ones that feel undermining and draining.* Most survivors look back from their own changed perspective at families who are still caught in the patterns that existed when they were children. And as they step out of the family system, they are confronted with the possibility that there will no longer be a place for them.

Before I told my family about the incest, I believed they would always

* For an example of how family members can support each other in healing, read Michelle and Artemis's story on page 446.

offer me unconditional love and nurturing. Afterwards, I had to tear down those false assumptions and replace them with reality.

Giving up the little girl's longing for security and protection was excruciating. Stepping outside of the shared beliefs of my family system and insisting on the truth was terrifying. I felt like a speck of dust floating all alone in a big empty universe.

Family members may differ greatly in how they respond to your disclosure of abuse, your healing, and your needs now. It's common for survivors to have one or more family members who support them and others who deny everything.

My brother has completely supported me. He always has. He's the one person who's been consistent in my whole family. He's been very compassionate toward me. He's told me he loves me, and that he knows my parents have always treated me badly. He says he's sorry about that. And he's offered me a place to stay if I ever need one.

My sister, on the other hand, has completely cut me out of her life. She doesn't want to talk to me. She thinks I'm nasty and I've ruined both my parents' lives by bringing this up. She says it never could have happened and that I'm crazy to say it did.

In a situation like this, it's particularly important not to consider your family as a conglomerate. You can decide to build on a strong connection with one or more relatives and limit or suspend contact with the rest.

MAKING THE MOST OF THE ALLIES IN YOUR FAMILY

If there are people in your family who respect you and genuinely want to support you, they can be valuable assets in your healing. You may have a sibling who shares your feelings, validates your reality, or can fill in gaps in your memory. You may have a mother who is as angry as you are that you were abused and wants to help you in any way she can. You may have an aunt, uncle, cousin, or grandparent who can offer empathy, information, and the love of someone who has known you for a long time. If this is the case, make use of those relationships.

There may be times when you feel that you need to separate from *everyone* in your family, but if you are fortunate enough to have a family—or part of a family—that can offer sincere concern in the context of a healthy relationship, it's in your best interests to take advantage of it.

One woman described her experience in allowing her mother to support her:

When I first remembered my brother's abuse, I tried to tell my mother, but she didn't get it. She listened, but then she just shoved it back in the drawer. I felt abandoned.

A couple of years later, I began to face it for real. But this time I didn't even want her to know. I blamed her for not listening, not *hearing* me the first time. I blamed her for not protecting me, for being unable to see what had gone on, pretty much for everything. I was so angry, I couldn't let her help me.

Over time, though, my anger at her has subsided. She has made an effort to change. She used to drown out my feelings with hers. Now she concentrates on mine. She listens when I tell her what I need. And there's a lot she knows about my childhood that I don't remember. She says things that help me piece it all together.

It's been a lot of work to get here, but I'm very glad to have her in my corner. Sometimes I can even ask her for a hug now.

It may take a substantial effort on both sides to build a healthy relationship or to repair one that's been damaged. But if someone in your family is willing and able to do that work, it's an opportunity that is likely to be deeply rewarding for both of you.*

Remember, though: you are the one who gets to decide whether such work is in your best interests, whether the person who offers is able to be helpful with no strings attached, and whether this is the healthy choice for *you.*

ASSESSING YOUR RELATIONSHIPS WITH FAMILY MEMBERS

It is up to you to decide how you want to relate to your family. It is not a requirement of healing that you work toward reconciliation. Nor is it always necessary to stop seeing your family altogether. One course of action is not more courageous than the other. You can choose either end of the spectrum or

anywhere in the middle, as long as your choice is based on what is genuinely in your best interests.

Look realistically at your relationship with each member of your family. Ask yourself:

- Do we have any contact now? Why? When? Is it because I want to, or is it out of obligation? Who initiates the contact?
- Have I told this person what happened to me? Does he or she acknowledge it? Is he or she supportive of my healing?
- How do I feel when we talk?
- Do I take more drugs, drink more alcohol, or eat too much or too little when we're together?
- Does this person criticize me, insult me, hurt my feelings, or show a lack of interest in my life?
- How do I feel after a visit? Depressed? Angry? Like I'm crazy? Nurtured and supported? Relaxed? Basically okay, but not great?
- What do I get from this relationship?

Look at the dynamics that exist between family members and at the role you play in the system. Is it comfortable, or is it something you want to change?. If yours was an incestuous family, is incest still going on? Just because you grew up and left home doesn't mean the incest has ended for you. Maybe your uncle doesn't come to your bed anymore, but if he comments on your figure and asks if you've "had any" lately, that kind of intrusion is still sexual abuse.

Contact with your family can throw you back into the reality you knew as a child, almost as though you'd traveled through a time warp. You know you're a thirty-five-year-old adult, but when you go home for the holidays you start feeling like a powerless, frightened

---

* Parents who are struggling to improve their relationships with adult children can benefit by reading a wonderful book, *Making Peace with Your Adult Child,* by Shauna Smith. See p. 570 of the Resource Guide.

I'M SAYING NO, MOMMA

by Laura Davis

ESTRANGE: 1. turning away in feeling, becoming distant or unfriendly; 2. to remove from customary environment or associations; 3. to arouse enmity or indifference when there had formerly been love, affection or friendliness; synonym, to wean.

WEAN: 1. to accustom (a child or young animal) to loss of mother's milk; 2. to detach affection from something long followed or desired. WEAN implies separation from something having a strong hold on one.

—Webster's Dictionary

Paul calls from Miami. He says I should forgive you and let go. Not hold a grudge.

Dotsy sends a postcard from Idaho: Your Mom is worried about you.

Dad says you called him, cross-continental, to ask if I'd had a nervous breakdown; seems there was no other way you could explain my letter. After all, how could a daughter in her right mind say she didn't want a relationship with her mother? How could your good little girl say no, not now, I'm not ready for you in my life?

I'll tell you how, Momma, I'll tell you how. Brick by careful brick, that's how, Momma. I've built this wall between us with careful, conscious precision. It is thick, my wall. Thick and nontransparent. I stand behind it and you cannot reach me. Its walls are smooth, Momma, flattened by ancient anger; its walls are caked with memory, bound with pitch, thick, black, and alive.

I stand back, separate from you for the first time ever, and inspect my work. What is the nature of this space I've created? What are its dimensions? What are its depths? How far can I travel inside before I come back round full face to you? What does it mean to be estranged? To take space? To create distance? What does it mean to set a boundary? To say no?

I'm saying no, Momma. I decide I like my wall.

It is not a wall of denial, of stasis, of immobility. It is a wall that grants permission. Behind its firm thick boundaries, there is movement. I stretch. I reach. I remember. What was given. What was denied. What never was there to begin with. What was good and whole and right. The lies that were told.

child. You may still be terrified of your abuser, when in reality he's a weak, seventy-year-old man. You may be plagued by nightmares or revert back to patterns of coping you abandoned long ago.

One woman was so upset by seeing her parents that she became suicidally depressed, got involved in car accidents, and was unable to function for weeks afterward. If you are shattered by the experience of being with your family, it is probably time to stop torturing yourself.

As you assess your relationship with your family, tally the good and the bad. What are the rewards? What is the price you pay? Look at what you want from each relationship. Are your expectations realistic?

If you let her, the child within will often choose to continue a destructive relationship solely in the hope that one day things might

For twenty-eight years, I never shared my pain with you. Only my successes, only how good life was, only the happy times. Never the sadness or fear or anger. I've been trying to make up for being different, Momma. Trying to win your love, your respect, your blessing. But I'm not trying now, Momma. I'm starting to let go.

You see, I've got this wall. They call it estrangement. I call it freedom. Behind its thick surface, I can feel and do and be, and I don't have to show you anything. I know I'm not the daughter you wanted, Momma. I've always known that. But with my wall close around me, I can see you're not the mother I wanted either, all-knowing, all-giving, all-protective. From behind my wall I can see things as they are, find my courage, and grieve for what's been lost. From behind this wall, tall and smooth and straight, I can stop striving for what I'll never have, and find room again for you in my heart.

And when I'm done, I can take it down, my wall. Brick by careful brick. So I can see you clear.

They call it estrangement. I call it loving.

get better. In order not to revictimize yourself, it is wiser to appraise your family with the distance and honesty only your adult self can provide.

SETTING THE GROUND RULES

You have a right to set ground rules. This means deciding if, when, and how you want to see the people in your family. Many survivors feel that if they open the channels at all, they have to open them all the way. When you were a child you had two options —to trust or not trust. Your options are broader now. If you choose to stay in contact with your family, you don't have to do so in any prescribed way, or in the way you've done in the past.

The first time I didn't send my mother a Mother's Day card, I thought for sure the sky would open up and God would strike me dead. Yet I couldn't maintain the facade. So I didn't send the card, and God didn't come to get me.

It can be a good idea to send family members a letter outlining the guidelines they must respect if you are to see them. You can choose to discuss certain things and not others. You can say that you want contact with them only when you initiate it. You can tell your mother that you want to see her, but only if the visit doesn't include your father. Or you can share information with your sister and ask her not to pass it on through the grapevine. There is no guarantee that these requests will be honored, but you have a right to ask, and then make choices based on the outcome.

There are many ways to set limits. You can get an unlisted phone number. You can insist that family members don't drop in without calling. Or you can not visit in person at all, limiting contact to phone calls or letters. The important thing is that you say no to any interaction that doesn't feel good to you.

Setting Limits: Leila's Story

My mother used to call me up at two in the morning and tell me she had just taken a bottle of pills and was going to die. I'd run over and call an ambulance and get her to the hospital. I did this on a monthly basis because I felt sorry for her. I knew what she'd been through. But I couldn't do it anymore.

One night I said, "This is the last time I'm ever coming here to make you throw up. If you decide you want to commit suicide, it's your decision. I'm going to have nothing to do with it. You can call me, but I won't come."

Before that, there had been this semblance of connectedness: "Gee, we're all women and we went through this together. Aren't men fucked? We have to stick together." It was real hard to give that up, because I needed to feel she was my ally. But I had to make the break. And you know what? She stopped attempting suicide. From that moment on, my life improved dramatically. I could almost see it in the daily things I did. I could bake bread better. Because I was relying on myself. I had a certain kind of faith in myself that I hadn't had before.

You've Got Two Choices: Dana's Story

Dana is a survivor whose mother and daughter were both molested. For more of her story, see page 295.

When my daughter, Christy, was five years old, she started asking, "Why did

I'm Glad I Did: Edith's Story

Edith Horning is a forty-seven-year-old personnel director who lives on a farm and raises horses. She's the mother of three grown children, and has made many changes in the way she's related to her own parents about the incest she experienced as a child.

I love my parents. And they love me. They love me the best they can. I happen to be a lot more fortunate than both my parents, in that my capacity for loving is far greater than theirs. They just don't have it.

For a long time I had more anger at my mother than I did toward my father. I felt the same way a lot of women do—you somehow always forgive the man because he's "weaker" and "can't help himself." But I expected my mother to be much stronger and to protect me.

As I got older and became a mother myself, I found out how little an ability to protect I had. I changed my feelings and became more compassionate toward my mother.

In the last couple of years, she has finally begun to acknowledge that there was incest. She's started to remember little pieces. A few years ago, she totally denied that it had ever happened. I told her, "You didn't listen to me any more this time than you did when I was nine."

And she said, "You never told me. You've never spoken to me about this."

And I said, "When I was nine years old, I came to you and said, 'Mom, Dad's coming into my bedroom, and he pulled down my pajamas.' And you said, 'How did you know it was a man?' And I said, 'Because I felt his whiskers on my leg.' And you said, 'No. That's a dream.' And mother, that was no dream. I was nine and I remember."

She said, "No, you never talked to me about this."

That was in November. In January, she called me on the phone and she said, "I remembered something. I remembered holding you by the hand and walking out of the house and walking all the way down the road, and getting clear down past the end of the corner, and realizing I had nowhere to go. And so I turned around and walked you back home again."

I said, "I'm glad to see that you can remember these things. Now you understand how I felt. Now you understand how it happened. You can't blame yourself. You just do the best you can at the time, Mom. When you're trapped, you're trapped." I really heard her. I could very easily see just how powerless my mother had been.

When I decided to go on television to talk about the incest, I went to my parents and told them. I didn't ask their permission. I just told them so they'd be aware of it. I told them I was going to be using my own name. And my mother said, "Aren't you going to turn your face or anything?"

And I said, "No, I'm not going to turn my face! What's the matter with you?"

"Well, people will *know*!"

"That's right. They sure will."

"Well, what will they think of me?" That was the first thing my Mom said. "What will people think of me?"

"They'll think you made a mistake, probably."

"Well, I don't know how you can do this."

And I said, "It won't be easy, but I'm going to do it."

When I told my father I was going on TV, he couldn't even get close to me, he was so scared. It just terrifies my father that I'm not weak anymore. Once it registered with him that I had taken charge, my dad became scared to death of me. All because I didn't ask him. I told him what I was going to do. I watched him get little. But I think it also registered that I wasn't out to beat him, to destroy him. I said, "Dad, this is going to be hard for you. It's going to be hard for me. But I don't want it to continue. If I can talk to people and I can stop one person, it's worth it."

When I went on TV I wasn't concerned with protecting my family. Why should I be? They never protected me. What the hell did they need protection for? They're all adults.

My kids knew. They weren't embarrassed for me. In fact they encouraged me to do it. I talked to the man who owns the business I work for and told him what I was going to do. And he said, "Edie, if you throw out a net and you catch one little fish, it's worth it. Do it!"

And I did. And I'm glad I did.

Daddy do these bad things to me? Nobody else has this kind of daddy." I explained that other people do have that kind of daddy, and that in fact, my own daddy did those kinds of things to me when I was little.

Soon after, Christy was visiting my mother. With a five-year-old's candor, she turned to her grandma and said, "My mommy said that her daddy did those same things to her that my daddy did to me."

To which her grandmother promptly replied, "What? *No!* Your mommy and her daddy never did any of those things! Oh no! *No!* Your mother's daddy loved her and he would have *never* done any of those bad things to her. You must be mistaken."

The next morning Christy reported the conversation to me. Angry and hurt, she said, "Your mommy said that your daddy didn't do those things."

I immediately called my mother: "Look, you've got two choices. You can either come back here and tell Christy the truth or you can just not see us anymore, because that's exactly the kind of lying that's gotten us into this situation. That's why it happened to you, that's why it happened to me, and that's why it happened to Christy. And I'll be damned if it's going to happen again."

My mother and I were both shocked by what I'd done. I'd never talked to her that way before. But that night my mother came over. We went out for tacos and while I went up to order the food, she talked to Christy. She said that sometimes when you remember things that really hurt a lot, it's easier just to pretend they didn't happen. And she said she was sorry she lied.

REPERCUSSIONS

Setting these kinds of limits may make you feel shaky and guilty. You are rejecting the status quo and insisting on what you need. It may be the first time you have ever said no to your family. It may be the first time anyone in your family has said no. If this is the case, you will probably be met with resistance. You may be called selfish or told you are wrecking lives because you "have an ax to grind."

Worst of all, you may find that your family cannot respect your needs, and you must choose between them and your own integrity. Standing up for yourself means running the risk of finding that you can't afford a relationship with your family anymore.

You deserve respect, support, and acknowledgment. You do not gain by remaining part of a family system that undermines your well-being. In fact, many survivors have made great strides in healing by cutting the cord.

But you do not have to make radical changes all at once. You have choices every step of the way. This is a process of testing and trying, evaluating and reevaluating. You can judge the success of any particular strategy or shift what you do as circumstances change. The essential thing is to stay aware that you have the right to make changes, to choose, and to set limits.

DEALING WITH THE ABUSER

The same issues that need to be considered in relating to your family of origin are also important in relating to former abusers.* Of course, you may not want any relationship at all. The abuser may have been a stranger or someone with whom you don't feel a connection. There may be a physical danger. The abuser may be a person you hate or simply someone you don't respect enough to warrant working on a relationship.

But even if the abuser has been through treatment and owned up to everything, it still doesn't mean that you should have contact if you don't want to. It is not your responsibility to be part of the abuser's healing process or life. If you do want a relationship, the possibility of building a healthy one will depend on how much the abuser is able or willing to change, to acknowledge responsibility, or to contribute to your healing.

Setting appropriate guidelines is absolutely essential if you choose to continue a relationship with a former abuser. You must be explicitly clear about what is and isn't acceptable. Unless the abuser has gone through a major transformation, you may need to specify things like the fact that it's not okay to make dirty jokes or to comment on someone's cleavage. You may want to avoid any physical contact, including hello hugs, goodbye kisses, or slaps on the back.

Inappropriate intimacy with the abuser can be harmful to you. One woman, who was a massage therapist, gave her ailing father a massage. The physical contact was devastating to her, and she was distressed for days afterward.

Setting these boundaries and sticking to them is not easy, but it is crucial.

---

* For information on confronting abusers, see "Disclosures and Confrontations" on p. 144.

The incest hasn't stopped, even now. It has stopped actively because I've stopped it. But her incestuous behavior hasn't stopped. She still will call me and say, "Suzanne, why don't you just come home for a week, and lie in my bed with me, and let me smoosh you like I used to." And I say, "Mom, that's what you have Dad for. I'm not here for that." I just cut it. Or if she kisses me on the lips, I stop it. But she'll still say, "What's wrong with that?" And I say, "It does not feel good to me." That's all I say. I've learned not to put myself on the defensive with her.

VISITS

Visiting your family should not be taken lightly. When you are actively in the process of healing from child sexual abuse, time with your family may seem more like work than a vacation. Stop doing it for the wrong reasons: because it's expected, because you have to prove you can do it, because you're supposed to, because one member of your family wants you to work things out with another, because you want some time off to relax.

If you do visit your family, it should be because you have made a decision that visiting is in your best interests. You should know why you're doing it. And you should prepare yourself thoroughly.

Ask yourself:

- Why do I want to visit?
- What do I hope to get out of it?
- Are my expectations realistic?
- Is this the right time for me to go? Is this

FOR ABUSERS: GUIDELINES FOR INTERACTING RESPECTFULLY WITH SURVIVORS

TO THE SURVIVOR:

Many survivors choose to break off all contact with their abusers. But some try to mend the rift. While this rarely results in a healthy relationship, the process of trying to come to resolution with the abuser can be a useful one for the survivor. If you are interacting with the abuser, you may want to set the following guidelines as a basis for your communication.

TO THE ABUSER:

Most abusers do not genuinely try to be helpful to survivors. Sometimes they make no pretense of trying to be helpful; other times they do things that make a show of being helpful, but which in actuality are not. Often their actions are tainted, so that they perpetuate the original dynamics in which the abuse occurred—the misuse of power. The abuse may no longer be sexual, but it's still abuse.

One abuser agreed to pay for his daughter's counseling after she threatened him with legal prosecution. Although he contracted to pay monthly, he was repeatedly overdue, sometimes as much as five months. This caused his daughter embarrassment as well as fear that if he didn't pay, she'd be forced to stop therapy. As a student, she could not pay for herself. Yet her father prided himself on his generosity and expected gratitude.

Looking as if you're helping is not the same as helping. If you really want to help, don't fool yourself. And don't try to fool the survivor. Follow these guidelines in your interactions:

Let the survivor control the relationship. She should choose if, when, and how much she wants to interact. Respect her limits, her boundaries, her pacing. Expect to comply with her needs, rather than asserting your own. For example, if she wants to meet with you, ask her where she would feel most comfortable. Be willing to travel, if necessary. Be willing to take off time from work, if needed.

Honor the survivor's need for distance. If she wants no contact, do not try to see her. If she wants only contact initiated by her, or only contact by letters or only under certain conditions, accept these with the attitude that they are necessary and reasonable.

Honor the survivor's anger. She not only has the right to be angry at you, but it is essential that she be angry at you. She has reason to be. Don't minimize or criticize her anger. Listen. Absorb what she has to say.

Acknowledge full responsibility for what you did and its effects. Make it clear that you know the abuse was entirely your fault. It was not something that happened between you, but rather something you did to her. Make it clear that you know that the effects of the abuse, the problems she continues to suffer from, are your responsibility.

Don't make any excuses. There are none.

Say you're sorry. Say that what you did was wrong.

Make a commitment that you will never act inappropriately again. Obviously this means not sexually abusing the survivor or anyone else. But it means not acting inappropriately in subtle ways as well. It means not telling jokes about sex to the survivor, not admiring her figure, not commenting on her sexuality (or anyone else's in her presence). It means not prolonging physical contact, such as kisses or hugs. If she chooses not to have any physical contact with you, respect that. Be scrupulously careful in your behavior, not only with the survivor, but with all people. Educate yourself about what is and what is not appropriate behavior. Stay aware.

Never use the survivor as a support person in your own struggles. You need your own support system to deal with this issue. If the survivor asks questions about what happened or asks for explanations, answer with the relevant information, but be aware that the survivor is not there to help you. You are there to help her. Don't shift the focus to your problems, past or present.

Go to therapy or into treatment yourself. This is the place to attend to your needs, your problems, your struggles. Find a knowledgeable counselor; join a support group where you will be challenged to confront yourself, not just patted on the back. Make the changes neces-

sary to become a respectful, trustworthy person.

Ask the survivor if and how you can be of help. This could include being available to talk about the abuse, if or when she wants to, acknowledging your responsibility to other family members, or providing financial support for therapy.

.If the effects of the abuse have limited the survivor's educational or vocational opportunities, she may ask you to make financial reparations. Many women find it extremely difficult to do the emotional work necessary for healing while working full time. In these circumstances, she may ask you to provide financial support for a time.

Do what she asks. Do it even if you don't want to. Do it even if you don't think you can. You're responding to a crisis you created long ago. Find a way.

Don't expect that you can make up for what you did. You can't. There's no way to effect justice. But this is *not* an excuse for not doing any of these things.

Don't expect the survivor to forgive you. If there is any forgiveness to be done, you must, through your own healing work, eventually forgive yourself.

You may or may not be able to heal your relationship with the survivor. That will depend both on your willingness and ability to change and on her decision whether a relationship with you is in her best interests, change or no change. And you must respect her decision. But if you act in accordance with these guidelines, you will definitely help the survivor in her healing.

what I need at this point in my healing process?

- How do I usually feel during and after a visit? Do I have reason to believe I'll feel the same or different this time?

When you do visit, make it on your own terms. You can visit at non-holiday times instead of the more loaded traditional ones. You can opt to stay in a motel instead of sleeping at your parents' house, or stop by for an afternoon instead of a week. You can bring a friend along for support. Or plan a visit on neutral turf or at your own home.

Visits are an opportunity to dig for facts, to unearth forgotten memories, to discover more about your history, to compare your memories with those of others, and to collaborate on putting together the whole picture. Sometimes a visit home is a chance to rebuild a broken relationship. Other times it is a validation that, yes, it really was (and still is) as bad as you remembered it. This kind of information is painful and you may not visit again as a result, but it is useful fuel for the healing process.

HOLIDAYS

Traditionally, holidays are times for extended families to come together and celebrate. In addition to whatever personal desires you have to enjoy the holidays with your family, there is enormous cultural pressure to do so. If your relationship with your family is strained, or if you are not seeing them at all, you may feel the loss acutely on holidays (the same can be true of birthdays or significant days of any kind). You may feel lonely and sad. You may be jealous that your friends are visiting their families and you're not. If you don't have close friends to be with, you may feel unloved and alone. You may even feel suicidal. You may be drawn to spend time with your family even though you have an intuition that it's not in your best interests.

You may be tempted to slide into patterns that put you in a compromised position. Be extra careful to protect yourself. All the guidelines for dealing with your family apply to holiday times as well. You are not required to give presents, send cards, visit, or do anything else that doesn't feel right for you. You still have the right—and responsibility—to make conscious choices. A good guideline is not to do anything during holidays that you wouldn't be comfortable doing at other times.

It's okay to feel your grief. You don't have to pretend to be having fun when you're not.

The first holiday after I stopped seeing my family was Thanksgiving. I went to a dinner at the house of an acquaintance and tried to act like I was having a good time, but I ached inside. When Christmas approached I knew I didn't want to do that again. I decided that I just wasn't going to do Christmas. I was in graduate school and I had an enormous amount of work due in January, so I decided to just ignore Christmas and work straight through the day. It turned out much better for me. I felt peaceful and productive.

If you no longer celebrate holidays with your family of origin (or even if you do sometimes), begin traditions of your own. Think back to your childhood. Were there holidays you especially liked? Are there parts of those holidays that you could incorporate into your own traditions? Are there ways you've seen other people celebrate that you'd like to try? Holidays are rituals in which we affirm our values and our relationships. Although most people follow customs established by their families, religion, or culture, it's possible for you to modify these or to create new ones with people of your own choosing.

> Passover has always been an important holiday for me. My grandfather, the patriarch of the family, presided over seders. He also molested me. I stopped going to family seders because I couldn't stand the idea of all my relatives sitting around talking about what a great man he was. So I make my own seders instead.
>
> I always invite the same close friends. We eat the traditional foods—matzoh, hard-boiled eggs, bitter herbs—and sing the traditional songs, but instead of using the customary service, we write our own each year. Since Passover commemorates the Jews' struggle for freedom, each of us talks about what the struggle for freedom means to us today. For me as a survivor, escaping from bondage has taken on a whole new meaning. Combining the old and the new feels liberating, which is what Passover is all about.

BUT HONEY, I LOVE YOU

When a relative who has abused you, not protected you, not believed you, or still doesn't support you in a wholehearted way says, "I love you," you are apt to feel confused and disturbed.

> It infuriated me that she could sit there, smile sweetly, and say, "Honey, I love you." That was her answer to everything—"But honey, I love you," in this weak, little sad voice.

You may sense that there is strong feeling behind those words, but also that there are strings attached. "Love" in your family may mean keeping silent or being bound by obligations you longer want to meet. Many survivors were even abused in the name of love.

Genuine love is a commitment to act in someone's best interests.

> When my mother tells me how much she loves me, and how sorry she is, I don't want to believe it. If I believe she *does* love me, then I have to make sense of the fact that she allowed such a terrible thing to happen to someone she loved. Even though I know, for her, that's love, I know that's not really love. When you love somebody, you'd kill for them. You do whatever's necessary. And she didn't do that. Her love is not the kind of love I can believe in. She doesn't have the instincts of the lioness for her cubs, and that's the kind of primal love I need.

This fierce, clear love isn't available to many survivors from their families. Instead you may be offered love that is smothering, manipulative, controlling, or desperate. Love that doesn't take into account your needs is not really worthwhile. And love that requires you to compromise your integrity, your values, or your healing isn't, ultimately, love.

Yet it can be terrifying to say no to any kind of love. You want it. The need for kinship and closeness is a basic human need. Even the songs tell you "All you need is love." If the love your family has to offer is the only kind of love you've ever known, it can be hard to trust that something better will take its place. When there is some real caring mixed in with the distorted need, it can be even more difficult to turn their love down. But when you start saying no to the kind of love that drains you, you open yourself to recognizing and receiving nourishing love.

DON'T BUY THE BULLSHIT

Family members often lack understanding or compassion for the work you are doing. Their outright accusations or naive blunders can be terrible. Sometimes the insidious nature of a relative who is trying to be supportive, but slips in a little jab now and then, can be harder to deal with than clearcut rejection.

With practice, you can recognize and reject these barbs immediately, before the first strains of self-doubt and confusion set in. To help, we have compiled a list of some of the worst (and most common) one-liners used on survivors by their families.

If you hear one of these, don't believe it. It doesn't matter that your mother says she has your best interests at heart, or that your grandmother has always given you good advice before. Their responses are most likely based on the fact that they are uncomfortable with what you are doing and want you to stop.

These stock lines don't have anything to do with reality, but you're bound to hear at least a few of them. When you do, remember, you're not alone. You read them here first.

- "It happened a long time ago. Why don't you leave it behind you and go on? Stop living in the past."
- "Now what *exactly* did he do?"
- "Your father [uncle, brother, grandfather] would never do such a thing."
- "You've always been crazy. Now you've gone and made this up."
- "You're just jumping on the incest bandwagon."
- "What do you expect me to do about it now?"
- "We only call those experiences to us that we need to grow."
- "It must be karma from a past life."
- "You must have been a very sexy little girl."
- "How did you bring this on yourself?"
- "Are you going to hold on to this forever?"
- "Now honey, it wasn't that bad."
- "It only happened once. What's the big deal?"
- "But he didn't penetrate you, did he?"
- "But didn't you enjoy it?"
- "Why didn't you stop it?"
- "Why didn't you tell me?"
- "I don't believe it. A mother could never do that to her child."
- "Give your brother a chance. He really misses you."
- "Forgive and forget."
- "Your therapist brainwashed you. She implanted these memories in your head."
- "You're the victim of 'false memory syndrome.'"
- "You must be a lesbian because your mother molested you."

- "You must be a lesbian because your father molested you."

Develop an instant bullshit deflector. When one of these comes your way, scoop it up and throw it back. Tell the person you never want to hear that particular bit of advice again.

GIVE IT TIME

When you first tell a relative that you were abused, it may be a shock. But sometimes a lukewarm reception will change to real support if you give people time to work through their initial feelings. If you don't write them off immediately, they may become your allies later on.

If it's not shock or denial, sometimes it's simply ignorance that keeps family members from being supportive. Someone who says, "But it happened twenty years ago. What difference could it make now?" may be totally unaware of the long-term effects of sexual abuse. While it's not your job to educate your relatives, providing a little information may turn a skeptic into a supporter. You might want to give them this book to read. Then, if they're still antagonistic, you'll know it's not because of a lack of information.

Sometimes people who cannot deal with your sexual abuse undergo major changes when the issue surfaces in their own lives. One survivor told her cousin that she'd been molested by their grandfather. The cousin abruptly broke off the relationship:

She left me when I needed her most. I was furious. I felt abandoned

and betrayed. We had no contact for many months, when I received a letter from her explaining that she hadn't been able to listen because she had been molested by him too. She said she was sorry and we met for lunch. Over Chinese food, she was ready to hear about everything that had happened to me—and about how angry I had been with her for leaving. She talked about her own fears and pain. And we recemented our bond more solidly than ever.

DON'T HARBOR UNREALISTIC HOPES

If you want to work out a relationship with someone in your family, it's a good idea to assess the odds. If your father has denied that he abused you for many years, there's little chance that he will significantly alter his outlook. As one woman put it, "He's seventy-two years old. I'm forty-six. I haven't gotten a response from my father in forty years. Why should he start now?"

On the other hand, it's not accurate to say that people never change. Anything is possible. It's like the lottery—we could all win a million dollars. But if you quit your job and start planning to spend the rest of your life on a South Sea island, you're foolish. The odds are simply against it.

SEPARATIONS

Separations can be a part of developing healthier relationships. With certain people in your family, there may have been nurturing as well as abuse or complicity in abuse. As you move along in your healing, you may want to reconnect with the positive aspects of the relationship that are still there. A period of separation can help you to sort out the good from the bad and determine exactly what, if anything, is salvageable. It can also help you to replace the child's longing with the realistic vision of the adult.

Separating from someone in your family should be based on your need to heal in a controlled environment, rather than on hope for a particular outcome. Although you may someday reconcile, it's self-defeating to separate and at the same time carry around a deep longing for the day when your relationship will transform. You control only your end of any relationship. Although you may want a healthy bond, the other person may not be willing or able to reciprocate. Expecting someone to change to meet your needs is an exercise in frustration and futility.

If you decide to make a separation for the sake of your own healing, you will have to let go, grieve, and move on. If you want to reconcile at some point in the future, you can try from your own willingness, knowing there are no guarantees. And if you decide that a permanent separation allows you to live a saner life, that's a responsible decision.

GIVING UP THE FANTASY

Painful as it is to cut off contact with family members, it can be even more painful to give up the fantasy of what your family could have been. In reality, your needs may never have been met, but the child inside has sustained a hope that maybe, maybe someday, your family would come through for you. One woman, the daughter of an abusive, alcoholic father, hadn't seen or talked to him in years when she got word that he was dying: "I was furious because I could no longer hope that he would love me."

Giving Up the Fantasy: Laura's Story

After a six-month estrangement, my mother came to visit me. I sat across from her and read her a letter I had written in her voice. It was the letter I wished I'd received from her during this heart-wrenching period.

Dearest Laurie:

I received your letter today. I'm so sorry you are in so much pain. It has been very difficult for me to believe what you've told me—until now—because I did not want to face the fact that my father could have hurt you that way. Frankly, for me denial has been the easiest way to deal with the unpleasant things in life. But now that I see how deeply this has affected you, I realize that I must step past my own denial and support you. I believe what you have told me. What my father did to you was an atrocity. No wonder it has so deeply affected your life. I know sometimes it must seem like it would have been better never to have remembered at all, but now that you have, you at least can put to rest some of the deep questions you've had about your life.

Laurie, I am so sorry it happened to you. I am sorry I didn't see it, sorry I didn't stop it, and I am sorry you are living with it still. My biggest regret is that I didn't protect you, but you have to remember, Laurie, such things were not even thought of then.

Unfortunately for both of us, nothing can be done about that now. Yet here we are in the present, two adult women. As your mother, I want to give you whatever love and nurturing I can to help you get through this thing. I'm not saying this to rush you. I know it will take time for you to heal from the effect this has had on your life. You've lived with this secret festering inside of you for more than twenty years, and that's got to have taken its toll. I want you to know, Laurie, that you have my full support for as long as it takes for us to lick this thing. He's not going to win, Laurie. You're not going to let him and neither am I. Whatever I can do for you, just let me know.

I also want to tell you that this last year has been one of the hardest years of my life. It has been hell for me to come to accept this about my father, to shatter the picture I had so carefully constructed of the man who raised me.

At times I hated you for bringing this horror into my life, but now I realize that it's not your fault—it's his. He's the one who did this to us. Now that I understand that, I've been able to let go of my anger and put myself in your shoes a little more. I never thought the day would come when I would say this to you, but I'm actually glad you told me. You've given me a chance to give you the kind of love and support I wish I could have given you then, when you couldn't fight back for yourself.

Laurie, I think you are incredibly brave to do this work. I am proud of you. Your willingness to face the truth of your life is an inspiration to me. I only hope I can face my

own life with as much grit and determination. For a while, Laurie, I was convinced that this incest thing would tear us apart and destroy all love between us. But now I know it is only with this kind of truth that we can forge the kind of healthy mother-daughter relationship that we have both always wanted. I truly believe this healing can bring us together.

All my love,
Mom

I had to stop many times as I read, I was crying so hard. When I finished, there was a long silence in the room. Then my mother turned to me and said she couldn't give that to me.

She said, "It's like the Laurie I love so much and want to comfort is sitting right there. And there's this other horrible monster next to her, who's making these accusations about my father."

I told her, "They're just one person, Mom. They're all me. It's a package deal. It's taken me over a year to accept and love that monster and I can't afford to split her off from me anymore, not even for you."

That exchange said it pretty clearly. I was not going to get what I wanted from my mother. She was not going to get what she wanted from me. I had to live my own life.

MAKING THE BREAK

I have no grandparents for my children. My mother is alive. My father is alive. I have grandparents who are alive, and they won't see me. I have aunts and uncles in the same town who won't see me. My sister won't see me.

And it's all because of the incest. I ache for an extended family.

It is painful to make a break with your family, but it is even more painful to keep waiting for a miracle.

One thirty-six-year-old survivor spent years trying to have decent visits with her mother. Each time the visit would fail, she'd berate herself: "Why can't I work it out with my mother?" Then she'd try again, always bolstered up with phone numbers of friends she could call for support. Again the visit would fail.

Finally she decided to stop seeing her mother: "I was sick of repeatedly putting myself in a situation in which I needed back-up reinforcements just to get through. I thought, Why am I doing this to myself? And I decided to give myself a break. I started doing more of what I liked to do, instead of always picking the hardest thing and forcing myself to do it."

This woman stopped torturing herself when she accepted the reality of her situation. "The best relationship I have with my mother is through letters. We write nice letters to each other. We cannot be in the same room, but at least I have a mother in letters."

Another survivor, who was molested by her older brothers, had made plans to visit her sister:

I wrote to my sister and I asked if I could have a party at her house when I came to visit. She said sure, send me a list of the people you want me to invite. So I did. She wrote back and said, "I don't think you should invite Mother because the last time you two were to-gether, it was very uncomfortable for me. And I think you should invite the boys." My brothers! She knows exactly what I'm going through. She said, "There isn't a time they don't ask after you. They love you so much. And I don't think you should invite your friends. They can see you anytime." It was crazy. So I wrote her back and said, "At your suggestion, I have rethought the whole visit. I am going to the coun-try instead."

One survivor, after years of going back and forth, finally came to the conclusion that she had "evolved past" her family altogether. "I have no family," she said. "They're still relating in that old destructive way, and I don't want anything to do with that. Life is too short."

The main factor in the decisions of these women was the respect they had for them-selves. Like them, you can be kind to yourself and take whatever course of action will give you the most peace.

MARKING THE OCCASION

When you experience a major loss, a rit-ual can help you integrate the change and move on. Giving up your family, and the an-guish that causes, deserves recognition.

One woman wrote up a divorce decree, officially terminating her relationship with her parents. Other women have changed their names, casting off any identification with the abuser. One survivor, who was sick of everyone reminding her how much she had loved her father, wrote a will specifying that she did not want her body to be buried in the family plot next to him.

Another woman, who was abused by her mother, created a mother-separation ritual:

As Mother's Day approached, I began to feel depressed and anxious, as if I was sinking into a deep hole. I knew I had to do something. I called the women in my incest support group for a ritual.

They brought candles, wine, and small gifts, tokens of their love for me. I cut a slit in a dress my mother had given me, in the Jewish tradition, a sign of mourning. I had a photo from childhood of me sitting on my mother's lap and I cut us apart with scissors.

Doing the ritual was a powerful marker. Things were not magically different afterwards, but at least I knew what I was shooting for.

Other rituals could include going to the desert, holding a wake, throwing a party, or making a scrapbook or photo album of what *was* good in your childhood. Pick something that has personal significance for you, that will acknowledge and honor your feelings and your decision.

COMING TO RESOLUTION

Resolving things with your family is never completely over. Although it can get much easier, you rarely become invulnerable. If you feel insecure, if your life circumstances change, if you forget the reasons you've set certain limits and consequently break them, you may experience another round of pain. But as time goes on, you will be affected less and you will make your way back to solid ground faster.

If your original family is not a source of enrichment in your life, put your energy into cultivating what you want from sources that can actually yield. Although you may have only one mother, one father, one sister, or one Aunt Bea, you can create an alternative family of your own choosing in the present. Look to your friends, the members of your incest group, your partner, or your children. Although they will not replace what you have lost, they can offer abundant opportunities for nurturing, closeness, and comfort. This is what makes a healthy family.

WRITING EXERCISE: YOUR FAMILY NOW

(See the basic method for writing exercises on page 32.)

What is satisfactory for you in relating to your family of origin now? What do you like? Who are your supporters? Whom do you enjoy being with? What do you get from your contact with them? What are the advantages in being with your family?

What isn't okay for you? What is destructive, irritating, infuriating, frightening, painful? Who are your adversaries? Whom do you feel bad being with? What are the disadvantages of being with your family?

CONSIDERING A LAWSUIT*

In the past decade it has become possible in many states for an adult survivor to file a personal injury lawsuit for sexual abuse that happened in childhood.† After centuries during which the abuse of children was condoned or tolerated, our legal system has begun to recognize the serious damage done by child sexual abuse and to offer survivors recourse through the courts.

Such a lawsuit offers a survivor an opportunity to speak the truth about what happened, to break the silence. She is able to confront the person who abused her in a public forum, to seek monetary compensation for therapy expenses, lost income, and emotional distress, and to ensure that the abuser is confronted, in some way, with the effects of what he or she did.

Socially, such suits have a beneficial effect by promoting greater recognition of the prevalence and harm of child sexual abuse. Mary Williams, a California attorney who represents adult survivors, explains:

---

* We want to thank attorney Mary R. Williams for her contribution to this section. Much of the information presented here is gleaned from interviews with her that were presented more fully in the first two editions of *The Courage to Heal.*

For people considering a lawsuit in California, Mary Williams can provide written materials explaining the statue of limitations. Write to her at: The Creamery Building, P.O. Box 1375, Point Reyes Stations, CA 94956-1375, or call (415) 663-9202.

† For an account of the history of these cases, see *Suing Child Sexual Abusers: A Legal Guide for Survivors and Their Supporters* and other resources listed in the "Legal Resources" section on p. 543 of the Resource Guide.

Ultimately, it's educational for society as a whole for these cases to come into the courts. The legal system is so important to the American consciousness. If victims of sexual abuse use the court system, then people can no longer accept abuse and not talk about it. Abusers can no longer count on not being confronted. And society cannot just sweep it under the rug.

Suing, however, is an arduous process for a survivor. It is notoriously slow, frustrating, grueling, and often expensive. Although the outcome may be worth the work and the stress, the toll a lawsuit takes should not be underestimated. If you are considering suing your perpetrator, it's essential that you think through your decision carefully, weighing the pros and cons, taking into account what you know about yourself, and looking honestly at what will be best for you. Some important questions to ask yourself are:

- Why do I want to sue? What do I hope to get out of it?
- What are my expectations? What do I hope to gain monetarily? Emotionally? Are these goals realistic?
- What are my chances of winning this suit? What might I have to give up in the process?
- How will I feel if I lose the lawsuit? Would such a defeat leave me feeling revictimized?
- How will a lawsuit affect my healing? Is it likely to help me feel empowered, strong, able to stand up for myself? Or is it more likely that I will feel attacked, undermined, or devastated by the process?

- Can I continue to make progress in my healing even while I pursue this lawsuit? Or is it probable that I will have to put my feelings on hold for an extended time?
- Do I have sufficient support in my life to sustain me through the legal process?
- Am I far enough along in my healing that I can withstand attacks on my credibility or challenges to my integrity?
- How will a lawsuit affect my life? Will I be able to carry out my responsibilities to my children? At work? In school? Can I include enough pleasurable, relaxing activities in my life to balance out the strain of a lawsuit? Or am I barely managing to cope as it is? Would a lawsuit push me into crisis?
- How would a lawsuit affect my relationships with my present family (partner, children, chosen family) as well as with members of my family of origin? Are these changes worth it?

Many survivors choose to sue because they want the abuser to admit what he or she has done and take responsiblity for it. But the court system is not designed to achieve that. Mary Williams explains:

Unfortunately, a lawsuit is not a great vehicle for getting someone to admit to something. What lawsuits are best able to do is to get money. A lawsuit is not likely to make the defendant feel differently or to apologize from his heart. Once you file a lawsuit, the defendant is going to fight it. He'll deny it and try to undercut your case.

But, Williams adds, the court system may provide other opportunities for empowerment:

The expectation that there's going to be some kind of emotional resolution is a false one, but a lawsuit does allow the survivor to go into the legal system and stand up to this person as an adult, as an equal, as another citizen who now has power of her own.

It is often a cathartic experience for victims to talk about the abuse, to say things that have been said only to a few people, and to say them in an adversarial situation where they're sitting across the table from someone who is being paid to cross-examine them. It's really an experience of standing up for yourself and saying the truth.

The aftermath of a lawsuit may be difficult as well as rewarding. Many survivors feel that it's been worth the effort, that they've grown emotionally, become stronger, and experienced greater personal power and self-esteem. Yet, as Mary Williams describes, there's often a feeling of disappointment and letdown at the same time:

With lawsuits, even if you win, you seldom win clearly and overwhelmingly, nor do you get everything you're entitled to. The process is always a compromise.

Another thing that can happen after a lawsuit is that the survivor suddenly has to deal with all the feelings that came up during the lawsuit, which she couldn't afford to feel fully while it was going on. Even though the lawsuit was resolved in her favor, the effects of the abuse haven't necessarily disappeared or become any

Box continues on page 320.

easier. The emotional reconstruction still has to be done.

But again, a lot of my clients also feel a tremendous sense of relief and victory. The lawsuit produces a healthy separation that can be a rite of passage for the survivor. He or she is often able, through this experience, to put closure on a certain aspect of their relationship to the abuser, and to move forward in life with more positive energy than before.

The decision to sue is a highly personal one. Depending on your situation, a lawsuit may or may not be something you want to pursue. Some survivors have never considered suing. Others have learned that the laws in their state or their own particular circumstances precluded the possibility.

If you are considering a lawsuit, it is important to recognize that the legal arena has become a battleground. As we explain in "Honoring the Truth" (see page 473), legal challenges to perpetrators have been a motivating factor in the current backlash against survivors. So if you go to court today, you will be entering the legal system at a time when your memories (and your therapist) are likely to be attacked by expert witnesses for the defense, when the media may challenge your credibility, and when your perpetrator may fight back vigorously, claiming that he has been falsely accused. This doesn't mean suits cannot be won—they can be—but it does mean that suing can be complex and demanding. And in cases in which there is little hope of proving that the abuse took place, it is unlikely that a trial will result in justice, vindication, or healing.

It's essential that survivors have the opportunity to seek justice through the courts. But whether or not this endeavor is right for you is a decision that should not be made lightly. Each survivor must weigh his or her decision carefully, with full consciousness of the risks and challenges involved, the likely impact on the process of healing, and a realistic understanding of what can and cannot be accomplished through the law.

COUNSELING

One counselor said to me, "You're at the center of your healing process. I'm just one of your tools." I really liked that. That's the way healing should be.

—Saphyre

The support of a skilled counselor can be extremely helpful in your healing. A good counselor is a compassionate witness to your healing. By offering consistent support, encouragement, hope, information, and insight, a counselor provides a safe space within which we can learn to accept ourselves. Laura explains:

When I couldn't believe in myself, when I didn't know if I could make it, my counselor believed in me. Week after week, she sat there, a loving witness to my pain and my progress. She loved me no matter what I did or said. For the first time in my life, I felt accepted as if I were valuable—not for what I did, but just for who I was. That was her greatest gift.

For many people, a counselor provides a safe place to spill out the secrets and pain—and the hopes—that have been held inside.

For me the most important thing about therapy is that there is someone who will listen to you. Freely. He won't talk back, or correct you, or interrupt, or tell you you're wrong, or undermine you in more subtle ways. You can say anything you want, you can say the things closest to your heart, the things you may never have told anyone, and it's all right.

Some people think a therapist will try to fix them, like an auto mechanic—tinker here, adjust there, change a part—and this will feel disruptive and invasive and troubling. But if it's a good therapeutic relationship, it's not like that. Ultimately you do get "fixed." You do get healed, but in the places you need to be and in a way that feels right. It's comforting and it's a relief.

For survivors who were hurt by the people closest to them, one of the most important things about seeing a therapist may be that you have an opportunity to trust again.

Trusting my counselor wasn't easy. It took a lot of work—on both our parts. When I look back on it now, I have to laugh sometimes at what I put her through. Once she was going on vacation and she said she'd be back in a week. I called her in seven days and she wasn't there. She stayed away nine days. I felt so betrayed, hurt and furious. When she got back, I confronted her. She explained that since it was a work week and two weekends, she just said a week, but she took a lot of time to acknowledge my feelings and she told me she'd be more precise in the future. It must have taken real patience on her part to apologize and promise to be more careful. But that's the kind of response I needed. And bit by bit, I really did learn to trust her.

There's a magic that takes place in therapy, a transformation. Feelings are reclaimed, ancient hurts are resolved, lives are re-envisioned, and the future opens up with possibility. What once seemed impossible and unattainable often comes within reach. Therapy can be a powerful vehicle for change.

CHOOSING A COUNSELOR

Be willing to put in a fair amount of effort to find a counselor. You don't have to go to the first person you see. Even if you are in crisis and feel you can't make it through the week if you don't get help, hold off on committing yourself to a long-term therapy relationship until you've looked around thoroughly.

Ask for recommendations from friends, other survivors, or family members. Battered women's shelters, rape crisis centers, parents' centers, and other women's programs are also likely places to get referrals.

You can save money and time by doing some preliminary screening on the phone. Counselors have different policies about this. Many will talk to you for ten or fifteen minutes on the phone for free.

Once you've narrowed down your choices over the telephone, talk in person to the two or three you liked most. One woman went to six counselors, one each week, until she found the person she wanted to work with.

When you're evaluating potential counselors, there are some guidelines you should keep in mind. It's important that your prospective counselor:

- never minimizes your experiences or your pain
- has information (or is willing to get infor-

mation) about the healing process for adults who were sexually abused as children

- keeps the focus on you, not on your abuser
- gives you room to explore your own history without trying to define it for you
- doesn't push for reconciliation or forgiveness
- doesn't want to have a friendship with you outside of counseling
- doesn't talk about his or her personal problems
- doesn't want to have a sexual relationship with you, now or ever in the future
- fully respects your feelings (grief, anger, rage, sadness, despair, joy)
- doesn't force you to do anything you don't want to do*
- encourages you to build a support system outside of therapy
- encourages your contact with other survivors of child sexual abuse
- teaches you skills for taking care of yourself
- is willing to discuss problems that occur in the therapy relationship
- is accountable for mistakes that he or she makes

Ask questions to get a sense of the counselor's attitudes, experience, and way of working. There may also be particular issues that matter to you. For instance, you may

---

* The only exceptions to this are if you are actively suicidal or are threatening to hurt someone else. If you disclose a situation in which a child is being abused today, your therapist will be mandated to report that abuse, whether you want it reported or not. When faced with a mandatory report, many counselors will help you become strong enough to do the reporting yourself.

want someone familiar with alcoholism or with eating disorders. Many survivors prefer working with a woman because they feel safer, because they were molested by a man, or because they are more comfortable discussing intimate feelings with a woman. Other women have benefited from working with male therapists because they wanted a safe relationship in which they could learn to trust a man. Choose whichever gender you want to work with. You may also prefer to choose a counselor of your race, economic background, sexual orientation, or religion.

As a nun I felt more comfortable going to a nun because we could talk about spiritual things. If you get the wrong counselor, they say, "Spiritual, smiritual. There is no God." My counselor was a nun herself. So I was able to join a group for incest and rape survivors that was made up of just nuns. That way we didn't have to talk about our marriage partners or our sexual partners. We all had the issue of being "good," and we had a lot of the same guilts. I would have been very nervous as a religious to talk about sexual things in a secular group. I would have been very conscious of the fact that I was a nun, and that that was fascinating to people. This group was safe. We could focus on what was important.

Your needs may not be this specialized and your options may vary depending on where you live. But it's worth trying to find the best person for you.

Once you've talked to several counselors, compare the way you felt when you were talking with each of them. Whom did you feel the strongest connection with? Where were you most at ease? Think about the way each person responded to your concerns. Compare their availability, philosophies, and cost.

When you're looking for a counselor, it's helpful to take the attitude that you are a consumer making an informed choice about the person you're hiring to work with you. Even though you're seeking counseling to fill an emotional need, being a consumer gives you certain rights: the right to determine the qualities you want in a therapist, the right to be treated with respect, the right to say no to any of the suggestions your therapist makes, the right to be satisfied with the services you're receiving, the right to freely discuss any problems that arise in therapy with your counselor, and the right to end a therapy relationship that isn't working for you.

IF YOU'VE BEEN AVOIDING COUNSELING

Although it's wise to choose carefully, don't insist on so many qualifications that no one can meet your criteria.

I kept picking counselors that I could easily get rid of. I went to see seven different counselors for either one or two sessions. I would go to great lengths to find people who worked far away from where I lived, so I could say, "Oh well, this is too far to drive."

I would pick nontraditional therapies because I didn't want to work on things. One time I picked a past-life counselor, and you know that wasn't what I needed to work on!

I'd make the initial appointment because I felt desperate. Within one or two visits, I wouldn't be quite that desperate, and so I'd quit.

Soledad wanted to see only a lesbian Chicana counselor who had worked with sexual abuse.* Since there was no one who met these specifications in her area, she could have talked herself out of going to therapy. But she decided getting help was more important. She compromised and found a skilled woman who has effectively facilitated her healing.

WHAT DOES EFFECTIVE COUNSELING FEEL LIKE?

When you work with a good counselor, you should feel understood and supported. You should feel warmth between you and your counselor. And that should happen early in the therapy process.

However, you can't judge whether it's good therapy by the way you feel in the moment. Some women experience counseling as a haven they can't wait to get to. Others dread every session and have to force themselves to go. One woman said, "There were times I was absolutely terrified of going to therapy. I don't know how I drove there, how I got out of my car, how I got through the door."

Counseling is not always comfortable, but you know you're with a good counselor if

---

* For more of Soledad's story, see p. 384.

you develop more and more skills in taking care of yourself as time goes on. Even if there's an initial period of strong dependency, you should eventually become more independent. Gizelle's counselor was able to do this for her:*

> I really owe a lot to my counselor. When I was struggling time and again and would say, "Where do I go from here? What should I do?" he would say, "Trust your process. Trust yourself. *You* know." The greatest gift he's given me is belief in myself. He constantly reflected to me my own knowing and my own power, my own ability to heal. He never gave me the answers. *He* never did the healing. It's very important to work with people who help you get back your power, who help you get back your trust in your body, in your instincts, in your gut, in your voice, in you.

Although your relationship with your therapist may be tremendously significant to you, it is essential that you don't relinquish all of your power in the counseling relationship. Remember that you are at the center of your life and your healing. A good counselor is only one of the many resources you will use.

IF YOU FEEL THERE'S A PROBLEM

If you don't feel respected, valued, or understood, or if your experience is being minimized or distorted, that's a sign that you're in bad therapy, or at least that there's a bad fit between you and the counselor. If you feel there is something wrong in the therapy relationship, or if you get upset or angry with your counselor, talk about it in your session. Afterward, you should feel you've been heard and understood. However, if your counselor discounts your feelings or responds defensively, then you're not getting the respect you need. Look elsewhere.

If you feel your therapist is pressuring you to say you were abused, you're seeing the wrong therapist. No one else can tell you whether or not you were abused. You are the expert in your own life. Find someone who will follow your lead, not insist they know your final destination.

If a counselor ever wants to have a sexual relationship with you, get out right away. Report the therapist to the appropriate licensing board. It is never okay for therapists to have romantic or sexual involvements with their clients.

If you have had a damaging experience with a counselor, you have a right to be angry, but don't let a negative therapy experience stop you from getting the help you need and deserve. There are a number of good books on abuse by counselors that can help to validate your feelings and support your healing. Before you commit yourself to another counseling relationship, think about what you want; take your time and utilize the resources available in order to protect yourself in the future.

---

* For more of Gizelle's story, see p. 461.

SUPPORT GROUPS

Being with other survivors is a critical part of the healing process, and joining a group can be an ideal way to work with other women who've been abused. Group work is particularly useful for dealing with shame, isolation, secrecy, and self-esteem. Talking with other survivors is helpful for problem-solving also. There's likely to be at least one other woman in the room who has suggestions for dealing with whatever issue you're facing.

In groups, survivors get together at a regularly scheduled time specifically to support each other in their healing. Groups can be organized for a set number of weeks or they can be ongoing. They can focus on a particular topic—such as anger or sexuality—or they can be more general. In leaderless groups (these usually are free), all members share responsibility for running the group. Groups led by a trained facilitator or counselor usually have a weekly or monthly fee.

Being with a group gives you the opportunity to be with survivors of child sexual abuse as they share their feelings, their struggles, and their triumphs. You see women who, in spite of their pain and problems, are strong, beautiful people with integrity. You can see that the abuse was not their fault, that they are not to blame. You can be outraged on their behalf and compassionate with their suffering—kindnesses you may not yet have extended to yourself. And as you realize that you are a lot like these other women—that you are one of them—you learn to see yourself in the same affirming light.

One survivor, Jennierose Lavender, explained the benefits she gained from being in a support group:

When I joined a group with other survivors, it was the first time I ever felt connected with anybody. All my life I had felt alone. I had never trusted anyone. I had always isolated myself. All those years in therapy, I had just played psychiatrist with them. I told them the kinds of things I knew they wanted to hear. I never could talk about my fears or what was really bothering me.

But now I wasn't alone anymore. There were other people who had the same kind of symptoms I did, for the same kinds of reasons. I started to reach out and make friends. It was an incredible relief.

Working in a group is the only helpful therapy I've gotten in my whole life, and I've been in therapy since I was six years old. That's forty-one years. Being in a group is better than being with a therapist because other survivors really understand—they weren't *taught* to understand. And hearing other people's stories has sparked things in my memory.

STANDARDS FOR A GOOD GROUP

A good support group should be a safe and respectful space in which each member is valued. Expectations should be clear, participants should share time and focus equitably, and no one should dominate or be excluded. You should feel accepted and able to speak honestly about your experience and your feelings. No one should be made to feel that she needs to exaggerate either her abuse or her pain to deserve attention. Because survivors share extremely vulnerable parts of themselves, support groups are not appropriate places for confrontations and criticism. Instead, the focus should be on each woman's individual and unique healing journey.

A MUTUAL JOURNEY

When you entrust a counselor to witness and support your healing, you are allowing that person to see you, to know you, and to touch your life in a profound way. The counselor should consider it an honor and a privilege—and should extend to you the best of his or her skills, experience, and compassion. For your part, you offer the willingness to face your past and to work honestly with your best efforts. The result is a collaboration in which you are able to heal, to grow, and to create a rich and satisfying life. As one survivor expressed it:

A therapist once said to me, "Psychotherapy is looking your destiny in the face and saying 'NO!'" The people who abused me would have left me feeling worthless or going insane. In therapy I got an outside, objective assessment, the chance to be heard, the chance to connect with supportive people and not be alone with fear or pain, or even joy.

I gained a sense of perspective that wasn't distorted. I found that the things I had been ridiculed for as a child were not indictments of me, but symptoms of abuse. I discovered that I was living in a situation where new rules apply: no one can hit or rape me and force me to suffer such brutality in silence.

But beyond that, I learned about human decency. I found out that the world is not only full of violent people, but that there are many or even more folks like me. For me therapy was a process of coming home, into the native land that had not been mine as a child. Therapy taught me that I felt bad about being an ugly duckling for so long because I was really a swan. What a gift!

Counseling is not the only context in which such healing can take place. Many survivors do their healing work in other ways—through art, music, writing, outdoor adventures, spirituality, and activism, to name a few. Survivors draw their support from friends, partners, family members, and other survivors. But for many, counseling is at the core of their support system, providing a safe and supportive haven that makes growth and transformation a reality.

PART FOUR

FOR SUPPORTERS

OF SURVIVORS

THE BASICS

Being a close supporter of a woman actively healing from child sexual abuse can be a challenge. While being part of a deep healing process holds the potential for tremendous growth and intimacy, it can also leave you feeling conflicted, overwhelmed, or resentful. You may be frightened or confused, unsure what to do, how to feel, or what to expect. These are natural and appropriate responses to a complex and trying human situation.

This is a time when it's important for you to take care of yourself. It's essential that you honor your own needs. If the survivor wants more than you are able to give, admit your limits. Encourage her to call on other resources. Take some breaks. Get help for yourself. Dealing with such raw pain is difficult, and you need a place where you can express your own fears and frustrations.

If you find yourself feeling extremely defensive or upset when the survivor talks about her abuse, you may be reacting from experiences you've repressed from your own past. This is very common. One person's pain frequently brings up hurts for another. Seek support in dealing with your own unresolved feelings. You are important too.

All intimate relationships—friends, couples, or family—have a lot in common. "For Partners" (page 337) offers specific suggestions that will help even if you're not in a partnered relationship with the survivor.

HOW TO HELP

When a survivor tells you that she was sexually abused as a child, she is entrusting you with a part of her life that is painful,

For Neil, Because You Asked
by Krishnabai

Stress, long my enemy,
visits me often
wearing long, full skirts
which harbour her children.
They creep out
when my back is turned.
They try to overtake me.

The eldest, Fear
is strong and cruel.
He jumps on my back,
arms around my throat
shrieks horrors in my ears,
and on fast feet I jump
out the window,
scream down the street
into the dark
horizon of night,
and only much later do I return
ragged, weeping, alone.

Here's how to care for me
when I'm with Fear:
move softly as approaching
a luna moth,
have gentle, calm eyes,
stay centered from my panic,
and, if we ever
reach this place of safety—
just hold me.

frightening, and vulnerable. These guidelines can help you honor that trust and assist her healing:

- **Believe the survivor.** Even if she sometimes doubts herself, even if her memories are vague, even if what she tells you sounds too extreme, believe her. Women rarely make up stories of abuse. Let her know that you are open to hearing anything she wishes to share, and that although it's painful and upsetting, you are willing to enter those difficult places with her and to receive her words with respect.

- **Join with the survivor in validating the damage.** All abuse is harmful. Even if it's not violent, overtly physical, or repeated, all abuse has serious consequences. There is no positive or neutral experience of sexual abuse.

- **Be clear that abuse is never the child's fault.** No child seduces an abuser. Children ask for affection and attention, not for sexual abuse. Even if a child responds sexually, even if she wasn't forced or didn't protest, it is still never the child's fault. It is always the responsibility of the adult not to be sexual with a child.

- **Educate yourself about sexual abuse and the healing process.** If you have a basic idea of what the survivor is going through, it will help you to be supportive. See the Resource Guide for suggested reading.

- **Don't sympathize with the abuser.** The survivor needs your absolute loyalty.

- **Validate the survivor's feelings: her anger, pain, and fear.** These are natural, healthy responses. She needs to feel them, express them, and be heard.

- **Express your compassion.** If you have feelings of outrage, compassion, pain for her pain, do share them. There is probably nothing more comforting than a genuine human response. Just make sure your feelings don't overwhelm hers.

- **Respect the time and space it takes to heal.** Healing is a slow process that can't be hurried.

- **Encourage the survivor to get support.** In addition to offering your own caring, encourage her to reach out to others. (See "Counseling," page 321.)
- **Get help if the survivor is suicidal.** Most survivors are not suicidal, but sometimes the pain of childhood abuse is so devastating that women want to kill themselves. If you are close to a survivor who is suicidal, get help immediately. (See "Dealing with Suicide," page 347.)

- **Accept that there will very likely be major changes in your relationship with the survivor as she heals.** She is changing, and as she does, you may need to change in response.
- **Resist seeing the survivor as a victim.** Continue to see her as a strong, courageous woman who is reclaiming her own life.

FOR FAMILY MEMBERS

Child sexual abuse is a difficult thing to face. When a survivor tells you that she was abused, you will have many strong feelings. You may feel guilty, enraged, appalled, or devastated. You may feel threatened or trapped. You may not believe the survivor.* You may feel attacked or blamed. You may feel deep compassion and sorrow for her pain. Or you may feel confused, hopeless, or even completely numb. If the abuser is (or was) a family member, the image you have of your family will be shaken. If the perpetrator is your husband, son, brother, or father, someone within your immediate family circle, you will be faced with agonizing choices.

You may have to make critical decisions about separation, divorce, family loyalty. Your life will be thrown into turmoil.

Although it is distressing to give up your image of your family, this is a crucial opportunity for everyone to face unhealthy patterns. If child sexual abuse is not dealt with, it often repeats itself generation after generation. It is a serious problem that affects the whole family, not just the survivor.

PARENTS WHO DIDN'T ABUSE

Although it is a terrible thing for a parent to realize that she (or he) has not protected a child, your opportunities to be a good parent are not over. When your daughter tells you that she was abused, or when she begins to work on her healing, you have an opportunity to be helpful. Don't deny your

---

* And with the claims of "false memories" so prominent in the media, you may be tempted to latch onto an explanation that says your daughter's memories of sexual abuse were implanted by a therapist. (See "Honoring the Truth," p. 473, for more.)

334

child's experience—or her pain. Don't allow yourself to be overwhelmed by guilt or regret for what you didn't do before. Your feelings need recognition and expression—and for that reason you should seek support for yourself—but don't lose sight of the chance to be an understanding parent to your adult child in the present. Your compassion, courage, and willingness to change are extremely valuable.

If the survivor feels you didn't protect her, she may be very angry at you. Although no one is ever responsible for someone else abusing a child, children have the right to expect to be protected by their parents and other caretakers.

If you are a mother, be aware that our society is more comfortable with anger directed at women than at men. Although a mother is responsible for failing to notice that her child is being abused or for not protecting her, she is not responsible for the abuse itself. The person who abuses the child is always to blame for that. (See "Working Through Mother Blame," on page 136.)

Accept the responsibility for not protecting your daughter. Apologize. Tell her you wish you had been awake enough to see what was going on, strong enough to recognize it, courageous enough to stand up for her. And then take her side now. Acknowledge her feelings rather than defending yourself or the abuser. Stand up for her now.

It's a good idea for you to get counseling to sort out your own complex feelings. Both individual counseling and a group with other parents whose children have been abused can be helpful.*

There are also a number of worthwhile books for parents of children who have been abused. A couple have been written for parents of adult children; the majority are intended for the parents of young or adolescent children. See the "For Family Members of Adult Survivors" and the "If Your Child Is Abused" sections of the Resource Guide (pages 570 and 577).

SIBLINGS

If your sister was abused by a relative, or if there were other abusive elements in your home (alcoholism, battering, neglect), you were affected by the same family dynamics. You too grew up in a family in which there was betrayal, secrecy, pain, and fear. One way or another, you suffered.

If you weren't sexually abused yourself, you may feel guilty. You may criticize yourself for not having protected your sister. It's common for those who escape abuse to blame themselves. Those who live through situations in which others are hurt or killed often feel guilt, question "Why me?" and struggle both emotionally and spiritually to come to terms with the injustice of tragedy. Whatever your feelings, you will need support. This is a stressful time for everyone.

If you were abused but have not dealt with your feelings, you may be threatened or angry when your sister speaks out, forcing you to face your own abuse. Don't criticize her for wanting to deal with this. Don't aban-

---

* See "Counseling," p. 321, for guidelines on screening for a therapist. Although you may not be a survivor yourself, you will still want to see someone sensitive to the subject of child sexual abuse.

don her. Instead, get help for yourself. Find a counselor who is knowledgeable about sexual abuse. You are a survivor too. You too deserve more than coping and Band-aids. You deserve to heal.

Since many children cope with abuse by blocking out the memory, it is possible that you were abused too. If you find yourself extremely frightened, confused, or angry at her when your sister brings up the issue, be open to the possibility that it may have happened to you.

Whether you were abused or not, you both grew up in the same family, and by talking together you can lend each other invaluable help. You may have a memory she needs. She may be able to fill in a piece of your puzzle. The functioning of many families is so distorted, so painful, so confusing, that survivors often find it hard to trust their memories. You can confirm for each other that things were as bad as they seemed. And that neither of you is crazy. For a survivor to have even *one* member of her family who validates her reality is invaluable. You are in a position to give a great gift, and the gain for you can be the healing of your own childhood wounds.*

---

* For a good example of what supportive siblings can do for each other's healing, see "Michelle and Artemis" on p. 446.

FOR PARTNERS

Unless you have your own psychological house in order, relating to a survivor opens up old wounds and challenges every facet of the way you live. My feelings toward Barb run the whole gamut from "What did I do to deserve a relationship with a screwed-up person like you?" to "If we can hang on and lick this, my life will be rich beyond measure."

—Phil Temples, husband of a survivor

The information in this chapter pertains to all couples—married and unmarried, heterosexual and lesbian. Although there are significant differences in cultural conditioning, power dynamics, and role expectations between heterosexual and lesbian couples, these differences are far outweighed by the common problems all couples face when one or both partners are survivors.

This chapter addresses the partners of survivors, but many of the suggestions will be equally useful to other family members and to the survivors themselves.

For more in-depth information for partners, we recommend Allies in Healing: When the Person You Love Was Sexually Abused as a Child. *See page 569 of the Resource Guide.*

Being the partner of someone actively healing from child sexual abuse has both problems and rewards, although the problems are often more obvious than the rewards.

Survivors commonly have difficulties with trust, intimacy, and sex, all of which have a direct impact on your relationship. Often, at least for a time, the survivor's problems and healing dominate your time together. Depending on the stage of the healing process the survivor is in, she may be angry, depressed, or totally preoccupied. She may be self-destructive or suicidal. (If the survivor is suicidal, see "Dealing with Suicide" on page 347.) She may have a great need for maintaining control in her life. Sometimes the abusive patterns from her original family are acted out with you or your children.

As a partner, you may not understand what is going on. You may feel inadequate because you can't fix things, guilty if you aren't 100 percent supportive. You may be isolated, with no one to talk to. Partners often feel frustrated at the amount of time healing takes. Sometimes you will have to continue to deal with the survivor's abusive family members. Other times, your own family history will be reawakened, accompanied by painful emotions. And all the while, your own needs may not be getting met.

If both you and your partner are survivors, your relationship can be affected in complex ways. Depending on how far along you are in the healing process, you may be able to offer each other tremendous support, reassurance, and understanding. On the other hand, you can intensify each other's struggles, trigger memories and old patterns, and otherwise get entangled in painful dynamics.

Since so many women have been abused,

WHERE ARE YOU NOW?

- You suspect your partner is a survivor but isn't aware of it yet.
- Your partner has just recognized that she's a survivor. She's starting to have memories, and you're totally bewildered.
- Your partner admits she was abused, but says it has nothing to do with your relationship or her life today. You think differently, but she refuses to discuss it.
- You understand that the survivor has a problem but don't think it has any connection with you. Up until now you may have thought it was all her responsibility. Now you're starting to wonder.

- Both you and the survivor have been working on these issues for a few years. You have good communication and a basic handle on these issues, but want help in dealing with a few problem areas.
- You want help with sex.
- You're just getting involved with someone who hands you this book and says she thinks you should look it over.
- You're on the verge of splitting up. This is your last resort.
- Your partner is suicidal. Your life is falling apart. Everything's in chaos. You don't know what to do.
- You've just separated from a woman who is a survivor and you want to understand why you broke up.

lesbian couples often find themselves in this situation. So do an increasing number of heterosexual couples, as more men are beginning to identify their childhood abuse. If both you and your partner are survivors, this will create both liabilities and opportunities. Be especially patient and compassionate with yourselves and each other, and consider couples counseling with an experienced therapist.

THE BENEFITS

There are powerful positive elements to being in a close relationship with someone healing from childhood sexual abuse, but sometimes these may be hard to see. At a workshop for partners of survivors, Ellen suggested that the participants write about the ways they could benefit from being in a relationship with a survivor—what were the opportunities for them? One man sat through the fifteen minutes allotted for this exercise, looking perplexed. At the end he said, "I'm really confused. I came here to learn how to help my wife with her problems and now I'm supposed to be finding my opportunities!?"

It may seem crazy to look for what is positive for you, personally, in a situation that causes you—and the survivor—a lot of pain and stress. But there are valuable aspects to being the partner of a survivor.

Being with someone actively engaged in the healing process means that you are in a growing relationship, not a stagnant one. One man said:

People unconsciously pick a mate where your meeting point is where you both need to grow, and that's definitely true for us. Around this issue of sexuality is where we're both wounded and we're both the most deaf to each other. There's no way I would dredge through my own shit as deep as I have if I didn't have to relate to Karen. If we each didn't have this problem, we wouldn't each be confronting our own shadow.

One partner found that her own problem area was learning to be separate:

She's good at autonomy. She knows how to take care of herself. She's not so good at intimacy. I'm good at intimacy. Give me a person and I'll merge. Being with her, I've had to learn to be independent.

Another partner grew in his capacity to express feelings:

As I look back over the last six months, I realize the tremendous personal growth we've both undergone. I've always lagged a bit behind in the communications department. But I'm now expressing feelings and allowing myself to experience emotions that never before would have been possible. At the height of an argument I can now recognize when I'm no longer mad, but instead very sad—and then I can cry.

If you haven't been used to thinking about your own feelings, your own fears, or the ways you were influenced by your childhood, you may initially feel uncomfortable with such a major focus on self-exploration. But even if this is unfamiliar to you, the emphasis on growth can provide you with valuable opportunities. And working together can bring you closer to your partner, build your foundation more solidly.

> When we've come through the rocky points, we were able to look at each other with pride and say "We did it!" It was a sense of mutual accomplishment. That's been a real special thing in our relationship.

Taking part in a deep healing process is a miracle and an inspiration. Although it's demanding, it is also a privilege. There are rewards both in the giving and in the receiving.

DON'T TAKE IT PERSONALLY

Intimacy is paradoxical in relationships with survivors, especially if they were abused by someone they were close to. Their love and trust were met with betrayal. Now, the more intimate a relationship becomes, the more it feels like "family," the scarier it is for the survivor. If you're unaware of this dynamic, the whole thing can look crazy.

Some survivors have had more superficial relationships in the past and have handled them relatively well. They may have managed short-term relationships, or even long-term ones, before they began to deal actively with the abuse. They kept their coping mechanisms intact and though some depth was sacrificed, things functioned.

If the two of you really love each other and yet the relationship is rocky, this does not mean that something is wrong. It's more likely to mean there's something very right— so right, in fact, that she's threatened. If both of you know that it is frightening for her to get close—and for good reason—then it's less likely you'll be diverted into dwelling on rejection, fighting, or breaking up.

Survivors always tell their partners, "Don't take it personally." This is extremely difficult because so much of it *is* personal.

> A lot of my fears sexually have always had to do with rejection. I'm a very threatening size and part of me has internalized those threatening pictures as who I am: "Okay, I'm a real monster." I began to believe that all the things that are frightening and injurious about maleness were embodied in me. Having Karen withdraw brought all those feelings right to the surface.

If the survivor withdraws, is angry, is sad, needs time alone, doesn't want to make love, all this affects you personally. And yet it is true that her behavior does not necessarily reflect her feelngs for you or for your relationship. In reality, your partner is either repeating coping behaviors from years before you ever met her, or she is doing what she needs to do to heal. It often has very little to do with you.

Maintaining a balance between sharing wholeheartedly in the process and keeping an appropriate sense of independence and separateness is one of the challenges of supporting a woman who is actively healing from child sexual abuse. Throughout, you will be trying to encourage her, nurture yourself, and create healthy patterns for a relationship that will serve you not only during this crisis, but throughout life.

OVERCOMING SHAME

One man at a workshop for partners asked Ellen, "Could you talk about shame?" So Ellen went on at length about survivors' shame for having been abused, for having experienced sexual arousal, for having needed attention, for the ways in which they coped. When she finally stopped, the partner looked at her blankly. "Am I getting to what you want?" Ellen asked.

"No," he said. "I mean the kind I felt today when I was coming to this workshop and I had to tell my co-workers where I was going. I didn't tell them. I made up something."

Yes. You may be ashamed too. You're not supposed to have problems. Your sex life is supposed to be terrific, your relationship perfect. You're not supposed to need counseling, workshops, or help.

Partners, as well as survivors, find obstacles that keep them from reaching out for support—or even from just being honest about where they're going. And shame is a major one. But you have nothing to be ashamed of. There is nothing shameful about loving a woman who is working to heal from trauma. There is nothing shameful about experiencing the problems that result from such abuse. There is nothing shameful about your own pain, anger, or fear.

GETTING SUPPORT

Just as survivors need support through the healing process, you need support as well. Some of this can come from the survivor, but the demands on her own healing are often too great for her to have a lot of energy left over to support you. Nor should you expect it. As one survivor put it: "If someone has a heart attack, you don't go into the hospital and go on and on about how upset *you* are about *their* heart attack. You talk about it with other people, and you act confident while you're with that person about their ability to heal. You have to approach survivors the same way."

Yet you need someone to listen to your pain, your fears, your frustrations, and your confusion. You need compassion too.

> For the partner, it's bewildering. There's no information. There's no way to cope with what seems like rejection. I would not have been able to do it, as dedicated as I was to making this relationship work, without knowledge of what was happening. I had a friend who was an incest survivor too. Talking to her about her feelings helped me understand what the impact of abuse can be.

It is essential that you have time when it's safe to express your feelings bluntly. You need to air your anger, your frustration, your despair. Sometimes you need to just stomp around and yell, "I can't take it anymore!" The survivor needs to hear these feelings from you too, but she probably doesn't need to hear them as frequently as you need to express them.

- **Talk to a counselor.** Couples counseling or individual therapy can provide you with essential support.
- **Seek out friends who are good listeners.** Before you do this, clarify with your part-

ner the specifics of what you can share and with whom. But within these guidelines, share. It's not healthy to be isolated with your feelings.

• **Find other partners of survivors.** Other partners can be a tremendous source of comfort and support. If there are workshops specifically for partners in your area, that's great. If not, your partner may know other survivors who have partners. Try calling a local counseling center for leads. If you're already in counseling, ask your counselor about starting a group for partners.

There still aren't many resources for partners, but it's worth the effort to build a support network. The chance to talk and to listen can be an incredible relief. As one man put it, "You think there's something wrong with you—that you're too demanding, too impatient—and then you hear everybody else feels that too. It's like the burden drops. You can stop thinking of yourself as a rapist just because you want sex. You can stop feeling so bad about yourself."

TAKING CARE OF YOURSELF

Although any caring person feels the pain of a loved one, excessive identification with the survivor's pain is not healthy. Some partners are more comfortable attending to the survivor's problems than to their own. If you played the caretaker role in your original family, you may be doing so now out of habit. Also, by immersing yourself in taking care of the survivor, you are shielded from facing your own issues.

If this has been your pattern, it will be a difficult but necessary change in perspective to make a distinction between your partner's feelings, wants, or needs and your own.* Do whatever it takes to get some time alone for yourself, to get to know yourself separately from your partner and her problems.

DO THINGS THAT MAKE YOU FEEL GOOD

Many, if not most, people look to their partners for their primary emotional contact and companionship. But while your partner is immersed in her own healing, she may not have the time, energy, ability, or desire to meet your needs. It's essential that as the partner of a survivor and also as an autonomous person, you not be totally dependent on your lover and your family for all your nurturance.

Start to make meaningful connections with people outside your relationship, and find fulfilling activities that are your own. Think about the things that make you feel good, and do these things regularly. If you have previously relied on shared experiences for pleasure, you may have to change your patterns in order to avoid feeling deprived and annoyed.

One partner said that she and her lover had always gone backpacking together, but recently her lover was so involved with other survivors and support groups that she didn't want to go away with her. The partner was

---

* Al-Anon, the support group for partners of alcoholics, can be a useful resource. Many partners have benefited from attending Al-Anon meetings, even if alcohol wasn't directly involved in their relationship.

disappointed, but decided to go backpacking with a friend. Although she missed her lover and felt some sadness that they weren't together, she was a lot happier backpacking with her friend than she would have been sitting home idle and lonely.

Ellen is the partner of a survivor and has gained by learning to take pleasure alone:

> Personally, I have a tendency toward workaholism. Evenings that I spend with my lover, I put on the telephone answering machine, close the door to my study, and relax. But if she is out or wants to be alone, I gravitate toward my desk and "get a little work done." Recently I realized what an unsatisfactory setup this is. It means that if she's unavailable, I am deprived not only of her company but also of a good time.
>
> In the past few months, I've been giving myself permission to relax in the evening when I'm alone. I can listen to the radio, embroider, or take myself to the movies. I can read a novel in bed. All things I rarely have time for during the busy days. I've found I like being home alone, listening to my sleeping daughter breathe in the next room, inviting the cat to my lap for petting. When I go to sleep, I feel nourished, whole, good about myself and my life.

BECOMING ALLIES

One of the important realities to keep in mind is that your partner did not create the difficulties you are both facing. One man said:

I've never blamed her for making the relationship difficult because of the incest. That seemed like such an obvious trap. It would just be terribly rude for me to think that. She didn't do it. It was her father who did it. Not her. She didn't have this little qualifications list when we got together. Neither of us knew this was coming. To me, it's just part of growing and trusting and opening doors, and that was what was behind one of them. That was just part of the package.

Although the abuse happened to the survivor, it affects your life and becomes your concern as well. Many partners get angry when they realize they have to deal with abuse, but they may be reluctant to express that anger. Ellen says this was true in her relationship:

> When my lover and I were in the midst of difficulties, she continually encouraged me to tell her when I was angry. "Don't store it up," she insisted. "I want to know when you're angry."
>
> But it was hard for me to express my anger. I wanted to be perfectly understanding, perfectly supportive. After all, wasn't I an expert in the healing process? Didn't I support hundreds of other women through it? How could I be angry at my own lover?
>
> But of course I *was* angry. I was both angry and supportive. I was a whole person, with many varied responses. And they were all valid and all needed expression, not just the understanding ones.

It's essential that throughout your struggles with all these issues, you communicate your feelings frankly and respectfully. Both you and your partner have valid feelings and needs. Neither of you is wrong or to blame. If you can see yourselves as allies with a common problem, rather than as adversaries in combat, it becomes possible to find ways to reconcile your differing needs.

COMMUNICATION

Communication is essential for a healthy relationship. It's important when things are going well, and it's critical when you face major difficulties. You need to tell your partner how you feel, what you think, what's going on inside you. And you need to hear the same from her. Communication is the basis for understanding, compassion, and creative problem solving.

On Communication: Roger

We got into this situation where the communication between us was getting more and more closed. Karen had been seeing a therapist for some time. She'd come back from therapy and I'd ask her how it went, and she'd say, "It's too painful to deal with. It's too much work. I don't want to talk about it." That keyed me into my stuff about feeling rejected: if she couldn't trust me, then I must really be a monster.

I needed her to communicate with me more. I needed her to pay more attention to what I needed. I needed just as much support and nurturing as I gave. I finally came to a point where I exploded. We call it the dynamite incident. I said to her, "General information isn't enough for me. I need you to tell me what you're going through. And you have to deal with what's happening to me too! I want communication and I'm not going to settle for no!" I knew I had to break through. It really caused fireworks because Karen felt threatened, but I couldn't keep letting the gap widen.

Things did change after that. We started talking more. And since then, I feel much more hopeful. I have some idea where she is and where she's going, and where we are in the process.

LEARNING TO ASK

Even with a good support system and other friends to talk with, there will be times when you want and need attention from your partner, and no one else will do. You may want time together, reassurance that you're loved, or help with some problem of your own. Whatever it is, you need to ask.

For many partners this is difficult. You may be afraid of making demands. You may feel the survivor is too fragile. But stating a need is not the same as making a demand. Stating your needs directly is the most effective way to communicate. But as one man explains, it's not always easy:

My habitual way of asking was to complain: "You haven't told me you loved me for ages," or "It's been four days since you've even wanted to make love. Monday night you were at class. Tuesday you went to the movies. . . ." Immediately my wife became defensive. She wanted to protect herself, not open up.

It felt too vulnerable for me to say, "I really need to be close to you," or "I'd like it if you'd rub my back," or "I've been feeling insecure. Would you tell me that you love me?" Coming forward with criticism was easier for me than exposing my simple need.

Even though you can't always get what you want, you increase your odds by asking clearly in a nonthreatening way. If, for example, you're not getting the attention you want, you might ask your partner to set aside one night a week to be with you—an evening to *not* talk about sexual abuse, to just have a relaxed time together. The rest of the week, you won't expect her to really be with you. If she feels able, she may agree. If not, you can ask if an hour might be possible or even ten minutes. The bottom line might be, "Are you able to give *anything* at this point?" Although at some critical times the answer may be no, it's likely that most of the time she will be able to agree to some minimal togetherness.

Some partners have struggled along for months or even years without ever finding out what the survivor could give. It may feel risky to ask exactly what you can and can't expect. Talking about it frankly—negotiating—can also feel strangely businesslike or cold. And you may be afraid of rejection. But the survivor may be relieved to hear clearly and uncritically what you need. And unless you talk together, you can't work out a solution.

As a bonus, sometimes just talking about a difficulty goes a long way toward dissolving it.

SETTING LIMITS

If you're committed to supporting your partner, that doesn't mean you're required to be available for every crisis or to take care of every need. There are limits to everything and you need to be responsive to your own. When you try to give beyond your capacity, there's usually a backlash of resentment that undercuts the value of what you've given. It's far better to admit honestly that you can't be there, to tell her that you love her and have faith in her, and to go on with your own life.

It's not realistic to expect yourself to be able to handle everything just because the survivor is healing from a major trauma. A relationship, even when one person is in crisis, involves two people, and you can't obscure yourself totally without damage to both of you.

You may not want to hear every detail of her healing process. Or you might not want to hear every detail, every time. One woman said, "She had some horrible things happen to her and sometimes I don't even want to know." This partner felt guilty for feeling that way, but no one is superhuman. You do your best, and then you have the right to say no, just as she does.

Everyone has different limits. Don't wait until you're over yours before you speak up. If you do, you're apt to be resentful, and it will make your communication less effective. Instead, speak up when you're approaching your limits.

DEALING WITH HER PAIN, GRIEF, AND DEPRESSION

Recovering from child sexual abuse entails feeling the pain and grief of early wounding. For some survivors, a generalized depression blankets everything. This can be very difficult for partners. As one partner put it, "It's hard to witness so much pain and be so helpless."

People tend to think they have to *do* something to help a person get over pain, but often there's not a lot you can do. Some of that pain is inevitable. Some of it is her work to transform. Your place is not to make it better—your place is to be a loving partner through hard times.

- **Listen.** Sit with her and let her talk.
- **Try to understand.** Be as compassionate as you can.
- **Ask her what she needs.** Offer extra comfort.
- **Don't ignore it.** Make room for her feelings.
- **Don't try to smooth it over and make it better.**
- **Reassure her.** Tell her it's okay to feel her feelings.
- **Get help yourself if you start feeling shaky.**
- **Be patient.**
- **Lighten her load when you can.** Take on extra housekeeping duties. Do more child care. Cook her a hot meal.

In doing these things, you not only help the survivor, but you give her a gift that may be new to her—the experience of a healthy, nurturing relationship.

CRISIS PERIODS

For many survivors, there is a time when pain eclipses every other feeling. These crisis periods often come when a survivor gets her first memories, initially faces the long-term effects of her abuse, or confronts the people who hurt her. If your partner is in a crisis stage of her healing, you will have your hands full. (See "The Emergency Stage" on page 72.) She may be unable to function, unable to meet any of your needs and few of her own.

It is extremely stressful to love someone who is in deep pain. Even if you're good at taking care of yourself, being with someone who's anguished has to affect you. On top of that, the survivor may be angry. She may blame you or pick fights with you. You may feel overwhelmed by the extras duties you've had to take on—reassuring your children, paying for therapy, covering for her financially if she can't work. And you may be frightened, unsure of what to do.

At one workshop, a man described his conflict and guilt as he was torn between taking care of his wife and taking care of his child: "It'll be in the middle of a Saturday afternoon and my wife will be totally hysterical. I want to comfort her, but our four-year-old daughter is there and she's affected by all of this. So I take my daughter out—to a shopping mall or something—but I feel so guilty. I'm not there supporting my wife. But I can't just leave the child."

Everyone in the group hastened to assure this man that he was doing the right thing. He was taking care of his child and giving his wife space to experience her feelings. Anyone who cares for the child of a distressed mother is supporting that mother. The partner was reassured that he wasn't abandoning his wife, but their lives were still in tumult. "It can happen any time, any day," he said.

"I know what you mean," another man said. "When I walk into the house I never know what I'll find. It's totally unpredictable."

And another: "I thought I had a reasonable relationship with a reasonable person."

The important thing to remember is that such a crisis will not last forever. It is part of her healing process. The best thing for you to do is make sure you both have help and find ways to take care of yourself.

DEALING WITH SUICIDE

If the survivor is talking about suicide, has attempted suicide, is taking large quantities of drugs or alcohol, is mutilating or injuring herself, or is driving recklessly, her life is in danger. Do not try to deal with this alone. Get help.

Call suicide prevention. Make sure you have the phone numbers of the survivor's therapist and support group members. Call them. If the survivor is isolated, take an active role in helping her find skilled support. Have her make a no-suicide agreement. Tell her you want her to contact you or her therapist before she tries to kill herself.

While it's impossible to stop a person from killing herself if she is determined to do so, these measures can help sustain the survivor through a time of acute despair.

(For more on preventing suicide, see "Don't Kill Yourself," pages 212–213.)

CONTROL

Survivors often have difficulty compromising or relinquishing control. It may seem to you that the survivor needs to control everything: when and if you make love, how you should raise the children, even down to details of everyday life—when and where you go out to eat, which movie to see, where to hang a picture on the wall. Sometimes this control will be obvious. Other times it will be less clear-cut—such as maintaining control through moodiness or preoccupation.

What you are up against is a survival mechanism that has been absolutely essential to her. By now it is a firmly entrenched habit. If you want to work toward balancing the control in your relationship, start by appreciating how fundamental her need for control is. She grew up being abused by an adult who was out of control. Now she feels it is crucial to maintain control over her life. It's only when the survivor knows that you understand the depth of her need for control that she will be able, gradually, to give it up.

Expect changes to go slowly, but do express your needs. For example, you can make it clear that you need something to change, but don't expect to set all the terms. If you want to spend more time with your partner, try saying "I need to spend more time with you. How can we do that?" instead of "You've got to quit your aerobics class. You're spending too many nights away from home."

When your partner is being particularly controlling, it may also help to ask if she wants to talk about what's going on. If she's feeling powerless in another area of her life, if something is frightening her, or if there's a crisis, her need for control may flare up. Often it helps just to recognize and talk about her fears.

TRUST

When children are sexually abused, their capacity to trust is shattered. Now this trust has to be consciously rebuilt. You can't just say "Trust me, come on and trust me already" and expect your partner to leap into the land of the trusting. If she could do it that easily, she would have done it already. To make the shift from not trusting to trusting, she must go step by step. (Read "Learning to Trust" on page 236.)

At the same time, *you* need to be conscious of the ways in which you are or are not trustworthy. Be scrupulously honest: In what ways can she trust you safely? In what ways are you careless or untrustworthy? Inconsiderate or scared? Is there an arena in which you feel confident that you can absolutely be trusted, where you can commit yourself to come through no matter what? For example, if you're supposed to be on time, would you be willing to get there ten minutes early rather than be five minutes late?

To establish trust, you must work together. Try making a specific offer: "I'll water your plants while you're on vacation. You can tell me in detail just what each plant requires and I'll do it carefully." Or, "Please trust me that if I offer to give you a massage, I won't try to seduce you into sex." Or, "I'd like to make a commitment to you to cook dinner on Mondays and Wednesdays since those are the days you work late. It won't always be a big deal, but there'll be something ready by the time you get home." You can add, "I really am reliable about this. Please risk it and trust me."

If you do come through, that will make an impression. And if you do this over and over, you will definitely build trust.

WILL THE REAL ABUSER PLEASE STAND UP?

It is common for survivors to see the person they're relating to as the abuser. Various things can trigger this identification: a similar gesture, an increase in closeness, sexual passion, anger. If you start to feel that the survivor isn't relating to you anymore, but rather to the abuser from her past, you need to stop and check. Ask her "What's happening? Did something scare you? Are you reminded of something?" Or more simply, "Where are you?"

Getting to know what the issues are, naming them, and tracing them back to their source will help differentiate the present from the past. One partner, Phil, describes a unique way he was able to do this for his wife:

For a long time Barb had asked me to grow a beard. She kept telling me how attractive it would look. I wasn't very keen about the prospects of a scraggly-looking face, but I started growing it.

About six months later, I told Barb I was thinking of whacking it off. She suddenly burst into tears. She told me that the hair on my face allowed her to maintain a reality check during certain times when flashbacks of her father molesting her interfered with our lovemaking (Barb's father was always clean-shaven).

I don't believe Barb fully understood the importance of my having a beard until that conversation. Certainly I didn't. And keeping my hair took on a totally different perspective for me. I now take a certain delight in experimenting with various cuts and trims. More importantly, I've found yet another way I can be there for Barb.

This determination to distinguish her husband, whom she loved and wanted to make love with, from her father, who had molested her, appeared in a guise neither of them consciously recognized at first.

IF THE SHOE FITS

At one workshop for partners, Ellen explained that survivors often identified their partner with the abuser, and one man said that yes, that was happening in his relationship. Ellen went on to talk about not taking it personally and supporting the survivor in differentiating between the two, but she failed to mention the fact that sometimes partners *are* abusive.

About a year after that workshop, the survivor who was married to this partner told Ellen that every time she had tried to get him to see that he was being abusive, he referred back to Ellen's statement that survivors often identify their partners with their abuser. And that became his excuse for not changing. Eventually, though, he was able to hear her and did join a group of men who batter. Their relationship improved dramatically after that.

This man, like many others, was not blatantly violent. But in subtle ways his behavior was threatening, and the power he wielded was destructive to their relationship.

Especially in heterosexual relationships, a power differential is built into the fabric of the relationship. A certain amount of condescension toward or power over women is accepted as normal in our society. Even if

you're not an overtly abusive man, it may be a real challenge to develop more equal power dynamics in your family, but it's essential if your relationship is to thrive.

Although they are generally more egalitarian, lesbian relationships are not immune to violence or threatening behavior. If there is any abuse in your relationship, you and your partner need help right away.*

HER FAMILY

Survivors usually have complicated feelings about their families. The mother who didn't protect her also tucked her in at night and sang lullabies to her. The brother who raped her was a victim of their parent's abuse too. It's natural for her feelings to be complex and difficult to sort out. And they may change more than once over the course of her healing.

Your feelings may be complicated too. You may feel loyalty or love for her family. If the abuser is someone you've respected, you may find it hard to see him now as the perpetrator of a terrible violation. You may not want to believe it's true. Or you may want the survivor to forgive the abuser or other relatives. You may want relations to go on as they always have.

But this is not possible. It is essential, in fact, that you do not in any way defend the abuser for past or present actions. It is up to the survivor, and the survivor alone, to deter-

---

* *Naming the Violence* by Kerry Lobel is an excellent resource on lesbian battering. See the "Domestic Violence, Rape, and Sexual Harassment" section on p. 567 of the Resource Guide.

mine what kind of relationship she wants to have with the abuser, with the people who didn't protect her, or with anyone in her family who doesn't respect her healing now.

If you feel an allegiance to the abuser, you need a place to talk about your feelings. But the survivor is not the one to whom you should turn for this help. She should not have to convince you that the abuser is to blame, or that she has a right to be angry.

If, on the other hand, you're so raging mad that you want to kill the abuser, it may be difficult to allow the survivor the room to sort through her own mixed feelings. Although it's essential that she not minimize what was done to her, it frequently takes some time for women to tap into their fury.

Sometimes partners of survivors feel that they shouldn't get angry at abusers or family members, especially if the survivor isn't angry yet. But your anger can be a helpful catalyst in awakening her own. She needs to hear that she has a right to her anger, that it's safe to be angry, and that you're angry that she was hurt.

Although it's important not to overwhelm her with your own reactions, your anger is appropriate, justified, and ultimately in her best interests. If she tells you that she doesn't want to hear it, respect her request, but find other people to talk to. You wouldn't be angry if you didn't care about her. It's part of love.

FAMILY VISITS AND ONGOING RELATIONSHIPS

Sometimes it's hard to understand why the survivor would want to continue a relationship with people who abused or neglected her. Yet ultimately it is her decision whether she wants any relationship with her family—and if so, what kind.

You, however, get to decide what your involvement will be. You don't have to subject yourself to humiliation, pretense, or danger. If the survivor wants you to continue to attend Friday night dinners at the home of the parent who abused her, if she wants you to pretend nothing happened, embrace them, and talk pleasantries, and if all this makes you incapable of digesting your chicken, you can decline. If the survivor wants the brother who abused her to visit for the weekend, you can negotiate the arrangement: he can visit during the day but sleep in a motel; you want it to be the weekend your children are at the Girl Scout sleep-out, or he can come, but you want to be free to speak your mind frankly.

If, however, the survivor wants to sever relations with the abuser or her family, you will have to go along with that decision even if it's not your preference. To continue to relate on friendly terms with someone who abused your partner, or who is buying into the family facade of denying or minimizing the abuse, is a betrayal in itself.

ACTIVE SUPPORT

There are many things you can do to actively support the survivor in dealing with her family. One partner reads the letters that come from her lover's relatives. She passes on any important information and then throws out the letter. That way the survivor doesn't have any unwanted contact. Another woman took this a step further, intercepting calls from her lover's father:

My lover was abused by her father. It had been many years since she had talked to him when he called one day while she was at work. He said he'd call back that evening. She was upset, felt invaded, and didn't want to talk to him. I wanted to answer the phone, but I was afraid she might see that as butting in

---

Conversation with My Lover's Father

Carol Anne Dwight wrote the following confrontational letter to her lover's dead abuser as a way to discharge her own anger:

Lloyd Edwards,

I want to talk to you for a moment. Could we step over there?

No. We don't need to go to another room. This is fine, thanks. I'm concerned about Rhonda, your daughter.

Lloyd Edwards, *you raped my lover* when she was eight years old.

You covered it up very thoroughly. You lied. You lied to Rhonda. You lied to the doctors. And you refused to discuss the matter later. You trivialized a major childhood trauma, an event that destroyed Rhonda's chance for a secure childhood and safe launch into the adult world. You stole all those years and happiness from her. And you had the unmitigated *gall* to disown her for behaviors we now know to be symptomatic of childhood sexual abuse, behaviors you actually caused.

Lloyd Edwards, you are responsible for all of that. You are responsible for her drug use. You are responsible for her prostitution. You are responsible for her difficulties with sex and intimacy. You denied her a childhood, ruined a large segment of her adult life, and made things harder for me too.

That's right. I as lover/life partner inherit some of the "fallout" from your acts.

No, I'm not finished yet. I'm afraid that you'll have to endure more insults, Mr. Rapist.

I hate you for having interfered in my lover's ability to trust me. I hate you for having hurt her, violated her, lied to her when she was utterly vulnerable. Most of all I hate you for being dead, beyond my reach or the reach of the law. How dare you escape this judgment!! Off scot-free, never to be exposed, humiliated, to atone, apologize, explain. How dare you be dead!

I hate you for the guilt I feel, trying desperately sometimes to avoid hurting Rhonda. I hate you for how careful I must be when I wish to be sensual/sexual with my lover. I hate you for making it so hard for me to persuade her to take care of herself. I hate you for making my burden so heavy in this relationship.

There is no forgiveness or pity from me. None of the good things you did will in any way compensate for the rape of Rhonda. The fact that you, too, may have been molested as a child will not lighten my judgment. Perhaps, if you were alive now, Rhonda would accept your apology, explanation, restitution, love—that would be her choice. If it were up to me, though, I'd prosecute.

Okay, I'm through now. But remember that Rhonda isn't finished. *She* may have something further to discuss.

and usurping her power. But I took the risk and asked, figuring the worst that could happen is that I'd look pushy.

As it turned out, she was grateful. It was the first time in her life that anyone asked to protect her, the first time anyone came forward without her having to drag it out of them. She was grateful and I felt good to be able to do it.

Phil regularly composes letters to his wife's parents and relatives. Then he mails them:

One of my coping mechanisms for my anger and frustration is writing confrontational letters to Barb's parents and other relatives. In fact, I have spent hours and hours in front of the word processor with a letter—polishing every insignificant word and phrase.

If there's a way you'd like to offer active support, first ask the survivor, so she can tell you if your suggestion would be helpful. If it's not what she wants, you don't have to feel hurt or rejected. You're a caring person who is willing to try, and she'll probably appreciate your intentions.

SEXUALITY

Beginning the Journey: Ellen

"I don't want you ever again to make love with me when you don't want to. I don't want you ever to pretend," I told my lover earnestly. We had been together for over a year. She was a survivor, and I knew that making love when she didn't want to was damaging.

She started to shake. "I don't think I can do that," she said, her voice almost a cry. "It's too hard. I don't think you could handle it either."

"I know it's essential that you say no when you want to say no. That you're honest with yourself and with me."

She looked straight into my eyes. "You don't know what you're asking for," she said.

I didn't.

But even if I had, I would have told her the same thing. Only more soberly, with less optimistic enthusiasm in my voice, for the mutual journey we've taken has been painful, demanding, and difficult. It's also been worth it.

PROBLEMS WITH SEX

For most couples in which one or both partners are healing from child sexual abuse, sex is particularly difficult. Since the means by which the survivor was abused were sexual, it makes sense that this would be an arena charged with conflict.

It will help you to be allied with the survivor if you understand the process of healing sexually. Many survivors have been split sexually—what they felt inside didn't match the way they acted on the outside. To heal, the survivor must stop doing anything she doesn't genuinely feel.

Healing sexually takes conscious time and attention. It requires stopping, slowing down, and reexamining everything, so that the survivor has time to integrate the feelings, memories, and associations that emerge.

This will probably have a radical effect on your sex life. The survivor may want no sex. She may want sex only under very controlled circumstances. She may want only certain sexual activities. She may want only to touch you and not be touched herself, or vice versa. She may want sex only if she initiates, only if you massage each other first, only if you have time to talk before or afterward. Sometimes it may seem to you that she wants sex only if the moon is new, it's snowing, *and* the kids are at summer camp.

The survivor may have difficulty staying present when you make love. One partner explained, "We'll be kissing and making out and then I get this eerie feeling that I'm all alone." She may have flashbacks to her original abuse. She may have to stop suddenly. She may go numb or have no desire whatsoever. If your partner has had orgasms, she may stop having them. Or she may cry hysterically when she comes, as she connects with powerful feelings of rage, horror, or sadness. She may become afraid of or disgusted by sex. Or she may vacillate. As one partner put it, "I feel like this oven getting turned on and off, but I don't know which way to turn."

Frustration: Roger's Story

There was a long time when we shuffled around to find out what was safe sexually. Karen set the standards. She began orchestrating what our lovemaking would involve, and I went along with that because I wanted to support the growth she needed.

It felt to me like there was this stone wall with this one little box in it where we could make love according to certain rules. Then, and only then, was it okay. For a while it felt real hopeless. The box kept getting smaller and smaller. It was very difficult

for me to be patient when I had no idea whether she was in the first 10 percent or the last 10 percent of working this out. I felt like she was saying, "I'm going to work on this stuff. You're just going to have to forget all about sex until I'm done. I'll call you and tell you when I'm through." I knew it could take years. It felt like it could take forever.

It seemed like my only options were either to shut down or to leave. I didn't want to leave. And the problem with shutting down was this: She finally gets through her stuff and there I would be, all shut down, and how do you break through the ice then?

In the beginning I just stuffed down my needs and said, "I'll wait my turn," but then I realized I had always put someone else in front of me, and my turn never came. I finally got to the point where I realized I couldn't keep sitting around patiently waiting, slam my dick into a drawer until she was through, and just forget it.

COMMUNICATION IS THE BEST FOREPLAY

When couples first admit that they have sexual difficulties, they often see only two options when sex isn't going well: pretend and continue to make love, or be honest and stop. Once the survivor is committed to honesty, she stops. At this point the partner is usually hurt or angry, and withdraws more or less. The survivor is left feeling guilty and alone in addition to whatever was bothering her in the first place.

This is a time for communication. Talk to each other. Ask questions. What's happening that is upsetting her? When did she go numb? When did she get scared? Did she have a flashback? But don't barrage her with questions. The survivor may not be ready to talk right away. She may need time to stay quiet with her feelings. She may want to wait a day or two. Or she may want to spill everything out immediately. The important thing is that the two of you figure out a way to discuss what happened.

One partner described the process with her lover, Jesse, this way:

> Eventually Jesse told me that she didn't want me to just turn away if she didn't want to make love, or if she spaced out while we were making love. She asked me to talk to her, to help her identify her feelings and to express them. We discovered that this communication right on the spot really helped.
>
> Jesse began to identify her feelings more precisely. Rather than say "I'm not sure if I want to make love," she'd say "I feel very closed right now. I'm afraid to open up and let you in." Often she discovered that it wasn't so much the sex that scared her, but the intimacy, the trusting.

If the survivor hasn't explained what she wants from you, ask. If she doesn't know, experiment together. For every survivor, what is frightening will be somewhat different. By communicating, you can explore the threatening aspects and find ways to move through them.

CREATIVE INTIMACY

Many of us are accustomed to getting our needs for intimacy met through sex. Sex is the only way we really feel loved. When sex is not an option, we're stymied. Yet there are times when simple holding or tender words can bring comfort and closeness. Soothing, rather than forced passion, may be more appropriate when you are ragged from a difficult day or are overly tired. As you begin to explore a variety of avenues for intimacy, you will feel less compulsive, freer, and more satisfied.

Look at the needs you meet through sex. We all need intimacy, touch, validation, companionship, affection, nurturing, pleasure, intensity, love, passion, release. See which of these needs you can meet in other ways.

If Not Sex, How About . . . : Ellen's Story

When my lover began to say no to sex on a regular basis, I quickly realized that it wasn't okay with me for her to simply say no, turn over, and go to sleep. I wanted *something*, even if I couldn't have sex. And the closer to sex the better. If she didn't want us to make love together, then maybe she could hold me while I made love to myself. If she couldn't do that, I wanted her to take a bath with me. If that was too threatening, maybe she could give me a massage. And if that was too much, then maybe we could go for a walk and hold hands. And so on.

Also I didn't want to have to ask for it. Asking and having her say no was difficult enough. I wanted the next move to be hers.

"I want you to offer me something," I told her, "anything you feel you can give. You can say 'No, I don't want to make love, but I'd like to kiss a little,' or 'No, but I love you very much,' or 'No, but I'll rub your back.'"

This was hard for her. When she said no she felt guilty. It was difficult to offer something else, and to her, the offerings felt pitifully small compared to actually having sex, which is what she knew I really wanted. Often when she said no, she was in her own turmoil—which was why she said no in the first place—and she resented having to deal with my feelings at all. Now I was asking her to give even when she didn't really want to, to stay aware that there were two of us in this relationship.

It didn't develop smoothly, but my lover gradually learned to offer something when she didn't want to make love. One morning after a particularly bad night she said, "Would you like me to make you breakfast?" I really didn't want her lousy breakfast. I wanted sex. But she had offered something, as much as she was capable of at the time. I knew she was sincere. "Yes," I said. And we ate omelettes together while Tina Turner sang "Let's Stay Together" on the radio. We both cried. And I learned that there were ways to be close, to feel nurtured and loved, that weren't sexual.

OKAY, I'VE DONE ALL THAT

Some needs simply can't be met in non-sexual ways. Some of what you want is sex, making love, that specific combination of you and your lover coming together with all your body parts engaged. Foot rubs aren't going to do it. You're frustrated and angry. Okay. Allow yourself to be frustrated and angry.

It's important to be clear about what you need even if you're not getting it at the time. Don't pretend to yourself that you're satisfied if you're not. Don't be dishonest with yourself about what you want or need. One partner, whose wife hadn't yet remembered her abuse, tells the following story:

There was a time early on in my marriage when my wife wanted to be permanently celibate, like Gandhi. Because I didn't know myself very well, I decided that if she wanted to be celibate, I would accept that. The way I put it to myself was that I loved *her,* that she was more important to me than the nature of our relationship.

This was very noble. It was also a complete failure. I was hurt, angry, and frustrated with myself and with her. It would have been far better if I could have been honest with both of us and said that although I loved her, I didn't want a celibate marriage. But I didn't know then that I was entitled to want or to need.

Your partner is trying to learn about herself, to learn what she does and doesn't want. This is an excellent time to explore for yourself what *you* need in a relationship. Keep in mind your image of the satisfying relationship you're working toward, even if you can't realize it in the present.

Healing sexually is usually a slow process, but as one partner said, "Going slow is a lot faster than not going at all."

MUTUAL HEALING

Few of us feel totally healthy, joyous, integrated, and free. As one survivor advised partners: "Be really up-front about your own damage. However you learned about sex as a child in this society, you're damaged. Explore it honestly."

Both survivors and partners have the opportunity to heal sexually.

The quality of my own experience of sexuality has improved dramatically since my lover and I began to work together on her healing. I can't ever just go through the motions anymore. Both of us are more present than ever. The sexual inhibitions and tense, blocked places I used to experience are much less present because I have had to become aware of myself. I've had to face my own fears and vulnerabilities. So, although I've assisted her, she's assisted me as well. Even speaking selfishly, it's been more than worth it.

DO I WANT TO BE IN THIS RELATIONSHIP?

Be realistic about your commitment to the relationship. Are you willing to hang in through some rough times? For how long? Is your bond strong enough to withstand the problems you're having?

If someone came to me and said, "I just found out my partner's dealing with incest. What should I do?" I'd say, "Seriously evaluate your relationship and how much you're willing to put out when you may not get much back in return. After that, make sure your partner gets professional help, and consider therapy for yourself too. It'll bring up a lot for you. But first, evaluate the relationship, because it's hell. You've got to be strong. You've got to be patient. You're going to get angry."

***

During the period where I felt a widening chasm, a lot of what I went on was just faith and commitment: "I promised to hang in with this no matter what, and damn it, I'm going to make it work." Our wedding vows said we would be together "through all the changes of our lives." I often remembered those exact words. Either I was going to eat those words, or I was going to back them up.

***

If someone had shown me the job description for being the partner of an incest survivor, I never would have signed up for the job.

Even if you are married or in a committed partnership, you still have a right to make choices about staying in the relationship. You can make the choice that you will stay no matter what. Or you can choose to reassess an earlier commitment. But if you feel trapped, your resentment is likely to poison the relationship.

She Has to Put Her Healing First: Ellen

There was a time when I was impatient for my lover to make changes in our sexual relationship. I wanted her to want me passionately. We weren't making love as often as I wanted, and I told her that I wouldn't mind the droughts if there were *some* times that we really made love a lot. She looked at me as if I was denser than she'd thought, and explained, not entirely without patience, "Ellen, if there were *some* times when I could make love a lot, there'd probably be a *lot* of times. The problem is that I can't yet feel that. I want to. But I can't leap from here to there. I have to go step by step."

I remember this talk clearly. We were sitting on the couch, facing each other. I finally realized that she was doing the best she could, she was going as fast as she could. She was in therapy. She was working on this stuff. She wasn't just fooling around.

"I want to change as much as you want me to," she continued. "More. You can always leave and get another lover. I've only got myself. I *have* to change. But I can't fake it anymore. I have to put my healing first even if it means losing you, which I very much don't want to do."

This was an important moment, because it set the priorities straight. She was right. She was on this healing journey and it was up to me whether or not I came along.

In that same talk she told me she could understand that I might not want to stay. "I wouldn't blame you," she said.

It was true. I didn't have to be with her. I could find another lover. If it was hard for me to stay, that made sense. It wasn't because I was a weak, lousy, or disloyal person. I was choosing to be part of a situation which was genuinely difficult, which everyone wouldn't choose, and which, after that talk, I felt appreciated for. Through my lover's understanding that I might want to leave, I felt I was given absolute freedom to choose. Not surprisingly, this drew us closer together, and I continually made the choice to stay.

ACKNOWLEDGING DOUBT

Most partners go through periods when they wonder whether they are doing the right thing, doubt their capacity to help the survivor, or question their overall commitment to the relationship. You may wonder if the survivor will heal or if the relationship will stabilize. Partners often question their capacity to deal with the deep pain that accompanies healing. One partner spoke of her lover's journals: "She says if I knew what was in those notebooks, I'd leave her. Sometimes I wonder myself."

You may worry that you're repeating a self-destructive pattern of your own. This might mean staying in a situation where your needs aren't getting met, staying in crisis, or concentrating on someone else's problems instead of your own. One partner, the child of an alcoholic, said, "I just don't think it's healthy for me to be waiting around for someone to change. That's what my childhood was all about."

When you have doubts, it's important to accept them and to talk about them. While it's good to let the survivor know what you're thinking, it's also important not to burden her excessively. Find other people to talk to.

Partners often feel guilty if they think of leaving. At one partners' workshop, a woman told Ellen, "I want to leave but I feel like I shouldn't. She's trying so hard."

Ellen replied, "Just because someone is trying doesn't mean you have to make a commitment to go on the journey with her. You can leave and wish her well. The only good reason to do this is because you really want to. It doesn't help her if you stay only because she needs somebody. Just because someone loves you or needs you doesn't mean you have to be there."

You're not necessarily a better person if you stay. You're not selfish or cruel if you decide to leave. The essential thing is to be honest. It's very useful to be honest with someone who's been abused, even if the truth is blunt and miserable. Most survivors have had to deal with too many lies already.

Admitting what you can handle, the extent of your commitment, is essential. It gives you both the best chance of growing together through this challenge. And if it becomes clear that you are not able or willing to meet each other's needs well enough to stay together, you then can separate in a way that's respectful, even with its pain.

SEPARATING

Sometimes you have both tried your best and it still isn't working out. Your needs are incompatible. You're fighting all the time. You keep going around on the same loops and you're stuck.

It's natural to feel stuck temporarily. No couples glide through the healing process smoothly. But if the bitter times are outweighing the progress, and if you feel that you're in each other's way more than you're being helpful friends, then you may want to consider a separation.

Separations need not be permanent. A separation of a week, a month, six months, or a year can sometimes give you both the room you need and actually prevent the need for permanent separation. Although separations are usually painful, at least in part, there is often a good deal of relief as well. Both people get the opportunity to try to meet their own needs and live their own lives without tripping over each other.

Separations, like most major decisions, work best when there is mutual agreement. Leaving the survivor in the middle of a crisis is not going to be beneficial for her. If she's just recovering memories, inundated with flashbacks, and terrified of being alone, she's not going to appreciate your rational words in favor of time apart. But if you both agree that you've tried everything else and it's time to try a separation, that can be a positive step, not only for each of you individually but for the relationship as well.

If you don't want to separate but need some way to acknowledge that the relationship is in crisis, an amended living-together contract can help. You might come up with an agreement like this: "For the next four months, we'll live together but we will be like two ships that pass in the night. That way you'll have space to heal, and I won't be hanging on your every step. This is different from our regular relationship."

PERMANENT SEPARATIONS

Working through the difficulties of healing from child sexual abuse sometimes causes more stress than a relationship can bear. A new relationship may not have enough foundation to hold up under the pressure. The coping patterns of both people may have dovetailed for so long that there's no way to sort them out. And one or both of you may have changed to the point where you no longer want to be together. Although a permanent separation or divorce is painful, staying together when you truly can't support each other, can't grow, and can't make peace is worse for both of you.

IF YOU STAY

There are no guarantees about the length of time healing will take for any survivor. But if your partner is actively working —and you are too—you can be assured that things will change. The problems you're confronting now won't be exactly the same as the ones you'll be dealing with six months or a year from now. You are not in a static situation. There will be transformation. Of course, she's not going to be perfectly healed at some specific moment in time. But then again, neither are you.

It's difficult to be patient when you're under stress. You're trying to work, raise kids, cope with her problems, cope with your own, change, and keep it all together without going crazy. But she needs to pace her own healing. You can encourage, but you can't rush her. You can say what you need and negotiate what's possible, but sometimes you're just going to have to wait.

And of course it helps to take breaks. One husband of a survivor said, "I'd be happy if I never heard the word 'growth' again." If you feel like this, it's time for a break. The survivor may not need one, but you do. Take a weekend off and go fishing. Buy a record that makes you feel like dancing, then play it a lot. Enjoy yourself. Don't grow.

IT'S WORTH IT

Moving together through the tight places, learning about each other's fears and insecurities, becoming more sensitive to each other and ourselves, is a lifelong process. If you consider this a long-term partnership, a few years of struggle is worth it.

It feels to me right now that what's coming through on the other side is a much more fulfilling and exciting relationship than the one we started with. It's made us close. I mean, you don't get close living in a bowl of cherries. It's coming through stuff together that makes the bond stronger. When you're not dealing with it, it seems like a mountain. In reality, it comes down to a smaller scale when you take it apart and work with it. In retrospect, it really is not a very long process. I mean, what's a couple of years?

And as one partner makes clear, things do change.

Being sexually abused isn't that unusual. The shocking thing is that it's so common that it almost isn't an appropriate way to delineate people anymore. What's important isn't that it happened to her, it's how she's dealt with it in her life. She's not a victim anymore. She's a survivor. I'm coming to her years after she's delved into all this. She's a well woman. I'm happy with her just the way she is.

ALL THAT IS FINE AND STRONG BETWEEN YOU

When there are serious problems, it's easy to concentrate so much on the difficulties that you lose sight of all that is fine and strong between you. Make time to enjoy what you really like in your relationship right now. Affirm those aspects to each other. In the midst of all this growth and change, remember to celebrate what you've got.

In the meantime, expect her to be powerful. Don't think of her as a victim. Don't see her as weak, sick, or permanently damaged. Instead, hold the attitude that she's a whole human being going through some difficult struggles. See her as courageous and determined. Concentrate on her strength and her spirit.

Reflecting the survivor's strengths back to her is a gift you can give throughout the healing process. Even if it's a time when she doesn't want your direct help, even if you're separated by distance or differing feelings, you can always hold in your mind the image of her as a healthy, vibrant person.

Healing from child sexual abuse is a heroic feat. She deserves your respect, confidence, and admiration.

PART FIVE

COURAGEOUS

WOMEN

AN INTRODUCTION

The sixteen stories in this section highlight particular aspects of the healing process. They represent a broad range of experience, and you will probably see parts of your own life reflected in them. We hope you will find at least one woman with whom you can identify.

The stories are not finished, because the lives are not finished. Each represents one fixed moment in time—the day the interview took place. Often when we sent copies of the interviews back to the survivors, they'd say, "But that's not me. So much has happened since then!" Like all of us, these women have continued to grow.

Take your time reading these stories. Give yourself a chance to digest each one, rather than reading them all at once. Let yourself feel. They are meant to be an inspiration, a touchstone, a reminder that healing is truly possible.

NAMES OR PSEUDONYMS: THE RIGHT TO CHOOSE

It's such a disappointment not to be able to use my own name. I've earned the right to own my words, my journey. I feel angry at the situation, denied what is mine by birthright—my name connected with my truth. Strange, so much of the journey has been a "naming" of shadows. And now I must place my own name back in the shadows . . .

—Gizelle

About half the women who share their stories here chose to use pseudonyms to maintain their privacy. After careful consideration, they decided it wasn't in their best interests to publicly come forward as survivors. For these women, using pseudonyms was a way to protect themselves and safeguard their healing.

The other women wanted to use their own names. They saw identifying themselves as a way to end the secrecy and shame that burden survivors of child sexual abuse. They also wanted, quite simply, to tell their story honestly—to name themselves, their abuser, the place where they lived, the facts of their lives. They'd lived with enough lies already.

As authors, we were committed to respecting each woman's decision. We wanted each woman's participation to be an empowering experience for her. However, we learned that it was not legally possible for a publisher to print a survivor's story with actual names and places if the abuser (and possibly other family members) was alive and identifiable.

This situation perpetuates the very hiding and silence that we are working to end. To tell women that they can't speak up, name their abuse and their abusers, and tell their stories in their own names without fear adds to the already formidable obstacles that women must overcome to break the silence.

We talked with the women who wanted to use their own names and together decided that we'd rather use the stories with pseudonyms and changes in identifying details than not include them at all. We all felt their value to survivors was so great that it was worth compromise, but we want to make clear that this is yet another violation of the rights of survivors. As with many of the laws and legal procedures regarding child sexual abuse, this operates once again to protect the abusers rather than the abused. And like the others, it must be changed.

JUDY GOLD

There's nothing as wonderful as starting to heal, waking up in the morning and knowing that nobody can hurt you if you don't let them.

Judy Gold is forty-five years old.* She is a musician and lives with her husband, Howard, in an upper-middle-class, predominantly Jewish suburb of New York. Howard is a businessman and works for his father-in-law in the garment industry. Judy and Howard have been married for twenty-five years and have four children, the eldest of whom is nineteen.

Of her childhood, Judy says: "My father's sister died in an insane asylum and I was named for her. I was always told I was going to end up just like her—bad and crazy. We were upper middle class. My mother was addicted to prescription

drugs. She was always hazy. Before she married my father, she had been a published author. It's too bad because she could have had a successful life and it ended up being a real zero. She's dead now.

"My father was a very violent man. He was like Dr. Jekyll and Mr. Hyde. He was loving toward us whenever our family was portrayed to the outside world. He used to march us out every Sunday night to a fancy restaurant for dinner. It was like Make Way for Ducklings. But what went on before we got into the car was a horror show.

"The world loved him. He set up scholarships; he helped build the local temple. He's given buildings to universities and hospitals. So no one would ever suspect what went on in that house.

"The only time I can remember him being loving was when he was in my bed. He would batter

_____

me at night and after he'd beat me up, he'd make me take his shoes off and kiss him goodnight. And then in the morning he'd climb in my bed and molest me. There was never any intercourse, but there was everything else.

"My first memories of being abused are tied in to my sister's birth, when I was six. The beatings continued till I went away to college, but the incest stopped when I was about twelve, when my baby sister turned six. That's always made me wonder if he moved on to her.

"Even though the actual abuse stopped when I reached puberty, the sexual innuendos never stopped. He's just sleazy, horrible. You wouldn't want to meet him. Yet, as I say, the whole world loves him."

How did the incest affect me? I've never really been in touch with me or my feelings. I was always real tough. If I ran fast enough and far enough, then I wouldn't have to think. I did a lot of drinking, a lot of drugs, a lot of fast living. I would drive at high speeds. I would think nothing of walking out at three in the morning in a deserted area. It was almost like I was tempting fate.

I had learned to tune out when my father beat me as a child. I never physically felt any pain. I used to say, "You'll never make me cry." And I never did. I allowed myself to feel anger, but never sadness or pain. It's what saved me, but it got out of control, the living out of my body. Spacing out was a very common thing for me. It wasn't until about a year and a half ago that I stopped doing that. I would be sitting talking to you, and I wouldn't be in my body. I used to say, "I turn into foam rubber." Everything went numb. My whole body would tingle, like your fingers going to sleep. Or my hearing would go off.

A dread that something bad was waiting for me has followed me most of my life. I have a morbid fear of the dark. I will never close my eyes in the shower. There are parts of my own house I am just beginning to go into.

THERE WAS ALWAYS A WALL AROUND ME

I could go anywhere and make friends, but I allowed people to get only so close. The minute you got closer, I turned you off. I felt I was filled with something evil, and that evil rubbed off on anyone I came into contact with.

Then I met Howard, who was my knight in shining armor. I was twenty-three. He was going to save me from all this craziness. Howard is the antithesis of my father. My survivor self knew I could not get into a relationship that would be a repeat of what I'd had with my father. Yet I know I've tried to goad him. I would test him. I'd say, "Go on, I know you want to hit me." And he never did. When I look back, I marvel at the composure he had.

Howard put such order into my life. And I really believed he was going to save me from the insane asylum. That's how the relationship began. Of course, things have changed. Things are much more realistic. As I began to work on this stuff, I was strong enough to say to Howard, "You know, I'm never again going to hold you accountable for my failures, but I'm never going to give you credit for my successes either." That was the beginning of the eroding of the white knight.

My sexuality has definitely been affected by the incest. I was uncomfortable having sex, but I never knew why. Every time Howard and I had sex in our marriage, I would wake him up and tell him I was sure someone was breaking into our house. And afterwards, I would get up out of bed, go to the kitchen and eat, and make like it had never happened: "Who me? Have sex?" And the strange thing is *I enjoyed the sex!* It was hard to get started, but once I got into it, I really enjoyed it. There were parts of the incest I enjoyed too, and that has been a really heavy trip for me. I mean, my body responded. It had to. But I'm not so quick to forgive that part of me.

I've never been able to have sex in the morning, obviously. Howard wouldn't dare touch me in the morning. We've had a lot of fights, mostly over sex. As much as I loved him and looked at him like he was going to save me, I never trusted him.

It was also very hard for me to hold my kids. They suffered because of what happened to me. I was not a nurturing mother. People see me as a wonderful mother. They marvel at how laid back I am in my parenting, but what they don't understand is that I was afraid to get close to those kids because I felt that I would infect them. So what they interpreted as giving my children independence was me being scared to death of them. I was scared to touch them.

If you asked people, they would tell you I was the most self-assured, self-confident, commanding, imposing woman. Once I started therapy, I would always complain, "I don't know who I am. People tell me I'm one thing, but I feel like I'm another." They see me as someone who has her whole life in order, because I never talked to anybody about what I really felt.

COME ON, ASK ME

When I stopped smoking, I gained thirty pounds in four months. Somebody gave me the name of this therapist who did hypnosis for overeating. I really believe that there are no accidents. I think I ate myself up to those thirty pounds for the purpose of seeking therapy. It was right there on the surface, waiting to come out.

I was almost provocative in the kinds of things I said to my therapist, like "Oh, you should know my family." In other words, "Ask me. Come on. I'll tell you if you ask me."

What was going to be five sessions has now become over four years. A couple of months into the therapy, he asked me to tell him about my father. I said he used to beat me up. And he said, "What else did he do to you?" And I said, "Nothing." And he said, again, "What else did he do to you?" And I said, "Oh, well, he crawled into my bed." And he said, "What else?" And I kept insisting there was nothing. And then he just asked me point-blank, "Did he ever touch you?" That started the whole thing. I finally admitted, "Yes, he touched me."

When we started using hypnosis, I got to the first memory. Then I started to remember incidents without the hypnosis. I got to the point where I could remember my father's precise smell. It took me two years to clearly remember what had happened.

The one thing that brought it all into focus—and it was the hardest thing—was a memory that I had always wet my pants. I used to hide all these sticky underpants in my closet as a little girl. And now I know I didn't pee in my pants at all. My father had ejaculated on me when I had them on, and I had saved all those underpants on the floor of my closet. My grandmother found piles of them in the closet and she showed them to my mother, who accused me of wetting my pants. I told her I hadn't done it, but she wouldn't believe me. She punished me for denying it, and he beat me for lying later the same night. As I pieced this together in therapy, I realized she had to have known the difference between urine and semen. It was the the worst memory I had. But it made it all very real.

My mother's death freed me up to remember all of this. I remember when my mother was dying, I talked about the beatings. I said, "Why didn't you stop him? How could you allow him to do those things to us?" And her answer was "What could I do?"

I had always adored my mother because she was so talented. And I felt such pity for her. But when I realized that she had known what was going on, I hated her. I even went to her grave and stomped on it. I was screaming at her. They could have locked me up then if they had seen me.

After I got through all the anger, I realized that she really was helpless. I'm sure that she had been a victim herself. And she sacrificed me so that she could live.

IF FOR NO OTHER REASON THAN SPITE, I FORCED MYSELF TO GET BETTER

When I first started remembering, I was very scattered. I was totally depressed. I gained a tremendous amount of weight. I didn't go out of the house. I became very solitary. I couldn't stop crying for a long time. I was making up for forty years of not crying. I could have been hospitalized at points. It was an effort to get out of bed in the morning. It was an effort to decide what to put on. I would go through periods of that and then periods of feverish activity. I would play the piano for hours on end, and then I wouldn't sit down at it again for months.

I didn't want anyone touching me. There was no sex. I had a tremendous amount of back pain. The psoriasis I'd always had got worse.

But the worst part was the terrible despair. I just felt like I was down in the sewer and I was never going to see daylight again. And I kept saying, "Why did I do this? Why did I open up Pandora's box?" I cursed myself because I could see no end in sight. I remember saying to my therapist, "Am I ever going to smile again?"

I felt like I was being battered from the inside. It was like a parade of demons, only the parade never stopped. I'd no sooner put one to bed than another one would come out to haunt me. There were a lot of nightmares, and I was always being chased by an unknown male.

I felt so close to crazy, but I kept saying to myself, "Are you going to let him win out? How can you let that prophecy come true?" If for no other reason than spite, I forced myself to get better. I was hell-bent on surviving, if only to show him that I was going to outlast him.

If I was to name one particular reason I got through it, it would be the anger. I was angry at myself first, for having delved into the subject. What did I need it for? I was angry at myself for having put on so much weight, for doing all those drugs. And then suddenly the anger starting being directed where it should have gone all along. And that anger—at him—is what fueled me to get well. When I would be raging, my therapist would say to me, "Hold on to that anger. That's your best friend." And he was right.

Then I had to grieve. That came toward the end of the process. I grieved for that little girl who never was. I never had a childhood, and I think that's what I mourned more than anything. For the longest time, I never understood what my therapist meant when he said, "Get in touch with the little girl. Feel her. Forgive her."

It took me a long time to understand that I hadn't done anything to cause the molestation. The little girl was not to blame. Even if I had lain there spread-eagled, naked, he was the adult, and I was the child, and not accountable. I finally believe that now. I've been able to forgive her.

I FOUND OUT I WASN'T ALONE

Along the way, there were little tiny victories that got me through the next day: like getting up, like getting out of bed, like saying "I'm going to go to an exercise class today." It was a victory to be able to make dinner for my family, to be able to be out there in the market with people.

Another thing that helped me was reading articles, books, anything I could get my hands on. I watched every program about incest. I kept saying, "It's got to get better, because other people have lived through this and survived." It helped to know I was not alone.

I have a very dear friend from my college days who I've kept in touch with all these years. She knew I was in therapy for eating, and she could see that I was gaining weight. About a year into my therapy we went out to lunch, and she said to me, "I

have to ask you a question. Were you ever sexually abused? You don't have to answer if you don't want to. I'm asking you because I was, and you sound just like me."

You could have knocked me over. I couldn't even get the word "yes" out. I just nodded my head and started sobbing. And that has been one of the greatest sources of healing for me.

IT'S *OUR* PROBLEM, HOWARD

It was two years into my therapy before I told Howard what was going on. I never told him before because I thought he would be repulsed by me. It never occurred to me that he might be angry with my father instead. Until that point, I'd just said to him, "I'm dealing with some very heavy issues, and I just don't feel free to discuss them with you." I let him know I was in trouble, but I wasn't going to tell him why. It was a nightmare. The fact that we're still married is amazing.

In order to tell Howard, I had to get drunk and drugged and angry. I just spit it all out: "Oh, yeah, let me tell you something. . . ." He was numb. He never said a word. I picked something up and I threw it at him. And I said, "Damn you, you give me a reaction. Do you hate me? Do you think I'm terrible? Do you think I'm dirty?" I was filling in the blanks. Everything I thought he should think of me, I told him.

He admits now that for a whole year he never really integrated the information. I don't think he believed a lot of it. He'd seen my father get violent, so he believed that part. But he didn't want to talk about the incest. I think he operated on the premise "If I don't talk about it, then it doesn't exist."

But I would force him to talk about it. I said, "Didn't you ever wonder why I always fooled around for hours to avoid coming to bed? Didn't you ever wonder why you couldn't touch me in the morning?"

I remember one time Howard said to me something about "my problem." And I said to him, "You don't understand. The minute I told you about this, it became *our* problem." It took him a long time to realize it was a problem we shared now. It was very hard for him. It still is. And it's doubly hard because he works with my father.

Once we started to talk about it, we talked all the time. I would sometimes say, "I can't talk about it anymore." Or, "Let's promise that on Tuesday and Thursday night we won't discuss it." We actually had to make appointments *not* to talk about it. Your brain can only absorb so much.

I still have battles with Howard over the incest because he is embarrassed by it. He would say things like "Be careful who you tell." And I would say, "Look, I don't care who knows. As long as I'm the one who tells them." And he would say, "You better be careful who you tell. Some people would love to get some dirt on you." He's ashamed. He'd rather I kept it a secret.

Howard is thrilled about the changes in me—that I'm off the drugs and off the cigarettes—but it's hard for him to give up control. He's been used to having the control in our relationship. And now he's had to give a lot of it up. He's given up all control in terms of sex.

Now it's when *I* want it and that's been very hard for him, but he's been wonderful about it. I've finally been honest. A lot of these problems came up because I was so dishonest. Now I can say to him, "I don't want you to touch me." I don't have to hang out in the bathroom for half an hour or get busy doing something. I used to say my greatest creative time was at night. That was just so I didn't have to go to bed.

I am just starting to realize that I am a very sexual human being. It's such a nice feeling to know that after I have sex I can go to sleep. I don't have to go in that kitchen and eat and pretend that it didn't happen, that it was somebody else in that bedroom responding.

It's taken a lot of hard work for us to stay together. There have been some real rough times. My way of dealing with most problems was to run away from them. And in a marriage, you just can't do that. Gradually we've learned to deal with problems right when they happen. And that's making us closer than ever.

I WANTED TO GET MY FATHER OUT OF MY LIFE

I'd thought about it for a year. My father was in the hospital. Fittingly, he had something wrong with his pecker. I thought, "Maybe they'll cut it off."

We went to visit him. He had on one of those hospital gowns with the back cut out. He purposely stood up and exposed himself to me. Then he said, "Judy darling, would you help me with this?" Finally at one point I said, "For Christ's sake, can't you put a bathrobe on?" He just lay in the bed and said, "Judy darling, would you pull the sheet up for me?" And I said, "Pull your own damn sheet up," and I walked out. That was the beginning of the end.

When Howard saw this, he couldn't believe it. He said, "If I ever doubted you, I never will again."

But still, it wasn't easy getting my father out of my life. My husband was in business with him. And I was still scared of him. I made a list of all the times I had to have contact with him, whether it was by phone or in person. And I thought, "What is one thing I could cut out? Is it maybe calling him on his birthday? Could I not have him come to my house for Thanksgiving dinner?" Well, I couldn't do that the first year, but I didn't call him on New Year's Eve to wish him a Happy New Year.

Every time I was able to cross something off the list, I'd feel terrific. The first time I didn't call him on his birthday, I cannot tell you my sense of elation. But it was very hard. I lived in fear that that phone was going to ring and he was going to yell, "Why didn't you call me on my birthday?"

I would rehearse—"If he does call me, what am I going to say?" I had the whole thing planned. At first I'd pretend it was a bad connection and yell into the phone, "HELLO? HELLO? It must be a bad connection. Call back." And then I'd take the phone off the hook and pretend the phone was out of order. Or I'd drop the phone if I heard his voice. I had lists of things I could do next to each phone. Doing that gave me courage. I would act it out with Howard. He would play my father, and I would practice what to say. I wrote out scripts and carried them in my wallet.

And finally my father did call, and he said, "What is going on between us? You never call me back. Do you have any intentions of calling me back?" And I said, "No." That was the end of it. I never said why.

Then his wife called and asked what was going on. She said, "He's so upset. He doesn't understand. Is it because he took you out of temple when you were nine years old and made you go home?" Can you believe this?

And I said, "You know, I'm not prepared to discuss this with you right now." She kept saying, "What did he ever do?" And I just repeated, "I have no intention of discussing this with you. Now if you want to talk about something else, I'd be more than happy to talk to you. But otherwise, we have nothing more to say to one another." And that was the end of it.

Do you know how long it took me to rehearse that? But when I could do it, what a victory! When I got him out of my life, the rest of the healing just fell into place. That was the moment when I knew that I really was in control of my life.

I'LL NEVER FORGIVE HIM

I have such venomous hate. I pray to God that he comes down with some terrible disease. I'd like him to get AIDS. That or Alzheimer's.

I can't wait for his funeral. You can bet I'm going to be the first one at that coffin to make sure he's really dead. I've even rehearsed what I'm going to say to people at the funeral when they say how wonderful he was: "I'm glad you have good memories of him. Isn't it nice that some people have nice memories of him." Things like that.

I always tell my children, "Don't ever hate. It's not worth having that kind of poison." But this hatred affects me in a positive way. Every time I think of how much I hate him, it gives me the strength to say, "You're never going to beat me." My hatred has helped me get well.

Maybe someday I'll look at him as a defenseless old man and think nothing. I doubt that. I'm not sure I want to get to that point.

IT WAS TIME TO REBUILD

Over time, I've come to accept what happened to me. I don't think there's any more to remember. And even if there is, so what? It can't be any worse than what I've already remembered. So what am I going to remember, one more night?

The incest happened. I can't change that. But I have the rest of my life ahead of me. I'm not going to live the way I lived the first forty years, because they weren't fun-filled years. But I don't have to. And that's what I've worked so hard for. I can change.

There was a point where I felt like I had gotten all the poison out and it was time to rebuild. It was a different pain. Now the healing has to do with dealing with my life: What do I do from here on in? How do I set things up that I'm not so rigid in what I expect from myself?

I finally know that I'm a nice person. I'm not that sleazy, slimy black goo I thought I was. It's nice to look in the mirror and say, "You're not ugly. You're not crazy."

And I like myself. I never liked myself before. I always thought that what they'd told me was true, that I was bad. But I wasn't bad. I was screaming for help and nobody heard.

A YEAR AND A HALF LATER

A year and a half after this interview, I was diagnosed with cancer. Getting sick really put everything in perspective. I believe I got the cancer because of all the years of stress, of shoving this down. Keeping the secret took its toll. The human body is like a stuff bag. If you keep shoving things in, you start to rip at the seams.

Cancer is the ultimate test of survival. I've had unbelievable support from my husband and kids. They just held me. That became a very important part of my healing. I learned what safe hugs are all about. It was important for me to keep fighting. I underwent radiation and chemotherapy. Compared to what I survived all those years, this was a piece of cake. Last month the doctor told me the cancer was entirely gone.

I am a survivor, and I'm going to live to dance on my father's grave.

EVA SMITH

You get tired of dealing with incest all the time. There's an ending point to everything. There's an ending point to life. Why can't there be an ending point to dealing with this shit?

Eva Smith is an African-American woman in her early thirties who lives in California.* She is a therapist and an artist. She lives with her two teen-age children. "I share this information with you as a gift of healing for other women. I am truly living my life now, after just surviving for so many years."

Between the ages of three and eight, I was molested by my great-uncle. From nine to fifteen, my stepfather molested me. I grew up just trying to live from day to day and survive, wishing the whole thing would

be over and stop. I used to pray my step-father would get struck by lightning. I wasn't above making a pact with the devil to get rid of him. *Anything.* And anything happened. I got pregnant.

I had always been a fat child. When I was thirteen, I weighed 188 pounds. And then I lost weight. So when I got pregnant, everybody just thought I was getting fat again. I'll never forget—I was going into my junior year in high school and my mother and I went shopping for clothes, and my mother came into the dressing room with me. She really was looking at me and she was saying, "You look different." And I said, "I'm just getting fat again." And she said,

* Eva Smith chose to use a pseudonym.

"I'm taking you to the doctor." That was in September and considering that my son was born in November, I must have been at least seven months pregnant, but all this was brand new to me.

When the doctor told my mother I was pregnant, she asked me who the father was, and I told her. She confronted my stepfather and he claimed that he knew nothing about it. Within a week we left him and went down South.

When I first realized I was pregnant, I attempted suicide. It was a hard time for me. *I* knew I needed therapy. I wish somebody else had realized it at the time!

My mother told me I didn't have to keep the child, that I could put it up for adoption or that she would raise it as her own. I chose to keep that child because it was the first thing that was ever mine.

I created a cover story about who the father was. I said he was some boy I'd been going with. I had to deal with a lot of put-downs from people, you know, 'cause I was fifteen and having this baby.

Because of all the things that happened to me, there was this question that used to haunt me, you know, "Why me?" Those were the years I call my trauma years. And I went out of the trauma years into being a battered wife.

I got married at seventeen. I was already pregnant with my daughter. My husband and I were the same age. I told my husband about my stepfather and that he was my son's father. If only I knew then what I know now! I would have never told him. Because he got jealous. Every time we argued, he'd bring that up. I was different kinds of whores and sluts and this and that.

We were into it before we ever got married. We used to argue once a week when we were going together, but not real physical kind of stuff. But after we were married, he had the license. You know, they pronounce you man and *wife,* not man and *woman.* To my way of thinking it gives men a free ticket to do whatever they want. So the battering started and increased till I couldn't take it anymore.

I left him after he'd taken a branch off a tree and beat me with it, but then I came back and went through what I call my three months of hell. I was making $1.79 an hour. I was paying all the bills, I paid the rent. I was buying all the food, all the clothes, even renting him a television. I got off work at 4:30. I was expected to catch the bus at 4:35, hit downtown at 5:00, change buses, and walk in the door at 5:20. If I walked in the door at 5:30, I got my ass kicked.

So in essence, he held my children hostage. He did lots of sadistic things to me during that time. I was on a large dose of Librium. My nerves were so bad, I was going through bouts of temporary blindness.

I was twenty then, and I tried to kill myself. I had gotten my prescription filled. I came home and I took about half the bottle. He found the bottle and he woke me up 'cause I was going off to la-la land. And he got me up and went and got my son, who was about four then. He sprayed Raid in his hair, then he took a lighter and held it over his head and said, "If you don't wake up, I'm gonna light his hair." I mean I was going through it. We didn't have a phone or anything. There's that isolation thing.

I decided to kill him.

It was a question of survival. I knew we couldn't live together without one of us killing the other. So I was going to kill him. We had this argument on a Monday and I had planned that Friday that when I got paid,

I'd pay the rent, the water bill, buy a gun, go home, walk in the door, scream, and kill him. Even now, I can say with conviction I was going to kill him.

And this woman who was like my second mother said, "You don't want that on your conscience the rest of your life." So I turned him over to the military because he'd gone AWOL. They took him to jail. I took my children to safety and moved out of the house in four days. I started divorce proceedings immediately.

When I got rid of my husband, all that weird stuff went away. I didn't have to take Librium any more. The blindness went away. The shaking went away. All of that went away.

So by the time I was twenty-one, I had been married, divorced, and had two children. When I moved to California, I had seven suitcases, two kids, and one hundred dollars. And Lord, I've come a long way from there.

I HAVE TOLD MY SON

My son will be eighteen this fall, and when he was thirteen, I told him who his father was. He had been asking questions on a regular basis. He wanted to know who he was, where did he come from, what was he about.

When he was younger, I'd told him my cover story—that his father was a teenager I had sex with. That was okay then, but as he got older, when he'd ask questions about his father, there'd be a hush in the whole room or people would change the subject. So he got the feeling there was this secret, and there were a number of people who were in on the secret, and he wasn't one of them.

There's no father listed on his birth certificate, so there was always this air of mystery. And at thirteen he just asked me in a much more straightforward way than he ever asked me before, so I told him.

Ahmal, the man I was involved with at that time, who was a father figure for my children, and I got together and discussed it very thoroughly. And then the three of us went into my bedroom. My son was trying to be grown up, wanting to have a cigarette. Everybody was cool, you know. I think it's important to say how I told it to him because I didn't make it a real heavy-duty kind of thing.

I'm a storyteller, and I just told it like you'd tell any kind of story to a child. I had parts in it that made him laugh. I told it in a way that wasn't condemning about my stepfather, because no matter how much pain he had brought into my life, the bottom line to this whole thing was this: this man was my son's biological father and whatever I told him was going to mold a certain part of him for the rest of his life. So it was important to me to not make my stepfather an ogre, to tell my son about it in such a way that he would not become as devastated as I was by it. Your children are more important than anything that may hurt you or the hate that you feel.

And so I dredged up every good memory about my stepfather that I could find. I really worked at making him very human. I talked about his shortcomings and the good things about him. I talked about his smile, 'cause he had a wonderful smile. I didn't go into the sexual abuse real heavy because that was not the important thing at that point. I talked about what he did to me and how young I was. I put a little drama in, 'cause there was plenty of drama in what happened, but I didn't make it a great big thing. And I talked about what it was like being pregnant with him. How I felt. I was fifteen. How that felt.

My son's first reaction was, "Wow, all of that happened to me!" And Ahmal said, "Hey, blood, check this out. None of that happened to you. It happened to your mother." And so my son had to deal with that. He had to weigh how this affected who he was as a person. He had to make sure he was never that type of male himself. It was a very difficult time for him. And it was a very, very hard time for me because he was trying to punish me for who his father was.

Slowly it has healed for my son. Now it's just a fact of being. I don't think he resents me for it. If anything, I think maybe he loves me a little more. He was a spirit that had to come here and that was the way he came.

IT'S MADE ME MORE COURAGEOUS AS A PARENT

Because of the things that happened to me, I was very open with my children about sex. I've always told them the truth. My children did not grow up talking about dick and pussy. They grew up talking about penis and vagina, you know, and had a very clear understanding about what sex was all about. I didn't want them to be in the dark about what happens when you stick a penis in a vagina.

My son was talking to this woman and he said, "My momma would beat me to death if I hit a woman." Oh good, he knows. He's going to have to have a certain amount of respect toward women. That's how he's been raised.

I USED TO CALL MYSELF THE THIRTY-TO-NINETY-DAY WONDER

I was only involved in relationships that lasted thirty-to-ninety days. On the ninety-first day the relationship would be over, you could give it up. And this went on for many, many years, until I met Ahmal, who was willing to really put in some time.

After I'd been involved with him for ninety days, I began to end the relationship. On the ninety-first day I was suddenly pissed off and acting different. And he said, "Okay, what's going on? I woke up this morning and you've changed, you know. What's happening?" I can remember saying to him, "Hey! After ninety days I don't know what to do! We're into the ninety-sixth day and I don't know how to relate to you." And you know, we worked to stay together. And I give him a lot of credit for that.

He was a very compassionate man. I could come home from group and share what I had done and what had come up for me and he wouldn't browbeat me about it. If he felt there was something more that I needed to explore, he'd help bring that out for me.

But I think when you go through sexual abuse you almost become a bottomless pit— this is what he used to say—of need. And that's what he became upset with, became frustrated with. After a year we broke up and that was a part of it. He's still very close to me, though. He's still an integral part of my life and the lives of my children.

What's important to me now is to be in a relationship with someone who has a certain amount of tenderness and compassion toward me, you know. I am a very strong sister. I admit it. But by the same token, I got this other little part that's kind of, you know, soft, and you know, like lace, and most people don't see it. Most men don't see it. So when I meet a man who sees that, I'm very drawn to him.

"OKAY, BODY, FEEL!"

I have always enjoyed my sexuality. But there have been these "little" issues that come up from time to time.

I'd be out of my body and not even aware of it. Tactilely, I was very numb. I had one lover who used to pinch me all the time, just so I could feel. He recognized how numb I was.

When I began to make love or masturbate, these pictures from my past would come up and that was a trip. It was erotic and it wasn't. It was my orientation to sex, so it got me off, but I always felt bad. I had a lot of guilt and shame about it. So when I began to have sex and these scenes would begin to bleed through, it would make me numb out. I could be with somebody I really cared for and liked. I could be having a real good time, and all of a sudden I'd just numb out.

I'd never tell my partners what was going on. I'd just continue what I was doing and lay up there and say, "Okay, body, feel! Toes, I want you to feel. Let's feel in the toes now. Okay, let's bring it up to the ankles." I used to do this, you know. I'd bring the feeling up. "Okay, fingers, let's feel. That's the way. C'mon arms, we're feeling now!" I used to do this so that I could be able to have some kind of feeling.

Most of the time I did have orgasms, but how far I would let the orgasms go was another thing. I could feel sexual pleasure to a certain extent, but I was afraid that it would make me crazy, so I would feel a little bit and then I would cut if off—you know, put on the brakes. Then there would be no more feeling.

I've worked on it metaphysically. I took out those pictures and I destroyed them. As I eliminated the pictures, so went the guilt and the shame. And I'm *very* happy about that. It's a miracle that I am a sexually active woman today and that I enjoy sex as much as I do. And I *do!*

I NEEDED TO SCREAM AND HOLLER AND YELL

Confronting, dealing with, and releasing anger has been the hardest part of healing for me. In a survivors group that I was in, all this anger came up. I needed to scream and holler and yell, but I didn't feel safe in the group. So what happened was, I didn't express it.

You know how women talk about falling apart and crying all the time? They're going from crying to anger and all that. Well, I did that in three days. It came close to breaking me 'cause I'd never realized the depth of that anger. I realized why I'd never let myself feel it either, 'cause it was so debilitating. All I could feel was this raging. I probably could have torn up sheets with my fingers. And to go between this anger and this crying. I had to leave work because I was always breaking into tears. But I couldn't stay at home either.

I went to a movie. I watched the movie with tears just streaming down. In the theater I could be out of control and no one would pay attention to me. I felt like there were little pieces of me all over the theater. I called this man who was like a brother to me. He picked me up and took me to the beach. I lay down in the sand and cried. I made these mounds of sand and pounded them. My head was hurting terribly. I couldn't take it anymore. So he took me to the hospital and they gave me a shot, something to relax me. I was okay after that—physically.

My advice to someone working on this stuff is to find working therapy as opposed to talking therapy. Talking doesn't truly release it. That's why people can be in therapy for twenty years, you know—because they just talk about it. Express it and release. If you need to scream and holler, that's what you need to do. So do it.

A TRIP BACK HOME

Recently I made a trip back home, and a lot of that had to do with making peace with all of that old bull, 'cause that's where the original sexual abuse began. I went down to look at the house where it all began. The house isn't there anymore because it burned down. I went there and thought about some of the things that had happened to me there, and I was able to leave it and not feel that I had to carry it anymore, like "Hey, that was then!"

I went to complete one cycle and to begin a new cycle for myself—making peace and coming to terms with what that whole area means to me. Before, whenever I went into that area, I don't care how sunny it was, it was cloudy for me. One of the things that happened on this trip was that this was erased. All of that for me has been lifted and it's gone. It was really quite wonderful that I could be there and not be upset.

JANEL ROBINSON

If I was talking to another teenager in my situation, I'd say, "Hang in there. It's tough, but it gets better. It may not seem like it, but it does. It's a process you have to go through."

Janel Robinson is nineteen years old.* She lives with her mother, stepfather, and fourteen-year-old brother, works part-time selling newspaper ads, and is completing her AS degree at her local community college. Janel studies computer science and would someday like to have a career helping other survivors of sexual abuse.

I was molested by two of my grandfathers. The first time, it started when I was two and went on until I was six. The only reason anybody found out was that I kept having bladder infections. The doctor found bruises in my vulva. That's how everything came out.

I remember being questioned with anatomical dolls, but I didn't really know what was going on. My mom stuck me into counseling for a little while, but I didn't like it. There was this big dark hallway we had to go through and it scared me, so after a while we stopped going.

My family handled the first molestation fairly well. My grandmother was shocked, but she helped with the prosecution. She said, "This is what we have to do. This is what's right." The whole family helped out. My grandfather was convicted and sent to jail.

---

* Janel chose to use a pseudonym.

When I was nine or ten, my cousin told me my other grandfather had been molesting her for years. At first, I didn't believe her. It was too shocking. I'd blocked out the earlier molest. But after she told me, I stopped and said, "Wait a minute! That happened to me before!"

My cousin went to my grandfather and said, "Tell her it's true." He said, "Okay. We're going to play a little game. Take off all your clothes." I just stood there in shock.

My grandfathers knew each other and they talked about the molestation. I guess he figured since it had happened to me already, it was okay to do it again.

He molested us for the next year. I kept telling my cousin, "We need to say something." Finally we made a plan to tell our parents the same weekend. I went home and told and she went home and didn't. Our grandfather was convicted and went to jail. And that whole side of the family resented me.

The hardest thing for me was that my parents wanted to stay on good terms with my grandfather and that side of the family. They pushed me to go over there for holidays and then I'd get shunned. It was awful.

My relatives hated me because I had put him in jail. One even implied I was the one who had initiated the molestation. He told me, "From now on you better mind your parents and be a good little girl."

That was the last time I went over there. I started staying home by myself on holidays. That's what started the healing process for me—taking a stance and saying, "I'm not going to put myself through that."

Everyone protected my grandfather. The family kept sweeping it under the rug. Even my cousin protected him. When he got out of jail, she and my brother continued to go to his house. He started molesting both of them again. And he was sent back to jail.

After he was convicted the second time, my parents finally came to the conclusion, "This is not right." They only have minimal contact with my grandfather now.

HOW THE ABUSE AFFECTED ME

I started acting out some time after the second molestation. I didn't know why. I didn't connect it to the molestation. I just thought I was a bad person who was going in the wrong direction.

I did drugs, marijuana, and LSD. I carved on myself. I was promiscuous. I didn't get along with anybody. I hated myself.

I remember being in the fifth grade and thinking of suicide.

By my freshman year in high school, I was doing a lot of cocaine. I did it to feel better about myself. I also thought I was fat and wanted to lose weight. But I was really skinny. That was another reason. When you do cocaine, you feel great. You're on top of the world. But when you come down, you feel awful, like you're the lowest person in the world.

When I was thirteen and coming down from cocaine, I tried to kill myself.

My mother and I had been arguing. I wanted to go out and she didn't want to let me. I was wearing a miniskirt and she said I looked like a slut. Something clicked in my brain. I said to myself, "Even my mom thinks I'm a slut. Everyone thinks I'm a slut because I was abused. So it's all my fault." Boom. I ran into the bathroom and slit my wrists. I didn't really realize what I was doing till I started bleeding all over the place. I didn't feel anything.

My mom didn't know what to do with me. She put me in bed and watched me all night long. Two days later, she took me to the emergency room and I was hospitalized.

STARTING TO HEAL

Being in the hospital was comforting. I'd hit such a bottom, I didn't resist it. It was a women's hospital. There were adults and teenagers there. The majority of women had been sexually abused. Sharing with them was really helpful. I was able to say, "Here's my story. This is what happened to me." That was a real turning point for me. I learned that I was not the only one. I started realizing I had a lot of problems and that they were related to the molestation.

It was almost like a type of school. All I did there was learn. I learned a lot about me. It was wonderful. I was still feeling confused and introverted and not so hot about myself, but at least I had some insight to work with.

After a month, my insurance ran out. My psychiatrist went on vacation and the person who took his place said, "You're out of here." My psychiatrist came back and said, "Where is she?" I wasn't supposed to be released, but they released me anyhow.

When I went home, I was really depressed. I wasn't eating or sleeping. I wasn't functioning. My mom said, "I don't know how to deal with this," and she put me in a group home. She said, "They can deal with you."

Initially we were going to do a six-week trial period—a kind of assessment. I thought, "Six weeks, no problem. That's half my summer vacation—I can deal with that." Six weeks passed and I said, "Okay, Mom.

I'm ready to come home." And she said, "No, you're not. We really aren't ready to deal with you." So I said, "Screw you," and stayed in the group home.

Three or four times we made a date for me to come home, and that day would roll around and pass. She kept saying I wasn't ready, that she didn't think she was ready. Looking back, I realize she didn't feel capable of dealing with me. She didn't think she could handle it if I had a really bad day and felt suicidal. I don't really blame her. Now. But at the time, I really resented it. It was really disappointing. I had to separate myself from my mom and say, "I'm my own person. I don't need to be so attached to you."

I was in a group home for a year. There were meetings twice a week. We saw psychologists and counselors and social workers. It was very structured and I think that was helpful. Looking back, I'm extremely thankful I was there.

After a year, I finally went home. At first my parents tried to structure everything —they overstructured it for the first couple of months. We argued a lot. My mom threatened to send me back to the group home. But after that, we laid out everything straight and said, "Here's your space. This is ours." We worked it out. I'm still living with them and it's great.

CONFRONTING MY GRANDFATHERS

While I was in the hospital, I decided I wanted to confront my first grandfather. He molested me from the time I was two until I was six, yet I only remembered three incidents. Obviously I'd repressed a lot because I lived with him for quite a while, and this was a regular thing that went on, probably every day. But I couldn't remember it, and that really scared me.

I found out he had cancer. I decided to confront him before he died. I wanted some closure. I wanted to find out what happened to me rather than spending lots of money on a hypnotist. So we had a confrontation. I talked to him for an hour. It was really scary. He told me just about everything that he had done to me.* He said, "I didn't do anything bad to you. You liked it. You kept coming back. I just gave you what you wanted." I said, "A two-year-old doesn't know what's right and wrong." He couldn't really say anything to that. When he died a couple of years ago, I was really glad I'd talked to him.

We sued my second grandfather. It wasn't my idea, but I felt good about it. My mother called me while I was in the hospital and said, "Guess what? We're suing your grandfather." She said, "If you can't get them to stay in jail long enough, the best way you can get them is where it really hurts—in their pocketbook." I knew the hospital was really expensive. I thought, "If this is going to put my parents in a financial bind, maybe this is what we should do."

It was a really long process. He made me go through a deposition. It lasted two or three hours. He had three different lawyers there. They didn't even want to let my mom in with me. It was really scary. I was only thirteen.

The deposition was almost like a court trial, the kind you see on TV. It was awful. They asked everything. I've blocked out a lot of it, but I remember them asking me if I was a virgin. He began to explain to me the process of losing your virginity and what happens with the breaking of the hymen. I was shocked. I thought, "How could this pertain to my grandfather molesting me?" I just looked at him and said, "That's none of your damn business." He asked me again, and the lawyers got into an argument.

They asked me every personal question in the book: what boyfriends I had, how my other grandfather molested me. They asked me more questions about my personal life than they did about the molestation. They tried to minimize the molestation, saying, "Isn't it true he only did this to you?" They made me feel really bad. When I walked out of there, I felt really small, like I was the bad person.

It's awful how the justice system makes victims feel that way. I think people being accused of the crime should go through that—not the victim. If the victim says, "This happened to me," why should they be questioned and bugged about it? It's just a tactic lawyers use to scare the victim. I don't think they should be allowed to do it.

I THINK THE SYSTEM IS REALLY SCREWY

The system—the criminal justice system, the social workers, the police—handle these things terribly. A lot of kids are abused, and the system says, "Okay, we're going to take you out of your home." Why do they have to take the kids out of the home? Why can't they put the abuser somewhere else? Why do they have to disrupt the child's life? While I was in the group home

---

* Janel's experience with her grandfather is unusual. Most perpetrators deny the abuse and aren't reliable sources for finding out what happened to you.

there were two or three girls I knew personally who had been in ten foster homes, two or three group homes, different shelters, juvenile hall, out on the street, thrown here, there, and everywhere. Personally, I don't think it's good for kids to be shuffled around like that.

When I was in the group home, I met this girl who was my age. We had the same status, we'd gone through a lot of the same stuff. Both of us had been abused. Neither of us had ever broken any laws. By the time she left the group home, she had a police record. She ended up killing herself.

That was really hard on me. She was a good friend. We were in exactly the same boat. She went in one direction and I went in the other. She came to the group home to get therapy and become more stable. I believe the system made her worse. She fell through the cracks. A lot of kids do.

WHERE I AM TODAY

Once I figured out that a lot of my problems stemmed from the abuse, I knew I needed to deal with them. I had a lot of determination. I wasn't going to let anybody or anything stop me.

I'm still healing. I'm not in as intense therapy as I was, but it still affects me. I still have trouble trusting people and trusting my own judgment.

For a while I had trouble being sexual. I'd look at my boyfriend's face and all of a sudden it would be my grandfather. It was awful. My boyfriend and I worked through that. It took quite a while, but he has a lot of patience. He listened. He went to counseling with me. We read books together. Anytime I'd have a memory or flashback, he'd be there. He'd listen and comfort me. Now my sex life is great.

I'm proud of coming as far as I have. I can say to myself, "Hey I survived that, and I'm still here."

Going through what I've gone through has made me a stronger person. I've converted the pain into tools and knowledge that I can apply to problems that come up now. I'm proud of that.

SOLEDAD

When it happened, I couldn't name it. And then when I got the words to be able to name it, I forgot. All I was left with was hatred for my father. For a long time, I thought that people were born hating their fathers.

Soledad is a twenty-eight-year-old Chicana who was severely abused by her father throughout her childhood.* For the past eleven years she has lived in Sonoma County, California. Today she is a high school counselor.

Soledad writes, "In this interview, I have spoken more of my biological parents (due to my feelings of betrayal and violation) than of my Tias and Tio, who were very much my parents, in the true sense of the word. Without them, I am convinced that my ultimate survival would not have been a reality, for I am certain that my life would have been beaten or suffocated out of me. To them I owe

my life. And because of them, I will struggle to keep it.

"I once read that we can give two things to children—one is a sense of roots and the other is a sense of wings. I now know my roots, my history. Now I am ready to fly towards the sun."

As was sometimes true for other women of color, it was particularly difficult for Soledad to entrust us—two white women—with her story. Because much of white America holds the stereotype that abuse happens only to "others," many women of color are reluctant to disclose their abuse for fear that it will reinforce already existing prejudices. Still others come from cultures that have a strong taboo against exposing "private" experiences.

---

* Soledad chose to use a pseudonym.

Pushing past these barriers to speak out is courageous.

Being Latina is real precious to me. However, part of the culture that I hate is the silence. As beautiful as our language is, we don't have words for this. Our history is passed orally, yet there's such silence in Latino families about this.

There was no talk of sex in the house, ever. It was all out on the streets. And how can you go to a woman you haven't been able to talk to about your damn period and tell her that her husband is raping you?

I think this kind of silence might be common, but I think it's especially true because my people feel so powerless in this culture, fearing authorities outside of the family. We had to stick together and protect each other from the system, and from the white people who control it. What other option did we have? We just had to keep it in. Admitting any problem would reflect badly on our whole culture.

And that's why it's still hard for me to talk about it. I don't want anyone to use this against people of color, because there are so many negative stereotypes of Latinos already. People are already more willing to trust white men than they are men of color. And I don't want to promote more mistrust of men of color. But this is how it happened for me and I feel I need to break the silence.

MY FATHER WAS LIKE A VOLCANIC ERUPTION

I was raised in an extended family in Los Angeles, in a hard-core ghetto. I'm the oldest of three kids. My dad worked on and off in factories. My mom worked in sweatshops until she became disabled. We not only lived in poverty, we *were* poverty.

I was beaten at least every other day for years. I hated that my parents beat us, but everybody around us got whipped, so that was just the way it was. At least when my mother beat us, we still had a feeling she loved us. And it hurt less.

My father was like a volcanic eruption. You wouldn't know when it was going to happen, but when it did, there was no stopping what was happening. He wore these steel-toed shoes for work, and he'd kick us everywhere, including the head. You could get arrested for kicking a dog like that.

When people smack you around the way my father did, it's hard to decide which is worse—that or the sexual abuse.

My father not only molested me, he molested all my cousins and all the girls in the neighborhood. The ones that I know, there are at least twenty-four. There are others I've thought about. People really trusted him with their kids. He was a great social manipulator and he knew how kids thought. It's amazing how one person can mess with so many kids.

From what I can tell, the sexual abuse with me started right when I was brought home from the hospital. I found out from another relative that for a long time he didn't even sleep with my mother. He slept with me when I was a little baby.

In the beginning there was a lot of fondling. He could be what you would call "gentle," but I would interpret that as being sneaky, because I knew that he could kill me too. If you already know that this man can kill you so easily, you're not going to say anything. And so I would just be frozen, with the feeling "Soon it will be over." But it got worse and worse.

The peak of it all was at about eight. That's when he first raped me. It was pretty regular after that, at least three times a week. It happened in a lot of different places. We lived in really small quarters. There was no privacy. So he'd tell me we had to go out for milk, or that we needed to go for a ride in the car. He really loved to take all the girls out for a ride. Most of this stuff happened in the car, a lot of it in the dark, so this left a blank for me because a lot of it I didn't see.

A lot of the raping happened from behind. When he abused me, he would talk to me in Spanish, threatening to cut my throat or cut my tongue out. So now, telling you my story in English is easier. Telling you in English keeps more emotional distance. I probably would be sobbing by now if I was describing what he had done in Spanish.

When I was thirteen the sexual abuse stopped. I had gotten more streetwise than ever, and he started to be fearful of me. He knew I was ready to die, that I would fight him to our graves if I had to.

I LIVED ON THE STREETS

I was very self-destructive in terms of drugs and fighting. I started taking drugs at nine. I started hustling. I did just about everything. I would do drugs and at the time I wouldn't even know what the hell it was that I was using. I didn't care. That went on until I was sixteen.

Fighting was an everyday occurrence on the streets. As we got bigger, the toys got more dangerous. I carried knives. I got into fights with people who carried knives. And some with guns. They would be tripping, too. You would never know if you would

come out of there alive. I thought this was just the way it was, and it was fine if I died with it.

Between what was happening to me at home with him and having to fight and live on the streets too, I always thought the only freedom would be to go to prison. Then I would be "free."

I always dealt with my life on an hour-by-hour basis. For a long time, I never did want to live. I'd be five and I'd think, "Maybe I won't live until I'm ten," and I would hope that that would be true. Or I'd get to be ten, and I'd think, "Okay, fifteen, max. That's as long as I'm going to live."

What other choices did I have? I grew up poor. I didn't know there were other worlds outside of this. I still have a hard time with the whole concept that you have control over your own destiny. Life was just the way it was, and the only way out of it was to kill myself or destroy myself or become like a vegetable. I never knew there was a way out.

I didn't have much self-esteem. Self-esteem wasn't a concept I learned till I went to college. With Chicanos, that can get confused with being pompous, and if you're being pompous, you're forgetting who you are and where you're from. I just didn't think too much about myself.

THERE WAS MORE TO LIFE THAN WHAT I KNEW

How I got out of that whole drug and fighting scene was that there was a teacher who took an interest in me when I was sixteen. I was always in and out of school and I was illiterate. And this woman did care about me. She thought that I had a good mind. She was scared of me, but she wanted to find out why I was the way I was. And I trusted her. I didn't tell her anything about the abuse, just that it was a bad situation at home. I think she knew what I was not telling her.

She started talking to me and just spending time with me. It mattered to her that I didn't destroy myself. And that made all the difference. There wasn't anyone before who had ever spent that kind of time with me.

Learning to read helped me see there was more to life than what I knew, and that in fact, this was not life. That was the beginning of my healing. It was the first time I thought that maybe I could survive without hustling. Maybe I could learn something from some magazine or some book and get some power from it. Get some options.

I was lucky. I got into an Upward Bound program. She helped me get into college. College was a real culture shock. I hadn't ever been around that many white people. I still couldn't read enough to understand the menus in the cafeteria. And I didn't know what any of the foods were. I not only didn't know what it was, I'd never heard the words "eggplant parmesan" before. But I stuck it out. I had to make it work for me.

I WAS BARELY KEEPING MYSELF ALIVE

Even though I succeeded in going to school and getting a job, I knew things weren't right inside. For a long time all I was doing was coming home and laying in my bed. Sometimes I'd turn the TV on, sometimes not. My dinner would be a bottle of Coke. Maybe I'd decide to have a real dinner, and I'd have a pint of ice cream. And that was my life. I'd never open these drapes, never would answer my phone. If anyone knocked on the door, I wouldn't even look to see who was there. I could care less who it was. I was barely keeping myself alive.

Because I wouldn't let anyone take care of me, I ate to comfort myself. I gained a lot of weight. I drank a lot. I remember one time in particular when I had no intention to fuck myself up, but that's just what I did. I drank shot after shot of tequila. I finished off half a bottle, and then I went for another. I think I would have died if my girlfriend hadn't found me on the floor and gotten help.

I never really believed that anyone loved me, so I felt kind of orphaned. I was self-sufficient. If I hadn't been, that would have been the end of me. It's prevented me from ever wanting anyone to take care of me. I will take care of myself and that's it. And if anyone needs to be taken care of, I will take care of them, but I will never let them take care of me. And that's kind of hard, 'cause I get sick too and I'll grow old.

I KNEW I WASN'T CRAZY AND THAT I NEEDED HELP

This whole thing got triggered by talking to a cousin of mine who had also been molested by my father. She called me up a year and a half ago and said, "Did you know that your dad molested my sisters?"

I said, "I never really thought about him that way. But it doesn't surprise me." I went to visit her to find out what had happened. We stayed up the whole night and the whole day to talk about it. It was painful, but I felt so vindicated the whole time. I knew I wasn't crazy. I knew there were reasons why I was destroying myself and why I hated him so much.

It was validating to know it happened to all of my cousins too. It's sad that it did. But if it had only just happened to me, I'd probably still be questioning it. If you're told you're crazy enough times, you really start to believe it.

From then on I couldn't stop thinking about what I knew. I started getting really obsessed. And I started to understand all these things. I started to wake up feeling powerful. I'd always had to carry a knife or be hustling to feel powerful before. All of a sudden, I had a belief in myself.

But at the same time, I got very depressed. It just seemed like one more heavy thing to cope with. It felt like another death. I needed help dealing with it. So I went to a Chicana therapist that I knew. I said, "God! I found this out. I talked to my cousin and then I remembered." I told her this had happened twenty years ago, that there were no kids around him now. Right while I was talking to her, she gets up and goes to the phone, and starts to call Child Protective Services.

Now that is my ultimate fear. First, I was just learning about this thing. And second of all, he has that fear about outside authorities, and if that car pulled up to his house, he would never live through that. And not that I especially wanted him to live, but I wouldn't want him to die in the hands of the system.

So she picked up the phone and she started saying, "Well, I have this situation here . . ." And I started saying, "What the hell are you doing? I swear to you there are no kids . . ."

And she said, "I need to talk to a supervisor." She just kept on. She asked how she was supposed to report this. And I was just shitting. Give me a break! What the hell are you fucking doing? I knew that they had to assess if there was someone in danger now.

What this person finally told her was that what she was reporting had happened twenty years ago, that there were no children in the home, and that they were overloaded and couldn't deal with situations that weren't definitely happening now.

That scared the shit out of me, but I still needed help. I couldn't handle what I was feeling. I had a definite picture in mind of the kind of person that could help me. I wanted a Chicana. I wanted a lesbian. I wanted this and that. I spent months and months looking, and I really couldn't find anyone who lived near me. And I didn't want to commute.

I could have been so damn picky that I never would have done it. That was my pattern. I would never have to be vulnerable and could just keep it in. And I couldn't do that anymore. Finally, I had to ask myself how much of this was my defenses in being scared to work on the molest issue. So finally I decided she had to be someone who had dealt with abuse. She couldn't be homophobic or racist, but I had to get started.

So finally I found this woman who's straight, middle class, white, but she's been good. She's been fucking good. I can't say a bad thing about her. I still wish I could have the other, but this is working for now.

I'M TRYING TO LEARN TO BE A LITTLE GIRL AGAIN

To be a healthy adult, I think you need to have been a child at one time. And I wasn't. I was always trying to be an adult. So now I'm an adult, and I'm trying to redo my childhood. It's totally reversed.

I'm trying to learn to be a little girl again. I have to find that softness that I lost or never was able to deal with. I have to cry those little girl tears. I have to feel what happened.

It's been painful. At first the only way I could relate to the little girl was by drawing pictures. Since I could always deal better with other people's problems than my own, she always came out looking really different from me. I'd think about the terrible things that had happened to her, and I would feel bad for the little girl in the picture, but I would separate her from me.

I've had to get under her skin, and that's when the process started getting hard. I've almost had to make myself regress. I've had to remember what it felt like to have a little body, to wear those little clothes.

I'VE HAD TO CHANGE PATTERNS AROUND SEX

I've always been more content being alone than with a lover, but I have had lovers since I was twelve, thirteen. I never felt I had the right to say, "No, I'm not interested in you. I don't want to be sexual with you." But they weren't relationships. They were just people to fill time with. I didn't know there was more to being a lover than just the sexual part.

It's always been important for me to control the whole sexual thing and to be really detached. I thought being soft was the same as being weak. When you're from the streets, you're just not vulnerable like that. You don't submit yourself to those feelings. At least you never let people know you have those feelings. I'd be hard and distant and cold, and now I can't even imagine why people wanted to be sexual and intimate with me.

A lot of times when I would have sex with someone and they would be coming, maybe they'd be making noise or breathing hard, I'd think to myself, "Oh, just get over it. How weak you are!" Because that's what I'd thought of my father.

I always made sure when I was sexual that I was really quiet. I was not having an orgasm because of anybody else. To me, having an orgasm was just like my body reacting to something. It had nothing to do with emotions. You know how you smack your knees to test how fast your reflexes are? Well, that's how I felt about sex. It's a crass way to describe it, but that's what coming was like for me. It was easy to be quiet. Some people call it being butch; I call it being really repressed. And that just came from that frozen little girl who was being molested and raped, waiting for it to be over soon.

The most important thing I've realized is that relationships can be different from how they have been for me. I'm really trying to turn that around, to let people in on an emotional level. I've been plenty in people's bodies, but not in their souls. I've finally been able to realize that just because you're being sexual with someone doesn't mean that you're being close with them.

I DIDN'T WANT TO HURT THE PEOPLE I LOVE

Another area that's been hard for me is dealing with my anger. Anger was always really easy access for me. It would come out like that! [She snaps her fingers.] But now that I have more information about *why* I'm angry, it's better. When I didn't have any information, the anger was explosive, just like my father's.

But I didn't want to hurt people I loved. I didn't even want to hurt people I didn't like. But it was hard to break that pattern. Whenever I started to have those feelings I'd stop and say, "I just want to beat the shit out of you right now!" It was hard to admit it. But it was a start. I'd be able to talk about the feelings of wanting to punch her out rather than doing it. It was a matter of starting to live my life watching what I did, because for a long time I hadn't ever watched any of it. Now I try to be more aware of where that behavior came from. I don't want to repeat what they did to me.

I think there's a lot of anger still pinned inside me, but I'm getting it out in better ways. I use my voice, and if the neighbors hear us, then fine. At least I'm not using my fists. I also have a couple of friends that I wrestle with. It's terrifying to be pinned, but it's an outlet for the rage. I've done weight lifting too. That really helped a lot.

I EXPECT TO CONFRONT MY FATHER BY THE END OF THE YEAR

Sometimes I think I'd like to confront him right in the middle of a party, right in front of all his friends. Other times I think I'll call him out to a park. I want to get it

through his head that he really lost something and someone special. A lot of people who were really special. He lost the opportunity to even be a father to me and to my sister or to be a trusted uncle to my cousins. I want him to know he has no claims on me as a daughter.

I also want to tell him that he was the one who gave me reason to hate him, and that I do not love him. That I never loved him. And whether he loves me or not doesn't matter. If he does love me in his own sick way, he can just stick it somewhere else. And I also want to tell him that I think he is a really sick man. This thing he probably figured didn't hurt anybody, hurt plenty.

Some people don't deserve a chance. I'd like to put my hands around his neck and say, "Remember, you used to do this to me?" I really want that opportunity to deal with him in the way he deserves to be dealt with. I have fantasies of mutilating him in the ways he threatened to do to us, beating him in the ways he used to beat us. I'd like to cut off his little *huevos*. I've had offers from people who said they'd go with me. But I've learned to respect life more than he ever did.

I'VE COME OUT OF MY SHELL STRONGER THAN I'VE EVER BEEN

I feel lighter, like a real burden has come off me. I literally felt less pressure in my chest and in my shoulders. I felt like I'd been walking around with twenty pounds of cement on my chest all my life. If I had run away from the pain, I don't think I'd ever have been able to shed that weight. I would still be destroying myself in some way.

It's a small thing, but I never had plants

before. It's just my way of trying to keep something other than me alive. It gives me a lot of pleasure. I grew up where there weren't too many flowers, right in the middle of the damn city.

I got my first plant about six months ago. Now I have all sorts of flowers on my porch. I have big bushes with purple flowers. I have big round pots with different flowers in them. I wanted color around me.

It's real Latina, all these colors. It reminds me a lot of my aunts.

It's a reason to live, really. I was scared about it at first. But now I know I can nurture them and keep them healthy. I make sure they don't have bugs. After I've been so rough in my life, I can still take care of something so delicate. Even though I've been knocked around, I can still keep them alive.

EVIE MALCOLM

Face a fear, and the death of that fear is certain.

Evie Malcolm is thirty-eight years old.* She lives in Boston, works as a secretary, and lives with her partner of thirteen years, Faith. She has spent the last eight years recovering from agoraphobia, which resulted from her experiences being molested by strangers in New York City.

"When people hear my story they say, 'Oh that happens to everyone who grows up in New York. What's the big deal?' It's so common, they accept it. When I was in eighth grade, the teacher asked all the girls if it ever happened to them, and every single girl raised her hand. Were we given any advice on how to deal with it? Were we told we could yell or kick or even say 'Stop'? No. It was totally expected and totally normalized. We learned that nothing could be done about it.

"But that doesn't make it tolerable for a child. That doesn't make it any less devastating. People say, 'That's just part of living in New York,' as though it's not bad if it happens to everyone. But the fact that it's so widespread makes it worse, not better."

I grew up in the suburbs of New York. My mother was a secretary who worked her way up to an administrative assistant position. My father is a businessman. They both grew up poor, leaving high school before they graduated, but they strove hard to be educated. Intelligence and scholastic ability were highly valued in my household. We were working class in reality, but rose through determination.

---

* Evie Malcolm chose to use a pseudonym.

My family was very old-fashioned. I was extremely protected. I was raised to be polite and respectful of authority. The abuse took place at a time when no young girl was encouraged to defend herself or be strong.

The first time, I was ten years old. I had taken my little brother to a children's matinee on a Saturday. A man sat down next to us, threw his coat on my lap, and started feeling me up. I said to my brother, "We've got to move." My brother complained, but we got up and switched seats. As soon as we were settled it happened again. I didn't know if it was someone else or the same man, but we got up again. The theater was crowded and I couldn't find any empty seats. By that time my brother was screaming. The usher told us we'd have to go back to our same seats or leave. So we left.

My brother screamed all the way home on the subway. I said, "I can't explain it, but when we get home, Mom and Dad will explain it to you." When we got home, I immediately told my parents. My mother turned away in disgust. My father started intellectualizing about the whole thing. They didn't do anything. They didn't explain it to my brother. They didn't say I was right to leave. They didn't offer to take us back to the movies the next day. I saw they were powerless against that man. And I learned I could never look to them for help. Somewhere inside I gave up.

Shortly after that, I passed the test to get into a public school for intellectually gifted girls. My new school started with seventh grade, so I was eleven when I began.

But I lived in Brooklyn and my new school was in Manhattan. And in order to get there I had to ride three different subways. And that's where the rest of the abuse happened. It started the second day of

school, during rush hour. I got on the train. I sat across from an old man. He was staring at me. And then I realized that he was exposing himself and masturbating. I thought he was crazy and insane and I was afraid that he was going to kill me. In my mind, only a lunatic would do something like that.

For the next six years, that kind of incident and much more—the grabbing and being molested in a crowd, the being followed from car to car—kept happening to me. I was very tall for my age, five foot nine. Yet I was childlike in appearance—no makeup, plain and childish clothes. I made an easy target.

Something happened almost every day. It was inevitable. And then after it happens a few times, it doesn't matter whether it happens or whether it doesn't—you have to get back into the exact same situation, and you think about it happening all the time. I had to get on that train five days a week for six years.

Quite a few of the incidents are burned into my brain. I call it being raped standing up in a crowd. It was as much rape as if there'd been actual penetration. And sometimes they got awfully close. One man stood near me masturbating with a vacant look on his face. He was smiling and his penis was completely out of his pants. With his free hand he took my arm, linking it in his—like friends walking down the street together. Just then the train got stuck in the tunnel. I felt completely trapped. In my head I was screaming, "Oh God, get me out of here." My whole self went up into my head. I felt completely disembodied.

Have you ever heard of deer who get on the road and get blinded by the headlights and they stop, and stand there, and the car hits them? What, is the deer wrong?

That's what happened to me in the subway. I'd never seen these things before. I just thought, "Oh my God," and froze. And it ran over me like a two-ton truck.

I doubt it was ever the same person. There are a million nasty men in the subways of New York. The majority were well dressed, they were coming from good neighborhoods, they were carrying briefcases. It was never a black or Hispanic man or a man of any other race but white. It wasn't poor old bums. It was all so-called normal men on their way to work, who casually took advantage of the opportunity. It was just like "Here's this young flesh. Reach out and grab it." You can molest a child so easily.

I never told anyone. I knew it was useless to tell my parents. Besides, my mother would have taken me out of my school, and I wanted to keep going. It was a tremendous honor. And I had every right to go. And I love the kid that kept going to that school. She didn't let those fuckers stop her.

A FULL-BLOWN PANIC ATTACK

I graduated when I was seventeen. I left the city and for five years I didn't come back. When I did, I started riding the subway again, and I started having panic attacks. I'd go down to the platform to wait for the train, and as soon as the doors to the subway would open, I'd have a full-blown panic attack with all the physical symptoms —I'd feel like I was going to die.

It's the kind of terror anyone would experience if they were being kidnapped, if they were about to be murdered. I don't know how to make it strong enough that it's about the worst feeling you can have. Every single body part feels threatened and the adrenaline is pumping in your body and you feel like a trapped rat. You want to run. You want to scream. You want to get out. And so I'd run out of the subway.

At that point I had no idea what was happening. I was twenty-two years old and I had no memory of what had happened to me as a kid riding the trains to school. It seemed like a panic that came out of the blue.

Over a period of years, I ended up not being able to ride the subways, then not being able to ride buses, then not being able to take cabs, then not being able to walk anywhere but to my college, ten blocks away. I could function at school and I could function at home, but I couldn't even go across the street for a cup of coffee.

Agoraphobia is like a mental cancer—it just extends into everything. At my worst, the panic attacks came on no matter what. I'd have several a day. And they're really debilitating. There's a lot of fatigue connected with agoraphobia. I was worried all the time. I developed a nervous bladder and a spastic colon. I have high blood pressure, and there's no history of that in my family. There isn't a part of my life it hasn't affected.

I WENT TO ALL KINDS OF THERAPISTS TO GET HELP

No one ever told me what was going on. No one ever told me I had agoraphobia. The therapists I went to didn't talk. You spill your guts and they never say anything. I just got worse and worse. I'd say, "I can't take trains anymore. Now I'm taking buses."

And then a year later, it was "Dr. Horowitz, I can't get on the bus anymore. I'm too frightened. What's happening?"

One doctor told me I was obsessive-compulsive and that he had a new medicine he wanted to give me for free, which means they don't know what it's going to do yet. I had to sign a release to take it. Not only couldn't I get out of my house on that medicine, I couldn't get off my couch. I was like a cucumber or a head of cauliflower. I got so depressed from that medication. I called Faith at work and I said, "You better come home. I'm thinking razor blades here. I don't want to kill myself, but it's all I can think of."

I finally self-diagnosed myself as agoraphobic after seeing a woman on the Tom Snyder show describe exactly what I experienced. I said, "Oh my God! That's me!" I called the station to get the number of one of the doctors who had been on the air with her. I ended up going to the Roosevelt clinic and getting help from some of the top people in New York.

I WASN'T ALONE

I went to phobic therapy three times a week for two and a half years. It was important for me to know there were other people suffering what I was suffering, that I wasn't alone. All my friends were phobics. Those women were very important to me. I worked on a phobic newsletter.

They teach you that fears don't come without thoughts. People usually say, "I was just in the supermarket and suddenly it hit me." It feels like it comes from nowhere, but there's always a trigger. It's your own thoughts. It's a command you're giving.

What you need to learn is, "What are the thoughts?" Then you can stop them. Then your body doesn't pump the adrenaline, your throat doesn't close up, your palms don't sweat, your legs don't get shaky, you don't feel like you're going to vomit.

I was lucky enough to hook up with a wonderful phobic therapist, who's called a "Helper." We did what's called contextual therapy. The purpose of contextual therapy is to get frightened, so you can feel the fear with another person who can help you reinterpret it and teach you to cope with it. You literally find the places where you're going to be afraid. If you're afraid of restaurants, you go to a restaurant.

You don't try to figure out why. You need to be able to function. If you can't get out of your house, a phobic therapist will come to your house, because obviously, how does the person get better if they can't get to the therapist's office?

My therapist's name was Sandy. We worked together for four years. She was completely fearless and warm. I owe most of my life to her.

Sandy got me out of my house again. She'd come over and walk out a little bit with me, walk me to the corner, go out to a restaurant. She asked me where I had the very worst panic attacks. I said, "On the subway." She said, "That's where we should start."

So we'd buy the tokens and go down there. We did it in small increments. It's sort of like someone who has a stroke and can't speak. They have the kind of therapist who teaches them how to speak again. Sandy taught me to be on the subway again.

At first we'd sit on the bench and watch the trains go by. That was all I could do. And she'd have me quantify the fear level from zero to ten. It would go up to an eight or nine, at which point my neck was stretched, my heart was pounding, I'd want to run. She would help me feel those feelings and not run. Then we'd get on the subway and ride one stop. And if I wanted to get out after one stop, I could. The important thing was for me to be in control.

When we got in a subway car and the doors shut—and that's a frightening moment for me—she would say, "Now what are you feeling?" And we would talk about it. Then she would say, "What are you thinking?" And I would say, "I'm not thinking anything. I'm just getting scared." And she would say again, "What are you thinking?" And it would be the same thing, over and over, until *I* could hear the thoughts. And the thoughts were saying, "You're trapped and you're going to die."

And she would say, "Look around. There are other people on the train. They're not trapped. You're not either. We can get off at the next stop. Whatever you want." She always restored the control to me, allowing me to break down in small pieces this huge problem of being unable to function in the world. Sandy made me feel there was no pressure or right timetable to get better. I was calling the shots. She was just there to help me.

And after an hour of working with her, I could come home just as proud from being able to ride the subway a couple of stops as someone who accomplished something at a high professional level at work. And I probably was using as much energy, intelligence, and commitment in what I was doing with Sandy as they did in their jobs.

THE GHOSTS OF THE MEN

After I'd worked with Sandy for a year and a half, I was able to get on the subways when I wasn't with her. On Thanksgiving that year, Faith and I were going to my parents' house for dinner. We had to ride the exact same route I had used when I was a kid coming home from school. When we got on the train, I had to ride in the first car, because my head was racing ahead to be on the other side of the tunnel. And she was saying, "Are you going to make it?" I was using every phobic technique they had taught me. I felt I was really driving that subway train with this incredibly powerful fear.

When we got to Brooklyn, the doors opened and I got off. I went up to a pillar, leaned against it, and I burst into tears. All of a sudden I was eleven years old. It wasn't a memory. It was a reexperiencing. The ghosts of all those men who molested me came around, and I sobbed and sobbed. Faith held me. I couldn't have cared less what people thought. It had taken a year and a half of healing for me to have the strength to remember.

I'M VERY PROUD OF WHAT I'VE DONE

Remembering the molestation and connecting it to the agoraphobia didn't suddenly cure me, but it did allow me to know it wasn't all coming out of the blue. I don't think anyone develops agoraphobia for no reason. I mean you don't just develop a fear of pigeons for nothing. Something happened to you with pigeons. Agoraphobia is so complex, it's hard to figure out exactly where it started, but I think it often has to do with sexual abuse.

Phobias are coping mechanisms, and though they limited me, I found I was sad to give them up. The day I could get on the bus without any phobic feelings, I felt really weird. It's like when a refrigerator goes off and you realize it's always been on. It was disorienting, and it was a loss. But the gains were so much bigger.

All my symptoms have gotten less, but they haven't gone away entirely. I liken it to turning the volume down on a radio. If the radio is blasting, then you can't function. If you turn the radio down to a moderate level, you can still hear it, but you can function. There are times when that panicky feeling in me is very low and I can ignore it. Other times it's stronger but I can push myself to ignore it. And then there are times when it overwhelms me.

I'm rebuilding my confidence slowly. The damage that's done to you when you're a kid, I don't know how much you get over it. I'm strong in my conviction that I want to be cured, but I'm not looking for a miracle. At the same time, I don't want to see a therapist who says, "You have to live with this." Maybe I will have to live with some of it, but I want to break through those limits as much as I can. I've worked very hard to do that and I'm very proud of what I've done.

I FOUGHT BACK AND I FEEL GREAT ABOUT IT

There was a man who exposed himself to me, my mother, and my aunt in front of Korvette's in New York a couple of years ago at Christmastime. A Salvation Army Santa Claus was standing right next to us. My aunt and my mother were talking about where to go to lunch. I was looking around, and out of the corner of my eye I saw this guy's face, and I just knew this man was exposing himself. He had the same spacy, faraway look on his face that the molesters in the subway had. I thought, "I can't believe this. This guy's jerking off in the middle of a Christmas crowd, in front of Santa Claus, no less!"

The man was standing very close to me, and the look on his face was getting more and more urgent. He was beating off to beat the band. I had a shoulder bag, and it was heavy, and I swung it at him, hitting him really hard in the head. He started hopping and jumping everywhere, trying to protect himself from the blows and trying to zip up his pants and trying to run, all at the same time. I screamed at him and ran after him, and I said very loudly, very publicly to my mother and my aunt, "That man was exposing himself to us, right here in front of Santa Claus!"

They were very supportive. They said, "That's awful! Good for you for chasing him away!" Their response was wonderful. I didn't feel the shame or the humiliation I'd felt in the subway. Because this time, I fought back. And this time I wasn't alone.

ANNA STEVENS

Q: How did dealing with incest affect the rest of your life?
A: What rest of my life?

Anna Stevens was born in Taiwan.* A dip-lomat's daughter, she grew up in ports around the world. Her background is a cross between English and Irish. Anna's family was well off and kept up appearances. Her mother was an alcoholic and a pill addict—there is extensive alcoholism on both sides of the family. Anna has one brother.

Anna says: "Everything in my house was de-signed to keep conflict from surfacing. No one ever admitted my mother was crazy, of course. No one ever raised their voice. Nothing was discussed. Everything was shrouded in denial and secrecy."

Anna was physically abused by a nanny when she was three. Her mother sexually abused her re-peatedly from the age of two until she was eleven. She masturbated Anna and used Anna's body to masturbate with. After her mother reached orgasm, she'd put Anna in a scalding bath or beat her. Anna learned to leave her body when the incest happened: "I watched it all through a kind of yel-low fog.

"I forgot what happened to me as I grew up, but I hated my mother with a poisonous hatred. I was completely nauseated by my mother's smell. And as an adolescent, if she touched me, I'd throw up. The flip side of my physical revulsion was some kind of sexual feelings."

Anna now lives in New York City and works as a carpenter. She writes poetry and is working on a novel. She is twenty-six and has been in recovery for alcoholism for the last year and a half.

---

* Anna Stevens wanted to use her own name, but couldn't for legal reasons.

The bottom-line effect of the incest for me was trust and not-trust. I felt zip trust for anybody. When I reached a certain level of closeness, I'd have anxiety attacks so bad I couldn't breathe. But I'd also flip to the opposite extreme. I'd just throw my trust at people—because it became so intolerable not to trust. That got me into dangerous situations, including getting raped. I had no blueprint for knowing who or how to trust. I only knew the extremes.

It's only been in the last couple of years that I've even been able to admit I wanted human company. From the age of four, my strongest fantasy was to go live on a desert island by myself and to be absolutely self-sufficient. My basic attitude toward life had always been that I'd be happier alone. And if I was kindly permitting you to be in my life, I wanted you to know it was only on probation.

The ironic thing is, I tell people incredibly intimate things very quickly. It's an appearance of intimacy. I'd hear myself saying these "really honest things." But I said them so many times that they were just blunt instruments. The other person would react like I was taking them into my confidence, but I knew it was all fake. It was just an appearance of belonging to the human race.

I didn't have any self-esteem. I had a mixture of arrogance and fear. I always felt I was dirty. Part of me believed I must have asked for it. I had responded physically. I was sure people could see it on me.

Adolescence was particularly terrible. I was growing breasts and becoming like my mother. I felt puberty was a direct consequence of what had happened with her. It was as if she was pulling it out of me, making me like her. I loathed any resemblance between us. I remember when I was four-teen, looking in the mirror and seeing her face in my face, and wanting to tear the skin off my face. I felt an incredible sense of vulnerability and exposure. I disguised myself as best I could in men's clothes.

I was always acting out. I was a kleptomaniac. I stole from the time I was eleven until I was caught shoplifting booze when I was fifteen. When I was caught having a lesbian affair with a married teacher, I was expelled from boarding school.

I lied all the time. I didn't tell lies to get out of trouble. I told them to erase difference, because I felt so weird. I'd lie so I could make connections with people. It was a case of having to invent circumstances because my own truths weren't good enough.

AND THEN THERE WAS THE SPLITTING

I remember sitting on a stone step when I was twelve or thirteen and feeling this click, and then this voice in my head saying, "Oh, my mind's split!" One voice, the one that was sarcastic and snide and savage, went and sat in the left-hand corner of the ceiling. It sat there, and watched and sneered. It never felt anything, except maybe a sarcastic kind of anger. The other voice was an incoherent out-of-control scream. A lot of the time, she was preverbal. I knew she was there. She came out in nightmares. She felt incredibly guilty and ashamed. I would get drunk, and then I would be slashing my wrists. I tried to kill myself twice by the time I was eighteen.

I had to give up splitting because it was another out. Booze had been an out. The suicide attempts had been an out. I had to give up all of them. And each time I chose not to use those options any longer, it was the beginning of another growth cycle.

It's still very hard for me not to split. It's just starting to heal. I talk to the different people inside myself and write it down on paper. I can give those parts of me voices. And I've been able to talk about it. I talk to my lover, and I talk at AA and Sexual Abuse Anonymous meetings.* Talking and writing has really helped heal the split.

I STARTED DRINKING WHEN I WAS TWELVE

I was an alcoholic drinker from the start. I drank alone. I kept a supply of booze I didn't like, in case I ever ran out. When I was sixteen, I was told I was an alcoholic. I thought that was ridiculous. After all, I only drank like my parents. But really I did it more drastically. I drank not to feel, and then when that became intolerable, I'd drink to feel. I did that for thirteen years.

I was always as rigidly controlled about my drinking as I was about everything in my life. But you can't control alcoholism in the long run. By the end I had such an incredible thirst for alcohol, it had become the most important thing in my life. I was terribly lonely and frightened. The thing that had helped me to control things was finally out of control. So I had to stop.

I'd always been sure I'd be dead by the time I reached twenty-five. Instead, that's when I went to AA and got sober. Going to AA was terrifying. My specialness was being taken away. My specialness had been being

---

* Sexual Abuse Anonymous is a program for incest survivors, modeled on AA. Anna helped start that program in New York City.

crazy. But there was also this tremendous relief. I don't think about my drinking in terms of wasted time. Partly that's because I got in fairly young. I'm actually very grateful that I'm an alcoholic because it got me into AA and that's been the basis for real growth.

TRUTHS I DIDN'T KNOW YET

When I put down drinking, the connection to the abuse was almost immediate. There'd been this black hole I'd inhabited at various points in my childhood. Once I got sober, that image began to obsess me again. I started to paint it. I drew all these strange pictures of children being pulled back into the womb.

I had this recurring dream when I was a child. I had it again when I first got sober. It was of a happy family on a speedboat, smiling in the sun. They all had on bright new clothes. I wanted to scream and I wasn't able to. There was a monster that was coming up under the water. And everyone was immobilized with these smiles on their faces. Everybody knew that the monster was there, but nobody could react at all.

After a month I went to see a therapist. The third session, I went into that black hole and remembered being abused by my nanny. I saw someone pushing a hairbrush into my vagina. Then I became the three-year-old. It was terrifying.

I knew the memories were true because I was remembering in German, and that was what the woman spoke. I only spoke German until I was six. I was completely bilingual. Then I forgot it all. My therapist said, "What's she saying to you?" And I said, "I don't know. I can't translate it."

That was the beginning. My therapist asked me if I thought there might have been any incest. She said lots of people make up stories like this because it's safer to say it's somebody outside of the family. And I said, "No." What I kept thinking was, "Not my father. Not with my father." I had never heard anything about incest with your mother. A part of me knew it, but it seemed so outlandish. And I was very practiced at denial.

When I first starting having actual memories of incest with my mother, I had a hard time believing them. It was over a year before I believed that it was my mother who raped me. But increasingly, and mostly through my writing, so many involuntary things I'd always said and done just suddenly fit into place. It was like writing a story. You know things are right when they start falling into place. I *knew* this story was right. Everywhere I turned with it, something just went, "Yes. Uh-huh. Yes."

There were so many things that I thought were lies, and I couldn't understand why I kept telling them. I would think, "That's a lie. Why do you say that?" Things like telling people "I don't know who I lost my virginity to." I knew perfectly well the first boy I had fucked, but I kept saying this other thing. Everything I habitually said has a story inside of it. Part of me was always telling the truth. I realize now that some of the lies I told weren't lies, they were just truths I didn't know yet.

THERE WAS NOWHERE TO HIDE

When I talk to incest survivors who've been abused by men, I'm always relieved that the effects are the same. I need to talk to other women who've been abused by their mothers in order to see what the differences are. But there hasn't been much opportunity. I've come across little snippets, mostly by women who were abused by both parents.

I didn't want my mother to know anything about me. I had the feeling that if she knew me, she'd be able to dismantle me and turn me into someone else. I was fighting for my right to exist at all as a separate self. My gut feeling about my mother was that she had reached so far inside my body that there was nowhere to hide.

I also had to accept that I was turned on by my mother. I had wanted contact with her—even if it was sexual contact. For a long time I felt like a collaborator. It was very hard to untangle my need for closeness from "I wanted it. I deserved it. I seduced her." I tried to protect her by taking on the blame myself.

I have had to accept that my mother is a part of me. Because she violated me when I was that young, my boundaries got fucked. Literally, they got fucked.

Because she was my mother and not my father, I think the separation issue is stronger. Even though other survivors talk about being colonized by their fathers, or that they were his toy or his doll, or that they can't get the dirt off, I haven't heard many people talk about the feeling of actually *being* their abuser, or just having them inside you. And that, I think, is really tied up with it being my mother. I mean I get really nauseous if I think about being born, because being born has sexual connotations for me.

It brings up such wells of self-destructiveness. I feel her in my throat. I feel I have to give birth to her, which means giving birth to the anger. There's a scream inside

Poem for My Mother's Birthday

Athena was born from the head of Zeus
you will be birthed in my throat
no wonder it hurts

you'll be born from my throat in a scream   in a
puke   the passage shredded and raw   like eating
too fast   like needing to shit   muscles ache to
spit you out

Athena was born from the head of Zeus

my pores bleed tar   my walls seep blood
I can smell it on my fingers like I saw it on
my panties   white   the kind that leave elastic
lines   midriff high   I saw it one Christmas morning
mother   your fingers tore it from me

Athena was born from the head of Zeus

and you   child monster child   your smell
in the hall   in my room   on my bed   on my hand
on my tongue   I swallowed it all   night against
night   if I close my eyes

Athena was born from the head of Zeus

I am afraid to scream   afraid you'll come   afraid
you won't   and the wet wolf's breath in my face
her gray eyes   telling my lies

Athena was born from the head of Zeus

and you mama you   your bulging eyes   your
hanging head   the dribble   the chin   the gray green
stench of you in my bed at night   I'll wash you
in vomit   I'll powder you with tears   I'll
hurl you to the crowd and turn away my ears

Athena was born from the head of Zeus
the cap of his skull gliding aside

While I   I was born in the slit of you   violet
violent blood black scab   torn into air
while you   your hands tangled in arteries   your
limbs poking lumps in my breast   in my elastic skin
you will be birthed in my throat
no wonder it hurts

me that I've wanted to scream forever. Just saying that is making my skin crawl right now. I feel revolted.

INCEST WAS STAMPED IN EVERY YARD OF MY CLOTH

During the first stage of dealing with incest, I was in shock. I fought for a long time about how much it was inside everything. I'd scream, "Enough already! Why the fuck doesn't it just get fixed?"

Eventually I had to accept that incest was stamped in absolutely every yard of my cloth. I had to understand that it was a part of my life, not just something to fix and get over. What happened gave me strengths as well as incapacities, and I am learning from it. It was only when I reached that level of acceptance that I could be patient with myself.

The second stage was developing enough trust in myself and in other people to put down the survival mechanisms that didn't work any longer. That's about healing from the splitting. It's about not repeating the same patterns in relationships. It's about taking risks I wouldn't have taken before. It's not quite so backward looking. I also feel strongly that part of the second stage is beginning to reach out to other people, to pass the strength on. That's what saves me from hopelessness.

HEALING SEXUALLY

My pattern was to get intensely involved sexually with someone for a few months. Then the intimacy would have built up to the point where it started to bring up real problems. Then I would cut off. I would decide the sex was no good, and I would leave the relationship. It never occurred to me that you could negotiate a sexual relationship, that you could take it apart and change it. It was either there or it wasn't. And if it wasn't there, I left.

When I first got sober, I realized that since I wasn't going to get involved with anyone for a while, I was going to get sexually frustrated if I didn't deal with masturbation. I had always felt that my masturbation was very ugly, and so in limited doses, I started to allow myself to touch parts of my body and just feel them. That was very difficult because I felt safer with other people touching me than I did with myself. I did not trust my own hands not to hurt me. I would masturbate in a sensual way, and then, all of a sudden, I would start thinking, "I have to orgasm now. I have to orgasm now!" And I would rev into these old fantasies that actually bored me, that actually took away from the pleasure but helped me orgasm fast. It was a feeling that I had to orgasm fast or I would hurt myself.

There were certain things I didn't want to do because they had happened with my mother. I didn't want anything to do with oral sex. I detested the nice romantic practice of bathing after sex. And before I could change any of those things, I had to accept that it was okay to have limits: "It's okay. Not everybody in the world likes oral sex."

I had to be clear with anyone I slept with: "These are things that I don't like, and they are in the course of changing. I will let you know what's okay and what isn't. My commitment to you is that I will let you know if something is upsetting, so you don't have to worry about it. And if you do freak me out inadvertently, I won't hate you forever."

Then I had to pay attention to times when I really *did* want to do those things. Doing them once didn't mean I always had to do them. And there are a whole lot of behaviors I use now which let me know I am not with my mother anymore. I can't orgasm if I can't make noise, because I had to be silent with her. I always call out the name of the person I'm with when I orgasm, because I need to know it's them and not her.

It's difficult for me to feel sexual when my partner isn't. As soon as my desire makes someone else feel uneasy, I want to crawl right back in my shell. I'm sure that has to do with my fear of being abusive. Not that I'm going to throw them down and rape them, but simply that my desire for them is abusive. And that's pretty obvious in its origins.

Surprisingly, I'm fairly accepting of my sexuality. Sex is something that I enjoy. All the exploration I've done I figured out on my own. And I feel proud of that. My experience of masturbation has really changed. It's much more sensual. The orgasms have grown. They're no longer just like a sneeze.

YOU DON'T GRADUATE

Healing is not a finite thing. You don't graduate. It's been a lot of work. The beginning of the healing process was a sequence of choosing not to kill myself, then beginning to write and let things through, and then getting sober. Next I came to understand that I only got what I could handle. And that was the beginning of a spiritual connection, the feeling that I am on a path and that I am being looked after. All I have to do is be with whatever is happening in the moment.

KYOS FEATHERDANCING

"What do you feel there is left for you to do?"

"Heal the earth. My mission in life is to heal the earth and all living things."

"Yeah, but is there anything left for you to do for your own healing?"

"That *is* for myself. I don't see my healing as separate from that."

Kyos Featherdancing is a thirty-four-year-old Native American woman, born and raised in a rural town in California's San Joaquin valley.* She now lives in the San Francisco Bay Area. Kyos works odd jobs as a landscaper and as a chef, but primarily she is a healer.

Her father was of the Caddo tribe, her mother a mixture of Choctaw and German. Kyos grew up poor. Her family picked cotton. Later her father became a welder and a plumber, and eventually he went to work for the nuclear industry. Kyos says, "He sold his soul and stopped being an Indian."

Kyos has two brothers and two sisters, all of whom were abused by her father.

The most sustaining influence in Kyos's childhood was her grandmother. From her Kyos learned the "old ways," which have remained the source of her survival and healing.

---

* Kyos Featherdancing is using her own name.

I THOUGHT IT WAS A GENTLE AND VERY LOVING RELATIONSHIP

From the time I was a baby until I was nine, I loved my father more than anything in the entire world. No one could say anything bad about him to me. His favorite thing was to suck my cunt when I was a baby. When I was three years old, I first remember him actually putting his prick into my vagina. That was something that we had between each other. He made me believe that every father did that with their daughter. So I believed that. And I became that. And I loved it, too.

My parents didn't let me go to other people's houses very much. I know now my father didn't want them knowing what he was doing. But when I was nine, I went to stay with a friend, and when it was time to go to bed, her father and mother tucked us in and gave us a kiss on the forehead and said, "Good night." I thought that was real strange. I kept wondering if anything else was going to happen. And finally I nudged my friend and said, "Hey, does your father come in and give you nookie?"

And she was like, "What? What are you talking about?" She told her parents about it, and they said we couldn't be friends anymore after that. That was the first time I realized not everybody had a father like that.

YOU DO WHAT YOU HAVE TO DO TO GET THROUGH IT

I became the woman my dad wanted me to be. I dressed how he told me to dress. I never went out of the house without makeup. I always shaved my legs. I shaved my underarms. I shaved my eyebrows and my legs around my cunt so I wouldn't look hairy. I shaved hair on my stomach. My dad taught me women were put here to be fucked by men, so that's the way I was. I began to be that to men in the neighborhood, to men in the streets, to the men in the office in that town. I had routes. I made money.

And my father sold me to his friends. I couldn't bring my friends to the house because they would end up in bed with him. He'd manipulate that somehow.

From nine to eighteen, I hated my father's guts and did every conniving thing I could think of, every conniving thing he taught me, and turned it around on him. I used his money. Made him buy me cars. Made him buy me good clothes. I got hooked on drugs, made him pay for it. I was strung out on junk by the time I was sixteen. I did speed. I dealt drugs to some of my teachers. I made grades that way. Some of them passed me to get rid of me. They didn't want to get hit or kicked in the balls. I was mean. No one could control me.

I hated myself completely. It was, "Okay, this is who you are. This is who he wants you to be. This is what you have to do, so just do it to get by." To me, that's what surviving is about. You do what you have to do to get through it until you can get out of it.

"YOU'RE GOING TO FIND OUT YOU HAVE A PATH"

When I was thirteen, I had an abortion. It was my father's child. He made it look like I was lying, and I was really angry. I started going to this Pentecostal church with my aunt. It was a place where I could go to scream and shout out my anger. She told me, "Give it all to the Lord." And that's what I did.

When I was fourteen or fifteen, I started hanging out with this black woman. She was my best friend. The woman took me in and mothered me like I'd never been mothered before. She'd take me down to the church and she'd jam on her piano. She gave me singing lessons, and the first thing she said to me was, "Sistah, you're gonna hafta open up your mouth and get ugly!" And from that point on, I just let it roar. I sang it out. Singing has been one of the most healing things for me. Singing and shouting and dancing in the spirit.

My father would forbid me to go to church. He was into all kinds of ugly spiritual things—black magic and all kinds of sorcery. That was one of the things that he put on me at a very young age. Different tribes do their own sorcery, their own ceremonials, but my dad used magic in very dark ways that are not to be done. I was into those things too, but I began breaking away from them.

My grandmother had taught me healing ways. She taught me a lot about my own self and about healing, about how to cook, how to clean. My grandmother lived the old ways. She had her blackberry bush. She did her rituals. She burned sage. She burned cedar. She had her path. I never forgot those ways. My dad forbade me to do them. He tried to keep me away from her. But she's alive in me. She always told me, "You're going to find out that you have a path and it's going to be different from who your father is." He tried to kill that, but he couldn't.

SOME HARD AND HEAVY THINGS CAME DOWN ON ME

I left home at eighteen. I'd run away before, but every time they'd pick me up and take me right back. I hung out with bikers and rowdies from the time I was twelve, and my father always made it look like I was the bad one and he was respectable. He had cousins and uncles that were pigs in that town and he did deals with one judge there. I learned real fast that he could get me locked up for a long time.

The day I turned eighteen, I split. It was about a month before I was going to graduate from high school. I was going to go to college and get into home eonomics. Being Indian, the government was going to pay for the whole thing. But a close friend of mine came home from Viet Nam and committed suicide and I couldn't go through with it. So I left with just the clothes on my back and an overnight change. I sold some dope and hitched to Chicago. I stayed in an all-night laundromat the first two weeks.

The next years were rowdy. I got into a biker's club. I was heavily into drugs. I didn't take a bath. I wore Levis for months on end. I was mean. Always drinking, always fighting, always in gang fights—*rowdy*.

After I left the bikers, I joined a Christian band. They were doing heroin addict programs and I ended up in a halfway house. Christians is the biggest way to get out of tight situations. I learned how to use it for my benefit. I got myself clean and stayed with the halfway house for quite a while. Then they sent me to do a street ministry in Boulder, Colorado. I was living with three other single Christian women. I fell in love with one of them and we got caught having an affair. I felt guilty and I started getting back on drugs again. And they kicked me out of the house.

I WANTED TO LOVE WOMEN

I moved to Denver to this boarding house. Ended up meeting all these lesbians, women who were into all kinds of healing. At that point, I was an alcoholic. I was back on drugs. I was just sick. I felt I was dying. I didn't want to be a Christian anymore, but I didn't know what direction to take.

I met this woman and we hitched to the Michigan Women's Music Festival. I'd never met so many healers in my life. I learned that being a lesbian is not just about sexuality. It has to do with healing power. It was the first time I was allowed to be a real woman, because churches do not allow this. I became aware of who I really was. Then I had a real clear picture of why my father wanted to destroy me. But it hadn't worked. I had survived.

YOUR HEART WILL NEVER LIE TO YOU

At that point I started healing on a different level than I had ever known before. I started cooking healthy foods. I was stretching. I was running. I was riding a ten-speed. I didn't do any more prescription drugs. I didn't do any more speed. I didn't do any more cocaine. I didn't go back to junk. For a while I kept drinking, then I quit. I had a lot of support. It was a good time for me. I was very impressed with the changes that I was making.

Then I met a woman who became my mentor. She taught me about group ther-

apy, primal screaming, and co-counseling. I added this to everything I knew from my grandmother, everything I had picked up from the earth.

This woman helped me to realize that I needed to have a relationship with myself before I could have a positive relationship with anyone else. So I became celibate for quite a long time, about nine years. I chose to be celibate because I didn't know how I wanted to be touched, or whether I wanted to be touched.

When I was younger I had relationships I would just call fucking relationships. I didn't know or care who I was fucking or who was fucking me. I had practiced this one pattern my whole life, that I had to be fucked in order to be loved. And that was a hard pattern to break.

I spent a lot of time alone, loving myself, touching myself in loving ways. I spent a lot of time hugging myself. Getting feelings back of sensuality rather than sexuality. Just lots of real comforting times with myself. Hot tubs. And sweating. I like to do sweat lodges with sage.

It was a time for my own personal therapy. I lived in the mountains for a while. I rented a room in the city for a while. I beat drums. I chanted. I wrote. I did anger work. I went to the woods and shouted and beat and screamed and cried and gave it to the wind. I did rituals for turning myself around and letting the earth heal me. I did rituals in the sun to burn the poisons out of me. I fasted. I drank spring water.

I had collected a lot of ideas about how to heal myself and I needed to be alone to do that healing. That time was really important. I learned how to have a relationship not only with myself, but also with the earth I love so dearly. When I need to be alone, I need to be alone with the earth. I get my energy and my answers from her.

I have everything I need to heal myself. That's what my grandmother taught me. She taught me how to follow my heart and my intuition. I have always had a vision of my grandmother's brown crinkly hand coming toward me to walk with me in that blackberry patch. She is my protector and has always been my protector. She taught me, "Trust your heart. Your heart will never lie to you."

That's one of the reasons I've never really been able to get therapy, because I don't believe therapists can give me the answers. I have everything I need to heal myself because no one knows my experience like I know it. I've turned myself around and nobody else could.

I DON'T NEED TO FORGIVE THAT BASTARD

A lot of people believe forgiveness is the ultimate healing. And to me, that's bullshit. The man doesn't deserve my forgiveness. *I* deserve my forgiveness. What I need to do is get right the fuck on with being right where I'm at with my anger. If you're looking to forgiveness as this goal, then you're still believing that lie that keeps you under control. That's what Christianity is about—keeping you under control.

And as far as freeing myself, I freed myself by saying, "Get out. I don't want you, and I will not be ruled by you, and I will not let you overwhelm my life."

I wrote this poem and sent it to my father:

To My Dad   *For Father's Day 1984*

To my Dad.
To the Daddy you never were.
Daddy, why?
Why didn't you teach me the ways of our
        people?
You only taught me how sucked in and
        limited you are,
and trapped in the white man's ways.
The earth is keeping me alive.
And you have chosen to die.
Didn't you realize,
Didn't you know that I would find out?
Did you think you could kill my powers?
My powers were louder than your white lies.
I have listened for a long time.
And I have heard.
Never been a child
Just born
Never been a child
Just fucked.
Didn't talk too much
Just watched a lot
Learned a whole lot.
Wild but tamed
Never been little
But I know how to play the game.
Mom always told me,
Your dad has needs
I can't meet them all
But you can, so be a good little girl,
he's been through a lot.
Anyway, you got it good.
My paleface mother
Stupid white woman.
Powerless bitch.
She gets what she wants by letting others
        shit on her.
It makes her feel like she's worth something,
and she's being a good wife.
Daddy sure loved her, according to her.

But Mom, what about all those other women
    in his life?
Oh, they're just friends of his, helpless
    women. He feels sorry for them,
And takes care of them. Most of them are
    widows.
Not to speak of me, my sisters, their friends
    and mine.
Great love, a father who takes care of every
    woman's needs.
Oh mighty fuck father fuck of best fuck of the
    world super stud
Save the Indian race, fuck the chief
Never satisfied
Had to fuck till it finally fell off.
Cancer, you say?
Are you satisfied?
Did you finally come Daddy?
I'm tired, leave me alone.

In rage and anger.
With hate,
Kyos

I don't have to get any revenge, because
the way he's done his magic, he's brought it
back on himself. He avoided the earth and
who he is, so now he's dying. He's got cancer. They've cut half of his stomach out and
his genitals. That's where it all started. And
that's where it's all ending for him.

GIVING IT TO THE WIND

I sometimes wonder when the work is
going to be finished. I don't think it ever
really is. It doesn't overwhelm me as much
as it used to. I used to cry and cry about it. It
felt like everything inside of me was collaps-
ing. I don't feel that way now. Some subjects
about this, I'm just cried out. I've let it go
and given it to the wind, and let the wind
heal it.

I'm excited about my life now. I'm excited about the healing I'm going to do next,
because it's going to be the ultimate freedom
that I've been wanting—the healing of my
spiritual life. I know now that I can truly be
a healer and that what I've lived through
doesn't have to hold me back. When it does,
I can control it. I can tell it to leave me
alone. I can spend time with it. Whatever I
choose. It doesn't have to hinder my walk
with the spirit.

LORRAINE WILLIAMS

Q: Was there any time in the process of healing that you lost hope that life was worth living?

A: Oh, about once a week.

Lorraine Williams is a twenty-two-year-old albino African-American woman.* She is legally blind, and her disability makes her extremely sensitive to the sun. Lorraine is a sociology student at a large eastern university.

Lorraine was the second child of five in an upper-class home. Her family was a religious one. Several of her relatives are ministers and missionaries.

Lorraine was abused by a brother and a cousin, though her primary abuser was her maternal grandfather. The incest with him started when

---

* Lorraine Williams wanted to use her own name, but couldn't for legal reasons.

Lorraine was fourteen and lasted until she left home at eighteen.

On being abused as a teenager, Lorraine says, "Being fourteen or fifteen years old had nothing to do with it. I could have been three for all the power I had." At fifteen, Lorraine became pregnant with her grandfather's child and a quiet abortion was arranged. Everyone denied he was the father.

In the course of confronting her grandfather and talking to other relatives, Lorraine learned that he also had sexually abused her mother, a sister, and a niece.

I was twenty years old when I actively started to deal with the incest. The first year there was a lot of groundbreaking, actually facing and pinpointing instances, saying "Yes, I am an incest survivor." Before that time, those words did not exist. Yet deep down I knew: "This happened to you, Lorraine." Once I admitted that to myself, everything came caving in. Life was therapy. I couldn't focus on anything else. I felt like I was going insane. But after the first six months, I realized I would live. I still didn't want to deal with all of this, but I knew I had to.

I CONFRONTED MY GRANDFATHER

In the second six months, I confronted my grandfather. I didn't plan to confront him. I was going to visit my mother and I had taken my friend, Debra, with me. My brother picked us up at the train station and then proceeded to drive to my grandfather's house "to get a few things."

I felt really set up. Debra said, "I won't let that bastard touch you." When I saw him, I was instantly repulsed. He was up to his old tricks, guilt-tripping me for not visiting him. I stood there, listening quietly. All of a sudden I started screaming at him, "Who do you think you are? Who do you think you are, trying to make me feel guilty? *You*, of all people! You who hurt me, who abused me, who molested me? Don't you think that's sick? Don't you think you've done anything wrong?"

He just laughed. He said he hadn't done anything wrong, but that it had been, as he called it, his right to "educate his girls." This angered me even more, because I realized he was probably going to die thinking he'd done nothing wrong. He didn't deny it at all! He called it "educating his girls"!

MY MOTHER WAS THE MOST DIFFICULT PERSON TO CONFRONT

I wrote my mother a letter and was absolutely crazed on the day I knew she was going to receive it. I was so overwrought I got on the wrong bus.

The letter was direct. It said that my grandfather had molested me for years because she hadn't done anything about it. That I was in therapy now to recover. It was a very detailed letter with lots of different instances spelled out. I told her that she was a fool if she couldn't believe me. Why the hell would I be going through therapy if nothing had happened? And I said that she was partly responsible.

I had always been the good girl in my family, the one that didn't cause any trouble. This is not what a good girl does. So I was terrified. She had denied it when I was a teenager. She was his daughter. I didn't know how she was going to react. I could only go by how she reacted previously. So I unplugged my phone.

When I finally plugged the phone back in, she called right away. It was six in the morning. I knew it was her. I just picked up the phone and said, "Yes, mother?"

I think the letter really got to her. My sister disclosed to her too, so she was getting it from both of us. She was very sympathetic and she cried. She didn't get angry. I was prepared for her to be angry, and I was unprepared when she wasn't. She believed me. She said she was so sorry she hadn't believed me before. Then she told me he had molested her too. She was very angry with him. She actually wanted to go kill her father. I remember saying, "It's not worth it, Mama. He's already dead as far as we're concerned."

Since then, she's been a good ally when I've confronted other family members. She and I have done a lot of work getting to know each other.

I'M NOT BEING SILENT

My grandmother didn't believe anything had happened and said that I had an overactive imagination. And if anything *had* happened, I should be over it by now. My sister, who's also a survivor, doesn't talk about it. She won't see my grandfather and won't let her child see him, but she won't talk about it either. My brother, who molested me when I was younger, blames me and sides with my grandfather. He feels nothing wrong happened.

Last Thanksgiving, I went to Pennsylvania to visit my mother. The family has a week-long celebration every time there's a holiday. Different people in the family have different creative pursuits. Some dance, some sing, some play an instrument. I'm the writer. I was to bring up some of my writings and read them.

I have a very large family. There were thirty people there. Only two of them—my mother and my brother—knew anything at that point. So there were twenty-eight people who knew nothing. Included among them were two of his other daughters.

I thought I had brought only "safe" pieces, and then I realized I had brought very volatile pieces. One of these dealt with the incest. I wavered back and forth about whether I should read it. I really didn't know if I would until the actual moment I got up there. I pulled it out and was trying to decide. And then I realized that I had brought that story for the specific purpose of reading it. I just said to myself, "Yes. These people need to know he's not the angel they've painted wings on."

So I said, "There really isn't anything that I can tell you to preface this story, except that by the time I finish reading it you'll know why I wrote it." I was scared. I was shaking and sweaty on the inside, saying, "You really can't do this!" But on the outside, all appearances were intact. And I read it:

NOVEMBER
by Lorraine Williams

It was November, the month each year that Grandmother went away. She took a week off from the family to attend the annual church convention in Memphis. It was my job to stay at the house that she and my grandfather shared, to cook and clean. The two operated a board and care home for emotionally disturbed men.

The year that I was seventeen I especially resented having to stay at the house. I fussed, fumed, and fought, trying to find a way out. I tried endlessly to convince my mother that she should be the one to stay at the house. I mean, they were her parents. I did not want to be alone with my grandfather. Finally defeated, I gave in. I created what I thought was an elaborate plan. I'd make my younger brother, then eight, sleep in the bed with me. For him, it was a way to stay up late and watch TV. For me, it was a small act of defense.

. . .

My grandmother always departed at night, because she said the flights were cheaper. I sat on her bed as she packed the last few things in her overnight case. We sat and talked as we waited for her sister's arrival. She, too, was a missionary.

"You'll take care of everything, won't you?" Grandmother asked, as she stood adjusting her hat in the mirror.

"Of course," I told her. I wondered if she knew just how well things would be cared for.

"If anyone calls, tell them that I'll be back next Wednesday."

"But that's ten days!" I said in shock. Usually she was only gone for a week.

"Three more days won't kill you."

"No, I suppose it won't." Inside however, I was already dead.

. . .

That night, after I'd gone to bed, my body jolted awake, feeling another next to it. Immediately I knew it was him. I tried to pretend I was asleep as his hands invaded me, probing. Inside I felt nauseous, sick, repulsed.

"Get up and come into my room," he demanded. I ignored him, refused to move.

"Dammit, get up or I'll do it here." I didn't want my little brother to see anything, so I rose and did as he said.

I followed him into his bedroom, separate from that of my grandmother, slid into the bed, and went back to sleep. I hoped that he would feel sorry for waking me and thus leave me alone.

I awoke once again to his hand pawing my body, trying intently to gain access. I fought him by clamping my legs shut and wearing flannel pajamas, my only defenses. I didn't want to be there, didn't want any of it to be happening. Silently, I began to cry. Anger, agony, and shame filtered through me, lingering. He continued in an attempt to force an entrance. I crying, he pushing, me feeling totally helpless.

"Open your legs," he whispered angrily.

"No," I said, knowing already that I was powerless.

"Well then, I'll just take what I want."

. . .

He pushed against me, pumping hard and harder again. My skin felt as if it were being bludgeoned, beaten. His body slapped against my own, making it feel like it was being stoned. Heavy breathing filled the room as he panted and exclaimed obscenities. His moans and words filled my ears, though I attempted to block them.

"I'm coming, baby please, please never leave me," I heard.

My only thoughts were that it was almost over. The steamy, slick semen contaminated me. It burned the insides of my vagina, reaching, it felt, far into my uterus. My tears lay in a puddle on each side of my head.

. . .

I rose like a zombie as he rolled off of me, leaving the room quickly, quietly. I went straight to the bathroom adjacent to my room, sat on the toilet, and sobbed uncontrollably. I sat there, still like a mannequin, for an endless amount of time. Finally I turned on the water in the tub. I made it hot, steamy hot, as hot as I could bear. I needed to cleanse the infection from my system. I scrubbed and rubbed, making my white skin pink. Afterward, exhausted, I returned to bed. I changed the sheets, making the bed clean once more.

Sleep did not come. I lay there motionless, awake, afraid to return to slumber. I listened to my brother's breathing, deciding it was easier being a boy. I watched as dawn crept into the deep blue sky. Watching until my eyes closed in some deep sleep.

Time came for me to get up and prepare for school. I dressed carefully, finding soft clothes to hug my body, for it still hurt. I saw my image in the mirror, very pale. I knew it was going to be a bad day. I went downstairs to breakfast, my brother and my grandfather already there. Grandfather had a smile on his face that read, "I got what I wanted from you. HA HA HA."

We said not a word to each other until I started to leave, when, as I was exiting the door, he said to me, "Have a good day."

* * *

I read the story. Everyone just sat there and didn't say anything. I looked up occasionally. Some of their faces were blank.

Some were horrified. Others were just awed. There was dead silence.

I followed it with a light poem, and they all discussed the poem, but no one said a word about the story. Afterwards, various individuals came up to me. One of my aunts was angry at him. My other aunt was furious at me, saying I had written a bunch of lies: "My father couldn't have done anything like that. My father is a good person." I was the bad person. A couple of my male cousins and uncles were very angry at him and supportive of me. I was really shaken up.

And then during the course of my visit there, my twelve-year-old cousin told me that after I'd done the reading, she had had a dream that he had molested her too. She remembered everything and was very upset, very afraid to tell her mother. So I did it with her. The three of us sat down and talked. We all ended up sitting there crying together.

It was an overwhelming visit.

But I'm glad I told in the manner I did, because it destroyed their image of me as the good one, as the one who was always nice. Having that spot in the family meant I couldn't be me, couldn't be independent. And I feel better about myself.

We have to speak out and break the silence, especially in our own families. I know I have been able to heal because I'm not being silent.

RANDI TAYLOR

I never saw anyone like me in the incest books. I never saw anyone who said she had a good relationship with her father. All the perpetrators looked like angry, ugly, mean people, and yet my father appeared to be a loving, charming, wonderful man. I loved and adored him. He treasured me. That made the whole thing even more insidious. My story needs to be told because women need to know their experience counts. There's no such thing as mild abuse.

Randi Taylor is thirty years old.* She is single, lives alone, and works as a restaurant manager in Seattle. Randi was raised in an upper-middle-class family. Her parents were English, Scottish, and German. Randi's father was an accountant; her mother a housewife. She has two sisters and two brothers.

Randi's parents were very liberal. She called them by their first names. They were "cool." They knew their children were smoking pot but never reprimanded them. They kept a keg of beer in the garage so the kids could invite their friends over to drink. There were no limits, no boundaries.

Randi was always Daddy's girl. She idolized him. The molestation occurred when Randi was twelve to fourteen, just as she was going through puberty. It was always in the guise of playing games and laughing.

---

* Randi Taylor wanted to use her own name, but couldn't for legal reasons.

My father and I would do a lot of ruckus, fun things together. I'd pour a glass of water on his head, and he'd pour a glass of water on mine. We'd be tickling and wrestling and chasing each other around the house. A lot of times while he was tickling me, he'd reach his hand around and cup my breast. I'd always scream at him not to do that, but my screams would get mixed up with all the laughter and hilarity and screaming that was already going on. I'd tell him to stop, and he'd say, "Oh gee, did I slip? I didn't mean to." It was in the same tone as someone who just poured a glass of water on you and said, "Oops! I didn't mean to do that." He made a mockery of it.

Whenever we rode in the car, I'd sit in the middle of the front seat. When we went around a sharp turn, my father would elbow my boobs. He'd do it on purpose, always with an exaggerated gesture. My sisters and I had a name for it. We said my father was "boobing" me.

Then there was a routine we went through every morning. I'd get up to brush my teeth, and when I came back to my room, I'd have to search in my closet and under my bed, because my father would be hiding there, waiting for me to undress. I knew he wanted to see me naked, so I'd have to chase him out before I changed my clothes. I had to protect myself from this Peeping Tom who was my father, but it was made into a game. It was just part of the Taylor family morning routine.

At one point my father took up a sudden interest in photography, but the only thing he wanted to photograph were his daughters. He made me wear a thin T-shirt and he shined a light from behind my boobs. He wanted a picture of my boobs showing through a filmy T-shirt. That one never quite came out right, so he talked me into taking off my shirt. He promised he wouldn't photograph my breasts—only my chest and shoulders above my breasts. But they were definitely erotic photos.

While he was doing the photos, his hands would get shaky. His breath would be louder than normal. He would be excited. It was very scary for me to see him that way. Here was this man I adored and something happened to him. He was out of control and I never knew how far he would go.

One time my mother was going to be away all day. I was home sick from school. And in the middle of the day, my father came home from work. I was very frightened. I said, "What are you doing here?" He was joking and smiling and happy. "Oh, I thought I'd come home to see you. I knew you were here by yourself not feeling good. I thought I'd spend a little time with you."

He'd brought home some felt-tipped pens, and the game he had in mind was to decorate my breasts. He made me pull up my nightgown and he drew on my body. He made my two breasts into eyes, and then he drew a nose and mouth below it. His hands were shaking and his breath was really hot while he was doing that. And all the time, he was joking and teasing. It was horrible for me. Yet it was the one experience that allowed me to feel anger at him later on. All the rest of it, I said to myself, "Oh, he just slipped accidentally." But this was clearly thought out ahead of time. It was the only time he ever did anything that no one else saw him do. The rest of it was all out in the open.

Soon after, when I was fourteen, he complained that I was never home anymore, that I was always off with my friends. I turned to him with anger and said, "Why do you think I never spend time at home anymore? It's because I'm always afraid of what you're going to do to me." That stopped him cold and he didn't touch me again after that. But an atmosphere of sexual jokes and innuendos continued.

I DIDN'T KNOW HOW TO SAY NO

Before he molested me, I was a happy child, a normal child. But after it happened, I started seeking out friends from the other side of town. I hung out with guys with motorcycles, the kind of guys who drank a lot, who had tattoos and dropped out of school. We stole cars and went joy-riding. I had a boyfriend who was a year older than me. I got pregnant the first time we had sex, when I was thirteen. He dumped me, and I was afraid to tell my parents. I wore a lot of baggy clothes. It was the style at the time. I was six months pregnant before they figured it out. It shows how little parenting was going on.

My mother and I went shopping for a new bra because my breasts were swelling. When she saw me nude in the dressing room, she knew, but she didn't say anything to me. Instead she came home and told my father. That night when I was in bed, he came into my room and said my mother had told him I might have a problem. He asked if I was pregnant. I said I was. He asked me when I'd had my last period. I said six months ago. He was shocked. He told me my mother had known I was pregnant because my breasts had changed, that the nipples were larger and the brown area around the nipples had gotten bigger and browner. Then he said he wanted to see. I protested.

He said he wouldn't touch me, and then he insisted I pull up my shirt. He stared at my breasts for a few minutes, and then let me pull my shirt down. I felt invaded and ashamed.

My parents never got angry at me for the pregnancy. They asked me what I wanted to do. I said I just wanted to get rid of it. I flew to New York with my mother to some sleazy hospital for a saline abortion. They injected saline to kill the baby and then they gave me a drug to induce labor. It was extremely painful. I gave birth to the baby more than twenty-four hours later. I had no idea what was happening. I remember the water broke and I thought that was it. I yelled for the nurses and told them it was over. I had no idea there would actually be a baby, or that it would be so big. I only knew that the abortion would get rid of this problem.

The nurses had me give birth into a bedpan. It was only then that I realized it was a baby. It wasn't just a thing. Then they took it away. I never found out if it was a girl or boy.

My mother visited me a couple of times, but she only sat there crying. She was frightened and didn't nurture me at all. She hadn't brought enough cash and her main concern was that she might have to spend the night in the hospital waiting room. I ended up feeling guilty that I'd caused her all this pain. I felt like a horrible person. And once we got home, it was never mentioned again.

I now see how the pregnancy was a direct result of being molested. I didn't know how to say no. My boyfriend told me he had biological needs and that all the other boys were getting it, that if I didn't give it to him, he was going to have to go somewhere else.

And I didn't think enough of myself to let him go. Having had the experience of my father being sexually out of control made me believe that boys had this need that had to be filled. And of course I had to fill it.

SELF-ABUSE AND ANXIETY ATTACKS

As a teenager, I smoked a lot of pot and took a lot of acid. I went through a period in my early twenties of eating compulsively and making myself throw up. I finally quit over-eating when I started doing cocaine. I no longer had any desire for food. The cocaine addiction only lasted a few months. I spent all kinds of money, and then I knew I had to stop. Then I started drinking too much.

But nothing worked to keep away the fear. I'd started having anxiety attacks when I was a teenager, but they got really bad when I was in my twenties. When I was twenty-four I had a nervous breakdown. I thought I was going crazy. I said to myself, "This is it. I'm over the edge. I need to be taken to the mental ward." I went to see a psychiatrist, but I couldn't afford to keep it up. Besides, it didn't seem to be helping.

The panic attacks kept increasing. They seemed to come from out of the blue. They were crippling. Adrenaline would rush through my whole system. My muscles would pump up, my arms would tighten, my whole body would start to sweat and shake. I'd feel like I was about to blank out. My vision would change. It's like looking at an overexposed photo. The world becomes this foreign place where everything is just white-washed.

The panic attacks happened most frequently when I was in the car. I'd be driving on the freeway and I'd feel like I was being forced to go faster than I wanted to go. When I had to pull up at a stop light, I'd feel completely trapped. I'd want to run the red light.

Sometimes I got the feeling that the sky was just too big. I wouldn't see it as blue sky but as infinity, as something that went on forever, that really had no boundaries. For me that had a lot to do with the lack of boundaries when I was growing up. I'd feel like I was going to be swallowed up by that vast, limitless sky. If I was walking in a field, I'd cover my head and crawl on the ground so I didn't float away into this limitless space. It was terrifying.

"IT WAS MOLESTATION"

One of my sisters is an alcoholic. When I was twenty-five, she got into AA. As part of her 12-step recovery program, she did an inventory of her life and had to tell someone about it. Part of her story dealt with our father. He'd never touched her when she was a teenager, aside from the photo sessions. But when she was twenty-two, they went on a trip together. They'd gotten drunk and had sex. Because of her age, my sister had always blamed herself.

When she talked about it in her inventory, the other person said, "My God, you were molested. That was incest. It wasn't your fault." My sister started reading books about incest, and then she came to me and said, "What Dad did to us was incest."

I said, "Maybe for you, but not for me. I love my father. He loves me. He never did anything to hurt me." But she gave me a bunch of books to read. And I started to think about it. I went back into counseling.

It took the longest time for me to

wholeheartedly believe that my experience counted. I felt like what happened to me was minor compared to what happened to other women. Molestation sounded like something horrible, and what happened to me didn't seem that horrible. My father just slipped once in a while.

I think it was the panic attacks—the fact that there was a direct result I could point to —that made me start to believe that he had done something wrong. They pushed me to break through that barrier of protecting my father, to face how terrified and angry I had been.

One day when I was driving, I started to panic. I was trying to talk myself down by saying "You don't have to scare yourself this way." And all of a sudden this thought popped into my brain: "You don't have to frighten yourself the way he frightened you the day he came home from work."

That's when I finally made the connection. I realized the phobias were the fears I had to suppress. It was like a suspense thriller, where the girl has trusted someone to protect her from the killer who's after her, and all of a sudden she finds out he is the killer. That's the kind of fear that was going on for me. My father, who was supposed to keep me safe from harm, *was* the harm.

I finally realized there had been damage done. For the first time in my life, I got angry at my father. He lost his hero status.

For a long time I stayed in the grief of having lost him. Looking at the reality of what happened meant losing the fond relationship I had with my father, and I wanted to hang on to that desperately.

AT FIRST I FELT SORRY FOR MY FATHER

My sister confronted my father a couple of years ago. She told him we were both in therapy. When she told me she'd talked to him, all I could think was "How is he going to handle it?" I felt sorry for him. I felt it was such a big burden for him to shoulder— that two of his daughters were in therapy. I thought the guilt would crush him. I'd taken care of my father's emotional needs for so long that it was hard for me to recognize that he was a sick person who did bad things.

My father's admitted to me that what he did was wrong. He knows there's nothing he can do to make it better, but says if there was, he'd do it. He says I'm still special to him, and that the only important thing is that I get better. For a while he called me quite regularly. I'd get angry at him over the phone and he'd apologize. But it wasn't really helping me. Finally I told him I didn't want to do that anymore. Just recently I wrote him a letter and said I didn't want to have contact with him for the time being. I was crying, but it felt terrific to write. It's hard because I don't know what kind of relationship I will have with my father when this is all over. I don't know what will be left. But at least I know I'm getting healthy.

ALICIA MENDOZA

I figure this thing is at least a camel, and that I'm over the first hump.

Alicia Mendoza is a thirty-one-year-old writer and teacher who lives in San Jose, California, with her husband, Joe.* They are newly married and are planning to have a child.

Alicia was born to a Venezuelan mother and a Jewish American father. She lived in Venezuela until she was thirteen, at which time her family moved to Minnesota, where her father had a university research position. Alicia has two younger brothers.

Alicia was physically abused by her mother. "She was an alcoholic, but I didn't realize it until I was nineteen, when she went to AA and quit. No one in the family had ever talked about her drink-

ing while I was growing up. We just called it 'Mama's temper.' "

At five, Alicia was sexually molested by her uncle Steve. "He was a medical student. He'd come home during the day and play doctor with me. Take my temperature vaginally. All kinds of innovative things like that." The abuse continued until she was nine, when he raped her in the middle of the night. After that it was more sporadic, and it stopped when her uncle moved to another city, when she was twelve.

Alicia grew up in a politically active leftist family, and she was a feminist and anti-war activist in her teens. She has been involved in many different progressive movements and organizations over the years. She sees her writing as an important part of that work.

Since early childhood, Alicia has written

---

* Alicia Mendoza chose to use a pseudonym.

poetry and stories. She has been published in magazines and anthologies, and has recently published a novel. She teaches literature and creative writing.

IT WAS SAFE TO REMEMBER IT AGAIN

The main way I coped with the incest was deciding not to remember it until it was safe. The main thing that made it safe was finally being in a relationship where I felt I could really count on my partner.

We were in couples therapy when I had my first flashback. I remembered the sensation of being molested, and I got a very clear image of the room. In fact, as the memory came back, I got more and more details of things in the room—there was a window here, and a dresser there, and always a person-size hole in the picture where my uncle should have been. He wasn't in the picture.

One of the objects I first remembered was the clock on the dresser. That was very significant in terms of letting the rest of the memory come through. For a couple of years, I'd had an inkling that something was there, because every time people started to talk about incest, my stomach would start churning. I think one of the reasons I held off remembering for as long as I did was that I was afraid that it might have been my father who molested me, and I have a very close relationship to him now. That was just too terrifying to face.

But when I saw the clock in that room, and saw what time it was, I knew I was waiting for my father to come home from work, so it couldn't have been him. And as soon as I realized my father couldn't have been in the room, it was safe to remember the rest of the incest. I had no attachment to protecting my uncle.

I kind of started with the margins of the memory and then worked my way in. More and more pieces kept fitting in. At first it was hard to believe them. I needed complete belief from the people around me, especially when I just had feelings and nothing to attach them to. Joe had to keep saying, "Trust your instincts. Trust your feelings. Trust your body. You're not making it up. These images are coming from somewhere."

I went to a workshop called "Healing from Hurts of Violence," and the leader said that there was a high correlation between children who wet their beds late and incest survivors. I wet my bed until I was twelve. And when I heard that, it was a piece of external evidence that opened up a new chunk of memories. Each time I got some confirmation that said "This might really be true, you know," another piece opened up.

As I dealt with the memories, there were repercussions in how I dealt with other parts of my life. I was able to face my mother's violence for the first time, because the underlying silence had been broken. Unlocking the incest unlocked other things too.

I COULDN'T TAKE A BREATH WITHOUT THINKING OF INCEST

Remembering the rape triggered the very worst period of the whole healing process. It felt like I was going to die. I couldn't take a breath without thinking about incest. In fact, it was a struggle to breathe a lot of the time. I had a few days where I just sat on the kitchen floor, rocking and holding myself. I don't think Joe really knew what to do.

There were times when I felt I would just start babbling. I made these subconscious connections when I was out on the street. *Everything* reminded me of incest. "Oh, look at that lamppost. Oh God—incest!" It was everywhere! The landscape was about incest. It took over my awareness all the time.

It felt like my body was inhabited by this thing that had happened in my childhood, that there wasn't a cell in my body that wasn't involved in it. The memories felt like they were invading me, in the same way my uncle had invaded my body. I spent a lot of time feeling like I was going to throw up. I was often out of my body. I'd feel like I was floating somewhere at the other end of the room. I couldn't feel anything below the neck. My brain was working, but my *legs?* "What legs?"

I had to keep reminding myself to sleep and eat. I had notes all over my house, saying, "When did you last eat? When did you last sleep?" I wasn't rigid about it. I just said, "To maintain basic health, I have to eat once a day and I have to go to bed at night. Even if I don't sleep, I have to lie down and rest every night."

The first few months after I remembered, I developed this pattern of waking up at four in the morning, every single morning. Four a.m. was the exact time he came in and raped me. I'd sit bolt upright in my bed every night, to the minute.

At the point when I was having a lot of flashbacks, I kept thinking I had the body of a nine-year-old child. I'd look at my body in the mirror and not recognize myself. Joe had to constantly remind me that I was not nine years old, but thirty, that I was in the present, that he was with me, and that he would never touch me against my will in any way. I needed constant reassurance. He had to say it over and over, like a broken record.

Right through the emergency stage, I felt dirty a lot. I got a bunch of vaginal infections. But I got through that pretty quick, because of the support I got from Joe. He would say, "You were a beautiful little girl. You are a beautiful woman now. Nothing he did to you could ever make you dirty." He just said things like that over and over again.

Gradually there was a shift in how I saw it. The temperature lowered, and I got past the point where it felt totally urgent to deal with it all the time. I started to be able to think about other things, to allow the incest to sit on the back burner.

I STARTED TO HAVE DREAMS WHERE I WAS TAKING POWER

I kept a record of all the dreams I had during that time. I had a dream where my uncle was sitting on a chair, and I went and sat on his lap. He got a hard-on, and then a little bit of semen dripped onto his pants. And I grabbed his pants and I said to Joe, who was standing right there, "Look! We have a stain!" And I rushed it to the lab. "Now we have proof!"

I had another dream about a doctor trying to molest me in his office. He said something terrible would happen if I told. And I told him that if he laid a finger on me, I was going to scream at the top of my lungs, scratch his eyes out, kick him in the balls, and tell absolutely everybody I knew. And the doctor collapsed in this powerless heap on the floor.

DEALING WITH INCEST HAS BROUGHT JOE AND ME CLOSER

Joe was tremendously willing to treat the whole subject as something he didn't know much about. He's really followed my lead. When I was intense about it, he'd be right there with me. When I wasn't talking about it as much, he'd back off and just check in with me about it periodically.

He was also willing to be experimental in helping me: "What would you like to do? Do you want to talk or not talk? Do you want me to touch you or not? Do you want me to hold you while certain feelings come up, or do you want me to leave you alone?"

He was doing co-counseling on his own, and we were in couples counseling together. I think that gave him the necessary support to talk about how it was affecting him.

Joe never doubted that I would get through it, and he kept expressing that. Somehow he was able to see past what was going on, to the potential for us if we worked together. He got real tired of it at various points along the way, but the long view enabled him to hang in through some pretty unpleasant times. It was a strain on the relationship, but it illuminated so many things. Things that were just annoying or frustrating to him about me before suddenly fit into a framework that made sense.

I know it's also brought things up for him—old hurts from his own childhood. It made him much more aware of the nuances of sexual power.

There were times in the process that I would forget he was Joe and react to him as "generic Man." He had never hurt me in any of those ways, but I would confuse his identity completely. We'd be lying in bed at night. I'd be trying to go to sleep, and I'd have to get up because I felt "I can't lie here with this male body. It's too terrifying."

That was really painful, because Joe was being tremendously supportive and loving through the whole thing. And the fact that he acted in such a contradictory way to what I expected was a real strong part of the healing process for me.

There was a point, right around the time we decided to get married, where I just decided that the relationship wasn't giving me anything I wanted, and that I should start from scratch with somebody else. It was terror about the intimacy. I had assumed that people wouldn't come through for me for so long. And here he was coming through for me, and what went along with that was a price tag of intimacy. I had to open up. I no longer had an excuse. There were no wrong actions on his part that I could blame for the lack of intimacy. So I had to let go of my defenses. I was absolutely terrified. And he stuck by me.

If I had to do it over again, I'd work on the incest more outside of the relationship. I didn't have a real strong support group to work with then. And I think it would have been better if he'd been in some kind of support group for partners. There was too much imbalance with him taking care of me. That's slowly started to shift, but I've been scared that if he wasn't taking care of me, he wouldn't want to be around me. And he's been scared that if I didn't need him, I wouldn't love him. Shifting that balance has been real tricky.

THE INCEST DID STRANGE THINGS TO MY SEXUALITY

I had a whole variety of problems. Because I didn't get much physical affection from my mother, I was very receptive to the physical cuddling from my uncle. Then when he violated me, I somehow made the connection that sex was the only way to get touched.

As an adult, I wanted to be made love to all the time. I would feel real stormy and out of control and freaked out if I couldn't get it. And at the same time, I didn't really want to make love to anyone else. I didn't want to bother. I didn't want to touch someone else. I particularly had trouble going anywhere near a penis. That's changed since I've been with Joe.

Another problem I had was that focusing any sort of special attention on sex made it impossible. Birthdays, anniversaries, any occasions that were supposed to be romantic would just ruin any chance for me to be sexual. I'd start fighting immediately. I'd sabotage it in any way I could. Or if we did try to make love, everything that was disturbing about sex would come up immediately. Something about it being romantic was just too huge a contradiction to what my initiation into sexuality was. All that pain would just surface in the face of it.

Also, when I was younger I had experienced sexual excitement with my uncle. As a result, I've felt there was something really shameless and animal-like about sexual pleasure. Like I was just an animal in heat whenever I had strong sexual feelings. With my uncle, I was constantly being put in a state of sexual arousal and then abandoned. I never had an orgasm. And as an adult I had a hard time having orgasms with a partner.

I'd always freeze up. Then I'd get angry at my partners for not being able to make me come. When it happened with Joe, he got really frustrated. So we went to couples counseling and got some basic information on touching one step at a time. It's only since I've worked on the incest that I've been able to have an orgasm while making love with someone else. I could by masturbating, but I'd never been willing to give someone else that much power over me before.

Once I started actively dealing with the incest, there were a lot of shifts in my sexuality. The way I moved down the street was different. I felt my body differently. I found myself acting real childlike when I was being sexual. Playing that out—talking in a little girl's voice, giggling a lot, wanting to play childhood games. My whole way of going for sexual contact changed.

I also had a lot of sexual dreams about my uncle, which I felt really guilty about. Sometimes in bed with Joe, I'd have flashbacks that horrified me. Other times they'd turn me on. Then I'd feel disgusted. I started having fantasies of going back as an adult and seducing my uncle. It was, "Hey, you think I was something when I was nine? You should see me now. I'm *hot* stuff. You better finish what you started, and this time, you better make it good!" It was a cross between wanting to confront him with the incest and wanting to initiate the whole thing myself, so that I would be the one in control. My feelings in these fantasies were very aggressive and hostile, and the images really turned me on. I felt fine on the inside about having them, but I didn't feel safe telling people.

I found myself getting turned on when I wrote about the incest. And I'd think, "God, this is really disgusting!" And when

I'd see girls who were the age I was when the abuse happened to me, I tended to imagine it happening to them. And sometimes that had a sexual charge too.

I found myself reacting to touch in different ways. Some touching that had been pleasurable felt like irritation. Specific gestures, expressions, or positions would put me into a nightmare state. My uncle used to cover my mouth with his hand. And if anyone got their hand anywhere near my mouth, even in the most playful way, I would panic. I only wanted to be held in a specific way. And if his arm went around my neck at all, I'd get violent.

Sometimes I'd continue to make love when that happened, but eventually I stopped doing that. That had more to do with Joe than it did with me. I wouldn't even have to say anything. He got real fine-tuned. There'd just be this little twitch in my body and he would pay really close attention. If I was shrinking away at all, he would stop and say, "You want to stop now?" in a cheerful "it's-fine-with-me-if-you-want-to-stop" voice. He was often the one to make the decision. I didn't have the strength to do it. I would just freeze and say to myself, "Well, I'll just close my eyes and then it will be over with soon," which is exactly what I did as a child. And Joe wouldn't let me get away with that.

My desire for sex would come and go, because I had the pattern of going after sex, and I also had the disgust. For a couple of weeks I just wouldn't want sex at all. And then I'd go in the other direction. I'd feel really urgent about making love. So we'd start making love, and I'd freeze up and say, "I can't do this." I went back and forth and back and forth for about six months.

One of the ways that affected the relationship was that Joe was really scared to make love to me. He was understandably wary, because half the time I'd run to the bathroom and start barfing, or suddenly push him away and start sobbing. It was nerve-wracking for him.

There was a point when it got real hard for him, when I didn't want to touch him. And because he'd been so understanding and respectful about my needs, I was able to see, "Oh, he's hurt because of this," instead of thinking, "He's angry. He wants to throw me down on the bed and rape me." When I saw he was being hurt, I was able to remember, "Oh, *this* is Joe. *That* was Steve. *This* one's my buddy." I wouldn't necessarily want to make love, but I was able to hold him or touch him in ways that would comfort him.

It was Joe's attitude that really helped me move through the feelings. I needed him to hang in there, to separate himself out enough not to take it personally when I was completely unpredictable around sex.

He also told me when he was upset. He managed to stay consistently supportive, but it was very hard on him. He was starting to wear thin with it at the point when I started to feel more comfortable.

All the work I've done has been really worth it to me. I feel I'm moving toward more and more power with my sexuality all the time.

HAVING A CHILD IS GOING TO BE HEALING

Another thing that's really shifted my feelings about sexuality has been thinking about having a child. It's the positive part of feeling like an animal. I've had feelings of power in my body since we started talking about it. And I think having a child is going to be really healing in itself. I expect it will be hard to watch my child being as vulnerable as I once was. I can even imagine wanting to be abusive myself, but I'm not afraid of acting those feelings out. I'm in such a supportive situation with people who talk so openly, I don't think I'll have anything to worry about.

S. R. BENJAMIN

My history no longer defines me. It's something I've gone through, not who
I am.

S. R. Benjamin grew up in the Midwest, raised by parents of German origin.* An only child, she was sadistically abused and tortured by her parents and other members of a child pornography and prostitution ring.

Now in her forties, Dr. Benjamin has a Ph.D. in biological chemistry from Yale University and works at a biotechnology company. She and her husband, Robert, have been married for many years.

S. R. Benjamin's father vehemently denies that he ever abused his daughter in any way and has attributed his daughter's view of events to an irreversible psychosis. He is a member of the False Memory Syndrome Foundation and has told SR he intends to supply them with the version of his family's history he has written. Such accounts are solicited and accepted by the FMS Foundation as legitimate sources for their research efforts.

Both of my parents were associated with a ring of criminals who exploited children for profit. To terrorize children into cooperating when they were filmed and sold, the ring used pseudo-religious rituals with satanic overtones.

The abuse started when I was very young—before I entered kindergarten. I was told that if I didn't hurt animals, I

---

* S. R. Benjamin wanted to use her own name, but couldn't for legal reasons.

would be hurt—or that if I refused to hurt one animal, an adult would kill another animal. I also have the standard memory many ritual abuse survivors have of coming to from a state of unconsciousness and seeing my hand held by the hand of an adult, wrapped around a knife that was stuck into what looked like a baby. Now, whether it was a doll or whether it was a baby, I don't know. Many tricks and deceptions were used in the rituals. But the important thing is that the people who were hurting me told me I had killed a baby, and I believed them. Once they accomplished that, it made it easier for them to control me.

Being sold to people began when I was in elementary school. If I didn't earn enough money, they'd use that as an excuse to hurt me or force me to watch other children being hurt.

The children would be sold in a big room like an auction, and the people who bought us would start to hurt us right there. The violence to the children escalated to such an extreme that the organizers had to take steps to keep us from being killed. And so they began auctioning animals along with the children so that people who were out of control with their violence could kill an animal instead of a child. Despite the horror, there was intense empathy between some of the animals and the children. We felt for each other.

During the selling, I saw a little girl die. I was in a car with her. The driver would take several children to drop off and pick up at different houses. The driver had picked up this little girl after she had been sold. Apparently she had been mortally injured by whoever had bought her and she went into convulsions and died in the car next to me. Her death was horrible. The adults in the car panicked. They drove to a deserted place near some woods with me, a little boy who was also in the car, and the little girl's body. They stripped off her polka-dot dress and dumped her in the woods.

These atrocities were not perpetrated by ignorant savages. My parents might have seemed strange, but they were educated and functional. So were the other criminals. Included in the group were a pediatrician, a psychologist, and an engineer who built the electrical torture devices. My mother participated mostly in the making of pornography, while my father was more involved with the prostitution, and both were involved in the sadistic ritual abuse. The ring was smart and sophisticated.

So was their use of torture. For prostitution, they need compliant children. They used many tortures: "the box," "the hole," "making the frog hop," "flying." I thought I was crazy remembering the names, but later I read accounts of political torture survivors whose captors used those same bizarre names for tortures. In "making the frog hop," I was stripped, wet with water, and placed on metal plates. When my captors electrified the plates, my muscles spasmed. Sometimes they would pile animal body parts on me, so that when my muscles convulsed from the electricity, the parts would go flying. I was also placed in a box with one wall that could be moved to crush whoever was inside. I was drugged with things that made me very ill, and when I agreed to do whatever they wanted me to do in front of the camera, I was injected with an antidote that made the sickness go away. Being repeatedly tortured produced such a feeling of pain, depletion, and terror about dying that I would do anything to make it stop. My captors counted on that.

And my parents made it clear to me that I was going through all this because it was my destiny and because it was all I deserved in life.

At the end of sixth grade, my mother died and my father started making me sleep with him every night. I never forgot that; I just discounted it.

When I was in seventh grade, my gym teacher tried to report her suspicion that I was being abused. She was stonewalled by the school system. That was also the year that I became pregnant from being raped, and my father and his mother forced me to have an abortion.

As an adult, I went back to see my seventh-grade English teacher. She told me, through tears, "The school officials told us you were upset by your mother's death and that we should leave you alone. But I knew you were upset about more than your mother dying."

HOW I COPED

I have lived most of my life, up until very recently, as a multiple. I remember splitting for the first time when I was about four and my father was trying to force me to sodomize my pet rabbit with a roofing nail. He got very angry when I refused, and finally, in a rage, he threw me down on the basement floor and raped me. When I came back to myself after the experience, there were three parts of me. These parts, I would learn later, had distinct names, ways of being, and traumatic histories. They were Benjamin—ageless, spiritual and protective; Bunny—little and worried; and Scarlet, the only female and the one who dealt with the sexual abuse. I coped through them, and

through what I learned from loving the animals who were hurt with me. The animals gave me a commitment to integrity and the sacred, which kept me from giving up or giving in, as much as possible under the circumstances.

As I got older, other things sustained me too. *Star Trek* was uplifting, showing a certain striving for integrity in the characters it presented, and an honoring of differences.

Another thing that helped was being invited to a major university to participate in a program for scientifically gifted students while I was in high school. It got me away from home—and the abuse—for two months. I worked at science and fell in puppy love. It was my first taste of freedom after a childhood of slavery.

After high school I left the state to get away, going back to the university that had sponsored the gifted program. There were puzzling but manageable phobias, and my desperation not to fail so that I wouldn't have to return home, but nothing indicated just how badly I'd been hurt. When I met my future husband, Robert, I got into therapy because I sensed there was something wrong with me that would affect my ability to have a good marriage. Nothing happened in that therapy. I just wasn't ready.

At the same time, I started seeing medical people at the university. It was the first time I'd been to doctors not associated with this ring of criminals, and they were starting to see some of the permanent physical damage from the abuse, much of which was unmistakably traumatic in origin. One doctor looked at the cigarette burn scars my father had left on my back and buttocks and asked me how I got them. Another said, "My God, these look like burn scars on your tongue.

What happened?" But I couldn't let myself know the memories. I couldn't say, "They stuck wires in my mouth and shocked me." So I said, "Nothing happened." And I went home crying, with a desperate sense of being unloved but not knowing where the feelings came from.

After Robert and I got married, sex was difficult, but basically things were quiet. They stayed that way after we moved to New Haven, where I was working on my Ph.D. at Yale. I now see those times as the lull before the storm—quiet years of internal stabilizing and getting ready for the real truth of my life.

When I was three-quarters of the way through graduate school, the shit hit the fan. I started having cryptic nightmares. I was scared to come home to a house with a basement, but I had no memory of torture in basements. I was scared of Robert. Sex became awful. I had an affair with another man, with whom I started having flashbacks. There were no images, just feelings of things being wrong, and of my being severely dislocated in time. Robert and I started therapy together.

SOMETHING TERRIBLE HAD HAPPENED TO ME

While we were going to couples therapy, I went into therapy myself. And in 1986 I went to my first workshop with other survivors of child sexual abuse. That was the turning point for me. By the workshop's end I realized that my oldest and most persistant fear—that something terrible had happened to me, far worse than incest—was true. I was starting to remember extremely bizarre abuse.

I went to more workshops, kept going to therapy, and the tornado came. I painted it as a thundering vortex gouging its way across a burning plain. Later the art would become graphic along with the flashbacks, which were becoming populated with faces I knew, and body pain.

I was falling apart, but I had done enough research that I didn't get kicked out of school. I managed to earn my degree, get a fellowship, and get accepted into a lab at Harvard for postdoctoral work.

While I was at Harvard I did the bulk of the horrible healing. The pain, grief, and memories prevented me from functioning. I'd go home limping and crying from the body memory of my father raping me and breaking my pelvis. Some memories were triggered by work. At one point I was doing DNA sequencing on a gene I had cloned, handling high-voltage power supplies and wires attached to the sequencing apparatus. I was just terrified to touch the machines, until I remembered being shocked, and then the fear subsided. Memory after memory was like that. Worse, there was no empathy where I worked. To this day I remain shocked by the cruelty and scapegoating that most of the other postdoctoral fellows directed towards me. I feel sad for them and for me. Only an injured person would choose to wound someone who is already hurt.

I WAS LEARNING WHAT THE PARTS MEANT

By this time, I was learning what the parts meant. I had always known the names Bunny, Scarlet, and Benjamin, but I hadn't dealt with being split. It was really brought home to me when a bodyworker suggested I draw the "imaginary playmates" I'd told her I had. Thank God, I drew them in my therapist's waiting room, right before an appointment. I showed him the freshly drawn pictures of children with rabbits' heads on their bodies. One was a young child lying on the bathroom floor, with blood coming out of the mouth and no neck, while a forest of belts fashioned into nooses hung over him. I knew my father had strangled me, and I knew the picture was of Bunny. Another was of an adolescent who had been beaten and raped—Scarlet—I'd known her name before I started school. And Benjamin was sitting on a teeter-totter on the first-grade playground. I asked my therapist, "What does this mean?" And we began exploring the different places inside me where the trauma lived.

When I finished my postdoctoral work, I accepted a position as an assistant professor at a university where I set up a laboratory, studying how organisms adapt to harsh environments. Ain't that a hoot! While there, I had my first memories of the pornography. And within a month, it went straight from there to prostitution to ritual abuse. I started drawing pictures of parts in the middle of a circle with candles and robed figures. By that time enough was known about ritual abuse that I had an idea what the pictures meant. So I said, "Hell, I'm only copying what others have said." But unfortunately, the pictures were originals.

The dynamic of having parts began to change for me. I'd go to therapy, and parts would talk about the abuse. A few hours later I'd be on the phone with my therapist saying, "I don't think that stuff with dogs really happened, and I'm not sure how real those lousy parts are, either." And within a

few minutes, there would be some part on the phone, saying, "Not only did *that* happen, but *this* happened too." When the barriers that kept the trauma compartmentalized began to crumble, it was wretchedly sad. Some parts didn't know other parts had been hurt—they had tried to protect those parts, or thought those parts had escaped unscathed. And there was bottomless grief when the truth of how pervasively parts had been abused came out.

THE WORST TORTURE

I'd had a feeling since childhood, of being a child myself and having killed children. I came to know this was not a bizarre, crazy thought—that I had been used as an instrument by my captors in their hurting and killing of animals and children. Some people call this "forced perpetration," but I think that term lays too much responsibility on the person who has been tortured. I was no different than an inanimate gun or belt in my captor's hands. Of course I didn't come to that belief immediately. My first response to those memories was "I should probably kill myself now as an act of protest and atonement." Yet I knew the decision to kill myself was a huge step, and I didn't want to be rash. I didn't want to die at all, but I was perfectly willing to, if it was right. So I spent an agony-filled summer talking to people I was close to and thinking hard. In the end I decided that, as sad as it was, I couldn't make anything better by dying now. It was the fate of those who had died to be dead, and mine to live with the worst kind of awareness I could imagine. I decided it had to be okay for me to live.

Anyone who wants to understand ritual

abuse must understand torture. And so I started reading accounts about coercion by groups of people—like in political prisons and the Holocaust. Amnesty International acknowledges that the most horrific thing you can do when you torture someone is force them to violate their deepest values. There's no more effective way to break a person. And when I began to appreciate that what had happened to me was torture, it got easier for me to look at it as something that had been done to me, not as something that I did. That I would "allow" my captors to maim an animal for every sip of water I took wasn't an indictment of me; it was an indictment of them because they never should have chained up a child and left her without water.

Ironically, one thing that helped me was an episode of *Star Trek: The Next Generation*. There was an episode where the stalwart captain of the *Enterprise* is tortured. And toward the very end of the episode, after he's been rehabilitated, he's speaking with the ship's psychologist, and he's talking about being in a room where there were four lights. And he was tortured and told that if he would say there were five lights, they would stop hurting him, give him food and water, and take the pain away. And here he is, sitting in command of the ship, still a person of power, and he says, "The shocking thing for me was that toward the end, I really believed that I could see five lights." He was broken to that point. And yet he was shown in this program as still being someone who had competence and integrity and who was in command. That show helped me redefine myself as someone who'd been tortured, but who wasn't permanently broken by it.

I started judging my life not by what had happened when I was tortured, but by how I lived my life afterwards. Did I hurt people? Did I hurt myself? Was I living with integrity and joy and richness?

Unfortunately, not many people understand this distinction. A priest I had been open with for over a year finally told me that I was guilty for the people I had hurt when I was a child and told me, "It is important for you to confess your crimes." When I pointed out that such a belief didn't take into account what tortured children experience, he asked, "But couldn't a child theoretically have held out?" This is the most sensitive area of my life and his was the worst wounding I have experienced as an adult. No less an authority on torture than Amnesty International states that with enough time and access, torturers can break anyone. Anyone! A person who is brokenhearted by the killing must be viewed differently than the perpetrators who choose to kill. The orientation of the heart speaks louder than actions forced by torture.

THE PHYSICAL DAMAGE CORROBORATED THE MEMORIES

By this time, I was acknowledging that the physical damage corroborated the memories. I found out that I had damage to the muscles in my legs, that both of my hip joints were damaged, and I had scar tissue on one side that suggested that my hip had actually been dislocated. The same was true of my left shoulder. My right shoulder also had damage. I didn't want to believe what I was being told, but it was undeniable.

One physical therapist tried to tell me I might have a birth defect that made my connective tissue abnormal. Since I'd just been teaching about connective tissue disorders, I knew this was extremely unlikely. I was aggravated that she was so desperate to deny what she was seeing—that there had been trauma. So I asked her how she would differentiate between a birth defect and trauma. She said that if I had a birth defect, the joints in my spine would be abnormal too. So I asked her to examine them. When she found them to be normal, she became distressed. In general, the medical community exhibits a deplorable inability to deal with child abuse.

When I finally found a physical therapist who could deal with what had actually happened to me, she helped me greatly. She told me I had muscle damage in my legs which was a large part of why I limped, along with the damage to my pelvis. And she told me that she could dislocate my left shoulder backwards and forwards just by pushing it, and that it would never be fully functional without surgery. I was shocked by how much damage she found. But she was positive about helping me, and with therapy I have been able to have less discomfort, to limp less, and to do more with my left arm.

INTEGRATION

Integration was one of the biggest changes I went through. I had made great effort to work on the trauma, but I had come to the belief that I would never integrate. After all, I was co-conscious and the parts were finally congenial. Then the changes started.

I began feeling my feet on the floor. I became exhausted but never came down with any illness. I began eating more and feeling warm for the first time, instead of always freezing cold. Parts were merging and becoming blurry, but I had no idea what was happening. And then one day I was on an airplane on a business trip and the plane hit turbulence. I hate that—it reminds me of the torture they called "flying." So I leaned back in my seat, figuring that there'd be another part along any minute, since that was how I coped with things that frightened me. When nothing happened, I figured I was just a little slow on the switch and pressed further back into the seat. And all of a sudden, I had the realization that nothing was going to happen, because there were no parts. The first thing I did was look at my watch to see how much longer I would have to be on that stinking plane.

That was the beginning of enormous changes. Time became important. It was a relentless march of seconds that might bring unendurable trauma at any minute, and I wouldn't be able to split and get away. I felt so trapped. There was no buffer between me and the world. I felt betrayed—I had never chosen to integrate. I had never needed any medicine before, but I scurried to pay a shrink $150 to get a few Valium for business flying. The panic attacks were outrageous and frequent—on and off planes, in public, and when I was alone. It took probably about a year for things to quiet down. Now being integrated is like walking with less of a limp after physical therapy—it may feel strange at times, but deep in my body it feels more "right" than the other way.

TIKKUN OLAM: REPAIRING THE WORLD —AND SOMETIMES BEING LAZY

There is a Jewish concept, *tikkun olam*, which means repairing the world, making things a little better. I try to do that. And I like the balance in the saying that "you are not required to complete the task, but neither are you at liberty to abstain from it."

From the time I was a young girl grieving for the murdered animals, I knew that what was done somehow damaged the world and went against what should be. I knew I cared. And that profound caring never stopped. I feel that deep childhood feeling now sometimes, when I am working in the lab, being with Robert, giving talks about prevention of child abuse. That feeling is a common thread that runs through the deepest parts of my life and defines God for me. It is a form of love that I feel. It keeps me going.

It is wonderful to be free and to be with Robert. Sometimes I resent having gone through so much pain to heal, given that the life I live now is sometimes painful, difficult, boring, or empty. Other times I relish living in what is a time of peace for me, where I can eat safe food and drink water, live in a house where I can stay dry and warm, get medical attention if I need it, watch children and animals and plants grow without their paths being violated. I can work for money, but without coercion. I can rest or even be lazy. I can make choices. These things are precious to me. My history is part of me, but it doesn't define me. Along with many others, I am a living and sensitive being dancing in a complex matrix of life, just like trees or rocks or oceans, robins or stars, insects or rabbits.

I was born into slavery. Now I am free. It is enough.

REASONS TO NOT KILL YOURSELF

by Mari Collings*

Because you deserve to live.

Because your life has value, whether or not you can see it,

because it was not your fault,

because you didn't choose to be battered and used,

because life itself is precious, because they were and are wrong,

because you are connected to each and every other ritual abuse survivor, and so your daily battle automatically gives others hope and strength.

Because you will feel better, eventually,

because each time you confront despair you get stronger, and you can't know now what you will ultimately be able to do with this new morsel of strength, what future battles you will be able to win,

because if you die today you will never again feel love for another human being, or trust, or gratitude; because you will never again see kindness and compassion in another's eyes.

Because if you die today you will never again see sunlight pouring through the leaves of a tree, or a bird take flight, or feel the quality of light in winter,

because the seconds do not cease their passing, because even if it feels like time has become an unbearably heavy stone, it has not, and you only have to endure,

because you have already won . . . you have known the cleverness and resiliency and courage and stubborn will to make it this far, and no one can take that away,

because the will to live is not a cruel punishment, even if it feels like that at times: it is a priceless gift.

Because your inner children need you, they have no one else and their need is so great, and because they deserve more than anyone to be healed and comforted: they are true heroes against impossible odds.

Because you owe your inner children, they are the reason you are here. If you die today you will erase the meaning of their suffering and incredible endurance, and that is too great a loss,

because you already have the skills to find your healing path; you have proven this over and over again,

because we need more warriors against this evil,

because we need survivors to offer testament against this horror and despair,

because no one knows better than you the meaning of suffering, and agony deepens the heart,

because you deserve the peace that will come after this battle is won, and it will be won, but only minute by minute . . . we must learn to let go of the unconquerable,

because we can all come together in later years to laugh in their faces; because we will be able to show them that even though they had all the power and strength and ruthless cunning, even though we were only helpless, innocent, dependent children, we will have beaten them at the game they so smugly thought they had mastered,

because I am furious that we have to suffer the pain of another's evil and filth,

because you too will one day feel fury,

because it is critical that you survive.

---

* "Reasons to Not Kill Yourself" is available as an 18" by 23" full-color poster illustrated by Kore Loy Wildrekinde McWhirter. Make checks payable to Survivorship, 3181 Mission St. #139, San Francisco, CA 94110. Send $15.

DIANE HUGS

Diane Hugs is a thirty-two-year-old writer who has been struggling with memories of her childhood abuse for the last ten years.* She's had multiple sclerosis for the last twelve. MS is a degenerative condition of the central nervous system, with symptoms that vary greatly from person to person. In Diane's case, she has been paraplegic for six years and legally blind for the past year. Diane connects her disease with the severe abuse she experienced, starting in infancy.

In the past two and a half years, Diane has become aware that she has multiple personalities—more than thirty of them, ranging in age from three to thirty. As she eloquently expresses, women with multiple personalities can heal.

---

* Diane Hugs is using her own name.

From the time I was a very young child, I had experiences which were so traumatic they split my personality wide open. There was no way for my young mind to cope with the brutality and random acts of sadism that I experienced. Instead, I completely forgot the incidents and created a totally new personality. Within two years, I went in and out of three such changes: from being an introverted, shy pacifist, to being the leader of a girls' gang that went after known rapists and child molesters, to becoming an academic scholar. Each of these personalities began without the old scars, without the old terror, without the anger. Each had her own coping mechanisms, approaching the world in a completely different way. I, as the core personality, was totally unaware of their existence. Every time I wiped the slate clean, a new and different personality would come out to take over so that I might survive. There were many times as a child when I questioned whether I would survive. The ultimate threat was always "I will kill you if you tell, if you . . . if you . . ."

It wasn't until I was much older that I realized I had multiple personalities—more than thirty of them. I also realized that I had blocks of time which I did not remember. I had always accepted that as being normal. I thought everyone occasionally spaced out and found themselves in another city or in the midst of a conversation with no idea what was being talked about.

Accepting each of these parts of myself and then integrating them into my personality is a long process. And it's often very painful, as each of these splits, each of these personalities, has memories and feelings separate from my own experience. So to integrate means to accept those feelings and to accept those memories which I have successfully blocked since I was a child. Sometimes, accepting how I coped in order to survive is extremely painful. Imagine integrating an eighteen-year-old part who is a prostitute when you've been a lesbian for over ten years.

Usually, when one of these personalities takes control, so to speak, I lose time. It seems to me as if seconds have gone by, when in reality minutes, hours, or a day has gone by with this other personality functioning in my place. As I begin to accept the feelings and the parts of me that have split off, instead of losing time with that particular personality, I hear a voice in my head which is that other personality talking. Sometimes it's totally against what I'm thinking or feeling, so I have a lot of inner arguments as part of the process of integration.

After the arguments comes a blending where I not only accept those parts of me, but am strengthened by the knowledge, the courage, whatever it is that each part holds. It's as if each personality holds a special part of my life, not only a painful part of my life. And each time I integrate one, I'm integrating another part of myself that adds to my understanding.

One of the major aspects of healing from childhood abuse is to begin to love yourself. With multiple personalities, this task is much more difficult, because I have to love parts of myself that have been so walled off, so blocked from the conscious personality, that I don't even know them. Over and over, I have to figure out ways to get through those walls so I can know other parts of me. Before I can love myself, I have to know myself.

MULTIPLE PERSONALITIES *

Multiple Personality Disorder (MPD) might—with equal accuracy—be called Multiple Personality Miracle (MPM). Because it is, indeed, a miracle that under conditions of extreme trauma, children find a way to survive. When there is no way to physically escape the pain, terror, and despair, children sometimes endure by escaping mentally, or dissociating.

---

* There is an increasing number of books, organizations, audio and videotapes, newsletters, and other resources for people with multiple personalities. See "Dissociation and Multiple Personalities" in the Resource Guide on page 563.

Since dissociating is something we all do to some extent, it's helpful to look at the process as a continuum. At one end are the mildest examples, such as highway hypnosis or an awareness of "the child within" as a part of oneself. At the other end is an internal system in which the dissociation has solidified through repeated abuse into distinct selves (which can be called personalities or alters) so that there is little, if any, awareness of what is going on with the others.

In between these two ends of the continuum there are many survivors who experience some degree of dissociation. For many people, the question "Do I have multiple personalities?" might more fruitfully be replaced with "To what extent do I have multiple personalities?"

Multiple personalities are a highly successful adaptation to otherwise intolerable pain. Even though the existence of separate alters may be difficult, disconcerting, or even horrifying to you, it's essential to remember that this ability—and these alters— are what got you through. The problem is not primarily one of fixing yourself because you have this "disorder," but rather of addressing and healing the trauma that made this adaptation necessary in the first place.

But before intentionally going back to retrieve memories, it's important to get to know the parts of yourself, to learn to communicate and cooperate internally in a healthy and respectful way, and to achieve a basic level of stability so that everyone can be reasonably safe. There are many ways to encourage and support internal communication. One of the simplest is to provide a journal in which all alters are invited to write or draw, or use a bulletin board on which any alter can put up a message.

Sometimes it's difficult for survivors with multiple personalities to accept and appreciate all their inner people. Some alters may appear hostile, weak, or in some other way disturbing to you. You may wish you could get rid of them—or even try to. But it's essential to remember that each and every one—no matter how problematic he or she may seem to you now—has played an important part in your survival. Everyone developed to fill a need and, given the limitations of the situation, they all fulfilled those roles in the best way they could. Everything you've done, even if it doesn't look like it makes sense now, has its own intrinsic logic, which is sane and rational.

Healing with multiple personalities is more complex than the healing process for survivors who have not separated into different selves. Each alter holds part of the experience and each needs to do the work of healing. Plus, all need to learn to work togther. However, there can be advantages too. There is the potential for an internal system of support and collaboration that can be very valuable. Many survivors with multiple personalities have internal helpers, wise healers, and inner guides, as well as alters who are good at going to work, driving, and taking care of business even in the midst of crisis and chaos.

As a creative and highly intelligent way of coping with and surviving extreme abuse, the ability to create distinct selves within ourselves is a formidable testimony to the resourcefulness of the human mind and spirit. As you learn to understand and respect the ways in which your mind has worked, not only to keep you alive, but to preserve and enhance your strengths and capacities, you can offer to yourself an attitude of acceptance, understanding, and honor.

KRISHNABAI

The first twenty-five years of my life were an experience of despair. They were just incredibly painful. There's something devastating about a child who does not feel loved. And I've really turned that around in my life. I have experienced healing and I just feel incredibly blessed.

Krishnabai is thirty-five years old.* She lives in the Boston area, does workshops for survivors, and works as a consultant.

Krishnabai grew up in a rural area of New Jersey. "I had no feeling of being part of a family. It was like being a member of a boarding house. Although I was close to my father, I had no relationship whatsoever with my mother."

When she was nine years old, Krishnabai was sexually abused one time by her great-uncle. As is true for many women, Krishnabai's sexual abuse was just one of the factors that shaped her early development. Her story clearly demonstrates the way sexual abuse can exacerbate already existing problems.

Krishnabai says she was psychotically depressed for most of the first twenty-five years of her

---

* Krishnabai is using her own name. She received the name "Krishnabai" while living in the ashram of Baba Muktananda. She changed her name legally and says, "It was a real release of the past. That name I had, which I don't even say anymore, is gone. It marks the end of an era. Using 'Krishnabai' makes me vulnerable, but it also gives me strength."

life. In the ten years since then, she has healed herself through a combination of therapy, reparenting, and spirituality.

I was molested once by my mother's uncle during the summer between fifth and sixth grades. I was already a very isolated, withdrawn child. My uncle got drunk one night and pounced on me, and started kissing me and feeling me up. I was unable to get away. He was in the process of getting undressed when my aunt walked in. She sent me to my room, yelled at him, and then came upstairs and said to me, "It's really obvious that no one loves you and you're just a sad little kid. I'm really sorry this happened, but you must never, ever tell anyone." And I didn't tell anyone for years.

I already had a very shaky foundation, and this just destroyed me. My mother had been unable to make any kind of emotional connection with me. She once said to me, "I should never have been a mother." She didn't know how to nurture, how to open up, how to express love. And so I already felt unlovable.

After the sexual abuse, my behavior took a radical turn toward the bizarre. I thought if people touched me it would kill me. I thought there were people in the trees. I thought there were cameras in the house, staring at me. I was getting messages from the universe. I had to plug my teddy bears into invisible oxygen tubes at night before I went to sleep, so they wouldn't suffocate. I had an incredible amount of ritualistic behavior going on, trying to control my environment. I started wearing black shroudy clothes. Weight, which was always an issue, became much worse. I was throwing up every morning.

I was very isolated. I went into therapy in ninth grade. I was given Librium. I continued having visions and hearing voices but I knew not to tell anyone about them.

I was bright and I excelled at school. I went to Europe between my junior and senior year of high school to study at the University of London. It was 1968. I got immersed in the hippie scene. I came back and I got into drugs and acting out sexually. I got into freedom. Everything just blew wide open, and it was supported by the times.

I went to college for a year, and then quit and moved to Boston. I got a job as a cashier. I lived in this hippie crash pad. You never knew who was going to be there. I have no idea how many people I fucked. It was just this continuous "Whatever you want is fine with me 'cause I don't know who 'me' is." I was totally bland, because I had killed my feelings. I got into drugs because they made me feel real. So I took a lot of them, including LSD.

I JUST CRUMBLED

When I was twenty my dad died, and I just crumbled. My dad had been my one link to the world. He had been a gentle and beautiful man, so when he died I just fell apart. I went into intensive therapy. They loaded me up on psychotropic drugs. They considered hospitalizing me.

I couldn't work. I was totally fogged out. I was put into a program through Massachusetts Rehabilitation. They put me in cooking school, figuring maybe I could function on that level if they trained me to be a cook. I ended up working as a cook in a snack bar at a mental hospital. There I was flipping hamburgers in this snack bar, and the patients started talking to me. They had decreased my drugs at that point, and my intellect got aroused. The clinical staff started to notice that these patients could talk to me, that there was a real relationship going on. And so I got invited onto the clinical staff.

I only worked the night shift, which was perfect, because no psychiatrist ever saw me. I dealt with people in their most difficult moments, which I could totally understand. It helped me so much to help them.

Right about that time, I got into a car accident. A drunken driver plowed into me. I went into the hospital and the doctor said, "Well, I think you're okay. But I don't want you to be alone for the night. Do you have a roommate?"

I said, "No."

And he said, "Do you have a friend you can call?"

I said "No."

He said, "Do you have any family you can call?"

I said, "No."

And he looked at me with this incredible compassion and said, "Is there anyone there for you in your life?"

And I thought about it, and I said, "No."

He ended up having me call a coworker to tell her what had happened. I went home and was terribly depressed. I decided to kill myself that night by hanging myself with the telephone cord, and just then, the woman I had called phoned to check in with me. She talked to me for two hours on the phone, and then came and got me. I started to tell her how I really felt. And she said, "I think you need to see somebody."

I went to this psychiatrist at the hospital where I worked, and I said, "Look, I need help, and I don't know how to get it." And so she agreed to take me on. And then in the process of unfolding me, she kind of went, "Oh, my God! We've got this person on our staff!"

She listened to me for maybe five sessions and she said, "Something is really wrong here. You've never experienced connection. You've never experienced happiness in your life. I think there's something going on with you biologically and I want to try some drugs on you." Well, I had nothing to lose.

She put me on Tofranil, which was a brand-new drug at that time. One day a few weeks later, I woke up and I felt really weird. It was about four in the afternoon. I'd worked the night before. I called her up and I said, "I don't know what's going on, but I feel really weird." And I kept talking, and she got really excited. And she said, "You've got to come right over here."

So I went over and she said to me, "You're starting to have feelings! I can't believe it! It's working! These are emotions you're feeling! This is what everybody has. Your TV is going from black-and-white to color and you don't understand because you've never seen color before."

We spent the next six months in therapy with her saying, "This is sadness. This is happiness." She described different feelings to me and helped put them in a framework that I could understand. I was like a baby looking out at the world and beginning to understand things for the first time. And my life really started to change.

When I got access to my feelings, the psychotic episodes dropped down a whole lot. Some kind of pressure was released. I started to have more energy. I was so hungry to explore the world. I decided to go back to school and I did.

"GO TO THIS WORKSHOP"

I was working full time at night and going to school during the day. I was living in this alienating group house. There'd been a woman who lived there once who got all kinds of neat junk mail. And she got a circular saying, "Our friends Robbie and Judith Gass are going to be offering a brand-new workshop called *Opening the Heart,* and we want to invite all of you to come."

That was when I heard my clear inner voice for the very first time. It said, "Go to this workshop." All I'd had up until then was real traditional psychotherapy. I was still on the medication. I was so-called stabilized. So I wrote them a letter, asking all kinds of questions about the schedule and what they'd be doing. And Robbie wrote back a letter that said, "Don't worry. Just come. Love, Robbie."

And I said to myself, "Oh my God! I can't do this." But I sent my money in and I got back this list: Bring a baby picture, a picture of your parents, a blindfold! I'm like really flipping out, but this little part of me pushed me to go. And so I did.

I was terrified. I was the first one to show up. I was totally going on faith and I didn't know what faith was. The whole weekend was the most incredible experience. There was singing, there was bioenergetic work, there was meditation. We did yoga, visualization, and a lot of work in pairs. It was an experience of people letting go of the gates in their heart, releasing the blocks that have kept them from feeling love.

We did this exercise where we were supposed to lie on the floor, reach up our arms, and call for our mothers. I couldn't do it. I was terrified. Judith sat down next to me and said, "Let me hold you. Let me put you on my lap." And she pulled me onto her lap, put her arms around me. I had never experienced such tenderness.

Here was this beautiful woman holding me like that. I cracked right open. I bawled my eyes out. And she rocked me and she held me for so long. Robbie came over and joined us. The two of them saw some potential in me that I was not able to see. And they made this commitment that weekend to hold on to me and help me with my healing.

AT SPRING HILL

About two months later, I went to visit them at Spring Hill.* Judith put her arms around me and said, "I want you to come live with us. I think it would be really good for you." And so I moved in in the spring of 1977. I was twenty-six years old. I lived in their house, in the room right beneath them.

Judith was like this barnacle. She hung on through all my acting out, all my fear, all my resistance. First I thought I was crazy.

---

* Spring Hill was a community and conference center in Ashby, Massachusetts, that sponsored the Opening the Heart workshops from the mid-1970s to 1998. These workshops supported personal growth by offering a safe and loving environment and a variety of tools and skills for change.

Then I thought they were crazy. My fears and doubts just got flushed right out of me.

Although I had made some progress before I came to Spring Hill, I was still a totally isolated person when I got there. I was functional in a work sense, but not in a people sense. I was terrified of people. I had no ability to have loving relationships. I was like this little bubble floating in the universe with no connection.

I was split, like pieces in a basket, and Robbie and Judith picked up the basket, took it to Spring Hill, dumped the pieces out on the floor, and started putting them together, like a puzzle. And then when there was enough that they could recognize the picture, they made contact with me and said, "Well, is this the kind of picture you want to be?"

I couldn't cooperate for a long time because I didn't understand what they were trying to do. There was no sense of "me" in there. They could see the "me," but I couldn't. I couldn't do it. I was like a baby.

Judith just kept hanging in there with me. She'd say, "You're going to get through this. You are this incredible being. You just need a little bit of love. You just didn't get enough love, and I'm going to help you with that." And I bonded with her, and with Robbie, and they became my parents.

They did things like come to my college graduation. They gave me big birthday parties. Judith helped me with my appearance. She got me to start bathing. They encouraged me to have fun and to develop a sense of humor. They kept telling me it was okay to be me, and that I was lovable. They reparented me, and they loved me into life. For that I feel they really gave me life. They really birthed me.

I lived with them twenty-four hours a day, and on top of that, Judith was my therapist. Life was going off and having therapy, and then coming back and watching them practice what she had just told me about. I finally saw that there were two people on the earth who were trustworthy and consistent. And I had never known that before.

I got off my medication. That was terrifying for me. I had to take the gamble that if I lost it and had a psychotic break, Judith would be there for me. And that I could survive without those drugs. Because they had become like a lifeline for me. So what I did was transfer that lifeline over to Judith. And it worked. They literally saved my life.*

"I'M NOT CRAZY ANYMORE"

One day, about six months after I came to Spring Hill, Judith and I had this amazing therapy session. She was trying to get me to talk about something that was real hard for me. I was shaking, and I felt myself losing grip with reality, and I kind of started to melt away. And she looked at me and she said, "Don't you understand? Your mother tried to kill your spirit. You did what you needed to do to survive. You did the right thing! You survived and now you can live."

This revelation swept through me. In-

---

* Krishnabai's experience living with Robbie and Judith Gass at Spring Hill was profoundly healing—and unique. Robbie and Judith Gass are exceptionally mature individuals who had the support of a residential healing community when they took Krishnabai in. Unfortunately, many other survivors have been offered what seemed like special opportunities for reparenting which have had disastrous repercussions. Therefore we do not recommend this kind of unusual involvement.

stead of seeing myself as unworthy, I realized that I had done the right thing. I burst into tears, and I hung onto her, and I started weeping, and I said, "I'm not crazy anymore."

I realized at that moment how far I had come. I felt the integration happening right then. And Judith burst into tears, and she rocked me. And at that point, for the first time, I knew that I had a future. That I had hope, that I could change my life, and that my destiny was not to be psychotic, alienated, and a complete wreck for the rest of my life. It was in my control to heal myself. The past was over, and this was the beginning of the future.

I TOO HAVE WALKED IN THE LAND OF DREAMS

I believe we come into the world to learn certain lessons. The universe is like a central data bank, and each of us is like a terminal. I think we get what we need. I feel very provided for. I feel a lot of gratitude. And it's a natural spillover to want to help other people.

I'll tell you of a healing experience I had in that regard. I was at Ellen's workshop. I wasn't really sure why I was going. I felt like the sexual abuse stuff had been pretty much laid to rest, yet I had this intuition to go. So I went. There was a woman there who was so badly abused that she was also psychotic. And during the first day of the workshop, she went into that psychotic place and was speaking out from there. I was watching her, and I knew where she was. Ellen was working with her, and then there was a cooling-off period.

What was true was this woman was in pieces, and she wasn't able to pull herself back together again. She was kind of like this mess all over the floor. I looked at her and I knew I could say something to her that would have a very healing effect. But it meant exposing my history to a group of women that I didn't know.

Finally I asked myself, "What's more important—your safety or helping her?" And I knew it was to help her. I took a deep breath, and I looked over at her, and I said, "I too have walked in the land of dreams, and I have become real. And I know that you too can become real."

Well, it just broke us both up. I spent the next three and a half days with her in my lap almost all the time. It was an incredible connection. It showed her that it was possible for her to heal. It created the first tangible sign of hope that she had ever had. And what it did for me, on a very concrete level, was show me that I was completely on the other side of the river, and that I could now turn around and offer my hand to someone else. It was the last piece of really knowing that I was whole.

And consequently, the bond that happened between us was so potent that it's very alive for both of us. I feel like she's my kid, and I would do anything for her, because I know, the way Judith knew for me, that there's a way out. And I have dedicated myself to being a guidepost for her. I think helping other people heal is very important in our own healing, keeping it all a circle.

MICHELLE AND
ARTEMIS

Because we're sisters, I think we blared through everything at an incredibly high intensity and speed. Having each other to bounce off of has really catalyzed things. As each one of us broke a barrier for ourselves, we broke a barrier for the other person.

Michelle Thomas is thirty-one years old.* She is a counselor and lives with her husband of four years, David, in Boulder, Colorado. Her sister Artemis is thirty-seven. She is a nurse and was recently divorced after a twelve-year marriage.

Michelle and Artemis grew up in Denver. They lived with their mother, their stepfather, and their younger sister, who is now twenty-five. Their stepfather worked for the military and earned a

good income, but they lived in poverty because he gambled. Frequently there was no food in the house.

Both parents were violent alcoholics, and both sexually abused the girls. Their mother abused them mostly in the context of "preparing" them for Ben, their stepfather. She was totally unpredictable—kind one minute and sadistic the next. He was particularly brutal in his abuse, often torturing the girls.

MICHELLE: When we were children we never talked about the abuse. It was almost as if we couldn't stand to look at each other—

---

* Michelle Thomas and Artemis wanted to use their own names, but couldn't for legal reasons.

446

you know, the victim hating the other victim syndrome.

ARTEMIS: You never knew what you were going to get from who, when. There was never a feeling of safety. When I was eleven, I had an abortion with my stepfather's child and almost died. Michelle was five years old and she was told to take care of me.

At the point of the abortion, I went amnesiac. I clinked out. I was standing at the living room window. It was raining and I just let go of any hold on reality and slipped into a gray fog. I just disappeared and nobody knew it. And I remember the intense feeling of isolation and hopelessness. That's when the splitting began.

There was a daytime Artemis and a nighttime Artemis. They did not know each other existed. The daytime Artemis was very sweet and accommodating. She was the Barbie Doll, whatever anybody needed or wanted me to be. And the other one, the nighttime Artemis, was just a dead person, like a beaten-up pulp of death. I remember I used to act out this thing with our cat. I would dress up in our mother's clothes and I would torture the shit out of this cat. And then I would throw it in the bathroom and lock the door. And then I would take my mother's clothes off and I'd be me, and I'd go take the cat out and really love it. I acted out the split continually. It was a ritual for me. I used to black out and not know how I'd gotten into certain places. Then suddenly I'd wake up and I'd be the daytime person. I only remember coming out of my fog once.

MICHELLE: That was the time we tried to kill our stepfather. I was seven and Artemis was thirteen. I basically talked her into it. I knew I was too small to do the job alone.

ARTEMIS: We made a pact, Michelle and I. Nighttime Artemis stuck a knife in his back when he was sleeping. We punctured his lung, but my mother's a nurse and he never went to the hospital. You know, live with a nurse and you can handle the abuse at home.

My sense of failure at that point was really amazing. I had come out of my fog to kill him for all of us, and I failed.

I remember the daytime Artemis asked my mother sometime in my teens, "I feel like I've tried to kill someone." And she said, "Artemis, you have such a wild imagination." And since the daytime Artemis really didn't remember what happened to the nighttime Artemis, the daytime bought it.

MICHELLE: My stepfather had my mom committed to a number of mental facilities. The message was, if you said anything or you crossed him in any way, it would be very easy for him to institutionalize any of us. And so it was progressively impressed upon us to not go to the outside.

ARTEMIS: And even when we did tell, no one believed us. Michelle told the principal in fifth grade. And I used to draw pictures of what was happening to me and leave them places. I got in a lot of trouble for drawing dirty pictures. I told people I baby-sat for. They'd just go on with their conversation as if I'd never said anything. I remember my exact thought: "I must be telling a lie. Why am I telling a lie?"

MICHELLE: I was just on a straight survival mode. I never did anything that would be your normal teenage routine. Life was very serious. I put myself through school.

I worked, I crammed my life as full as I possibly could with outside stimulus. I was a zombie, just going through the motions of being alive.

And then there was my tough guy. We grew up in a tough neighborhood. I always used that as a cover: "I was just a hard kid because of where I grew up." Yet I never got into dope. I needed control much too much to allow myself to get stoned or drunk.

I was very withdrawn. I made sure that nobody knew me. And at the same time, I bounced around in a lot of relationships. There was a revolving door on my bedroom. That lasted until I met David.

I never split like Artemis did. I just stayed there and kicked ass as hard as I could. I made sure that the house ran at least on some existence level. As early as nine I did most of the shopping. I would always come in after the fact and clean up the mess, clean the blood off the kitchen floor, make sure my mom was going to survive, whatever.

ARTEMIS: My coping was very different. I learned the tremendous capabilities of the mind. I could keep myself from feeling pain. I took a lot of drugs. Nothing that addicted me—just so I stayed in the ozone. I screwed around. I hated men. I hated myself.

As an adult, I was either docile and helpless or I would fly into violent rages and get ugly as hell. I'd fix the house up very nice, and I'd try so hard to do things beautiful for myself and for my husband. But I couldn't handle it for long. He'd come home and the house would be in shambles. I would have demolished it.

And my husband would say, "Why did you do it?" And I'd say, "I don't know why."

Things would trigger me off and I'd run down the street just screaming. Or I'd be in a car and kick the windshield in or try to jump out. At this point I hadn't remembered anything about the abuse.

Once I took a knife to my husband. I realized later I was acting out the whole stabbing incident with my stepfather. And then I would turn around and be very nice. That's how split I was. Looking back, I have no idea how I was able to function as a nurse for all those years.

DON'T YOU KNOW I'M POISON?

MICHELLE: In sex I was always the controller and there was always a very fine knife edge between pain and pleasure. I would say where it was going to go, and when it was going to go, and how far.

I had an almost sadistic desire to watch the other person come to a point of pain. I knew how to string it out to a fine degree where they weren't sure if they were in pain or whether it was just slightly pleasurable. I would toy with other people to the point of being cruel. I had been extremely well trained. I was very adept at it.

I had lots of denial about being vulnerable and feminine. It wasn't until I came into a soft relationship with a strong woman that I learned not to be in that dominant role in sex. From her I learned to touch and to feel because it was safe.

ARTEMIS: I was never cruel or sadistic sexually. I was always just the victim. I would seduce a lot of people into bed, and then I'd disappear and not feel anything. I also had a big appetite for sex, a lot of actual physical desire, which confused me, and I hated it. It was the most disgusting, degrading thing to actually want sex.

With my husband, who was a very gentle man, I got more destructive. It was like "Don't love me. Don't you know I'm poison?" I would often get hysterical and start beating at him, screaming "I'm a whore. I'm a whore. Can't you see how ugly I am?"

And then he'd say, "Artemis, no." Because he loved me, he sincerely loved me. He'd say that and I'd go into absolute hysteria. I'd go about definitely proving to him how evil I was. I'd start smashing everything in the room or myself with a knife or everything in the room with a knife. It would then be a matter of him trying to save us both.

He'd say, "Artemis, don't close off to me. I'll stay right here till you're ready, but don't close off." And then he'd say, "Okay, can I reach out to you?" And he'd gradually reach out to me, and then slowly I'd be able to climb out of this hole I was in and reach out to him.

MICHELLE: When I first remembered the abuse, I went through long periods of "Don't touch me." Then when I started feeling sexual again, I tried to go back and do the same kind of sexual controlling I had always done with David, and it didn't work. I'd crack up laughing in the middle of it.

My domination and cruelty had been connected to my fear of feeling. People set up scenarios to keep from feeling particular things. If you're going to go to that elaborate way of making sure that you don't feel something soft, something's going on.

I didn't make serious changes in my sexuality until I was willing to make a commitment to my partner around monogamy. I mean monogamy was the equivalent of being imprisoned. It had the potential of a man being in control of me again. But it wasn't until I made that commitment that I was able to explore my own feelings of sexuality and sensuality.

ARTEMIS: And I remember coming to a place where I let myself admit that I loved my huband. That was a big taboo. I mean, you can let a man beat you, you can let him rape you, you can hate him, but you can't love a man. Sincerely care for a man? That was against all the rules of the universe and God was going to strike me down for sure. It's almost like that was more humiliating than being raped and being beaten and tortured. That fresh, wonderful feeling of just loving him. And I did love him.

IF I HAD BEEN ALONE, I WOULD NEVER HAVE BELIEVED IT

ARTEMIS: Before I even began remembering the abuse, I had a dream in which a friend stood at my bedroom window with a long scroll and said, "You have to remember Artemis. You have to remember." And I had no idea what I was supposed to remember.

MICHELLE: I always remembered the alcohol and the neglect. But I didn't remember anything about the sexual abuse until I was in a very safe relationship. David and

I were driving from Boulder to Denver. All of a sudden I saw my stepfather's face and knew what had happened. His face just kind of hung outside the window, and when I turned to look at David, he was Ben. I remember going very white and afraid, and throughout the rest of that night, I progressively became more conscious of what that fear and those feelings were. I knew why I hated him so much.

After I started remembering, I lost a couple of jobs because I couldn't handle being in the outside world. I virtually did not leave my house for three months. I thought I was insane. I would find myself sitting in a room and hearing my stepfather and my mother, or hearing scenes before I saw pictures. And I thought, "This is it. You're crazy, kid. You're hearing voices so you are possessed."

ARTEMIS: That thing of being possessed and being of the devil was something we were always told: "Devil's daughter. Devil's child. You're evil, and someday everybody's going to find out how evil you are."

MICHELLE: For the first couple of years, I didn't have any pictures. I knew that I had been sexually abused by my stepfather. I didn't know to what degree. I just started becoming aware that my actions toward other people, the way I would respond to things, everything I did from breathing onward, seemed related to what had happened as a child. There wasn't a part of me I liked.

ARTEMIS: I was the opposite of Michelle. I didn't start remembering until everything

that was secure around me left. My husband and I separated.

Our youngest sister got married. Michelle and I were driving home from the wedding. I don't remember what led up to it, but Michelle looked at me and said, "Did anything happen to you?"

And I said, "No, nothing ever happened to me. But I always had these dreams." And so I told her the dreams and she looked me straight in the face and said, "Those were not dreams, Artemis." And it just cracked. It was like a lightning bolt hit me and my head opened up. And I knew. My God, they were not dreams.

That night I did not sleep. I kept the light on all night, and just remembered. I had no control over the memories. But I had done a lot of meditation, so I knew there was some part of my brain where I could sit in a calm and neutral place. In the midst of experiencing it very intensely, I climbed into that one little corner of myself that could view it neutrally.

MICHELLE: You get to the point where you realize that the memory is only a memory. You already lived through it the first time, and it can't hurt you anymore. And if you can just take the observer role and watch it, then the fear of going crazy goes away. But that fear was there for the longest time.

I remember coming up against a picture and fighting it for days: "No, I'm not going to see this. Because if I see this, I'll go crazy. If I see this, I'll disapear." And finally I came to a place where I knew I needed to see the pictures, and I would actually chase after them.

I believed the memories right away,

but believing another human being could do those things to a child was where the doubt came in.

ARTEMIS: I never would have believed the memories if I hadn't been able to call Michelle and tell her, "This is what happened." And she'd say, "Yes, it did happen. And here's the other part of it." Between the two of us we were able to put the puzzle pieces together.

MICHELLE: For a long time, I didn't realize how bad these things were. It had been such a way of life that I just accepted it. It wasn't until I could bounce it off somebody else and see their reaction that it sank in.

ARTEMIS: There were times I felt I was going to go under with the memories. The agony was so awful, and the aloneness. The feeling was, nobody loves someone who needs. Everyone is afraid of the rawness of pure human need, so don't let anybody see.

But finally I said, "Fuck it! I'm going to look myself and I'm not going to be afraid to let anyone else see." Because everybody's human. So I just dove into that aloneness completely, and dove all the way through it until I was no longer afraid of the intensity of my need as a human being.

FACING THE SHAME

ARTEMIS: I've done everything in the damn book that's wrong, or had it done to me. And I realize the integrity of who I am in the face of all that. I'd worn that cloak of shame and it branded itself into my skin. But I found out that I could take it off,

even if it meant taking my skin off along with it. I could grow back new skin that was healthy and good.

What helped me do that was allowing myself to be deeply loved. I allowed myself to be loved in the places where I felt the ugliest and most ashamed of myself. And I don't mean physical places.

MICHELLE: I'm in a marriage where there's total, unconditional love—to do the most horrible rotten things you can do to a person and to have them be accepting of you, and love that ugliness in you, until you yourself can love that ugliness. And that ugliness and that shame turns into something very soft and very warm and very beautiful inside of yourself.

The particular incident I'm thinking of is the time I was staying at Artemis's house. I remember reading, for the third time, *If I Die Before I Wake*. I was by myself. And I was in a total state of agony and numbness at the same time, if you can do that. The world could have disappeared and I wouldn't have known it. I was feeling the shame and the ugliness that had surrounded my life so intensely, and feeling horribly alone, like I had no right to be alive because I was the carrier of all this horrendous atrocity. And that day, I dove into that self-destructiveness because I knew I had to or I would never get to the other side.

There were knives in the house, which were my favorite tool as a child. As a kid I would sit and carve and just watch the blood to know I was alive. There are scars on my body and I have no idea where they came from. I couldn't tell you which ones I inflicted and which ones were inflicted upon me. When I was twelve, I realized I could kill myself, so I quit. This was the first time since then that I'd had that feeling again. And so I got myself out of the house.

I walked to the top of a steep cliff, watching the ocean and thinking about different ways that I could kill myself. I thought about jumping off the cliff. I thought of this whole series of things, one, to intensify the pain, and two, to get away from it. And I looked down and I happened to be sitting right in the middle of poison oak.

I remember very vividly thinking about my mother, thinking that staying alive didn't matter because she never loved me. She never cared. I finally faced that I'd never had a mother, and I never would.

And so, sobbing, I just picked up handfuls of poison oak and rubbed it into my skin from head to toe. After doing that I felt better. There was always a release with the carving—and this time with the poison oak—because somebody on the outside could see the pain that was a constant on the inside.

And then I went and sat on the steps outside Artemis's house and waited until somebody came home. And I told both David and Artemis what I had done.

ARTEMIS: You risked being vulnerable and we both were there for you. I think that was the day you lost your hard guy.

MICHELLE: Yeah. I did. You just loved me. Even with what I had done. So to heal shame, you just dive right into that shame and you risk letting somebody love you inside of that.

WE LITERALLY RERAISED OURSELVES

ARTEMIS: Bringing my two selves together was a long, slow process. There was a time when I had to go back to being a young child. I had to learn to feel and reach out and touch the world. For a while I went around and touched everything. It was so magical just to feel things that were soft. It was magical that I could feel my feet in shoes, my legs in my pants, how the cloth felt on my body. And be able to say, "It's safe to feel." Just the thing of feeling a pencil on paper. I was ecstatic.

MICHELLE: That's the intense integration process that happens. You raise that two-year-old to a five-year-old and then you bring the five-year-old up. You have to function in the outside world as an adult, but part of you inside is growing up. Remember the little notes we'd write and leave around the house?

ARTEMIS: Oh, yeah: "It's okay to feel safe in my room. It's okay to feel safe in my house." All these little reminders. I also remember when I became aware that I took up space. I had volume. I was not just a thought. I was not just flat; there was a behind to me, a side to me. And other people took up space too, and there was space between us through which we could reach. At first that was extremely threatening because that also meant there was a space between us that they could hurt me in.

NO LONGER WOULD ABUSE BE THE CAUSE AND MY LIFE THE EFFECT

MICHELLE: I had always considered myself a chalkboard that somebody erased really fast. And there was a little scratch of a piece of chalk here, and here. If you've ever had a sloppy teacher, you know what that looks like. And I was angry about that. I wanted to know where I'd been in this life. Yet there was a fear. What if it's just too horrible? And it *was* horrible. It was pretty damn close.

And then you get to the point of "Well, I lived through it once and it didn't kill me. Somehow I managed to survive it that time and I had a hell of lot less resources than I do now. It's time to face it."

So you face, and you face, and you face, and you continue to face each aspect of yourself. You have to remember and claim each individual experience. Acknowledge that it happened. Acknowledge that you lived through it.

I realized why I would always position my bed in a particular part of the room. I realized there wasn't an aspect of my life that wasn't somehow a response to the abuse. The way I walked. The way I breathed. There was nothing about me, at some point during this healing process, that I haven't confronted and changed. I have totally metamorphosed.

And then I had to face that person who was my mother. And there was a period of "I hate you because you did that." And "Why did you do that?" You ask, "Was there some way as a child I unknowingly invited all of that?" And you come up with the answer, "No, there's no way."

And then I blamed my mother for being in her own agony so much that she wasn't willing to challenge herself, if for no other reason than to save her kids.

And you hate. And you hurt. And you hate yourself. And you hate the mess

that you're in. And you'd love to run away. And I think as the stages progress, there are parts of the cycle that recur. Each time it *looks* like you're going through the same thing, but it's elevated just a little bit. And you have to come to a position of trust that "Okay, I'm facing this thing again. There's a reason I need to face it from this particular position. There's something I didn't learn before."

Then I stepped out of my own life to see where my stepfather was coming from. He had also been sexually and physically abused by his parents. My mother told me that. And I know that she had been abused. I slowly started to see the other people's positions in the whole play. And once I did that, I was able to make that quantum leap of no longer identifying with my past.

ARTEMIS: For me the decision not to identify with the past was a decision, not just a change I went through in the healing process. I had to make a quantum leap that I was no longer going to have the abuse be the cause and my life be the effect. And to say "I am me, whole and complete." I'm able to do that because now I do have an identity, a whole person that I have given birth to, that the people who love me have given birth to.

MICHELLE: The identification as an abused person can be a prison in itself. I had to say, "I'm just going to risk who I am here and now, without that identity." It's almost a rebirthing. You change your birthright.

ARTEMIS: It's like "Where are you *now*? *Right now* you have to choose what standpoint you are going to live life from." And it's a constant choice. Every time I'm in a situation where I start acting in those same patterns and my mind says, "I need this security, I need these ways of manipulation, and it's because of what happened to me," I have to say, "No! *No!*" Sometimes I'll be in a state of terrible limbo because I'm not sure what to do instead.

It's still a constant decision for me. I've been alive for thirty-seven years and the groove on that record is pretty deep, but I pick up that needle and move it over.

For me the hardest part was letting go of the right to hate. It was letting go of the right to be confused and messed up because of what had happened to me. Because I did have a right to those things. And they were treasures, but if I wanted to heal all the way, I had to give them up.

I mean I grew up waking up in the morning in a pool of my own vomit and my own blood. And I grew up having to wake myself up in the morning, having to clean myself up and get ready for school alone. I lived it. I grew up being raped at knifepoint by somebody I was supposed to be able to trust. I had a right to hate. I had a right to get even. And I did!

Until finally I realized, "I'm destroying myself because of this. As long as I hold on to my right to hate, I am limiting myself. I'm the only one who's putting the prison walls around me now. Because there's no one raping me anymore. There's nobody torturing me anymore. I am surrounded now by nothing but loving people." I realized I loved myself too much to keep myself in that prison, and so I let go of my hate for *me*. It was a real inside job.

I experienced some damn heavy things and I've come through it. I've come through with an intense love for myself and an intense amount of love even for that man who was called my stepfather. I have struggled intensely, and I have come into a state of real forgiveness, to the point where I feel love for him. I have never seen him again, but I don't feel fear anymore. It goes all the way straight through me, clean.

MICHELLE: But you can't fake it. There's a fine line between denial and moving on. You can't forgive someone until you're ready. I went through a phase of trying to be magnanimous and forgive before I was ready, and I got smacked right in the face with it. It was like a boomerang.

There is no way to move on without total acceptance of each place where you are. You have to accept yourself as the awakener, as the victim, as not wanting to be the victim, and then as the survivor. And you have to go through all the pain and agony and pride of being that survivor before you can move beyond that to warrior status.

Each step becomes a sweater that you wear and it keeps you warm and it keeps you safe until you grow out of it. Then the sweater gets tight and starts pinching you. You say, "I'm never going to let go of this sweater." And it's not until that sweater becomes so outrageously uncomfortable that you just *have* to take it off that you take a chance that maybe you'll find something else to take its place. You have to be willing to accept the next void, at any given point in time, in order to be able to fill it.

ARTEMIS: I had a sense, even when I was in the deepest hell, of something that said

"I'll get you out of this. Don't worry. Trust me." I don't know what to call it. I don't know if that's called spiritual awakening. But I trusted it. And that for me is where the healing really happened. When I felt connected to that part of myself, it healed the rest of me.

MICHELLE: I didn't go to much therapy. I wasn't inclined that way, to be honest, because I haven't found anybody who could stay ahead of me. "How am I going to give my trust over to somebody to guide me when I don't feel they're any more capable than I am?" Mostly I've utilized my own resources. I can process and analyze things up one side and down the other. And my stubbornness really helped.

ARTEMIS: I didn't go to therapy either. Because as a teenager it meant someone trying to throw me in the hospital and put me on drugs. And when I did try counseling they identified me so much as a victim that I could hardly get past their image of me.

But even though I didn't go to therapy, I did not do it alone. I had people around me who had deep insights into me as a person, who knew the reality of my intrinsic self, who were able to hold it for me even when I couldn't hold it for myself. Their belief in me was like a magnet which pulled me through.

I realized I didn't want to be loved *because* I had survived these things. I want to be loved and cared for for who I am. And it's a fine line. I'm not ashamed of what happened to me. But I don't want

that to be an excuse through which someone loves me. Or the only reason I can say, "I need."

When I need, I immediately lapse into that person who was desperately needy and could not have any of those needs filled. I want to be able to say "I need" because I'm a woman alive *today,* without having to throw myself back into being the victim. I want to risk coming as a person needing *now,* because I'm a human being, not because of what happened to me.

COMING OVER THE RISE

MICHELLE: I think when I learned that I could have a sense of humor, that it was okay to laugh at things, that it was okay to be joyful in the world, was when I started having hope.

Now there's amusement in my life. I realized there were things in life that were actually designed to be enjoyable, that I didn't always have to struggle at being alive. It's like coming over a rise and all of a sudden you see in the horizon a world that you've never experienced before. You have no idea what's going to happen to you. It's all brand-new. The world starts opening up. You slow down enough to feel the trees. To notice light and shade and shadow. To notice sounds. And to start expanding your life in other ways. And that's an even bigger challenge than the one you just came from.

Incest is not a taboo. Talking about it is a taboo.

Mary McGrath is forty-eight years old.* She grew up in Nevada. She is Scottish and French. Raised as a fundamentalist, she went to Lutheran churches throughout her teen years and early adulthood. At age twenty she married an alcoholic, and she stayed in that marriage for almost twenty years. She has five grown children. After leaving her husband, Mary came out as a lesbian. She now lives with her lover of two years and earns her living as a massage therapist.

Mary has one sister. They were both molested by their stepfather. The incest started when Mary was seven and continued through her teen years.

The two girls shared a room, and they would

talk about what was going on: "Because we could give each other support, we were clear from the beginning that he was the bad guy, so we never had the confusion many victims have."

Three years after our stepfather started molesting us, we told our mother. Mother had a classic reaction: "You never liked him. He's so good to you. You're just making this up." Years later, when I was in my thirties, she told us she had believed us and had in fact told him to stop.

Sometime in high school the molestation stopped, but he still used to stand in the doorway and watch us dress, or leave us weird notes. His intrusive behavior continues even to this day if we're not really strong about setting limits and boundaries. Mother

---

* Mary McGrath chose to use a pseudonym.

stayed married to him until she died last year. So we had to keep dealing with him.

I never had a warm relationship with my mother. It was mostly "Don't rock the boat." "Present this facade to the world and Mother will be happy." I never forgot the incest, but I did minimize it to please my mother for many years.

LIFE WAS DOING

I developed a victim stance in life. I married an alcoholic. Like a martyr I said, "You put up with. You hang in there." There was a whole lot of "I'll wait and see if this helps." I'd say, "It must be me. It must be how I keep house. It must be how I take care of the kids." I just kept waiting, and blaming myself. I was a co-alcoholic. I thought I could fix it: "I'll love him and he'll be fine."

My greatest denial of the incest had been presenting myself as this happy, bubbly kid. I did the same thing with my own family when I grew up. I presented myself to the world as a self-assured, fun, together person. "It doesn't matter what's really going on. Keep up appearances."

I did the same thing with the alcoholism that I did with the incest: Be active in church, be friendly with the neighbors. People were dumbfounded when they found out we had a problem.

I kept everything totally superficial. Life was doing. You got up and did what you had to around the house. You figured out bills and shopping and getting through the day. There were brief moments of intimacy, but intimacy wasn't something I thought of, or understood, or realized I needed.

The main exception was my sister. Be-cause of our common experience, I could be more real with her. And then there were my kids. I got a lot of my needs for closeness met with my kids. I still do, but that's shifted. I know now I can't own my kids.

MY BODY IS AS MUCH A PART OF ME AS MY HEAD AND HEART

I didn't feel associated with my body for many years. I was really all mental until my mid-thirties. I've brought my center down out of my head after ten years of body work. Now I know my body is as much a part of me as my head or my heart. And as I've gotten in touch with my body, I've gotten in touch with my feelings and vice versa.

I had been totally alienated from my feelings. That's how I protected myself all those years. It took me forever to feel a feeling, much less express it. People would say to me, "How do you feel?" and I'd say, "Well, I think . . ." It was like learning a totally different language. It was a process of getting things intellectually, then at a feeling level, and finally being able to act from that position.

I did not view myself as a sexual person. I was a virgin when I married. My sexual relationship in my marriage was good compared to other marriages I knew. I was orgasmic. My sex life seemed satisfactory to me. But I was shut down in terms of being able to *be* a sexual person. Sex was something you *did* and once in a while you enjoyed it. The message was "Don't be a sexual person," or "Be one, but only in a compartmentalized way." I mean, obviously, if I was going to get married, I was going to have sex.

There were prescribed things that were okay, but I wasn't willing to explore. My husband wasn't complaining. He was happy with the number of times we had sex. So there was nothing pushing me to move those boundaries. And that's how it was throughout an eighteen-year marriage.

COMING OUT

As my marriage ended, I fell in love with a woman, and that was like the change between night and day. There's change that comes slow and you work on it, and then there's change that's like a complete reversal. The very first time I was with this woman, I had no inhibitions, no guardedness.

I guess I thought, "If I can do this (be with a woman at all), then I can let this side of me down." I didn't have any problem feeling it was sick or immoral. I knew there would be problems as far as how the world perceived me, but I didn't have any other issues with lesbianism, even though I'd been a churchgoer all that time. It was like being let out of a cage, and suddenly I was in touch with a part of me that I didn't even know was there.

Now I enjoy my sexuality tremendously. If I feel it, I express it. Even if it's a hug or a kiss on the ear. I won't ever shut it down again. It's not that my lover always has to respond. It's just that I won't ever say, "I can't show this part of myself. She's had a hard day at the office." Life is so much more of a turn-on being in touch with that. I don't mean wanting sex ten times a day. I mean responding to things, visually and tactilely. It's put me in touch with my senses.

I WAS IN AND OUT OF THERAPY MOST OF THE TIME

Phase one of my healing was sharing it with my sister, never letting the memory get too far away from us. Phase two started when I was thirty-seven years old, and it's involved a good ten years of healing. During that time, if I felt like I needed to do body work, I'd work with a body work therapist. If I felt like I needed something else, I'd find the right person for that.

My first therapy experience was very cerebral, very verbal. We worked on feelings, but it was elementary. It probably was all I could handle. My therapist was a warm, nurturing, supportive person, and that's really what I needed at the time.

The second time, I was in couples therapy with my woman lover. That was a problem-solving kind of therapy.

At one point I did some body therapy work. I don't know if I would have made that leap if I hadn't been training to be a body worker myself. I knew those therapies existed, and I was willing to try it. But it was real scary.

I did work on a mat, trying to get in touch with the feelings in my body when my stepfather was about to molest me. I did lots of screaming and kicking. I remember at the time thinking, "This is dumb." But it helped me feel different *in* my body. I had real severe muscle spasms in my back on and off for years. They were crippling. They're almost totally gone now.

I did some rage work with Elisabeth Kübler-Ross. I used to think, "You've been through this and you can't even feel rage? You have no rage? I find that hard to believe!" But I was just terrified—knowing I couldn't feel it, but that it was there.

Elisabeth Kübler-Ross tends to attract people who have had trauma in their lives. There were people who had been battered as children, people who had lost children through murder and accidents, all kinds of things.

She has people work in a large group with telephone books and rubber hoses. Her basic theory is that if feelings aren't expressed, they're internalized, and that's what contributes to us being physically sick and having pain. And as we release our feelings, we begin to heal.

Doing the actual rage work wasn't scary. In fact, it was very exciting. It's such a safe environment with so much love, you have the feeling you can do or say anything. It's okay if you bash in your stepfather's face with a rubber hose. I remember thinking, "This isn't so bad. This isn't going to kill anybody." Every once in a while I'd stop, look around the room, and think, "No way, that didn't come from me!" I had totally shredded a Denver phone book, just obliterated it, and still more to come. I'd have to catch my breath or blow my nose, and I remember looking at the devastation and thinking, "My God! That was all inside!" I was flabbergasted at how much rage there was.

After all that release, I started having powerful dreams. In one, I was lying in bed as a teenager. I felt my stepdad was in the room. I'd always thought if I could only scream, I could stop it. And in the dream, I did. I literally did. I let out a piercing, bloodcurdling scream. I was able to scream and stop it.

I HAVE TAKEN CONTROL

There were times when I thought I was through the whole healing process. About fifteen of those times! I'd say to myself, "Now I've done incest. Now I'm through." I understand, finally, that you never really get to the end. Not until you die.

For instance, my mother's death brought up the whole new thing: What do I do with my stepfather now that she's dead? Do I take responsibility for his connection with the children? What limits do I set, and what do I do if he doesn't honor those limits?

I don't want a warm, friendly relationship with him. I don't. Even if he hadn't been my incest offender, I still wouldn't want it. What I'd like to have—the ideal—would be no funny energy with him, where I could see him, say hello and talk on a surface level, and not feel I have to watch where I stand. I still feel real vulnerable. I have to be constantly on guard: "Is he going to try to corner me and talk about something that will make me feel weird?"

He doesn't ever quit. I would tell him not to hug me, and so he would sit *way* down on the other end of the couch and pout. In front of a roomful of my children he would say, "I *hope* this is acceptable."

When my mother died, my stepfather starting sending me and my sister incest articles. I thought, "This might be his convoluted way of saying 'I'm sorry,'" but my feeling was, "This is more incest offense. If he has something to say, he needs to learn to say it. And if he's working through something, then the victim is not who he works it through with. He goes to the shrink and he pays good money. I'm not going to be his therapist."

I sent the article back and I said, "I have never been real clear with you about what the boundaries were. Now I'm going to spell them out. The boundaries are no hugging, no touching except for a handshake. No discussion or information about sex, sexual preference, incest, sexual assault of any kind. What is acceptable is, 'How is your job going? How are the kids? What's the weather?' It has to be within these boundaries; watch my lips. And if you cannot honor this, then I am ready to discontinue communication with you." I also told him, "I am not willing to work this through with you. If indeed you are trying to say 'I'm sorry,' then you need to get a therapist to do that with you." I put all that in a letter. My sister did the same thing, and we mailed them to him.

I got no reply, except my usual little Christmas check. That's been all.

I think the most important thing for incest families is to have no more secrets and no more "We're not going to talk about this." To keep silent is to continue to protect the offender. Part of the result of his abusive behavior is that he has to deal with the consequences within his own family. Not only for the sake of that family, but for the sake of ending incest in America, we need to quit having any secrets about it at all.

We need to quit taking care of anybody. If Mother can't handle it that's her problem. If the incest offender can't handle it, that's his problem. We as survivors have to do what we have to do.

HEALING IS SOMETHING I'VE INTEGRATED INTO MY LIFE

A big part of healing for me has been learning that I have power and options. I decided I didn't like not being responsible for my own life: "If he would just stop drinking. If she would only get her shit together." That was nice in one way—there was always someone else to blame. But it kept me stuck. Finally I got tired of blaming. I decided I wasn't going to be a victim anymore. And instead of saying "I want to survive this," I started to say "I want my life to be different." I wanted more than just to be able to go back to my hometown without throwing up. I wanted to make real changes.

I take a lot of responsibility for my own healing. It's been pretty continuous, not like a roller coaster, more like a steady level with a couple of high peaks. One thing that's been helpful to me lately is not to try so hard. What I say to myself is "I don't have to *do* anything, but I have to *be* open to my feelings and not shut down." *Trying* shut me down. It kept me feeling bad about myself: "I'm not doing enough. I'm not doing it right." I don't feel I have to push through things anymore. I just have to be open. Healing isn't separate anymore. It's just a regular part of life.

GIZELLE

Though I still become caught in fear and anger, each day I become more aware of the power I possess to choose love. The most powerful words given me during this painful process of healing came from Martin Luther King, Sr.: "No matter what you do to me, I will not give you the power to make me hate."

Gizelle is forty-two years old and lives in Santa Cruz, California.* She was born in Newton, Massachusetts, the second of four girls in an Italian Catholic family. Her father was a surgeon at a prominent New England hospital. Gizelle was dressed in Saks Fifth Avenue clothes, had ballet and piano lessons, and was sent to private schools and expensive colleges.

Gizelle has been married and divorced twice, and has a sixteen-year-old daughter, Adrienne. Gizelle has suffered much of her life with disabling illness. Just three and a half months before this interview took place, she remembered the violent rape she experienced at age three. She now understands that this caused the emotional and physical problems she has had all her life.†

---

* Gizelle wanted to use her own name, but couldn't for legal reasons. Of her pseudonym Gizelle says, "The name I have chosen belongs to a Canadian friend, a woman who is making her own healing journey from sexual abuse. Her story and mine are not the same; however, I have chosen her name (with her permission) so that I can honor yet another brave and beautiful woman. This lessens the pain of having my own name deleted."

---

† Since this interview, Gizelle has remembered other incidents of molestation that continued throughout her childhood.

461

I WAS SOUND ASLEEP IN MY ROOM

It was soon after I was born that my father went away to Burma and spent two years in a MASH unit in the jungle, putting together blown-up bodies. When he came back, he was unable to work. He was in a lot of emotional difficulty. One of his best friends had committed suicide right after the war.

I really don't think my mother and he could relate when he came home. They hadn't seen each other in almost three years. She was expecting her husband to come home, and that's not really what came back.

And I was very small. All I had in my mind were pictures of Daddy. I was very open and very loving. And so, as I gather from my mother, he spent a great deal of time taking care of me. I was his human link to affection and comfort.

The rape happened the month of my third birthday, right after he returned. I was sound asleep in my bedroom. I woke up with my father's penis in my mouth. The impact of it thrust my head back and literally cut off my wind and I thought I was dying. I didn't know what was in my mouth. I didn't know what a penis was. I just woke up with this whatever-it-was shoved down my throat, suffocating, gagging.

And then he took his penis out of my mouth and began raping me vaginally. As soon as his penis left my mouth, I threw up. I didn't make a sound. I remember him banging, trying to get into me, and then he ripped me open and actually entered me and I let out a terrified scream. Within seconds he was gone, and I was alone and the room was empty.

And then within seconds after that, my mother came into the room and put on the light. She found me lying in bed covered with blood and vomit all over the sheets. And she went into immediate hysteric denial. She wouldn't compute. She refused to compute. So what she computed, in her craziness, was that I had done this to me. That I had somehow done this to myself.

She started screaming at me, "Bad, evil, wicked child." Even at that point, I still had my knowledge that I hadn't done this. I knew my father had been the one who had done it by his smell and the whole feel of him, even though it was dark.

And so I screamed back to my mother, "Mommy I didn't do it. I didn't do it. It was Daddy." Then my mother was hitting me, over and over again. "Don't you ever say that again. You lying, evil, dirty, filthy child." She just kept hitting me and hitting me.

She cleaned up the sheets, put me back in bed. She was still screaming, she was still hysterical. Through a lot of the beating I maintained, "I didn't do it, Mommy. I didn't do it." It's amazing that at age three, in the face of being raped and beaten, I was able to say that I was innocent.

Then my mother left the room. She was still screaming at my father. He hit her across the face, said for her to go to her room. "I'll take care of it." And then the next memory I have is my father, whose office was downstairs in our house, sewing my vagina back up, without any anesthetic. I was never taken to the hospital.

He put me back into bed. Then he left the room and I was alone. And I remember feeling my bed was all sticky and wet. That must have been the blood. I was a little girl, and I was thinking, "I'm a bad girl. I got my bed all sticky and wet." So by then I was beginning to buy the other reality.

Suddenly, as I was lying there, my grandmother, who was living with us, came quietly creeping down the hall and into my room. She put her hand on my head. My feeling as I reexperienced it was that if my grandmother had not come in and put her hand on my head, I was going into this no-man's-land where I might never come back. But when she put her hand on my head, it brought me back. I kept saying "Nanny, I'm a bad girl." She didn't say a word. She just kept stroking my head.

The next morning my mother and father went away on a vacation. I was left with my grandmother. I remember going to get out of bed. I wanted to play. But I couldn't move and I couldn't get out of bed. I said to my grandmother, "What happened? I can't get out of bed. I hurt." And her message to me was "Don't talk about it. Pretend it didn't happen. I'll take care of you. It'll go away." So I forgot it.

IT ALL FITS NOW

The effects of the abuse manifested through my body. I sleepwalked. I had high fevers that were life-threatening. And they could never find a cause. I had nightmares. I had severe asthma. I would just stop breathing. I was at the doctor's all the time. I was in the bed, always sick. My legs were turned out so badly that I could not walk without tripping over my own feet. I had to wear corrective shoes. It all fits now.

I had a great deal of compulsive behavior as a child. I structured my world so incredibly. I had to open and close doors twice and I'd have to hear them click. I had to do everything in pairs. I made everybody re-peat things twice and I repeated everything twice. I developed a compulsive head spasm. The feeling was always that something was out of place and that if I could just shake my head, everything would click back into focus. It was always a feeling that something was just out of whack. So I developed all of these things to give some shape to my reality, to create some boundaries and some safety.

I split my father into two different people, because there was no other way to sit across the breakfast table from him. The man who came down and sat at the kitchen table was my father. The man who came in the middle of the night and molested me was a shadow. I made him into someone else.

And as I split him into two, I split myself into two. There was the little girl whose father taught her to ride a bike, who got A's and became a perfectionist. And then there was the little girl who played in the attic, felt that she was dying, wanted to commit suicide, had nightmares. But I never could speak of her. Her voice had been taken away.

I felt caught, trapped in my body. That's continued into adulthood. I never heard any messages from my body. I would be really sick and I'd stagger around and go to work. I made a lifetime dedication of not listening to my body, because if I had, I would have had to hear that I was raped, and I couldn't do that and survive.

I developed an eating disorder when I was eighteen, which they now call anorexia nervosa. I was at college. I felt obese if I weighed over ninety-five pounds. When I ate, I would eat alone. I would never let anyone see me eat. I'd starve myself. I'd have a hard-boiled egg and half a piece of toast and that would be my quota for the day. And I would do that for three or four days. Then I would go to the store for a quart of ice cream and eat it all in one sitting.

I understand now it was a terror of becoming a woman. That was just the age when I was beginning to integrate my sexuality. As I started to go out with men, the terror was there. There was no way to deal with it but to somehow stop myself from being a woman. If you stop eating, you don't have hips, you don't have breasts, your periods stop. You are not a woman; therefore you can't have sex, you can't be raped.

It wasn't until I was twenty-three and I got pregnant with my daughter that I began to eat like a normal human being. Having a healthy child became the most important thing to me, and so I taught myself to eat right.

I OWE MY DAUGHTER MY LIFE

From the moment my daughter was born, my instincts kicked in, and I was able to nurture her and be intimate with her. Somehow my love and my desire that this child would not be hurt were strong enough to overcome the obstacles that stopped me in other areas of my life. And I don't know how. I literally can say I owe my daughter my life because she awakened that ability to mother. Time and again, when for myself I would have died, I chose to live for her. I knew that somehow this had to stop with me and that I would not pass it on to my daughter. And I didn't even know what the "it" was.

I remember very distinctly that when my daughter was the age I had been when I was raped, I began to distance myself from her. She came to me in tears and said,

"Mommy, you don't like me anymore." I put my arms around her and I said, "Adrienne, you've got to understand. Something happened to Mommy when she was very little. And you remind me of what happened. It's not you. You're fine. I love you. It's me. There's something in Mommy. I was hurt very badly when I was young, and that's why I'm not holding you." That's all I could tell her. I didn't even remember the rape at the time.

I COULDN'T GO ON

When Adrienne was five, I developed chronic back and hip problems. I became crippled by the pain. It got worse and worse. I was in and out of the hospital for back surgery. I lost the feeling in my left leg. I was in traction. And I was a single mother when this was happening.

I knew it was all connected to what was happening emotionally, so I went for counseling. But whatever I did, I was besieged with terror associated with severe nerve pain in my pelvis. I had anxiety attacks so bad I couldn't move. I was in severe depression. I cried all the time. I couldn't even read a book. I couldn't sleep. I couldn't eat.

One morning, when I was thirty-eight and my daughter was almost twelve, I took a lot of pills. I never said anything to anybody. I just knew I couldn't go on in the kind of pain I was in, that I had tried everything I could think of. As I said, it was not just the physical pain, but the terror that hooked into the physical pain. The two completely overwhelmed me.

That suicide attempt didn't work, and I went into counseling again. The pain got worse and worse. I started receiving epidural blocks, which alleviated some of the pain. And they gave me antidepressants.

All through this, I was working with my dreams. I went to an American Indian power circle and something happened, like a dam breaking, and I started crying. There was an older Mexican-Indian woman there who worked with me. I did Lomi body work —a combination of breath and deep tissue massage. And I started moving through some of the pain.

And then everything froze and I began to get severe nerve pain in my neck, and a terror that was as bad as the terror around the pain in my pelvis. It totally immobilized me again. I couldn't even mother during that time. My daughter was mothering me. I felt like I was destroying my daughter's life. I felt guilty for being alive. I made the decision once again to kill myself. That led to suicide attempt number four.

This time all I can say is that my survival was a miracle. I took enough pills and alcohol to kill me twice over. I said a prayer just before I took the drugs. It was "I no longer can live and believe in a God of suffering." One of my last acts was to tear that God down, and I said, "If there is another reason for me being alive besides extended suffering, then I surrender into your hands."

I was not found for twenty-four hours. That was how I planned it. I was in a motel and the maid found me. I was in a coma. And they rushed me to the hospital. They said I wasn't going to live, and that if I did live, I wouldn't have a brain.

The doctors did a last-ditch measure where they took all the blood out of my body and recirculated it through a charcoal screen, and then put it back in my body. It worked, and I started to stabilize. The third day of the coma they said I would live, but that I might be a basket case. And then on the seventh day, I came out of the coma.

I had a vision as I was coming out of the coma which has stayed with me through my entire healing process. I had a vision of a tree which was in blossom. All over the tree were the most incredibly beautiful flowers I had ever seen in my life. And the tree was growing out of the desert.

I came out of the coma and I did have a brain.

Unbeknownst to me, my daughter had sat by my bed for seven days and seven nights. She was driving herself to the hospital. She was fourteen years old at the time. It was her life force that connected with mine and brought me back. I felt it the minute I came to. That was a year and a half ago.

WE BOTH NEEDED HELP

The psychiatrist gave me a list of counselors I could see and sent me home. I looked at Adrienne and I saw that she had no energy left whatsoever, that she had used every ounce she had to bring me back. So I took her by the hand and got in the car and drove down to the Parents Center and walked in the door and said, "We both need counseling. We both need help." I hooked my daughter up immediately. She had a lot of anger about the situation and we had to work that out.

Then I looked at the list the psychiatrist had given to me and I called a therapist and got started. I hooked up with Frank Lanou, who has been my counselor and guide through this whole thing.*

---

* Frank Lanou is using his own name.

It was his belief in my strength that kept me moving forward. He'd say, "Look at what you've done. You're an incredibly strong woman." Time and time again when I lost belief in my healing, Frank would say: "Trust your process, *allow* it to lead you. *Trust* yourself, listen to yourself." The greatest gift Frank gave me was his unwavering faith in the wisdom and power of my own healing spirit. He listened so carefully to my feelings that I began to trust them, which led me to my discovery.

By spring I knew I was getting very close. The anxiety attacks were overwhelming again. A psychiatrist friend suggested I go back on antidepressants and I said, "No, I'm not going to put this to sleep again. If I do, it's going to kill me."

I asked Adrienne's stepfather if she could move in with him for a while. I said, "Look, I've *got* to do this. And it's too hard on Adrienne." The three of us talked about it, and she went to live with him.

OH MY GOD, IT'S MY FATHER

It was during that same month that I started to have the flashbacks. I was in the hospital getting my last siege of tests. I had needles stuck in my back. They had me on a drug and I started freaking out. I started calling everybody motherfuckers, trying to pull the needles out, screaming, "Stop it now. Get out of my body. Take the needles out! I don't want to do it anymore." They had to hold me down to finish the test.

When I got back to my room, I somehow had the presence of mind to know that I was having flashbacks. I called Frank and he came to the hospital. I was extremely suicidal. All I could say was, "Frank, it's con-nected with the drug. I'm having flashbacks and I don't know what's happening." So I told the doctor to discontinue the drug, and I checked myself out of the hospital.

Within a week, Frank and I did a five-hour session and it all came up. We used a drug called MDMA as a therapeutic tool.* I had been reading about this drug, and how it specifically worked in cases of severe repression by lowering the level of fear. And I said, "Frank, I want to use this, because whatever this is, I can't get close enough. The terror is too great." And Frank, who had never used drugs in his therapy, said, "I'll be with you."

The night before I planned to take the drug, I gave him a tape to listen to. I make a tape of all my dreams as soon as I wake up. And I just pulled one tape out, and I didn't even know what was on it, and I said, "Frank, my gut says for you to listen to this tape because the key is in it."

On the tape was a dream where I had been raped and I was a little girl. This little girl who was autistic keeps saying, "I love you, Daddy. I love you, Daddy." And everybody thinks she's crazy or retarded. And I tell the people who come to take her away: "There's nothing wrong with her mind. She's been severely traumatized. If you take her and put her in a mental hospital, she'll never recover. She's got to stay with me because I have the key to her healing." And at the very end of the dream, I say, "I feel like

---

* Although Gizelle had a powerful healing experience, MDMA is not always helpful in recovering memories. Other women have had negligible or negative reactions resulting in severe emotional stress. When Gizelle used MDMA it was legal and she had the support of a skilled therapist. At present, use of the drug is illegal.

I've been raped." They're the last words on the tape.

So Frank comes to the session with this tape. I took the MDMA and within twenty minutes, it all started coming up. First I said, "I feel numb." Then I said, "I feel trapped." Then I said, "I see this little girl, but she's on the other side of a screen and I can't get to her." We worked out how to get to the little girl. And as soon as I got to her, I said, "Frank, this sounds crazy, but I feel like I'm being raped. That's the feeling in my body." And then I said, "Who would do this to me?" And then the next moment, I said, "Oh my God, it's my father." And every part of my body just knew it.

But even then, the denial was so strong. Frank said to me, "What's happening?" And I said, "I don't know!" And then I'd go into hysteria where I couldn't breathe. And then I'd start choking. And then I would go numb and I wouldn't feel anything. We went around like that for three hours. I said to Frank, "You know what I'm feeling? I feel like I'm lying."

The next day, I called my father and said, "Dad, something happened between you and me. I was three years old and I was really hurt. Tell me! Tell me what it was." And he immediately said, "Nothing," but his voice started getting really shaky and weird. So then I said to him, "I know something happened. It was after you came back from the war, Dad. I know something happened."

So he rattled off all these things: "Well, there was one time I gave you a shot. And I started coming near you and you started screaming so bad I couldn't give it to you." And I said, "Nope, Dad. That wasn't it." And he said, "Well, there was a time you had a really bad asthma attack and we had to take you to the hospital and put you in an oxygen tent." And I said, "Nope." And he said, "I have all these things it could be, and you're not listening to me." And I said, "I'm listening, but they aren't what happened." It ended by him saying he would think about it. He said, "I'll talk with your mother and we'll see if we can come up with what it could have been."

Then I started feeling crazy. I felt that way on and off until the second MDMA session, when I had total recall. Within five hours the whole thing just came back, three-dimensional and solid. I remembered it all—not only the rape, but what my mother said, my grandmother, the doors opening and closing, who did what, when, how, where, exact words. It's all on tape. I'm talking like a three-year-old. And then I'm my mother, using my mother's voice, her exact tone of voice, the words she was using. It's like it's all recorded in your skin, in your body.

This time I believed it right away. I knew it wasn't the drug. It was the kind of feeling that can't be denied. Every time I'd take a breath it went right to my core. I knew this was what I'd been looking for. It was instant click. This is it!! I got it!

"DAD, YOU MOLESTED ME"

After I discovered the details of the rape, I called up my father again and said, "Dad, I know what happened. You molested me." I nearly vomited getting the words out. And he said I was wrong. And I said to him, "Dad, I want you to know that I understand the context in which it happened. I understand you'd just come back from the war. My heart is breaking because I know the torment you were in at the time, and I know that you loved me. But I need to heal this."

Then he reversed everything he had said to me about the war, and he said, "There was nothing wrong with my mind when I came back from the war. I was perfectly fine. There has never been anything wrong with my mind. You're crazy."

Then my mother got on the phone and she was hysterical: "How can you say this about your father? How can you possibly say this?" And I said, "Mother, those are the exact words you screamed at me forty years ago. And they didn't make it go away then. And they can't make it go away now. This is what happened, Mom. I was molested. And your denial and my denial is not going to change it." She screamed that I was crazy and I needed to be institutionalized. And then she hung up the phone.

Then my father sent me a photograph. It was of me, before the molestation happened. I'm sitting on my mother's lap on a swing in the backyard. It was yellowed. He must have carried it in his wallet all those years. And he enclosed a postcard I had written as a teenager when he had sent me to Europe, saying I was having a wonderful time. And he enclosed a picture of the church. All in one letter! And he said, "See this little girl. See how happy she was. Does this look like a girl who was molested? And does this postcard sound like it comes from someone who's miserable? You were a very happy child growing up. An evil psychiatrist has implanted a hypnotic suggestion into your mind. As your father, and as a professional, I *demand* that you get a new psychiatrist, an *M.D.* And I want a letter from him stating that you are in his care. If you do not do this immediately, I will sever all further relationship with you. Love, Dad."

I wrote back and said, "First of all, it was not hypnotic implantation. I remember being molested. It's that simple. I remember how and when and where it happened. It's instant recall, Dad. Secondly, I'm not going to change counselors." I told my father that I was going to heal this wound, and that I'd do it with him or without him.

I'm glad I confronted him when I did. The initial step of picking up that phone and saying "I know" was empowering to me. It's moved me very quickly. I got on with my own healing, without wasting a lot of time fantasizing that my father would help me.

I NEEDED SOMEONE TO LISTEN

The immediate thing when I first realized I was molested was a feeling "I've got to talk." My mouth went twenty-four hours a day. I felt if I couldn't talk about it, I'd go crazy. When you have been sexually abused and your voice has been taken away, the child in you needs to speak. My child had been silenced for forty years. I began to hear her crying out in me: "Someone has to listen to me. No one's ever listened to me. No one's ever believed me." And that was her first need—to be listened to—if she was going to heal.

By that time, I had made a few good friends who stood by me. I started with a very sparse network of support, which has since spiraled, one person at a time. I felt so blessed with the support I had. I went home and made a list of all my dearest friends, female and male, and I said, "This is what I'm discovering. And I need someone to listen. I'm calling all my friends. I'm going to structure seven days, and I want you to tell me what day you can come, and if you can give me a commitment to come every Monday between two and four, it'd be great." And people came through. I talked and I talked. About my feelings. About the molestation. About my health. About my suicides. About my father. Giving it form. Giving it shape. Naming it. Feeling it. I just needed to have someone listen to me.

HEALING WITH MEN

If you can't be with men when you're healing, it's fine. You may need to get your power back with women. But there's a real treasure in doing some healing with men. It allows you to directly and dynamically work out your feelings toward your abuser. If you're able to speak your truths with a male friend, and hold your own, and ask for comfort, there's a real empowerment there, because you're doing it with the gender that has taken your power.

And for the man, it makes him aware of this whole issue and how it's affected women. It encourages him to look at himself and to start his own healing if he's out of balance.

Anybody that sits with you during your healing is going to start healing themselves. It just works that way. It will be a healing for him, and hopefully he'll take it to another man. And that's how it will spread.

It has to. Because now it's "We rape your children in war. You rape our children in war. We throw a bomb at you. You throw a bomb at us." And if we as women stop at the stage where we're out just to cut off the nuts of all our persecutors, we're stopping short of our goal to heal ourselves, the earth, our children, and our world.

Men are out of synch and they need to be healed. We can't keep them out. We have to heal ourselves, but we need to bring them into the circle to be healed. If the men don't get healed, rape is going to continue. And they can't be healed through hatred. It's a vision I have.

I JUST KEEP BREATHING

I've gone through periods in the healing process where the terror is so great that I avoid breathing. I breathe very shallowly to avoid breathing into the pain. But then I have to lie down and breathe into it. When I breathe into it, I feel like I want to throw up.

What I've learned is to use my hands to massage any place that's tight or blocked. I breathe from my diaphragm and I use my hands to release the energy. If I feel a block in my throat, I put one hand there and another hand on my solar plexus. And I try to feel the channel between those two points. Then I'll put my hand over my heart, or on top of my head. It's pure instinct when I do it.

And as I breathe, I give my breath a sound. I just let out whatever sound comes out of my mouth. I don't plan it. I let my body speak. I give my child a voice. Because I was orally molested, my throat will often close up when I do this. It's like the penis is in my mouth again, and I'll gag or choke. Then I put my hand on my throat and keep my throat as open as I can, as I make the sound. Sometimes it comes out like the child is crying or like a lullaby, like the mother in me responding to my child's cry.

Music is another thing that's helped. I got a Walkman and I change the music on it all the time. Whatever sounds my child needs to hear—sometimes it's Bach's Mass in B Minor, all the angels in heaven singing through my ears, other times it may be gentle music, or sound of the ocean, or wolves howling. I've extended that into the use of my own voice. I don't know what to call it—it's not really singing, it's not really choking, it's just letting the sound out—but I do it now almost everyday. I do it with drums, or I do it with rattles. Music is very powerful—the ability to move it out through sound. There's a lot of power there to heal.

MY OUTRAGE COMES FROM LOVE

I had to learn to honor all my feelings, especially the anger and the outrage. I was outraged not only against my father, but against all of the men who are doing this.

This friend of mine said, "You know that you created this because you are the creator of your universe and your soul set this energy in motion. So take responsibility for it and stop mewling and whining and bellyaching about it. Just forgive and go on."

And I got *so* pissed! I was just choked with anger. When you're feeling anger, you need to honor that. If you try to get to the forgiveness before you deal with the anger, you're going to fuck the whole thing up. You have to work from where you are in your belly, not from where you think you should be in your head.

I go through real revenge periods. I imagine walking into my parents' house with a shotgun aimed right at my father's balls. "Okay, Dad. Don't move an inch. Not one step, you sucker. I'm gonna take 'em off one at a time. And I'm gonna take my sweet time about it, too!"

But at the same time, I believe that the only way to stop abuse is to come from a consciousness of love and forgiveness. Hate cannot be stopped with hate. Abuse cannot be stopped with abuse. That does not mean you don't stop the people who are doing this, or that you stop prosecuting them. But you do it from a place of love. If I didn't feel love for the child in me who had been raped, I would not have this outrage.

Sometimes I sit here and feel such compassion for my father, I weep. Other times I see myself taking a gun and shooting his balls off. I am letting it all come right on through. And the more I allow all of it to come up, the more I find myself moving toward love. The more I block the rage, the more I stay stuck. And so for me they're both right there. I reconcile it by saying I trust the process. I trust the validity of my outrage. The outrage is because I honor and value and love life.

SHE ALMOST LOST HER MOTHER

The incest affected every aspect of my relationship with Adrienne. We both went through a lot of sadness, a lot of aching. She almost lost her mother to madness and to suicide.

Everything would have been better if I'd known this twenty years ago. The one thing I couldn't give my daughter was my happiness, my love of myself. I was able to give her a love for herself, a feeling for her strength, but there was a lot of joy we were never able to share. I weep for that. However, it's coming. It's down the road.

And you know, I see all I couldn't give her and she sees all I gave her. That's a blessing. My daughter is a very strong, creative, emotionally healthy human being. I feel proud to watch her becoming a strong woman who refuses to be compromised or silenced.

My first feeling was not to tell Adrienne about the rape, to protect my father, who is her grandfather. And then I thought, "No, that's where this is passed on. This is the denial that allows this to happen. My daughter has a right to know the truth of what's going on."

So I sat down with her and told her, and she wept with me. We both sat there and cried. One of her first responses was, "How were you able to survive that and not become evil yourself?" And I didn't have an answer.

The rifts in our relationship are already mending. I do my work. She does her work. When we get together, each time it's shifting and moving, and there's a mutual healing and a mutual honoring that's starting to happen. She's doing a lot of writing about my attempted suicide, about my surgeries, about her love for me, about her anger, the whole nine yards. We share our writings. We talk. If I can mend me, we can mend the relationship. All I have to do is heal myself. In the process of healing myself, the relationship can heal.

EVERYTHING IN ME HAS CHANGED

Since it's come out, it's been the difference of night and day, of living in hell and living on the earth. Everything in me has changed—my perceptions of myself, of others, of the earth, of my power, of my strength, of my abilities, of my sanity—everything. It's been so fast, I can't believe it. In just three and a half months, there's incredible healing.

For so much of my life, I have fought death wishes. Now I feel grounded, very connected to the earth, very determined to stay. The purpose of my living is to help other men and women heal this, to give it a voice. Nothing is going to take me off of this one. Before, the thing that kept me here, despite all the pain and agony, was my daughter, and then even that wasn't enough.

My strength and energy to deal with my life is returning. My neck has begun to unlock. I've begun to feel a looseness in my hips that I never felt before. I feel life moving through my body. I walk around and say, "God, this is what life is about!" I am just deluged with feelings in my body—of warmth, of movement, of connectedness. I've never had them before. There is nothing that can't be healed in the spirit of life.

I really can't tell you how far my body can heal. I know I'll be able to free up my neck and the strength in my arms. As far as my back goes, there's been a lot of cutting down there, so I'm not sure. But I do know that I will heal physically enough to be able to lead a productive, full, and happy life, even if I have residual pain.

THERE'S A GREAT DEAL OF MAGIC IN THIS HEALING PROCESS

When I get into a crisis now, instead of saying, "Oh my God, I'm never going to heal," I see that it's like layers, and the more I work with it, the more they keep coming around. And even though it's like "But I was feeling good two days ago and now I'm shaking and crying and I can't sleep," I'm beginning to see that I'm not coming back to the same place, I'm coming back at a different level. It's a circling, an up and down, and I have to be with it, and ride it, and trust it. When I reach the next level where the tears are, where the fear is, where the tiredness is, I have to trust in my life energy —that where I am is where I need to be. And by being there as fully as I possibly can, I move to the next step.

I feel there's a great deal of magic involved in this healing process. And what I mean by magic is that the old ways of healing, that have been lost, are waking up. I'm awakening in my cells a lot of that old knowledge. It comes from the earth, from the spirit of the earth. It's the knowledge of women who have healed through the centuries. It's very mysterious and it's very in our gut. It doesn't come from books. It doesn't come from medicine. It doesn't channel through churches, or through yoga teachers, or through anything like that. It's ancient traditions that were passed down from mother to daughter until they were lost through witch hunts and the systematic elimination of women healers.

This knowledge connects with the ca-pacity to heal the rift that has the world in crisis, that has us in danger of extinction. It's the healing power of mother earth. It's been taken away and lost. And She's coming back through us now.

Sometimes when I think that one man can molest thirty children, I feel hopeless. When I get in that space, I have to get in contact with the power of the Mother. She could line up a hundred bleeding women and Her power could touch each of those women and they could heal. Only She is more powerful than the forces of destruction and death.

To me She is the sweetest force, the most gentle healing force there is. She's so sweet it's almost too much to take, it's almost unbearable. And She's very powerful. This is the kind of healing force that heals so gently. It's like a feather. And I feel very strongly that She is what's needed to heal me and to heal all the destruction upon this earth.

PART SIX

HONORING THE TRUTH: A RESPONSE TO THE BACKLASH

"Honoring the Truth" is a response to the current backlash against adult survivors of child sexual abuse. If you've watched TV, listened to the radio, or read newspapers or magazines in the past two years, it's likely that you've heard about the "false memory syndrome" and have witnessed attacks on survivors' memories and credibility. It is these attacks we are responding to here.

As in the rest of *The Courage to Heal,* we have included the experiences of survivors as well as practical self-help information. Unlike the rest of the book, however, we also incorporate here the work of therapists, researchers, and other experts—and more than a hundred footnotes—to place this backlash in a historical and political perspective.*

A number of survivors and professionals have read "Honoring the Truth." Most appreciated having clear information and an analysis of the issues. One

---

* In writing *The Courage to Heal,* we listened to survivors of child sexual abuse and presented what we learned in a clear, practical, and respectful way. In writing "Honoring the Truth," we again listened to survivors, as well as therapists who work with survivors, researchers, and other professionals and activists whose views have very much informed our thinking. We thank all of you who have written and spoken—publicly and privately. We also thank all those who contributed to this section by generously sharing both information and feedback. See the Acknowledgments on p. 9.

survivor wrote to us, "I felt a lot of the cloudiness of the issue fall away—I felt reassured and validated." Another said, "I am not as likely to get sucked into the fear and doubt that the backlash is trying to perpetuate." Yet this same survivor said it had been a lot harder to read than she had thought it would be:

> If I had read this in 1988 at the beginning of my healing, I would have been overwhelmed and fearful. Hell, it is five years later and I'm still a bit overwhelmed. It is difficult to hear that there is an entire organization working against me and my healing. For me, survivor work is basically something I do on my own. It isn't political; it isn't a matter of social responsibility; it's simply living or not living. Now, however, I understand that there is much more at stake. Staying in my closet of isolation was certainly challenged by reading it.

There is material in "Honoring the Truth" that may be deeply disturbing to you. We have included information about the patterns and behavior of perpetrators. We have also documented the extensive backlash against survivors. This information may feel distressing or overwhelming to you. Memories and feelings from your original abuse could be restimulated. For this reason, we want to stress that reading this section is *not* a required part of the healing process. The way you read it—or whether you read it at all—is up to you. If you're struggling to keep your equilibrium as it is, you may not want to delve into information that could distress you further. If, on the other hand, the backlash has already upset you, you may feel less threatened if you educate yourself about the forces behind it.

If material disseminated by the backlash has you confused, worried, or angry, you may want to turn right to the suggestions in "Personal Strategies for Dealing with the Backlash" on page 522 or to "Rachel's Story" on page 524. If you're looking for a social, political, or historical perspective, start at the beginning. Throughout, we present accurate information about sexual abuse, memory, the impact of trauma, and healing.

As with the rest of *The Courage to Heal,* check in with yourself as you read. If you find yourself spacing out or feeling overwhelmed, take a break, put the book down, or turn to a different section. Skip any parts that contain more information than you want. Read a little bit now and more later. Or save this entire section for another time. The choice is up to you.

THE EMERGING BACKLASH

Since 1992 we have watched with growing concern the emerging backlash against survivors of child sexual abuse, their supporters, and the significant social progress they have made made. There has been a barrage of articles, magazine stories, and radio and TV talk shows that have attacked the credibility of sexual abuse survivors, their therapists, and support books such as *The Courage to Heal.* Headlines like "Repressed Memories, Ruined Lives," "Beware the Incest Survivor Machine," and "When Memory Holds a Family Hostage" have appeared in newspapers across the country.[1] A typical article began:

> This is a series about people who say it didn't happen, people whose grown children entered psychotherapy or counseling and ended up accusing their parents of incest or even satanic ritual abuse. Speaking in the past tense of families that were once close and loving—but now are ripped to shreds—these parents believe their pain is because of a type of treatment gone awry: recovered memory therapy.[2]

Another started even more bluntly:

> You've raised them, praised them, wiped their tears and noses, and finally bid your kids farewell on their voyage to adulthood. Now they're back . . . to accuse you of rape.[3]

Many of those who challenge the credibility of survivors claim that recovered memories of child sexual abuse are untrue, that substantial numbers of people are falsely accused, and that those who say they are survivors often have been misled—or even brainwashed—by naive or manipulative therapists, authors, and book publishers.

Initially we thought the wisest response was to ignore these attacks, that the obvious truth of child sexual abuse would prevail. But to our dismay, highly biased stories, lacking in historical context or political analysis, kept appearing in major newspapers across the country. Story after story passed off nearly identical quotes, distortions, and misinformation as fact. *The Courage to Heal* and other books were quoted out of context. Studies on the nature of memory were misrepresented. Extreme cases of abuse were presented as the norm so as to provoke disbelief about child sexual abuse. And stories of family strife were almost always told from the perspective of the people accused.

Most of the coverage has been extremely adversarial, belittling survivors, depicting them as gullible victims, vengeful children, or simply crazy. Unfortunately, survivors have heard this all too often.

As the backlash became a major media event, we began to hear from survivors, many of them alarmed by this nationwide assault on their integrity. One survivor wrote:

---

[1] *The San Jose Mercury News,* October 11, 1992, p. 21; *The New York Times Book Review,* January 3, 1993, p. 1; and *The San Francisco Examiner,* April 4, 1993, p. A-15.

[2] *San Francisco Examiner,* April 4, 1993, p. A-15.

[3] *The Cleveland Plain Dealer,* May 17, 1992.

I was shocked and angered at the attacks against survivors and those who support survivors. The articles attacked so much of what I have gained strength from.

Some survivors have been deeply distressed by the hostility of the backlash. Others, especially those far along in their healing, have not been personally shaken by these attacks. They recognize the serious threat that such attitudes pose, but they have been able to maintain their equilibrium in the midst of this storm.

But for those new to the healing process or just beginning to sort through their histories, these public attacks on their credibility have been particularly devastating. To be suffering from intrusive flashbacks and frightening memories and then to be told that you're making it up—not just by your family, but by the national media—can make you feel that you are under siege. One survivor said simply, "It's horrible to be uncovering memories in the face of a society that's attacking you."

The questions raised by the backlash feed on the self-doubts that are a natural part of the healing process. Many survivors have spent their lives pretending the abuse didn't happen, wishing it hadn't happened, or hearing their families tell them that they're crazy. In such circumstances it can be exceedingly difficult to accept and believe that the abuse really took place.[4] And now, bombarded with

reports of "false memories," survivors may find it even harder to trust themselves.

The fact that the public debate mirrors so much of the pain that survivors have known in their families makes it even more difficult. One woman explained, "For me this all goes back to my childhood, when I tried to tell and nobody believed me." Another said:

This is a new page in my family's sick history. My father has gotten wind of this. He's called a family meeting and he wants to take a lie detector test. It's such a joke. We haven't had a family meeting in thirty years. We've never been a family.

For many survivors, it's as if the abuse were happening all over again. Only this time, it's not just their own families; it's talk-show programs on the radio, it's television, it's newspaper articles, neighbors, and sometimes even friends. The trauma is retriggered, and feelings about the original abuse come rushing to the surface. One survivor explained:

I feel like there's this sword of Damocles hanging over my head and the rope keeps fraying, and at any moment the sword is going to drop. It feels dangerous and scary, just like the original abuse.

Many survivors have been concerned about the impact this public wave of denial will have on their healing. They've expressed how excruciating it is to have their hard work in healing—and in changing the attitudes in our culture—undermined. One woman said:

---

[4] For a more thorough description of the role of doubt in the healing process, see "Believing It Happened," on p. 96. And if you find yourself doubting your memories, see p. 78.

The attacks being made on survivors and those who help them really scare me. It is frightening to think that therapists and people who help survivors could come under such pressure—legal and otherwise—that they would no longer be able to provide their services. It feels like a real war.

And another:

The recent surge of attacks may cause an untold number of survivors to continue to suffer in silence, thereby protecting their abusers . . . and effectively perpetuating the already out-of-control cycle of abuse in this country.

Other survivors have been angry and asked what they could do to fight back. Still others have asked us, as authors of *The Courage to Heal,* for support and leadership:

On Saturday, I got a letter from my father urging me to "put aside my anger and bias" and read a pile of crap he sent me about "false memories." For me, receiving the materials felt like an assault. I am hoping you can make a public response to some of this trash.

It was because of letters like these, and out of concern for the impact of this backlash on all survivors, that we decided to respond.

Our goals here are fourfold. First, we want to reassure you and offer you support —to remind you that you can trust yourself, your perceptions, your body, your memories —and to let you know, once more, that you're not alone. Second, by putting this current backlash into historical perspective and analyzing some of its tactics, we hope to give you a deeper understanding and insight into the nature of these attacks. Third, we want to help you cope with any personal impact you may be feeling. If you are confused, are questioning your memories, or are angry and want to know what you can do, we'll offer specific suggestions. And finally, we will recommend some future directions for moving forward in a positive and respectful way.

A LITTLE HISTORY

Since 1860, child abuse has been discovered and then discredited every 35 years by the most visionary clinicians of the day, each faced with the alternative of denouncing the discovery or succumbing to scorn and disgrace.[5]

—Roland Summit

This is not the first time survivors of child sexual abuse have been told they were lying, misguided, vindictive, imagining it, wanting it, or just plain crazy.

Early in his career, Sigmund Freud identified child sexual abuse as the cause of much mental and emotional illness in adulthood. By listening to his patients (a revolutionary idea in itself), he learned that many of the women and men he was treating had been sexually traumatized.[6] Many had initial amnesia for the trauma, but when they were

---

[5] Roland Summit, "The Centrality of Victimization: Regaining the Focal Point of Recovery for Survivors of Child Sexual Abuse," *Psychiatric Clinics of North America* 12, no. 2 (June 1989), p. 427. (Roland Summit is clinical associate professor of psychiatry at the UCLA School of Medicine.)

[6] Freud published his findings, "The Aetiology of Hysteria," in 1896. His theory was based on his work with twelve women and six men.

able to recall the events and talk about them, their contemporary symptoms subsided. When he put forth this discovery, Freud was criticized and ridiculed by his colleagues. Ultimately he recanted, and proposed instead that his patients had either fantasized the sex or had desired it.[7] Thus scientific knowledge was put on a fast train backwards, and sexually abused children—and the adults they grew up to be—were left bereft.[8]

But Freud is not the only pioneer whose discoveries of child abuse were rejected. Even earlier, in 1860, French forensic physician Ambroise Tardieu published an exposé on battered children and later one on rape and child sexual abuse. His findings were immediately denounced by his contemporaries.

Also in France, Pierre Janet independently came to the same conclusions as Freud. He learned that the severe physical, mental, and emotional symptoms from which his patients suffered were caused by early trauma. He, too, was unsuccessful in convincing the medical profession, though he never recanted.

Freud's student Sandor Ferenczi confirmed not only that child sexual abuse could lead to severe psychological distress, but also that being listened to and comforted is healing. He spoke out on behalf of his patients until his death in 1933, yet his brilliant insights were never accepted.

In 1870 Josephine Butler campaigned against child prostitution, comparing the traffic in young girls to the slave trade. She was harassed by the London police and assaulted by the owners of brothels. Although her cause was supported by other prominent crusaders in Europe and in the United States, it wasn't until 1910 that the U.S. Congress passed the Mann Act, forbidding the transport of women and children across state lines for sexual exploitation.[9]

In 1946, when John Caffey discovered the physical evidence of child battering by means of x-rays, people still would not accept that abuse took place. They preferred to believe in genetic bone problems rather than face the reality that these children had been beaten. It was not until 1962, with the publication of "The Battered Child Syn-

---

[7] Jean Goodwin, in "Credibility Problems in Multiple Personality Disorder Patients and Abused Children," in *Childhood Antecedents of Multiple Personality,* ed. Richard P. Kluft (Washington, D.C.: American Psychiatric Press, 1985), p. 6, points out that "Freud published several cases in which a patient's account of prior sexual abuse was corroborated by a co-victim, a witness or by the adult participant. He never published a case of a corroborated false account of sexual abuse. Yet, Freud later expressed embarrassment at his 'credulity' in having believed stories of sexual seduction in childhood."

[8] The first to publish on Freud's recanting of his theories was Florence Rush, in her article "Freud and the Sexual Abuse of Children," in *Chrysalis,* a feminist journal, in 1977. Her subsequent book, *The Best Kept Secret: Sexual Abuse of Children,* Jeffrey Masson's *The Assault on Truth: Freud's Suppression of the Seduction Theory,* and Judith L. Herman's *Trauma and Recovery* also extensively document this early history. For further information, see descriptions of these titles in the Resource Guide.

[9] Roland Summit documents Butler's, Tardieu's, and Ferenczi's work in "Hidden Victims, Hidden Pain: Societal Avoidance of Child Sexual Abuse," in *Lasting Effects of Child Sexual Abuse,* eds. Gail Elizabeth Wyatt and Gloria Johnson Powell (Newbury Park, CA: Sage, 1988), pp. 45–50.

For a fuller account of Josephine Butler's work, see Florence Rush, *The Best Kept Secret.* For more about Ferenczi, see Jeffery Masson, *The Assault on Truth,* and for more on Janet, see B. A. van der Kolk and O. van der Hart, "Pierre Janet and the Breakdown of Adaptation in Psychological Trauma," *American Journal of Psychiatry* 146 (1989): 1530–40 (summarized in Judith Herman's *Trauma and Recovery*).

drome," that child battering was finally recognized.[10]

The acknowledgment of sexual abuse has met similar, if not greater, resistance. Even when there were clear physical signs of incest, doctors refused to identify sexual abuse. Instead they fabricated rationales such as "victim promiscuity; congenital problems, such as absence of the hymen; or the consequences of excessive masturbation."[11]

Until the 1980s, emerging accounts of child sexual abuse were met primarily with denial, minimization, and blaming the victim. In the first three-quarters of this century, sexual abuse was primarily considered the fault of the child. In 1907 Karl Abraham described a nine-year-old girl who had been led into the woods by a neighbor who then attempted to rape her. The child fought off the man and managed to run away, but Abraham wrote that she had "allowed herself to be seduced" and had "allowed him to go a long way in carrying out his purpose before she freed herself from him and ran off. It's not to be wondered at that this child kept the occurrence secret."[12]

In 1937 Loretta Bender and Adam Blau

wrote, "These children undoubtedly do not deserve completely the cloak of innocence with which they have been endowed by moralists, social reformers and legislators." Referring to the children's "unusually charming and attractive . . . personalities," they went on to conclude that "the child might have been the actual seducer rather than the one innocently seduced."[13]

And in 1953, Alfred Kinsey and his fellow researchers documented the prevalence of child sexual abuse but minimized its impact. In a sample of over one thousand women, one in four reported sexual abuse. Eighty percent of these said they had been frightened by the encounters, but Kinsey and his colleagues discounted their accounts, writing, "It is difficult to understand why a child, except for its cultural conditioning, should be disturbed at having its genitalia touched." They went on to express their belief that penalties for perpetrators were overly harsh: "In many instances the law, in the course of punishing the offender, does more damage to more persons than was ever done by the individual in his illicit sexual activity."[14]

In 1962 Eugene Revitch and Rosalie Weiss wrote, "The majority of pedophiles are harmless individuals and their victims are

[10] C. H. Kempe, F. N. Silverman, B. F. Steele, W. Droegmuller, and H. Silver, "The Battered Child Syndrome," *Journal of the American Medical Association* 181 (1962), pp. 17–24.

[11] Jean Goodwin, "Rediscovering Sadism," in *Rediscovering Childhood Trauma* (Washington D.C.: American Psychiatric Press, 1993), pp. 90–91.

[12] Karl Abraham, "The Experiencing of Sexual Traumas as a Form of Sexual Activity," in *Selected Papers* (London: Hogarth, 1927), pp. 50–53. This and the following examples are drawn from Anna C. Salter's *Treating Child Sex Offenders and Victims: A Practical Guide* (Newbury Park, CA: Sage Publications, 1988), pp. 22–40, in which

she documents this history of denial, victim-bashing, and mother blame.

[13] Loretta Bender and Adam Blau, "The Reaction of Children to Sexual Relations With Adults," *The American Journal of Orthopsychiatry* (October 1937), p. 514. As cited by Anna Salter.

[14] Alfred C. Kinsey, et al., *Sexual Behavior in the Human Female* (Philadelphia: Saunders, 1953) pp. 121 and 20. As cited by Anna Salter.

482 / HONORING THE TRUTH

usually known to be aggressive and seductive children."[15]

And when sexual abuse was not being blamed on the victim, it was blamed on the mother. In 1966 Noel Lustig and his colleagues said that mothers of incest victims were really the ones responsible for the abuse: "While rejecting their husbands sexually and generating in them considerable sexual frustration and tension, they played conspicuous roles in directing the husbands' sexual energies toward the daughters."[16]

Numerous authors have concluded that mothers *want* their daughters to take over their sexual duties. In 1979 Blair and Rita Justice concluded that by "inviting the daughter to take over her role, she [the mother] is suggesting that the daughter also become her mate's sexual partner." Mothers, they went on to state, were to blame for incest because they were "weak, dependent, indifferent, absent, depressed or promiscuous."[17]

In recent years, the whole family has been held responsible for the perpetrator's actions. As late as 1983, Adele Mayer wrote, "In father-daughter incest, the entire family is involved and each member is active in perpetrating the abuse."[18]

Interestingly, while some professionals were blaming everyone but the perpetrator, others were insisting that child sexual abuse didn't happen at all—or only very rarely. As late as the 1970s many clinicians were still taught that incest was extremely rare, affecting only one in a million children.[19]

Considering this history, our present ability to recognize and confront child sexual abuse is nothing short of phenomenal.

The advances of the past twenty years are a direct outgrowth of the women's liberation movement that gained force in the 1970s. Women courageously spoke out about rape and battering, wrote books analyzing the ways in which our society condoned such violence, and worked to establish battered women's shelters and rape crisis centers. Simultaneously, a few pioneering clinicians and researchers, both men and women, were beginning to study child sexual abuse and set up models for treatment. It was from this visionary thinking—and grassroots activism —that the current movement to end child sexual abuse was built.[20]

---

[15] Eugene Revitch and Rosalie G. Weiss, "The Pedophiliac Offender," *Diseases of the Nervous System* 23 (1962), p. 78. As cited by Anna Salter.

[16] Noel Lustig, et al., "Incest: A Family Group Survival Pattern," *Archives of General Psychiatry* 14, (1966), p. 34. As cited by Anna Salter.

[17] Blair Justice and Rita Justice, *The Broken Taboo* (New York: Human Services, 1979), p. 34. As cited by Anna Salter.

[18] Adele Mayer, *Incest: A Treatment Manual for Therapy with Victims, Spouses and Offenders* (Holmes Beach, FL: Learning Publications, 1983), p. 22. As cited by Anna Salter.

[19] I. B. Weiner, "Father-Daughter Incest: A Clinical Report," *Psychiatric Quarterly* 36, no. 1 (1962), pp. 607–632. And S. K. Weinberg, *Incest Behavior* (New York: Citadel, 1955, 1976). As cited by Anna Salter.

[20] Some of the pioneers whose work our present movement is built upon are Diana Russell (*The Politics of Rape*, 1975), Susan Brownmiller (*Against Our Will*, 1975), Suzanne Sgroi ("Sexual Molestation of Children: The Last Frontier in Child Abuse," 1975), Ann Burgess and Lynda Holmstrom ("*Sexual Trauma of Children and Adolescents*," 1975), A. Nicholas Groth (co-author with the previous three of *Sexual Assault of Children and Adolescents*, 1978), Sandra Butler (*The Conspiracy of Silence*, 1978),

We began to insist that children be protected, survivors be supported, and perpetrators be held responsible for their acts. This monumental advance in our willingness to be aware, to care, and to respond has come about only in the past two decades—most visibly in the past decade. This is the first time in history that children and adults who were sexually abused have been listened to, respected, and believed.

Adult survivors of child sexual abuse now have a voice and the power of community. Survivors are educating the medical profession, mental health workers, teachers, law enforcement officers, and the media. Laws are being changed. As a nation we are stunned to learn that our children are being harmed in great numbers. We have begun to break through our collective wall of denial—a wall that has been at least as hard as the Berlin Wall to bring down. This is revolutionary change, and such change does not come without opposition.

There is a documented history of backlash against every progressive movement to redress the rights of the disenfranchised and oppressed. No significant steps are won without it. Although the attacks on survivors of child sexual abuse are extremely upsetting,

they are also an indication of the substantial social progress we have made. Our movement has attained sufficient momentum, visibility, and clout to attract such opposition.

The current backlash is in direct response to the activism of survivors. It was not until survivors started challenging and changing the laws regarding the accountability of perpetrators—and suing their abusers—that claims of "false memory syndrome" started to appear. (See page 495 for more.)

And this denial, although it has a new name and a new face, is really the same old thing. Judith Herman, associate clinical professor of psychiatry at Harvard Medical School, explains:

> For the past twenty years, women have been speaking out about sexual violence, and men have been coming up with denials, evasions, and excuses. We have been told that women lie, exaggerate, and fantasize. Now [we're being told] that women are *brainwashed* . . . Once again, those of us who have labored for years to overcome public denial find ourselves debating victims' credibility. How many times do we have to go over the same ground?[21]

WHO SUPPORTS THE BACKLASH

The supporters of the backlash are varied. Some people get involved because they *are* indeed innocent and have been falsely accused. But for many others the backlash pro-

---

Kee McFarlane (*Sexual Abuse of Children*, 1978), Karen Meiselman (*Incest*, 1978), Louise Armstrong (*Kiss Daddy Goodnight*, 1978), David Finkelhor (*Sexually Victimized Children*, 1979), Florence Rush (*The Best Kept Secret*, 1980), Linda Sanford (*The Silent Children*, 1980), Judith Herman (*Father-Daughter Incest*, 1981), Susan Griffin (*Pornography and Silence*, 1981), Jean Goodwin (*Sexual Abuse: Incest Victims and Their Families*, 1982), Roland Summit ("The Child Sexual Abuse Accommodation Syndrome," 1983), Henry Giarretto, founder of Parents United (1972), and researcher and practitioner Lucy Berliner.

---

[21] Judith Herman, "Backtalk," *Mother Jones* (March/April 1993), p. 3.

vides a convenient cover. Abusers, obviously, would be eager to take advantage of any group whose mission is to vindicate those accused of abuse. Likewise, pedophiles and pedophile advocacy groups, such as the René Guyon Society and NAMBLA, stand to benefit from the silencing of survivors.[22]

Spouses who are unable to face the fact that their partner abused their child have embraced the idea that many reports of sexual abuse are false. Family members and well-meaning friends often find it more tolerable to believe in false accusations than to accept that someone they know and love could have abused a child.

Among professionals, a number of those who endorse the "false memory" theory have little or no clinical experience with survivors. Some have specialized in unrelated areas and are uninformed about the impact of trauma or the patterns of perpetrators. Others have been moved by the obvious pain of accused parents who, whether or not they abused their children, are clearly suffering. Still others, concerned with issues of suggestibility, have erroneously gone on to challenge the credibility of all survivors who remember their abuse as adults. And finally, those who serve as expert witnesses for the defense of accused perpetrators have a clear professional and financial stake in discrediting survivors.

Journalists have played a role as well. By presenting sensationalized and distorted stories, they have legitimized a climate of disbelief. Anna Salter, adjunct professor of pediatrics at Dartmouth Medical School, has served as an expert witness for child victims and has been shocked by the subsequent media coverage:

I've been in court on cases that I didn't recognize on television. That happened to me last year. When they told me the case I was seeing on television was the case I'd testified in, it was hard for me to believe it. A reporter decided that this was a case of overzealous prosecutors, that the father was falsely accused. The reporter completely neglected to bring forth the man's history of molesting children. Yes, you would have gotten incensed by what was presented on TV. The problem is it had nothing to do with the facts of the case.[23]

Why do so many journalists present one-sided, erroneous accounts? The subject is dramatic and controversial. It sells papers, improves ratings, makes great sound bites. It grabs the attention of even the most jaded reader.

The appeal of these stories, however, goes far beyond our national obsession with sex, violence, and broken families. Anti-survivor propaganda has found a receptive audience with the public at large. People read about the "false memory syndrome" and are readily convinced. Why? Because denying the reality of child sexual abuse appeals to a

---

[22] The René Guyon Society is an organization that advocates sex between adults and children. Their motto is "Sex before eight or else it's too late." NAMBLA is the North American Man-Boy Love Association. Although the backlash as a whole does not endorse pedophilia, there are occasions on which these lines blur. See p. 493 for more.

[23] Anna Salter, interview by Laura Davis, September 16, 1993.

basic human need: the need to distance ourselves from human cruelty.

It is painful to face the reality that so many children were—and continue to be—severely abused. There are times when the stories we hear are so horrible, we want to deny their truth. It is far easier to call it fantasy, manipulation, fabrication; easier to say that someone has been brainwashed into believing they were abused than to face the possibility that this person endured such torments as a child.

But we know—history has taught us—that atrocities happen. We have only to think of recent history—the Holocaust, the gassing of the Kurds, the massacre at My Lai, the rape of women in Bosnia—to illustrate the extent of human cruelty and our reluctance to confront it.

Today there are groups who propound the belief that the Holocaust didn't happen; that documents such as Anne Frank's diary were fabricated; that Auschwitz, Dachau, and Bergen-Belsen did not exist.[24] How much easier to smother the truth of an individual's personal torture.

This is not to say that our movement is beyond reproach. Any time there is such massive social progress, serious and harmful mistakes are inevitably made. Children have been retraumatized in courtrooms, interviewing procedures have been flawed, and

[24] A Roper poll, sponsored by the U.S. Holocaust Memorial Council and the B'nai B'rith Anti-Defamation League in 1993, found that 22% of adults and 20% of high school students say it's possible the Holocaust never happened. For a thorough and thoughtful analysis of Holocaust denial, see Deborah Lipstadt's *Denying the Holocaust: The Growing Assault on Truth and Memory* (New York: The Free Press, 1993).

families have been reunited prematurely. Some therapists working with adult survivors have pushed clients to acknowledge abuse or have attributed problems to abuse that did not occur. False allegations have been made. Such transgressions need to be confronted and challenged, but in no way do they diminish the pain suffered by the vast majority of men and women who are coming forward to say they were sexually abused or the integrity of the dedicated professionals who work with them.

THE TRUTH ABOUT THE BACKLASH

When you watch shows or read reports about "false memories," you may feel angry and betrayed but not know how to respond. When the coverage of this debate is filled with interviews with well-credentialed experts, sympathetic portrayals of accused parents, and scientific-sounding evidence about the nature of memory, it can sometimes be hard to keep your equilibrium. By analyzing the claims of the "false memory" argument and examining the organizations behind the backlash, we hope to give you a clearer perspective on these attacks and to provide information you can use to respond effectively.

There is no such thing as a "false memory syndrome."

The cornerstone of the current backlash is the promotion of the concept of a "false memory syndrome." In fact, no such syndrome exists, as psychotherapist Karen Olio makes clear:

"Syndrome" usually refers to a documented group of signs and symptoms that characterize a particular abnormality. In this case, however, there have been no clinical trials, no scientifically controlled comparison groups, no research to document or quantify the phenomena. "Syndrome" is used simply to create an aura of scientific legitimacy . . . The creation of an "official" label seeks to establish by its mere existence the legitimacy of a phenomenon that has yet to be verified.[25]

Mary Harvey, director of the Victims of Violence Program at Cambridge Hospital, concurs:

There is no such thing as a "false memory syndrome." There is psychosis; there is hallucination and delusion, and there is outright lying and malingering. There is also bad clinical practice. There is, however, no "false memory syndrome" and no evidence to support the proposition that such a syndrome— or a "genuine memory syndrome" for that matter—ought to be placed in our DSM-IV lexicon of psychiatric diagnoses.[26]

Seventeen distinguished academic researchers in the fields of memory and trauma were so concerned about the use of the term "false memory syndrome" that they wrote a letter to the *APS* [*American Psychological Society*] *Observer:*

We, a group of researchers from diverse areas, share a common concern for the responsibility of psychology as a science. . . . While we strongly support research aimed at understanding the veracity of memory, we urge a more even-handed approach to this topic. In particular, we object to the term "false memory syndrome," a non-psychological term originated by a private foundation whose stated purpose is to support accused parents.[27]

Psychiatrist Judith Herman adds: "The very name FMS is prejudicial and misleading: there is no such syndrome, and we have no evidence that the reported memories are false. We know only that they are disputed."[28]

The "false memory syndrome," then, has been created, not by scientific research, but through the use of highly emotional anecdotal reports and an effective public relations campaign.

When Pamela Freyd, Executive Director

---

[25] Karen Olio, "The Truth Behind the False Memory Syndrome," *Minneapolis Papers: Selections from the 31st Annual ITAA Conference* (October 15, 1993), ed. Norman L. James, p. 295. (Available through Family Violence Sexual Assault Institute, 1310 Clinic Drive, Tyler, TX 75701.)

[26] Mary R. Harvey, "Principles of Practice with Remembering Adults," keynote address at the 9th Annual Abuse and Victimization Conference, at the Family Violence Program of Children's Hospital and Harvard Medical School, Boston, April 1993.

The DSM-IV is the forthcoming fourth edition of

the American Psychiatric Association's *Diagnostic and Statistical Manual.*

[27] "Letters to the Editor," *APS Observer* (March 1993), p. 23.

[28] Judith L. Herman, "Adult Memories of Childhood Trauma: Current Controversies," position paper presented at the annual meeting of the American Psychiatric Association, May 26, 1993.

of the False Memory Syndrome Foundation, was interviewed by David Calof in *Treating Abuse Today,* she was unable to provide even a basic definition of "false memory syndrome," excusing her inability by saying she was not a clinician. When Calof insisted that the Executive Director of a national organization would be expected to know such information, Freyd responded in the following exchange:

TAT: If I was talking to the Executive Director of the Muscular Dystrophy Association, who presumably is also not a clinician, I'll bet he or she could give me the signs and symptoms of muscular dystrophy. But in the case of false memory syndrome, so far no one seems to be able to say.

FREYD: Gotcha. I'm in agreement with you. There are some soft areas here that need to be clarified.[29]

The False Memory Syndrome Foundation is an advocacy group for people who say that they have been falsely accused of child abuse.

The group most frequently cited in promoting the idea of "false memories" is the False Memory Syndrome (FMS) Foundation. Despite their official-sounding title, this foundation is not primarily a scientific research organization; rather, it is an advocacy group for people who say that they have been falsely accused of child sexual abuse.[30]

The foundation prints dramatic accounts about women who say they were mistreated by unethical and incompetent therapists. These stories are presented as though they represented the customary practices of counselors who work with survivors. The foundation disparages the contributions of both individual survivors and those who have worked to support them. When interviewed for newspapers, magazines, or talk shows, members of the organization and its scientific advisory board repeatedly debunk the testimony of survivors.

The FMS Foundation presents information that is out of context, and distorted. Psychiatrist Richard Lowenstein, a past president of the International Society for the Study of Multiple Personality and Dissociation, explains:

The FMS Foundation's written materials are selective, biased, and incomplete in their fragmentary reviews of selected articles and books in the childhood trauma literature. [Their] main

[29] David L. Calof, "A Conversation with Pamela Freyd, Ph.D., Co-founder and Executive Director, False Memory Syndrome Foundation, Inc. Part I," *Treating Abuse Today* 3, no. 3, 39.

[30] Although the FMS Foundation's mission statement says they will sponsor scientific and medical research into the existence and cause of false memory syndrome, the only research we are aware of is their member surveys in which members of the Foundation provide their version of their family's history and current events, socioeconomic status, and information about their children's therapists.

Clinical psychologist Pamela Birrell questions the objectivity of such research: "Can the goals of objectivity in science be met by an organization that appears dedicated to proving that memories of abuse are false? How many of you give the same credence to research on the effects of smoking done by the American Tobacco Institute compared to the same research . . . supported by neutral grants at universities." (Pamela J. Birrell, Open letter to board members of the FMS Foundation, September 1, 1993).

goal is media propaganda dressed up in the garb of apparent objectivity."[31]

The FMS Foundation has an advisory board of well-credentialed professionals from prominent universities. However, a founding member of this board (who has since resigned) has engaged in questionable practices designed to intimidate therapists, and squelch academic debate.[32]

The FMS Foundation has distributed questionnaires to accused parents, requesting information about their adult child's therapist.[33] Their literature has encouraged parents to file complaints against these therapists with state licensing boards, professional associations, and in California, even with the Victims of Crime Program.[34]

Although they concede that "parents would seem to have no cause for malpractice against the therapist," they go on to suggest that "the parent may have a cause for libel and slander or for tortious interference with a family relationship." As if such challenges to therapists were not sufficient, they go on to propose the possibility that parents usurp legal control over the entirety of their adult children's lives: "Lastly, and even more remotely, the parent may take the legal position that the accusing child is incompetent and seek guardianship proceedings."[35] Psychiatrist Richard Kluft believes that the use of such tactics diminishes the legitimate concerns of the FMS Foundation:

> My argument with the FMS people is not their point of view. It's that they advocate hurtful means of repair. . . . This group is trying to intimidate those who work in the abuse fields by saying in essence, "If you and a patient conclude they've been abused when they didn't say so in the first place, we're coming after you—and a lawsuit will take up a lot of your life.". . . That's why I'm so dead set against this group.[36]

---

[31] Richard Lowenstein, *ISSMP&D News* volume 10, no. 6 (December 1992), pp. 1–2.

[32] Psychologist Anna Salter has been sued in California and Wisconsin for criticizing former FMS Foundation advisory board member Ralph Underwager (in both cases, the charges were dismissed by the judges before trial). Underwager has appealed. Attorney Patricia Toth and a number of others involved in a TV show critical of Underwager have also been sued by Underwager in Illinois, Virginia, and Maryland. Those cases are on hold, pending the outcome of the appeals. In one deposition, Underwager acknowledged hiring a private investigator to get information on a monograph Anna Salter was writing, *Accuracy of Expert Testimony in Child Sexual Abuse Cases: A Case Study of Ralph Underwager and Hollida Wakefield* (Deposition of Ralph Underwager, Ralph Underwager and Hollida Wakefield vs. Anna Salter and Patricia Toth, Madison, WI, April 15, 1993, Case No. 92-C-0229-S). That private investigator called Anna Salter, pretending to be an attorney in a custody case involving allegations of child sexual abuse (transcript of telephone conversation between Dan Lundy, private investigator, and Anna Salter 10/23/89, pp. 1–9, Exhibit D). He tape-recorded the phone call and it was later used as evidence in a defamation suit Ralph Underwager filed against Anna Salter.

[33] "Therapist information," part C of survey no. 92.1, distributed by the FMS Foundation in October 1992.

[34] In the April 6, 1993, *FMS Foundation Newsletter*, this admonition to report complaints was presented as an unsigned request from FMS contacts in California.

[35] "Legal Aspects of False Memory Syndrome," written and distributed by FMS Foundation (June 1992), p. 3.

[36] Richard P. Kluft, "Advanced Treatment of Multiple Personality Disorder," lecture presented on December 4–5, 1992, in Oakland, CA by Westword Institute.

The FMS Foundation was started by one set of parents after their daughter confronted them about having been sexually abused.

The FMS Foundation was founded largely by one set of parents, Pamela and Peter Freyd, who claim that accusations of sexual abuse by their adult daughter, Jennifer Freyd, are false. As psychotherapist David Calof put it, "There is persuasive evidence that this organization grew out of one family's feud that's overgrown its boundaries and come into the popular culture."[37]

One week after she entered therapy in 1990, Jennifer Freyd, professor of psychology at the University of Oregon, recovered memories of sexual abuse by her father, Peter Freyd. She confronted her parents about the incest, and they denied it. Six months later, her mother, Pamela Freyd, published "How Could This Happen? Coping with a False Accusation of Incest and Rape" under the pseudonym Jane Doe.[38] The article contained personal information about Jennifer—some of which was inaccurate, much of which was embarrassing—and Pamela Freyd sent copies of the Jane Doe article, along with letters clearly indicating that she was the author, to her daughter's colleagues. Among the recipients were members of Jennifer Freyd's own department at the university, where she was being con-

sidered for a promotion to full professorship.[39]

The following winter, Pamela Freyd founded the FMS Foundation, and since then she has crisscrossed the country promoting the idea of "false memories" and talking about the destruction of families through false allegations.

In the meantime, Jennifer chose not to speak publicly about her childhood abuse or about her mother's role in founding the FMS Foundation, as she still hoped for a private resolution of these matters. Finally, in 1993 she broke her silence and told her side of the story, stating, "I have already lost so much of my privacy, and in such an unclear and distorted way, that I have come to desire clarity and public truth as the lesser of two undesirable situations."

Jennifer Freyd reported that she was sexually abused by her father from the time she was three or four years old until she was sixteen. Although the sexual abuse ended when she was a teenager, Jennifer detailed a

---

[37] David Calof, speaking at the Fifth Anniversary Eastern Regional Conference on Abuse and Multiple Personalities, June 3–8, 1993, Alexandria, VA.

[38] Jane Doe, "How Could This Happen? Coping with a False Accusation of Incest and Rape," *Issues in Child Abuse Accusations* [Ralph Underwager's journal] 3, no. 3 (Summer 1991), pp. 154–165.

[39] Peter Freyd acknowledged to Jennifer that aspects of the Jane Doe story were fictitious. In an electronic mail letter he wrote that a reporter he knew thought he could "put together stuff from the Jane Doe article and the Darryl Sifford columns, but in both cases fictional elements were deliberately inserted." As quoted by Jennifer Freyd, "Theoretical and Personal Perspectives on the Delayed Memory Debate," presentation for The Center for Mental Health at Foote Hospital's Continuing Education Conference "Controversies Around Recovered Memories of Incest and Ritualistic Abuse," August 7, 1993, Ann Arbor, MI. Jennifer Freyd's story, as told here, is taken from this paper as well as the interview she did with the *The Oregonian* (August 8, 1993). Information was also drawn from Steven Fried's "War of Remembrance," in *Philadelphia* (January 1994). The full text of Jennifer Freyd's speech is available by writing to *Moving Forward*, P.O. Box 4426, Arlington, VA 22204.

continuing pattern of sexualized talk, boundary violations, and invasive and demeaning treatment that continued into her adult years. She described her father showing her a replica of his penis and testicles that he displayed in the living room. She recounted being humiliated in front of visitors by her father's excessively sexual comments. And when she tried to discuss a memory of sexual abuse with her parents, she related that her mother's reaction was that the memory had to be false because if it were true, their dog would have made a lot of noise . . . as the dog always joined, apparently noisily, in human sexual events.

Jennifer Freyd described a family in which denial, minimization, and distortion were commonplace. Throughout her growing-up years, her father was an active alcoholic; he was eventually hospitalized for alcoholism in the early 1980s.[40] She related that during her childhood, her father "sometimes discussed his own experiences of being sexually abused as an eleven-year-old boy. He discussed these experiences, however, not in terms of 'abuse' but in terms of precocious sexuality, calling himself a 'kept boy.' "[41]

The Freyds have made every effort to discredit Jennifer's testimony. And as she explains, attempts to discredit her are not totally new:

> My father told various people that I was brain damaged at various times throughout my childhood and adult years. I was reminded of this theory of brain damage by a family friend who had heard it from my father while I was a graduate student at Stanford University on a National Science Foundation Graduate Fellowship.[42]

It is hard for Jennifer Freyd to understand why her father would say such things—or why he would be believed:

> I am flabbergasted that my memory is considered "false" and my alcoholic father's memory is considered rational and sane. . . . Is my father more credible than me because I have a history of lying or not having a firm grasp on reality? No, I am a scientist whose empirical work has been replicated in laboratories around this country and Europe, and until the last few years of parental invasion I enjoyed an excellent professional reputation without any scandal attached to my name. . . .
>
> Am I not believed because I am a woman? A "female in her thirties" as some of the newspaper articles seem to

---

[40] Both Peter and Pamela Freyd have publicly acknowledged that Peter was hospitalized for alcoholism in 1982. Peter contends, however, that his drinking never affected his family. "Memories of A Disputed Past," *The Oregonian* (August 8, 1993), p. L6.

[41] Peter Freyd himself confirms that he had a sexual relationship with a pedophile when he was nine. At about the same time, Peter met his future wife, Pamela, whose mother married Peter's father, making Peter and Pam stepbrother and stepsister. From Steven Fried, "War of Remembrance," *Philadelphia* (January 1994), p. 151.

[42] Jennifer Freyd's father is not the only one of her parents to malign her intelligence or her sanity. In a newspaper article published in the Portland *Oregonian* the day after Jennifer's public disclosure (August 8, 1993), Pamela Freyd is quoted as saying of Jennifer, "By thinking of her as temporarily deranged, I have been able to keep feelings of love alive."

emphasize? Am I therefore a hopeless hysteric by definition? . . . Indeed why is my parents' denial at all credible? In the end, is it precisely because I *was* abused that I am to be discredited despite my personal and professional success?

Most incomprehensible to Jennifer is Peter and Pamela Freyd's invitation to her to join the advisory board of the foundation, an organization whose very existence is predicated on discounting her reality. In a letter expressing surprise that she declined, Peter Freyd revealed, "I still insist on thinking of our Newsletter, indeed the whole project, as being primarily a way of communicating with our daughters."[43]

The idea that the FMS Foundation is seen by its founders as a way to communicate with their daughters is alarming. As Jennifer states:

> The weight of a whole Foundation stands behind my mother's frenzied denial of my reality. . . . For my parents' sake I hope they can find a way to look inward, to do their own healing, instead of waging a kind of war at the national level.

The FMS Foundation is only the latest incarnation of the backlash against victims and survivors of child sexual abuse.

Although the foundation grew directly out of the pain and dysfunction of one family, it did not arise in a vacuum. The backlash had been gaining momentum for some time.

In 1984 Victims of Child Abuse Laws (VOCAL) was established in Minneapolis to champion the rights of the accused in child abuse cases, claiming that children's allegations of sexual abuse are frequently false and that children do not make credible witnesses.[44]

VOCAL was born in the aftermath of a highly publicized child sexual abuse trial in Jordan, Minnesota. In that case, accusations of sadistic ritual abuse of dozens of children led to one conviction, two acquittals, and charges being dropped for twenty-one other defendants. Because this was the first trial involving such massive and unprecedented allegations, the investigation was flawed and questions remain, but it's clear that children had been abused.[45]

In his book *The Battle and the Backlash*, David Hechler dates the origin of the backlash to the Jordan case and specifically to

---

[43] Electronic-mail letter from Peter Freyd to Jennifer Freyd on November 11, 1992.

[44] VOCAL newsletters include information on cases and attorneys, book reviews, conference reports, and writings from those accused and convicted of child abuse—sometimes from jail. And VOCAL regularly sent "courtesy" newsletters to prisoners. Reported by David Hechler, *The Battle and the Backlash: The Child Sexual Abuse War* (Lexington, MA: D. C. Heath, 1988), pp. 118–119.

[45] A state commission investigating the case concluded that some of the charges could have been successfully prosecuted if they hadn't been dropped. The commission wrote, "Those defendants who were guilty went free, and those who were innocent were left without the opportunity to clear their names. Those children who were victims became victims once again. The commission has concluded that the wholesale dismissal of the twenty-one cases was not justified." (Report to Governor Rudy Perpich, Commission Established by Executive Order No. 85–10 Concerning Kathleen Morris, Scott County Attorney, pp. 52–53.) Cited by David Hechler, p. 115.

September 19, 1984, the day Lois and Robert Bentz were acquitted of abusing their son and four other children.[46] One month later, VOCAL had its first organizing meeting in Minneapolis. Robert and Lois Bentz and another Jordan defendant were on VOCAL's first board of directors.[47] Psychologist Ralph Underwager, expert witness in the Bentz trial, participated in VOCAL's initial meetings, acted as the group's first public spokesman,[48] and spoke at VOCAL's first four national conferences.[49]

Underwager and his wife, psychologist Hollida Wakefield, went on to publish *Issues in Child Abuse Accusations,* a journal that primarily prints articles supporting the idea that most sexual abuse allegations are false. Underwager was also pivotal in the formation of the FMS Foundation. Its original membership was drawn from a list of 202 families who had contacted him through his Institute for Psychological Therapies.[50] And he served as an advisory board member of the foundation until the summer of 1993. (See page 494

for more on the circumstances of his resignation.)

VOCAL and the FMS Foundation take much the same stance. VOCAL claims that children aren't credible witnesses, that they are too young and are prone to fantasy. The FMS Foundation says adult survivors shouldn't be believed because they've been misled by manipulative, therapists. VOCAL accuses investigators of asking leading questions to get children to "admit" to abuse that never really happened. The FMS Foundation says therapists brainwash adult clients. VOCAL accuses child protective workers—or "child savers" as they call them—of incompetence and says they're responsible for breaking up families. The FMS Foundation similarly accuses therapists—and self-help books—of doing the same. Both groups talk about "witch hunts" and "child abuse hysteria," and claim it is impossible for defendants to get a fair trial in sex abuse cases because there's a presumption of guilt rather than innocence. Both groups say they are as concerned about the guilty going free as they are the innocent being falsely accused, but publish only articles dealing with false accusations. And neither group has a way to tell which of their members are falsely accused—and which are guilty.[51]

---

[46] David Hechler reports that the Bentzes' six-year-old son testified from the stand that his parents *had* sexually abused him. Hechler writes, "When asked by a defense attorney if he feared his father would sodomize him, the child turned to his father and said, 'You won't do that no more, right?' " Hechler, *Battle,* p. 111.

[47] Hechler, *Battle,* p. 119.

[48] "Defense Advocates Visit," *Update,* American Prosecutors Research Institute, National Center for the Prosecution of Child Abuse, vol. 1, no. 4 (August 1988).

[49] Glenn Cooly, "Disavowing Memory," *NOW: Toronto's Weekly News and Entertainment Voice* 12, no. 5 (October 1–7, 1992), p. 18.

[50] *FMS Foundation Newsletter,* February 29, 1992.

---

[51] David Hechler reports that Leslie Wimberly, California coordinator for VOCAL, acknowledges that her group has supported people through their trials who were later convicted of child molestation. She says, however, that VOCAL has also expelled members with prior child abuse convictions. When asked specifically if VOCAL had a way to know whether its members were guilty or not, she responded, "Neither does the Boy Scouts, or church groups, or the general public. I mean, you could be a child molester for all I know, right? See? I mean, that's a silly question, isn't it?"

According to Hechler, Gerald Maloney, who served

Both VOCAL and the FMS Foundation make some legitimate claims. False allegations have occurred, some investigators have asked leading questions, and therapists have, on occasion, misconstrued a client's history. But the extent of these problems has been greatly exaggerated by both groups, who

---

as the VOCAL coordinator for Washington State, was a convicted child molester (Hechler, *Battle*, pp. 124–125).

FMS Foundation co-founder and executive director Pamela Freyd has repeatedly acknowledged that the FMS Foundation also has no way to tell whether its members are really falsely accused. When asked in an interview if members of the Foundation could be perpetrators of sexual abuse Freyd responded, "Of course. We are not clairvoyant" (Lana Lawrence, "Backlash: A Look at the Abuse Related Amnesia and Delayed Memory Controversy," *Moving Forward* 2, no. 4, p. 14).

In an interview in *Treating Abuse Today*, Freyd stated: "I have said from the beginning, we don't know the truth or falsity of any story. . . . There is no way we can know the truth or falsity of events to which we're not a party."

Later in the same interview, when the subject of the anonymous list of 2000 "false memory families" came up, the following dialogue ensued:

TAT: But at this time you really cannot tell us with any degree of certainty whether or not any of those individuals on your anonymous list are perpetrators or not?

FREYD: I don't like the use of that term.

TAT: How about whether they have committed sexual offenses? You apparently cannot tell us that.

FREYD: Not without some validation.

TAT: Precisely. So you don't know for sure at this time.

FREYD: I'm going to ask you: How do you know that? Or, how am I to know if you have stopped beating your grandmother? How do you prove or show negatives?

TAT: I'm not talking about negatives, I'm talking about testing for possible existence of alcoholic blackouts, dissociative disorders, sociopathology. Those aren't negatives.

then go on to draw distorted conclusions that they use to manipulate public opinion.

Although particular organizations like VOCAL and the FMS Foundation may rise and fall, the backlash is likely to continue to evolve—and to find supporters—in other incarnations. Until we as a culture face the reality of sexual abuse, our collective denial will continue to feed—and need—such groups.[52]

Both VOCAL and the FMS Foundation have ties to people whose views on child sexual abuse are alarming.

LeRoy Schultz, a featured speaker at VOCAL's first two national conferences and an editor for Ralph Underwager's *Issues in Child Abuse Accusations,* has written about the

---

FREYD: Absolutely. You're right.

(David Calof, "A Conversation with Pamela Freyd, Ph.D. Co-Founder and Executive Director, False Memory Syndrome Foundation, Inc. Part I," *Treating Abuse Today* 3, no. 3, pp. 34–39.)

[52] A more extreme group defending the "falsely accused" is The Coalition of Concerned Citizens in Seattle. David Hechler interviewed its founder, Marilyn Gunther. She said, "The primary function we perform is not to determine whether these people are guilty or not guilty, but whether or not these people have received due process in their case." Of the eight hundred cases she had reviewed so far, she said she didn't know of a single case where the person accused had lied, but she acknowledged that it could have happened. When asked about molesters, Gunther said, "Sometimes they make excellent parents. There are a lot of people who sexually offend their own children who are excellent parents, despite that one little hangup. It's not as if they abuse them all the time. It may be two or three times a week over a prolonged period." She went on to say that children weren't necessarily damaged by the experience. "Usually all they require is to be told, 'Hey, it wasn't your fault, and we're going to see that it doesn't happen again. Forget about it.' " As reported by David Hechler, in *Battle*, pp. 125–126.

possibility of consensual sex between adults and children.[53] Of child victims, Schultz writes, "Their cooperation is usually needed to at least initiate the sex act, if not complete it." He goes on to say that police and other reports "do not adequately explain the portion of guilt that may be attributable to the victim." And finally Schultz states, "So great can the role of the victim be in sex offenses that many should be considered offenders themselves."[54]

Richard Gardner, a professor of child psychiatry at Columbia University and a frequent expert witness for the defense in child abuse cases, has appeared numerous times on television promoting the idea of a "false memory syndrome." In an article published by Underwager's *Issues in Child Abuse Accusations*, he writes,

> Sexual activities between adults and children are a universal phenomenon. . . . Such encounters are *not* necessarily traumatic. The determinant as to whether the experience will be traumatic is the social attitude toward these encounters. As Hamlet said: "There is nothing either good or bad, but thinking makes it so."
>
> Of relevance here is the belief by many of these therapists that a sexual encounter between an adult and a child —no matter how short, no matter how tender, loving and non-painful—automatically and predictably must be psychologically traumatic to the child. This belief justifies lengthy, ongoing therapy. . . . Obviously, if the therapist did not take this position, then she would not be able to enjoy the financial rewards attendant to this belief.[55]

Ralph Underwager and his wife were interviewed in *PAIDIKA: The Journal of Paedophilia,* published in the Netherlands. In response to the question "Is choosing paedophilia for you a responsible choice for the individual?," Underwager replied:

> Certainly it is responsible. What I have been struck by as I have come to know more about and understand people who choose paedophilia is that they let themselves be too much defined by other people. That is usually an essentially negative definition. Paedophiles spend a lot of time and energy defending their choice. I don't think that a paedophile needs to do that. Paedophiles can boldly and courageously affirm what they choose. They can say that what they want is to find the best way to love. I am also a theologian and as a theologian I believe it is God's will that there be closeness and intimacy, unity of the flesh, between people. A paedophile can say: "This closeness is possible for me within the choices that I've made." . . .

[53] Hechler, *Battle*, pp. 126–127.

[54] Leroy G. Schultz, "Interviewing the sex offender's victim," *The Journal of Criminal Law, Criminology and Police Science* 50, pp. 448–452. As cited by Anna Salter in *Accuracy of Expert Testimony in Child Sexual Abuse Cases: A Case Study of Ralph Underwager and Hollida Wakefield*, p. 8.

[55] Richard A. Gardner, "Belated Realization of Child Sexual Abuse by an Adult," *Issues in Child Abuse Accusations*, 4, no. 4 (Fall 1992), p. 191.

What I think is that paedophiles can make the assertion that the pursuit of intimacy and love is what they choose. With boldness they can say, "I believe this is in fact part of God's will."[56]

When this interview came to the attention of survivors, their supporters, and subsequently the media in the summer of 1993, Underwager resigned from the FMS Foundation advisory board. However, his wife still serves on its advisory board.

A primary motivation for the backlash is the establishment of a legal defense for those accused of child sexual abuse.

Over the past decade, survivors have begun to lobby the legislatures in all fifty states to make it possible for adult survivors to bring civil suits against their perpetrators for abuse they suffered in childhood.[57] It was only when these legislative and judicial reforms began to take place that we started to hear about the "false memory syndrome." Judith Herman believes these suits, and the po-

litical activism that enabled them to occur, are the motivating force behind the current memory controversy:

I believe that the intense popular and professional interest in this question is not fueled by a sudden fascination with academic memory research. Rather, the debate is being driven by forensic questions. We are witnessing a struggle over issues of accountability.

Up until very recently, sexual assaults in general, and sexual abuse of children in particular, have been essentially perfect crimes.... Victims have been effectively denied access to the justice system, and perpetrators have been practically assured of impunity. As a result of feminist consciousness-raising and legal reforms, recently some victims have begun to hold perpetrators accountable for their crimes.... This is a very real threat to the power and privilege of perpetrators. It is natural to expect that they will fight back.[58]

This struggle over the credibility of abuse victims is not new. In fact, the history of the backlash corresponds directly to the evolution of defense arguments in child sex abuse cases. Patricia Toth, executive director of the National Center for the Prosecution of Child Abuse, says, "Twenty years ago, there weren't a large number of cases of abuse—either physical or sexual—being criminally prosecuted. It happened every now and then, but they were few and far between. If a family member was involved, it was left up to

[56] "Interview: Hollida Wakefield and Ralph Underwager," conducted in Amsterdam in June 1991 by Joseph Geraci, published in *Paidika: The Journal of Paedophilia* 3, no. 1 (Winter 1993).

Additional quotations—equally outrageous—from this interview are included in *Moving Forward: A Newsjournal for Survivors of Sexual Abuse and Those Who Care for Them* 2, no. 4, p. 13, along with an accounting of the FMS Foundation's initial responses to these revelations. Subsequent issues of *Moving Forward* follow up on further developments.

[57] See "Considering a Lawsuit" on p. 318 and "Legal Resources" on p. 546 of the Resource Guide for more information on these suits.

[58] Herman, "Adult Memories of Childhood Trauma," p. 7.

the civil system to remove the child from the home. Parents weren't convicted of crimes, but they might lose custody of their children." [59]

Toth says the emergence of rape crisis centers, and the increased attention given to adult rape cases, led to more focus on child sexual abuse. "Children started showing up as victims. Ten to fifteen years ago, you began to see the first specialized child abuse units in police departments and prosecutors' offices. Victim witness programs became more plentiful and started to devote more attention to children as victims. All of this converged. We started taking child abuse cases more seriously. And as we began to file more cases and get more convictions, the people who found themselves in the position of being accused, some of whom had means, got more serious about fighting back."

Initial defenses in sexual abuse cases were rather unsophisticated. "The first defenses were things like 'I'm a good person. I couldn't have done it.' Now that there's more recognition that abusers don't have to look like monsters, the defense has moved on to other arguments."

As more cases were filed that involved suspected abuse of groups of children, the defenses evolved. "When a group of children all describe similar activities by the same suspect, they could no longer say, 'This kid just has something against this suspect. That's why she's making it up.' So they resorted to, 'These ideas were planted in the kids' heads.' The 'suggestibility of children' defense has really grown with this backlash."

Laurie Braga, who co-directs the National Foundation for Children with her husband, Joseph Braga, explains how the development of false memory rhetoric—and the FMS Foundation—is a logical extension of this battle over the viability of children's testimony in sexual abuse cases:

Those of us who were working to establish the credibility of abused kids in court were glad when adult survivors began coming forward in large numbers. We felt that their stories would give credibility to kids as witnesses. The backlash feared the same. So it was a natural progression for them to attack not only kids as witnesses, but adults too. [60]

Clearly, there has been much legal maneuvering in abuse cases to save perpetrators from conviction. Yet Patricia Toth says that some of the questions that have been raised are legitimate: "Not all of the issues raised are bogus. I think there are some folks that got carried away, who got careless in their investigation and preparation of cases. People cut corners—they're 'experts' after all—they can 'just tell' if a child's been abused—so why shouldn't they be able to testify to that effect? Those kinds of attitudes lead to mistakes being made. We've had to step back and say, 'Whoa. Wait a minute. What *are* we doing? Where do we need to improve?' And when they're wrong, we need to *show* that

[59] Patricia Toth, interview by Laura Davis, September 16, 1993.

[60] Laurie Braga, interview by Laura Davis, September 13, 1993.

they're wrong, not just with an emotional reaction, but with facts, with research, with solid evidence."[61]

Although the legitimate rights of defendants must be upheld, this should not be achieved by sacrificing children. We disagree vehemently with the philosophy of those expert witnesses for the defense who are in sympathy with the principle that "it is better to let 100 guilty men go free than to convict one innocent man."[62]

One person wrongly convicted is a tragedy. But a hundred perpetrators allowed to continue to abuse what could be thousands of children is *not* less of a tragedy.[63] The viola-

tion of children must be considered to be at least as serious as the violation of the rights of adults. Because children are more vulnerable than adults, they need and deserve the fullest possible protection.

Progress has been made, both in protecting children and in establishing legal options for adult survivors. As Patricia Toth concludes, "If these cases weren't being treated as serious crimes, there wouldn't have been a backlash. It's a measure of our success."

In reality, false claims of sexual abuse are uncommon.

As with every other crime, false denials are much more common than false accusations—and, tragically, real child sexual abuse is all too frequent.

According to the best measures available, as many as one in three girls and one in six boys are sexually abused as children. In a survey of a random sample of over nine hundred women in San Francisco, sociologist Diana Russell found that 38 percent had been sexually abused before the age of eighteen. Of these, 28 percent had been seriously abused before the age of fourteen.[64]

Bud Lewis, director of a *Los Angeles Times* poll that questioned 2,627 men and women nationally, found that 22 percent (27 percent of the women and 16 percent of the men) said they'd been sexually abused as chil-

---

[61] For an example of how one defense expert's testimony was scrutinized, see p. 512.

[62] Richard A. Gardner, *The Parental Alienation Syndrome and the Differentiation Between Fabricated and Genuine Child Sex Abuse* (Cresskill, N.J.: Creative Therapeutics, 1987), pp. 175–176. Richard Gardner writes that he endorses this principle for two reasons. "First, I am in sympathy with the aforementioned American legal principle. Second . . . many perpetrators are so shaken and sobered by the investigations into their sexual activities that they 'cease and desist' from further molestation of children, even though exonerated." This last assumption—that abusers stop abusing solely because they are investigated—is not supported by the vast majority of people working with perpetrators. To the contrary, without intervention by the criminal justice system and court-mandated therapy, it is highly unusual for perpetrators to stop. Even in the most successful treatment programs, the recidivism rate is still quite high.

As quoted in the *Los Angeles Times* (February 11, 1985, p. 14), Ralph Underwager takes this idea of protecting the accused even further. He says, "It is more desirable that a thousand children in abuse situations are not discovered than it is for one innocent person to be convicted wrongly."

[63] For information on the number of children one child molester can molest, see footnote 83 on p. 501.

[64] Diana E. H. Russell, "The Incidence and Prevalence of Intrafamilial and Extrafamilial Sexual Abuse of Female Children," *Child Abuse and Neglect: The International Journal* 7, no. 2, pp. 133–139. Reprinted in *Sexual Exploitation: Rape, Child Sexual Abuse and Workplace Harassment* (Beverly Hills: Sage Publications, 1984).

dren.[65] If these numbers are applied to the present population, there are as many as 38 million adult survivors of child sexual abuse today.[66]

Despite the advances that have been made, most abuse continues to go unreported. Less than 10 percent of child sexual abuse cases come to the attention of child protection agencies or the police.[67] Yet inflated claims about the number of false allegations are now commonplace. In cases involving children, these claims are often based on the number of "unfounded" or "unsubstantiated" cases. These terms, however, do not necessarily mean that an accusation is false. Patricia Toth explains that "unfounded" only means that—for whatever reason—the abuse couldn't be proved:

"Unfounded" or "unsubstantiated" can mean that it was false, but it can also mean a variety of other things. In most cases, child protective services only has responsibility for familial or caretaker abuse. If the abuser doesn't fit into those categories, for their purposes, it's unfounded. If you have an infant who has gonorrhea of the throat and can't talk, with no eyewitnesses and no confession, you can be pretty darn sure that child was sexually abused—but you might not be able to identify the offender—and it's unfounded. Or you might have a totally overloaded caseworker who has fifty cases to investigate in a month, so she picks up the phone and says, "We have a report that you abused your child. Is that true?' " And they say, "It's not true.' " And the caseworker says, "Thank you." It's unfounded—because they don't have the skills or resources to properly investigate. Or the report comes in, they try to find the family, and the family has moved to another jurisdiction. Again, unfounded.[68]

Clearly, it is erroneous to use the rate of unfounded cases to assess the number of people falsely accused. Similar misrepresentations are made in cases involving adult survivors. Just because a case isn't successful in court—or a prosecutor declines to prosecute—doesn't necessarily mean the abuse didn't happen. It only means that there wasn't enough evidence to prove it in court. (See "Legal principles do not apply to healing," p. 505.)

This is not to say that false allegations don't exist. They do. But they are not at all the norm. John Briere, associate professor of psychiatry at the University of Southern California School of Medicine, writes:

---

[65] *Los Angeles Times,* August 25, 1985, p. 1. One-third of those who were abused said they'd never told anyone about the abuse before being asked in the survey. Of those who told, 70% said no effective action was taken.

[66] For an in-depth analysis of prevalence studies for child sexual abuse, see David Finkelhor, *A Sourcebook on Child Sexual Abuse* (Newbury Park, CA: Sage Publications, 1986); Anna Salter, *Treating Child Sex Offenders and Victims;* and D. G. Kilpatrick, C. M. Edmunds, and A. K. Seymour, *Rape in America: A Report to the Nation,* (National Victim Center, Arlington, VA, 1992). Also see John Crewdson, *By Silence Betrayed: Sexual Abuse of Children in America* (Boston: Little, Brown, 1988).

[67] In the *Los Angeles Times* poll, only 3% had reported the incident to the police or other public agency. In Diana Russell's 1984 study, less than 5% of the sexual abuse had been reported.

---

[68] Toth interview, September 16, 1993.

I do assume that some small number of people—by virtue of their injury, confusion or despair—will say things that may not be true.[69]

Any given individual reporting repressed memories may be prey to the same afflictions found in the rest of the human race, including psychosis, confusion, desperation, and misrepresentation.[70]

Those who wish to discount and disbelieve abuse survivors grab onto these few cases where there may in fact be incorrect memories and publicize these as obvious examples of why everyone should be disbelieved.[71]

False claims of sexual abuse do exist, but compared to the astronomical numbers of survivors who truly were abused, such claims represent only a minuscule percentage of survivors' accounts. Even if all five thousand families who've contacted the FMS Foundation were indeed falsely accused, that amounts to only .01%—or one one-hundredth of a percent of the estimated number of adult survivors of child sexual abuse in this country.[72]

Perpetrators rarely tell the truth about what they've done.

While it's likely that some who claim to be falsely accused are innocent of the charges against them, it is clear that pedophiles and abusers have much to gain from not telling the truth.

And you can't tell the innocent from the guilty by looking. Lawrence Klein, clinical director of the Wood County Mental Health Center in Bowling Green, Ohio, explains:

The striking thing about sexual offenders is that the vast majority of them are not striking. Contrary to our expectations they bear no outwardly distinguishing features. They look the same as our neighbors and members of our families. . . . They commonly function in an apparently normal, unremarkable way. Yet they routinely commit acts of chilling insensitivity, egocentricity and destructiveness.[73]

Child abusers come from every walk of life, as Brian Abbott, executive director of the Giarretto Institute, makes clear:[74]

Offenders run the gamut of every socioeconomic and ethnic group. I've seen guys who dig ditches or are on unemployment, as well as people who are

---

[69] Margo Silk Forest, "An Interview with John Briere, Ph.D.," *Treating Abuse Today,* 3, no. 1, p. 22.

[70] John Briere, "Adult Memories of Childhood Trauma: Current Controversies," abridged and revised version of a presentation to the American Psychiatric Association, San Francisco, CA, May 26, 1993, p. 3.

[71] Forest, "Interview with John Briere."

[72] As of August 1993, 5,000 families had called the FMS Foundation (FMS Foundation fundraising letter, September 21, 1993).

[73] Lawrence R. Klein, "Perpetration Issues in the Treatment of Survivors of Child Sexual Abuse," presented at the Eighth Regional Conference on Trauma, Dissociation, and Multiple Personality, Cuyahoga Falls, Ohio, April 1993, p. 6.

[74] The Giarretto Institute is the home of Parents United, a nationwide organization that works with abusers, spouses, children in incest families, and adults molested as children. See p. 540 of the Resource Guide.

pillars of the community—attorneys, doctors, people who are doing extremely well in their lives.[75]

Many of the abusers we've met have been charming, personable people.[76] If we didn't know better, we too would have said, "He [or she] could never have done such a thing." Most abusers aren't monsters. Even the ones who've done monstrous things are often successful and well liked in the rest of their lives, as psychologist Anna Salter illustrates:

> Several times I have seen members of a community write letters or sign petitions insisting the police had the wrong man, only to have the offender eventually confess.[77]

A well-publicized example is Sol Wachtler, sixty-two-year-old former Chief Judge for the New York State Court of Appeals. In April 1993, he pled guilty to charges that he threatened to kidnap the fourteen-year-old daughter of his former lover, a well-known and influential Republican fundraiser. Numerous phone calls and letters came to light during the FBI investigation, in which Wachtler spelled out the sexual perversions he planned to inflict on the girl. All this while he was serving as a respected judge and was campaigning for a Senate nomination.[78]

How could this happen? How can someone serve as an esteemed judge, run for Congress, and at the same time plan an elaborate reign of sexual harassment and terrorism? Psychiatrist and medical historian Robert Jay Lifton has come up with a concept called "doubling" to explain this capacity to lead a double life.

Lifton studied Nazi doctors who participated in the Holocaust. He wanted to understand how men could kill, torture human subjects in "medical experiments," select who was to live and who was to die, and then go home, attend church, and play with their children. To explain their seemingly unthinkable behavior, Lifton came up with the idea of "doubling," a dissociative defense that enabled the doctors simultaneously to commit heinous acts and to maintain their respectable place in society.[79]

Lawrence Klein explains the capacity of sexual offenders to live a dual life in a similar way. He says every offender has a "Kingdom" in his mind, a place that gives him the license to abuse:

> The KINGDOM quite simply is a place in the perpetrator's mind where

---

[75] Brian Abbott, interview by Laura Davis, September 9, 1993.

[76] This is one of the arguments given by FMS Foundation founder Pamela Freyd when asked how she knows her group isn't harboring perpetrators. See p. 507.

[77] Anna Salter, *Transforming Trauma: A Guide to Treating Sexual Abuse* (Newbury Park: Sage Publications, in press, 1994), chapter 1.

[78] Information drawn from Lawrence Klein, "When In Doubt," a presentation for the Center for Mental Health at Foote Hospital's Continuing Education Conference "Controversies Around Recovered Memories of Incest and Ritualistic Abuse," August 7, 1993, in Ann Arbor, MI; and from Lucinda Franks, "To Catch A Judge: How the F.B.I. Tracked Sol Wachtler," *The New Yorker* (December 21, 1992), pp. 58–66.

[79] Klein, "When In Doubt." See Lifton's book *The Nazi Doctors* (New York: Basic Books, 1986) for more on this phenomenon.

he as King can do anything he pleases; when, where, how, and with whom he pleases. As King, he defines reality. He creates the rules that govern. . . . All others are things that exist for his ownership and pleasure. . . . From the Kingdom, perpetrators cannot see beyond their own needs. . . .

A perpetrator lives a double life. There is the life of the Real World, a world that for the perpetrator has long been bereft of meaningful and genuine human contact. Then, there is the Revised World, or the world of the Kingdom. Over years of experience the perpetrator learns to pass unobtrusively between the two realms. Quite typically, the perpetrator is viewed by associates as an unremarkable, law abiding citizen. . . .

Perpetrators do not stop their pattern of abuse until they renounce the Kingdom, and strive to embrace humanity. . . . When this happens, in almost all instances, it follows criminal prosecution. Only the jolt of pending incarceration can counter the allure of solitary gratification, in an individual who has lost faith in the viability of human relationships.[80]

Psychologist Brian Abbott works extensively with sexual abusers, particularly incest offenders. Ninety percent of the abusers in his program are ordered to attend by the courts as a condition of probation or bail. A large percentage have not yet been convicted

of any crime, but Abbott says that in his experience, false accusations are rare. What he finds commonplace is denial:

Denial runs from absolute denial, "I didn't do it," "The child was abused but it wasn't me," to minimization, "It wasn't that serious," to rationalizing, "The child seduced me," or "I was drunk or high." If you define denial broadly like that, I see it with every offender who walks in the door.[81]

Even when faced with clear and irrefutable proof, many offenders continue to deny that they did it, often with great emotion and conviction.[82] And their denial frequently continues even after they are convicted and jailed for child sexual abuse.[83]

---

[80] Lawrence Klein, "Therapists' Page," *Many Voices* (December 1989), pp. 3–4.

[81] Abbott interview, September 9, 1993.

[82] In *Transforming Trauma*, Anna Salter tells the story of a 14-year-old sexual offender who thoroughly denied abusing a young girl even though the evidence against him was compelling. This boy was charged with sexual assault after grabbing a female classmate while walking her home from school, knocking her down, and threatening her with a knife. The whole event was witnessed by a friend of the offender, who testified against his schoolmate. A number of other children reported similar incidents with the same offender. Salter writes: "The examiner had 34 documents on her desk which testified to her client's previous deviant sexual behavior and his prediliction for knives. He admitted to owning 28." Yet the youth "denied he had assaulted his classmate on the walk home, denied that he had ever assaulted or intimidated anyone, denied other sexually deviant behaviors, denied any deviant fantasies, denied that he had ever had a single non-deviant sexual thought or fantasy, and denied that he had masturbated. He further volunteered that he had never held his penis while urinating."

[83] In a 1983 study J. S. Wormith investigated 205 sex offenders, one-third of whom were child molesters. Even

Brian Abbott says offenders often get so psychologically invested in maintaining their denial that they can't break through it:

> They may have convinced significant people in their lives—their wives, extended family, employers, preachers—that they didn't commit the offense. Now they've got this whole chorus of people saying, "We know he didn't do it." When you have that kind of strong alliance supporting you, it makes it much more difficult to admit what you've done. Sometimes "I know he didn't do it" is said so often, the of-

fender begins to believe that's the reality of his situation.[84]

There are other reasons abusers deny what they've done. They can't face it, they feel ashamed, they hope to get away with it, or they don't believe it was wrong. And some are just afraid. One survivor related the following story:

> My father sexually abused me when I was eleven. When I confronted him about it initially, he denied it. But several years later, he admitted what he had done and even filled in some of the information I didn't know. Because of that, we were able to start healing the relationship. In a counseling session, I asked him why he had denied it at first. He said simply, "I was scared."

The backlash reinforces denial.

Mary Jo Barrett, director of training at the Center for Contextual Change in Skokie, Illinois, says there are four stages of denial an offender needs to work through before he or she can be accountable for the abuse and can prevent further perpetrations:

> The first level is denial of the facts: "I didn't do it. It never happened. She's lying." The second stage is denial of awareness: "Maybe something happened, but I don't remember it." The third stage is denial of impact: "I didn't hurt her." And the last stage is denial of responsibility, "It happened, but she made me do it."[85]

---

after being convicted and incarcerated, only two-thirds admitted their crimes. Even then, they usually admitted only to the offense they were caught for, denying any other sexual abuse.

When offenders are granted immunity for sex crimes that haven't yet been disclosed, their level of self-disclosed reports rises dramatically. In a 1991 study, Mark Weinrott and Maureen Saylor interviewed rapists and child molesters who were currently in prison for their crimes. The 67 child molesters interviewed were known to have molested 136 children. When questioned with a guarantee of immunity, however, they admitted to more than 8,000 sexual offenses against almost 1,000 children.

And when offenders are guaranteed both anonymity and confidentiality, their own reports of sexual offenses go up astronomically. In 1987 Gene Abel and his colleagues studied over 500 sex offenders, offering them protections far exceeding those in previous studies. The 377 extrafamilial child molesters in the sample were responsible for 48,297 acts against a total of 27,416 victims. The 203 incest offenders in the group committed 15,668 acts against 361 victims. Abel also found that the chances of getting caught for child molestation were a meager 3%.

These and other studies are described more fully in chapter 1 of Anna Salter's *Transforming Trauma*.

---

[84] Abbott interview, September 9, 1993.

[85] Mary Jo Barrett, interview by Laura Davis, November 11, 1993.

In a gradual therapy process that eventually includes the whole family, Barrett and her colleagues help the offender break through each level of denial:

> The denial is always to try to make the truth more comfortable, to protect them from the pain of acknowledging what they've done. If the offender is denying the facts, we don't start by focusing on the facts. Rather we look at the offender's social, political, cultural, economic and religious background, as well as his own family history. We ask: "Did he have trauma in his own family? Was he emotionally abandoned? Does he prescribe to a patriarchal belief system which demeans women and children?" Basically, we assess, "Does he have the variables which would make him vulnerable to being a sex offender?" And we say to the offender, "According to what you're saying, you could have been vulnerable to turning to children." And gradually, he or she is able to acknowledge that the abuse might have occurred.

When denial is on the level of awareness, Barrett asks her clients, "What would happen to you if you found out you did this? What do you have to lose by remembering? What do you have to gain?" Gains, Barrett points out, are things like having real power for the first time:

> . . . the power that comes from having genuine human connections rather than from hurting others; the benefit of trying to help their child for the first time, the benefit of not getting cut off and being totally isolated and alone, the benefit of not going to their graves with the secret.
> We also ask them, "What would your child have to gain by making this up? Why would your daughter have a dream, wake up and believe she was sexually abused? If that happened to me, I'd just rub my eyes and say, 'Wow, what a really bad dream.' "

The third level, denial of impact, is addressed through a confrontation with the victim—at a point when the offender is ready to listen and to recognize the pain the survivor has experienced. And the acknowledgment of responsibility usually follows closely once the perpetrator begins to feel empathy with the victim.

"The process is very slow," Barrett says, "But I've seen real metamorphosis if they stick with it." About half the time, survivors are able to maintain their own integrity—knowing they were traumatized—while still retaining a piece of their family relationship. For Barrett such resolutions are deeply gratifying: "It's been miraculous seeing adult survivors and their families change together."

In the past year, however, Barrett has worked with several families in which the parents came to therapy already steeped in backlash beliefs. These families have been much harder to work with.

Barrett points out that similar stages of denial are common in all members of the family, not just the offender. The survivor, for instance, may deny that the abuse took place, may forget or have dissociated the experience, may minimize the impact the abuse has had on her life, or may blame herself instead of putting the responsibility where it belongs—with the perpetrator.

Before, parents came in and it was just about their family and the facts of their lives. But now they come in with a pathological take on their kid: "You've been brainwashed." So no matter what happens, the parents say, "You're under the influence of your therapist. You're under the influence of a 12-step program. You're under the influence of *The Courage to Heal.* You were a wonderful, happy child until all this happened to you." They're doing exactly what they accuse their kids of doing—buying a party line and swallowing it whole. Such polarization stops the healing. It's made my work much harder.

Barrett says the worst thing about the false memory doctrine is that it retraumatizes the victim: "There's no empathy for the survivor. And lack of empathy is one of the main reasons the abuse happened in the first place."[86]

Mark Schwartz, co-director of the Masters and Johnson Sexual Trauma and Compulsivity Programs, says he too has watched the propagation of the "false memory argument" reinforce the denial of perpetrators:

In our perpetrators' program, many individuals who had previously acknowledged their perpetrations have begun carrying around "false memory" articles to fuel their denial, resulting in more perpetrations.[87]

It is imperative that we create a climate in which people who commit abuse can acknowledge what they've done and be accountable for their actions rather than be bolstered by rhetoric that further reinforces their denial.

Reports of families "destroyed by false allegations" tell only one side of the story.

The typical profile of a survivor, as presented by the backlash, is that of a well-educated woman in her thirties, who had a basically happy childhood and then invented a history of sexual abuse to explain her contemporary problems and get back at her parents.

In these accounts, it's always the parents who categorize the childhood as happy. They pull out family albums filled with photos of smiling children and talk about how wonderful things were until their daughter, or occasionally their son, came under the influence of a villainous therapist and suddenly began making these accusations "out of the blue." This depiction of therapists as evil manipulators allows the parents to blame someone other than themselves, or their child, for their current distress and conveniently makes the family the victim rather than the source of the problem. The lingering question "Why would my wonderfully happy, well-adjusted child level such serious charges against me?" goes unanswered.

---

[86] Mary Jo Barrett and Terry S. Trepper's book, *Systemic Treatment of Incest: A Therapeutic Handbook* (New York: Brunner/Mazel, 1989), is a useful guide for therapists working with families in which incest has taken place. It presents a positive and effective method of helping abusers and their spouses break through their denial, make necessary changes, and stop the sexual abuse. However, some statements in the book can be misleading if taken out of context. Therefore, it is important to consider the book in its entirety.

[87] Mark F. Schwartz, "False Memory Blues," *Masters and Johnson Report* 2, no. 1 (Summer 1993), p. 3.

The adult children, meanwhile, are rarely heard from in these reports. But many of them have spoken or written to us, and they do not characterize their childhoods as happy.[88] Instead, they describe years of trauma—much of which can be corroborated—as well as years of inner suffering. And many explain that, contrary to their parents' claims, they remembered their abuse without help from a therapist—or never forgot it:

> It drives me crazy that my parents keep going around saying how my survivors' group put these ideas in my head. Why would I have gone to a survivors' group if I wasn't abused? I didn't need a therapist to convince me I was abused. I went for help *because* I was abused. And the part about how I'd always been such a happy child is pitiful. I'd always been a successful functioner. I looked good. But I wrote in my diary at age ten that I wanted to die, and my first suicide attempt was the next year.

Legal principles do not apply to healing.

Survivors have been criticized for making claims of abuse without enough evidence. Because they don't have the kind of proof that would be required to win a lawsuit, survivors are condemned for saying that they were abused, limiting contact with their families, or protecting their children from potential abuse.

Irate parents, and the professionals who defend them, rely on principles that pertain to the law, such as "You're innocent until proven guilty," to censure the choices of survivors. These parents complain that their adult children won't tell them exactly what they're accused of, won't admit them into their therapy, or continue to see them. But choices about how one conducts one's life are not bound by legal principles. We are all entitled to live our lives as we see fit, without providing evidence to justify our choices.

Healing—and simply living one's life—is very different from suing in a court of law. Yet this obvious difference is often obscured in the media coverage of the backlash and sometimes in professional circles.

In a lawsuit, stringent standards of proof are necessary. We have a legal system that attempts to protect each party's rights while pursuing justice. This is as it should be. However, outside the legal arena, adults have the right to explore their own history and to make their own choices without providing proof, evidence, or even an explanation. In healthy relationships, people naturally want to discuss their motives and feelings when making changes that affect others. But in relationships marred by abuse, such honesty is often impossible.

Most survivors repeatedly try to work things out with their families, hoping for healing and reconciliation. It's only after coming up against intractable patterns of denial, minimizing, and continued abuse that they make the agonizing decision to pull away from their families.

When there are rifts in families that can't be mended, it's always a loss with much suffering involved. But some survivors have found that continuing contact with their parents or other family members is destructive to their mental health and to their ability to create positive, satisfying lives.

---

[88] See Jennifer Freyd's story on p. 489 for an example.

Being an incest survivor does not offer enough advantages to encourage anyone to "jump on the bandwagon."

Those who seek to invalidate survivors like to claim that incest has become an attractive club to join, that people claim to be survivors in order to get attention, sympathy, approval from therapists, or to create an excuse for their contemporary problems.

In reality, survivors usually minimize the abuse they experienced or pretend it didn't happen, rather than make up or exaggerate histories of abuse. It's excruciating to know that people you loved and trusted could have betrayed you in such a profound way.

Most survivors are not eager to name their abuse. On the contrary—they avoid facing the rigors of the healing process for as long as they can. As Judith Herman and Mary Harvey point out, recovering memories is so agonizing that survivors hold on to their denial for as long as possible:

> When traumatic memories break into awareness, distress can be overwhelming. Survivors . . . tend to cling to their doubts long past the point where most impartial observers would be convinced. That is why many therapists and self-help books encourage survivors to have confidence in their suspicions.[89]

In fact, as psychologist Christine Courtois points out, many survivors who do remember childhood abuse wish they didn't:

> Those with access to memory usually wish to forget, repress, or minimize

what they know. Those with absent, hazy, or fragmented memory are usually desperate to remember, until memory returns. They then move to the position of survivors with memory: they want to forget.[90]

Identifying as an incest survivor confers very few privileges. It does name a reason for an often complex and dizzying array of problems, but naming the root cause as abuse is only the beginning of the healing process. The responsibility for healing, inevitably, lies with the survivor. No one else can accomplish the arduous work of healing, feel the feelings, and make the changes needed to create a healthy life in the present. Although healing is ultimately rewarding and worth the work, it is not something one would choose if it weren't absolutely necessary.

One survivor, who has spent years struggling to heal from the wounds of her childhood, finds the charge that she made up the abuse not only absurd but painful. "Why," she asked simply, "do we have to fight to hold on to something we wish would go away?"

The propagation of the "false memory" theory reinforces some very old and powerful stereotypes about gender, class, and race.

The first stereotype is that of women as pawns: weak, gullible, and so impressionable that reading a book about sexual abuse or having a therapist suggest that they might

[89] Judith L. Herman and Mary R. Harvey, "The False Memory Debate: Social Science or Social Backlash?," *The Harvard Mental Health Letter* 9, no. 10 (April 1993), p. 5.

[90] Christine A. Courtois, "The Memory Retrieval Process in Incest Survivor Therapy," *Journal of Child Sexual Abuse* 1, no. 1 (1992), pp. 15–16.

have been sexually abused would be enough to convince them of a reality not their own. This stereotype is not only false; it's a gross insult to women, telling us we don't have the power or sense to know what happened to us. We do not believe most women are so easily led or manipulated.

Supporters of the backlash frequently talk about child sex abuse "hysteria." In Freud's time, "hysteria" was a legitimate term used to describe a condition of severe emotional and mental distress. The word has since acquired such negative implications and has been applied to women in such insulting ways that we suggest it's long past time when "hysterical" can be responsibly used to describe women's testimony. Clearly, supporters of the backlash have chosen this word for its inflammatory effect.

Another erroneous stereotype is that abuse doesn't happen in affluent white families. According to a fact sheet put out by the False Memory Syndrome Foundation in June 1992, the median income level of parents who join their organization is over $60,000. More than half are college-educated, and 25 percent have advanced degrees.[91] In one newsletter, founder Pamela Freyd responded to charges that her group might be harboring abusers:

> How do we know we are not representing pedophiles?
>
> This question keeps coming up,

and it is critically important to our image and to our ability to get things done. . . . One person suggested that I take a camera to meetings so that when the opportunity for going public presented itself, we could suggest representatives who would have the best image. . . .

If I had taken a camera to any of the three meetings held here in Philadelphia, I would have been hard put to know whom to photograph. We are a good looking bunch of people: graying hair, well-dressed, healthy, smiling. The similarity of stories is astounding, so script-like and formulaic that doubts dissolve after chats with a few families. Just about every person who has attended is someone you would likely find interesting and want to count as a friend.[92]

The implication is that well-to-do, good-looking people couldn't possibly have abused their children. This contradicts well-established facts about abusers.[93]

Although they aren't always identified as such, the families presented in the media as victims of the "false memory syndrome" have all been white. The message here is that real abuse takes place in poor families, in African-American, Latino, Asian, and Native American families, but that "false memories" are to blame for the disintegration of well-to-do white families. This implication is both racist

---

[91] In a study of families served by the FMS Foundation, 92.2% reported that the accusing child grew up in a "middle," "upper middle," or "upper" class home; 7.2% reported their socioeconomic status as "lower middle" class; and only .7% said they were "lower" class (*FMS Foundation Newsletter*, May 3, 1993, p. 9).

[92] *FMS Foundation Newsletter*, February 29, 1992.

[93] See p. 499. Anna Salter further discusses this issue specifically in regard to members of the FMS Foundation in *Transforming Trauma*, chapter 1.

and false. Abuse crosses all lines of race, class, and gender.[94]

It is unusual for therapists to convince their clients that abuse took place when it didn't.

The core of the "false memory" argument is that fictitious memories of child sexual abuse are implanted in the minds of impressionable patients by overeager, manipulative, or greedy therapists, and that they use coercive mind-control techniques to do so.

This is not how responsible therapists work. The foundation of good therapy is a respectful relationship in which the therapist provides a safe space, genuine caring, and support. Good therapists don't lead—they follow their clients into the difficult and painful places they need to go. In doing so, their clients are empowered to do their own healing work, to uncover their own history, to find their own truth. As Judith Herman explains, "Psychotherapy is a collaborative effort, not a form of totalitarian indoctrination."[95]

If it were really possible for therapists to create new memories in their clients, survivors of child sexual abuse *would*, in fact, probably be the first to sign up. As one survivor put it, "If it is so common and so easily accomplished to alter or even implant memories, where can I get some new ones? Mine are all too real and sickening and frankly, I'm tired of them."

This is not to say that there aren't bad or even abusive therapists. Unethical therapists have forced hospitalizations, overmedicated their patients, had sex with clients, and perpetrated a variety of other abuses. But such practitioners are not representative of the mental health profession as a whole.[96]

All therapists, even good ones, do sometimes make mistakes. In the past, these mistakes—at least those relative to survivors—had more to do with minimizing and denying abuse than seeing it where it didn't exist. Even now, many therapists are reluctant to explore a history of abuse with their clients.[97]

As awareness of sexual abuse has become more widespread, however, therapists sometimes have made the opposite mistake: concluding a client was abused before that person had a chance to explore this possibility herself. But even then, it is very unusual for clients to take on every suggestion a therapist makes. One woman, who'd come from a violent alcoholic home but who'd never been sexually abused, related the following story:

> Two times now, I've been in therapy with counselors who've told me I have all the symptoms of someone who's been sexually abused. One of them kept pushing at me. It made me

---

[94] For documentation of the universality of child sexual abuse, see David Finkelhor and Larry Baron, "High-Risk Children," in Finkelhor, *Sourcebook on Child Sexual Abuse*, pp. 60–88.

[95] Herman, "Backtalk," p. 4.

[96] For resources on dealing with abuse by therapists, see p. 550 of the Resource Guide.

[97] And that reluctance is growing. Faced with attacks on their professional judgment and the threat of legal action and ethics charges by irate parents, a growing number of therapists are finding themselves in conflict between protecting themselves and following the best interests of their clients.

mad. I'd given the matter a lot of thought, and I knew it wasn't what happened to me. A lot of other things happened—but not sexual abuse. So I told her to leave it alone, and finally she backed off.

When a therapist inaccurately surmises that someone has been sexually abused as a child, it is a serious error of grave concern. It has the potential to damage both the client and the family involved. Families who have suffered this kind of pain deserve acknowledgment and compassion.

Women who say they were misled in therapy, and that the abuse they once claimed never really happened, call themselves "recanters." A number of these women report being mistreated through hospitalization, excessive and inappropriate drugs, and authoritarian and invasive methods that far exceeded simply asking the question "Were you ever sexually abused as a child?" or even the more leading "You show all the signs of being sexually abused. I think you were." Recanters have described not just being asked if they were abused but feeling coerced by their therapists into coming up with a story of abuse. Some report that they made up a story, either to please their therapist or to fit in with members of their group. Only later, as time went by, did they begin to believe these stories themselves.

Some recanters talk about being subjected to mind control and feel as if they're recovering from being involved in a cult. Interestingly, a sizable number of recanters say they were involved in cults or cultlike groups at an earlier time in their lives. An article in a newsletter for recanters explored this common link in the histories of many of its readers:

We often share the *same vulnerabilities of high idealism, dependency weaknesses, basic resistance to change, spiritual hunger.* A cult experience offers us a tempting escape from the hostile pain of the real world, a black and white answer, a righteous us-against-them stance. There was a desperate inner structure to be gained from our idealistic battle against perceived "perpetrators" and "abusers." [98]

The experience of these women is painful and must be acknowledged. However, it does not hold true for the majority of people who recover memories of child sexual abuse during therapy.

In their July 1993 newsletter, the FMS Foundation reported there were sixty women who said that the sexual abuse they initially described never took place. Even if all sixty cases were accurate, they represent only a tiny fraction of the millions of actual survivors of child sexual abuse.

Confronting one's abuser and family is one of the most painful, frightening things a survivor faces. As with children's disclosures, it is possible that some recantations are a result of enormous family pressures rather than an erroneous accusation. It is also of interest that a number of recanters acknowledge that they *were* sexually abused; what they now say is that their accusations snowballed beyond the truth, implicating people who did not actually abuse them.

There need be no schism between survivors and recanters. It is imperative that re-

---

[98] *The Retractor: Newsletter for Survivors of Recovered Memory Therapy* (Fall 1993), p. 2.

canters speak out and tell their stories. But it is equally important that they do so without attacking all survivors of child sexual abuse, the validity of their memories, and the important social gains that have been made.

Therapy is rarely the sole or primary trigger for memories of child sexual abuse.

Proponents of the "false memory syndrome" promote the belief that most adult survivors regain their memories of child sexual abuse at the instigation of a therapist. This is not true. Many survivors never see a therapist at all. They struggle along as best they can without coming to terms with the abuse, or they work through their pain without the aid of a counselor. Of those who do seek therapy, many already know about the abuse. Either they've always remembered it and they now are ready to seek help, or something else has triggered the memories and they need help coping with the fallout.

There are three factors that are usually present when adults (or adolescents) recall abuse they have previously blocked out: distance from the original abuse, a life circumstance that leads to the letting down of normal defenses, and an external event that restimulates the memory.[99] These factors can exist in a good therapeutic relationship, and therefore some survivors do uncover abuse while in therapy. But recall of child

---

[99] Discussed by Karen Olio and William Cornell in "Therapeutic Relationship as the Foundation for Treatment with Adult Survivors of Sexual Abuse," *Psychotherapy* 30, no. 3 (in press). (Available through Family Violence Sexual Assault Institute, 1310 Clinic Drive, Tyler, TX 75701.) Also see Christine Courtois, *Healing the Incest Wound* (New York: W. W. Norton, 1988).

sexual abuse is far more common in other circumstances.

Life transitions—puberty, childbirth, a commitment to an intimate relationship, the death of a parent, retirement, moving, menopause, aging, divorce, losses of any kind—frequently trigger memories. So does sobriety. Medical treatment—a trip to the dentist, an exam by a gynecologist or urologist, surgery or other invasive medical procedures—can also jar loose buried feelings and images. Adult experiences of victimization—a rape, a robbery, being fired from a job—often stir up memories of earlier violations. Parents sometimes remember their own abuse when their child is abused or when that child reaches the age they were when they were first abused. Survivors may also remember while making love, exercising, or getting massaged—when they use their bodies in a new way.

Of course any of these life events may occur while a survivor is in therapy. And a survivor may seek therapy for help in coping with such events. But a therapist's question, or even suggestion, about sexual abuse is rarely the only or most significant reason for memories to emerge.

There is a lot more to determining whether someone is a survivor than a single memory.

The "false memory" argument hinges on the assumption that an assessment of child sexual abuse is based solely or primarily on memory. But that isn't true. Long-term trauma is reflected in the daily lives of many survivors. For some the injury is obvious—they have suffered from severe and debilitating symptoms for many years. Some have permanent physical damage that is unmistakably traumatic in origin.[100] Other survivors have been successful at creating highly functional lives, but their inner world is self-hating or full of pain. These effects, which have frequently been present for years prior to uncovering a sexual abuse history, are not created in a therapist's office.

Reconstructing a history of child sexual abuse is a complex process based on a whole constellation of symptoms, of which memory is just a part. Phobias, flashbacks, intrusive imagery, chronic patterns of denial and dissociation, flooding of feelings, spontaneous regression, startle reflexes, numbness in the body, and terror of sex may all point to a history of trauma in childhood.[101]

Those who say memories of sexual abuse can be implanted fail to explain the presence of these symptoms. A therapist cannot induce you to jump out of your skin every time someone comes up behind you. "False memories" cannot explain why you see your abuser's face when you climax (see Rachel's story on page 524), why you're terrified of subway cars (see Evie Malcolm's story on page 392), why you carve into your body (see Michelle and Artemis on page 446), or why you wake up terrified every morning at 4:00 a.m. (see Alicia Mendoza's story on page 421). These and hundreds of other distressing patterns fall through the cracks of the "false memory" theory and are, unfortunately, often explained by an all-too-real history of child sexual abuse.

Memory research is being distorted to validate the idea of a "false memory syndrome."

The research cited to validate the existence of a "false memory syndrome" consists largely of studies designed to learn about variations in normal memory and to assess the accuracy of eyewitness accounts of incidents such as car accidents. Such studies show that memory is fallible and that people are often in error when they report what happened. However, this research does not apply to traumatic amnesia. To say that the errors in ordinary memory prove that fictitious memories of child sexual abuse can be implanted by therapists violates a basic tenet of science: Findings pertaining to one specific set of circumstances and one population cannot be assumed to hold true for a different set of circumstances and a different population.[102]

One of the examples most often cited to prove the idea of a "false memory syndrome" is a study by Elizabeth Loftus, professor of psychology at the University of Washington and a member of the FMS Foundation advisory board. With the help of family members who insisted that a bogus event was real, Loftus was able to convince five subjects that they'd been lost in a shopping mall when they were children.

However, being briefly lost is in the realm of common childhood experience. There is no evidence that memories of something foreign, traumatic, and repugnant to

---

[100] See S. R. Benjamin's story on p. 428.

[101] As described by Karen Olio, "The Truth Behind the False Memory Syndrome," p. 299.

[102] Discussed by Karen A. Olio and William F. Cornell, "Making Meaning, Not Monsters: Reflections on the Delayed Memory Controversy," *Journal of Child Sexual Abuse*, Vol. 3 (3), 1994. (Available in *Trauma, Amnesia, and the Denial of Abuse*, edited by Robert Falconer. See listing on p. 555 of the Resource Guide or order directly through the Haworth Press (800) 342-9678).

us, like sexual abuse, could be similarly implanted. Psychiatrist Richard Kluft speculates on this question:

> We might think the academicians have won the day. . . . However, there are some reasons for skepticism about skepticism about allegations of sexual abuse. Is Loftus' laboratory equivalent to the family bedroom? Is the picture of an automobile accident equivalent to the imagery of a penis coming right at you? Is sitting in a nice air-conditioned university classroom the equivalent of being forcefully penetrated? Is it possible that the memories might be laid down a little differently?[103]

In a letter to Karen Olio about the relevance of this study to survivors of child sexual abuse, Loftus herself wrote, "Being lost in a shopping mall is completely different from being sexually abused. . . . I've never tried to say they were the same."[104] Loftus's research, like the other studies cited as evidence of a "false memory syndrome," have little relevance to traumatic memories of child sexual abuse.

Expert witnesses for the defense in sexual abuse cases have also given extremely misleading testimony about memory research. Anna Salter studied Hollida Wakefield and Ralph Underwager's book, *Accusations of Child Sexual Abuse,* as well as transcripts of Underwager's testimony:

> I took a look at his transcript and I was horrified. He was talking about research I knew and books that I knew. He was saying things like, "All research in this volume demonstrates that children are very suggestible." In fact, the book mentioned a *number* of studies on suggestibility. Some found children were more suggestible than adults, some the same. At least one found that adults were more suggestible. One author summed up by saying, "No systematic relationship between age and suggestibility has been consistently documented." That was in direct opposition to what Underwager said.
>
> That's when I became aware that nobody was going back and looking at the academic scaffolding for this.[105]

Under the auspices of the New England Association of Child Welfare Directors and Commissioners, Salter wrote a monograph, *Accuracy of Expert Testimony in Child Sexual Abuse Cases: A Case Study of Ralph Underwager and Hollida Wakefield,* in which she examined more than five hundred articles to which Underwager referred in his book and in his court testimony.[106] She found a multitude of factual errors, both minor and serious:

> In their book, Underwager and Wakefield cite a study that they say was done with younger and older children. Actually, the study was done with college students. Errors like that in court

---

[103] Kluft, "Advanced Treatment of Multiple Personality Disorder."

[104] Elizabeth Loftus in a personal communication to Karen Olio, November 1, 1992, as cited by Olio and Cornell, "Making Meaning, Not Monsters."

[105] Salter interview, September 16, 1993.

[106] This monograph is available from Anna Salter, Ph.D., Midwest Center for Psychotherapy and Sex Therapy, 426 S. Yellowstone Dr., Suite 225, Madison, WI 53719, (608) 829-3880; fax: (608) 829-1422.

testimony in cases where the safety and security of children are at stake, is horrifying. . . . Cases of child sexual abuse are sometimes won or lost based on expert testimony.[107]

Expert witnesses often come to court citing research they do not bring with them. By the time the other side can track down the research to see if the claims are accurate, the trial may be over. Salter writes:

If the defendant is acquitted on the basis of inaccurate expert testimony, there is no appeal. The defense may appeal a conviction, but the prosecution cannot appeal an acquittal. Thus it is very important that psychologists, psychiatrists, and social workers testify as accurately as possible in these cases. It is not too much to say that justice depends on it.[108]

WHAT WE DO AND DON'T KNOW ABOUT MEMORY

There are many unanswered questions about trauma and memory, but whether traumatic amnesia exists is not one of them. The fact that people experience amnesia for traumatic events is—or should be—beyond dispute. It has been documented not only in cases of child sexual abuse but among war veterans, battered women, prisoners of war, and others who have suffered severe ongoing trauma.[109] Psychotherapist David Calof, who has worked with more than four hundred abuse survivors, explains:

What stood out in many of these cases . . . were symptoms common to other trauma victims, including survivors of such public horrors as the bombing of Dresden, the camps at Auschwitz, the massacred villages of Vietnam, Guatemala and Bosnia, the killing fields of Cambodia and the torture chambers of Brazil. Like survivors of these public

---

[107] Salter interview, September 16, 1993. Ralph Underwager's testimony has been partially or wholly excluded in at least nine instances. In *State v. Deloch,* 1990 WL 48536 (Minn. 1990) (slip opinion) the Court of Appeals ruled, "The record does not establish that the scientific basis for [Dr. Underwager's memory] theory is reliable and broadly accepted in its field." In *Oregon v. Herrick* (trial court decision) the court held that "Dr. Underwager did inadequate research. His preparation was inadequate and therefore it's lacking in sound foundation." And in *People v. Chuck* (New York State, April 26, 1988) the trial court held that Dr. Underwager was "not qualified to render any opinion as to whether or not [the victim] was sexually molested."

[108] Salter, *Accuracy of Expert Testimony,* p. 3.

---

[109] See Joel Osler Brende and Erwin Randolph Parson, *Vietnam Veterans: The Road to Recovery* (New York: Plenum Press, 1985); Judith Lewis Herman, *Trauma and Recovery* (New York: HarperCollins, 1992); Bessel A. van der Kolk, *Psychological Trauma* (Washington, D.C.: American Psychiatric Press, 1987); Jean Goodwin, "Rediscovering Sadism," in *Rediscovering Childhood Trauma* (Washington, D.C.: American Psychiatric Press, 1993), and "Credibility Problems in Multiple Personality Disorder Patients and Abused Children," in *Childhood Antecedents of Multiple Personality Disorder,* ed. Richard Kluft (Washington, D.C.: American Psychiatric Press, 1985); and Frank W. Putnam, Jr., "Dissociation as a Response to Extreme Trauma," also in *Childhood Antecedents of Multiple Personality Disorder.*

traumas, my clients had dissociative symptoms, such as sleepwalking and memory disturbances, as well as signs of post-traumatic stress, such as flashbacks, sleep disturbances and nightmares. They wanted to be anonymous, or were socially withdrawn. They were depressed or had other mood disturbances. They often tended to minimize or rationalize painful present realities, and they suffered from feelings of numbness, emptiness and unreality.

Unlike the survivors of publicly acknowledged disasters, however, they did not know *why* they felt that way. Their memories of the traumas were often fragmented into bewildering mosaics or missing altogether. Often, they were veterans of intensely private wars that had taken place in barns, attics and suburban houses with the blinds drawn. Their wounds were never reported in newspapers or discussed with family members. There were rarely any witnesses other than the people who hurt them. . . . their childhood rapes and beatings were encoded into memory in fragments, in a state of terror, when their hearts and minds were flooded with adrenaline. They didn't remember them the way one remembers a walk in the park, and they doubted the fragments they did recall.[110]

There is increasing documentation of traumatic amnesia specific to survivors of child sexual abuse. In the much-publicized Father James Porter case, a Catholic priest admitted to sexually abusing between fifty and one hundred children. As adults, many of these survivors experienced amnesia, including Frank Fitzpatrick, the first man to come forward.[111]

Psychologist John Briere and therapist Jon Conte studied 450 survivors (420 women and 30 men) regarding amnesia for sexual abuse incidents. Fifty-nine percent of the survivors identified some period in their lives, before age eighteen, when they had no memory of their abuse. Amnesia was most common when the abuse took place at an early age, was extended over time, included multiple perpetrators, or was violent.[112]

Linda Meyer Williams, research associate professor at the Family Violence Research Laboratory at the University of New Hampshire, studied traumatic amnesia by interviewing 129 women who as children had reported sexual abuse and had been brought to the hospital emergency room for treatment and for the collection of forensic evidence. At the time of the original abuse, the girls and their families were all interviewed and information about the abuse was carefully documented. Seventeen years later, 38 percent, more than one in three, did not remember the abuse or chose not to disclose it.[113]

---

[110] David Calof, "Facing the Truth About False Memory," *The Family Therapy Networker* 17, no. 5 (September/October 1993), pp. 40–41.

[111] See Elinor Burkett and Frank Bruni, *A Gospel of Shame: Child Sexual Abuse and the Catholic Church* (p. 560 of the Resource Guide) for a thorough accounting of the Father James Porter case.

[112] John Briere and Jon Conte, "Self-Reported Amnesia for Abuse in Adults Molested as Children," *Journal of Traumatic Stress* 6, no. 1 (1993), pp. 21–31.

[113] Linda Meyer Williams, "Recall of Childhood Trauma: A Prospective Study of Women's Memories of Child Sex-

In a study by psychiatrist Judith Herman and psychotherapist Emily Schatzow of fifty-three clients, most of whom had recovered memories of child sexual abuse, 74 percent were able to find corroborating evidence. Most of these got confirmation from family members who knew about the abuse. Some found diaries or photos, talked to other victims, or had perpetrators who admitted what they had done. (In several instances, the perpetrator even tried to reinitiate sex!) Nine percent found evidence that strongly suggested sexual abuse but was not conclusive, and 11 percent did not try to confirm their memories. Only 6 percent could not find any supportive corroboration.[114] In their ability to find corroboration, there was no difference between the women who'd always remembered their abuse and those whose memories had been repressed.[115]

All too often, recovered memories are substantiated through the discovery that a child is being abused in the present by the same person who abused the adult survivor in the past.[116] Frequently this tragic turn of events is the only thing that finally brings families to acknowledge that the adult survivor is telling the truth. As one survivor described:

> I'd told my mother. I'd told my brothers. And my sisters-in-law. I'd screamed at them to keep my niece and nephews away from my father. They thought I was a raving lunatic. My mother believed me for about two weeks and then she collapsed. She couldn't face it. And nobody did anything. Now it's too late. The kids have all been abused and finally, everyone believes me.

This is not to say that memory is always 100 percent accurate. We know for a fact that

---

ual Abuse," *Journal of Consulting and Clinical Psychology,* 62(6), 1167–1176. The authors state that their research suggests that most of the women who didn't disclose the abuse in fact did not remember it. They write: "Most of the women told the interviewer about many other very personal matters—such as information on other sexual, physical and emotional abuse suffered in childhood . . . so it is unlikely that embarrassment was the reason that so many women did not tell about the 'index' abuse. Of the women who *did not recall* the child sexual abuse which brought them into the study, 68% told the interviewer about *other sexual assaults* (clearly involving different perpetrators and circumstances) that they experienced in childhood." (This article and others reporting findings from the same are available from Linda Williams, Director of Research, The Stone Center, 106 Central St., Wellesley, MA 02181, (781) 283–2834, fax (781) 283–3646.)

[114] Judith Herman and Emily Schatzow, "Recovery and Verification of Memories of Childhood Sexual Trauma," *Psychoanalytic Psychology* 4. no. 1 (1987), pp. 1-14. (For a copy of this article, write to the Women's Mental Health Collective, 61 Roseland St., Somerville, MA 02143.)

In describing this study, Judith Herman added the following caveat: "I'd like to emphasize that the choice to take this action properly belongs to the survivors, not to therapists, researchers or anyone else. We may not impose a search for corroborating evidence upon our patients, as some have suggested, simply to satisfy *our* wish for certainty."

[115] Judith Herman, "Adult Memories of Childhood Trauma," p. 5.

[116] See *The Hidden Legacy: Uncovering, Confronting and Healing Three Generations of Incest* by Barbara Smith Hamilton (Fort Bragg, CA: Cypress House, 1992) for an illustration of how unacknowledged sexual abuse can devastate an entire family. Also interesting in this account is that some of the survivors always remembered (including the author, a grandmother), others regained memories as they healed, and some continue to have memory gaps.

it is not. Researchers Ulric Neisser and Nicole Harsh, for example, found that many people were mistaken in their recounting of where they were and what they were doing when the *Challenger* crashed. None, however, were mistaken about the fact that the *Challenger* crashed and the astronauts died.[117]

So too in memories of child sexual abuse. It is inevitable that survivors will remember the details of their abuse with some degree of inaccuracy. Time sequences may be mixed up, multiple incidents may be telescoped into a single incident, whole portions of incidents may be missing, and the events before and after may be blurred. But the core of the memory, its emotional felt truth, has its own authenticity. (See "The Essential Truth of Memory" on page 89 for more.) One survivor explained:

> There's a lot I'm pretty sure I'll never have straight. After all, it began before I can remember. I mean, there was never a time *before* the abuse. So a lot of it's blurred. And I honestly don't think it'll ever come into focus. But I've

gotten clear on the essentials—what I need to know to do my healing work and get on with my life. I know the main cast of perpetrators. I know the extent of the damage. Maybe I'll get more bits and pieces as time goes on, but if I don't, it doesn't matter. The cards are on the table—which is a relief.

BUT HOW COULD YOU FORGET A THING LIKE THAT?

Even though you may intellectually understand the relationship between sexual abuse and traumatic amnesia, you may still have trouble imagining that it's possible to "forget" something as significant as sexual abuse for twenty or thirty years. One survivor, who'd always remembered her incest vividly, could not comprehend how anyone could forget such violations. It was a struggle for her to believe the stories she heard from women who didn't remember their abuse until adulthood.

> Over the years I've been in several support groups for incest survivors and used to wonder about the women who were in the process of recovering memories of their abuse. After all, I could remember all the abuse I suffered. Why couldn't these survivors describe their abuse in the same vivid way? For instance, I can recall the exact pattern of the dress I was wearing at age nine when my grandfather pushed me down on the bed. Although I wanted to support these other women, I found it difficult.
>
> However, the day after I confronted my grandfather about his

---

[117] Ulric Neisser and Nicole Harsch, "Phantom Flashbulbs: False Recollections on Hearing News About Challenger," in *Affect and Accuracy in Recall: Studies of "Flashbulb" Memories*, eds. Eugene Winograd and Ulric Neisser (New York: Cambridge University Press, 1992).

Although there has been enormous skepticism from the backlash that memories of abuse that took place decades ago could be accurately recalled, there is, in fact, research to suggest the opposite. Fran H. Norris and Krzysztof Kaniasty ("Reliability of Delayed Self-Reports in Disaster Research," *Journal of Traumatic Stress* 5, no. 4 (1992), p. 586) found that while memories of ordinary events are continually modified by new experiences, distorted, and sometimes forgotten altogether, memories of events that have a major impact on our lives are more likely to retain striking accuracy.

abuse, I remembered an incident that happened when I was five. It came back to me with the same kind of vivid detail I've always recalled about the other times he molested me. I now believe in suppressed memories, but I think it is very difficult to understand this phenomenon if you have not experienced it yourself.

MEMORY AND ABUSERS

In all this debate about memory, much has been said about survivors' memories but little about the memories of the abusers. Since there are so many unknowns about memory, then why aren't those who claim to be "falsely accused" questioning their own memories of the past? As one survivor wrote:

It's perfectly rational to believe that parents who are abusive might repress the memories of the abuse and then deny it. Some of the anger I read in the parents' stories sounded like the anger of being discovered, rather than the anger of being accused of a wrong they did not commit.[118]

Perpetrators have a strong and clear motivation to bury what they've done. Psychologist John Rhead speculated on this probability in a letter he wrote to the director of the FMS Foundation:

Recently a man I was working with recalled an event in which he was the abuser, and it reminded me how much more of an incentive the abuser has to falsify memories. When I attempt to imagine having abused one of my children I am filled with an anguish I can scarcely describe. . . . It seems to me that the anguish associated with having been the betrayer has to be at least as great as that of having been the betrayed. . . .

The parent probably has already [felt] such deep and powerful love for their offspring that to integrate those feelings with an awareness of having betrayed the child would be difficult to say the least. . . . I expect that the parent would be particularly vulnerable to . . . conjuring up a memory of a warm and loving relationship with their child, uncomplicated by memory of the abuse and betrayal.[119]

Many offenders were victims of child sexual abuse themselves. Their subsequent perpetration against children is sometimes a reenactment of what they themselves experienced. They may or may not be aware of their own childhood trauma or connect it to their abuse of children now. But the patterns of denial, repression, or even complete amnesia that helped them cope with their own violation may limit their capacity to acknowledge and face their abusive behavior now.

Most therapists who work with offenders observe that denial operates more frequently than actual amnesia when it comes to their abuse of children. But in some cases this

---

[118] Màiri Mc Fall, *Mama Bears News and Notes*, vol. 10, no. 3, April/May 1993.

[119] John Rhead, letter to Pamela Freyd at the FMS Foundation, June 1, 1992.

suppression of awareness is so strong, the offender really thinks he didn't do it. As psychologist Brian Abbott explains:

> Most offenders are aware of what they're doing while they're committing the sexual offense, but there's a feeling of disgust, shame and guilt associated with it. In order to preserve some feeling of self-worth, the offender forgets what he has done. By not remembering, he doesn't have to be faced with those disgusting, shameful feelings about his behavior. Some offenders literally bury it in their mind to the point where they're not consciously aware of it anymore.[120]

In light of this, it's easy to see how even those whose perpetration has been clearly proven could still continue to believe in, and proclaim, their innocence.

FACING SADISTIC RITUAL ABUSE

> If there is even a small chance that one ritual abuse claim is true, we owe it to all potential victims to explore the problem of ritual abuse in greater depth.
>
> —Margaret Smith[121]

Some of the propaganda of the backlash has attempted to discredit survivors' stories by ridiculing their reports of extreme abuse, including the torture of sadistic ritual abuse.[122] It is understandable that as a society and as individuals, we are reluctant to face such atrocities, but our inability to believe is what leaves victims vulnerable and survivors bereft of compassion—or even acknowledgment. Elie Wiesel, renowned author and survivor of the Holocaust, was recently interviewed by Oprah Winfrey. In response to her exclamation of how "unbelievable" his experiences were, Wiesel responded, "The enemy counted on the disbelief of the world."[123]

This is the situation we face now, and the dangers of our collective denial are grave. Psychologist Susan Van Benschoten says:

> To realize the danger in not taking patients' accounts of satanic abuse seriously, one only has to consider instances in which reports of atrocities were initially denied and later found to be true. Two vivid examples from this century are the tragedy at Jonestown, Guyana, and the Holocaust. In both instances, accounts of the events unfolding were

[120] Abbott interview, September 9, 1993.

[121] Margaret Smith, *Ritual Abuse: What It Is, Why It Happens, and How to Help* (San Francisco: HarperSanFrancisco, 1993), p. vii.

[122] In *Rediscovering Childhood Trauma* (pp. 95–111), Jean Goodwin proposes that we use the term "sadistic abuse" to name the "extreme and severe acts of interpersonal violence which in the 1980s came to be described as 'ritual abuse.'" Discussing sadism through history, Goodwin concludes that the term "sadistic abuse," being more inclusive, allows us to place this abuse within a context we already recognize: "If we understand ritual abuse as simply one of many forms of sadistic abuse, then other, more readily available data bases become relevant, including surveys of sadistic criminals, studies of users of sadomasochistic pornography, studies of war criminals, and descriptions of perpetrators of extreme family violence."

[123] *Oprah*, July 16, 1993.

available long before they were be-lieved.[124]

Although stories of sadistic ritual abuse are horrifying in the magnitude and perversity of the abuse, they are really not implausible considering the documented crimes we hear about every day. Chrystine Oksana, in her book *Safe Passage to Healing: A Guide for Survivors of Ritual Abuse,* explains:

> Everything found in ritual abuse collectively (physical abuse, emotional abuse, sexual abuse, incest, sadistic violence, murder, drugs, deception, manipulation, conditioning based on punishment, and unbridled veneration of power) is known to occur independently in our society. We also know that it is a tragically common occurrence for people in our society to organize to abuse others in pursuit of power (think of neo-Nazis and the Ku Klux Klan). Ritual abuse combines all of the above. It is organized abuse, carried out by a group for the purpose of achieving power. The abuse aims to break a victim's spirit and to gain the ultimate in power—absolute control over another human being.[125]

This does not mean that every detail of a survivor's disclosure is sure to be accurate.

In fact, when we are dealing with such extreme trauma, it is likely that there will be confusions, distortions, and reports of events that could not literally be true.

One survivor, for example, told her therapist that while she was being abused, a woman was killed. Her therapist had no way of knowing what literally took place, but she knew this survivor was telling her story as best she could. As this survivor was able to face more of her history, she recovered enough information to determine that while she was being abused, her perpetrators had shown a "snuff" film in which a woman was, indeed, murdered. In her child's mind—in this ordeal of extreme pain and terror—the images on the screen seemed to be happening in the room.

Distortions like this are due, in part, to the nature of memory in situations of great pain and fear. But such distortions are also deliberately created by the perpetrators. Illusion is often used in sadistic ritual abuse in order to terrify, silence, or otherwise control the victim, as well as to lessen a survivor's credibility should she or he seek help. For example, one survivor was told that she was going to be operated on and that a bomb would be put in her stomach. She was threatened that if she ever told anyone about what had been done to her, the bomb would go off, killing her. They told her that if she even thought about telling, she'd feel sick to her stomach, nauseous. Then she was drugged, superficially cut, and when she woke up, she saw blood and believed she had been operated on.

Psychologist Mark Schwartz explains:

> Children see things through children's eyes; but regardless of "what happened," whatever was coded in the

---

[124] Susan C. Van Benschoten, "Multiple Personality Disorder and Satanic Ritual Abuse: The Issue of Credibility," *Dissociation 3,* no. 1 (March 1990), p. 25.

[125] Chrystine Oksana, *Safe Passage to Healing: A Guide for Survivors of Ritual Abuse* (New York: HarperCollins, 1994), preface.

child's perception and memory defined the traumatic experience. For example, if a child believes he's seen someone killed, even if that person survives and is alive, the trauma can be as intense as if a death had occurred.[126]

Under conditions of torture and terror, people dissociate to protect their minds from the total perception of the horror they're subjected to. This pain, fear, and dissociation, combined with drugs, intentional brainwashing, and the use of illusion, make some degree of distortion almost inevitable. However, as Susan Van Benschoten explains, none of this lessens the ordeal of the survivor, the essential truth of her disclosure, or the heinousness of the abuse:

> An experience is no less traumatic when it does not conform completely to literal reality. Neither can the perpetrated act be considered less brutal and inhumane, simply because the format may involve techniques such as illusion or the forced witnessing of another's abuse.[127]

Some of the media coverage of sadistic ritual abuse has been particularly misleading. For example, in the McMartin day-care trial, preschool children testified that they were taken through underground tunnels and then sexually abused. The jury acquitted the teachers accused of abuse, and the press highlighted the fact that no tunnels had been found. The media concluded that millions of dollars in public funds had been wasted and that there was no proof of any abuse at the McMartin preschool. In 1990, long after the trial was over and the school had been sold, the parents of the children hired Gary Stickel, an archaeologist who teaches at the University of California at Los Angeles, to excavate the site. Using directions given by two of the children, Stickel found a tunnel exactly where the children said it would be. The tunnel he excavated, which ran between two classrooms, had been dug sometime after 1967, when the McMartin preschool opened. It had been filled in with debris.[128]

The finding of the tunnel sheds a totally different light on the trial and on the children's claims. As Gary Stickel explains, "The defense used the fact that no tunnels were found as a major element in discrediting the children's testimony. Finding the tunnel supports the credibility of the children. If they were right about the tunnels they could have been right about everything else they said."[129] Yet the finding of the tunnel was barely mentioned in the press. Some people's denial went so far as to suggest that the tunnel was actually a rabbit burrow!

There is much outcry from skeptics that

---

[126] Schwartz, "False Memory Blues," p. 3.

[127] Van Benschoten, "Multiple Personality Disorder and Satanic Ritual Abuse," p. 27.

[128] The tunnel ran across the north axis of the school, between classroom #4 and classroom #3, and continued to an entrance under the west wall of the building. It was full of junk and debris—pieces of board, concrete slabs, and cans. Stickel said the most bizarre thing he found in the tunnel were four large containers, one and a half to two feet high, one made of crockery, two of metal, and the fourth a black iron cauldron that he said "would have made a good Halloween prop." All four were standing upright and had obviously been placed by someone in the middle of the tunnel.

[129] Gary Stickel, interview by Laura Davis, September 17, 1993.

there is no evidence of sadistic ritual abuse, but evidence has been found. Tunnels with cauldrons and debris are definitely not rabbit burrows. Animal mutilation and sacrifice exist. The U.S. Supreme Court recently passed judgment that such sacrifice as part of religious practices is legal.[130] Child pornography and child prostitution are a $2.5 billion-a-year business.[131] Children are filmed and photographed in violent and sadistic acts.[132]

We know that horrifying acts have been perpetrated on children, but this knowledge is so distressing that we try to explain it away. In Rupert, Idaho, the body of an infant girl was discovered in a remote rural area. According to a report in the *Los Angeles Times*, she had been "dismembered, disemboweled, possibly skinned, and burned." When a local nine-year-old boy described having seen a

baby sacrificed and burned—as well as relating his own sexual abuse, which included frequent mentions of the devil—the possibility of sadistic ritual abuse was obvious. But authorities concluded that the boy had made up his story and fabricated their own far-fetched explanation of a baby "who died of pneumonia and then was discarded and set on fire by a scared family illegally in the country to work the Idaho crops." One official even proposed that "predatory animals could have mutilated the body."[133]

Yet sadistic crime, including crime involving satanic belief systems, exists. Larry Jones, a police lieutenant in Boise, Idaho, reminds us:

> We've got confessed killers on death row throughout the country who have said they killed because they worshipped Satan. We've got child molesters who have confessed that their satanic belief system places a positive value on torturing children. . . . Any detective knows there are unsolved murders in every jurisdiction around the country.[134]

---

[130] *Church of the Lukumi Babalu Aye, Inc. et al vs. City of Hialeah*. Decided June 11, 1993 (93 Daily Journal D.A.R. 7368).

[131] Sadistic ritual abuse is one of the most effective tools for controlling children and rendering them compliant so they can be exploited in prostitution and pornography. See S. R. Benjamin's story on p. 428.

[132] Kenneth J. Herrmann, Jr., and M. J. Jupp, "A Request for Concern: The Sexual Exploitation of Children," testimony before the U.S. Attorney General's Commission on Pornography, November 20, 1985. Also in Kenneth Herrmann's "Children Sexually Exploited for Profit: A Plea for a New Social Work Priority," *Social Work* (November–December 1987), p. 523. Herrmann reports: "There are about 100,000 to 300,000 child prostitutes in the United States. Thousands more are victimized by pornographers. . . . [Worldwide] children have been stolen, purchased from parents and others, found as street children, and adopted legally and illegally for the purpose of sexual exploitation. These children are used for pornography and prostitution; are abused, tortured, murdered . . ."

[133] Reported by Leslie Bennetts in "Nightmares on Main Street," *Vanity Fair* (June 1993), p. 62.

[134] Ibid.
One of the common challenges from those who reject the idea of sadistic ritual abuse is "Where are the bones?" Referring to a study of sadistic sex offenders by P. E. Dietz, R. R. Hazelwood, and J. Warren, "The Sexually Sadistic Criminal and His Offenses," Jean Goodwin addresses this issue in *Rediscovering Childhood Trauma* (pp. 106–7): "In view of the difficulty of finding bodies to document ritual abuse, it is of interest that concealment of the bodies of victims was admitted by 20 of the 30 offenders [of sexually sadistic violence]." Goodwin goes on to ask, "How dangerous are these 30 sadistic offenders? Only 22 of the 30 had killed, but those 22

Idaho and Illinois have passed legislation that defines the ritual abuse of children and establishes provisions for its investigation and prosecution.[135] And sadistic abuse cases *have* been successfully prosecuted. One example, documented by Jan Hollingsworth in *Unspeakable Acts*, is the Country Walk daycare case in which Frank and Iliana Fuster were convicted. Although Frank Fuster continued to deny the massive evidence against him—even from prison—his wife, Iliana, confirmed that children had been assaulted sexually, including oral and anal penetration. They were drugged, urinated on, forced to eat feces, tied in bondage, and subjected to perverted rituals. Some of what the children reported sounded fantastic at first, but it all had its own horrifying cohesiveness. For example, some children told that Frank had "pennies" put in his bottom. At the trial, Iliana testified that she would powder Frank's genitals, diaper him in a bedsheet, and give him suppositories wrapped in copper-colored foil.[136]

None of us want to believe such stories, but for the sake of the survivors we must.

There are adult survivors of sadistic ritual abuse who bear the long-term damage of torture and abuse in their bodies—so much so that doctors who treat them now as adults are at first stymied, and then appalled by the residual damage.[137] And of course the emotional, mental, and spiritual devastation is profound.

Sadistic ritual abuse exists. We don't yet know how prevalent it is. We don't know that every report is accurate. But we do know that survivors are suffering from its effects. It is painful—devastating—to face this reality. But unless we face it, we allow it to continue. The Talmud asks: "To look away from evil: Is this not the sin of all good people?"

PERSONAL STRATEGIES FOR DEALING WITH THE BACKLASH

It can be valuable and empowering to read information that reveals the truth about the backlash. But if you're feeling angry, scared, hurt, or betrayed, you may also need help in taking care of yourself in the midst of such hostility.

As with all the other aspects of the healing process, you come first—your feelings, your needs, your choices. If you're confused or full of doubt, this section will offer you guidance in sorting through your feelings. If you're angry and want to fight back, we'll include some suggestions for responding effectively.

To begin, here are some general guidelines for maintaining your balance:

---

had logged 187 known murder victims . . . 5 of the men accounted for 122 of the murders. . . . Forty-three percent . . . had victimized children. Torture techniques included weapons, painful insertion, beating, electric shock, burning, amputation, cutting, and threatening with animals." Also, 60% of those who were parents admitted to incest. And 30% had "impeccable reputations as solid citizens."

[135] House Bill No. 817 was passed in Idaho in 1990. Public Act #87-1167 was signed into law in Illinois on September 18, 1992. Ritual abuse laws have also been passed in Louisiana and Missouri. Legislation is currently being considered in California.

[136] Jan Hollingsworth, *Unspeakable Acts* (New York: Congdon & Weed, 1986).

[137] See S. R. Benjamin's story on p. 428.

Get support for dealing with your feelings.

The attitudes and opinions propagated by the backlash may be reminiscent of your original abuse. Even survivors who are far along in their healing have been shaken and restimulated by this material. If this is happening to you, it's critical that you get support to work through your feelings.

Protect yourself.

You don't have to read every newspaper article or listen to every television show that reports on "false memories." If the material is difficult for you, give yourself a break and avoid it.

Keep telling your story to those you love and trust.

Don't let yourself be silenced. Your life experience is valid, and it needs to be shared with those who can listen with respect and compassion.

IF YOU'RE DOUBTING YOURSELF

Have patience toward all that is unresolved in your heart and . . . try to love the questions themselves.
— Rainer Maria Rilke[138]

When you've been told for your whole life that you're crazy, bad, and wrong, and then your daily newspaper questions your very capacity to remember and name what happened to you, it may become exceedingly difficult to hold on to the validity of your experience, or even to believe in your right to search for the truth of your past.

Yet this is a most crucial right for survivors, for all people: the freedom to explore and to understand their history. You have the capacity to know and name your own experience. And certainly you know more about your life than anyone else—you lived it. No author, book, therapist, expert, research psychologist, backlash group, newspaper article, or family member can tell you whether or not you were abused or if your memories are valid. You are the expert on your life. Honor your own truth.

If you are questioning your memories, the following guidelines can be of help.

Remember that doubt is often part of the healing process.

Moving into and out of denial is a natural part of the healing process.[139] Periodically having doubts does not necessarily mean that your memories aren't reliable or that the events in question did not really occur. Even survivors whose memories have been verified by external evidence may have times when they struggle to believe they were really abused. Very few people who truly think that they were sexually abused later find out they weren't. Although it is possible your doubt means it didn't happen, it's more likely that it's just a normal part of the healing process.

Look at the times doubts come up.

If doubts come up after you read a particularly nasty article, when you visit your parents, or right after you have intense memories, it's likely your doubts are related to

---

[138] Rainer Maria Rilke, *Letters to a Young Poet* (New York: Random House, 1984).

[139] See "Believing It Happened" on p. 96.

HOW THE BACKLASH HAS AFFECTED ME: RACHEL'S STORY

Rachel is a thirty-year-old survivor who was sexually abused by her father.* Although she has always remembered some aspects of her abuse, new memories surfaced when she stopped drinking six years ago. The backlash has angered and upset Rachel so much that she has decided to speak out publicly.

I was devastated by the incest for so many years. It was like I had this big stain on my life. I kept trying to whitewash it, but it was like the kind of paint where everything bleeds through.

I started drinking when I was twelve. I did whatever drugs I could get my hands on —cocaine, crank, speed. I smoked pot, dropped acid, and stole prescription drugs from my parents. When I was seventeen, I joined the army to get away from my family. My whole life was lived in bars.

I was like a chameleon. Whatever situation I was in, I could adapt myself to fit it. I could be whoever you wanted me to be because I had no idea who I was.

I was into wild sex. But when I was emotionally intimate with someone, I couldn't perform. I'd have sex and then throw up. Or I'd have an orgasm and picture my father in the room. I didn't know why.

I never had amnesia about the fact that my father was a pornography addict. I al-

---

* Rachel wanted to use her own name, but couldn't for legal reasons.

ways remember him reading it to me or making me look at it. He had pornographic tapes he made me listen to. When he grabbed a towel and a magazine and went into the bathroom, I knew what he was doing in there. But I did forget for years that sometimes I was in that bathroom with him.

I got sober when I was twenty-four. It changed the world for me.

About a year later, I had a very clear memory of an incident with my father. He was touching my breasts and I could see his hands—the fingernail that was broken and his hairy fingers and his hairy arms. It was very vivid.

I had flashbacks for the next six months. They were almost continuous. I had a lot of body memories. I had absolutely no question in my mind that they were true. I *knew*.

After a couple of years, I went to see my father. I still hadn't said anything to anyone in my family, but I think he sensed that something was going on with me. He sat me down at the kitchen table and started telling me how abused he had been when he was a kid, about how his father used to hit him and hold his hands over the fire. And how he had to sleep in the same bed with his father after his mother died. He kept saying how abused he'd been. He didn't specifically say sexual abuse, but I knew that's what he meant. And this is a person I'd never talked to before. I had never had a conversation with my father before, not once in my whole entire life.

At about that same time, my older sister called to ask if I was going to Thanksgiving dinner. I still hadn't said anything about what was going on, so I told her, "No, I just can't handle seeing Dad." It was no secret that he'd emotionally and verbally abused us, to the point of decimating us. All of us have been suicidal at some point in our lives. And she said, "Yeah, I know. He's a real pain in the ass." Then I started crying. I said, "There's stuff that happened between me and Dad that nobody knows about." That's all I said. And she broke down crying and asked, "Did he sexually abuse you?" I couldn't believe she asked me that. I was crying and I said, "Yes." And she said, "He did it to me, too."

WHY ARE THEY TRYING TO TAKE MY HEALING AWAY FROM ME?

When I first heard about the "false memory syndrome," it felt really personal. I couldn't believe the audacity of these people to actually try to tell me what my experience was, to say that my experience wasn't valid or truthful. I was really angry.

Then I got scared. I still vacillate between anger and fear. On a core level, what I felt was, "These people are trying to get away with what they've done. These people are trying to make me a liar."

I've felt like I've been about eight years old, on and off, for the last nine months. That's how bad it's been. I feel like a little kid who's having to tell and tell and tell because nobody is really listening. Every day I have to try to settle that little kid down. And that's really hard. It's hard to show up in my adult life when I'm feeling like a child.

The survivor in me gets very pissed off, ready to go to any length to challenge these people, to take what they say, turn it back around on them, and expose it for what it

really is. But the wounded child in me is freaking out and scurrying for protection, trying to find a good place to hide from all this. It's been really difficult.

I was doing really well before all this came up. I'd gotten to the stage where I didn't feel small anymore. I was in my body. I didn't dissociate anymore. I was in touch with my feelings. I was no longer afraid of what was inside of me. I was about to stop therapy.

It's like opening up a wound that had a really nice scar on it. It was all healed over nicely. And all this talk and baiting by the FMS has quite effectively torn that open.

I HOLD THEM RESPONSIBLE

The dynamic in my family was divide and conquer—my father kept us all separate, strangers to each other. This backlash operates on the same principles. Everybody in the greater family of incest and child sexual abuse survivors had been talking and telling each other what they knew. There's power in the truth. If everybody tells what they know, then there can't be any secrets anymore. And the closer we got to the truth, the more these people tried to throw up a smokescreen to disguise it. And the lengths to which they'll go to throw up that smokescreen is what is so scary to me.

Because I'd already done a lot of healing, the backlash hasn't affected me as severely as it has some other people. And because of that, I feel obligated to reach out to survivors who aren't as far along as I am. Like my sister, who just told. Or people who

Box continues on page 526.

want to tell and can't. My mother is an incest survivor. She told my sister about it nine months ago. She had never told anyone else, and now I don't know if she will. And I hold those who've joined the backlash accountable for that. For the silencing of my mother.

I'm sure there are some people in these backlash groups who are innocent. Statistically, that would have to happen. But morally, I think these people should question what they're doing. How do you know that the guy next to you is not a perpetrator? How do you know that the leader of the group is not, in fact, guilty? It seems to me if these people had any conscience, that somewhere these thoughts would have to creep in: "I know I'm innocent, but what if this person next to me at this meeting really did molest his child?"

Regardless of whether particular individuals are innocent or not, they're perpetrating abuse just by aligning themselves with these backlash groups like the FMS. What these groups espouse is full of hate. Why can't they say instead, "Some people get falsely accused, but we're not going to denounce an entire movement over it."

THE BACKLASH IS PUTTING CHILDREN IN DANGER

The backlash hasn't caused me to doubt my memories, to think, "This never happened to me," but I have had doubts like, "Maybe I should never have told." My sister has doubted that it ever happened to her, even though she clearly remembers. Her husband is an alcoholic and doesn't believe her. She lives two blocks from my parents and my mother's been feeding her all this stuff: "They say your therapist can really mess you up."

My sister still wants contact with my mother because my mother helps out with the grandchildren. And here I am telling her, "Mom didn't protect us. What makes you think she's going to protect your kids?" My sister went over there one day and found my dad sitting at the table reading a *Playboy* with her little girls. She wants to protect her children, but she's really struggling.

And now with all this publicity about false memories, my father is playing on her doubts. And that's jeopardizing my nieces. All three of them are exactly at the age that my father, who's a pedophile, happens to prefer. I find it appalling that this backlash is giving my father a soapbox to stand on. Right there in my own family you can see it —the backlash is putting children in danger.

Children are so disposable in our culture. They're just treated like trash. This backlash is protecting an ingrained and established system of abuse. And that's why I don't think it's anywhere near over. That's why survivors need to mobilize—for each other and for society at large. We really need to be strong because this is not just about what happened to me as a child. It's much bigger than that. It's about what could happen to our children if we're not careful.

these influences. If they persist even when you're calm and centered in yourself, there may be more reason to think you may have at least part of your story wrong. Yet even if you find that some of the things you believed are not true, it doesn't mean that all of your memories are unreliable. It's possible to be mistaken about one incident while remembering other events accurately. (See "The Essential Truth of Memory" on page 89 for more.)

Know that there's a reason for your pain.

If you're experiencing the level of anguish common to survivors of sexual abuse, there is some legitimate reason for that distress. It may not be sexual abuse; but there's something there for you to identify and address. You're not crazy to be feeling so much pain.

Heal from the things you are certain of.

For example, if you're sure you were emotionally abused but you're not certain if there was any sexual abuse, focus on healing from the emotional abuse. You'll be making progress in your healing even if you don't yet have a way to pin down other events that might have taken place.

It's okay if you're not sure.

Although you may feel under pressure to know exactly what happened, it may take time for you to discover the truth. Give yourself that time. It's okay to not know everything yet.

Don't affirm anything you're not ready to affirm.

If you're not sure whether you were sexually abused, don't feel pressured to say that you were—or that you weren't. You may need time and space to figure it out for yourself. People who pressure you either way—and this may include your therapist, your incest support group, or the people in your family—are not helping you. Talk instead with people who will hear your questions, respect your struggle to know, and give you the time to find out. Minimize your contact with those who insist it be one way or the other.

Assess your own therapeutic relationships.

If you're in therapy, talk about your doubts with your therapist. If your therapist is supportive, open to your questioning, and doesn't try to force answers on you, then you can feel confident that you're getting ethical help in exploring your history.

If you're in group therapy, you should feel that there's room for you to share your own experience, as it happened, without elaborating on it in any way. You should never feel that you need to stretch the truth or outdo someone else's story in order to be acknowledged. Whatever your childhood experience, it should be respected and taken seriously. And if you're not certain about what happened to you, there shouldn't be pressure in the group for you to identify yourself as a survivor prematurely.

If you never really thought you were abused and your therapist insisted that you were, or if you thought you had to make up a story and now you don't know if it's true, you're going to need sophisticated and capable help. A consultation or second opinion can often help clarify the situation. Make sure you choose someone who doesn't have an investment either in validating your memories or in proving you were misled. Work with someone capable of keeping an open mind until your true history becomes clear.

One woman, upset by a prominent series of newspaper articles promoting the idea of "false memories," talked about her search to find her own truth:

> I went to my incest survivor's group and said, "These articles are driving me crazy. I feel like I'm going nuts. I really don't know if I belong here. I don't know if it was sexual abuse." I wanted to quit the group, but since I was still having flashbacks, I decided to stay until I figured it out.
>
> I went into a shell. I clammed up. I didn't know what to do with the feelings. I meditated and sat with the paradox.
>
> Finally, I realized it was important for me to work this through. I had quit therapy, so I went to a new therapist. I told him, "For four years I've been uncovering the trauma that happened to me. It looks like sexual abuse. It feels like sexual abuse. And yet I'm also struggling with what the false memory people are out there saying. I want you to honor that I'm living a paradox. I want you to help me figure out if I really was sexually abused. I'm ready to go deeper into the confusion, but I need your help. I don't want you to make a judgment one way or the other or to tell me what you think happened to me. I want you to help me own my experiences and memories." And with him, I feel like there's room to explore it.

Look for corroboration only if you want it.

Even if you never come up with absolute proof to confirm your memories, corroboration of some kind may be available. In Rachel's family, for instance (see page 524), everyone knew that her father was emotionally abusive and exposed his children to pornography. Although this does not prove that he molested her, it certainly is consistent with Rachel's memories and gives them outside validation.

Verifying abuse is not always a direct process. Relatively few abusers admit what they did. And often family members didn't know the abuse was going on or don't want to acknowledge it now. But if you look clearly at your history, you may find information that helps you figure out what took place. Reexamining family photo albums, old diaries, or family stories may give you clues about your past. Sometimes talking to people who were there—family members, old friends, teachers, school counselors, or neighbors—can yield valuable insights. School and medical records may also contain revealing information.

This kind of information gathering, however, may involve risks. You may not find anything concrete to help you, and emotionally, the experience of going back to your childhood home and talking to people who knew you as a child can shake you to your roots. It's essential that you undertake such an investigation only when you're ready, and only if you truly want to—not because you feel pressured into coming up with "proof." Such a search is definitely not a required part of the healing process.[140]

---

[140] See Lana Lawrence and Mary Anne Reilly, "Corroboration and Evaluation of Delayed Memories of Abuse," *Moving Forward* 2, no. 4, pp. 15–16, and "Research Your Childhood," on pp. 228–30 of *The Courage to Heal Workbook*. Both offer specific advice on how to assess the pos-

Unless you are suing your abuser, you need only enough corroboration to satisfy yourself, not the standard of evidence required to convict someone in a court of law. (For more on this, see page 505.)

If your family keeps bringing up the topic of "false memories," it's okay to set limits.

If your family sends you articles about gullible women being brainwashed by therapists or tries to engage you in debates about the validity of your memories, it's okay to protect yourself. If you don't want to read the articles, you can throw them away. If you don't want to talk about your memories, you can change the topic or end the conversation. You have options. Learning to exercise them is an important part of healing.

Even if you're not sure about what happened to you, you can still limit or discontinue contact with your family if you need to. Though it may be difficult for you and for them, you're not victimizing someone by setting limits or even separating from them. Do what's best for you. Take as much time as you need.[141] (For more on separating from your family, see "Legal principles do not apply to healing" on page 505.)

Hold off on confronting your abuser or disclosing the abuse to family members who are likely to be extremely upset.

Don't talk with your family about the abuse until you're ready. If you're uncertain about what happened, if you're still sorting through possibilities, it's usually best to postpone any confrontations. Wait until you're more clear and then assess whether or not a disclosure or confrontation is in your best interests.[142]

If you've already told your family or confronted someone with abuse and now you're not sure, there's no shame in being honest. Depending on what's best for you, you can tell those involved that you're no longer sure or you can wait until you feel more certain to talk to them. In the meantime, it's your choice whether you continue to have contact or take some time away to get clear. And when you come to your own truth, talk about it with people you trust. If you've been in error or made mistakes, acknowledge them. Although it may be very difficult, honest sharing is at the very core of the healing process.

The whole survivors' movement does not rest on your shoulders.

If, upon further exploration, you become clear that you were not sexually abused, it's okay for you to claim that truth. You are not letting anyone down because you don't share a particular trauma. The whole survivors' movement does not rest on your shoulders.

---

sible benefits and dangers of investigating your history, how to prepare, get support, protect yourself, and how to gather information.

[141] "Disclosures and Confrontations" on p. 144 and "Families of Origin" on p. 299 provide extensive information on dealing with your family of origin, as does *The Courage to Heal Workbook.*

---

[142] If children are at risk, you will have to consider their protection as well as your own needs. (See p. 152 for more.)

Your experience does not invalidate the experience of other survivors. Just because you were mistaken doesn't mean that they are. There's room for you—and for them—to have had different experiences. Respect their courage and integrity, and expect them to respect yours.

Remember, you can trust yourself.

Above all, trust your own sense of who you are and what your experiences have been. If the healing process is about anything, it's about learning to trust yourself, your feelings, your reality.

You are the best judge of what happened to you. Continue to value your own knowing, even if that changes as you discover more.

IF YOU WANT TO FIGHT BACK

Many survivors are concerned about how the current climate of disbelief will affect other survivors and children who are being abused today. If you want to take action to counteract the negative images of survivors being portrayed in the media, here are some suggestions.

Get informed.

Although your own personal experience is valid in itself, it can help to have information available from other sources, particularly if you're dealing with the media. There's quite a bit of relevant research and analysis that you can use to refute some of the claims of the backlash. Many of the studies, books, and articles cited in the footnotes in this chapter are rich sources of information. Fur-

ther resources are included in the Resource Guide on page 564.

Write back.

Members of the backlash groups are enthusiastic about writing letters, making phone calls, and organizing. They contact the media, establish phone trees, and print newsletters. It's essential that survivors and their supporters also organize and speak out in great numbers. Every time a misleading or biased article is printed in the newspaper, there should be an avalanche of letters to the editor, setting forth the truth. Use your pen or your word processor to write a letter of protest, or dash off a postcard to set the record straight. Call your local radio and television stations, as well as the national ones—both in response to shows you find offensive and to encourage them to air shows on the truth about abuse.

Speak out.

What the supporters of the backlash want most of all is for you to keep your mouth shut. There's a real need for survivors to stay visible and to continue telling the truth of their lives. If you're feeling centered and stable enough to handle the public arena, this can be a powerful way to fight back. But don't feel pressured to take a public stance if it doesn't feel right to you.

Organize locally.

Get together with other survivors and supporters in your area. Strategize about the best responses to particular articles and radio and TV shows. Track the activities of the backlash groups in your area, look at the things they're targeting, and brainstorm the best ways to respond. Share information and ideas. It's less scary, and more powerful, to respond with the power of a group behind you.

Join an organization that is responding to the backlash.

Many organizations, both regional and national, are working to counteract the backlash. Groups that provide services for survivors, offer information and resources, work for legal reform, or support other efforts toward recognizing and stopping child sexual abuse all may be good vehicles for confronting the current backlash. If you want to contribute your energies and efforts toward this work, call or write to some of the groups included in the Resource Guide.

Remember, it's okay if you don't do anything.

Many survivors see the need to do something, but because they're still in the vulnerable stages of their own healing, they're not yet in a position to respond themselves. That's fine. Your own healing is your first responsibility. As you grow stronger, you can share that strength, but it's crucial that you take care of yourself first. As author and activist Sandra Butler says, "For a woman in this culture, to take herself and her life seriously is the first act of politics."[143]

FUTURE VISIONS

The strides we've made in recognizing and dealing with child sexual abuse in the past fifteen years have been both positive and far-reaching. As a society we have begun to assert the right of children to grow up free from battering, emotional abuse, and sexual terrorism. We have challenged the status quo—children as property—and as a result, our hard-fought gains are being attacked. The current backlash against survivors of child sexual abuse is a destructive, undermining force, and the use of that force has been intentional.

We are at a crossroads. As a society we can continue to fight for the integrity of every child and the healing of every survivor, or we can give in to our collective denial and once again bury the truth.

It is crucial that we reaffirm our commitment to children, to adults who've been abused, and to stopping the abuse that is still going on. We have progressed from silence about abuse to awareness. Yet there is still formidable work to be done. Children continue to be abused in appallingly large numbers, adult survivors continue to suffer, and families struggle to come to terms with these violations. To meet this challenge, therapists, law enforcement officials, and the courts need continuing education and training.

Our academic institutions need to address the massive problem of child sexual abuse.[144] Counselors and other professionals must be taught how to assist survivors through the healing process in a respectful, compassionate, and skilled way.

---

[143] Personal communication, October 10, 1993.

[144] Only in the last few years have universities begun to offer instruction in this field. As recently as 1989,

We need to establish an environment where survivors of child sexual abuse can come forward and be believed and where the protection of children is a priority. We need to create a climate that encourages honesty rather than defensiveness, where people who have abused can acknowledge their behavior and be accountable, rather than join an organization that further reinforces their denial. We need to provide programs in which offenders can get help in stopping their abuse of children as well as help in their own healing.

This is essential. Educating the public, helping survivors heal, and prosecuting abusers are all very necessary, but we must also stop people from abusing. Treatment for offenders, especially juvenile offenders, is critical.[145]

In the courtroom we need to establish safeguards to ensure accuracy in expert witness testimony. Nonbiased standards for the evaluation, investigation, and prosecution of child abuse cases must be implemented as well.

We need to differentiate more clearly between the legal arena and the private arenas of therapy and healing. The healing process has its own integrity, which should not be judged by forensic considerations.

We need more research on memory, traumatic amnesia, and how best to treat people who've suffered trauma. We need to ensure that such research is not manipulated toward political ends but instead is rooted in open-mindedness and a genuine search for the truth.

We must reaffirm that survivors of child sexual abuse are the true experts on their experience. Many professionals have spoken out eloquently on behalf of survivors—and many others have insulted, pathologized, or dismissed them. Yet in the midst of all this debate *about* survivors, we need to remember that our greatest understanding comes not in listening to professionals, but to the survivors themselves. As psychiatrist Roland Summit reminds us:

> Survivors can lead us, one by one, into the oblivion of their past, but only if we are willing to follow. . . . We have to consider that even the distorted recollections of someone who has survived the journey might be more reliable than the beautiful engravings of landlocked geographers.[146]

THE WORLD SPLIT OPEN

Once the truth is exposed, regardless of how much anyone tries to cover it up again,

---

when we lectured to counselors, we'd ask groups comprised of psychologists, marriage, family and child counselors, social workers, doctors, nurses, and even a few psychiatrists. "How many of you ever had the opportunity, during the course of your education, to take classes in working with survivors of child sexual abuse?" On a good day, four out of four hundred raised their hands.

[145] The Safer Society Program has published an excellent series of books and resources for work with perpetrators. See p. 541 of the Resource Guide.

---

[146] Roland Summit, "Hidden Victims, Hidden Pain: Societal Avoidance of Child Sexual Abuse," *Lasting Effects of Child Sexual Abuse,* eds. Gail Elizabeth Wyatt and Gloria Johnson Powell (Newbury Park, CA: Sage Publications, 1988), p. 52.

things can never be the same. Survivors have had the courage to speak what had been unspeakable. As poet Muriel Rukeyser wrote, "What would happen if one woman told the truth about her life . . . the world would split open."[147] And in fact, it has. The world has split open, revealing that millions of children have been sexually abused and that those children—those who survive—grow up into adults who suffer, but who also retain enormous strength and integrity. And we will not be silenced. Psychologist John Briere says:

> The thing that gives me . . . hope is that just as when women [won] the vote, or when slaves learned to read, or—at whatever level—when those who are disempowered are given important new tools, the culture can never return to its former state of ignorance or denial. . . . Because a vast number of survivors have found a voice, no amount of what is now trendy disbelief will silence them.[148]

As a culture we are learning the value of remembering, of witnessing, of commemorating. We are creating memorials that allow us to acknowledge tragedies, to mourn, and to learn. We have the Vietnam Veterans Memorial and the Names Project's AIDS quilt. We have The United States Holocaust Memorial Museum. At its dedication on April 22, 1993, Elie Wiesel spoke:

> The essence of this tragedy is that it can never be fully communicated. . . . And yet, we are duty-bound to try. Not to do so would mean to forget. To forget would mean to kill the victims a second time. . . . Memory is not only a victory over time, it is also a triumph over injustice.[149]

The poet Marge Piercy wrote, "Memory is the simplest form of prayer."[150] Maybe this is why attacks on our memories affect us so deeply—because memory is such an integral part of our being, of our healing, of our social change, and even of our prayer.

One never moves forward without opposition. All worthwhile social struggles take time and commitment on the part of many people, whether it's preserving our environment, ending discrimination, achieving peace and justice, or ending child sexual abuse. When the struggle is difficult, we like to remember the words of educator and nonviolent activist, Danilo Dolci:

> There are moments when things go well and one feels encouraged. There are difficult moments and one feels overwhelmed. But it's senseless to speak of optimism and pessimism. The only important thing is to know that if one works well in a potato field, the potatoes will grow.

---

[147] From "Kathe Kollwitz," in *The Collected Poems of Muriel Rukeyser* (New York: McGraw-Hill, 1982).

[148] Forest, "Interview with John Briere," p. 21.

[149] Elie Wiesel, "For the Dead and the Living, We Must Bear Witness," *Bostonia*, 2 (Summer 1993), p. 15.

[150] Marge Piercy, "Black Mountain," in *Available Light* (New York: Knopf, 1988).

If one works well among men [and women, we would add], they will grow——that's reality. The rest is smoke. It's important to know that words don't move mountains. Work, exacting work, moves mountains.

Survivors of child sexual abuse and their supporters are willing to do that work. We've come too far to stop now.

RESOURCE GUIDE

Dear Readers:

We've once again updated the Resource Guide, adding many new books, videos, newsletters, and organizations. We've also reorganized the listings so that they're easier to find. However, since many bridge more than one category, try skimming through other related sections if you don't find what you're looking for right away.

This updated Resource Guide reflects changes in the way we communicate with each other. We've added fax numbers, e-mail addresses, and web sites. New and of special interest to survivors are resources for dealing with the "false memory" controversy, a guide to finding help on the Internet, and advice on finding a survivor pen pal. The sections on legal resources and clergy abuse are expanded, and there are more listings for parents whose children have been abused, as well as youth who've molested other children. Our listings for

counselors and other professionals have been augmented, too. Throughout, we've highlighted some resources we don't want you to miss.

Most of the books we list here are available in bookstores. If you can't find them on the shelves, you can ask the store to special-order them. We've included the addresses of small presses, either in the listing itself or in the back of the Resource Guide, so you also have the option of ordering directly from the publisher.

Although there are many sources for buying books, as authors we encourage you to support your local independent bookstore. Although you may be able to buy some books a little cheaper elsewhere, it's the independent booksellers that make it possible for us to have access to a wide range of ideas. If we don't want to limit our reading to what will sell well in the mainstream, it's critical that we patronize independent bookstores so they can continue to survive.

Although many of the books listed here are new and most are currently in print, we've retained some valuable out-of-print titles because you may be able to find them in libraries.

We've also updated listings for a wide variety of national organizations. These listings are intended as suggestions about where to look for help, not endorsements. When selecting an information source, organization, or program, use the same care you would in choosing a therapist.

Resource guides go out-of-date quickly. By the time you read this, some of the information may already be outdated. Publishers fold; books go in and out of print; organizations change their names, move, or go under. New resources develop all the time. Because of this, we will continue to update the Resource Guide every couple of years. And we'd like your help.

If a book is out of print, a phone number is no longer operating, a web site has disappeared, an organization is not very helpful (or is disrespectful), drop us a note. If we've excluded your favorite book, tell us why you loved it. If there's a new resource you'd like us to consider for the next edition, please send information or a review copy.

Write to: Courage to Heal Resources, P.O. Box 5296, Santa Cruz, CA 95063. We'll consider your suggestions carefully, but unfortunately we won't be able to answer your letters personally.

In the spirit of healing,
Ellen Bass and Laura Davis
January 1998

P.S. We greatly appreciate the many survivors, counselors, authors, publishers, and others who helped us update this Resource Guide. In particular we'd like to thank Anita Montero and Molly Fisk of The Healing Woman, Eileen King of One Voice/ ACAA, Euan Bear of the Safer Society Foundation, the women of Full Circle and Herland Books, Joyce Boaz of Varied Directions, Anne-Marie Eriksson, Marge Eide, Donna Covello, Kerry Ellison, Marcia Cohen Spiegel, and Mike Lew. We applaud Teri Cosentino, who put in endless hours inputing text on her computer. We give kudos to the staff at Bookshop Santa Cruz, who generously provided us with countless biographical details. Most of all, we'd like to thank our fabulous researcher, Shana Ross, whose intelligence, persistence, and humor made this work possible.

CONTENTS

FINDING HELP, BUILDING COMMUNITY

HOTLINES

RAINN
(800) 656-HOPE

The Rape, Abuse and Incest National Network (RAINN) operates a free 24-hour-a-day hotline for survivors of all kinds of sexual assault, including sexual abuse, rape, and domestic violence. When you call RAINN, a computer instantly connects you to the nearest rape crisis center. At least 1,000 trained counselors are available to answer calls. All calls are confidential and will not show up on your phone bill.

Childhelp USA National Child Abuse Hotline
(800) 4-A-CHILD
(800) 422-4453

Counselors are available 24 hours a day offering crisis intervention, information regarding child abuse, resources for adult and child survivors, help with parenting, and referrals to agencies across North America.

National Domestic Violence/Abuse Hotline
(800) 799-SAFE
(800) 799-7233
(800) 787-3224 TDD

This 24-hour-a-day hotline is staffed by trained volunteers who can connect you with help in your own community, including emergency services and shelters, information about counseling for adults and children, and assistance reporting abuse. They have access to translators for 150 languages.

COMPUTER NETWORKING

Survivors on the Internet [1]
Adapted from an article by Kerry Leigh Ellison

Web sites, newsgroups, and electronic mail are all potential tools for healing, activism, and building our survivor community. If you don't have a computer or you need help getting started, check with your local library. Many have public computer terminals and a librarian may be able to walk you through the process. It will be helpful if you bring along addresses of web sites, also called URLs (Uniform Resource Locators) that interest you.

Web Sites

There are hundreds of web sites of interest to survivors at all stages of healing. Most are set up and maintained by survivors. You can locate referrals for therapists and support groups, study the latest research, read poetry, or lobby Congress for better laws.

Often people look for sites using search engines like Yahoo! and AltaVista. However, this may leave you with thousands of sites to consider. A better way to find survivor resources is to go directly to one of the addresses listed below. All have numerous links to other sites.

Chat and News Groups

Chat groups allow you to interact with people who are online and newsgroups allow you to send messages that others can read whenever they log on. You can also "browse" or just read public messages. There is a great potential for survivors to reach out and support each other through these channels, but there are inherent problems, too. Chat rooms can be a magnet for voyeurs or perpetrators who may dominate the conversation. "Flaming," a form of Internet harassment, is not uncommon.

Bulletin boards and Usenet news groups have gotten better ratings from survivors, although there, too, you may encounter some off-beat information and unwelcome ads. However, it is possible to meet others with similar interests through bulletin boards. Together you can form private E-mail groups, which function like closed, mutual support groups.

---

[1] A longer version of this article first appeared in *The Healing Woman* (November–December 1997). It is reprinted here with the permission of the author and *The Healing Woman.*

19 TOP WEB SITES

1. Sexual Assault Info Page
   **http://www.cs.utk.edu/~bartley/
   saInfoPage.html**
   Extensive links for survivors of child sexual abuse
   as well as information on a wide variety of topics
   including rape, law, domestic violence, men's resources, and self-defense.

2. The Survivors Page
   http://www.sehlat.com/survs.html
   Chock full; lots of information and links to chat
   rooms, resources on self-injury, pregnancy, and
   sexual harassment in schools; also things that are
   fun and comforting.

3. I.S.N.R.I. Incest Survivors Resource Network International
   http://www.zianet.com/ISRNI
   Extensive resources and links for survivors. Information about clergy abuse and for male survivors.
   Includes list of groups and newsletters outside of
   North America.

4. M.A.L.E. Men Assisting Leading & Educating
   http://www.malesurvivor.org/Index2.html
   Chat rooms, articles, and extensive links to a diver-
   sity of abuse-related resources (not just for men).

5. Jim Hopper
   http://www.jimhopper.com
   A comprehensive source of information about recovered memory issues, including scientific research and scholarly resources.

6. Recovered Memory Page
   **http://cgi-user.brown.edu/Departments/
   Taubman_Center/Recovmem/
   Archive.html**
   A survivor and scholar's collection of corroborated
   cases of recovered memory. Related research and
   publications on traumatic amnesia.

7. Susan K. Smith, Attorney at Law—Civil Litigation
   and Claims for Victims of Sexual Abuse
   http://www.2.imagine.com/smithlaw
   Resources for lawyers and survivors considering
   filing civil suits, state-by-state information on the
   statute of limitations, and links to lawyer referrals.

8. Discord's Abuse Survivors' Resources
   http://www.tezcat.com/~tina/psych.html
   Extensive links to newsgroups of interest to survivors, as well as many general resources.

9. Canadian Online chat
   **http://www.worldchat.com/public/asarc/
   welcome.htm**
   Self-help support to survivors of sexual abuse. Excellent links. Includes bulletin boards for survivors,
   therapists, partners, family members, and other
   support people.

10. Partners and Allies of Sexual Assault Survivors Re-
    source List
    **http://idealist.com/wounded_healer/
    allies.shtml**
    A compilation of resources for partners and allies

of incest, rape, and sexual abuse survivors. Newsgroups, chat rooms, bibliography.

11. On The Road to Healing
    **http://www.connect.ab.ca./~emsmythe/
    index.htm**
    A Canadian survivor's personal home page with
    good links, including information and resources
    for disabled survivors.

12. Help the Children (Pandora's Box)
    **http://pages.prodigy.com/faulkner/
    help1.htm**
    Advocacy for child abuse prevention, child protec-
    tion, and resources for protective parents.

13. Children: Abuse and Protection
    **http://www.radix.net/~mschelling/
    children.html**
    Extensive links dealing with child abuse prevention,
    sexual abuse, abduction, foster care, parenting,
    and more. Includes "scum" page with state-by-
    state lists and photos of sex offenders and dead-
    beat dads.

14. S.E.S.A.M.E.—Survivors of Educator Sexual Abuse
    and Misconduct Emerge
    **http://home.earthlink.net/~jaye/
    index.html**
    S.E.S.A.M.E. is a voice for the prevention of sexual
    abuse and harassment of students. Includes sto-
    ries, advocacy, and general information.

15. Not Victims
    http://www.smalltime.com/notvictims
    A good site for information on eating disorders,
    chronic pain, sexual abuse, depression and much
    more.

16. N.O.M.S.V.—The National Organization on
    Male Sexual Victimization
    http://www.NOMSV.org
    Articles, resources, newsletters, conference infor-
    mation and great links to sites of interest to male
    survivors.

17. P.A.S.A.—People Against Sexual Abuse
    **http://www.echonyc.com/~pasa/library/
    talk_about_it.html**
    Resources for male survivors. Also resources for the
    deaf community of survivors and information to
    help the hearing better serve deaf survivors.

18. The Santa Cruz Ritual Abuse Task Force
    http://members.cruzio.com/~ratf
    Help with grass roots organizing; many links to sites
    dealing with activism and ritual abuse.

19. S.A.D.M.—Sexual Abuse, Dissociation & Multiple
    Personality Disorder Group
    http://www.golden.net/~soul/sadm.html
    Private, confidential e-mail listserv group. Anyone
    who has experienced child sexual abuse associ-
    ated with dissociation or multiple personality can
    join a variety of interactive groups where you can
    talk to other survivors. Support for partners and al-
    lies as well. Great music and graphics.

Electronic or E-mail

E-mail can be sent to one person or many people. It's a great way to communicate quickly and to disperse information broadly. However, it's important to remember that electronic communication is not private.

Mailing lists are a promising means of survivor activism. One person may gather articles, news items, or action alerts, and then forward them automatically to subscribers. Once the list is set up, forwarding may be automated and addresses kept confidential.

The "backlash" has several mailing lists. When pro-survivor coverage appears in the media, the word goes out and false memory proponents inundate the publication or network with electronic protest mail, phone calls, or letters. Consumer complaints get heard. Lists are clearly effective tools for advocacy and grass roots organizing. We can use them, too.

One Voice/ACAA (American Coalition for Abuse Awareness) runs two information lists for survivors and child advocates. One list monitors the backlash, the other covers the media and news of conferences, research, and legislation. E-mail Eileen King at ACAADC@aol.com for more information.

A Word of Caution

There are wonderful resources for survivors on the Internet. However, the Net is fluid; sites come and go and may change from day to day. Also, be aware that there are no guarantees of truth on the Internet. Anyone can have a soapbox. There are false memory, pornographic and anti-survivor sites. And not everyone is who they claim to be. If at any time you feel unsafe or invalidated, remember you can leave. Use your own judgment.

ORGANIZATIONS

There are more organizations listed under specific topics.

Child Sexual Abuse Strategic Action Project, 2 Massasoit St., San Francisco, CA 94110, (415) 285-6658.

The Strategic Action Project is working toward a cohesive movement to end child sexual abuse and empower survivors through community organizing, survivor leadership and mobilization, legal and legislative efforts, and public education. They address child sexual abuse not only as an individual and mental health issue, but also as a community and societal issue.

Family Violence and Sexual Assault Institute (FVSAI), 1121 ESE Loop 323, Suite 130, Tyler, TX 75701, (903) 534-5100; fax (903) 534-5454; e-mail: fvsai@iamerica.net or on the web:
http://www.gatekeep.net/fvsai/index.html

This excellent clearinghouse is set up to increase networking, education, training, and dissemination for various facets of family violence and sexual abuse. Sponsors annual International Conference on Children Exposed to Family Violence. Their services also include a book club, data bases accessible by computer, and the semi-annual publication *Family Violence and Sexual Assault Bulletin* (sample issue is free). Membership is $30/year.

Giarretto Institute, 232 Gish Rd., San Jose, CA 95112, (408) 453-7616; fax (408) 453-9064; e-mail: giarretto@earthlink.net or on the web:
http://www.giarretto.org

The Institute sponsors Parents United International, a sexual abuse treatment program that includes individual therapy, group therapy, and a guided self-help component. The program offers healing for child victims, non-offending parents, offenders, and adults molested as children. There are chapters nationwide.

Gift From Within, RR1 Box 5158, Camden, ME 04843, (800) 888-5236; fax (207) 236-4512; joyceb3955@aol.com or on the web:
http://www.sourcemaine.com/gift

Develops and disseminates educational materials, including videos, books, and a resource catalog for people suffering from PTSD and those who work with them. Offers phone/pen/e-mail pal services for isolated trauma survivors.

Incest Resources at The Women's Center, 46 Pleasant St., Cambridge, MA 02139, (617) 354-8807 (TTY/V).

Founded in 1980 by and for adult survivors of incest. Provides information and referrals for survivors and professionals nationally. Offers excellent resources, such as *Starting from Scratch: The Incest Resources Group Model*, a manual for organizing survivor support groups, listings of self-help groups and agencies throughout the country, and many booklets, including "Inside Out: Therapeutic Bodywork for Incest Survivors," "Picture This! Rage Release for Incest Survivors," and more. They also have resource lists for male survivors, survivors of female-perpetrated abuse, ritual abuse survivors, non-offending parents, and more.

Incest Survivors Resource Network International, P.O. Box 7375, Las Cruces, NM 88006-7375, (505) 521-4260 (2–4 p.m. or 11–12 p.m. EST Monday–Saturday); e-mail: IRSNI@zianet.com or on the web: http://www.zianet.com/ISRNI

> Survivor-run educational resource. Founded in 1983 as a Quaker peace witness, ISRNI has operated the first international helpline for incest survivors and professionals answered only by incest survivors. It continues especially to encourage calls from survivors of mother-son incest.

King County Sexual Assault Resource Center, P.O. Box 300, Renton, WA 98057, (425) 226-5062; fax (425) 235-7422.

> This politically sensitive, groundbreaking agency provides publications, programs, and counseling for sexual assault prevention and treatment. They are the source of many excellent resources in this field.

National Organization for Victims Assistance (NOVA), 1757 Park Rd. NW, Washington, D.C. 20010, (202) 232-6682 (24-hour crisis line); fax (202) 462-2255; e-mail: nova@trynova.org or on the web: http://www.access.digex.net/~nova

> NOVA is an advocacy organization for crime victims. Sponsors training seminars, educational programs, and conferences; provides a 24-hour information and referral line.

National Victim Center, 2111 Wilson Blvd. #300, Arlington, VA 22201, (800) FYI-CALL, (703) 276-2880; fax (703) 276-2889 or on the web: http://www.nvc.org

> NVC is a national center for victims of violence. They offer networking, information, referrals, a newsletter, a manual for starting self-help programs, and a national organization directory. They work extensively with the way the media deals with victims of violent crime and are currently collecting information on ritualistic child abuse, including referrals.

One Voice: The National Alliance for Abuse Awareness and its public policy project, The American Coalition for Abuse Awareness (ACAA), P.O. Box 27958, Washington, D.C. 20038-7958, (202) 667-1160 or (202) 462-4688; fax (202) 462-4689; e-mail: OVoiceDC@aol.com or ACAADC@aol.com or on the web: http://www.sover.net/%7Eschwcof/newshead.html

> **One Voice/ACAA is a national alliance of survivors, their supporters, child advocates, and health care and legal professionals working together to educate the public, the media, and congressional representatives on child abuse, the right to seek redress through the courts, and access to appropriate treatment. It has a national resource line, provides legal referrals, and distributes a press kit packet on abuse, trauma, and memory, as well as the videos of Marilyn Van Derbur.**

The Safer Society Foundation, Inc. (SSFI), P.O. Box 340, Brandon, VT 05733, (802) 247-3132; fax (802) 247-4233; referral line (802) 247-5141 (M, W, F 1:00–4:30 P.M. EST) or on the web: http://safersociety.org

> **SSFI is a national research, advocacy, and referral center on the prevention and treatment of sexual abuse. They publish excellent groundbreaking literature, audiotapes, and videocassettes, including the best resources for youthful sex offenders. They maintain a computerized nationwide directory of agencies, institutions, and individuals who provide specialized assessment and treatment for youthful and adult sex offenders.**

The Sidran Foundation, 2328 W. Joppa Rd., #15, Lutherville, MD 21093, (410) 825-8888; fax (410) 337-0747; e-mail: sidran@access.digex.net or on the web at http://www.sidran.org

> A public interest organization devoted to advocacy, public education, and research on behalf of persons with trauma-generated psychiatric problems. Focuses on post-traumatic and dissociative disorders. They produce the *Sidran Foundation Bookshelf*, an excellent annotated catalogue of books about multiple personalities.

STOP IT NOW! P.O. Box 495, Haydenville, MA 01039, (413) 268-3096; Helpline: (888) PREVENT or (888) 773-8368; e-mail: info@stopitnow.com or on the web: http://www.stopitnow.com/

> **STOP IT NOW! addresses the causes of child sexual abuse through a media campaign encouraging potential abusers to seek help, challenging abusers to stop the abuse and get treatment, working with families and friends to confront abusers, and building a social climate that says "We will no longer tolerate the sexual abuse of children."**
>
> **No prevention program has ever directly asked abusers to step forward or asked adults to confront abusers. STOP IT NOW! VERMONT is a pilot program to test this idea. Based on its success, STOP IT NOW! will be expanded nationally.**

SELF-HELP GROUPS

American Self-Help Clearinghouse, Northwest Covenant Center, 25 Pocono Rd., Denville, NJ 07834, (201) 625-9565, TDD: (201) 625-9053; fax (201) 625-8848; e-mail: ashc@bc.cybernex. net or on the web: http://www.cmhc.com/selfhelp

This clearinghouse provides resources and information for people interested in *all kinds* of self-help groups, including survivors of sexual abuse. It maintains a database of over 700 national self-help headquarters and groups in the U.S. and Canada. Send a self-addressed stamped envelope for guidelines for starting a self-help group. An excellent directory, *The Self-Help Source Book: Finding and Forming Mutual Aid Self-Help Groups*, is available for $9.

Survivors of Incest Anonymous (SIA), P.O. Box 21817, Baltimore, MD 21222-6817, (410) 282-3400.

A twelve-step self-help peer program for incest survivors and supporters. They offer extensive literature (free if you can't afford it) and a bimonthly newsletter, *The Bulletin*. They also have a pen pal program.

To locate groups in your area, request a directory of meetings. For written information send a self-addressed double-stamped envelope.

Sexual Assault Recovery Anonymous (SARA), P.O. Box 16, Surrey, British Columbia, Canada V3T 4W4, (604) 584-2626; fax (604) 584-2888.

Based on a twelve-step model, SARA provides crisis intervention and therapeutic support to victims of sexual assault and incest through mutual-aid peer groups. Also provides prevention and educational materials. Their "Group Guidelines" discusses starting a self-help group and how to keep groups from getting caught in power struggles or otherwise going astray.

To Tell the Truth: Speak Out! About Incest and Sexual Abuse, c/o Survivor Connections, Inc. 52 Lydon Rd. Cranston, RI 02905-1121; (401) 941-2548; e-mail: totellthetruth@hotmail.com or on the web: http://www.angelfire.com/ri/totellthetruth

Sponsors an annual international Speak Out! in cities around the world on the first Saturday in October. Contact them for information on producing an event or participating.

NEWSLETTERS

There are also newsletters listed under specific topics.

Ask Us! published by ASK, Inc. (Abused Survivors Know). P.O. Box 10756, Burke, VA 22009, (703) 281-7468; fax (703) 978-7395.

Highlights advocacy efforts on behalf of survivors. Welcomes submissions of poetry, writings, or artwork.

For Crying Out Loud. The Survivor's Newsletter Collective, c/o The Women's Center, 46 Pleasant St., Cambridge, MA 02139.

This fine quarterly newsletter is by and for women with a sexual abuse history; $10/year.

Write To Tell. Anne Cox, 7909 Walerga Road, Suite 112-107, Antelope, CA 95843, (916) 725-9490 T–TH (11 A.M.–4 P.M.); e-mail: thecpac@calweb.com or on the web: http://www.thecpac.com/tell.html

A quarterly forum for survivors, partners, and supporters to share their writing. Send a self-addressed, stamped envelope for more information.

Voices for Survivors Support Society. 27A-250 Willingdon Ave., Burnaby, British Columbia, Canada V5C 5E9; (604) 298-4516.

A quarterly newsletter that welcomes articles, poetry, letters and artwork.

THE HEALING WOMAN

The Healing Woman Foundation is an organization for women survivors of childhood sexual abuse whose purpose is to provide information, self-help, and support. They are a good starting place to find resources of all kinds, as well as a rich source of inspiration for advanced healing.

The Healing Woman has produced many excellent audiotapes from their conferences and by its founder, Margot Silk Forrest, including Now That You've Got Your Life Back, What Are You Going To Do With It?, Panel on Advanced Healing, and Songs of Inspiration, Poetry, Laughter. They mail-order healing books, tapes, and CD's. They also offer a pen pal program which connects survivors with others of similar interests. They are best known for their excellent newsletter:

The Healing Woman: The International Newsletter for Women Survivors of Childhood Sexual Abuse.

A monthly for women survivors of child sexual abuse. Intelligent and supportive, each issue features self-help articles, interviews, creative writings, inspiring quotations, information on recent research, new laws and court cases, resources, and book reviews. $30/year, low income $15/year. Send a self-addressed stamped envelope for contributor's guidelines.

The Healing Woman is continually seeking volunteers to help both locally and nationally with conferences, events, and communication.

For more information, contact: The Healing Woman Foundation, P.O. Box 28040, San Jose, CA 95159, (408) 246-1788; fax (408) 247-4309; e-mail: HealingW@healingwoman.org or on the web: http://www.healingwoman.org

---

VOICES in Action, Inc., P.O. Box 148309, Chicago, IL 60614-8309, (800) 7-VOICE-8; (773) 327-1500 (international calls). All calls will be returned collect. Fax (773) 327-4590; e-mail: voices@voices-action.org or on the web: http://www.voices-action.org

National network of incest survivors and supporters, founded in 1980. Free referrals to therapists, legal resources, agencies, and self-help groups. Members receive a survival packet of excellent resource material and a subscription to The Chorus. You can also attend an annual conference, take part in group leader training, and participate in special interest support groups, the real core of VOICES. There are more than a hundred groups dealing with topics such as mother abuse, multiple personalities, abuse by priests, and abuse by sadistic perpetrators. These support groups correspond in a systematic way and operate under strict confidentiality. VOICES runs on membership fees, but no one is turned away for lack of funds.

LEGAL RESOURCES

ORGANIZATIONS

One Voice: The National Alliance for Abuse Awareness, P.O. Box 27958, Washington, D.C. 20038-7958, (202) 667-1160 or (202) 462-4688; fax (202) 462-4689; e-mail: OVoiceDC@aol.com

Distributes a guide for survivors considering litigation and an attorney referral list.

Child Sexual Abuse Law Center, c/o Mary Williams, The Creamery Building, P.O. Box 1375, Point Reyes Station, CA 94956-1375, (415) 663-9202; fax (415) 663-1907.

Provides comprehensive, up-to-date legal and scientific resources and assistance to attorneys working with victims of childhood sexual abuse in criminal, civil, and family law and juvenile dependency arenas throughout the country.

NOW Legal Defense and Education Fund, 99 Hudson St., New York, NY 10013.

A clearinghouse for information on the legal rights of adult survivors of incest and child sexual abuse. Provides an excellent packet of information on legal issues and options for $5. NOW-LDEF does not han-

PEN PAL PROGRAMS

These pen pal programs can help connect survivors with others of similar interests.

The Healing Woman Foundation, P.O. Box 28040, San Jose, CA 95159, (408) 246-1788; fax (408) 247-4309; e-mail: HealingW@healingwoman.org or on the web: http://www.healingwoman.org/

Gift From Within, RR1 Box 5158, Camden ME 04843, (800) 888-5236 or (207) 236-6051; fax (207) 236-4512; e-mail: joyceb@midcoast.com or on the web at http://www.sourcemaine.com/gift

Survivors of Incest Anonymous (SIA), P.O. Box 21817, Baltimore, MD 21222-6817, (410) 282-3400.

SurvivorShip: A Forum on Survival of Ritual Abuse, Torture & Mind Control, 3181 Mission St. #139, San Francisco, CA 94110-4515, (707) 279-1209; e-mail: svship@bigfoot.com or on the web: http://www.ctsserver.com/~svship/

VOICES in Action, Inc., P.O. Box 148309, Chicago, IL 60614-8309, (800) 7-VOICE-8; (773) 327-1500 (international calls). All calls will be returned collect. Fax (773) 327-4590; e-mail: voices@voicesaction.org or on the web: http://www.voices-action.org

---

dle cases itself, but they do provide written referrals to lawyers. No phone calls please.

WEB SITE

Susan K. Smith, Attorney at Law, Civil Litigation and Claims for Victims of Sexual Abuse has a web site of interest to survivors:
http://www.2.imagine.com/smithlaw
> On-line resources for lawyers and survivors considering filing civil suits, state-by-state information on the statute of limitations, and links to lawyer referrals.

BOOKS

Brent, Elizabeth. *Long and Mature Considerations: A Legal Guide for Adult Survivors of Child Sexual Abuse*, 1997. (Available for $12 from One Voice, P.O. Box 27958, Washington, D.C. 20038, (202) 667-1160.)
> Essential reading for any survivor exploring legal options. Contrasts the legal and therapeutic definitions of sexual abuse, looks at potential consequences of taking legal action, examines survivors' legal options, and explores activism as an alternative to legal action. Comprehensive and well written.

Crnich, Joseph and Kimberly. *Suing Child Sexual Abusers: A Legal Guide for Survivors and Their Supporters*, 1992. (Available for $16 from One Voice, P.O. Box 27958, Washington, D.C. 20038, (202) 667-1160.)

A user-friendly guide for adult survivors who are considering suing their perpetrators. Full of pertinent information and helpful advice.

Myers, John. *A Mother's Nightmare—Incest: A Practical Legal Guide for Parents and Professionals.* Thousand Oaks, CA: Sage, 1997.
> Written by a law professor, this book is a valuable resource for mothers who are trying to protect their kids. Discusses the ways the legal system may fail at achieving "justice" and explores the complexities of taking child sexual abuse cases to court.

The Incest Resources Legal Packet. Incest Resources, 46 Pleasant St., Cambridge, MA 02139.
> Includes information and resources about civil suits and criminal prosecution for survivors and nonoffending parents, as well as resources for survivors of abuse by clergy and other professionals. It also contains materials which address the backlash by "false memory" proponents. Available for $18.95.

ATTORNEYS

Greg Meyers, at Pratt, Thomas, Pearce, Upting and Walker, 16 Charlotte St., Drawer 22247, Charleston, SC 29413-2247, (803) 727-2200.
> Can provide written guidelines for adult survivors who are considering suing perpetrators, as well as referrals.

Michael S. Morey, Lakeside Plaza, 8 N. State St., Suite 301, Lake Oswego, OR 97034, (503) 636-6001; fax: (503) 636-8512; e-mail: morey.lawfirm@worldnet.att.net

> Offers a resource packet for survivors based on many years of experience handling civil suits for survivors in Oregon, Washington, California, and Alaska. Also can provide resource information for survivors, attorneys, and therapists to counter attacks by the False Memory Syndrome Foundation.

Mark E. Roseman, 505 S. Main St., Suite 720, Orange, CA 92868, (714) 547-8801; fax: (714) 547-2735; e-mail: meroseman@aol.com

> Offers free brief consultation to survivors wanting to know more about their potential legal rights. Handout available: "Sexual Abuse Litigation: Common Questions and Answers."

G. Dana Scruggs, 340 Soquel Ave., #205, Santa Cruz, CA 95062, (831) 457-3700.

> Write or call to receive a copy of *Information and Guidelines for Survivors Contemplating Legal Action Against Their Perpetrators.* Please allow two weeks.

SEXUAL ABUSE AND HEALING

ABOUT SEXUAL ABUSE

Armstrong, Louise. *Rocking the Cradle of Sexual Politics: What Happened When Women Said Incest.* New York: Addison-Wesley, 1994.

> Although Armstrong spends much of this book disparaging the recovery movement and adult survivors' focus on individual healing, she also presents much that is of value. She carefully traces the history and permutations of the backlash, highlights the terrible injustices done to abused children and the mothers who try to protect them, and urges us to make stopping further sexual abuse a priority.

Bloom, Sandra. *Creating Sanctuary: Toward the Evolution of Sane Societies.* New York: Routledge, 1997.

> This study of a unique psychiatric program to treat survivors goes beyond helping the individual to address the social wounds in our society that require healing. A much-needed call to action.

Butler, Sandra. *Conspiracy of Silence: The Trauma of Incest.* Volcano, CA: Volcano Press, 1978, 1996.

> **A classic. Feminist analysis of child sexual abuse.**

SURVIVORS OF CHILDHOOD SEXUAL ABUSE: AN ANNOTATED LIST OF BOOKS
by Marge Eide

Marge Eide, an academic librarian and survivor, has compiled a comprehensive bibliography of books about sexual abuse or of particular interest to survivors and their families, therapists, friends, and colleagues. This valuable resource documents the vast number of books that have been written about abuse during the past fifteen years.

To order, send $10 to Marge Eide, 1206 Franklin Blvd., Ann Arbor, MI 48103.

Ernst, Sheila, and Lucy Goodwin. *In Our Own Hands: A Book of Self-Help Therapy.* N. Pomfret, VT: Trafalgar Square (P.O. Box 257, North Pomfret, VT 05053, (800) 423-4525), 1981, 1997.

> Guidelines for starting a self-help group. Gives clear guidelines for picking a therapist. Feminist analysis of encounter groups, bodywork, massage, dance, psychodrama, gestalt, regression, and dream work. Practical exercises for each.

Finkelhor, David. *Sexually Victimized Children.* New York: Free Press, 1979, 1981.

> Results of a landmark study on sex between adults and children. Combines survivors' accounts with data in a readable style. *Child Sexual Abuse: New Theory and Research* and *A Sourcebook on Child Sexual Abuse* are among his follow-up books.

Herman, Judith. *Trauma and Recovery.* New York: Basic Books, 1992, 1997.

> **A brilliant and compassionate synthesis of our understanding of the impact of trauma including the experiences of battered women, sexually abused children, war veterans, and prisoners of war. Herman's *Father-Daughter Incest* (1981) was one of the first to deal with incest from a feminist perspective.**

Masson, Geoffrey. *The Assault on Truth: Freud's Suppression of the Seduction Theory.* New York: Farrar, Straus and Giroux, 1984.

> This book challenges Freud's seduction theory; it

sent shock waves through the psychoanalytic community. Currently out of print.

Miller, Alice. *Thou Shalt Not Be Aware: Society's Betrayal of the Child*. New York: Penguin Books, 1986, 1991.

Miller brilliantly rips apart the Oedipal theory and shows that sexual abuse is real. Required reading for every therapist. Miller has written a number of other excellent books including: *The Drama of the Gifted Child* (1981), *For Your Own Good* (1983), *Banished Knowledge* (1990), *The Untouched Key* (1991), and *Breaking Down the Wall of Silence* (1997).

Rush, Florence. *The Best Kept Secret: Sexual Abuse of Children*. Englewood Cliffs, NJ: Prentice Hall, 1980.

A lucid feminist analysis of child sexual abuse from biblical times to the present. Rush was the first to expose the Freudian cover-up. Currently out of print.

Russell, Diana E. H. *Behind Closed Doors in White South Africa: Incest Survivors Tell Their Stories*. New York: St. Martin's Press, 1997.

Personal accounts as told by the survivors, with analyses of important incest-related issues. Compares the exploitation of girls by white male relatives with the exploitation of black people. Russell's first book, *The Secret Trauma: Incest in the Lives of Girls and Women* (1986) was the first to present extensive research on the prevalence of incest. Currently out of print.

Video

Counting the Cost. Cavalcade Productions, P.O. Box 2480, Nevada City, CA 95959, (800) 345-5530.

Bessel van der Kolk, along with clinicians, researchers and trauma survivors, explores the complex impact of severe childhood trauma in this 30-minute video for survivors.

SURVIVORS SPEAK OUT

Alleyne, Vanessa. *There Were Times I Thought I Was Crazy: A Black Woman's Story of Incest*. Toronto: Sister Vision (P.O. Box 217 Station E, Toronto, Ontario, Canada M6H 4E2, (800) 243-0138; fax: (416) 595-0627, e-mail: sisvis @web.net), 1997.

A painfully honest memoir that tells how the denial of her family and community almost made her believe she was crazy, and ultimately, how she began to heal.

Armstrong, Louise. *Kiss Daddy Goodnight: Ten Years Later*. New York: Pocket Books 1987.

An updated version of the classic speak-out on father-daughter incest. Challenges us to consider why incest is still going on.

Bass, Ellen, and Louise Thornton, eds. *I Never Told Anyone: Writings by Women Survivors of Child Sexual Abuse*. New York: HarperCollins, 1983, 1991.

These personal accounts of childhood abuse will let you know you're not alone.

Camille, Pamela. *Step on a Crack (You Break Your Father's Back)*. Chimney Rock, CO: Freedom Lights Press (P.O. Box 10257, Zephyr Cove, NV 89448), 1988.

A tough, funny, down-to-earth account of a young girl's journey from abuse to healing—and happiness. Good advice to survivors throughout.

Cartier, Marie. *I Am Your Daughter, Not Your Lover*. San Diego: Clothespin Fever Press (Available from Dialogus Press, Box 815761, Dallas, TX 75381, (800) 686-9484), 1994.

A brave document—poetry of resilience, perseverance and renewal.

Claman, Elizabeth, ed. *Writing Our Way Out of the Dark: An Anthology by Child Abuse Survivors*. Eugene, OR: Queen of Swords Press (P.O. Box 3646, Eugene, OR 97403), 1995.

This strong collection of poems, stories, and essays is by women and men who are survivors of all kinds of abuse. Many fine writers are included.

Cutting, Linda Katherine. *Memory Slips: A Memoir of Music and Healing*. New York: HarperCollins, 1997.

Cutting, a concert pianist, lost her ability to remember her music when she recovered memories of abuse. This book chronicles her struggle to regain herself and her music. A gripping, beautifully written memoir. Because music is so integral to this story, the audio version is particularly compelling.

Danica, Elly. *Don't. A Woman's Word*. Pittsburgh: Cleis Press (P.O. Box 14684, San Francisco, CA 94114; (415) 575-4700; fax (415) 575-4705; e-mail: cleis@aol.com), 1988.

A gripping account from a survivor of sexual abuse and child pornography. A very hard book to read. Currently out of print. The sequel, *Beyond Don't: Dreaming Past the Dark* (gynergy books, P.O. Box 2023, Charlottetown, P.E.I. Canada C1A 7N7, 1996) talks about what happened to Danica once she published *Don't* and became a public incest survivor. Includes a response to the backlash and an eloquent call to activism.

Donaforte, Laura. *I Remembered Myself: The Journal of a Survivor of Childhood Sexual Abuse.* **Self-published, 1982.**
This window into Laura's life tells the day-to-day struggles, pain, and triumphs of healing and offers a survivor's sense of humor, and hope. To order, send $7 to P.O. Box 914, Ukiah, CA 95482.

Franklin, Eileen, and William Wright. *Sins Of The Father: The Landmark Franklin Case: A Daughter, A Memory and A Murder.* New York: Crown Publishers, 1991.
Eileen Franklin's highly publicized story of witnessing her father kill her childhood friend. This book ends with the trial, but the case later became a rallying point for the FMS, George Franklin's sentence was overturned on technical grounds, and he went on to sue Eileen Franklin. A story with great political and legal impact. (Available through the Healing Woman, P.O. Box 28040, San Jose, CA 95159, (408) 246-1788.)

Fraser, Sylvia. *My Father's House: A Memoir of Incest and Healing.* New York: Harper & Row, 1987.
A stunning memoir—beautifully written, heart-wrenching, and ultimately healing. Currently out of print.

Hamilton, Barbara Small. *The Hidden Legacy: Uncovering, Confronting, and Healing Three Generations of Incest.* Fort Bragg, CA: Cypress House (155 Cypress St., Fort Bragg, CA 95437; (800) 773-7722; fax (707) 964-7531), 1993.
From the vantage point of her early seventies, Hamilton focuses an unflinching eye on the abuse that marred her childhood and the horrifying discovery that the tragic pattern was repeating for her children and grandchildren. Audio version available from: *The Hidden Legacy,* P.O. Box 401, Pacific Grove, CA 93950, (800) 500-1020; e-mail: Hlegacy@aol.com.

Harrison, Kathryn. *The Kiss.* New York: Random House, 1996.
A memoir of Harrison's incestuous relationship with her father that led her to the brink of insanity.

McLennan, Karen Jacobsen. *Nature's Ban: Women's Incest Literature.* **Boston: Northeastern University Press, 1996.**
An eloquent anthology from the 12th century to the present. In an era in which women's writing about incest is still often trivialized by the literary establishment, this is a powerful achievement.

McNaron, Toni, and Yarrow Morgan. *Voices in the Night: Women Speaking About Incest.* Pittsburgh: Cleis Press (P.O. Box 14684, San Francisco, CA 94114; (415) 575-4700; fax (415) 575-4705; e-mail: cleis@aol.com), 1982.
Women tell their stories. Includes mother-daughter incest.

Mirikitani, Janis, ed. *Watch Out! We're Talking: Speaking Out About Incest and Abuse.* San Francisco: Glide Word Press (Glide Memorial Methodist Church, 330 Ellis St., Room 203, San Francisco, CA 94102), 1993.
Essays, poems, and life stories from women and men who've been sexually abused. Many of the contributors, who were poor, homeless, or in recovery, were not comfortable with writing; their first-person accounts were drawn from a careful process of interview, transcription, and approval. As a result, there are many important voices we usually don't hear in this kind of anthology.

Morris, Michelle. *If I Should Die Before I Wake.* **New York: Dell, 1982.**
A harrowing fictional account of one child's experience of incest. Guaranteed to evoke feelings. Make sure there's someone around you can talk to when you're through. Currently out of print.

Peterson, Betsy. *Dancing with Daddy.* New York: Bantam, 1991.
A moving memoir of incest and recovery. Currently out of print.

Portwood, Pamela, et al. *Rebirth of Power: Overcoming the Effects of Sexual Abuse Through the Experiences of Others.* Racine, WI: Mother Courage (1667 Douglas Ave., Racine, WI 53404; (414) 637-2227; fax (414) 637-8242; e-mail: mocourage@aol.com), 1987.
A wonderfully creative collection of writings by sexual abuse survivors.

Randall, Margaret. *This Is About Incest.* Ithaca, NY: Firebrand Books (141 The Commons, Ithaca, NY 14850; (800) 663-1766), 1987.
Well known as a witness to Latin American progressive movements, Margaret Randall documents her own healing from her grandfather's incestuous assaults through words and photographs. *Memory Says Yes* follows with more poetry.

Silverman, Sue William. *Because I Remember Terror Father, I Remember You*. Athens, GA: University of Georgia, 1996.

> Award-winning memoir. Terrifying and heartening.

Wisechild, Louise. *The Obsidian Mirror: An Adult Healing from Incest*. Seattle: Seal Press, 1988, 1992.

> **A powerful description of healing from the inside out. Vividly describes the process of remembering and connecting with inner children. Graphic descriptions of abuse, however; you may need support. Wisechild has also written two other excellent books, *The Mother I Carry* and *She Who Was Lost Is Remembered*.**

Films and Videos

There are more films and videos listed under specific topics.

Healing Sexual Abuse: The Recovery Process. Varied Directions, 18 Mt. Battie Street, Camden, ME 04843, (800) 888-5236; fax (207) 236-4512; e-mail: Joyceb3955@aol.com

> This one-hour videotape sensitively interviews survivors and talks about the healing process. Hosted by Eliana Gil; features Ellen Bass and Dan Sexton. Accompanied by a useful resource guide.

Incest: Speaking the Deadly Secret. People Productions Video, 1737 15th Street, Boulder, CO 80302, (303) 449-6086.

> Despite the sensational title, this is a topnotch video. Sensitive and well produced. Survivors use art and writing to talk about their pain and their healing. If you want to get inside a survivor's feelings, watch this tape.

Renee Has a Secret . . . She Was Sexually Abused. RISK, P.O. Box 756, Brentwood, CA 94513, (510) 634-4902.

> This 25-minute video is a good introduction to the issue of sexual abuse for parents, teachers, and others concerned. $29.95 includes shipping and handling.

Scared Silent. Stone Associates, 2714 Pico Blvd., #215 Santa Monica, CA 90405, (310) 450-9244.

> This documentary, produced by Oprah Winfrey, is probably the most widely viewed show on incest. Available for $8.50.

A Story of Hope. Marilyn Van Derbur, P.O. Box 61099, Denver, CO 80206.

> Videotapes and audiocassettes available of several

THE NATIONAL FILM BOARD OF CANADA

The Family Violence Film and Video Collection, National Clearinghouse on Family Violence, 18th Floor, Jeanne Mance Building, Tunney's Pasture, Ottawa, Ontario, Canada K1A 1B4, (800) 267-1291; fax (613) 941-8930; TTY (800) 561-5643 or on the web: http://www.hc-sc.gc.ca/nc-cn

> That wonderful institution, the National Film Board of Canada, puts out an incredible catalogue of all the audiovisuals available in North America that deal with family violence. Many are U.S. films. Catalogue is bilingual in English and French.

---

inspirational talks given by Marilyn Van Derbur and her husband, Larry Atler. *A Story of Hope* is $27.50. Write for information.

To a Safer Place. National Film Board of Canada, P.O. Box 6100, Station Centre-ville, Montreal, Quebec, Canada H3C 3H5, (800) 267-7710; fax (514) 283-7564.

> This award-winning hour-long film shows one survivor's path toward healing. It follows Shirley Turcotte, a survivor of father-daughter incest, as she returns to her home town and confronts her family. Available on video and in 16 mm.

"Why God—Why Me?" Varied Directions, 18 Mt. Battie Street, Camden, ME 04843, (800) 888-5236; fax (207) 236-4512; e-mail: Joyceb3955@aol.com

> A painful, emotionally charged film that focuses on the trauma caused by child sexual abuse. The film tells the story of a woman in rural Maine who was sexually abused by the men in her family and later married a man who abused her children. A facilitator's guide is also available.

ON HEALING

Bassoff, Evelyn S. *Mothering Ourselves: Help and Healing for Adult Daughters*. New York: Plume, 1992.

> A warm, insightful book that suggests ways in which women can get the nurturing they need to lead full, healthy lives.

BEGINNING BOOKS

Bass, Ellen, and Laura Davis. *Beginning to Heal: A First Book for Survivors of Child Sexual Abuse.* New York: HarperCollins, 1993.

>An easy-to-read introduction to the healing process based on *The Courage to Heal.* Especially useful for new readers, those new to English, teens, and anyone needing a shorter, less intensive beginning. Also on audiotape.

Daugherty, Lynn B. *Why Me? Help for Victims of Child Sexual Abuse (even if they are adults now).* Racine, WI: Mother Courage Press (1667 Douglas Ave., Racine, WI 53404; (414) 637-2227; fax (414) 637-8242; e-mail: mocourage@aol.com), 1984.

>A good, simple beginning book for child, teen, and adult survivors.

Gil, Eliana. *Outgrowing the Pain: A Book for and about Adults Abused as Children.* New York: Dell, 1983, 1988.

>A good overview of the healing process for all kinds of abuse. Cartoon illustrations and simple, clear text. A helpful place to begin. Available in Spanish through Launch Press.

Go Gently: A Collection of Writings to Support and Guide Women Beginning Their Recovery from Childhood Sexual Abuse.

>Inspirational and informative articles from past issues of *The Healing Woman.* Available from The Healing Woman, P.O. Box 28040, San Jose, CA 95159, (408) 246-1788.

Bear, Euan, with Peter Dimock. *Adults Molested as Children: A Survivor's Manual for Women and Men.* Brandon, VT: Safer Society Press, 1988.

>Excellent. A simple straightforward approach to healing for both men and women.

HEALING BOOKS ESPECIALLY FOR TEENS

Lee, Sharice A. *The Survivor's Guide.* Thousand Oaks, CA: Sage, 1995.

>Written to educate adolescent girls about the effects of abuse, this small book will help young survivors understand that their reactions and difficulties are normal and they're not alone.

Wright, Leslie Bailey, and Mindy B. Loiselle. *Shining Through: Pulling It Together.* Orwell, VT: Safer Society Press, 1994.

>**An excellent, empowering book and workbook written especially for teenage survivors. Highly recommended.**

Blume, E. Sue. *Secret Survivors: Uncovering Incest and Its Aftereffects in Women.* New York: Ballantine, 1990, 1997.

>Clearly delineates and describes the long-term effects of incest. Can help survivors discover that their experiences and reactions make sense.

Braddock, Carolyn J. *Body Voices: Using the Power of Breath, Sound and Movement to Heal and Create New Boundaries.* Berkeley: Page Mill Press (2716 Ninth St., Berkeley, CA 94710, (510) 848-3600), 1995, 1997.

>An approach to integrating body, mind, and spirit for survivors. Includes guided sessions in which you learn to listen to the voices of your body to unlock feelings.

Bronson, Catherine. *Growing Through the Pain: The Incest Survivor's Companion.* New York: Prentice Hall/Parkside, 1989, 1992.

>Six women intimately describe their healing process.

Caruso, Beverly. *Healing: A Handbook for Adult Victims of Child Sexual Abuse.* Self-published, 1986.

>Well-organized, clear information on the basics: shame, self-esteem, sexuality, boundaries, and anger. Concretely contradicts false beliefs caused by abuse. To order, send $12.95 to Beverly Caruso, 2829 Inglewood Ave., S. Minneapolis, MN 55416.

WHAT MAKES US STRONG?

Coffey, Rebecca. *Unspeakable Truths and Happy Endings: Human Cruelty and The New Trauma Therapy.* Lutherville, MD: Sidran Press, 1998.

This book is unique in that it explores the genuine similarities between diverse types of traumatic experiences. Brings much needed intelligence to the discussion of trauma therapy.

Higgins, Gina O'Connell. *Resilient Adults: Overcoming a Cruel Past.* San Francisco: Jossey-Bass, 1994, 1996.

An inspiring study of forty adults who came from families judged to be "severely, extremely or catastrophically stressful," who went on to have stable, successful love relationships, as well as positive experiences with work and parenting.

Rhodes, Ginger, and Richard Rhodes. *Trying to Get Some Dignity: Stories of Triumph Over Childhood Abuse.* New York: William Morrow, 1996.

After the publication of his gripping memoir, *A Hole in the World,* Richard Rhodes corresponded with hundreds of survivors of childhood abuse. He and his wife, Ginger, chose twenty survivors to interview in depth. Filled with uplifting accounts of creative, original strategies for survival.

Sanford, Linda. *Strong at the Broken Places: Overcoming the Trauma of Childhood Abuse.* New York: Random House, 1990.

Studies transformation in the lives of twenty survivors. Clearly focuses on the positive lives survivors can create out of the devastation of their childhoods. Empowering and empathetic. Currently out of print.

Davis, Laura. *The Courage to Heal Workbook.* New York: HarperCollins, 1990.

Diverse in-depth exercises for women and men. Designed for both individual survivors and groups. Emphasizes skills in building your support system and learning to take care of yourself. Includes exercises dealing with the stages of healing outlined in *The Courage to Heal*, as well as sexual healing.

Engel, Beverly. *The Right to Innocence: Healing the Trauma of Child Sexual Abuse.* New York: Ballantine, 1989, 1991.

A recovery guide for adult survivors. Full of sensible, nurturing ideas for healing.

Fredrickson, Renee. *Repressed Memories: A Journey to Recovery from Sexual Abuse.* New York: Simon & Schuster, 1992.

Clinical expertise combined with good storytelling. Lots of valuable, practical information about recovering memories of sexual abuse.

Katherine, Anne. *Boundaries: Where You End and I Begin.* New York: Simon & Schuster, 1991.

Explains what healthy boundaries are, how to recognize violations, and how to protect yourself. Straightforward and practical.

Levine, Peter, with Ann Frederick. *Waking the Tiger: Healing Trauma: The Innate Capacity to Transform Traumatic Experiences.* Berkeley, CA: North Atlantic Books (P.O. Box 12327, Berkeley, CA 94712), 1997.

A fascinating book based on the premise that the body holds the key to healing. Levine believes that human beings, like all animals, have a deep and instinctual capacity to overcome traumatic experiences. His book provides guidelines for tapping into our bodies' natural capacities.

Maltz, Wendy. *The Sexual Healing Journey: A Guide for Survivors of Sexual Abuse.* New York: HarperCollins, 1991.

This comprehensive resource assists survivors in understanding the impact of sexual abuse on sexuality and learning how to create a new approach to intimate touch and sexual sharing. Maltz's first book (with Beverly Holman), *Incest and Sexuality* (1987) is an excellent resource for working through sexual (and other) problems. It includes lots of examples from work with teenagers.

Poston, Carol, and Karen Lison. *Reclaiming Our Lives: Hope for Adult Survivors of Incest.* New York: Bantam, 1989.

Nicely written, supportive healing guide by a survi-

WILDERNESS PROGRAMS FOR SURVIVORS

These programs use outdoor activities to teach survivors body awareness, trust, boundary setting, self-confidence, communication, and staying present. Physically based activities can be a powerful addition to therapy because they encourage healing on a body level.

Most outdoor programs require that you be involved in ongoing therapy before enrolling because the courses can bring up strong feelings. It's important that you have a support system to go home to. Also, talk to leaders of the program before you enroll to make sure the program fits your particular needs and stage of healing.

Association for Experiential Education (A.E.E.), 2885 Aurora #28, Boulder, CO.80303-2252, (303) 440-8844.

The AEE provides information about experience-based adventure activities for educational and therapeutic purposes. Their directory of 250 existing programs costs $18.50.

Outward Bound Women of Courage Programs
These wilderness courses for survivors of sexual assault, incest, and domestic violence provide opportunities for survivors to build self-confidence and self-esteem, practice safe risk-taking, get in touch with their bodies, and develop trust and support within a group. Financial assistance available.

Women of Courage Program, North Carolina Outward Bound, 2582 Riceville Road, Asheville, NC 28805, (800) 209-9773 ext. 112.

Women of Courage Program, Canadian Outward Bound, 150 Laird Dr., Suite 302, Toronto, Ontario, Canada M4G 3V7, (888) 688-9273; fax (416) 421-9062.

Woodswomen: Adventure Travel for Women of All Ages, 25 West Diamond Lake Rd., Minneapolis, MN 55419, (800) 279-0555.

Although they don't have trips specifically for survivors, their all-women trips are worth knowing about. They include biking, canoeing, climbing, rafting, trekking, skiing, and scuba diving, and range from relaxing vacations to strenuous outdoor adventures.

---

vor and a therapist. Outlines a healing process that explores issues of trust, power, control, and intimacy.

Schmidt, K. Louise. *Transforming Abuse: Nonviolent Resistance and Recovery.* Philadelphia: New Society, 1995.

A strong, respectful stance that offers a theory and method of recovery grounded in the connections between feminism and nonviolence. A challenging, inspiring book.

HEALING THROUGH THE ARTS

ART BOOKS, ART SHOWS, VIDEOS, AND PERFORMANCES

Abuse: Part 1. The Loss of Abundance, Part 2. The Art of Healing. Brazen Video (Available from Wisconsin Committee to Prevent Child Abuse, 214 N. Hamilton St., Madison, WI 53703, (608) 256-3374. $25 purchase or $10 rental).

This special film combines a social and political awareness with artistic expression. Part 1 explores the roots of abuse through interviews, art, song, and performance. Part 2 documents a project of healing through art. Both men and women survivors of many races and cultures are included.

The Art of Healing, organized by Judy Wilbur-Albertson c/o Sexual Assault Support Services, 7 Junkins Ave., Portsmouth, NH 03801.

An exhibit of over 400 works of art by women survivors. Work is by professional and nonprofessional artists in a variety of mediums. Too large to travel, the exhibit has been preserved in slides and on videotape. The videotape includes survivors speaking about the creative process of healing. The expanding slide collection now has grown to over 1,500 works. Powerful consciousness-raising and educational tools.

The Banner Project, Wisconsin Committee to Prevent Child Abuse, 214 N. Hamilton St. Madison, WI 53703 (attn: Sally Casper), (608) 256-3374; fax (608) 256-3378; e-mail: wcpca@juno.com

Initiated in 1989, this expanding national art project demonstrates the strength and courage of survivors. Individual survivors (women, men, and children) create 8½″ by 11″ panels using their handprint as the central motif. The panels are then sewn together. Currently there are 1100 panels and 11 banners available for display internationally ($10 usage fee plus shipping). For guidelines on making a panel, see p. 332 of *The Courage to Heal Workbook* or contact The Banner Project.

The Clothesline Project, P.O. Box 727, East Dennis, MA 02641, (508) 385-7004; fax (508) 385-7100.

A display of shirts created by survivors of violence or their loved ones. Each shirt tells a woman's story through words, pictures, and other decorative art, bearing witness to violence against women and its impact on society. Simply seeing the Clothesline can be validating for a woman who feels isolated and ashamed. More than 500 individual Clotheslines have been formed across the country and internationally.

INCEST: Remember and Tell, written and choreographed by Wendy Hoffman. Available through Varied Directions, 18 Mt. Battie Street, Camden ME 04843; (800) 888-5236; fax (207) 236-4512; e-mail: Joyceb3955@aol.com

This multimedia performance is available on videotape. It tells the story of a young girl who is raped and whose family denies the abuse, but who, as she grows into adulthood, will not be silenced. She tells, sheds her self-hatred, and goes on to reclaim her body, mind, and life.

In Light We Grow. Written and performed by G. Diane Hill. Words Unlimited, P.O. Box 11, Austin, MN 55912, (507) 437-6927; fax (507) 437-6927; e-mail: kastutzm @wolf.co.net

This moving one-woman show employs three unique characters—the Cleaning Lady, Lecture Lady, and Little Girl—to educate audiences about sexual abuse and healing. Compassionate and accessible, this videotaped performance is appropriate for survivors, counselors, and all concerned.

Books

E., Nancy. *Once I Was a Child and There Was Much Pain: A Glimpse into the Soul of an Incest Survivor.* San Francisco: Frog in the Well Press (P.O. Box 170052, San Francisco, CA 94117), 1988.

A breathtaking collection of drawings by a survivor. Powerful.

Wisechild, Louise. *She Who Was Lost Is Remembered: Healing from Incest Through Creativity.* Seattle: Seal Press, 1991.

A wonderful, inspiring anthology that presents the work of more than thirty visual artists, musicians, and writers, along with essays by each contributor on how she used creativity to heal. Fifty illustrations.

Hopkins, Khristine. *SURVIVORS: Experiences of Childhood Sexual Abuse and Healing.* Berkeley, CA: Celestial Arts (P.O. Box 7123, Berkeley, CA 94707), 1994.

This award-winning exhibit of hand-colored photographs and text consists of visual metaphors that express the experiences of women members of a survivors group. The *Chicago Tribune* called it "intimate and deeply moving." In addition to the book, a video is available through Tempest Press, P.O. Box 1438, Provincetown, MA 02657. Send a self-addressed stamped envelope for a brochure.

WRITING AND DRAWING AS HEALING TOOLS

Organizations

The National Association for Poetry Therapy, P.O. Box 551, Port Washington, NY 11050, (516) 944-9791 or on the web: www.poetrytherapy.org

A multidisciplinary organization for those who work with poetry, journals, literature, creative writing and language arts for growth and healing. Annual conferences, quarterly journal, and regional meetings.

The Center for Journal Therapy, P.O. Box 963, Arvada, CO 80001, (888) 421-2298 or on the web at www.journaltherapy.com

Dedicated to healing through writing. Offers training, consultation, and facilitation. Workshops are available in many cities.

Books

Adams, Kathleen. *Journal to the Self: Twenty-two Paths to Personal Growth*. New York: Warner Books, 1990.

> A gem for those of us who "get it out on paper" when we're searching to find our heart. Her excellent follow-up, *The Way of the Journal: A Journal Therapy Workbook for Healing* (1993), is specifically designed for sexual abuse survivors and for people diagnosed with dissociative disorders.

Cameron, Julia. *The Artist's Way: A Spiritual Path to Higher Creativity*. New York: J. P. Tarcher, 1992.

> This practical, personal guide offers a simple twelve-week program to recover your creative energy, even if it's long lost. Since its publication, it has given rise to a remarkable number of peer support groups practicing the principles contained in the book.

Capacchione, Lucia. *The Picture of Health: Healing Your Life with Art*. Santa Monica, CA: Hay House (P.O. Box 2212, Santa Monica, CA 90406), 1990.

> A beautiful handbook and guide to art therapy. Capaccione has a number of other excellent titles, including *Recovery and Your Inner Child*, *The Power of Your Other Hand*, *The Creative Journal*, and *The Creative Journal for Teens and Children*.

Cohen, Barry M., Mary-Michola Barnes, and Anita B. Rankin. *Managing Traumatic Stress Through Art: Drawing From The Center*. Lutherville, MD: Sidran Press, 1995.

> **Accessible art exercises that can help with an array of issues such as self-care, emotional health, and present day life skills. Excellent for survivors and therapists.**

Edwards, Betty. *Drawing on the Right Side of the Brain*. Los Angeles: J. P. Tarcher, 1979.

> A classic on developing your creativity. A friendly, readable companion. The sequel, *Drawing on the Artist Within: A Guide to Innovation, Imagination, and Creativity*, is equally worthwhile.

Goldberg, Natalie. *Wild Mind*. New York: Bantam, 1990.

> A remarkably wise and lovely follow-up to her underground Zen writing classic, *Writing Down the Bones*. *Living Color: A Writer Paints Her World* is a beautifully illustrated, inspiring book about Goldberg's development as a painter.

Lamott, Anne. *Bird by Bird: Some Instructions on Writing and Life*. New York: Doubleday, 1994.

> The funniest book on writing. Excellent advice, wise, kind, and thoroughly entertaining.

Metzger, Deena. *Writing for Your Life: A Guide and Companion to the Inner Worlds*. San Francisco: Harper San Francisco, 1992.

> **A deep and valuable book by an extraordinary life teacher.**

Mines, Stephanie. *Sexual Abuse/Sacred Wound: Transforming Deep Trauma*. Barrytown, NY: Barrytown Ltd. (Available through the Tara Program, 2910 County Road 67, Boulder, CO 80303; (303) 499-9990; e-mail: TARA.mines@mcione.com); 1996.

> A rich guide for healing through the expressive arts. Abounds with creative suggestions and a wonderful sense of possibility.

Newman, Leslea. *Writing from the Heart: Inspiration and Exercises for Women Who Want to Write*. Freedom, CA: Crossing Press 1993.

> **Down-to-earth commonsense advice and encouragement.**

Rico, Gabriele. *Writing the Natural Way*. Los Angeles: J. P. Tarcher, 1986.

> An innovative approach to writing (and fun ways to sneak past your censors).

SARK. *Succulent Wild Woman: Dancing With Your Wonder-Full Self!*, New York: Simon & Schuster, 1997.

> SARK's books invite you to celebrate yourself, to enjoy and experience the woman you are right now, with no improvements. Delightful. See also *Living Juicy*, *Inspiration Sandwich*, *A Creative Companion*, and others.

HEALING MUSIC

Joan Baez. *Play Me Backwards*. Virgin Records.
The title song—about sadistic ritual abuse—is stunningly powerful. Joan Baez at her best.

Nancy Day. *Survivor*. Nancy Day, P.O. Box 5743, Burlington, VT 05402.

> Honest songs about abuse and recovery. Also, listen to "Memory Lane" on her new CD *Born to Live*—a laugh-out-loud spoof on the FMS.

Robert Gass and On Wings of Song. *Trust in Love*. Spring Hill Music, Box 800, Boulder, CO 80306, (303) 938-1188.

> Healing music from the heart. Also many other inspiring albums, including *Many Blessings, Songs of Healing*, and *Om Namaha Shivaya*.

Ruth Huber and Kate McLennan. *Trailblazers*. Trailblazers, 7209 Grover Ave., Austin, TX 78757.

> Uplifting songs for adult children.

Tom Hunter. *Bits and Pieces*. Song Growing Co., 1225 E. Sunset Dr. #518, Bellingham, WA 98226.

> Includes a lullaby for grown-ups, "Rock Me to Sleep," that survivors love (and love to have sung to them).

Janis Ian. *Breaking Silence.* **Columbia Records.**

> **Title cut is one of the best on the subject. Inspiring.**

Judith May. *Heal the Broken Wing*. Yes You May! Music, P.O. Box 31539, San Francisco, CA 94131-0539.

> Deep emotion and beautiful music. Also, *Rising Again*, a celebration of the Divine.

Cathy Munsey. *NO MORE! Songs of Healing*. Heart Wings, 46 Charles Rd., Winchester, MA 01890.

> A focus on healing and empowerment.

Shaina Noll. *Bread For the Journey.* **Sing Heart Productions. Available in record stores or through** *The Healing Woman*, **P.O. Box 28040, San Jose, CA 95159, (408) 246-1788.**

> **A well-chosen collection of beautiful songs, including our personal favorite, "How Could Anyone" (How could anyone ever tell you that you're anything less than beautiful?)**

Fred Small. *I Will Stand Fast.* **Rounder Records, 1 Camp St., Cambridge, MA 02140, (800) 44-DISCS.**

> **Title song is the theme song for partners everywhere. Small's album** *Jaguar* **features a powerful, evocative song about incest, "Light in the Hall."**

Jim Weiss. *Good Night.* **Greathall Productions, P.O. Box 813, Benicia, CA 94510, (800) 477-6234; fax (707) 745-5820.**

> **Jim Weiss is a fabulous storyteller. These stories are soothing, comforting and dreamy visualizations. They put us to sleep every time.**

SURVIVORS' MEMORIES AND THE DENIAL OF ABUSE

In recent years, the validity of survivors' memories has been questioned by proponents of the "false memory syndrome," the media, and the general public. A number of excellent resources have emerged which respond directly to this challenge. The articles, books, videos, and web sites listed below provide a sane response to the continued attacks on the credibility of survivors and their therapists, while documenting the wealth of emerging research on memory and trauma.

Clear, thoughtful information about traumatic amnesia and the complexity of memory can be gleaned from the resources below. Most are written with therapists in mind, but can be useful and informative for survivors as well.

WEB SITES

In an area of inquiry that is new and groundbreaking, the Internet is often the best source for current information. The following web sites provide up-to-date research and resources on recovered memory issues:

Jim Hopper's Page
http://www.jimhopper.com

> A comprehensive source of information about recovered memory issues, including scientific research and scholarly resources.

Recovered Memory Page
http://cgi-user.brown.edu/Departments/ Taubman_Center/Recovmem/Archive.html

> A survivor and scholar's collection of corroborated cases of recovered memory. Related research and publications on traumatic amnesia.

ORGANIZATIONS

AAA: Accuracy About Abuse, P.O. Box 3125, London NW3 5QB, phone: 0171-431-5539; fax: 0171-433-3101; e-mail: morr@aaastar.demon.co.uk

> This informative monthly newsletter published by activist Marjorie Orr documents current events about the backlash against survivors and the controversy about survivors' memories in Great Britain, the U.S., and elsewhere in the world. An up-to-date global perspective.

One Voice: The National Alliance for Abuse Awareness and its public policy project, The American Coalition for Abuse Awareness (ACAA), P.O. Box 27958, Washington, D.C. 20038-7958, (202) 667-1160 or (202) 462-4688; fax (202) 462-4689; e-mail: OVoiceDC@aol.com or ACAADC @aol.com or on the web:
http://www.sover.net/%7Eschwcof/newshead.html
One Voice/ACAA is a national alliance of survivors, advocates, and helping professionals working together to counteract the forces of the backlash.

BOOKS

Contratto, Susan, and M. Janice Gutfreund, eds. *A Feminist Clinician's Guide to the Memory Debate.* New York: Haworth Press, 1996.
A collection of articles integrating clinical, political, legal, and ethical issues. Informative and intelligent.

Falconer, Robert, et al., eds. *Trauma, Amnesia, and the Denial of Abuse.* Tyler, TX: Family Violence and Sexual Assault Institute (1121 ESE Loop 323, Suite 130, Tyler, TX 75701; (903) 534-5100; fax (903) 534-5454; e-mail: fvsai@iamerica.net or on the web:
http://www.gatekeep.net/fvsai/index.html), 1995.
A collection of some of the most important articles about memory, abuse and the current controversies by prominent professionals such as Judith Herman, Bessel van der Kolk, David Finkelhor, John Briere, David Calof, Karen Olio and others.

Freyd, Jennifer. *Betrayal Trauma: The Logic of Forgetting Childhood Abuse.* Cambridge: Harvard University Press, 1996.
Cognitive psychologist Jennifer Freyd explores the issues of memory and amnesia when children are sexually abused by a trusted adult. Includes a careful review of recent research, as well as a discussion of the current social, historic and linguistic context. (Though Freyd's parents founded the False Memory Syndrome Foundation, she includes her personal history only briefly in the afterword.)

Herman, Judith. *Trauma and Recovery.* New York: Basic Books. 1992.
A brilliant, essential book that looks at the impact of trauma on battered women, sexually abused children, war veterans, and prisoners of war. Includes clear information about how trauma affects memory.

Knopp, Fay Honey, and Anna Rose Benson. *A Primer on the Complexities of Traumatic Memory of Childhood Sexual Abuse: A Psychobiological Approach.* Brandon, VT: Safer Society Press, 1996.
This well-written book examines the physiological processes of the brain in storing, retaining, and remembering traumatic experience. A major contribution to the field that makes very complex material clear.

Pope, Kenneth S., and Laura S. Brown. *Recovered Memories of Abuse: Assessment, Therapy, Forensics.* Washington, D.C.: American Psychological Association, 1996.
One of the best resources on the topic to date. Brings together a review of the research, pragmatic guidelines for clinicians, and guidance on forensic issues. Sane and practical.

Reviere, Susan L. *Memory of Childhood Trauma: A Clinician's Guide to the Literature.* New York: Guilford Press, 1996.
Distills current scientific research on childhood trauma and memory to present a much needed resource.

**Whitfield, Charles. *Memory and Abuse: Remembering and Healing the Effects of Trauma.* Deerfield Beach, FL: Health Communications (3201 SW 15th St. Deerfield Beach, FL 33442, (800) 851-9100; fax (954) 360-0034; e-mail: hci books@aol.com or on the web:
http://www.hci-online.com), 1995.**
Written for both survivors and helping professionals, this book clarifies what we know about traumatic memory. Whitfield discusses the factors involved in remembering and forgetting personal history, substantiates the existence of delayed memory, and suggests ways to sort out true from untrue memory. Throughout, Whitfield analyzes the history, politics and claims of "false memory" proponents and puts the backlash against survivors in perspective. Most readable memory book for the layperson.

JOURNALS & ARTICLES

***Treating Abuse Today: Survivorship, Treatment and Trends.* P.O. Box 3030, Lancaster, PA 17604-3030, (717) 569-3636; fax (717) 581-1355; e-mail: TreatAbuse@aol. com**
A bimonthly journal that explores current treatment issues and trends in the sexual abuse field. Excellent

continuing coverage of "false memory" controversy with many valuable back issues on different aspects of the topic. $39/year.

The Healing Woman, P.O. Box 28040, San Jose, CA 95159, (408) 246-1788.

A special issue, "Surviving the Backlash" (August 1993), is available for $3. A second, longer issue, "The Backlash in Perspective" (March/April 1998), is available for $6.

Backus, John, and Barbara Stannard. "Your Memories Are Not False: A Reply to the False Memory Foundation."

Send a self-addressed long envelope with 55¢ postage to Barbara Una Stannard, P.O. Box 16014, San Francisco, CA 94116.

AUDIO AND VIDEOTAPES

The Science and Politics of Recovered Memories. Lutherville, MD: Sidran Press, 1997.

An audiotape of an excellent symposium presented at the American Psychological Association. Speakers include: Jennifer Hoult, a survivor who successfully sued her father; Ross Cheit, a therapist who's established a database of corroborated recovered memory cases; Jennifer Freyd, professor of psychology at the University of Oregon and daughter of the FMS founders; David Calof, editor emeritus of *Treating Abuse Today* and therapist under siege; Anna Salter, author and therapist; and Laura Brown, clinical and forensic psychologist. A call to activism that is not to be missed. $17.50.

True/Not True: When Memories Can Be Trusted. Cavalcade Productions, P.O. Box 2480, Nevada City, CA 95959, (800) 345-5530.

Bessel van der Kolk, a leading trauma researcher, lucidly and elegantly speaks about how people remember—and don't remember—extraordinary trauma. Survivors of trauma also share their experiences. This video makes a complex subject easy to understand.

SPECIAL TOPICS

ABUSE BY WOMEN

Elliott, Michele, ed. *Female Sexual Abuse of Children.* New York: Guilford Press, 1994.

This important and challenging collection of articles includes chapters for professionals working with both survivors and offenders, as well as men and women survivors' accounts of their experiences.

Evert, Kathy, and Inie Bijerk. *When You're Ready: A Woman's Guide to Healing from Childhood Physical and Sexual Abuse by Her Mother.* Walnut Creek, CA: Launch Press, 1988.

One woman's story. A powerful resource for women molested by their mothers.

Harrison, Kathryn. *Thicker Than Water.* New York: Random House, 1991.

A beautifully written novel about a girl molested and neglected by her mother and raped by her father. Full of truth, vivid detail, and unforgettable images. Although some things are disturbing—like the girl's blaming herself for "allowing" her father's abuse to happen—this book is still a haunting story. Currently out of print.

Rosencrans, Bobbie. *The Last Secret: Daughters Sexually Abused by Mothers.* Brandon, VT: Safer Society Press, 1997.

Groundbreaking research, including testimony from 93 women. A significant and insightful work.

Sexton, Linda Gray. *Mirror Images.* New York: Doubleday, 1985.

Novel that centers on the healing of a teenage victim of mother-daughter incest. Currently out of print.

Wisechild, Louise. *The Mother I Carry: A Memoir of Healing from Emotional Abuse.* Seattle: Seal Press, 1993.

Powerful, honest, beautifully written look at emotional abuse by a mother.

Video

Alper, Mara. *Stories No One Wants to Hear.* Distributed by Varied Directions, 18 Mt. Battie Street, Camden ME 04843; (800) 888-5236; fax (207) 236-4512; e-mail: Joyceb 3955@aol.com

Women speak out on mother-daughter incest. An important video whose power is diluted by the fact that not all the women appear on camera.

ABUSE BY SIBLINGS

Barnes, Liz. *hand me downs.* San Francisco: Spinsters/ Aunt Lute (P.O. Box 410687, San Francisco, CA 94141- 0687; (800) 949-4883; fax: (415) 826-8300; e-mail: books @auntlute.com or on the web: http://www.best.com/~auntlute/), 1985.

> A delightful autobiographical novel written from the point of view of a spunky five-year-old who is abused by her brother. (Currently out of print; available from the author at 2 Asta Terrace, Santa Fe, NM 87505, for $10.)

Cole, Autumn, and Becca Brin Manlove. *Brother-Sister Sexual Abuse: It Happens and It Hurts. A Book for Sister Survivors.* Beccautumn Books ($9.95 from Autumn Cole, Range Mental Health Center, Box 1188, Virginia, MN 55792; (218) 365-5019), 1991.

> Based on Autumn Cole's doctoral dissertation, this clear and simple book validates the feelings, experiences, and healing needs of women who were molested by their brothers.

Fleming, Kathleen. *Lovers in the Present Afternoon.* Tallahassee, FL: Naiad Press (P.O. Box 10543; Tallahassee, FL 32302; (800) 533-1973; fax: (850) 539-5965; e-mail: naiadpress@aol.com or on the web: http://www.naiadpress.com), 1984.

> Well-written lesbian novel deals with incest by a brother.

O'Brien, Michael. *Characteristics of Adolescent Male Sibling Incest Offenders: Preliminary Findings.* Brandon, VT: Safer Society Press, 1991.

> This study compares sibling incest offenders with two other adolescent sex-offender groups. Points to gaps in judicial and social service policy regarding sibling incest offenders.

Wiehe, Vernon. *The Brother/Sister Hurt: Recognizing The Effects of Sibling Abuse.* Brandon, VT: Safer Society Press, 1997.

> **A guide to acknowledging and healing from sibling abuse, with a chapter on sexual abuse. Also see Wiehe's other books, *Perilous Rivalry: When Siblings Become Abusive* (1991) and *Sibling Abuse: Hidden Physical, Emotional, and Sexual Trauma* (1990, 1997) which defines the forms and causes of sibling abuse and gives guidelines for preventing and stopping it.**

Video

Once Can Hurt A Lifetime. One Voice, 1835 K St., NW, Washington, D.C. 20006, (202) 667-1160; fax (202) 462-4689. $27.50.

> This excellent video by Marilyn Van Derbur focuses on the damage that results when a sibling or trusted teen sexually violates a child. It is intended for both children and adults, victims and offenders, for the purpose of education and prevention.

FOR MALE SURVIVORS

There are several web sites for male survivors listed on p. 539.

Bass, Ellen, and Kate Kaufman. *Free Your Mind: The Book for Gay, Lesbian, and Bisexual Youth—and Their Allies.* New York: HarperCollins, 1996.

> Boys who have been sexually abused may be vulnerable to further exploitation and young gay men are especially vulnerable. This affirming book helps young people develop strong self-esteem which is the best protection against further abuse.

Berendzen, Richard. *Come Here: A Man Overcomes the Tragic Aftermath of Childhood Sexual Abuse.* New York: Villard Books, 1993.

> A famous astronomer and academician tells the story of sexual abuse at the hands of his mother. He repressed all memory of the abuse for over fifty years.

Estrada, Hank. *Recovery for Male Victims of Child Abuse.* Santa Fe, NM: Red Rabbit Press (P.O. Box 968, Truth or Consequences, NM 87901; (505) 894-4092; fax (505) 894-4100; e-mail: redrabbit@zianet.com), 1990, 1993.

> An informative and inspiring interview with a male survivor which includes an extensive resource bibliography of articles, books, and periodicals regarding male victimization and healing. To order, send $12 payable to Hank Estrada c/o Red Rabbit Press.

Grubman-Black, Stephen. *Broken Boys/Mending Men: Recovery from Child Sexual Abuse.* New York: Ballantine Books, 1990, 1997.

> Full of firsthand accounts of men sexually abused as children, this healing book written by a male survivor is simple, clear, and helpful.

Hoffman, Richard. *Half the House: A Memoir.* **New York: Harcourt Brace & Company, 1995.**

> **Beautifully written memoir about a working-class childhood that included sexual abuse by a coach as well as other family tragedies. This memoir led to the arrest of the perpetrator thirty years later.**

Hunter, Mic. *Abused Boys: The Neglected Victims of Sexual Abuse. Healing for the Man Molested as a Child.* New York: Fawcett Books, 1990.

> Solid, well researched. The follow-up, *The Sexually Abused Male,* is an excellent two-volume collection of professional articles.

Isensee, Rik. *Growing Up Gay in a Dysfunctional Family: A Guide for Gay Men Reclaiming Their Lives.* New York: Prentice Hall, 1991.

> Validates ways in which growing up gay in a homophobic society and being abused as a child create a double trauma, and offers specific suggestions for understanding and working through the problems involved. Warm, intelligent, and sure to be of real help. Currently out of print.

King, Neal. *Speaking Our Truth: Voices of Courage and Healing for Male Survivors of Childhood Sexual Abuse.* **New York: HarperCollins, 1995.**

> **A moving collection of first-person testimonies.**

Lew, Mike. *Victims No Longer: Men Recovering from Incest.* New York: HarperCollins, 1988, 1990.

> **Solid, clear, warm information and encouragement for men healing from child sexual abuse. This comprehensive, groundbreaking book was the first to talk about male survivors as survivors, not just potential perpetrators. It helped launch the male survivor movement.**

Mendel, Matthew Parynik. *The Male Survivor: The Impact of Sexual Abuse.* Thousand Oaks, CA: Sage, 1995.

> Based on a national survey, these findings present a sobering study of the victimization of boys. Examines the societal beliefs that have led to an underrecognition of male sexual abuse. Written for professionals.

Miletski, Hani. *Mother-Son Incest: The Unthinkable Broken Taboo.* Brandon, VT: Safer Society Press, 1995.

> This booklet presents an overview of the current research available on mother-son incest.

Mura, David. *A Male Grief: Notes on Pornography and Addiction.* Minneapolis, MN: Milkweed Editions (P.O. Box 3226, Minneapolis, MN 55403), 1987.

> A moving, poetic essay that explores why so many men are addicted to pornography. Powerful, provocative, beautifully written, this book can help anyone trapped in sexually compulsive behaviors. Currently out of print.

Porter, Eugene. *Treating the Young Male Victim of Sexual Assault: Issues and Intervention Strategies.* Brandon, VT: Safer Society Press, 1986.

> A good basic book on identification and treatment of young male victims.

Rhodes, Richard. *A Hole in the World: An American Boyhood.* **New York: Simon & Schuster, 1990.**

> **A magnificent autobiography by a renowned scientist about horrible abuse in his childhood. Currently out of print.**

Sonkin, Daniel. *Wounded Boys, Heroic Men: A Man's Guide to Recovering from Child Abuse.* Holbrook, MA: Adams (260 Center Street, Holbrook, MA 02343), 1998.

> A simple, straightforward guide for men who were hurt as children. Especially good for men not versed in the language of feelings or recovery.

Thomas, T. *Men Surviving Incest: A Survivor Shares the Recovery Process.* Rockville, MD: Launch Press, 1990.

> A male survivor tells his story. Focuses on twelve-step recovery.

Wright, Leslie Bailey, and Mindy B. Loiselle. *Back On Track: Boys Dealing With Sexual Abuse.* **Brandon, VT: Safer Society Press, 1997.**

> **Excellent, simply written. Helps boys (age 10 and up) recognize their feelings and take steps toward healing.**

Videos

Big Boys Don't Cry. KGW-TV. (Available from Public Affairs Office, KGW-TV, 1501 SW Jefferson, Portland, OR 97201, (503) 226-5184.)

> This documentary addresses adult male survivor issues, treatment for boy victims, juvenile and adult offenders, prevention and political activism. Segments on an adult survivor group are especially moving. Although this video has many positive aspects, we'd prefer a program on male survivors that didn't feel obliged to talk about perpetrators, too.

Four Men Speak Out On Surviving Child Sexual Abuse. Varied Directions, 18 Mt. Battie Street, Camden, ME 04843;

(800) 888-5236; fax (207) 236-4512; e-mail: Joyceb 3955@aol.com

Four male survivors tell their own stories, addressing the long-term effects of abuse, trust, telling, homophobia, and healing. A discussion guide accompanies the videotape.

ABUSE BY HELPING PROFESSIONALS

Chesler, Phyllis. *Women and Madness.* New York: Four Walls, Eight Windows (Available from Publishers Group West, (800) 788-3123), 1989, 1997.

A classic.

Gabbard, Glen, ed. *Sexual Exploitation within Professional Relationships.* Washington, D.C.: American Psychiatric Press, 1989.

An excellent collection of articles that deal with sexual misconduct by social workers, counselors, sex therapists, doctors, teachers, hospital staff, lawyers, and clergy. Guidelines for healing victims of abuse by professionals.

Gonsiorek, John C., ed. *Breach of Trust: Sexual Exploitation by Health Care Professionals and Clergy.* Thousand Oaks, CA: Sage, 1995.

An important collection of articles, including current research, accounts by victims, legal perspectives, and prevention training.

Peterson, Marilyn. *At Personal Risk: Boundary Violations in Professional-Client Relationships.* New York: W. W. Norton, 1992.

A fascinating book that explores the dynamics of professional boundary violations. Examines the obstacles faced by both clients and professionals in coming to a responsible, healthy resolution of such violations.

ABUSE BY THERAPISTS

Organization

BASTA! Boston Associates to Stop Treatment Abuse, 528 Franklin St., Cambridge, MA 02139, (617) 661-4667.

Offers workshops, support groups, consultation, advocacy, literature, training for professionals, and other resources for people abused by helping pro-

fessionals. Referrals to practitioners and support groups.

Books

Bates, Carolyn, and Annette Brodsky. *Sex in the Therapy Hour: A Case of Professional Incest.* New York: Guilford Press, 1989, 1993.

A woman tells the story of abuse by her therapist and the frustrating experience of suing for malpractice.

Minnesota Coalition Against Sexual Assault. *It's Never OK: A Handbook for Victims and Victim Advocates on Sexual Exploitation by Counselors and Therapists.* **Minneapolis, MN: Minnesota Coalition Against Sexual Assault (2344 Nicolett Avenue #170-A, Minneapolis, MN 55404-3352).**

This excellent booklet and its companion, a handbook for professionals, are clear and supportive. They can be ordered by writing to the address above.

Rutter, Peter. *Sex in the Forbidden Zone.* New York: Ballantine, 1989, 1997.

A psychiatrist analyzes why so many men in power sexually exploit the women they're entrusted to help. See also *Sex, Power and Boundaries* (1996) and *Understanding and Preventing Sexual Harassment* (1997).

Siegel, Shirley. *What to Do When Psychotherapy Goes Wrong.* Tukwila, WA: Stop Abuse by Counselors Publishing (5651 So. 144th, Tukwila, WA 98168), 1991.

A straightforward, powerful advocacy guide for clients hurt in therapeutic relationships. Defines therapist abuse and suggests ways to fight back. Includes a client's bill of rights.

ABUSE BY TEACHERS

S.E.S.A.M.E.: Survivors of Educator Sexual Abuse and Misconduct Emerge: A Voice for the Prevention of Sexual Harassment of Students by Teachers and Other School Staff, 681 Rt. 7A, Copake, NY 12156, (518) 329-1265; fax (518) 329-0127; e-mail: sesame-w@taconic.net or on the web:
http://home.earthlink.net/~jaye/index.html

SESAME's goals are to increase public awareness, to foster the recovery of victims and survivors, to encourage the reporting of offenders, to institute child-centered sexual harassment policies, and to

promote the adoption of a professional code of ethics. Quarterly newsletter.

ABUSE BY CLERGY

Organizations

The Linkup, 1412 West Argyle #2, Chicago, IL 60640; (773) 334-2296; fax (773) 334-0274; e-mail: ilinkup@aol. com or on the web: http://www.the linkup.com
The primary goal of The Linkup is to prevent clergy abuse and to empower its survivors to overcome its traumatic effects. Encourages religious institutions to make a concerted effort to prevent clergy abuse, to report it whenever it occurs, to hold perpetrators accountable, and to treat victims with compassion. Also sponsors a national education campaign for parents, teachers, and students in parochial schools.

Survivors Network for Those Who, as Children, Were Sexually Abused by Priests (SNAP), 8025 S. Honore, Chicago, IL 60620, (312) 483-1059 or on the web: http://www.teleport.com/~snapmail/index.html
Grassroots organization provides self-help support and resources. Organizes politically to challenge the church to better deal with priests' sexual abuse and misconduct.

Survivor Connections Inc., 52 Lyndon Rd., Cranston, RI 02905-1121, (401) 941-2548 or on the web: http://www.angelfire.com/ri/survivorconnections
Frank Fitzpatrick, a survivor of abuse by Father James Porter, started this activist organization for survivors of clergy abuse and those who support them. It's now expanded to include incest survivors and survivors of abuse by therapists, doctors, and other offenders. Activities include telephone peer support and advice, educational forums, legislative reform, and support for civil lawsuits and criminal prosecution. A quarterly newsletter, *The Survivor Activist,* is available, as is a national database of perpetrators.

Books

Burkett, Elinor, and Frank Bruni. *A Gospel of Shame: Child Sexual Abuse and the Catholic Church.* New York: Viking, 1993.
A well-documented look at child sexual abuse by priests within the Catholic church and the unwill-

ingness of church officials to deal with it. Currently out of print.

A Clergy Abuse Survivors' Resource Packet, Center for Women and Religion, Graduate Theological Union, 2400 Ridge Rd., Berkeley, CA 94709.
This helpful collection of articles and other information is available for $5.

Fortune, Marie. *Is Nothing Sacred? When Sex Invades the Pastoral Relationship.* San Francisco: Harper & Row, 1989.
Case study of sexual abuse by a pastoral counselor.

Fribert, Nils C. *Before the Fall: Preventing Pastoral Sexual Abuse.* Collegeville, MN: The Liturgical Press (St. John's Abbey, P.O. Box 7500, Collegeville, MN 56321-7500; (800) 858-5450; fax (800) 445-5899), 1998.
Addressed to church and seminary leaders, this book presents strategies for preventing sexual abuse by priests and other church workers.

Harris, Michael. *Unholy Orders.* New York: Viking, 1994.
Exposes Newfoundland debacle of abuse by over 400 priests.

Site, Richard. *Sex, Power and Priest.* New York: Brunner/ Mazel, 1996.
A priest and psychologist talks to the Roman Catholic community about abuse by priests. Provides historical context.

Shupe, Anson. *In the Name of All That's Holy.* Westport, CT: Greenwood Publishing, 1995.
A priest and psychologist talks to the Roman-Catholic community about abuse by priests. Provides historical context.

RELIGIOUS CONCERNS

Organization

The Center for the Prevention of Sexual and Domestic Violence, 936 N 34th Street, Suite 200, Seattle, WA 98103, (206) 634-1903; fax (206) 634-0115; e-mail: cpsdv@cpsdv.org or on the web: http://www.cpsdv.org
Founded by Rev. Marie Fortune, the Center is an inter-religious educational ministry serving both the religious and secular communities. Provides excellent literature, books, videos, trainings, conferences and consultation, and is responsible for groundbreaking work in family violence issues. They publish *Working Together to Prevent Sexual and Domestic*

Violence, an excellent quarterly newsjournal for advocates and religious professionals who work with survivors; $25/year.

Videos

These are just a few of the fine videos available through The Center for the Prevention of Sexual and Domestic Violence (936 N 34th Street, Suite 200, Seattle, WA 98103, (206) 634-1903; fax (206) 634-0115). Each comes with a study guide.

Hear Their Cries: Religious Responses to Child Abuse.
A training program for clergy of all faiths, lay leaders, educators, seminary students, and child welfare agencies.

To Save a Life: Ending Domestic Violence in Jewish Families.
A 35-minute videotape intended for abused Jewish women, Jewish leaders, and helping professionals.

Not In My Congregation.
The story of one congregation faced with sexual misconduct by its religious leader.

For Christian Women

Fortune, Marie M. *Sexual Violence: The Unmentionable Sin: An Ethical and Pastoral Perspective.* **New York: Pilgrim Press (700 Prospect Ave. East, Cleveland, OH 44115; (216) 736-3700; fax (216) 736-3703), 1983.**
Written from a Christian and feminist point of view, this groundbreaking book looks at the reasons the church has ignored sexual abuse and rape, and explains why and how it must be dealt with now. Fortune also has an excellent curriculum for running church-based family violence workshops, *Violence in the Family: A Workshop Curriculum for Clergy and Other Helpers* (1991), and a pamphlet for battered women, *Keeping the Faith: Guidance for Christian Women Facing Abuse* (1987, 1995).

Leehan, James. *Pastoral Care for Survivors of Family Abuse.* Louisville, KY: Westminster/John Knox Press (100 Witherspoon St., Louisville, KY 40202-1396 (800) 523-1631), 1989.
A Christian educator and counselor addresses the role of religious leaders in dealing with family violence. Effectively analyzes biblical prescriptions like "Spare the rod and spoil the child" which are sometimes used to rationalize child abuse. *A Defiant Hope: Spirituality for Survivors of Family Abuse* looks at religious and spiritual resources for healing from family violence.

Reid, Kathryn Goering, with Marie Fortune. *Preventing Child Sexual Abuse: A Curriculum for Children Ages Nine Through Twelve.* Cleveland, OH: United Church Press (700 Prospect Ave. East, Cleveland, OH 44115-1100, (800) 537-3394; e-mail: ucpress@ucc.org), 1989.
An excellent resource that interweaves secular materials with biblical resources. Ideal for use in Sunday School or other religious education programs.

Reilly, Patricia Lynn. *A God Who Looks Like Me: Discovering a Woman-Affirming Spirituality.* New York: Ballantine, 1995.
Personal accounts interwoven with the collective history of how women's stories have been buried in the Hebrew Scriptures and the Christian Bible. Filled with inspiring exercises and practical suggestions.

Rossetti, Stephen J. *A Tragic Grace: The Catholic Church and Child Sexual Abuse.* Collegeville, MN: Liturgical Press (St. John's Abbey, P.O. Box 7500, Collegeville, MN 56321-7500; (612) 363-2213), 1996.
An honest, direct discussion which offers concrete suggestions for how to understand and deal with the subject.

Volcano Press Staff. *Family Violence and Religion: An Interfaith Resource Guide.* Volcano, CA: Volcano Press, 1995.
An excellent collection of articles that deal with battering from a religious perspective. Also discusses battering in African-American, Hispanic and Asian families. Includes valuable material on elder abuse.

NEWSLETTER

Dancing Sarah's Circle: A Support Letter for Christians Healing Sexual Abuse, Assault and Incest, Box 296, Bottineau, ND 58318.
This newsletter seeks to "engage the resources of faith in proclaiming hope and healing to survivors of sexual abuse . . . to prevent sexual violation in church and society, and to foster strong local survivor communities." Quarterly. $22/year.

For Mormon Women

Daniels, April, and Carol Scott. *Paperdolls: Healing from Sexual Abuse in Mormon Neighborhoods.* San Diego: Recovery Publications (1201 Knoxville St., San Diego, CA 92110-3718), 1992.

A compelling, inspiring story of sexual abuse, sex rings, and healing in a Mormon context. Currently out of print.

For Jewish Women

Goldberg, Lilith. "Surviving Incest in a Holocaust Family," in *Lilith* (Winter 1993). *Lilith* is at 250 West 57th St., Suite 2432, New York, NY 10107, or call (212) 757-0818.

Lilith is a feminist Jewish quarterly. Subscriptions are $18/year. This issue is out of print, but the article is available for $2.50.

Green, Lilian. *Ordinary Wonders: Living Recovery from Sexual Abuse.* Toronto: Women's Press (Suite 233, 517 College St., Toronto, Canada M6G 4A2), 1992.

An intimate story of sexual abuse and healing in a "nice Jewish family." Told through journal entries in both poetry and prose.

"Roundtable: Jewish Women Talk About Surviving Incest," in *Bridges: A Journal for Jewish Feminists and Our Friends* (Spring 1991). *Bridges* is at P.O. Box 24839, Eugene OR 97402, (541) 935-5720; e-mail: ckinberg@pond.net or on the web: www.pond.net/~ckinberg/bridges)

An excellent discussion by Jewish survivors of sexual abuse. *Bridges* deals thoughtfully with politics, religion, and Jewish women's lives. This back issue is $10. *Bridges* is published twice a year; $15/year, more if you can afford it, less if you can't.

SADISTIC RITUAL ABUSE

Organizations

Healing Hearts Project/Bay Area Women Against Rape, 357 MacArthur Blvd., Oakland, CA 94610, (510) 465-3890.

This organization offers an annotated bibliography, an excellent library of audiotapes of training conferences, and an information packet that includes referrals for both professionals and ritual abuse survivors. The information packet costs $6.

SurvivorShip: A Forum on Survival of Ritual Abuse, Torture & Mind Control, 3181 Mission St. #139, San Francisco, CA 94110-4515, (707) 279-1209; e-mail: svship

@bigfoot.com or on the web: http://www.ctsserver.com/~svship

SurvivorShip provides resources and referrals, a confidential pen pal service, a weekly e-mail uselist, seminars, and a series of intelligent, helpful booklets, including *Dear Survivorship: Some Frequently Asked Questions.*

The Survivorship Journal includes articles by both professionals and survivors on all aspects of ritual abuse including therapeutic strategies, poetry, and art, with special sections devoted to adults, teens, children, partners, and children of survivors. *The Life Boat* is a separate pullout section for children. Quarterly.

Books

Beckylane. *Where the Rivers Join: A Personal Account of Healing from Ritual Abuse.* Vancouver: Press Gang (Available from LPC at (800) 243-0138 or on the web at http://www.coolbooks.com), 1995.

A poetic journal of extreme violence and healing. Painful to read, yet a testament to courage and hope.

Oksana, Chrystine. *Safe Passage to Healing: A Guide for Survivors of Ritual Abuse.* New York: HarperCollins, 1994.

A comprehensive, compassionate, practical guide to healing written by a survivor. Currently out of print.

Ritual Abuse: Definitions, Glossary, The Use of Mind Control. Los Angeles County Commission for Women, 1989.

Brief, excellent pamphlet. This is a good overview. Send $5 to 383 Hall of Administration, 500 W. Temple St., Los Angeles, CA 90012. Free to survivors.

Ross, Colin. *Satanic Ritual Abuse: Principles of Treatment.* Toronto: University of Toronto Press, 1995.

Valuable guidelines for therapists, as well as a thoughtful discussion about Satanism that attempts to reduce the polarization of the current debate. The afterword by Elizabeth Loftus (a proponent of "false memory syndrome") is perplexing in that she dismisses much of Ross's perspective as well as his treatment recommendations.

Scarry, Elaine. *The Body in Pain: The Making and Unmaking of the World.* New York: Oxford University Press, 1986.

This book explains the experience of being tortured. Although it focuses on political torture, it clearly reflects the experience of survivors who have been tortured in sadistic ritual abuse.

Spencer, Judith. *Suffer the Child.* New York: Pocket Books, 1989.

A powerful firsthand account of sadistic ritual abuse and resulting multiple personalities. Her 1997 book, *Satan's High Priest: A True Story* is a gripping case history of a cult that shows the way dissociation and amnesia is created in child victims.

StarDancer, L. J. *Turtleboy and Jet the Wonderpup! A Therapeutic Comic for Ritual Abuse Survivors.*

In comic-book style (that readers can color), a story of a child's heroic fight against ritual abuse. The graphic details can trigger painful memories. Read with support, please. Caryn StarDancer also has a book of poetry, *Returning to Herself,* about healing from sadistic ritual abuse. Order from StarDancer, P.O. Box 1284, Lakeport, CA 95453. *Turtleboy* is $7; *Returning to Herself* is $9.

Newsletters

Survivors of Abusive Rituals (S.O.A.R.) P.O. Box 532067, Indianapolis IN 46253-2067, (317) 767-3992.

Bimonthly newsletter in which ritual abuse survivors can share their stories, memories, fears, feelings, and questions.

S.M.A.R.T. P.O. Box 60577, Florence, MA 01062; e-mail: smartnews@aol.com or on the web:
http://members.aol.com/SMARTNEWS/index2.html

S.M.A.R.T. is a bimonthly newsletter for those interested in ritual abuse and its connection to secret societies. $12/year. For a sample newsletter, resource list, or order form visit URL:
http://members.aol.com/SMARTNEWS

Video

Coming Home: Recovery from Satanic Ritual Abuse. Varied Directions, 18 Mt. Battie St., Camden, ME 04843, (800) 888-5236.

Rev. Barnard J. Bush and Dr. Barbara Jackson talk about healing spiritually from satanic ritual abuse. Rev. Bush's theology may not match yours in all aspects and he is a bit dismissive of what psychology has to offer, but he still presents a perspective of much value. Dr. Jackson, a survivor, speaks so eloquently of her own experience and its spiritual implications that she transcends any doctrine.

DISSOCIATION AND MULTIPLE PERSONALITIES

This section includes resources for both survivors and therapists.

Organization

International Society for the Study of Dissociation (ISSD), 4700 West Lake Ave., Glenview, IL 60025-1485, (847) 375-4718; e-mail: info@issd.org or on the web: http://www.issd.org/

ISSD is the primary professional organization for therapists who work with dissociative disorders. Membership includes conferences, a bimonthly newsletter, *ISSD News,* bibliographies and reference lists. Also publishes the quarterly journal, *Dissociation.*

Books

Braun, Bennett. *Treatment of Multiple Personality Disorder.* Washington, D.C.: American Psychiatric Press, 1986.

Written for therapists, but still informative for the layperson.

Casey, Joan Francis, and Lynn Wilson. *The Flock: An Autobiography of a Multiple Personality.* New York: Fawcett, 1991, 1992.

A knockout of a memoir. Beautifully written, gripping, yet not sensationalized. Casey's recollections are juxtaposed with her therapist's notes on their sessions together. This is a hard book to put down.

Clell, Madison. *Cuckoo.* Eugene, OR: Green Door Studios (P.O. Box 12150, Eugene, OR 97440 or e-mail: door@cruzio.com), 1996.

An intriguing comic book by a survivor about her experiences with dissociative identity disorder. Quarterly. $12/year; single issues, $3.

Cohen, Barry, Esther Giller, and Lynn W., eds. *Multiple Personality Disorder from the Inside Out.* Lutherville, MD: Sidran Press, 1991.

Compiled by a therapist, a survivor, and a family member, this unique book talks about MPD from the perspective of those who live with it. Includes contributions from 150 people diagnosed with multiple personalities, as well as their significant others. Includes a listing of MPD treatment programs and a good resource section. Helpful, hopeful, and practi-

cal. Everyone concerned with multiple personalities should have a copy.

Gil, Eliana. *United We Stand: A Book for People with Multiple Personalities*. Walnut Creek: Launch Press, 1990.

>A wonderful simple cartoon book that explains multiple personalities and dissociation. A refreshing break from sensationalism.

Hocking, Phoenix J. (formerly Sandra J. Hocking). *37 to One: Living as an Integrated Multiple*. Brandon, VT: Safer Society Press, 1996.

>Inspiring for survivors facing the possibility of integration. Her earlier book, *Living With Your Selves: A Survivor Manual for People with Multiple Personalities* (1992) is short, clear and full of useful information—and even a little humor. Also see *Someone I Know Has Multiple Personalities: A Book for Significant Others, Family, Friends and Caring Professionals*.

Kluft, Richard. *Childhood Antecedents of Multiple Personality*. Washington, D.C.: American Psychiatric Press, 1985.

>Clinical discussion of multiple personality development and treatment. Also see his book *Incest-Related Syndromes of Adult Psychopathology*.

Putnam, Frank. *Diagnosis and Treatment of Multiple Personality Disorder*. New York: Guilford Press, 1989.

>Written for professionals, but useful for the lay reader as well. An excellent overview with clear guidelines and many practical strategies. Putnam's new book, *Dissociation in Children and Adolescents: A Developmental Approach* (1997), is comprehensive and well written.

Ross, Colin. *Multiple Personality Disorder: Diagnosis, Clinical Features and Treatment*. New York: John Wiley, 1989.

>An excellent resource for professionals. *The Osiris Complex: Case-Studies in Multiple Personality Disorder* (1994) demonstrates, through engaging stories from treatment, how virtually all psychiatric symptoms are a result of trauma.

The Troops for Truddi Chase. *When Rabbit Howls*. New York: Jove Publications, 1987, 1990.

>**Truddi Chase first developed multiple personalities when her stepfather raped her at age two. Written by her numerous selves during therapy, this book intimately shows how the mind works to cope with the horror of sexual abuse. This book can be very hard to read.**

W., Lynn, ed. *Mending Ourselves: Expressions of Healing and Self-Integration*. Cincinnati: Many Voices Press (P.O. Box 2639, Cincinnati, OH 45201-2639), 1993.

>An anthology of writings by the readers of *Many Voices*, dealing with their experiences of integration. Available for $15.95. A second volume, *Poems to Our Therapists*, includes poetry and art about survivors' relationships with their therapists. Available for $13.

Whitman, Tammy Colleen and Susan C. Shore. *The Multiple's Guide to Harmonized Family Living: A Healthy Alternative (or Prelude) to Integration*. Marina Del Rey, CA: Artistic Endeavors Publishing (P.O. Box 10224-P, Marina Del Rey, CA 90292).

>A self-directed healing manual for transforming inner systems into productive, harmonized families by the editor and publisher of the newsletter, M.U.L.T.I.P.L.E.

Newsletter

***Many Voices: Words of Hope for People Recovering from Trauma and Dissociation*, P.O. Box 2639, Cincinnati, OH 45201-2639, (513) 751-8020; fax (513) 751-8060; e-mail: LynnWatMV@aol.com (put MV in the subject line).**

>**Features self-help articles, a therapist's page, and a page for partners. Currently soliciting material for multicultural and international sections. Bimonthly.**

Videos

The Hope of Recovery. Varied Directions. 18 Mt. Battie St., Camden, ME 04843, (800) 888-5236.

>Three women with multiple personalities talk about their healing process. Articulate, moving, informative, and hopeful.

The following videos are all from Cavalcade Productions, P.O. Box 2480, Nevada City, CA 95959, (800) 345-5530.

Sessions and Sandtrays.

>Therapist Roberta Sachs is filmed working with survivors with multiple personalities. This 1991 film is powerful, educational, and inspiring. Designed to train professionals, it can also be validating and educational for people with multiple personalities. But it contains emotionally charged material, so view with caution. Cavalcade has also produced videos on mastering traumatic memories and on identifying and treating multiple personalities in children.

Treating the Dissociative Client: Stabilization and *Trauma Work.*

In this video series, a number of leaders in the field, including Peter Barach, James Chu, Christine Courtois, Richard Kluft, and Bessel van der Kolk, share their clinical insights. *Stabilization* emphasizes the importance of working toward safety, stability and symptom reduction before moving into trauma work. *Trauma Work* examines how therapists can help clients to process the traumatic events that have dominated their lives.

Working With Difficult Alters.

Some alters in MPD systems may identify with the perpetrators of their abuse, becoming hostile or self-injuring. Yet they were often the most hurt and are in need of healing. Therapist David Calof demonstrates how to work with such alters in this clear and compassionate video.

TAKING CARE OF YOURSELF NOW

HEALTH

The Boston Women's Health Book Collective. *The New Our Bodies, Ourselves.* New York: Touchstone Books, 1984, 1996.

New and expanded. The complete sourcebook on women's health-care issues from birthing to aging, from violence against women to occupational health hazards.

Black, Claudia. *It Will Never Happen to Me: Children of Alcoholics.* Denver: MAC Publishing (321 High School Rd. NE #346, Bainbridge Island, WA 98110, (800) 698-0148; e-mail: seeblack@nwlink.com or on the web: http//:www.claudiablack.com), 1981.

A groundbreaking book. Black has also published a workbook for adults, *Repeat After Me,* and *Double Duty,* which examines the struggles of adult children from homes where chemical dependency and another factor—such as physical disability, sexual abuse, being gay or lesbian—make recovery more complex.

Chernin, Kim. *The Obsession: Reflections on the Tyranny of Slenderness.* New York: Harper & Row, 1981.

An incisive, well-researched analysis of women's obsession with weight and body size. Also see her follow-up, *The Hungry Self: Women, Eating and Identity.*

SELF-INJURY

Trautmann, Kristy, and Robin Connors. *Understanding Self-Injury: A Workbook for Adults.* Pittsburgh: Pittsburgh Action Against Rape (81 South 19th St., Pittsburgh, PA 15203), 1994.

Honest, non-blaming, and informative, this workbook helps survivors understand self-injury and live more comfortably and safely with it. Offers alternatives for changing or stopping the injuring behavior.

The Cutting Edge: A Newsletter for Women Living With Self-Inflicted Violence. P.O. Box 20819, Cleveland, OH 44120.

Quarterly newsletter. Publishes only women's artwork and writing, but all are welcome to subscribe. Subscriptions on a donation basis.

Understanding Self-Injury. Cavalcade Productions, P.O. Box 2480, Nevada City, CA 95959, (800) 345-5530.

Geared toward survivors, this 30-minute video discusses the forms and functions of self harm, including interviews with trauma survivors who have self-injured.

Davis, Martha, Elizabeth Robins Eshelman, and Matthew McKay. *The Relaxation and Stress Reduction Workbook.* Oakland, CA: New Harbinger Publications (5674 Shattuck Ave., Oakland, CA 94609, (800) 748-6273; fax (510) 652-5472; e-mail: newharbpub@aol.com or on the web: http://www.newharbinger.com), 1982, 1995.

Practical step-by-step guidebook includes relaxation, self-hypnosis, meditation, imagination, nutrition, coping skills, assertiveness training, biofeedback, breathing, time management, exercise, and more.

Hutchinson, Marcia Germaine. *Transforming Body Image.* Freedom, CA: Crossing Press, 1985, 1998.

Every woman should read this book. Step-by-step exercises to help you integrate your body, mind, and self-image, and to begin to love and accept yourself just the way you are.

SELF-ESTEEM BOOSTERS

Clarke, Jean Illsley, and Carol Gesme. *Affirmation Ovals: 139 Ways to Give and Get Affirmations.* Plymouth, MN: Daisy Press (16535 9th Avenue N., Plymouth, MN 55447, (612) 473-1840), 1988.

> Wonderful reminders of the positive messages children should receive at each stage of their development. Great model for parents and for anyone striving to build self-esteem. Every survivor should have a set to play with ($9.50 for ovals and accompanying handbook). Daisy Press also offers an excellent variety of tapes, training materials, and other resources for building self-esteem.

Johnson, Carol A. *Self-Esteem Comes in All Sizes: How to Be Happy and Healthy at Your Natural Weight.* New York: Doubleday, 1995.

> A gift for women who want to feel good about themseves just the way they are.

Northrup, Christiane. *Women's Bodies, Women's Wisdom: Creating Physical and Emotional Health and Healing.* New York: Bantam, 1994.

> A practical holistic approach to healing that empowers women to take control of their physical, emotional, and spiritual health.

Radomsky, Nellie A. *Lost Voices: Women, Chronic Pain, and Abuse.* Binghamton, NY: Haworth Press, 1995.

> An enlightening exploration into the roots of chronic pain and healing by a family physician. Should be required reading for every doctor and a valuable resource for sufferers of chronic pain.

Roth, Geneen. *Feeding the Hungry Heart: The Experience of Compulsive Eating.* New York: Penguin, 1982.

> Looks at bingeing, hunger, body image, and nourishment as issues far deeper than food. Her second book, *Breaking Free from Compulsive Eating*, offers the best practical guidelines for stopping compulsive eating. Also see *Why Weight?*, a self-help workbook and *When Food Is Love*, on intimacy.

Schoenfielder, Lisa, and Barb Wieser. *Shadow on a Tightrope: Writings by Women on Fat Oppression.* San Francisco:

WOMEN, WORK AND ABUSE

Murphy, Patricia A. *Making the Connection: Women, Work and Abuse.* Delray Beach, FL: St. Lucie Press (2000 Corporate Blvd. NW, Boca Raton, FL 33431-9868, (800) 272-7737; fax (800) 374-3401; e-mail: orders@crcpress.com or on the web: http://www.crcpress.com), 1993.

> A vocational rehabilitation counselor looks at the way abuse undermines women's career choices. This groundbreaking book explores specialized vocational rehabilitation counseling as part of the healing process. The follow-up companion book, *A Career and Life Planning Guide for Women Survivors: Making the Connections Workbook* is a well-designed empowering tool for any woman who wants to understand the connection between her abuse, her problems with work, and her future vocational goals.

Aunt Lute (P.O. Box 410687, San Francisco, CA 94141-0687, (800) 949-4883; fax: (415) 826-8300; e-mail: books @auntlute.com or on the web: http://www.best.com/~auntlute/), 1983.

> A powerful anthology of stories, articles, and poems from the Fat Liberation Movement.

Villarosa, Linda, ed. *Body and Soul: The Black Women's Guide to Physical and Emotional Well-Being.* New York: HarperCollins, 1994.

> Clear, straight-from-the-heart self-help book addressing such issues as how Black women feel about their bodies, how to deal with doctors, the role of spirituality in well-being, the role of Black history and politics, facing abortion, sexual abuse, AIDS, loving Black men and Black women, coping with violence, and raising children.

White, Evelyn C. *The Black Woman's Health Book: Speaking for Ourselves.* Seattle: Seal Press, 1991, 1994.

> This diverse range of essays give a comprehensive picture of health issues faced by Black women. Essential reading.

White, Joycelyn, and Marissa C. Martinez, eds. *The Lesbian Health Book: Caring for Ourselves.* Seattle: Seal Press, 1997.

> Empowering collection of personal essays on a wide

array of topics, including breast cancer, childbirth, AIDS, menopause, and more.

DOMESTIC VIOLENCE, RAPE AND SEXUAL HARASSMENT

There are also relevant resources listed under "Religious Concerns."

Organizations

National Coalition Against Sexual Assault (NCASA), 125 N. Enola Dr., Enola, PA 17025, (717) 728-9764; fax (717) 732-1575 or on the web at http://www.achiever.com/freehmpg/ncas

NCASA is a national network of rape crisis centers, counseling services, educational programs, women's shelters, and concerned individuals. NCASA acts as an advocate on public policy issues, and works to share services for survivors, to encourage prevention, and to create an informed public. It tracks survivor and backlash issues.

The National Resource Center on Domestic Violence (NRC), 6400 Flank Dr., Suite 1300, Harrisburg, PA 17112-2778, (800) 537-2238; TTY (800) 553-2508; fax (717) 545-9456.

Focusing on civil and criminal justice, child protection and custody, and health care, NRC works to strengthen support for battered women and their children. Through their toll-free information line they provide information for government agencies, policy leaders, the media and other professionals. They assist communities nationally with technical assistance, training, and program development.

Books

Brewster, Susan. *To Be an Anchor in the Storm: A Guide for Families and Friends of Abused Women*. New York: Ballantine, 1997.

Written by a psychotherapist who was stalked and battered by an ex-boyfriend, this book lets family and friends know how they can *really* help—by being an anchor in the storm rather than a rescuer who magically fixes everything. This advice applies well to supporters of survivors of child sexual abuse as well.

Brownmiller, Susan. *Against Our Will: Men, Women and Rape*. New York: Bantam, 1975.

A comprehensive history and analysis of rape. A classic.

Carosella, Cynthia. *Who's Afraid of the Dark: A Forum of Truth, Support, and Assurance for Those Affected by Rape*. New York: HarperCollins, 1995.

Thirty rape survivors openly share the ways they cope with the long-term effects of rape. Together, they are powerful proof that it is possible to regain trust, hope, and self-esteem.

Griffin, Susan. *Pornography and Silence: Culture's Revenge Against Nature*. New York: Harper & Row, 1981.

Explores the ways pornography is woven through the texture of our society and the role it plays in undermining our basic humanity. Griffin's *Women and Nature*, a beautifully written classic, parallels the violation of women with the continuing violation of the Earth. *Rape: The Power of Consciousness* is a series of powerful essays.

Island, David, and Patrick Letellier. *Men Who Beat the Men Who Love Them: Battered Gay Men and Domestic Violence*. New York: Haworth Press, 1991.

An important silence broken. Includes both theory and practical help.

Ledray, Linda. *Recovering from Rape*. New York: Henry Holt, 1986.

A compassionate book that addresses the immediate aftermath, as well as the long-term effects. Recommended by rape crisis centers.

Lobel, Kerry, ed. *Naming the Violence: Speaking Out About Lesbian Battering*. Seattle: Seal Press, 1986.

Another silence broken. Includes personal stories, a look at the homophobia that has kept lesbians from seeking help, and suggestions for services.

Martin, Del. *Battered Wives*. New York: Pocket Books, 1976, 1990.

The pioneering book that first framed the problem of wife-beating. Still the best overview available.

McAllister, Pam, ed. *Reweaving the Web of Life: Feminism and Nonviolence*. Philadelphia: New Society, 1982.

A well-written and challenging collection of writings by feminists on nonviolence. "By combining our rage with compassion, we live the revolution every day."

NiCarthy, Ginny. *Getting Free: You Can End Abuse and Take Back Your Life*. Seattle: Seal Press, 1982, 1997.

A must for any woman wanting to leave an abusive partner. Valuable information on both practical and emotional issues. Expanded edition has sections on lesbian abuse, teen abuse, and emotional abuse. Available on audiotape and also in an excellent easy-to-read edition, *You Can Be Free.* NiCarthy's *The Ones Who Got Away: Women Who Left Abusive Partners* (1987) is a powerful chronicle of battered women who've left abusive spouses.

Sonkin, Daniel Jay, and Michael Durphy. *Learning to Live Without Violence.* Volcano, CA: Volcano Press, 1989, 1997.

Designed as a handbook for men who batter women, this excellent, practical guide can help anyone who wants to deal with anger more effectively. Also available on audiocassette.

Sumrall, Amber Coverdale, and Dena Taylor. *Sexual Harassment: Women Speak Out.* Freedom, CA: Crossing Press, 1992.

A collection of personal testimonies compiled as a response to Anita Hill. Many excellent writers and inspiring stories.

White, Evelyn C. *Chain Chain Change: For Black Women Dealing with Physical and Emotional Abuse.* Seattle: Seal Press, 1985.

A direct, clearly written, valuable resource.

Zambrano, Myrna M. *Mejor Sola Que Mal Acompanada: Para la Mujer Gopeada/For the Latina in an Abusive Relationship.* Seattle: Seal Press, 1985.

Bilingual. Excellent sections on institutionalized racism and the barriers that Latinas face in getting help.

SEXUALITY

There are also relevant books in the section "For Partners and Couples."

Blank, Joani. *The Playbook for Women About Sex.* San Francisco: Down There Press (938 Howard St., Ste. 101, San Francisco, CA 94103, (800) 289-8423; e-mail: goodvibe@well.com or on the web: http://www.goodvibes.com), 1982.

A nonthreatening, fun place to start a loving relationship with yourself. There is also a *Playbook for Men About Sex.* Blank's new book, *Femalia* (1993), features color photographs of women's genitals. If you've ever wondered if yours are "normal," here's beautiful reassurance.

MAIL-ORDER SOURCES FOR VIBRATORS, SEX TOYS, AND OTHER BOOKS ON SEX

Eve's Garden, 119 West 57th St, #1201, New York, NY 10019, (800) 848-3837 or on the web: http://www.evesgarden.com for an online catalogue.

"We grow pleasurable things for women." Send $3 for a mail-order catalogue.

Open Enterprises, 938 Howard Street, Suite 101, San Francisco, CA 94103, (800) 289-8423; e-mail: goodvibe@well.com or on the web: http://www.goodvibes.com

Open Enterprises has three excellent free mail-order catalogues: one for Good Vibrations (which sells sex toys), one for Down There Press, and one for their topnotch Sexuality Library.

Dodson, Betty. *Sex for One.* New York: Crown, 1986, 1996.

A beautifully illustrated sex-positive guide to masturbation. Dodson's video, *Celebrating Orgasm: Women's Private Selfloving Sessions,* shows five women (ages 26 to 62) practice and achieve orgasm through a step-by-step process. (The book can be ordered for $15.50, the video for $43, from Betty Dodson, Box 1933, Murray Hill Station, New York, NY 10156).

Engel, Beverly. *Raising Your Sexual Self-Esteem: How to Feel Better About Your Sexuality and Yourself.* New York: Fawcett, 1995.

A clear, compassionate book that helps you gain confidence, enjoyment and pleasure in your sexual life.

Fortune, Marie M. *Love Does No Harm: Sexual Ethics for the Rest of Us.* New York: Continuum, 1995.

A straightforward guide to ethical decision-making in intimate relationships for people of all ages and sexual orientations. Grounded in religious values, but applicable for everyone, with an intelligent social and political understanding.

Kasl, Charlotte Advise. *Women, Sex, and Addiction: A Search for Love and Power.* New York: HarperCollins, 1989, 1990.

> Well documented and politically astute. Kasl speaks with depth, and compassion. *Many Roads, One Journey* (1993) presents a feminist alternative to the twelve-step model for women in recovery. Her newest books, *101 Ways to Find Joy* (1994) and *A Home for the Heart : Creating Intimacy and Community in Our Everyday Lives* (1997) are gems of inspiration.

Loulan, JoAnn. *Lesbian Sex.* San Francisco: Spinsters Ink (East 1st Street #330, Duluth, MN 55802, (218) 727-3222; fax (218) 727-3119; e-mail: spinsters@aol.com or on the web: http://www.lesbian.org/spinsters-ink), 1984.

> A good read about sexuality, sexual problems, and healing for *all* women, not just lesbians. Sections on sex and disability, sobriety, sexual abuse, motherhood, aging, and youth. The follow-up, *Lesbian Passion,* has a chapter for partners.

Maltz, Wendy. *The Sexual Healing Journey: A Guide for Survivors of Sexual Abuse.* **New York: HarperCollins, 1991.**

> **This comprehensive resource helps survivors understand the impact of sexual abuse on sexuality and learn how to create a new approach to intimate touch and sexual sharing. Will help thousands reclaim their sexuality. Maltz's first book (with Beverly Holman),** *Incest and Sexuality* **(1987), is also excellent.**

Maltz, Wendy, and Suzie Boss. *In the Garden of Desire: The Intimate World of Women's Sexual Fantasies.* New York: Broadway Books, 1998.

> An informative and often entertaining look at where sexual fantasies come from, how they function and what they mean. Special chapters devoted to understanding and healing unwanted fantasies caused by abuse. Maltz's *Passionate Hearts: The Poetry of Sexual Love* (1996) celebrates sexual intimacy based on caring, safety and respect.

Mariechild, Diane, and Marcelina Martin. *Lesbian Sacred Sexuality.* Oakland: Wingbow Press (7900 Edgewater Dr., Oakland, CA 94621, (800) 999-4650), 1995.

> A beautiful exploration of opening to the sacred— and healing—in sexuality, in text and photographs.

FOR SUPPORTERS OF SURVIVORS

FOR PARTNERS AND COUPLES

There are also relevant books listed in "Sexuality."

Cameron, Grant. *What About Me? A Guide for Men Helping Female Partners Deal with Childhood Sexual Abuse.* Carp, Ontario: Creative Bound (P.O. Box 424, Carp, Ontario, Canada K0A 1L0, (800) 287-8610), 1994.

> A distillation of what Cameron learned while helping his wife recover from abuse. Talks openly about sex, suicide, anger, nightmares, and gaining trust. Supportive and honest.

Davis, Laura. *Allies in Healing: When the Person You Love Was Sexually Abused as a Child.* **New York: HarperCollins, 1991.**

> **A clear, supportive, and comprehensive guide for partners who are struggling to take care of themselves and the survivors they love. Full of helpful anecdotes, useful suggestions, and powerful first-hand stories. Also available on cassette.**

Engel, Beverly. *Partners in Recovery: How Mates, Lovers & Other Prosurvivors Can Learn to Support and Cope with Adult Survivors of Childhood Sexual Abuse.* New York: Fawcett, 1991, 1993.

> Good advice on how to be supportive to survivors as well as how to take care of yourself.

Gil, Eliana. *Outgrowing the Pain Together: A Book for Partners and Spouses of Adults Abused as Children.* New York: Dell Bantam Doubleday, 1992.

> An eloquent, optimistic introduction to issues for partners of survivors.

Hendrix, Harville. *Getting the Love You Want: A Guide for Couples.* New York: Harper & Row, 1990.

> Beginning with the premise that we all choose partners with whom we can work through our childhood pain, this excellent guide helps couples create a conscious partnership in which both partners can heal from old hurts.

Lerner, Harriet. *The Dance of Anger: A Woman's Guide to Changing the Patterns of Intimate Relationships.* New York: Harper & Row, 1986, 1989.

> Practical suggestions on handling anger and making meaningful changes in relationships. Lerner has also written *The Dance of Intimacy* (1990) and *The Dance of Deception: A Guide to Authenticity and Truth-Telling in Women's Relationships* (1994).

Mason, Patience H. C. *Recovering from the War: A Woman's Guide to Helping Your Vietnam Vet, Your Family and Yourself.* New York: Penguin, 1990.

> This book focuses on the Vietnam experience but offers valuable information on post-traumatic stress and being the partner of someone who's lived in a war zone—and survivors certainly qualify.

Strong, Maggie. *Mainstay: For the Well Spouse of the Chronically Ill.* New York: Penguin, 1989.

> Written by a woman whose husband has multiple sclerosis, this powerful, practical, and beautifully written book raises many issues and feelings that will ring true for partners of survivors as well. Currently out of print.

Videos

Partners in Healing: Couples Overcoming the Sexual Repercussions of Incest. Independent Video Services, 401 E. 10th Ave. Suite #160, Eugene, OR. 97401, (800) 678-3455.

> In this useful video, Wendy Maltz interviews several white heterosexual couples about the effects of abuse on their sex lives. Includes practical suggestions. A follow-up video, *Relearning Touch: Healing Techniques for Couples,* shows couples using a series of gradated touch exercises to reintroduce intimate touch into their relationships. A practical, non-threatening approach.

Partners Surviving: My Partner Was Sexually Abused. Lutherville, MD: Sidran Press.

> Five partners, representing a diversity of backgrounds and lifestyles, talk about the ups and downs of life with survivors. A support group in a video box.

FOR FAMILY MEMBERS OF ADULT SURVIVORS

Organization

The Family Dialogue Project, The Center for Contextual Change, 9239 Gross Point Rd., Skokie, IL 60077, (847) 676-4447.

> The Family Dialogue Project, founded by Mary Jo Barrett, is a national resource center for families seeking mediation in response to allegations of sexual abuse. Family Dialogue is an alternative to legal confrontation and attack which helps families find common ground from which they can grapple with these difficult issues.

Books

Engel, Beverly. *Families in Recovery: Working Together to Heal the Damage of Childhood Sexual Abuse.* Los Angeles: Lowell House, 1994.

> A straightforward guidebook for family members of survivors, intended to bring families together and help them recover from the devastation of abuse. Frank, sensible advice. Currently out of print.

Landry, Dorothy Beaulieu. *Family Fallout: A Handbook for Families of Adult Sexual Abuse Survivors.* Brandon, VT: Safer Society Press, 1991.

> A clear, comforting, and useful book for parents, siblings, partners, and children of adult survivors.

Smith, Shauna. *Making Peace with Your Adult Child.* New York: HarperCollins, 1991, 1993.

> **A recovery book that encourages cross-generational healing. Written for parents who are struggling to heal painful rifts with their adult children. Wise, compassionate, and accessible. A great gift book.**

FOR COUNSELORS AND OTHER HELPING PROFESSIONALS

Professional Associations

American Professional Society on the Abuse of Children (APSAC), 407 S. Dearborn #1300, Chicago, IL 60605, (312) 554-0166.

> APSAC is a 5000-member interdisciplinary professional society for people working in the field of child maltreatment. Membership includes subscriptions to *The APSAC Advisor* and *The Journal of Child Maltreatment,* discounts on conferences, tapes, and publications, and the opportunity to participate in state chapters and in task forces establishing national practice guidelines.

Kempe National Center for the Prevention and Treatment of Child Abuse and Neglect, 1825 Marion St., Denver, CO 80218, (303) 864-5252; fax (303) 329-3523; e-mail: BrossDonald@tchden.org or on the web: http://kempecenter.org

> A clinically-based research and demonstration center which focuses on child abuse treatment, training

GROUP WORK WITH SURVIVORS

Chew, Judy. *Women Survivors of Childhood Sexual Abuse: Healing Through Group Work: Beyond Survival.* Binghamton, NY: Haworth Press, 1998.

>This handbook for counselors presents clear, usable guidelines for running a thirteen-session incest survivor's group. Sessions are balanced between education, self-expression, skill building, and empowerment.

Courtois, Christine. *Workshop Models for Family Life Education: Adult Survivors of Child Sexual Abuse.* Milwaukee, WI: Families International, Inc. (414) 359-1040, 1993.

>A clear-cut eight-session model for psychoeducational survivor workshops that balance emotional awareness with intellectual understanding. Goals are to help survivors understand the dynamics and effects of child sexual abuse.

Webb, Laura Pisone, and James Leehan. *Group Treatment for Adult Survivors of Abuse: A Manual for Practitioners.* Thousand Oaks, CA: Sage, 1996.

>An excellent manual on group work with survivors. Clearly delineates advantages of group work as well as potential problems. Includes guidelines for self-care for therapists.

Yamamoto-Nading, DeAnn, and Gayle Stringer. *A Healing Celebration: A Manual for Facilitators of Therapeutic Support Groups for Women Who Are Adult Survivors of Childhood Sexual Abuse.* Renton, WA: King County Sexual Assault Resource Center (P.O. Box 300, Renton, WA 98057, (425) 226-5062; fax (425) 235-7422), 1991.

>An empowering, useful guide for facilitating groups for survivors. Accessible, clear, and ready to use.

and research. The program is committed to multidisciplinary approaches to improving the recognition, treatment, and prevention of all forms of abuse and neglect.

Books

There are also books for professionals under specific subject areas.

Briere, John. *Therapy for Adults Molested as Children: Beyond Survival.* New York: Springer, 1989, 1996.

>A clinically solid book on doing therapy with survivors that is politically sensitive and empowering. Guidelines for running groups are included. See also *Child Abuse Trauma: Theory and Treatment of the Lasting Effects* (1992) and *Assessing and Treating Victims of Violence* (1994).

Calof, David L., with Robin Simons. *The Couple Who Became Each Other: And Other Tales of Healing from a Hypnotherapist's Casebook.* New York: Bantam, 1996.

>Fascinating stories that show how clinical hypnosis harnesses the mind's natural healing powers. Reads like a novel.

Classen, Catherine. *Treating Women Molested in Childhood.* San Francisco: Jossey-Bass, 1995.

>This clearly written collection of articles provides treatment guidelines for crisis management, individual therapy, group work, couples counseling, hypnosis, and assessing a client's history without under- or overestimating the possibility of sexual abuse.

Courtois, Christine. *Healing the Incest Wound: Adult Survivors in Therapy.* New York: W. W. Norton, 1988.

>A feminist psychologist writes a top-notch guidebook for therapists on healing.

Crowder, Adrienne. *Opening the Door: A Treatment Model for Therapy with Male Survivors of Sexual Abuse.* New York: Brunner/Mazel, 1995.

>Based on the work of 41 therapists, presents approaches and interventions helpful to male survivors in group and individual therapy. Good resources.

Fontes, Lisa Aronson. *Sexual Abuse in Nine North American Cultures: Treatment and Prevention.* Thousand Oaks, CA: Sage, 1995.

>**A fascinating exploration of the role culture plays in allowing, preventing and treating sexual abuse in nine cultures: Cambodian, African-American, Seventh Day Adventist, gay and lesbian, Asian, Pacific Islander and Filipino American, Puerto Rican, Jew-**

ish, and Anglo-American. **Full of practical guidelines for professionals.**

Gil, Eliana. *Treatment of Adult Survivors of Childhood Abuse.* Walnut Creek, CA: Launch Press, 1988.

Clear guidelines for working with survivors, including memory work, group therapy, dissociation and multiple personalities, and post-traumatic stress disorder. Excellent. See also Gil's other books, *Systemic Treatment of Families Who Abuse* (1995) and *Treating Abused Adolescents* (1996).

Gonsiorek, John, ed. *A Guide to Psychotherapy with Gay and Lesbian Clients.* New York: Haworth Press, 1985.

A landmark work that provides insight into the special needs gay men and lesbians bring to the therapy setting.

Herman, Judith. *Trauma and Recovery.* New York: Basic Books, 1993.

A brilliant, compassionate synthesis of our understanding of the impact of trauma, including the experiences of battered women, sexually abused children, war veterans, and prisoners of war. Everyone who works with survivors must read this book.

Holiman, Marjorie. *From Violence Toward Love: One Therapist's Journey.* New York: W.W. Norton, 1997.

A courageous, fascinating memoir by a therapist about her personal and professional experiences with interpersonal violence. Offers compelling and compassionate insights into the world of violence.

Hunter, Mic, and Jim Struve. *The Ethical Use of Touch in Psychotherapy,* Thousand Oaks, CA: Sage, 1988.

This much-needed book argues that touch—a basic human need—is intrinsic to the healing process. It asks therapists to re-examine prohibitions against touch and offers guidelines for its integration into talk therapy.

Hunter's *Adult Survivors of Sexual Abuse: Treatment Innovations* (1995) is a collection of thoughtful articles on sexual dysfunction and compulsivity, partners of survivors, and chemical dependency.

Laidlaw, Toni Ann, Cheryl Malmo et al. *Healing Voices: Feminist Approaches to Therapy with Women.* San Francisco: Jossey-Bass, 1992.

An excellent, diverse collection of essays on a variety of empowering healing techniques, including group therapy, Native storytelling, dream analysis, bodywork, imagery, and hypnosis. Strategies for working with sexual abuse, compulsive eating, violence in Native communities, adult children of alcoholics, and more. Each approach covered includes a therapist's essay and a first-person account by a client who benefited from the approach.

Rogers, Annie G. *A Shining Affliction: A Story of Harm and Healing in Psychotherapy.* New York: Penguin, 1995.

A therapist working with a severely disturbed five-year-old victim of abuse finds herself drawn into her own mental breakdown and history of abuse. A moving account of a true-life double healing through psychotherapy.

Salter, Anna. *Transforming Trauma: A Guide to Treating Sexual Abuse.* Newbury Park, CA: Sage, 1994.

Extremely well researched and astute. Her prior book, *Treating Child Sex Offenders and Victims* (1988), is also informative and excellent.

Schwartz, Mark F., and Leigh Cohn. *Sexual Abuse and Eating Disorders.* New York: Brunner/Mazel, 1996.

A collection of academic articles which include prev-

FOR MEDICAL PROFESSIONALS

***The Missing Link: A Guide to Better Health Care for Men and Women and An Invaluable Tool: A Guide to Better Health Care for Women.* One Voice, 1835 K St., NW, Washington, D.C. 20006. $27.50 each.**

Marilyn Van Derbur has produced these excellent videos (and training manuals) to educate medical professionals about the importance of child abuse or trauma in diagnosing and treating adult medical problems. Should be required viewing for every medical professional.

Radomsky, Nellie A. *Lost Voices: Women, Chronic Pain, and Abuse.* Binghamton, NY: Haworth Press, 1995.

An enlightening exploration into the roots of chronic pain and healing by a family physician. Should be required reading for every doctor and a valuable resource for sufferers of chronic pain.

VICARIOUS TRAUMATIZATION

Pearlman, Laurie Anne, and Karen W. Saakvitne. *Trauma and the Therapist: Countertransference and Vicarious Traumatization in Psychotherapy with Incest Survivors.* New York: W.W. Norton, 1995.

> A scholarly book which addresses the impact of trauma work on *the therapist.* Important for all therapists who work with survivors. See also *Psychological Trauma and the Adult Survivor: Theory, Therapy and Transformation,* a book that is respectful, intelligent and full of insight (co-authored with Lisa I. McCann).

Vicarious Traumatization: The Cost of Empathy and Transforming the Pain. Cavalcade Productions, P.O. Box 2480, Nevada City, CA 95959, (800) 345-5530.

> The cumulative impact of clients' stories and reenactments can carry enormous emotional costs for therapists. Laurie Anne Pearlman and Karen Saakvitne of the Traumatic Stress Institute describe the effects of vicarious traumatization and ways to deal with it.

When Helping Hurts: Sustaining Trauma Workers. Varied Directions, 18 Mt. Battie Street, Camden ME 04843, (800) 888-5236; fax (207) 236-4512; e-mail: Joyceb3955@aol.com

> A video in support of trauma workers, both professional and volunteer, who may be suffering from "compassion fatigue."

alence data, treatment ideas, and an analysis of the reluctance many professionals have in accepting the prevalence of sexual abuse in women with eating disorders.

Sgroi, Suzanne. *Handbook of Clinical Intervention in Child Sexual Abuse.* Lexington, MA: Free Press, 1982.

> Excellent guidance for treatment and coordination in handling child sex abuse cases. Sgroi has also written *Vulnerable Populations* (1988), two volumes on sexual abuse treatment and evaluation for sexually abused children, adult survivors, and mentally retarded adults.

Shapiro, Francine, and Margot Silk Forrest. *EMDR: The Breakthrough Therapy for Overcoming Anxiety, Stress, and Trauma.* New York: HarperCollins, 1997.

> A well-written, fascinating book of case studies that illustrate the transformations made possible by EMDR (Eye Movement Desensitization and Reprocessing).

Simonds, Susan L. *Bridging the Silence: Nonverbal Modalities in the Treatment of Adult Survivors of Childhood Sexual Abuse.* **New York: W.W. Norton, 1994.**

> **A wealth of practical and theoretical information on integrating creative art therapies into healing.**

Sue, Derald Wing, and David Sue. *Counseling the Culturally Different.* New York: John Wiley, 1990.

> Helps counselors overcome obstacles in working with someone from a different cultural background than their own. Includes chapters focusing on Native Americans, Asians, African-Americans, and Hispanics.

van der Kolk, Bessel A., Alexander C. McFarlane, and Lars Weisaeth, eds. *Traumatic Stress: The Effects of Overwhelming Experience on Mind, Body, and Society.* New York: Guilford Press, 1996.

> Comprehensive summary of our current state of knowledge from leading authorities around the world. An education in itself.

Westerlund, Elaine. *Women's Sexuality After Childhood Incest.* New York: W. W. Norton, 1992.

> A therapist's study on the sexual attitudes and experiences of women who've been sexually abused. Through statistics and first-person accounts, Westerlund explores issues of body image, reproduction, sexual orientation, and sexual functioning. Includes a treatment model for healing which enables counselors and survivors to address sexuality issues as a team.

Professional Journals

Family Therapy Networker, 8528 Bradford Road, Silver Springs, MD 20901, (301) 589-6536.

> A bimonthly magazine featuring in-depth, informative, well-written articles that cover breaking and sometimes controversial treatment issues.

Family Violence and Sexual Assault Bulletin, 1121 East SE Loop 323, Suite 130, Tyler, TX 75701, (903) 534-5100.

> Reviews materials on family violence, announces

conferences, and acts as a clearinghouse for information. Quarterly.

Journal of Child Sexual Abuse, Haworth Press, 10 Alice St., Binghamton, NY 13904-1580, (800) 342-9678.

This interdisciplinary journal addresses research, clinical, and legal issues, prevention programs, and work with child, adolescent, and adult survivors. Quarterly.

Journal of Interpersonal Violence, Sage, 2455 Teller Rd., Thousand Oaks, CA 91320, (805) 499-0721; fax (805) 499-0871.

"Insightfully explores the disturbing, controversial, and sensitive subjects of today's violent society." Includes commentary, case conferences, practice updates, articles, book reviews, and a yearly index. Bimonthly.

Treating Abuse Today: Survivorship, Treatment and Trends, P.O. Box 3030, Lancaster, PA 17604-3030, (717) 569-3636; fax (717) 581-1355; e-mail: TreatAbuse@aol.com

A journal that explores current treatment issues in the sexual abuse field. Articles, in-depth interviews, case reports, conference listings, book reviews, and more. Includes alternative therapies such as bodywork, art, psychodrama, and movement. Refreshing in its political perspective, accessible language, and respect for survivors. Excellent coverage of "false memory" controversy. Bimonthly.

Violence and Victims, Springer Publications, 536 Broadway, New York, NY 10012, (212) 431-4370.

Forums for the latest developments in interdisciplinary theories, research, policy, clinical practice, legal notes, and social services. Quarterly.

Women and Therapy, Haworth Press, 10 Alice St., Binghamton, NY 13904, (800) 342-9678.

Focuses on issues that especially affect women. Offers effective interventions as alternatives to traditional treatment and speaks to the particular needs of feminist therapists. Quarterly.

SAFE, STRONG, AND FREE

PARENTING

Clunis, Merilee D., and G. Dorsey Green. *The Lesbian Parenting Book: A Guide to Creating Families and Raising Children*. Seattle: Seal Press, 1995.

Divided into two sections—one about the myriad ways lesbians become parents and about what makes our families special; the other full of developmentally sound parenting advice. A great all-around resource.

Davis, Laura, and Janis Keyser. *Becoming the Parent You Want to Be: A Sourcebook of Strategies for the First Five Years*. New York: Broadway Books, 1997.

A comprehensive sourcebook that respects parents and kids. Helps you envision and embody your own vision of parenting. Realistic, inspiring, mulitcultural.

Engel, Beverly. *Beyond the Birds and the Bees: Fostering Your Child's Healthy Sexual Development in Today's World*. New York: Pocket Books, 1997.

Addresses a wide range of issues, including sex education, understanding your own sexual issues and their impact on your child, and helping to prevent abuse. Although Engel takes some positions we disagree with, there's much of value here.

Faber, Adele, and Elaine Mazlish. *How to Talk So Kids Will Listen and Listen So Kids Will Talk*. New York: Avon, 1982, 1991.

Excellent, respectful, intelligent. Will bring about more cooperation from children than all the yelling and pleading in the world. Their other books, *Siblings Without Rivalry* (1988), *Liberated Parents, Liberated Children* (1990), and *How to Be the Parent You Always Wanted to Be* (1992), are also great.

Grevatt, Marge. *We Can Break the Cycle: A Mother's Handbook for Sexual Abuse Survivors*. Cleveland: Orange Blossom Press (Available from Center for Cooperative Action, 4115 Bridge Ave., Cleveland, OH 44113, (216) 651-1266), 1997.

This small pamphlet, written with the help of survivors who are mothers, talks about how to care for ourselves while caring for our children. It addresses the pitfalls that can affect survivors as they become parents, offering support and encouragement.

Kabat-Zinn. *Everyday Blessings: The Inner Work of Mindful Parenting*. New York: Hyperion, 1997.

A practical, poetic and spiritual guide to the inner life of parenting. Inspiration on being in the moment, fully present with our children.

(continued on page 577)

ESPECIALLY FOR CHILDREN

Bass, Ellen. *I Like You to Make Jokes with Me, But I Don't Want You to Touch Me.* Durham, NC: Lollipop Power Books (Available for $7 from Carolina Wren Press, 120 Morris St., Durham, NC 27701), 1981, 1993.

> A gentle picture book. Sara is a little girl who learns to tell a man that, though she wants to be his friend, she doesn't want him to touch her. Bilingual in Spanish and English.

Blank, Joani. *The Playbook for Kids About Sex.* San Francisco: Down There Press (938 Howard St. Ste. 101, San Francisco, CA 94103, (800) 289-8423; e-mail: goodvibe@well.com or on the web: http://www.goodvibes.com), 1980.

> A nonbiased body-loving sex education workbook for children "whose bodies have not started to change into grown-ups' bodies." Every child should have a copy of this and Blank's *A Kid's First Book About Sex.*

Freeman, Lory. *It's MY Body.* Seattle: Parenting Press (P.O. Box 75267, Seattle, WA 98125, (800) 992-6657; fax (206) 364-0702; e-mail: office@parentingpress.com or on the web: http://www.parentingpress.com), 1986.

> A picture book for preschoolers with an accompanying parent's discussion guide. Also available in Spanish.

Gardner-Loulan, JoAnn, Bonnie Lopez, and Marcia Quackenbush. *Period.* Volcano, CA: Volcano Press, 1981, 1991.

> Clear, well-illustrated information for girls. A book that will give girls a strong, self-confident feeling about menstruation and their bodies. Also in Spanish. A parents' guide is also available.

Harris, Robie, with illustrations by Michael Emberley. *It's Perfectly Normal.* Cambridge, MA: Candlewick Press (2067 Massachusetts Ave., Cambridge, MA 02140, (617) 661-3330), 1995.

> **A clear, user-friendly book on bodies, growing up, sex and sexual health. Fabulous illustrations. For pre-adolescents or anyone who wants accessible information about how our bodies work. Not to be missed.**

Jukes, Mavis. *It's a Girl Thing: How to Stay Healthy, Safe and In Charge.* New York: Knopf, 1996.

> A kid-friendly guide to puberty and early adolescence. Talks about getting your period, physical and mental health, diet and eating disorders, drinking, drugs, crushes, dating, sex, birth control, sexual abuse, and more.

Marvel Comics and National Committee for the Prevention of Child Abuse. *Spider Man and Power Pack.* New York: Marvel Comics Group (available for $1.60 each, plus shipping, through the National Committee to Prevent Child Abuse, Fulfillment Center, 200 State Rd., South Deerfield, MA 01373-0200, (800) 835-2671; fax (800) 499-6464), 1984.

> Abuse prevention in a comic-book form. There are three other comics in the series.

***New Moon: The Magazine for Girls and Their Dreams.* (P.O. Box 3620, Duluth, MN 55803-3520, (800) 381-4743; fax (218) 728-0314; e-mail: newmoon@computerpro.com or on the web: http://www.newmoon.org)**

> **A fabulous alternative to traditional "teen" magazines. Full of relevant information, great stories, women's history, and stories of girls' lives around the world. A must for girls age 8 & up. *New Moon Network: For Adults Who Care About Girls* is also available.**

Polese, Carolyn. *Promise Not to Tell.* New York: Plenum, 1985.

> A book for eight- to twelve-year-olds. This moving, beautifully illustrated story encourages children to tell if they are being abused.

ESPECIALLY FOR TEENAGERS

Two fine books especially for teen survivors healing from sexual abuse are on page 549.

Bass, Ellen, and Kate Kaufman. *Free Your Mind: The Book for Gay, Lesbian, and Bisexual Youth—and Their Allies.* New York: HarperCollins, 1996.

> A refreshing change from the barrage of books focusing on the despair and suffering of lesbian, gay, and bisexual youth. This comprehensive, practical guide supports youth to stand up, speak out, and know their own worth.

Bell, Ruth. *Changing Bodies, Changing Lives: A Book for Teens About Sex and Relationships.* New York: Vintage, 1980, 1988.

> An anti-sexist, no-nonsense guide for teens. Clear definitions of sexual violence. An all-around reference book that every teen should have access to.

Berg, Elizabeth. *Durable Goods.* New York: Avon Books, 1993.

> A beautifully written coming-of-age novel. Twelve-year-old Katie is facing her growing-up crisis on a Texas army base after her mother has died.

Coman, Carolyn. *What Jamie Saw.* Volcano, CA: Volcano Press, 1996.

> A gripping young adult novella about a nine-year-old boy who witnesses family violence. Dramatically portrays the impact of violence and documents what it takes to start a new life.

Hughes, K. Wind, and Linda Wolf. *Daughters of the Moon, Sisters of the Sun.* Stony Creek, CT: New Society Publishers, 1997.

> Vivid, real stories from forty teenage girls about their coming of age, accompanied by interviews with accomplished women mentors including poet Maya Angelou, the Indigo Girls, Native American leader Wilma Mankiller, activist Angela Advise and others.

King County Sexual Assault Resource Center. *Top Secret: Sexual Assault Information for Teenagers Only.* King County Sexual Assault Resource Center (P.O. Box 300, Renton, WA 98057, (425) 226-5062; fax (425) 235-7422), 1982.

> A well-designed, informative booklet written for teens. Great for classroom use. Bulk discounts and a discussion guide for teachers also available. Also, Gayle Stringer's *What's the Big Deal?*

Sexual Harassment Information for Teens, is a terrific illustrated booklet with enlightening information that every young person—male and female —could benefit from.

Kuklin, Susan. *Speaking Out: Teenagers Take On Race, Sex, and Identity.* New York: G.P. Putnam's Sons, 1993.

> This book of first-person stories documents the feelings and experiences of teenagers at a large multicultural high school in New York City.

Levy, Barrie, ed. *Dating Violence: Young Women in Danger.* Seattle: Seal Press, 1991.

> **This excellent anthology includes firsthand accounts and essays dealing with intervention, prevention, and the politics of the emotional, physical, and sexual violence facing young women. The follow-up, *In Love and Danger* (1993) is a teen's guide to breaking free of abusive relationships.**

Mufson, Susan, and Rachel Kranz. *Straight Talk About Date Rape.* New York: Facts on File (11 Penn Plaza, NY, NY 10001, (800) 322-8755), 1997.

> Provides information about sexual assault by acquaintances and friends and offers ways to avoid, and, if necessary, deal with unwanted sexual encounters. The *Straight Talk* series has other good books for young people including *Straight Talk About Post-Traumatic Stress Disorder.*

Rubin, Nancy, and a cast of hundreds. *Ask Me If I Care: Voices from an American High School.* Berkeley, CA: Ten Speed Press (P.O. Box 7123, Berkeley, CA 94707, (800) 841-2665), 1994.

> **A remarkable teacher from Berkeley High School gets students to write about their real lives—on topics ranging from racial identity to death, from sexual orientation to sexual abuse. Powerful and moving.**

Voight, Cynthia. *When She Hollers.* New York: Scholastic, 1994.

> This young adult novel by an award-winning author is an emotionally brutal portrait of one day in the life of a teenager who decides to fight back against her adoptive father's abuse. It's an intense book—not for all young survivors, but excellent.

Kurcinka, Mary. *Raising Your Spirited Child*. New York: HarperCollins, 1992.

> An invaluable resource for parents who have a child who is more active, emotional or otherwise intense. One reading can shift your perspective on your challenging child forever. Highly recommended.

von der Zande, Irene, with Santa Cruz Toddler Care Center Staff. *1, 2, 3 . . . The Toddler Years: A Practical Guide for Parents and Caregivers*. Santa Cruz Toddler Care Center (1738 16th Ave., Santa Cruz, CA 95062), 1986, 1993.

> A wonderful resource for all adults who have small children in their lives. Respectful, clear, great on limit-setting and empowerment.

PREVENTION RESOURCES FOR PARENTS

Adams, Caren, and Jennifer Fay. *No More Secrets: Protecting Your Child from Sexual Assault*. San Luis Obispo, CA: Impact Publishers (P.O. Box 1094, San Luis Obispo, CA 93406, (805) 543-5911), 1981.

> A fine practical guide.

Fay, Jennifer, et al. *"He Told Me Not to Tell."* Renton, WA: King County Sexual Assault Resource Center (P.O. Box 300, Renton, WA 98057, (425) 226-5062; fax (425) 235-7422), 1979.

> A parents' guide for talking to children about sexual assault. This clear, direct booklet is also available in Spanish. Also available from King County is DeAnn Yamamoto's *Especially for Parents of Adolescents* for parents of teens who have been sexually abused.

Krazier, Sheryll Kerns. *The Safe Child Book*. New York: Fireside, 1985, 1996.

> This is a clear, practical guide for teaching children skills to protect themselves. Reassuring, direct language.

Levy, Barrie, and Patricia Occhiuzzo Giggans. *What Parents Need to Know About Dating Violence*. Seattle: Seal Press, 1995.

> Drawing on real-life experiences, this book offers straightforward advice to parents who are concerned about teenagers in abusive dating relationships.

Sanford, Linda. *The Silent Children: A Parent's Guide to the Prevention of Child Sexual Abuse*. New York: McGraw-Hill, 1980.

> Detailed and practical. Resources for single parents, parents of children with disabilities, parents who are Asian, Native American, African-American, and Hispanic. Most comprehensive of the parents' guides. Currently out of print.

Wittet, Scott, and Debbie Wong. *Helping Your Child to Be Safe*. Renton, WA: King County Sexual Assault Resource Center (P.O. Box 300, Renton, WA 98057, (425) 226-5062; fax (425) 235-7422), 1987.

> Excellent education and prevention booklets for Southeast Asian refugees to the United States. In English, Chinese, Vietnamese, Cambodian, and Lao. Also helpful is an illustrated booklet, *Be Aware, Be Safe*, for S.E. Asian teens themselves.

IF YOUR CHILD IS ABUSED

Organizations and Web Sites

Alliance for the Rights of Children (ARCH), P.O. Box 3826 Merrifield, VA 22116, (703) 255-2643; (800) 636-4998; fax (703) 255-4653.

> This organization, set up in 1988 to support Dr. Elizabeth Morgan in her fight to protect her daughter, currently coordinates media efforts on behalf of protective parents and educates judges and CPS workers involved in child custody cases.

Justice for Children, 412 Main St., Suite 400 Houston, TX 77002, (713) 225-4357.

> With chapters in ten states, Justice for Children works to protect abused children from further abuse when existing agencies fail to help. Operates a hotline that guides those reporting abuse through the maze of government agencies, monitors court proceedings, conducts community forums, and provides information and assistance to elected officials on legislative issues.

Mothers Against Sexual Abuse (MASA), 503$^{1}/_{2}$ S. Myrtle Ave., #9, Monrovia, CA 91016, (626) 305-1986; fax (626) 305-5190; e-mail: masa@interinc.com or on the web: http://interinc.com/MASA

> Offers public education, support for nonoffending parents, networking, and legislative activism. A newsletter, *Protect the Children*, is also available.

WHEN CHILDREN MOLEST

These resources can be helpful to both parents and counselors.

ORGANIZATION

The Safer Society Foundation, Inc. (SSFI), P.O. Box 340, Brandon, VT 05733, (802) 247-3132; (fax) (802) 247-4233; referral line (802) 247-5141 (M, W, F 1:00–4:30 EST) or on the web: http://safersociety.org

> SSFI maintains a nationwide directory of agencies, institutions, and individuals who provide specialized assessment and treatment for youthful and adult sex offenders. SSFI also publishes many useful resources for helping young sex offenders.

BOOKS

Allred, Terri, and Gary Burns. Stop! Just for Kids: For Kids with Sexual Touching Problems by Kids with Sexual Touching Problems. Brandon, VT: Safer Society Press, 1997.

> **Written by a group of boys in a treatment program for young offenders. Faces the hard issues with candor and hope. Easy to read.**

Araji, Sharon. *Sexually Aggressive Children: Coming to Understand Them.* Thousand Oaks, CA: Sage, 1997.

> A comprehensive overview of sexual abuse perpetrated by children. Araji explores the causes of such abuse and identifies nine treatment models for dealing with sexually aggressive kids. Written for professionals.

Cunningham, Carolyn, and Kee McFarlane. *When Children Molest Children: Group Treatment Strategies for Young Sexual Abusers.* Brandon, VT: Safer Society Press, 1991.

> A therapeutic manual for working with "abuse-reactive" children, ages five to twelve, who are acting out sexually. A follow-up by this same team, *Steps to Healthy Touching: A Treatment Workbook for Kids Who Have Problems with Sexually Inappropriate Behavior,* is a 12-step workbook designed to help kids, aged five through twelve, who

have acted out sexually with younger children. Available from Kidsrights, 10100 Park Cedar Drive, Charlotte, NC 28210, (800) 892-KIDS.

Cunningham, Carolyn, and Kee McFarlane. *When Children Abuse: Group Treatment Strategies for Children with Impulse Control Problems.* Brandon, VT: Safer Society Press, 1996.

> Valuable compilation of therapeutic exercises and activities. Useful also for teachers and school counselors.

Gil, Eliana. A Guide for Parents of Children Who Molest. Rockville, MD: Launch Press, 1987, 1995.

> **Clear, simple, and compassionate. A must.**

Gil, Eliana, and Toni Cavanagh Johnson. *Sexualized Children: Assessment and Treatment of Sexualized Children and Children Who Molest.* Rockville, MD: Launch Press, 1993.

> A comprehensive look at the problem of sexually aggressive children. Clearly differentiates between age-appropriate sex play and molesting behaviors.

Hunter, Mic. *Child Survivors and Perpetrators of Sexual Abuse: Treatment Innovations.* Thousand Oaks, CA: Sage, 1995.

> The first half of this book for professionals deals with treatment of sexually abused boys, inpatient treatment of adolescent survivors and ritual abuse. The second half presents treatment strategies for abuse-reactive kids and their parents.

Ogawa, Brian. *To Tell the Truth.* Volcano, CA: Volcano Press, 1997.

> A full-color illustrated book for children eight years and older to help guide them through the criminal justice system. Excellent resource for children who have to testify in court.

Pithers, William, Alison Gray, Carolyn Cunningham, and Sandy Lane. *From Trauma to Understanding: A Guide for Parents of Children with Sexual Behavior Problems.* Brandon, VT: Safer Society Press, 1993.

> This pamphlet informs, reassures, and gives hope to parents.

"Reach Me, Inc.," P.O. Box 891341, Houston, TX 77289, (409) 935-5183; fax (409) 935-5183 or on the web: http://www.angelfire.com/tx/reachme

> Offers legal, psychiatric and medical help for parents and children. Especially helpful for protective mothers if the case becomes difficult. Skilled at working with Child Protective Services. Web site includes links to kids' games and entertainment.

SOC-UM (Safeguarding Our Children United Mothers), 1878 West 11th Street, Tracy, CA 95376, (209) 832-5703 or on the web: http://www.soc-um.org

> Dedicated to public awareness, children's education, and assistance to children who've been abused. They distribute an elementary school curriculum which can be downloaded from the Internet or requested by mail or phone.

Books

Adams, Caren. *Helping Your Child Recover from Sexual Abuse.* Seattle: University of Washington Press (P.O. Box 50096, Seattle, WA 98145-5096; (206) 543-4050; fax (206) 543-3932), 1987, 1992.

> **Practical guidance for parents in the days and months after a child is abused. Information for parents is on one side of the page and sample conversations and activities for parents and kids to do together are on the other. Invaluable.**

Ashley, Sandi. *The Missing Voice: Writings by Mothers of Incest Victims.* Dubuque, IA: Kendall-Hunt, 1992.

> Twelve women tell their stories. Currently out of print.

Golder, Christine. *If It Happens to Your Child It Happens to You! A Parent's Help-Source for Sexual Assault.* Saratoga, CA: R & E Publishers (P.O. Box 2008, Saratoga, CA 95070), 1987.

> This large pamphlet deals effectively with many crucial parental concerns.

Hagan, Kathleen, and Joyce Case. *When Your Child Has Been Molested.* San Francisco: Jossey-Bass, 1988, 1997.

> Simple, clear, and helpful.

Johnson, Janis Tyler. *Mothers of Incest Survivors: Another Side of the Story.* Bloomington, IN: Indiana University Press, 1992.

> A study based on firsthand accounts of six mothers whose daughters were abused by their fathers or stepfathers. Gives mothers a voice and challenges the stereotype of the collusive mother.

Matsakis, Aphrodite. *When the Bough Breaks: A Helping Guide for Parents of Sexually Abused Children.* Oakland: New Harbinger Publications (distributed by Varied Directions, 18 Mt. Battie Street, Camden, ME 04843, (800) 888-4236; fax (207) 236-4512; e-mail: Joyceb3955@aol.com), 1991.

> A compassionate guide full of exercises, examples and strategies for helping children. Written by a therapist whose daughter was sexually abused.

Myers, John. *A Mother's Nightmare—Incest: A Practical Legal Guide for Parents and Professionals.* Thousand Oaks, CA: Sage, 1997.

> **Written by a law professor, this book is a valuable resource for mothers who are trying to protect their kids. Discusses the ways the legal system sometimes fails and explores the complexities of taking child sexual abuse cases to court.**

Ogawa, Brian. *To Tell the Truth.* Volcano, CA: Volcano Press, 1997.

> **A full-color illustrated book for children eight years and older to help guide them through the criminal justice system. Excellent resource for children who have to testify in court.**

RESOURCES FOR TEACHERS AND OTHER ADVOCATES OF CHILDREN

Organizations

KIDPOWER•TEENPOWER•FULLPOWER, P.O. Box 1212, Santa Cruz, CA 95061, (408) 426-4407, Voice-mail USA (800) 467-6997, fax (408) 426-4480; e-mail: safety @kidpower.org or on the web: http://www.fullpower.org

> KIDPOWER was formed in 1989 to help people of all ages stay safe, act wisely, and believe in themselves. Workshops include training for children, teens, adults, families, and schools in boundary setting, conflict resolution, and full-force self-defense techniques. Contact them for a center near you or to bring a program to your community.

The National Child Rights Alliance, P.O. Box 422, Ellenville, NY 12428, (914) 647-3670; e-mail: JLenzer1@Comp Serve.com or on the web: http://linux.hartford.edu/~jerry/ncra.html

SEXUAL ASSAULT PREVENTION FOR PEOPLE WITH DISABILITIES

Garbarino, James, Patrick Brookhouser, and Karen Authier. *Special Children Special Risks. The Maltreatment of Children with Disabilities.* New York: Aldine de Gruyter (200 Saw Mill River Rd., Hawthorne, NY 10532), 1987.

A collection of clinical essays on a critical topic.

Plummer, Carol. *Preventing Sexual Abuse: Activities and Strategies for Those Working with Children in Special Populations.* Holmes Beach, FL: Learning Publications (P.O. Box 1338, Holmes Beach, FL 34218, (800) 222-1525; fax (941) 778-6818; e-mail: lpi@bhip. infi.net or on the web: http://www.bhip.infi.net/~lpi), 1984.

A curriculum guide for teaching prevention skills to children in grades K to 12. Includes section on parent education and teacher training, role plays, and other suggested activities. Includes guidelines for working with developmentally disabled children.

Shaman, Ellen. *Choices: Sexual Assault Prevention for Persons with Disabilities.* Seattle: The Disabilities Project of Seattle Rape Relief (1825 South Jackson, Suite 102, Seattle, WA 98144, (206) 325-5531 TTY/Voice), 1985.

Three self-help workbooks for people with physical disabilities, hearing, and visual impairments. The workbook on visual impairments is available in Braille, large print, and on cassette. $5 each or $10 for the whole set.

Charting New Waters and *Double Jeopardy.* The Family Violence Film and Video Collection, National Clearinghouse on Family Violence, 18th Floor, Jeanne Mance Building, Tunney's Pasture, Ottawa, Ontario, Canada K1A 1B4, (800) 267-1291; fax (613) 941-8930; TTY (800) 561-5643 or on the web: http://www.hc-sc.gc.ca/nc-cn

These videos deal with the issue of violence in disabled women's lives. A useful resource for teaching caregivers, social workers, advocates and criminal justice personnel how to deal with these situations in a respectful, appropriate manner. In *Double Jeopardy,* disabled women who are victims of family violence tell their stories.

An international organization of youth rights activists. NCRA works to defend the following rights for young people: the right to liberty, safety, survival, education, free speech, nondiscrimination, and free choice. An annual Youth Summit addresses issues from child abuse to AIDS to child labor. NCRA also publishes a fine newsletter, *The Freedom Voice,* which covers many issues relevant to survivors.

National Committee for the Prevention of Child Abuse, 332 S. Michigan Ave. #1600, Chicago, IL 60604; (312) 663-3520; fax (312) 939-8962 or on the web: http://www.childabuse.org/index.html

This national organization is committed to preventing child abuse in all its forms through education, research, public awareness, and advocacy. Fifty-two national chapters provide grass-roots leadership on the local level. Their Healthy Families America program promotes positive parenting, child development and health.

Their web site includes parenting tips, child abuse facts, and excellent links on adult survivor issues, children's legal rights, parenting, adoption and more. Contacts for all fifty states and culture-specific organizations are included as well.

Books

Fortune, Marie M. *Sexual Abuse Prevention: A Study for Teenagers.* New York: Pilgrim Press (700 Prospect Ave. East, Cleveland, OH 44115, (216) 736-3700; fax (216) 736-3703), 1984.

This excellent training guide outlines a five-session course of study for teenagers on sexual abuse. A must for anyone working with adolescents.

Gil, Eliana. *The Healing Power of Play: Working with Abused Children.* Rockville, MD: Launch Press, 1991.

Treatment issues for people who work with abused children.

Reid, Kathryn Goering, with Marie Fortune. *Preventing Child Sexual Abuse: A Curriculum for Children Ages Nine Through Twelve.* New York: Pilgrim Press (700 Prospect Ave. East, Cleveland, OH 44115, (216) 736-3700; fax (216) 736-3703), 1990.

> An excellent prevention curriculum which interweaves secular materials with biblical resources. Ideal for use in Sunday school or other religious education programs.

Mail-Order Catalogs and Educational Materials

ACT for Kids, Spokane Sexual Assault Center, Rape Crisis Network, 7 South Howard, Suite 200, Spokane, WA 99201, (509) 747-8224; fax (509) 747-0609; e-mail: sales @actforkids.org or on the web: http://www.actforkids.org

> **Produces books, videos, and other educational materials for children, parents, teachers, and professionals who work with abused children. Of particular note is *My Very Own Book About Me* (in Spanish and English), a personal safety workbook, *How to Survive the Sexual Abuse of Your Child*, and *Giant Steps*, a self-esteem curriculum for kids.**

At-Risk Resources, P.O. Box 760, Plainview, NY 11803-0760, (800) 99-YOUTH; fax (516) 349-5521; e-mail: info@at-risk.com or on the web: http://www.at-risk.com

> Educational posters, pamphlets, coloring books, library resources, multimedia, and videos about drugs, sexual abuse, self-esteem, and values.

Childswork, Childsplay: A Catalog Addressing the Social and Emotional Needs of Children and Adolescents, (800) 962-1141; fax (201) 583-3644 or on the web: http://www.Childswork.com

> A catalogue of books, tapes, posters, and games to help children with a variety of problems ranging from sibling rivalry to attention deficit disorder to sexual abuse. Especially good resources for dealing with anger and conflict resolution.

ETR Associates, P.O. Box 1830, Santa Cruz, CA 95061-1830, (800) 321-4407; fax (800) 435-8483 or on the web: http://www.etr.org

> Publishes a large variety of fine educational books and pamphlets on topics including sexual harassment, dating violence, and sexual abuse.

FOR INSPIRATION

Allison, Dorothy. *Bastard Out of Carolina.* New York: Plume, 1992.

> A powerhouse of a book. A beautifully written, painfully gripping story of poverty and abuse in rural North Carolina.

Angelou, Maya. *I Know Why the Caged Bird Sings.* New York: Bantam, 1980, 1983.

> A moving portrayal of incest and its effects. A wonderful autobiography that celebrates life.

Davis, Nancy. *Therapeutic Stories to Heal Abused Children* and *Therapeutic Stories That Teach and Heal.* Nancy Davis, 9836 Natick Rd., Burke, VA 22015, (703) 978-4321; e-mail: tellerofstories@juno.com

> Originally written for therapists, these wonderful looseleaf books are full of healing bedtime stories and pictures to color. These books are expensive; maybe you could share the cost with your support group.

Fisk, Molly. *Surrender.* Salt Water Poetry, P.O. Box 592, Stinson Beach, CA 94970 or on the web at www.oro.net/~molly. Available for $14.

> This audiotape features poems about love, sex, small towns, child abuse, and the solace of the natural world from the editor of *The Healing Woman.*

Flagg, Fannie. *Fried Green Tomatoes at the Whistle Stop Cafe.* New York: Fawcett, 1988, 1997.

> A funny and wise book about the things that are important to life. Every woman we know who's read this book—from twelve to sixty-five—has loved it.

Garden, Nancy. *Lark in the Morning.* New York: Farrar, Straus and Giroux, 1991.

> A fine young adult novel about two abused children who run away and the young woman who finds them. The children are brave and resourceful.

Gibbons, Kaye. *Ellen Foster.* New York: Vintage Books. 1988, 1997.

> The story of a young girl who overcomes adversity with considerable spunk.

Groening, Matt. *Childhood Is Hell.* New York: Pantheon Books, 1983.

> Terrific cartoons.

Hanauer, Cathi. *My Sister's Bones.* New York: Doubleday, 1996.

Well-written novel about a young woman dealing with anorexia.

Harrison, Kathryn. *Exposure*. New York: Warner, 1993, 1994.

A well-written and disturbing novel about a woman violated by her father's erotic photographs of her.

Karr, Mary. *The Liar's Club: A Memoir*. New York: Viking, 1995.

A vivid, intense memoir. Exceptionally well written, full of grit, humor, and love.

Kingsolver, Barbara. *The Bean Trees*. HarperCollins, 1988, 1991.

A wonderful novel about finding yourself, healing an abused child, and the power of love in a new "found" family. Her other fiction includes *Pigs In Heaven* and *Animal Dreams.*.

Laux, Dorianne. *Awake*. Brockport, NY: Boa Editions (92 Park Ave., Brockport, NY 14420, (716) 546-3410), 1990.

A fine poet—and survivor—writes about her childhood and her life. Highly recommended.

LeGuin, Ursula. *A Wizard of Earthsea*. New York: Bantam, 1975, 1994.

Compelling fantasy about a young man's quest to seek out and conquer the frightening shadows that chase him. Survivors of sexual abuse will have no trouble identifying with his denial, his search, and his recovery.

McKinley, Robin. *Deerskin*. New York: Ace Books, 1993.

A fierce and beautiful tale of sexual abuse and healing told in the fantasy genre—complete with princess, prince, castles, and even a dragon.

Morrison, Toni. *The Bluest Eye*. New York: Plume, 1970, 1994.

A beautiful novel about a young survivor from an extraordinary novelist.

O'Brien, Edna. *Down By the River*. New York: Farrar, Straus and Giroux, 1997.

Moving, lyrical novel about a young Irish girl who seeks an abortion after finding herself pregnant through incest. Based on an actual 1992 case that came before Ireland's Supreme Court.

Olds, Sharon. *The Gold Cell*. New York: Knopf, 1988.

One of the finest poets writing today, Olds captures the range of feelings in complex family relationships. See also *Satan Says, The Dead and the Living, The Father,* and *The Wellspring*.

Salter, Anna. *Shiny Water*. New York: Pocket Books, 1997.

Written by a therapist with long experience with both victims and offenders, this fine mystery about a child sexual assault custody case features detective Michael Stone, a female forensic psychologist. See also *Fault Lines* about a sadistic sex offender and a victim with PTSD. Graphic and terrifying.

Smiley, Jane. *A Thousand Acres*. New York: Fawcett, 1992.

A finely written story of complex people in a family whose foundation was undermined by sexual abuse.

Walker, Alice. *The Color Purple*. New York: Washington Square Press, 1982, 1998.

A young woman's letters to God. A passionate human story of triumph through adversity.

Watson, Larry. *Montana 1948*. New York: Simon & Schuster, 1993.

Told from the point of view of an adolescent boy, this beautifully written novel portrays a family's struggle when it is discovered that one of its members is guilty of sexual abuse. Shows small-town life and the tensions of class and race between whites and Native Americans.

Williams, Reverend Cecil, and Janice Mirikitani. *I've Got Something to Say About This Big Trouble: Children of the Tenderloin Speak Out*. Glide Word Press (Glide Memorial Methodist Church, 330 Ellis St., Room 203, San Francisco, CA 94102), 1989.

Drawings, poetry, rap poems, and stories by children from the Tenderloin district of San Francisco. Children speak for themselves about crack, homelessness, and being poor. From the introduction by Maya Angelou: "Despite the many ways we have abandoned them, their poems still dance with hope for our acceptance." Available for $14.

SMALL PRESS ADDRESSES

Many of the excellent, groundbreaking books listed in this bibliography have been published by small, feminist, and alternative presses. These presses generally can't afford to advertise much and have limited access to mainstream bookstores, so you may have to go to a little more trouble to find their books. You can order directly from them, go to a feminist or recovery bookstore, or order through a specialty bookstore, such as Full Circle Books (see below).

The following presses have been cited more than two times in the Resource Guide. Most of them will send you a free catalogue so you can find out about the other fine titles they offer.

Brunner/Mazel, 1900 Frost Rd. #101, Bristol, PA 19007, (800) 821-8312; fax (215) 785-5515; e-mail: bkorders@tandfpa.com

Crossing Press, P.O. Box 1048, Freedom, CA 95019, (800) 777-1048; fax: (800) 549-0020; e-mail: Crossing@aol.com or on the web: http://www.crossing press.com

Guilford Press, 72 Spring St., New York, NY 10012, (800) 365-7006; fax (212) 966-6708 or on the web: http://www.guilford.com

Haworth Press, 10 Alice St., Binghamton, NY 13904, (800) 342-9678; fax (800) 895-0582; e-mail: getinfo @haworth.com or on the web: http://www.haworth.com

Jossey-Bass Publishers, 350 Sansome St., San Francisco, CA 94104-1342, (800) 956-7739.

Launch Press, P.O. Box 5629, Rockville, MD 20855, (800) 321-9167.

New Society Publishers, P.O. Box 189, Gabriola Island, BC, Canada V0R 1X0, (800) 567-6772 or on the web: http://www.newsociety.com

Safer Society Press, P.O. Box 340 Brandon, VT 05733, (802) 247-3132; fax (802) 247-4233 or on the web: http://safersociety.org

Sage Publications, 2455 Teller Road, Newbury Park, CA 91320, (805) 499-0721; (805) 499-0871; e-mail: order@sagepub.com or on the web: http://www.sagepub.com

Seal Press, 3131 Western Ave #410, Seattle, WA 98121, (800) 754-0271; fax (206) 285-9410; e-mail: sealpress@scn.org or on the web: http://www.sealpress.com

Volcano Press, P.O. Box 270, Volcano, CA 95689, (209) 296-3445; fax: (209) 296-4995; e-mail: info @volcanopress.com or on the web: http://www.volcanopress.com

Note: An excellent mail-order source for hard-to-find abuse-related books is Full Circle Books in Albuquerque, New Mexico. For their extensive annotated catalogue on healing from sexual and family violence, access them online at http://www.bookgrrls.com/fcb. For a printout of the catalogue, send $10 to Full Circle Books, 2205 Silver SE, Albuquerque, NM 87106, or call (800) 951-0053.

THE COURAGE TO HEAL: A TRIBUTE
by Ellen Bass*

We were five in a plaid dress with a sash and a little white collar.
We were nine, it was after school in the garage, the smell
of motor oil and cut grass through the open window.
We were twelve, fourteen, sixteen in our own beds, in seersucker pajamas,
the rain pelting down and running through the gutters.

It was a neighbor, a priest, a stranger, our father, our mother.
It was every day. It was when he got drunk.
It was before our class trip to the state capital. When our mother
was in the hospital giving birth. Just once.

We were left for dead.
We were barely scratched.
We were found in a coal bin, so wild they couldn't catch us to wash, to comb our hair.
Nothing showed.

We lay at the bottom of the stairs. We found ourselves
looking down from a corner of the ceiling.
We found ourselves out in the limb of the maple tree,
in the night sky, up in the stars, where it was cool and there was so much empty space.
We found ourselves in our own beds. It was morning
and our clothes were laid out neatly on the chair,
our mothers prompting us to come for breakfast.

We told an English teacher with straight brown hair
clasped at the nape with a silver barrette.
We told our mother who slapped us once across the face and closed herself like a fist.
We told by carving our skin like a pumpkin.
We never told.

We slept clutching a plaster statue of the Virgin Mary.
By day, we couldn't concentrate. The long division
on the blackboard smeared in our minds.
We memorized everything. Our handwriting
an exact replica of Palmer cursive, only smaller.

We ate to erect a bulwark. We wouldn't eat.
We didn't want bodies. We didn't want to be part of the
food chain—eater or eaten.
We took enough pills to kill a horse.
We were in coma for a month. And emerged in rage.
We smiled. We smiled. We were drunk
the first six years of our daughter's life.
We held our son's hand over a candle.
We somehow knew how to mother. That
gave us joy.

Deciding to heal was a choice. The first one
we ever clearly made. We didn't decide.
The alternatives just became too painful.
We cried every day. We only cried once
but it went on for a year. We never cried.
We gave up and drove a motorcycle into a guard rail.
We threw a chair through the window.
We stood on the steps of the psychiatric unit

weeping about something we couldn't remember.
We remembered everything it seemed, each
detail etched into the soft organ of our minds.

We blamed ourselves because he gave us a bicycle.
We blamed ourselves because we didn't stop it.
We blamed ourselves because our bodies responded.

We stopped blaming ourselves. We beat
a hundred pillows and tore up a year's worth of the Sunday *Times*.
We filled forty notebooks with writing that dug through the pages like a plow.
We said once in a quiet voice, *I'm angry.*

We told our stories and we were believed.
We told our stories and our families denied it. *Never
were we left alone like that. It couldn't have happened.*
We told our stories and the faces that listened told theirs.

Once, we held out one fingertip to a woman with kind eyes
and she touched the pad of her finger to ours—for a moment.
Once we were rocked in a safe lap and someone smoothed
back our hair with a tenderness not even we could deny.

But that wasn't the end of it. It went on and on
beyond what we'd imagined, beyond what we'd signed up for.
We sat in fear like in our own urine. Our hearts
aching in our hollowed-out chests and down our empty arms.
We thought we would not survive.
Like stroke patients, we had to learn everything anew.
We saw how it had seeped into the corners of our lives like smoke.
Nothing was untainted, except the tough kernel we were born with,
the seed of who we could have been, could still be.

We reclaimed our bodies, inch by precious inch.
Feeling our own skin, astonished, like touching a newborn.
We tried out trust, like experimenting with drugs.
We went back to school. We took a vacation.
We spoke the truth. We did what we wanted.
We learned to sleep. We ate when we were hungry.

We woke in the morning, willing. We wanted
to be alive. We were hungry for all we'd missed.
We took it with eager, patient, or tentative hands
but we took it. We made a cup of tea
in our own kitchen and drank it at a blue table
on which we'd set a small bouquet of daffodils.

---

* Syracuse Cultural Workers asked Ellen to write a poem about the healing journey that could be made into an inspiring poster for survivors. This poem—a tribute to the survivors who have shared their stories, their struggles, and their healing—is available as a beautiful full-color poster for $14 (plus $4.95 shipping) from Syracuse Cultural Workers, P.O. Box 6367, Syracuse, NY 13217, (315) 474–1132; fax: (877) 265-5399.

INDEX

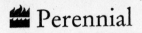 **Perennial**   **HarperCollins***Publishers*

To receive Laura Davis' free newsletter; to learn more about her books, workshops, and lectures; or to join her online healing community, visit WWW.LAURADAVIS.NET

Books by Laura Davis (and Ellen Bass):

I Thought We'd Never Speak Again: *The Road from Estrangement to Reconciliation*
ISBN 0-06-019762-5 (HarperCollins hardcover by Laura Davis)

All of us carry the painful burden of relationships that have been sundered by betrayal, distrust, anger, and misunderstanding. In this groundbreaking new book, Laura Davis examines what tears people apart, what keeps them estranged, and lays out the steps by which they can mend broken relationships and find wholeness.

To find out whether reconciliation is possible or desirable for you, visit www.lauradavis.net/neverspeak2.asp

The Courage to Heal: *A Guide for Women Survivors of Child Sexual Abuse*
ISBN 0-06-095066-8 (paperback by Ellen Bass and Laura Davis) • ISBN 0-898-45833-1 (audio)

First published in 1988, this million-copy bestseller (now in its third edition) is an inspiring, comprehensive guide offering hope and encouragement to anyone who was sexually abused as a child. By taking readers step-by-step through the healing process with clarity, compassion, and a deep respect for each survivor's journey, *The Courage to Heal* can change your life and convince you that healing is possible—even for you.

The Courage to Heal Workbook: *For Women and Men Survivors of Child Sexual Abuse*
ISBN 0-06-096437-5 (paperback by Laura Davis)

This groundbreaking companion to *The Courage to Heal* is an innovative, inspiring, and in-depth workbook containing checklists, open-ended questions, writing exercises, art projects, and activities that take survivors of child sexual abuse (or anyone suffering the effects of trauma) through the key aspects of the healing process.

Allies in Healing: *When the Person You Love Was Sexually Abused as a Child*
ISBN 0-06-096883-4 (paperback by Laura Davis)

Based on in-depth interviews, *Allies in Healing* speaks directly to the confusion, anger, bewilderment, and frustration of the partners of child sexual abuse survivors—girlfriends, boyfriends, spouses, and lovers—offering practical advice on deepening compassion, improving communication, and developing healing as a shared activity.

Beginning to Heal: *A First Book for Survivors of Child Sexual Abuse*
ISBN 0-06-096927-X (paperback by Ellen Bass and Laura Davis)

This gentle introduction to the healing process is perfect for teenagers, people in crisis, or anyone who wants to begin their journey of healing from sexual abuse.

Available wherever books are sold, or call 1-800-331-3761 to order.